# DESTINATION LONDON

P9-DMJ-099

A hundred movies, books, and Masterpiece Theatre productions have prepared you for London's quintessentially British brew of history, royalty, dignity, and civility. Even before you arrive, its images are imprinted on your consciousness. The dome of St. Paul's is iconically familiar. So are the Tower Guards, Big Ben, and the Thames. Go for a walk along the light-strung riverbank at dusk before an evening of theater, taking in the breathtaking view of the Houses of Parliament. Spend the day visiting royal palaces and museums, stuffed full of priceless treasures and works of art. Or go shopping, browsing through the luxurious department stores that dot the city, the famous bespoke tailor shops, and the trendy boutiques around Covent Garden. Then unwind with a wonderfully inventive meal at one of the city's fine restaurants. You'll soon understand why so many visitors have loved the city for so long, since before the nursery-rhyme bridge fell down—and why, of all the world's travel destinations, London may be the most revisited. Have a fabulous trip!

Tim Jarrell, Publisher

# CONTENTS

FATHER'S DAY 6/19/05
GABBY?

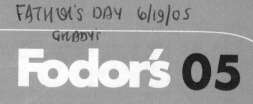

# LONDON

Where to Stay & Eat
for All Budgets

Must-See Sights
& Local Secrets

Ratings You Can Trust

Fodor's Travel Publications   New York, Toronto, London, Sydney, Auckland
www.fodors.com

**FODOR'S LONDON 2005**
**Editor:** Nuha E. Ansari

**Editorial Production:** Jacinta O'Halloran
**Editorial Contributors:** Rob Andrews, Catherine Belonogoff, Jacqueline Brown, Collin Campbell, Julius Honnor, Julie Tomasz, Amy Wang, Alex Wijeratna
**Maps:** David Lindroth *cartographer;* Bob Blake and Rebecca Baer, *map editors*
**Design:** Fabrizio La Rocca, *creative director;* Guido Caroti, *art director;* Melanie Marin, *senior photo editor*
**Production/Manufacturing:** Angela L. McLean
**Cover Photo** (Beefeaters stand guard at the Tower of London): Charles & Josette Lenars/Corbis

## SPECIAL SALES

This book is available for special discounts for bulk purchases for sales promotions or premiums. Special editions, including personalized covers, excerpts of existing books, and corporate imprints, can be created in large quantities for special needs. For more information, write to Special Markets/Premium Sales, 1745 Broadway, MD 6-2, New York, NY 10019, or e-mail specialmarkets@randomhouse.com.

## AN IMPORTANT TIP & AN INVITATION

Although all prices, opening times, and other details in this book are based on information supplied to us at press time, changes occur all the time in the travel world, and Fodor's cannot accept responsibility for facts that become outdated or for inadvertent errors or omissions. So **always confirm information when it matters,** especially if you're making a detour to visit a specific place. Your experiences—positive and negative—matter to us. If we have missed or misstated something, **please write to us.** We follow up on all suggestions. Contact the London editor at editors@fodors.com or c/o Fodor's at 1745 Broadway, New York, New York 10019.

PRINTED IN THE UNITED STATES OF AMERICA

10 9 8 7 6 5 4 3 2 1

## Maps

## CloseUps

# ABOUT THIS BOOK

The best source for travel advice is a like-minded friend who's just been where you're headed. But with or without that friend, you'll be in great shape to find your way around your destination once you learn to find your way around your Fodor's guide.

**SELECTION**

Our goal is to cover the best properties, sights, and activities in their category, as well as the most interesting areas to visit. We make a point of including local food-lovers' hot spots as well as neighborhood options, and we avoid all that's touristy unless it's really worth your time. You can go on the assumption that everything in this book is recommended wholeheartedly by our writers and editors. Flip to On the Road with Fodor's to learn more about who they are. It goes without saying that no property pays to be included.

**RATINGS**

Orange stars ★ denote sights and properties that our editors and writers consider the very best in the area covered by the entire book. These, the best of the best, are listed in the Fodor's Choice section in the front of the book. Black stars ★ highlight the sights and properties we deem Highly Recommended, the don't-miss sights within any neighborhood. Sights with numbered map bullets ❶ in the margins tend to be more important than those without bullets.

**SPECIAL SPOTS**

Pleasures & Pastimes focus on experiences that reveal the spirit of London. Also watch for Off the Beaten Path sights. Some are out of the way, some are quirky, and all are worthwhile. When the munchies hit, look for Need a Break? suggestions.

**TIME IT RIGHT**

Check On the Calendar up front and chapters' Timing sections for weather and crowd overviews and best days and times to visit.

**SEE IT ALL**

Use Fodor's exclusive Great Itineraries as a model for your trip. Good Walks in the Exploring chapter guides you to important sights in each neighborhood; ► indicates the starting points of walks and itineraries in the text and on the map.

**BUDGET WELL**

Hotel and restaurant price categories £–£££££ are defined in the opening pages of the **Where to Stay** and **Where to Eat** chapters—expect to find a balanced selection for every budget. For attractions, we always give standard adult admission fees; reductions are usually available for children, students, and senior citizens.

**BASIC INFO**

Smart Travel Tips lists travel essentials for the city. To find the best way to get around, see the transportation section; see individual modes of travel ("Car Travel," "Train Travel") for details.

**ON THE MAPS**

Maps throughout the book show you what's where and help you find your way around. Black and orange numbered bullets ❶❶ in the text correlate to bullets on maps.

| | |
|---|---|
| **BACKGROUND** | We give background information within the chapters in the course of explaining sights as well as in CloseUp boxes and in Understanding London at the end of the book. To get in the mood, review Books & Movies. |
| **FIND IT FAST** | Within the Exploring London chapter, sights are grouped by neighborhood, arranged in a roughly clockwise direction starting with Westminster, at the heart of the city. Where to Eat and Where to Stay are also organized by neighborhood, but alphabetically—Where to Eat is further divided by cuisine type. Nightlife & the Arts and Sports & the Outdoors are arranged alphabetically by entertainment type. In Shopping, a description of the city's main shopping districts is followed by a list of specialty shops grouped according to their focus. Side Trips from London explores Bath, Brighton, Cambridge, Canterbury, Oxford, Stratford-upon-Avon, and Windsor Castle. |
| **DON'T FORGET** | Restaurants are open for lunch and dinner daily unless we state otherwise; we mention dress only when there's a specific requirement and reservations only when they're essential or not accepted—it's always best to book ahead. Hotels have private baths, phone, TVs, and air-conditioning and operate on the European Plan (a.k.a. EP, meaning without meals). We always list facilities but not whether you'll be charged extra to use them, so when pricing accommodations, find out what's included. |
| **SYMBOLS** | |

**Many Listings**

★ Fodor's Choice
★ Highly recommended
⊠ Physical address
✛ Directions
🕮 Mailing address
☎ Telephone
🖷 Fax
⊕ On the Web
✉ E-mail
🎟 Admission fee
☉ Open/closed times
🏴 Start of walk/itinerary
Ⓤ Underground tube station
🖃 Credit cards

**Hotels & Restaurants**

🏨 Hotel
🛏 Number of rooms

🛏 Facilities
🍽 Meal plans
✕ Restaurant
🍷 Reservations
👔 Dress code
🚬 Smoking
🍸 BYOB
✕🏨 Hotel with restaurant that warrants a visit

**Other**

🐾 Family-friendly
🛈 Contact information
⇨ See also
⊠ Branch address
☞ Take note

A trip takes you out of yourself. Concerns of life at home completely disappear, driven away by more immediate thoughts—about, say, what marvels will beguile the next day, or where you'll have dinner. That's where Fodor's comes in. We make sure that you know all your options, so that you don't miss something that's around the next bend just because you didn't know it was there. Because the best memories of your trip might well have nothing to do with what you came to London to see, we guide you to sights large and small all over the city. You might set out to visit Buckingham Palace, but back at home you find yourself unable to forget the August sunshine in St. James's Park, or an early-morning visit to Borough Market. With Fodor's at your side, serendipitous discoveries are never far away.

Our success in showing you every corner of London is a credit to our extraordinary writers. Although there's no substitute for travel advice from a good friend who knows your style, our contributors are the next best thing—the kind of people you would poll for travel advice if you knew them.

Longtime Fodor's contributor Robert Andrews loves warm beer and soggy moors, but hates shopping malls and the sort of weather when you're not sure if it's raining. He lives in Bristol and traveled to nearby Bath to update it for our Side Trips chapter.

Born and raised in San Francisco, Catherine Belonogoff started travel writing during her college days at UC Berkeley when she wrote part of the Fodor's UpClose Los Angeles guide. She also contributes to Fodor's Great Britain. Her research this year included checking out many new good-value lodgings in London. Catherine currently resides in north London and for this edition, she updated the Where to Stay chapter, Smart Travel Tips, the Side Trips to Oxford and Cambridge, and the Books & Movies section.

No matter how many historical and cultured cities she has explored across Europe, writer and editor Jacqueline Brown declares there are equal treasures not far from her own doorstep. A London resident for more than 20 years, she has found both the best and the quirkiest places, as her Fodor's Around London with Kids testifies. Jacqueline has updated the Exploring and Shopping chapters of this book.

Julius Honnor has traveled widely but now lives in London. He has written or updated several guidebooks and is a contributor to Fodor's Great Britain. For this book he updated the Sports & the Outdoors chapters as well as the Brighton and Canterbury Side Trips.

A former Fodor's editor and incorrigible globe trotter, Julie Tomasz currently lives in London. When she's not taking in the latest show at her local pub theater or kicking up her heels at the Soho bars, Julie works as a freelance writer and editor.

London born and bred, Alex Wijeratna is a stalwart of Notting Hill. With English and Sri Lankan roots, Alex is well aware that London's true flavor lies in its ethnic diversity. He has written mainly for newspapers, including the London Times. And he's gratified that London has emerged as a top-notch foodie city. For this edition, he updated the Where to Eat chapter.

## Westminster & Royal London

All things start at Westminster, where there is as much history in a few acres as there is in many entire cities. The ancient Westminster Abbey, crammed with memorials and monuments to the great and the good, can blind you to the spectacular Gothic splendor surrounding you. Whitehall is both an avenue and the heartbeat of the British government; here is the prime minister's official residence, No. 10 Downing Street, and the Horse Guards, where two mounted sentries of the Queen's guard provide a memorable image. Whitehall leads to Trafalgar Square and the incomparable National Gallery, with the National Portrait Gallery just next door. From the grand Admiralty Arch, the Mall leads straight to Buckingham Palace, as unprepossessing on the outside as it is sumptuous inside. The streets are wide and the vistas are long—the perfect backdrop for the pomp and pageantry of royal occasions.

## Belgravia

Just a short carriage ride from Buckingham Palace is London's most splendidly aristocratic enclave, with block after block of grand, porticoed mansions. Built in the mid-1800s, it is residential, untouched by neon, with an authentic vintage patina. Most of its streets are lined with terraced row houses, all painted Wedgwood-china white (to signify they remain the property of the Duke of Westminster). Pedigree-proud locations include Belgrave Square, Grosvenor Crescent, and Belgrave Place. Also check out the chic alleyways, called "mews."

## Bloomsbury

The literary set that made the name Bloomsbury world famous has left hardly a trace, but this remains the heart of learned London. The University of London is here; so are the Law Courts and the British Museum. With the British Library parked just north at St. Pancras, a greater number of books can probably be found in Bloomsbury than in all the rest of London. Virginia Woolf and T. S. Eliot would be pleased to note that some of London's most beautiful domestic architecture, elegant houses that would have been familiar to Dr. Johnson, still line the area's prim squares. At one, Charles Dickens worked on *Oliver Twist* at a tall upright clerk's desk.

## Chelsea

Chelsea has always beckoned to freethinkers and hipsters—from Sir Thomas More to Isadora Duncan (she couldn't find a place to stay her first night, so she decamped to the graveyard at Chelsea Old Church, which natives *still* insist is a lovely place to stay). Major sights include Christopher Wren's magisterial Royal Hospital, the site of the Chelsea Flower Show, Cheyne Walk, where Henry James and Dante Gabriel Rossetti once lived and the King's Road, whose boutiques gave birth to the paisleyed '60s and the pink-haired punk '70s.

## The City

Known as "the Square Mile," the City is to London what Wall Street is to Manhattan. As the site of the Celtic settlement the Romans called Londinium, this is the oldest part of London. Unfortunately, thanks to blocks of high-rise apartments and steel skyscrapers, it looks like the newest part. Yet, within and around the capital-C City are some of London's most memorable attractions, including St. Paul's Cathedral and storybook Tower Bridge. Charles and Diana tied the knot at St. Paul's but they could have found other equally beautiful options here—St. Bride's (its distinctive multitiered spire gave rise to today's wedding cakes), St. Giles Without Cripplegate, and St. Mary-le-Bow. The legendary Tower of London is at the east border of the City.

### Covent Garden

Just east of Soho, Covent Garden is one of the busiest, most raffishly enjoyable parts of the city. Continental-style open-air cafés create a very un-English environment. Warehouses, once cavernous and grim, now accommodate fashion boutiques and a huge variety of shops favored by the trendy. A network of narrow streets, arcades, and pedestrian malls, the area is dominated by the Piazza, the scene of a food market in the 1830s and a flower market in the 1870s. Today the indoor-outdoor complex overflows with clothing shops and crafts stalls, and the remodernized Royal Opera House opens onto the Piazza.

### Docklands

The epicenter of London's modern growth is the Isle of Dogs, once a neighborhood fit only for canines. Now you'll find the space-age architecture (Canary Wharf's No. 1 Canada Square being the most prominent, literally), waterways from the old docks, and the nifty overhead electric Docklands Light Railway linking buildings to wharves. The Museum in Docklands traces the history of this quarter. The Thames Barrier strides across the river, between the east end on the north bank and Greenwich on the south bank, and its visitor center and pedestrian walkway presents an exciting panorama.

### The East End

The 19th-century slums, immortalized by Charles Dickens and the evocative etchings of Gustave Doré, are a relic of the past. Today the area possesses a haunting beauty and a warm spirit of humor and friendliness. On Sunday you'll find 21st-century versions of the medieval fair: Spitalfields Market and Petticoat Lane. Other fascinating sights include the Geffrye Museum, an overlooked cluster of wonderful historic interiors; Hawksmoor's Christ Church; and the Blind Beggar, the Victorian den of iniquity where Salvation Army founder William Booth was moved to preach his first sermon. Off the main thoroughfare, tap into the true pulse of East End life by exploring the lanes and alleys that still make up one of the world's most fascinating melting pots. Down by the river, sprawling eastward from Tower Bridge, the old docks have been regenerated into a modern landscape of glittering office developments.

### Greenwich

A quick 8-mi jaunt down the Thames will bring you past the National Maritime Museum and the *Cutty Sark* to Greenwich's Old Royal Observatory, where, if time stood still, all the world's timepieces would be off. When you tire of straddling the hemispheres at the Greenwich Meridian, take a stroll through the acres of parkland or, on weekends, the crafts and antiques markets. Sir Christopher Wren's Royal Naval College and Inigo Jones's Queen House both scale architectural heights, while Richard Rogers's now-closed Millennium Dome encapsulates modern style, for better or worse. The pretty streets of Greenwich house numerous bookstores and antiques shops.

## Hampstead

One of the great glories of England is the English village, and on the northern outskirts of London you'll find one of the most fetching: Hampstead. The classic Georgian houses, picturesque streets, cafés, and delis attract arts and media types and the plain wealthy. An amble along Church Row—possibly the finest terrace of 18th-century houses in London—will prove the pulling power of the area. London's most beautiful Vermeer painting is on view at Kenwood House (whose park hosts grand concerts and fireworks in summer). You can visit the Freud Museum and the Keats House, where the poet penned his immortal "Ode to a Nightingale." Or go bird-watching in the 800-plus emerald acres of Hampstead Heath.

## Hyde Park, Kensington Gardens

Together with St. James's Park and Green Park, these beautiful, leafy, breathing spaces run to almost 600 acres. The handsome trees and quiet walks will refresh you as thoroughly as these grounds refreshed Henry VIII centuries ago after a hard day's shenanigans. In the Regency era, splendid horseflesh and equipages were the grand attraction; today, the soapbox orators at Hyde Park Corner (most oratorical on Sunday mornings) remain grand entertainment. Sooner or later everyone heads to the Long Water in Kensington Gardens for one of London's most beloved sights: the Peter Pan statue. Then circumnavigate the Round Pond or swim in the Serpentine Lido.

## Knightsbridge & Kensington

Within the district's cavalcade of streets lined with decorous houses are small, sleepy squares; delightful pubs nestled away in back lanes; and antiques shops, their windows aglow with the luminous colors of oil paintings. Not surprisingly, the capital's snazziest department stores, Harrods and Harvey Nichols, are also here. Head first for the area's main attraction, the great museum complex of South Kensington. Raphael and Constable canvases, Ossie Clark couture, and William Morris chairs beckon at the Victoria & Albert Museum, a showcase for the decorative arts. Next to the V&A come two museums devoted to science, including the Natural History Museum. Most delightful are two historic homes: Leighton House, Lord Leighton's stunning Persian extravaganza, and the Linley Sambourne House, whose elegant Edwardian interiors were featured in *A Room with a View*. Regroup at Kensington Palace—its state rooms and royal dress collection are open for viewing—then repair to its elegant Orangery for a pot of Earl Grey.

## Notting Hill & Holland Park

These are two of London's most fashionable and coveted residential areas. Notting Hill, around Portobello Road, is a trendsetting square mile of multiethnicity, galleries, small and exciting shops, and see-and-be-seen-in restaurants. The style-watching media dubbed the natives—musicians, novelists, and fashion plates—"Notting Hillbillies." If Notting Hill is for the young, neighboring Holland Park is entirely the opposite—the area's leafy streets are full of expensive white-stucco Victorians and lead to bucolic Holland Park itself.

## Regent's Park

Helping to frame the northern border of the city, Regent's Park is home to the much-loved zoo and Regent's Park Open-Air Theatre. A walk around the perimeter of the park is a must for devotees of classical architecture; the payoff is a view of John Nash's Terraces, a grandiose series of white-stucco terraced houses, built around 1810 for the "People of Quality" who demanded London homes as nearly as possible resembling their grand country estates. In summer be sure to take in the rose-bedecked Queen Mary's Gardens. Next, head over to the open-air theater for, perhaps, a picture-perfect performance of *A Midsummer Night's Dream*.

## St. James's & Mayfair

St. James's and Mayfair form the core of the West End, the city's smartest and most desirable central area, where there is no shortage of history and gorgeous architecture, custom-built for ogling the lifestyles of London's rich and famous. Although many will say Mayfair is only a state of mind, the heart of Mayfair has shifted from the 19th-century's Park Lane to Carlos Place and Mount Street. Of course, the shops of New and Old Bond streets lure the wealthy, but the window-shopping is free. Mayfair is primarily residential, with two public grand houses to see: Apsley House, the Duke of Wellington's home, and, on elegant Manchester Square, the Wallace Collection, situated in a palatial town house filled with old master paintings and fine French furniture. The district of St. James's—named after the centuries-old palace that lies at its center—remains the ultimate enclave of the old-fashioned gentleman's London. Here you'll find Pall Mall, with its many noted clubs, including the Reform Club, and Jermyn Street, where you can shop like the Duke of Windsor.

## Soho & Theatreland

Once known infamously as London's red-light district, Soho these days is more stylish than seedy—now it's populated with film and record bigwigs (Sir Paul McCartney's offices are here). The area is not especially rich architecturally, but it is nonetheless intriguing. The density of Continental residents around quaint Soho Square means some of London's best restaurants—whether pricey Italian, budget Chinese, or the latest opening—are in the vicinity. Shaftesbury Avenue cuts through the southern part of Soho; this is Theatreland, where you'll find almost 50 West End theaters. It's beloved of those who admire Shakespeare, Maggie Smith, and *Phantom*. To the south lie Leicester Square, London's answer to Times Square, and Charing Cross Road, the bibliophile's dream.

## The South Bank

Totally rebuilt after the bombs of World War II flattened the remains of medieval Southwark (only a few stones of the Bishop of Winchester's Palace still stand), the South Bank has undergone a renaissance. If William Shakespeare returned today, however, he would be delighted to find a complete reconstruction of his Globe Theatre, not far from where the original closed in 1642. In fact, this side of the Thames—walk along the riverside embankment for great views of the city—has become a perch for diehard culture vultures: the Design Museum is here, as is the gigantic Tate Modern gallery, a new use for an old power station. The Millennium Bridge is a picturesque pedestrian walkway to St. Paul's Cathedral. Nearby is the South Bank Arts Complex—with its Royal National Theatre and Royal Festival Hall. And who can resist the London Dungeon—a waxwork extravaganza featuring blood 'n' guts—where "a perfectly horrible experience" is guaranteed. Towering over all is the British Airways London Eye, the tallest observation wheel in Europe.

## The Thames Upstream

The most powerful palaces—Chiswick, Kew Palace and Gardens, Osterley Park, Richmond, and Putney—were linked closely to London by the river. A river cruise along Old Father Thames to some of these famous places, enveloped with serenity and rolling greenery, makes an idyllic retreat from the city on a sweltering summer day. Stroll around and just enjoy the rural air or find your way out of the famous maze at Hampton Court Palace, England's version of Versailles.

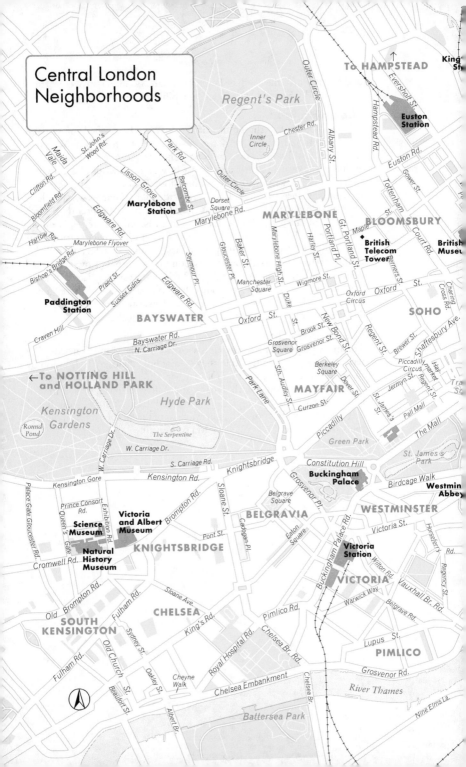

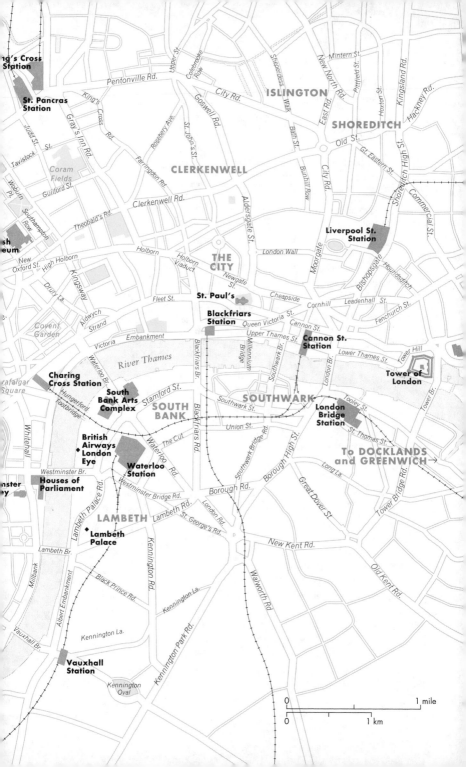

## London in 5 Days

Use the efficient itineraries below to keep you on track as you explore both the famous sights and those off the beaten path. Although you'll need those red double-decker buses and the Underground to cover long distances, you'll soon discover how London rewards those who stroll its streets. Shuffle the itinerary segments with the closing hours, listed below, in mind.

## DAY 1

Spend your first day in Royal London, which contains much that is historic and traditional in British life. Get an early start at medieval Westminster Abbey—if Prince Charles becomes king, this is where he will be crowned. After an hour exploring the abbey, make the 15-minute walk (or Tube it from Westminster to St. James's Park) to catch the Changing of the Guard at 11:20, outside Buckingham Palace. Optimally you need to get there by 10:45. In season an alternative option is to tour the palace. Next stroll down the Mall, enjoying the view the monarch sees when she rides in her gilded coach to open Parliament every year. Passing King George IV's glorious Carlton House Terrace, walk through the Admiralty Arch into Trafalgar Square, the very center of the city. Spend an hour or two in the National Gallery or go instead to nearby St. Martin's Place and the National Portrait Gallery, a visual who's who of England. From Trafalgar Square, head south to Whitehall, which is lined with grand government buildings, the Banqueting House, outside of which King Charles I was beheaded, and the Horse Guards Parade (Her Majesty's mounted guardsmen make a great photo op). Head past 10 Downing Street,

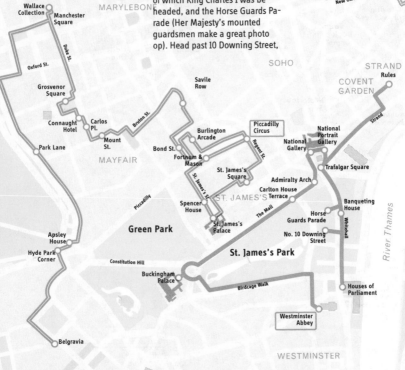

the prime minister's residence, to the Houses of Parliament. To see them, you have two options: either wait in line for the limited seats available in the Strangers Gallery of either house (use the St. Stephen's Entrance opposite the abbey) or prebook a tour, which shows off the state rooms. Eventually you'll hear Big Ben signaling the approaching dinner hour. It's best to do this tour on Tuesday or Wednesday. From August through March, the Changing of the Guard (usually a daily event) occurs only every other day; check schedules. Buckingham Palace is open daily in season—from late August to early October. When the Houses of Parliament are open to visitors, the House of Lords is closed from Thursday to Sunday, the House of Commons from Friday to Sunday; times are complex, so check the schedule in Chapter 1.

Treasure), then explore bookish Bloomsbury, including the Dickens House Museum and the British Library (on Euston Road, 10 blocks north), perhaps tracking the spirit of Virginia Woolf on Bedford, Russell, and Bloomsbury squares. Now head southeast to visit the Regency delight that is Sir John Soane's Museum at Lincoln's Inn. Continue south to Fleet Street, then east to 17th-century St. Paul's Cathedral, the city's presiding spirit. Wander south to Blackfriars Bridge and cross the Thames to Southwark; stop at the Tate Modern art gallery or take in a play at Shakespeare's Globe Theatre. At day's end, journey along Old Father Thames either east to Le Pont de la Tour or west to the OXO Tower for a riverside dinner. Don't plan on doing Day 2 on Sunday, when both the Dickens House Museum and Sir John Soane's Museum are closed. Note that Shakespeare's Globe stages plays in the open-air theater only from May to September.

Square, then continue on to palatial Spencer House, which once housed the ancestors of the late Princess Diana. From Piccadilly travel north for some ritzy window-shopping on Bond Street, in the Burlington Arcade, and along Savile Row, continuing on through Mayfair via Mount Street, Carlos Place—tea at the Connaught Hotel, anyone?—and Grosvenor Square. From here take Duke Street north to view the superb paintings at the Wallace Collection on Manchester Square. Keep going south to Park Lane and, just before Hyde Park Corner, visit Apsley House, by the Duke of Wellington's mansion. To the southwest is the splendidly aristocratic enclave of Belgravia. Apsley House is closed on Monday, and Spencer House is open only on Sunday.

## DAY FOUR

London legends populate this itinerary. First take a break from the city and travel up to its most famous "village," Hampstead. After taking in the picturesque houses, chic cafés, and Church Row—London's most complete Georgian street—move on to Abbey Road (if you're a Beatlemaniac), in nearby St. John's Wood. Then take the Tube down to Baker Street and visit the Sherlock Holmes Museum or Madame Tussaud's (a must for kids). Go north

Fleet St.    St. Paul's Cathedral

Blackfriars

THE CITY

Blackfriars Bridge    River Thames

OXO Tower    Tate Modern    Shakespeare's Globe Theatre

Southwark St.

SOUTHWARK

Tooley St.    Tower Bridge

Le Pont de la Tour

On Sunday the Banqueting House is closed, and Westminster Abbey (except for the museum) is open only to those attending services.

## DAY 2

Think of this day as London 101—a tour of the city's postcard sights. Begin at the British Museum (home of the Elgin Marbles, the Rosetta Stone, and the Sutton Hoo

## DAY 3

Explore St. James's and Mayfair, the core of London's posh West End. From Piccadilly Circus go west on Piccadilly to splurge on breakfast at the Queen's grocers, Fortnum & Mason. For a brush with royalty, detour several blocks to view the outside of Prince Charles's Tudor-era home, St. James's Palace near St. James's

### MAP KEY

Day 1
Day 2
Day 3

to Regent's Park and its elegant
Cumberland Terrace and Chester
Terrace. In the afternoon take the
Tube to Tower Hill and the Tower of
London to see the Crown Jewels
and the Tower Ravens. At dusk
cross the street to the Tower Hill
Tube stop to pick up a spine-chill-
ing Jack the Ripper Mystery Walk
through the East End.
Note that the East End Jack the
Ripper tours begin at 7 PM.

## DAY FIVE

This segment of your itinerary is
all about shopping, history, and
priceless art. Begin at the "museum mile" of South Kensington.
See either the Victoria & Albert
Museum, or, if you have children,
opt for the Natural History Museum or the Science Museum.
Head up Brompton Road for lunch
in Knightsbridge and shopping at

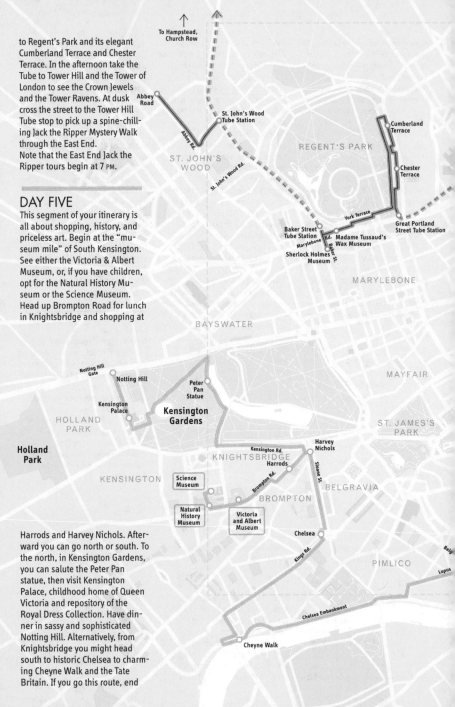

Harrods and Harvey Nichols. Afterward you can go north or south. To
the north, in Kensington Gardens,
you can salute the Peter Pan
statue, then visit Kensington
Palace, childhood home of Queen
Victoria and repository of the
Royal Dress Collection. Have dinner in sassy and sophisticated
Notting Hill. Alternatively, from
Knightsbridge you might head
south to historic Chelsea to charming Cheyne Walk and the Tate
Britain. If you go this route, end

the day by seeing a play or musical in the West End's Theatreland. Any day is fine for this tour.

## If You Have More Time

Spectacular day trips lie upriver and down. To the east of central London is Greenwich, with attractions such as the *Cutty Sark*, a 19th-century clipper, and the not-to-be-missed National Maritime Museum. Westward on the Thames from London lie destinations that take you back, not forward, in time: Chiswick House; Kew Gardens; Syon House; and sprawling Hampton Court Palace, half rose-red Tudor brick, half serenely classical.

Apsley House. You're in posh Mayfair now, so stroll to the Burlington Arcade and Bond Street for some shopping, then head north to view the treasures at the Wallace Collection. From Marble Arch take the Tube to Kensington High Street and Kensington Palace. After touring the historic palace, repair to its Orangery for tea. Finish the day by seeing a play.

## A KID'S DAY OUT

Get an early start with a Tube ride to the Tower of London, where you can see the Beefeater guards (plus its resident ravens). Across the street see the lively presentation about the Thames in the Tower Bridge. Cross to the south bank and hang a left toward Butler's

Wharf for lunch. If you have teens, stop on Tooley Street at the London Dungeon, a hoot of a horror waxworks show. Recross the river to catch a ferry at Tower Pier for a 15-minute cruise to Waterloo Pier (or, as far as Westminster Pier, from which you can walk across Westminster Bridge and then backtrack to Waterloo Pier; if it's raining, tube it from Tower Hill to Waterloo Station). On the way, watch a film at the BFI London IMAX Cinema; ride British Airways London Eye, the world's largest observation wheel; and tour the London Aquarium.

## If You Have 3 Days

Follow the itineraries for Days 1 and 2 above; then begin your third day at the legend-haunted Tower of London. After a morning tour, take the Tube or a taxi to Hyde Park Circle to see one of London's most spectacular town houses,

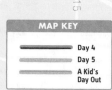

| MAP KEY | |
|---|---|
| ▬▬▬▬ | Day 4 |
| ▬▬▬▬ | Day 5 |
| ▬▬▬▬ | A Kid's Day Out |

# World Time Zones

Numbers below vertical bands relate each zone to Greenwich Mean Time (0 hrs.).
Local times frequently differ from these general indications,
as indicated by light-face numbers on map.

| | | | |
|---|---|---|---|
| Algiers .............**5** | Istanbul ............**16** | Mecca ..............**23** | Vienna .............**11** |
| Athens .............**17** | Jerusalem ..........**18** | Moscow ............**21** | Warsaw ............**12** |
| Baghdad ...........**22** | Johannesburg .......**20** | Nairobi ............**19** | Zürich ..............**7** |
| Berlin .............**10** | Lisbon .............**4** | Paris ...............**6** | |
| Budapest ..........**13** | London | Reykjavík ..........**1** | |
| Copenhagen ........**9** | (Greenwich) ........**3** | Rome ..............**15** | |
| Dublin .............**2** | Madrid ............**14** | Stockholm ..........**8** | |

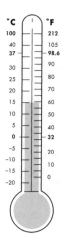

The heaviest tourist season in Britain runs mid-April through mid-October, with another peak around Christmas—though the tide never really ebbs. Spring is the time to see the countryside and the royal London parks and gardens at their freshest; early summer to catch the roses and full garden splendor; fall to enjoy near-ideal exploring conditions. The British take their vacations mainly in July and August, and the resorts are crowded. London in summer, however, though full of visitors, is also full of interesting things to see and do. But be warned: air-conditioning is rarely found in places other than department stores, modern restaurants, hotels, and cinemas in London, and in a hot summer you'll swelter. Winter can be rather dismal and is frequently wet and usually cold, but all the theaters, concerts, and exhibitions go full speed.

## Climate

London's weather has always been contrary, and in recent years it has proved red-hot and cool by turns. It is virtually impossible to forecast what the pattern might be, but you can be fairly certain that it will not be what you expect. The main feature of the British weather is that it is generally mild—with some savage exceptions, especially in summer. It is also fairly damp—though even that has been changing in recent years, with the odd bout of drought. The following are the average daily maximum and minimum temperatures for London.

Forecasts **Weather Channel** ⊕ www.weather.com.

## LONDON

| Jan. | 43F | 6C | May | 62F | 17C | Sept. | 65F | 19C |
|---|---|---|---|---|---|---|---|---|
| | 36 | 2 | | 47 | 8 | | 52 | 11 |
| Feb. | 44F | 7C | June | 69F | 20C | Oct. | 58F | 14C |
| | 36 | 2 | | 53 | 12 | | 46 | 8 |
| Mar. | 50F | 10C | July | 71F | 22C | Nov. | 50F | 10C |
| | 38 | 3 | | 56 | 14 | | 42 | 5 |
| Apr. | 56F | 13C | Aug. | 71F | 21C | Dec. | 45F | 7C |
| | 42 | 6 | | 56 | 13 | | 38 | 4 |

# ON THE CALENDAR

Top seasonal events in and around London include the Chelsea Flower Show in May; Derby Day at Epsom Racecourse, Wimbledon Lawn Tennis Championships and Henley Regatta in June; and the London Arts Season from February through March, which combines many events in theater, art, and music with good deals on hotels and meals out.

There is a complete list of ticket agencies in *Britain Events,* available in person only from the Britain Visitor Centre. When in London, check the weekly magazine *Time Out,* available at newsstands, for an ongoing calendar of special events. Or, for 60 pence per minute, call London Tourist Board's Visitorcall service, which offers the latest on events throughout the city.

## ONGOING

| | |
|---|---|
| Mar. 17–28 & Sept. 15–24 | The Chelsea Antiques Fair is a twice-yearly fair with a wide range of pre-1830 pieces for sale. ✉ *Old Town Hall, King's Rd., Chelsea SW3 4PW* ☎ *01444/482514.* |
| Late May– Late Aug. | Glyndebourne Festival Opera is a unique opportunity to see international stars in a bucolic setting. Tickets go fast and early booking starts on May 2. ✉ *Glyndebourne Festival Opera, Box 2624, Lewes, Sussex BN8 5UW* ☎ *01273/813813.* |
| Late May– Late Aug. | Shakespeare Under the Stars gives you the chance to see the Bard's plays performed at Regent's Park Open-Air Theatre. Performances are usually Monday–Saturday at 8 PM, with matinees on Wednesday, Thursday, and Saturday. ✉ *Inner Circle, Regent's Park NW1* ☎ *020/7486–2431.* |
| Mid-June– Early Sept. | Kenwood Lakeside Concerts offers fireworks and classical concerts under the stars in the park of London's regal stately house. ✉ *Kenwood House, Hampstead La., Hampstead NW3* ☎ *020/7973–3427.* |
| Mid-July– Mid-Sept. | Henry Wood Promenade Concerts is a marvelous series of concerts at the Royal Albert Hall. ✉ *Box Office, Royal Albert Hall, Kensington Gore, Kensington SW7 2AP* ☎ *020/7589–8212.* |

## WINTER

| | |
|---|---|
| Dec. | The Olympia International Show Jumping Championships (☎ 0870/733–0733), an international equestrian competition, takes place in Olympia's Grand Hall. |
| Dec. 31 | New Year's Eve at Trafalgar Square is a huge, freezing, sometimes drunken slosh through the fountains to celebrate the new year. Unorganized by any official body, it's held in the ceremonial heart of London under an enormous Christmas tree, which is a gift from the |

people of Norway and set up from early December to early January. Unlike Americans, however, most Brits celebrate New Year's Eve at home.

| | |
|---|---|
| Jan. 1 | The London Parade is a good ole U.S.-style extravaganza complete with cheerleaders, floats, and marching bands, and led by the Lord Mayor of London. It starts on the south side of Westminster Bridge at noon, passing Parliament Square, Whitehall, Trafalgar Square, Lower Regent Street, Piccadilly, and finishing in Berkeley Square around 3 PM. No tickets are required. |
| Jan. 31 | Charles I Commemoration is held on the anniversary of the monarch's execution and brings out Londoners dressed in 17th-century garb for a march tracing his last walk from St. James's Palace to the Banqueting House in Whitehall. |
| Late Mar. | Head of the River Boat Race offers the spectacle of 420 eight-man crews from Oxford and Cambridge universities dipping their 6,720 oars in the Thames as they race from Mortlake to Putney. The best view is from Surrey Bank above Chiswick Bridge (Tube to Chiswick); check *Time Out* for the starting time, which depends on the tide. The Oxford versus Cambridge University Boat Race takes place often the week after, over the same 4½-mi course, carrying on a tradition going back to around 1829. In 1912 both boats sank spectacularly. |
| Late Mar. | British Antique Dealers' Association Fair, the newest of the major fairs, is large and prestigious, with many affordable pieces. ✉ *Duke of York's Headquarters, King's Rd., Chelsea SW3* ☎ 020/7589–6108. |
| **SPRING** | |
| Mid-Apr. | London Marathon is a New York–style marathon through London's streets. Runners from 68 countries start in Greenwich and Blackheath at 9–9:30 AM, then run via Docklands and Canary Wharf, the Tower of London and Parliament Square to finish in the Mall. |
| Apr. 21 | Queen's Birthday earns a showy 41-gun salute at Hyde Park. In June, Elizabeth II's ceremonial b-day is celebrated by Trooping the Colour. |
| Mid-May | Punch and Judy Festival is held on the second Sunday in May and offers a May Fayre Procession in the morning, services at St. Paul's Church, then puppet shows until dusk. A lovely event for children of all ages. ✉ *Covent Garden Piazza, London WC2* ☎ 020/7375–0441. |
| Mid-May | Royal Windsor Horse Show (☎ 0870/121–5370) is a major show-jumping event attended by some members of the Royal Family. |

| | |
|---|---|
| May 23–26 | Chelsea Flower Show, Britain's most prestigious flower show covers 22 acres and is always graced by the Royals. ⊠ *Royal Hospital Rd., Chelsea SW3* ☎ *0870/906–3781.* |
| Early June | Beating Retreat by the Guards Massed Bands is when more than 500 musicians parade at Horse Guards, Whitehall. *Tickets from* ⊠ *Household Division Fund, Horse Guards, Westminster SW1A 2AX* ☎ *020/7414–2271.* |
| Early June | Derby Day is the best-known event on the horse-racing calendar. *Information from United Racecourses Ltd.* ⊠ *Epsom Downs Racecourse, Epsom, Surrey KT18 5LQ* ☎ *013727/26311.* |
| Mid-June | The Grosvenor House Antiques Fair is one of the most prestigious antiques fairs in Britain. ⊠ *Grosvenor House Hotel, Park La., Mayfair W1A 3AA* ☎ *020/7399–8100.* |
| Mid-June | Royal Meeting at Ascot brings the horsey set and their enormous hats out in force the third week in June (Tuesday–Friday; Thursday is the high-fashion Ladies Day). General admission is available but reserve months in advance; write for tickets to the Royal Enclosure (you must be sponsored). ⊘ *Protocol Office, American Embassy, 24 Grosvenor Sq., London W1A 1AE General admission:* ⊠ *Ascot Racecourse, Ascot, Berkshire SL5 7JN* ☎ *01344/876876.* |
| Mid-June | Trooping the Colour, Queen Elizabeth's colorful official birthday parade, is held at Horse Guards, Whitehall, usually on the second or third Saturday of June. Write for tickets *only* between January 1 and February 28, enclosing a self-addressed stamped envelope. ⊠ *Ticket Office, Headquarters, Household Division, Horse Guards, Westminster SW1A 2AX* ☎ *020/7414–2479.* |
| **SUMMER** | |
| Late June–Early July | Henley Royal Regatta (☎01491/572153), an international rowing event and top social occasion, takes place at Henley-upon-Thames, Oxfordshire. |
| Late June–Early July | The Wimbledon Lawn Tennis Championships are held at the All England Lawn Tennis and Croquet Club in Wimbledon. Write early to enter the lottery for tickets for Centre and Number One courts; tickets for outside courts are available daily at the gate. ⊠ *Church Rd., Wimbledon SW19 5AE* ☎ *020/8946–2244.* |
| Early July | Hampton Court Palace Flower Show is a five-day event that nearly rivals the Chelsea Flower Show for glamour. ⊠ *East Molesey* ☎ *020/7834–4333, 0870/906–3791 ticket agency.* |
| Late Aug. | Notting Hill Carnival (☎ 020/8964–0544) is one of the liveliest street festivals in England. Caribbean foods, reggae music, and street parades are part of the swirling event, usually held on the last Sunday and Monday in August. |

| FALL | |
|---|---|
| Sept. | Open House (☎ 020/7267–7697) is a rare one-day chance to view historic London interiors of buildings usually closed to the public, organized by Architectural Dialogue. |
| Early Oct. | Pearly Harvest Festival Service draws a crowd of costermongers to the Church of St. Martin-in-the-Fields on the first Sunday in October. The Pearly Kings and Queens strut their famous costumes. ✉ *Trafalgar Sq., Covent Garden WC2* ☎ *020/7930–0089.* |
| Early Nov. | London to Brighton Veteran Car Run (☎ 01753/681736) is a run from Hyde Park in London to Brighton in East Sussex. |
| Early Nov. | Lord Mayor's Procession and Show (☎ 020/7332–1456) is a procession for the lord mayor's inauguration that takes place from the Guildhall in the City to the Royal Courts of Justice. |
| Early Nov. | Remembrance Sunday, the Sunday closest to November 11, commemorates all those who have suffered and died in war. There's a ceremony at the Cenotaph in Whitehall, and the Queen and other dignitaries lay wreaths on the monument. |
| Nov. 5 | Guy Fawkes Day celebrates a foiled 1605 attempt to blow up Parliament. Fireworks are presented throughout London, but the place to be is the bonfire festivity on Primrose Hill near Camden Town. |

# PLEASURES & PASTIMES

## Food, Glorious Food: The Delights of Dining
London today ranks among the world's top dining scenes. This is largely thanks to a wave of superstar chefs such as Marco Pierre White and Gordon Ramsay, and style guru and restaurateur Sir Terence Conran, who transformed stodgy, unimaginative British cooking and stiff, traditional restaurants into vibrant, hip culinary hot spots. A fresh approach to food preparation precipitated this restaurant revolution—a cuisine that most refer to as "Modern British."

Savvy Londoners looking for a dinner bargain go for the nearest tandoori house—Indian food has gone from a cliché to national-dish territory. Londoners have now enlarged their purview to encompass most of the world's cuisines. In the space of two weeks, diners can cover as much tongue-tingling ground as in a two-week package tour of exotic, far-flung places.

So many people are eating ethnic that the indigenous caff (the British all-day diner)—which serves such grab-and-gulp goodies as fish-and-chips, or eggs, bacon, black pudding, mushrooms, toast, baked beans, and ketchup—is becoming less and less common in central London. Today, such native delicacies as the cockles, winkles, and jellied eels found in the cockney stalls of the East End appear as just one more exotic cuisine among many.

## Cheers! The Pub Experience
Londoners could no more live without their "local" than they could forgo dinner. The pub—or public house, to give it its full title—is ingrained in the British psyche as social center, bolt-hole, second home. Pub culture—revolving around pints, pool, darts, screened soccer and sports—is still male dominated; however, as a result of the gentrification trend by the major breweries (which own most pubs), transforming many ancient smoke- and spit-stained dives into fantasy Edwardian drawing rooms, women have been entering their welcoming doors in increasing numbers. The move has been toward female-friendly spaces, identified by large picture windows, more mirrors, candles, good food, and hardwood floors. The social function is the same: these are English pubs, but not as Londoners formerly knew them.

When on a London pub crawl, you must remember one thing: arcane licensing laws forbid the serving of alcohol after 11 PM (10:30 on Sunday; there are different rules for restaurants)—a circumstance you see in action at 10 minutes to 11, when the "last orders" bell signals a stampede to the bar. After many decades, however, some relaxation of these unpopular laws is in evidence with weekend "extensions" being granted, especially in Soho, plus a slew of clubs/bars/pubs that get around them by charging a moderate cover after 11 PM.

## Theater

An evening taking in a play is a vital element of any trip to London. Most people head first for the West End, the city's fabled "Theatreland." Here, you might catch screen actors doing star turns, fabulous musical revivals such as *My Fair Lady,* more than one Andrew Lloyd Webber extravaganza, and Agatha Christie's apparently immortal *The Mousetrap,* which opened in 1955. Then there is that great mainstay, Shakespeare. Shakespeare supplies the backbone to the theatrical life of the city; there's hardly been a day since the one on which the Bard breathed his last when one of his plays, in some shape or form, was not being performed. Indeed, London remains a theatergoer's town. Spain has its bullfights, Italy its opera, Britain its theater.

## Music

London has four world-class orchestras. The London Symphony Orchestra is in residence at the Barbican Centre, while the London Philharmonic lives at the Royal Festival Hall—one of the finest concert halls in Europe. Between the Barbican and the South Bank, there are concert performances almost every night of the year. The Barbican also presents chamber music concerts in partnership with such celebrated orchestras as the City of London Sinfonia. The Royal Albert Hall during the Promenade Concert season ("The Proms," July–September) is a don't-miss pleasure. Also look for the lunchtime concerts held throughout the city in either smaller concert halls, arts-center foyers, or churches; they usually cost less than £5 or are free. St. John's, Smith Square, and St. Martin-in-the-Fields are the major venues for these, and they also present evening concerts.

## Ballet & Opera

The two key players in London's opera scene are the Royal Opera House in Covent Garden and the more innovative English National Opera, which presents English-language productions at the London Coliseum. The Royal Opera House's current theater has undergone a monumental renovation, and the building has been very well received. The renowned Royal Ballet, which performs classical and contemporary repertoire, now has a permanent home in the Royal Opera House's spectacular state-of-the-art Victorian theater.

## Best Foot Forward: Walking Through London

London is a great walking city because so many of its real treasures are untouted: tiny alleyways barely visible on the map, garden squares, churchyards, shop windows, sudden vistas of skyline or park. It is, however, big—very big. And often rather damp. With the obvious precautions of comfortable, weatherproof shoes and an umbrella, this activity might well become your favorite pastime.

# FODOR'S CHOICE

The sights, restaurants, hotels, and other travel experiences on these pages are our editors' top picks—our Fodor's Choices. They're the best of their type in London—not to be missed and always worth your time. In the chapters that follow, you will find all the details.

## LODGING

**£££££** | **Covent Garden Hotel.** Painted silks, ottomans, and off-duty celebrities are the stars of this stylish hotel.

**£££££** | **The Dorchester.** Off-the-scale opulence *and* charm with 1,500 square yards of gold leaf and 1,100 square yards of marble in the heart of Mayfair.

**£££££** | **The Lanesborough.** You'll get your own butler for your stay at this stylish, luxurious hotel on Hyde Park Corner.

**£££££** | **Mandarin Oriental Hyde Park.** Unbeatable service is the highlight of this 1880s hotel between Knightsbridge and Hyde Park.

**£££££** | **Milestone Hotel & Apartments.** Across the street from Kensington Gardens, this Victorian brick masterpiece offers impeccable personal service.

**£££££** | **One Aldwych.** The ultimate in 21st-century style, and the swimming pool has underwater music.

**£££–££££** | **Miller's Residence.** Like living in an issue of *World of Interiors*, this small house in Notting Hill is a veritable gallery of antiques.

**£££–££££** | **The Portobello.** An eccentric Notting Hill hotel with antique rooms, including one with a round bed and Victorian bathing machine.

## BUDGET LODGING

**££** | **Arosfa Hotel.** Once the house of pre-Raphaelite artist John Everett Millais, it's now a family-run, comfortable B&B.

**££** | **County Hall Travel Inn Capital.** What it lacks in trendy decor, it makes up for with an enviable riverside location and a low price.

**££** | **Hampstead Village Guesthouse.** This chic bohemian house on a residential street in the village atmosphere of north London offers a home away from home with a Victorian decor.

**££** | **St. Margaret's.** Near the British Museum and in a quiet, dignified area of London, this guesthouse is run by an extremely friendly and helpful Italian family.

**£** | **Alhambra Hotel.** Here's one of the best bargains in Bloomsbury; rooms are small but definitely good value.

| | |
|---|---|
| £ | **Portobello Gold.** This funky, alternative accommodation resides on London's best known antiques shopping street. |

## RESTAURANTS

| | |
|---|---|
| ££££–£££££ | **River Café.** London's superstar Italian restaurant, which started a revolution with its single-estate olive oils and glorious, fresh ingredients. |
| £££–£££££ | **Club Gascon.** The tapas-style new French cuisine is served on a slab of rock, rather than on a plate at this sexy scene restaurant. |
| ££–£££££ | **Locanda Locatelli.** The food here is incredibly accomplished—superb risottos, silky handmade pastas, beautiful desserts. |
| ££££ | **Gordon Ramsay at Claridge's.** Nobody does it better than this hot spot's eponymous French-inspired chef, so most book six months in advance. |
| ££££ | **Sketch.** Dine in the astronomical Lecture Room restaurant, or go disco-dining in the much cheaper Gallery, and check out the tearoom, art space, bookshop, and two bars, East and West. |
| £££–££££ | **The Cow.** A chic gastro-pub, the Cow serves oysters, salmon cakes, and baked brill downstairs, and Anglo-French specialties upstairs, to a trendy Notting Hill crowd. |
| £££–££££ | **St. John.** The ultra-British cooking at this converted smokehouse favors strange animal-parts and can be intimidating, but rest assured: it is all delicious. |
| ££–££££ | **E&O.** The name stands for Eastern and Oriental, and the Pan-Asian cuisine is an intelligent mix of Chinese, Japanese, Vietnamese, and Thai. |
| ££–££££ | **The Ivy.** The theater set eats Caesar salad, kedgeree, bubble and squeak, salmon cakes, and baked Alaska here, in an art deco setting. |
| ££–££££ | **Momo.** Mourad Mazouz—Momo to friends—storms beau London with his Casbah-like North African restaurant behind Regent Street. |
| ££–££££ | **Racine.** This excellent addition to the Brompton Road dining scene serves classics like steak au poivre with Bearnaise sauce, or chilled cucumber-and-mint soup, and does them with panache. |
| £££ | **Providores.** Kiwi Peter Gordon scores a perfect 10 with his Pacific Rim fusion food at Providores in ever-so-trendy Marylebone. |
| ££–£££ | **Baltic.** Come here for dinner before a play at the Young Vic—you'll find a bustling vodka-party playground and a good spot for an East European meal in sexy surroundings. |
| ££–£££ | **Electric Brasserie.** There's nowhere better than the Electric on market day at Portobello; there's great people-watching while you restore yourself with chunky sandwiches, steaks, and salads. |

| ££–£££ | **Le Caprice.** This glamorous place has stood the test of time—the food is great, the surroundings even better. |
|---|---|
| ££–£££ | **The Wolseley.** You might actually feel as if you're in Europe here, feasting on Wiener schnitzel, Hungarian goulash, and apple strudel. |

## BUDGET RESTAURANTS

| £–££ | **Chelsea Bun Diner.** This hybrid of an American diner and British greasy spoon serves huge portions of comfort food. |
|---|---|
| £–££ | **The Eagle.** It's the gastro-pub of gastro-pubs, serving good-value Portuguese-Spanish food. |
| £–££ | **Konditor & Cook.** This cafeteria in the Young Vic theater serves great lunches, but the pies and cakes are the real standouts. |
| £ | **Coffee Cup.** A Hampstead landmark for about as long as anyone can remember, this smoky café is lovable, cheap, and packed. |

## AFTER HOURS

| **American Bar, St. James's.** The bartender mixes superb martinis, amid a chin-dropping array of sporting mementos. |
|---|
| **Cadogan Hotel Bar, Knightsbridge.** Take a break from your Knightsbridge shopping spree at this elegant bar with its late-Victorian interior. |
| **Fabric, East End.** London hipsters flock to the sprawling, subterranean Fabric for the best DJs, and live music on Friday. |
| **Library Bar, Knightsbridge.** This exquisite bar at the Lanesborough Hotel offers a remarkable collection of vintage cognacs. |
| **Revolution, Soho.** You'll find obscure premium vodkas here, from Russia, Poland, and Finland. |
| **Sanctuary, Soho.** There's something for everyone here: dance to pumping house music downstairs, sip cocktails in the wood-paneled bar, or sing along to show tunes around the grand piano. |

## MUSEUMS

| **Apsley House.** Unmissable, in every sense, is the gigantic Canova statue of a naked Napoléon Bonaparte, which presides over the grand staircase at No. 1 London. |
|---|
| **British Museum.** You could move into this grand pile and never tire of all that it has to offer, from the Rosetta Stone to the Elgin Marbles, and superb Mesopotamian antiquities. |
| **National Gallery.** Da Vincis, Rubenses, and Rembrandts fill the rooms here—the richest trove of old master paintings in Britain. |

**Natural History Museum.** The ornate French Romanesque–style terra-cotta facade depicts extant creatures to the left of the entrance, extinct ones to the right. Inside, it's a house of wonders for you and the kids.

**The Queen's Gallery.** A splendid temple for Her Majesty's collection of art, the gallery comprises acquisitions made by the monarchy over the years.

**Science Museum.** Don't be led into thinking this is kids'-only territory—there's plenty here for all ages, including the Wellcome Wing, devoted to contemporary science, medicine, and technology, which also includes a 450-seat IMAX cinema.

**Somerset House.** The Courtauld Institute Gallery, the Gilbert Collection, and the Hermitage Rooms are all here, in this grand Italianate building by William Chambers.

**Tate Britain.** Works by British artists from the 16th century to the present are on display here, including a wonderful collection of Turners.

**Tate Modern.** The converted Bankside Power Station is the largest modern art gallery in the world.

## OUTDOOR ACTIVITIES

**Derby Day, Surrey.** One of the world's greatest horse races, Derby Day is an important social event on the London calendar.

**Ice-Skating at Somerset House, Covent Garden.** The setting of the rink is hard to beat, in the grand courtyard of this central London palace.

**Lord's Cricket Ground, St. John's Wood.** That most gentlemanly of all games has been played here since 1811; spend a relaxing day watching a county match.

**The Serpentine, Hyde Park.** Go boating in a canoe or a rowboat, or swim in the Lido, which on a hot day in summer is surreally reminiscent of the seaside.

**Wimbledon Lawn Tennis Championships.** If you're lucky enough to get tickets, you're in for some great tennis, gorgeous strawberries and cream, and of course, pouring rain.

## PARKS & GARDENS

**Hampstead Heath.** A wild park, where wolves once roamed, it spreads for miles to the north—from its top, there are stunning views for miles to the city.

**Kensington Gardens.** More formal than Hyde Park, the gardens contain the famous statue of Peter Pan and the Victorian extravaganza that is the Albert Memorial.

**St. James's Park.** With three palaces at its borders, this is the most royal of the royal parks, and also the most ornamental.

## PERFORMING ARTS

**Donmar Warehouse.** Hollywood stars are often cast members in the Donmar's innovative productions of new plays, or reinterpretations of old classics.

**Open Air Theatre, Regent's Park.** On a warm summer evening, classical theater here is hard to beat for magical adventure.

**Ronnie Scott's, Soho.** Since the '60s, this legendary jazz club has attracted big names. The food isn't great, and it's always crowded, but the mood can't be beat.

**Royal Opera House, Covent Garden.** Watch the biggest stars perform in the extravagant Victorian auditorium, or listen to a concert in the splendid Vilar Floral Hall.

**Sadler's Wells, Islington.** The Random Dance Company and Ballet Rambert put on performances at this lovely modern theater.

**Shakespeare's Globe, South Bank.** London at its Wellsian time-machine best, this open-to-the-skies reconstruction of Shakespeare's beloved "Wooden O" transports you back to Elizabethan London.

**Soho Theatre, Soho.** This innovative theater offers excellent comedy shows by established acts and award-winning new comedians.

**Union Chapel, Islington.** The beauty of the space and its impressive multicultural programming has made this one of London's most interesting musical venues.

**Wigmore Hall, Marylebone.** This intimate chamber music venue has glorious acoustics and an Arts-and-Crafts painted cupola.

## QUINTESSENTIAL LONDON

**Beatles' Magical Mystery Tour.** This wonderful stroll down Memory Lane offered by Original London Walks includes the London Palladium, No. 3 Savile Row (the Fab Four's London headquarters), and Abbey Road.

**Changing of the Guard.** Adding a dash of red to the gloomiest of London days, the colorful regiments of guards march in front of Buckingham Palace as the band plays.

**Houses of Parliament at Sunset.** Cross the Thames to Jubilee Gardens to see this view of London at its storybook best.

**Sunday Afternoon at Speakers' Corner, Hyde Park.** A space especially reserved for anyone with anything that must be said publicly makes for great entertainment. Speakers seem to be most oratorical on Sunday afternoons.

**Tower Bridge at Night.** A dramatically floodlit Tower Bridge confronts you as you come out of the Design Museum on a winter's night. Have your camera ready.

**Westminster Abbey.** Nearly all of England's monarchs have been crowned here, amid great heraldic splendor; many are buried here, too.

## SHOPPING

**Borough Market.** A wonderful farmers' market and foodies' paradise with whole grain, organic everything.

**Butler & Wilson.** Irresistible costume jewelry in diamanté, French gilt, and pearls, as well as some great vintage gowns.

**Cutler & Gross.** Bold, creative, witty eyewear in plastic or metal, and vintage spectacles of all shapes and sizes.

**Floris.** A real old-fashioned apothecary, Floris has glass and Spanish mahogany showcases filled with gorgeous perfumes.

**Fortnum & Mason.** The Queen's grocer, and one of London's most elegant food halls; you'll find some wonderful gifts here.

**Foyles.** After more than a hundred years in the business, there's a new look to this labyrinthine secondhand bookstore and London institution.

**Harrods.** Not just a department store, but a London monument and museum.

**Hatchards.** One of London's most atmospheric bookshops, with wooden bookshelves and a winding staircase.

**Liberty.** Famous principally for its classic Liberty prints and William Morris fabric designs; you may well find an original gift here.

**Portobello Market.** The bargains are to be found on the Ladbroke Grove end of the market, and the best flea market is under Westway.

# SMART TRAVEL TIPS

*Finding out about your destination before you leave home means you won't squander time organizing everyday minutiae once you've arrived. You'll be more streetwise when you hit the ground as well, better prepared to explore the aspects of London that drew you here in the first place. The organizations in this section can provide information to supplement this guide; contact them for up-to-the-minute details, and consult the A to Z sections that end the Side Trips from London for facts on the various topics as they relate to the areas around London. Happy landings!*

## ADDRESSES

Central London and its surrounding districts are divided into 32 boroughs—33, counting the City of London. More useful for finding your way around, however, are the subdivisions of London into postal districts. Throughout the guide we've given the full postal code for most listings. The first one or two letters give the location: N means north, NW means northwest, etc. Don't expect the numbering to be logical, however. You won't, for example, find W2 next to W3. The general rule is that the lower numbers, such as W1 or SW1, are closest to the city center.

## AIR TRAVEL TO & FROM LONDON

### BOOKING

When you book, look for nonstop flights and remember that "direct" flights stop at least once. Try to avoid connecting flights, which require a change of plane. Two airlines may operate a connecting flight jointly, so ask whether your airline operates every segment of the trip; you may find that the carrier you prefer flies you only part of the way. To find more booking tips and to check prices and make online flight reservations, log on to www.fodors.com.

### CARRIERS

**British Airways** is the national flag carrier and offers mostly nonstop flights from 18 U.S. cities to Heathrow and Gatwick airports, along with flights to Manchester,

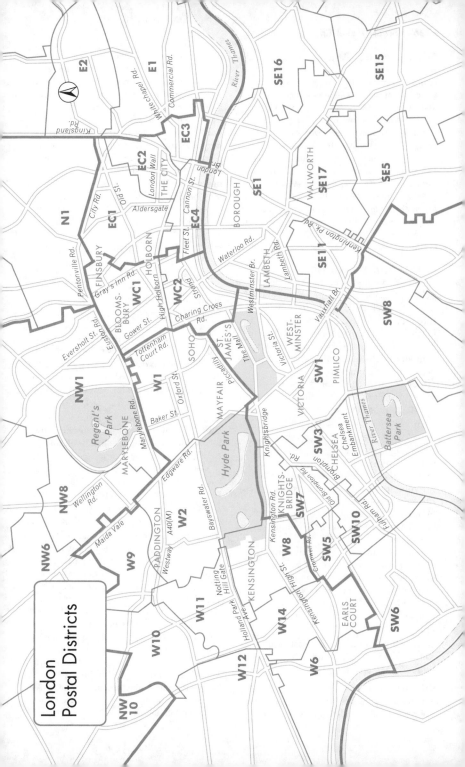

London
Postal Districts

Birmingham, and Glasgow. As the leading British carrier, it has a vast program of discount airfare-hotel packages.

**⁊ To & From London American Airlines** ☏ 800/433-7300, 020/7365-0777 in London to Heathrow, Gatwick. **British Airways** ☏ 800/247-9297, 0870/850-9850 in London to Heathrow, Gatwick. **Continental** ☏ 800/231-0856, 01293/776464 or 0845/607-6760 in London to Gatwick. **Delta** ☏ 800/241-4141, 0800/414767 in London to Gatwick. **Northwest Airlines** ☏ 800/447-4747, 0870/507-4074 in London to Gatwick. **United** ☏ 800/538-2929, 0845/844-4777 in London to Heathrow. **US Airways** ☏ 800/622-1015, 0845/600-3300 in London to Gatwick. **Virgin Atlantic** ☏ 800/862-8621, 01293/450150 in London to Heathrow, Gatwick.

### CHECK-IN & BOARDING

Always **find out your carrier's check-in policy.** Plan to arrive at the airport about two hours before your scheduled departure time for domestic flights and 2½ to 3 hours before international flights. You may need to arrive earlier if you're flying from one of the busier airports or during peak air-traffic times. To avoid delays at airport-security checkpoints, try not to wear any metal. Jewelry, belt and other buckles, steel-toe shoes, barrettes, and underwire bras are among the items that can set off detectors.

Assuming that not everyone with a ticket will show up, airlines routinely overbook planes. When everyone does, airlines ask for volunteers to give up their seats. In return, these volunteers usually get a several-hundred-dollar flight voucher, which can be used toward the purchase of another ticket, and are rebooked on the next flight out. If there are not enough volunteers, the airline must choose who will be denied boarding. The first to get bumped are passengers who checked in late and those flying on discounted tickets, so get to the gate and check in as early as possible, especially during peak periods.

Always **bring a government-issued photo ID** to the airport; even when it's not required, a passport is best.

### CUTTING COSTS

The least expensive airfares to London are priced for round-trip travel and must

usually be purchased in advance. Airlines generally allow you to change your return date for a fee; most low-fare tickets, however, are nonrefundable. It's smart to call a number of airlines and check the Internet; when you are quoted a good price, book it on the spot—the same fare may not be available the next day, or even the next hour. Always check different routings and look into using alternate airports. Also, price off-peak flights, which may be significantly less expensive than others. Travel agents, especially low-fare specialists ( ⇨ Discounts & Deals), are helpful.

Consolidators are another good source. They buy tickets for scheduled flights at reduced rates from the airlines, then sell them at prices that beat the best fare available directly from the airlines. (Many also offer reduced car-rental and hotel rates.) Sometimes you can even get your money back if you need to return the ticket. Carefully read the fine print detailing penalties for changes and cancellations, purchase the ticket with a credit card, and confirm your consolidator reservation with the airline.

When you fly as a courier, you trade your checked-luggage space for a ticket deeply subsidized by a courier service. There are restrictions on when you can book and how long you can stay. Some courier companies list with membership organizations, such as the Air Courier Association and the International Association of Air Travel Couriers; these require you to become a member before you can book a flight.

Many airlines, singly or in collaboration, offer discount air passes that allow foreigners to travel economically in a particular country or region. These visitor passes usually must be reserved and purchased before you leave home. Information about passes often can be found on most airlines' international Web pages, which tend to be aimed at travelers from outside the carrier's home country. Also, try typing the name of the pass into a search engine, or search for "pass" within the carrier's Web site.

**⁊ Consolidators AirlineConsolidator.com** ☏ 888/468-5385 ⊕ www.airlineconsolidator.com, for international tickets. **Best Fares** ☏ 800/880-1234 or

800/576-8255 ⊕ www.bestfares.com; $59.90 annual membership. **Cheap Tickets** ☎ 800/377-1000 or 800/652-4327 ⊕ www.cheaptickets.com. **Expedia** ☎ 800/397-3342 or 404/728-8787 ⊕ www.expedia.com. **Hotwire** ☎ 866/468-9473 or 920/330-9418 ⊕ www.hotwire.com. **Now Voyager Travel** ⊠ 45 W. 21st St., Suite 5A, New York, NY 10010 ☎ 212/459-1616 ⊟ 212/243-2711 ⊕ www.nowvoyagertravel.com. **Onetravel.com** ⊕ www.onetravel.com. **Orbitz** ☎ 888/656-4546 ⊕ www.orbitz.com. **Priceline.com** ⊕ www.priceline.com. **Travelocity** ☎ 888/709-5983, 877/282-2925 in Canada, 0870/876-3876 in the U.K. ⊕ www.travelocity.com.

🚪 Courier Resources **Air Courier Association/Cheaptrips.com** ☎ 800/280-5973 or 800/282-1202 ⊕ www.aircourier.org or www.cheaptrips.com; $34 annual membership. **International Association of Air Travel Couriers** ☎ 308/632-3273 ⊕ www.courier.org; $45 annual membership.

## ENJOYING THE FLIGHT

State your seat preference when purchasing your ticket, and then repeat it when you confirm and when you check in. For more legroom, you can request one of the few emergency-aisle seats at check-in, if you're capable of moving obstacles comparable in weight to an airplane exit door (usually between 35 pounds and 60 pounds)—a Federal Aviation Administration requirement of passengers in these seats. Seats behind a bulkhead also offer more legroom, but they don't have underseat storage. Don't sit in the row in front of the emergency aisle or in front of a bulkhead, where seats may not recline.

Ask the airline whether a snack or meal is served on the flight. If you have dietary concerns, request special meals when booking. These can be vegetarian, low-cholesterol, or kosher, for example. It's a good idea to pack some healthful snacks and a small (plastic) bottle of water in your carry-on bag. On long flights, try to maintain a normal routine, to help fight jet lag. At night, get some sleep. By day, eat light meals, drink water (not alcohol), and **move around the cabin** to stretch your legs. For additional jet-lag tips consult *Fodor's FYI: Travel Fit & Healthy* (available at bookstores everywhere).

Smoking policies vary from carrier to carrier. Many airlines prohibit smoking on all of their flights; others allow smoking only on certain routes or certain departures. Ask your carrier about its policy.

## FLYING TIMES

Flying time to London is about 6½ hours from New York, 7½ hours from Chicago, 11 hours from San Francisco, and 21½ hours from Sydney.

## HOW TO COMPLAIN

If your baggage goes astray or your flight goes awry, complain right away. Most carriers require that you **file a claim immediately.** The Aviation Consumer Protection Division of the Department of Transportation publishes *Fly-Rights*, which discusses airlines and consumer issues and is available online. You can also find articles and information on mytravelrights.com, the Web site of the nonprofit Consumer Travel Rights Center.

🚪 Airline Complaints **Aviation Consumer Protection Division** ⊠ U.S. Department of Transportation, Office of Aviation Enforcement and Proceedings, C-75, Room 4107, 400 7th St. SW, Washington, DC 20590 ☎ 202/366-2220 ⊕ airconsumer.ost.dot.gov. **Federal Aviation Administration Consumer Hotline** ⊠ For inquiries: FAA, 800 Independence Ave. SW, Washington, DC 20591 ☎ 800/322-7873 ⊕ www.faa.gov.

## RECONFIRMING

Check the status of your flight before you leave for the airport. You can do this on your carrier's Web site, by linking to a flight-status checker (many Web booking services offer these), or by calling your carrier or travel agent. Always confirm international flights at least 72 hours ahead of the scheduled departure time.

## AIRPORTS & TRANSFERS

International flights to London arrive at either Heathrow Airport (LHR), 15 mi west of London, or at Gatwick Airport (LGW), 27 mi south of the capital. Most flights from the United States go to Heathrow, which is the busiest and is divided into four terminals, with Terminals 3 and 4 handling transatlantic flights (British Airways uses Terminal 4).

Gatwick is London's second gateway. It has grown from a European airport into an airport that serves 21 scheduled U.S. destinations. A third, state-of-the-art airport, Stansted (STN), is 35 mi east of the city. It handles mainly European and domestic traffic, although there is also scheduled service from New York. The cost of hotels and car rentals varies little between Heathrow and Gatwick.

🛈 **Airport Information Gatwick Airport** ☎ 0870/000-2468. **Heathrow Airport** ☎ 0870/000-0123. **Stansted Airport** ☎ 0870/000-0303.

## AIRPORT TRANSFERS

London has excellent bus and train connections between its airports and downtown. If you're arriving at Heathrow, you can pick up a map and fare schedule at a Transport for London (TfL) Information Centre (in Terminals 1 and 2). Train service is direct and there are multistop train routes; the downside to this mode of transport is having to move around on escalators and connecting subways with luggage. Airport link buses may ease the luggage factor and drop you closer to central hotels, but they are subject to London traffic, which can be horrendous. Taxis can be more convenient, but beware that prices can go through the roof. Airport Travel Line has transfer information and takes advance booking for transfers between airports and into London.

Heathrow by Bus: Airbus A2 takes 1½ hours and costs £7 one-way and £10 round-trip. It leaves for King's Cross, with stops at Notting Hill Gate, Bayswater, Marble Arch, Marylebone Road, Euston, and Russell Square, every 30 minutes 5:30 AM–9:45 PM, but there are around 14 stops along the route, so it can be tedious. The N9 night bus runs every half hour from midnight to 4:30 AM to Trafalgar Square, takes an hour, and costs £1. For the same price and a journey closer to an hour, National Express buses leave every hour to Victoria Coach Station direct from 5:40 AM to 9:30 PM.

Heathrow by Train: The cheap, direct route into London is via the Piccadilly line of the Underground (London's extensive subway system, or "Tube"). Trains run every four to eight minutes from all four terminals from early morning until just before midnight; the 50-minute trip into central London costs £3.70 one-way and connects with other central Tube lines. The Heathrow Express train is comfortable and very convenient, speeding into London Paddington in 15 minutes, but is more expensive than the Tube. Standard one-way tickets cost £12 (£24 round-trip) and £20 for first class (more space). Book ahead for a discount ticket. Service is daily from 5:10 AM (5:50 AM on Sunday) to 11:40 PM (10:50 AM on Sunday), with departures every 15 minutes. At Paddington, you can use the Hotel Express bus to get to a number of central London hotels for £2.

Gatwick by Bus: Hourly service runs for Gatwick's south terminal to Victoria Station with stops at Hooley, Coulsdon, Mitcham, Streatham, Stockwell, and Pimlico. The journey take 90 minutes and costs £10 one-way.

Gatwick by Train: Fast, nonstop Gatwick Express leaves for Victoria Station every 15 minutes 5:15 AM–midnight. Trains leave Gatwick every 20 minutes 5:20 AM–6:05 AM, then at 5, 20, 35 and 50 minutes past the hour, until the last departure at 1:35 AM. The 30-minute trip costs £11 one-way, £21.50 round-trip. The Thameslinks train runs practically all day and all night to King's Cross, London Bridge, and Blackfriars stations; departures are every 15 to 30 minutes and the journey takes almost one hour. Tickets are about £9.80 one-way.

Stansted by Bus: Hourly bus service on Airbus A6 (24 hours a day) to Victoria Coach Station costs £8 one-way, £10 round-trip and takes about 1 hour and 40 minutes. Stops include Golders Green, Finchley Road, St. John's Wood, Baker Street, Marble Arch, and Hyde Park Corner.

Stansted by Train: The 45-minute journey on Stansted Express to Liverpool Street Station with a stop at Tottenham Hale runs every 15 minutes 8 AM–5 PM weekdays, and every 30 minutes 5 PM–midnight and 6 AM–8 AM weekdays, and all day on weekends. The trip costs £13 one-way, £21 round-trip.

Heathrow, Gatwick, and Stansted by Taxi: Taxis can get caught in traffic; the trip from Heathrow, for example, can take more than an hour and costs at least £35. From Gatwick, the taxi fare is at least £70 with a journey time of about an hour and a half. From Stansted, the £75 journey takes a little over an hour. Your hotel may be able to recommend a car service for airport transfers. Charges are usually about £35 to any airport. Add a tip of 10 to 15% to the basic fare.

🚖 Taxis & Shuttles **National Express Airbus** ☎ 0870/580-8080. **Gatwick Express** ☎ 0870/530-1530. **Heathrow Express** ☎ 0845/600-1515. **Stansted Express and Thameslink** ☎ 0845/748-4950. **Taxi at Stansted Airport** ☎ 01279/662444. **Taxi at Gatwick Airport** ☎ 0800/747737. **Taxi at Heathrow** ☎ 020/8745-7487.

🚖 Transfer Information **Airport Travel Line** ☎ 0870/574-7777.

## DUTY-FREE SHOPPING

Heathrow, Gatwick, and Stansted have an overwhelming selection of duty-free shops, but the tax-free advantages are for travelers departing the United Kingdom for a country outside the European Union. For allowances, *see* Customs & Duties.

## BIKE TRAVEL

### BIKES IN FLIGHT

Most airlines accommodate bikes as luggage, provided they are dismantled and boxed; check with individual airlines about packing requirements. Some airlines sell bike boxes, which are often free at bike shops, for about $20 (bike bags can be considerably more expensive). International travelers often can substitute a bike for a piece of checked luggage at no charge; otherwise, the cost is about $100. Most U.S. and Canadian airlines charge $40–$80 each way.

## BUSINESS HOURS

Generally, businesses are closed on Sunday and national (bank) holidays (⇨ Holidays). New Year's Day is a national holiday, but many major stores are open for the annual sales reductions. Many restaurants are closed over the Christmas period.

## BANKS & OFFICES

Banks are open weekdays 9:30–4:30; offices, 9:30–5:30.

## GAS STATIONS

Most gas stations in central London are open seven days, 24 hours. As you get farther out of town, and off trunk and major roads, hours vary considerably depending on the gas company, but are usually 8 AM–8 PM.

## MUSEUMS & SIGHTS

The major national museums and galleries are open daily, with shorter hours on weekends than weekdays. But there is a trend toward longer hours, such as one late-night opening a week.

## PHARMACIES

Pharmacies are called chemists and are open, for the most part, Monday–Saturday 9:30 AM–5:30 PM. The leading chain drugstore, Boots, is open until 6 PM (the Oxford Street and Piccadilly Circus branches are also open Sunday and until 8 PM Thursday). Bliss Chemist at 5 Marble Arch has the longest opening hours, from 9 AM–midnight.

## SHOPS

Shops and offices in central London tend to keep longer hours than those in the surrounding districts. Usual business hours are Monday–Saturday 9 AM–5:30 PM. In the main shopping streets of Oxford Street, Kensington High Street, and Knightsbridge, hours are 9:30 AM–6 PM, with late-night opening hours in Oxford Street on Thursday until 7:30–8 PM, and in the latter areas, on Wednesday. Many small general stores and newsagents stay open on Sunday; some chain and fashion stores in the tourist areas of Oxford Street and Piccadilly (and out-of-town shopping malls) also remain open.

## BUS TRAVEL TO & FROM LONDON

National Express is the largest British coach operator and the nearest equivalent to Greyhound. It's fast (particularly its Rapide services, which do not detour to make pickups and have steward service for refreshments) and comfortable (all coaches have washroom facilities on board). Services depart mainly from Victoria Coach Station, a well-signposted short walk behind Victoria mainline rail station. The departures and main information point is situated on the corner of Buckingham Palace Road; the arrivals point is opposite at Elizabeth Bridge. It's wise to arrive at least 30 minutes before departure so as to locate the correct exit gate (it's an extremely busy place at peak holiday and weekends). Smoking is not permitted on board.

Green Line serves the counties surrounding London, as well as airports. Bus stops (there is no garage) are on Buckingham Palace Road, between Victoria mainline station and Victoria Coach Station.

### FARES & SCHEDULES
Tickets can be bought from the Victoria, Heathrow, or Gatwick coach stations by phone with a credit card, via the National Express Web site, or from travel agencies. Apex tickets save money on standard fares, and traveling midweek is cheaper than over weekends and at holiday periods. Tourist Trail Passes, sold by British Travel International, make great savings if you plan to tour Britain, and they can be bought in advance. Prices run from £49 for two days of unlimited travel within three days to £205 for 15 days of unlimited travel within two months. The Discount Coachcard for students costs £10 and qualifies you for 20% to 30% off many standard fares over a one-year period.

🚌 Bus Information **British Travel International** ☎ 800/327–6097. **Green Line** ☎ 0870/608–7261. **National Express** ☎ 0870/580–8080 ⊕ www. gobycoach.com. **Victoria Coach Station** ☎ 020/ 7730–3499.

## BUS TRAVEL WITHIN LONDON
The red Transport for London (TfL) buses, which travel all over town, have been joined by the bright colors of other private bus companies that cover the suburbs. Bus stops are clearly indicated; the main stops have a red TfL symbol on a plain white background. When the word "Request" is written across the sign, you must flag the bus down. Each numbered route is listed

on the main stop, and buses have a large number on the front with their end destination. Not all buses run the full route at all times; check with the driver or conductor. If you want to decipher the numbers, pick up a free bus guide at a TfL Travel Information Centre (at Euston, Liverpool Street, Piccadilly Circus, and Victoria Tube stations, at West Croydon bus station, and at Heathrow Airport). Buses are a good way of seeing the town, particularly if you plan to hop on and off to cover many sights, but **don't take a bus if you are in a hurry.** To get off, pull the cord running above the windows on old buses, or press the button by the exit. Expect to get a little squashed during rush hours, from 8 AM to 9:30 AM and 4:30 PM to 6:30 PM.

Night Buses, denoted by the prefix "N" to their route numbers, run from 11 PM to 5 AM on a more restricted route than day buses. Fares are slightly higher, and One Day Travelcards are not accepted. Avoid sitting alone on the top deck of a Night Bus; it gives a mugger an ideal opportunity. All night buses run by request stop so flag them down if you are waiting or push the button if you want to alight.

### FARES & SCHEDULES
All journeys within the central zone are £1, and all others outside are 70p. Travel from the outer to the central zone costs £1. If you plan to make a number of journeys in one day, consider buying a Travelcard ( ⇨ Underground Tube Travel) good for both Tube and bus travel or a £2 One-Day bus pass, valid on all buses in zones 1–4. Traveling without a valid ticket makes you liable for a fine (£10 at press time). Buses are supposed to swing by every five or six minutes, but, in reality, you may wait longer.

### PAYING
In central London, you must pay before you board the bus. Automated ticket kiosks are set up at these bus stops, which are clearly marked with a yellow sign "Buy tickets before boarding." Otherwise, you can buy tickets at most central London tube stations as well as at newsagents, and shops that display the sign "Buy Your Travelcards & Bus Passes Here." Outside

the central zone, payment may be made to the driver as you enter (exact change is best so as to avoid incurring the driver's wrath). On some of the old buses, a conductor issues you a ticket.

🚏 **Transport for London** ☎ 020/7222-1234.

## CAMERAS & PHOTOGRAPHY

Don't be surprised if you're asked not to take pictures during theater, ballet, or opera productions, and in galleries, museums, and stately homes. Locals are generally happy to feature in your photos, but it's polite to ask if they mind before fixing the lens. There are many must-take sights in London, but guards on horseback in Whitehall and Big Ben top the list. The *Kodak Guide to Shooting Great Travel Pictures* (available at bookstores everywhere) is loaded with tips.

🚏 **Photo Help Kodak Information Center** ☎ 800/242-2424 ⊕ www.kodak.com.

## EQUIPMENT PRECAUTIONS

**Don't pack film or equipment in checked luggage,** where it is much more susceptible to damage. X-ray machines used to view checked luggage are extremely powerful and therefore are likely to ruin your film. Try to ask for hand inspection of film, which becomes clouded after repeated exposure to airport X-ray machines, and keep videotapes and computer disks away from metal detectors. Always keep film, tape, and computer disks out of the sun. Carry an extra supply of batteries, and be prepared to turn on your camera, camcorder, or laptop to prove to airport security personnel that the device is real.

## FILM & DEVELOPING

Film is available from pharmacies, newsagents, and supermarkets, as well as photographic stores. Kodak and Agfa are the most common brands, and prices range £2–£4 for a roll of 36-exposure color print film. Larger drugstore branches and photographic stores stock the Advantix line. These stores provide 24-hour film developing services.

## VIDEOS

Videos from the U.S. are not compatible with British and European models. If you're bringing your own video-camcorder, bring a supply of cassettes as well.

## CAR RENTAL

Rental rates in London vary widely and are expensive, beginning at £50 ($80) a day and £200 ($320) a week for a small economy car (such as a subcompact General Motors Vauxhall, Corsa, or Renault Clio), usually with manual transmission. Air-conditioning and unlimited mileage generally come with the larger-size automatic cars.

🚏 **Major Agencies Alamo** ☎ 800/522-9696 ⊕ www.alamo.com. **Avis** ☎ 800/331-1084, 800/879-2847 in Canada,0870/606-0100 in the U.K., 02/9353-9000 in Australia, 09/526-2847 in New Zealand ⊕ www.avis.com. **Budget** ☎ 800/527-0700, 0870/156-5656 in the U.K. ⊕ www.budget.com. **Dollar** ☎ 800/800-6000, 0800/085-4578 in the U.K. ⊕ www.dollar.com. **Hertz** ☎ 800/654-3001, 800/263-0600 in Canada, 0870/844-8844 in the U.K., 02/9669-2444 in Australia, 09/256-8690 in New Zealand ⊕ www.hertz.com. **National Car Rental** ☎ 800/227-7368, 0870/600-6666 in the U.K. ⊕ www.nationalcar.com.

## CUTTING COSTS

For a good deal, book through a travel agent who will shop around. Do look into wholesalers, companies that do not own fleets but rent in bulk from those that do and often offer better rates than traditional car-rental operations. Prices are best during off-peak periods. Rentals booked through wholesalers often must be paid for before you leave home.

🚏 **Local Agencies 1car1** ✉ 82 Caledonian Rd., London N1 9DN ☎ 020/7427-2368 🖷 020/7237-6459 ⊕ www.1car1.com. **Easy Car** ☎ 0906/333-3333, 60p per minute within U.K. ⊕ www.easycar.com. **Enterprise** ✉ 466-480 Edgware Rd., London W2 1EL ☎ 020/7723-4800. **Europcar** ✉ 245 Warwick Rd., London W14 8PX ☎ 020/7751-1770.

🚏 **Wholesalers Auto Europe** ☎ 207/842-2000 or 800/223-5555 🖷 207/842-2222 ⊕ www.autoeurope.com. **Destination Europe Resources** (DER) ✉ 9501 W. Devon Ave., Rosemont, IL 60018 ☎ 800/782-2424 🖷 800/282-7474 ⊕ www.der.com. **Europe by Car** ☎ 212/581-3040 or 800/223-1516 🖷 212/246-1458 ⊕ www.europebycar.com. **Holiday Auto** ☎ 0870/400-4482 ⊕ www.holidayautos.

co.uk.Kemwel ☎ 877/820–0668 or 800/678–0678
🖷 207/842–2147 ⊕ www.kemwel.com.

## INSURANCE

When driving a rented car you are generally responsible for any damage to or loss of the vehicle. Collision policies that car-rental companies sell for European rentals typically do not cover stolen vehicles. Before you rent—and purchase collision or theft coverage—see what coverage you already have under the terms of your personal auto-insurance policy and credit cards.

## REQUIREMENTS & RESTRICTIONS

An International Driver's Permit is a good idea; it's available from the American (A. A.A.) or Canadian Automobile Association and, in the United Kingdom, from the Automobile Association (A.A.) or Royal Automobile Club (R.A.C.). International permits are universally recognized, and having one may save you a problem with the local authorities.

## SURCHARGES

Before you pick up a car in one city and leave it in another, ask about drop-off charges or one-way service fees, which can be substantial. Also inquire about early-return policies; some rental agencies charge extra if you return the car before the time specified in your contract while others give you a refund for the days not used. To avoid a hefty refueling fee, fill the tank just before you turn in the car, but be aware that gas stations near the rental outlet may overcharge. It's almost never a deal to buy the tank of gas that's in the car when you rent it; the understanding is that you'll return it empty, but some fuel usually remains.

## CAR TRAVEL

In London your United States driver's license is acceptable (as long as you are over 23 years old, with no endorsements or driving convictions). If you have a driver's license from a country other than the United States, it may not be recognized in the United Kingdom. International driving permits (IDPs) are available from the American and Canadian automobile associations and, in the United Kingdom, from the Automobile Association and Royal

Automobile Club. These international permits, valid only in conjunction with your regular driver's license, are universally recognized; having one may save you a problem with local authorities.

The best advice on driving in London is: don't. London's streets are a winding mass of chaos, made worse by one-way streets. Parking is also restrictive and expensive, and traffic is tediously slow at most times of the day; during rush hours—from 8 AM to 9:30 AM and 4:30 PM to 6:30 PM—it often grinds to a standstill, particularly on Friday, when everyone wants to leave town. City center shopping areas are to be avoided, including the roads feeding Oxford Street, Kensington, and Knightsbridge. Other main roads into the city center are also busy, such as King's Cross and Euston in the north. Watch out also for cyclists and motorcycle couriers who weave between cars and pedestrians and seem to come out of nowhere.

Remember that Britain drives on the left, and the rest of Europe on the right. Therefore, you may want to leave your rented car in Britain and pick up a left-side drive if you cross the Channel ( ⇨ The Channel Tunnel).

## CONGESTION CHARGE

Designed to reduce traffic through central London, a congestion charge has been instituted. Vehicles (with some exemptions) entering central London on weekdays from 7 AM to 6:30 PM (excluding public holidays) have to pay a £5 per day fee; it can be paid up to 90 days in advance, or on the day you need it. Day-, week-, month-, and year-long passes are available on the Web site, at gas stations, parking lots (car parks), by mail, by phone, by SMS text message, and at BT Internet kiosks. Traffic signs designate the entrance to congestion areas, and cameras read car license plates and send the information to a database. Drivers who don't pay the congestion charge by midnight after the day of driving are penalized £80, which is reduced to £40 if paid within 14 days.
🖪 Congestion Charge Customer Service ⬧ Box 2985, Coventry CV7 8ZR ☎ 0845/900–1234 ⊕ www. cclondon.com.

## EMERGENCY SERVICES

The general procedure for a breakdown is the following: position the red hazard triangle (which should be in the trunk of the car) a few paces away from the rear of the car. Leave the hazard warning lights on. If you are on a highway (motorway), emergency roadside telephone booths are positioned at intervals within walking distance. Contact the car rental company, or an auto club. The main automobile help-groups in the United Kingdom are the Automobile Association (A.A.) and the Royal Automobile Club (R.A.C.). If you're a member of the American Automobile Association (A.A.A.) check your membership details before you depart for Britain as, under a reciprocal agreement, roadside assistance in the United Kingdom should cost you nothing. You can join and receive roadside assistance from the A.A. on the spot, but the charge is higher—around £75—than a simple membership fee.

🚗 **American Automobile Association** ☎ 800/564-6222. **Australian Automobile Association** ☎ 02/6247-7311. **Automobile Association** ☎ 0870/550-0600, 0800/887766 for emergency roadside assistance. **Canadian Automobile Association** ☎ 613/247-0117. **New Zealand Automobile Association** ☎ 09/377-4660. **Royal Automobile Club** ☎ 0870/572-2722.

## GASOLINE

Gasoline (petrol) is sold in liters and is increasingly expensive (85p per liter at press time). Unleaded petrol is predominant, denoted by green pump lines. Premium and Super Premium are the two varieties, and most cars run on regular premium. Supermarket pumps usually offer the best value, although they are often on the edge of the central city. You won't find too many service stations in the center of town; these are generally on main, multicarriageway trunk roads out of the center. Service is self-serve, except in small villages, and these gas stations are likely to be closed on Sunday and late evening. Most accept major credit cards.

## PARKING

During the day—and probably at all times—it's safest to believe that you can park nowhere except at a meter, in a garage, or where you are sure there are no lines or signs; otherwise, you run the risk of a towing cost of about £100 or a wheel clamp, which costs about the same, since you pay to have the clamp removed plus the cost of the one or two tickets you'll have earned first. Restrictions are indicated by the NO WAITING parking signpost on the sidewalk (these restrictions vary from street to street), and restricted areas include single yellow lines or double yellow lines. Parking at a bus stop or in a red-line bus lane is also restricted. It's illegal to park on the sidewalk, across entrances, or on white zigzag lines approaching a pedestrian crossing.

Meters have an insatiable hunger in the inner city—a 20p piece buys just six minutes—and some will only permit a two-hour stay. Meters take 10p, 20p, 50p, and £1 coins. In the evening, after restrictions end, meter bays are free. Daytime, take advantage of the many N.C.P. parking lots in the center of town, which are often better value (about £2.50–£3 per hour, up to 8 hours). A London street map should have the parking lots marked.

## RULES OF THE ROAD

If you must risk life and limb and drive in London, note that the speed limit is 30 mph in the royal parks, as well as in all streets—unless you see the large 40 mph signs (and small repeater signs attached to lampposts) found only in the suburbs. Other basic rules: pedestrians have right-of-way on "zebra" crossings (black and white stripes that stretch across the street between two Belisha beacons—orange-flashing globe lights on posts) and it's illegal to pass another vehicle at a zebra crossing. At other crossings pedestrians must yield to traffic, but they do have right-of-way over traffic turning left at controlled crossings—if they have the nerve.

Traffic lights sometimes have arrows directing left or right turns; try to catch a glimpse of the road markings in time, and don't get into the turn lane if you mean to go straight ahead. A right turn is not permitted on a red light. On designated bus lanes a sign at the beginning and end gives the time restrictions for use—usually during peak hours—if you are caught, you could be fined. The use of horns is prohibited between 11:30 PM and 7 AM. Seat belts are to be worn by law in the front and the back seats. Drunk-driving laws are strictly enforced and it is far safer to avoid alcohol altogether. The legal limit is 80 milligrams of alcohol, which roughly translated means two units of alcohol—two glasses of wine, one pint of beer, or one glass of whiskey.

## THE CHANNEL TUNNEL

Short of flying, taking the "Chunnel" is the fastest way to cross the English Channel: 35 minutes from Folkestone to Calais, 60 minutes from motorway to motorway, or 2 hours and 40 minutes from London's Waterloo Station to Paris's Gare du Nord.
**⑦ Car Transport Eurotunnel** ☎ 0870/535-3535 in the U.K., 070/223210 in Belgium, 03-21-00-61-00 in France ⊕ www.eurotunnel.com. **French Motorail/ Rail Europe** ☎ 0870/241-5415 ⊕ www.raileurope. co.uk.
**⑦ Passenger Service Eurostar** ☎ 1233/617575, 0870/518-6186 in the U.K. ⊕ www.eurostar.co.uk. **Rail Europe** ☎ 800/942-4866 or 800/274-8724, 0870/584-8848 U.K. inquiries and credit-card bookings ⊕ www.raileurope.com.

## CHILDREN IN LONDON

There's a kaleidoscope of activity for children to enjoy in London, and museums and major attractions have made great strides in special interactive features and exhibitions (particularly in summer and Christmas holidays). At many museums children now enjoy free admission, and between the great establishments there are masses of green spaces in the London parks. During the school holiday time, bookstores run story times; cinemas, concert halls, and theaters have plenty of programs to watch—and join in on. When packing, include things to keep children busy en route.

Up-to-date information is available in the section devoted to children's listings in the weekly magazine *Time Out* (£2.30), available at newsagents and bookstores. *Fodor's Around London with Kids* (available in

bookstores everywhere) can help you plan your days together.

If you are renting a car, don't forget to arrange for a car seat when you reserve. For general advice about traveling with children, consult *Fodor's FYI: Travel with Your Baby* (available in bookstores everywhere).
**⑦ Local Information Kids Out!** ☎ 020/7813-6018. **Londonline** ☎ 09068/663344 Children's London, calls cost 60p/min from a U.K. phone ⊕ www. kidslovelondon.com.

### BABYSITTING

**⑦ Agencies The Babysitting Co.** ✉ 130 Greyhound Rd., London W6 8JU ☎ 020/7385-5111. **Nanny Connection** ✉ Collier House, 163-169 Brompton Rd., London SW3 1PY ☎ 020/7591-4488. **The Nanny Service** ✉ 6 Nottingham St., London W1M 3RB ☎ 020/7935-3515. **Pippa Pop-ins** ✉ 430 Fulham Rd., London SW6 ☎ 020/7385-2458. **Universal Aunts** ✉ Box 304, London SW4 0NN ☎ 020/7738-8937.

### FLYING

When booking, confirm carry-on allowances if you're traveling with infants. In general, for babies charged 10% to 50% of the adult fare you are allowed one carry-on bag and a collapsible stroller; if the flight is full, the stroller may have to be checked or you may be limited to less.

Experts agree that it's a good idea to use safety seats aloft for children weighing less than 40 pounds. Airlines set their own policies: if you use a safety seat, U.S. carriers usually require that the child be ticketed, even if he or she is young enough to ride free, because the seats must be strapped into regular seats. And even if you pay the full adult fare for the seat, it may be worth it, especially on longer trips. Do **check your airline's policy about using safety seats during takeoff and landing.** Safety seats are not allowed everywhere in the plane, so get your seat assignments as early as possible.

When reserving, request children's meals or a freestanding bassinet (not available at all airlines) if you need them. But note that bulkhead seats, where you must sit to use the bassinet, may lack an overhead bin or storage space on the floor.

## LODGING

Most hotels in London allow children under a certain age to stay in their parents' room at no extra charge, but others charge for them as extra adults; be sure to find out the cutoff age for children's discounts.

The following hotels offer family rooms and/or cots, babysitting service, and children's portions and high chairs in the restaurant.

🔢 **Best Choices Edward Lear** ✉ 30 Seymour St., Bayswater, W1H 5WD ☎ 020/7402-5401. **City Inn Westminster** ✉ 30 John Islip St., Westminster, SW1P 4DD ☎ 020/7630-1000. **22 Jermyn Street** ✉ 22 Jermyn St., St. James's, SW1Y 6HL ☎ 020/7734-2353, 800/682-7808 in U.S. **The Landmark** ✉ 222 Marylebone Rd., Marylebone, NW1 6JQ ☎ 020/7631-8000.

## SIGHTS & ATTRACTIONS

The Tower of London, Tower Bridge Experience, London Dungeon, Madame Tussaud's, the Natural History Museum, and Pollock's Toy Museum are just a handful of sights to excite children. Places that are especially appealing to children are indicated by a rubber-duckie icon (🦆) in the margin.

## TRANSPORTATION

On trains and buses, children pay half or reduced fares; children under five go for free. Car rental companies may have child seats available. By law, where there are seat belts in front and back, children must use them, but it is the responsibility of the driver to ensure that they do. Children do not need a child seat if they are over age five and are 1.5 meters (4.9 feet) in height, but they must wear an adult seat belt. Children must be three to sit in the front seat, and if under 1.5 meters in height will need a child seat or adult strap, whichever is available.

## COMPUTERS ON THE ROAD

If you're traveling with a laptop, carry a spare battery and adapter: new batteries and replacement adapters are expensive, although if you do need to replace them head to Tottenham Court Road (W1), which is lined with computer specialists. John Lewis department store and Selfridges, on Oxford Street (W1), also carry a limited range. Never plug your computer into any socket before asking about surge protection. Some hotels do not have built-in current stabilizers, and extreme electrical fluctuations and surges can short your adapter or even destroy your computer. IBM sells an invaluable pen-size modem tester that plugs into a telephone jack to check if the line is safe to use.

## CONCIERGES

Concierges, found in many hotels, can help you with theater tickets and dinner reservations: a good one with connections may be able to get you seats for a hot show or prime-time dinner reservations at the restaurant of the moment. You can also turn to your hotel's concierge for help with travel arrangements, sightseeing plans, services ranging from aromatherapy to zipper repair, and emergencies. **Always tip** a concierge who has been of assistance (⇨ Tipping).

## CONSUMER PROTECTION

Whether you're shopping for gifts or purchasing travel services, **pay with a major credit card** whenever possible, so you can cancel payment or get reimbursed if there's a problem (and you can provide documentation). If you're doing business with a particular company for the first time, contact your local Better Business Bureau and the attorney general's offices in your state and (for U.S. businesses) the company's home state as well. Have any complaints been filed? Finally, if you're buying a package or tour, always consider travel insurance that includes default coverage (⇨ Insurance).

🔢 **BBBs Council of Better Business Bureaus** ✉ 4200 Wilson Blvd., Suite 800, Arlington, VA 22203 ☎ 703/276-0100 🖷 703/525-8277 ⊕ www.bbb.org.

## CUSTOMS & DUTIES

When shopping abroad, keep receipts for all purchases. Upon reentering the country, **be ready to show customs officials what you've bought.** Pack purchases together in an easily accessible place. If you think a duty is incorrect, appeal the assessment. If you object to the way your clearance was handled, note the inspector's badge number. In either case, first ask to see a supervisor. If the problem isn't resolved, write to the appropriate authorities, beginning with the port director at your point of entry.

### IN AUSTRALIA

Australian residents who are 18 or older may bring home A$400 worth of souvenirs and gifts (including jewelry), 250 cigarettes or 250 grams of cigars or other tobacco products, and 1,125 ml of alcohol (including wine, beer, and spirits). Residents under 18 may bring back A$200 worth of goods. Members of the same family traveling together may pool their allowances. Prohibited items include meat products. Seeds, plants, and fruits need to be declared upon arrival.

🚩 **Australian Customs Service** ⌦ Regional Director, Box 8, Sydney, NSW 2001 ☎ 02/9213–2000 or 1300/363263, 02/9364–7222 or 1800/020–504 quarantine-inquiry line 🖨 02/9213–4043 ⊕ www.customs.gov.au.

### IN CANADA

Canadian residents who have been out of Canada for at least seven days may bring in C$750 worth of goods duty-free. If you've been away fewer than seven days but more than 48 hours, the duty-free allowance drops to C$200. If your trip lasts 24 to 48 hours, the allowance is C$50. You may not pool allowances with family members. Goods claimed under the C$750 exemption may follow you by mail; those claimed under the lesser exemptions must accompany you. Alcohol and tobacco products may be included in the seven-day and 48-hour exemptions but not in the 24-hour exemption. If you meet the age requirements of the province or territory through which you reenter Canada, you may bring in, duty-free, 1.5 liters of wine or 1.14 liters (40 imperial ounces) of liquor or 24 12-ounce cans or bottles of beer or ale. Also, if you meet the local age requirement for tobacco products, you may bring in, duty-free, 200 cigarettes and 50 cigars. Check ahead of time with the Canada Customs and Revenue Agency or the Department of Agriculture for policies

regarding meat products, seeds, plants, and fruits.

You may send an unlimited number of gifts (only one gift per recipient, however) worth up to C$60 each duty-free to Canada. Label the package UNSOLICITED GIFT—VALUE UNDER $60. Alcohol and tobacco are excluded.

🚩 **Canada Customs and Revenue Agency** ⌦ 2265 St. Laurent Blvd., Ottawa, Ontario K1G 4K3 ☎ 800/461–9999 in Canada, 204/983–3500 or 506/636–5064 ⊕ www.ccra.gc.ca.

### IN NEW ZEALAND

All homeward-bound residents may bring back NZ$700 worth of souvenirs and gifts; passengers may not pool their allowances, and children can claim only the concession on goods intended for their own use. For those 17 or older, the duty-free allowance also includes 4.5 liters of wine or beer; one 1,125-ml bottle of spirits; and either 200 cigarettes, 250 grams of tobacco, 50 cigars, or a combination of the three up to 250 grams. Meat products, seeds, plants, and fruits must be declared upon arrival to the Agricultural Services Department.

🚩 **New Zealand Customs** ⌦ Head office: The Customhouse, 17–21 Whitmore St., Box 2218, Wellington ☎ 09/300–5399 or 0800/428–786 ⊕ www.customs.govt.nz.

### IN THE U.K.

There are two levels of duty-free allowance for entering Britain: one for goods bought outside the European Union (EU) and the other for goods bought within the EU.

Of goods bought outside the EU you may import duty-free: 200 cigarettes or 100 cigarillos or 50 cigars or 250 grams of tobacco; two liters of table wine and, in addition, (a) one liter of alcohol over 22% by volume (most spirits), (b) two liters of alcohol under 22% by volume (fortified or sparkling wine or liqueurs), or (c) two more liters of table wine; 60 ml of perfume; ¼ liter (250 ml) of toilet water; and other goods up to a value of £145, but not more than 50 liters of beer or 25 cigarette lighters.

Of goods bought within the EU, you should not exceed (unless you can prove they are for personal use): 3,200 cigarettes, 400 cigarillos, 200 cigars, and 1 kilogram of tobacco, plus 10 liters of spirits, 20 liters of fortified wine, 90 liters of wine, and 110 liters of beer.

Pets (dogs and cats) can be brought in to the United Kingdom from the United States without six months' quarantine, provided that the animal meets all the PETS (Pet Travel Scheme) requirements. The process takes about six months to complete and involves detailed steps. Other pets have to undergo a lengthy quarantine, and penalties for breaking this law are severe and strictly enforced. Fresh meats, plants and vegetables, unpasteurized milk, controlled drugs, and firearms and ammunition may not be brought into the United Kingdom.

🄵 **HM Customs and Excise** ✉ Valiant House, 365 High Rd., Wembley, Middlesex HA96AY ☎ 0208/929-0152 or 0845/010-9000 ⊕ www.hmce.gov.uk.

## IN THE U.S.

U.S. residents who have been out of the country for at least 48 hours may bring home, for personal use, $800 worth of foreign goods duty-free, as long as they haven't used the $800 allowance or any part of it in the past 30 days. This exemption may include one liter of alcohol (for travelers 21 and older), 200 cigarettes, and 100 non-Cuban cigars. Family members from the same household who are traveling together may pool their $800 personal exemptions. For fewer than 48 hours, the duty-free allowance drops to $200, which may include 50 cigarettes, 10 non-Cuban cigars, and 150 ml of alcohol (or 150 ml of perfume containing alcohol). The $200 allowance cannot be combined with other individuals' exemptions, and if you exceed it, the full value of all the goods will be taxed. Antiques, which U.S. Customs and Border Protection defines as objects more than 100 years old, enter duty-free, as do original works of art done entirely by hand, including paintings, drawings, and sculptures. This doesn't apply to folk art or handicrafts, which are in general dutiable.

You may also send packages home duty-free, with a limit of one parcel per addressee per day (except alcohol or tobacco products or perfume worth more than $5). You can mail up to $200 worth of goods for personal use; label the package PERSONAL USE and attach a list of its contents and their retail value. If the package contains your used personal belongings, mark it AMERICAN GOODS RETURNED to avoid paying duties. You may send up to $100 worth of goods as a gift; mark the package UNSOLICITED GIFT. Mailed items do not affect your duty-free allowance on your return.

To avoid paying duty on foreign-made high-ticket items you already own and will take on your trip, register them with Customs before you leave the country. Consider filing a Certificate of Registration for laptops, cameras, watches, and other digital devices identified with serial numbers or other permanent markings; you can keep the certificate for other trips. Otherwise, bring a sales receipt or insurance form to show that you owned the item before you left the United States.

For more about duties, restricted items, and other information about international travel, check out U.S. Customs and Border Protection's online brochure, *Know Before You Go.*

🄵 **U.S. Customs and Border Protection** ✉ For inquiries and equipment registration, 1300 Pennsylvania Ave. NW, Washington, DC 20229 ☎ 877/287-8667 or 202/354-1000 ⊕ www.cbp.gov ✉ For complaints, Customer Satisfaction Unit, 1300 Pennsylvania Ave. NW, Room 5.2C, Washington, DC 20229.

## DISABILITIES & ACCESSIBILITY

Compared to New York City, London has a way to go in helping people with disabilities, but it's moving toward making the city more accessible. Many of the tourist attractions and hotels are updating facilities, although traveling around is a problem. Here are organizations to help and advise.

🄵 **Local Resources Artsline** ☎ 020/7388-2227 ⊕ www.artslineonline.com. **Can Be Done** ✉ 7-11 Kensington High St., London, W8 5NP ☎ 020/8907-2400 ⊕ www.canbedone.co.uk. **DIAL** ☎ 01302/310-123 ⊕ www.dialuk.org.uk. **Holiday**

Care ✉ 7th fl. Sunley House, 4 Bedford Pk., Croydon, Surrey CR0 2AP ☎ 0845/124 9971 ⊕ www.holidaycare.org.uk. **Transport for London's Unit for Disabled Passengers** ✉ 172 Buckingham Palace Rd., London SW1W 9TN ☎ 020/7918-3312. **Royal Association for Disability and Rehabilitation** (RADAR) ✉ 12 City Forum, 250 City Rd., London EC1V 8AF ☎ 020/7250-3222. **Tripscope** ☎ 020/8580-7021. **Wheelchair Travel & Access Mini Buses** ✉ 1 Johnston Green, Guildford Surrey, GU2 6XS ☎ 01483/237668 ⊕ www.wheelchair-travel.co.uk.

## LODGING
If you book directly through Holiday Care, rates at some hotels with special facilities can be discounted.

◪ Best Choices **Copthorne Tara Hotel** ✉ Scarsdale Pl., Kensington, W8 ☎ 020/7937-7211. **Novotel London Tower Bridge** ✉ 10 Pepys St., City, EC3N 2NR ☎ 020/7265-6000.

## RESERVATIONS
When discussing accessibility with an operator or reservations agent, ask hard questions. Are there any stairs, inside *or* out? Are there grab bars next to the toilet *and* in the shower/tub? How wide is the doorway to the room? To the bathroom? For the most extensive facilities meeting the latest legal specifications, opt for newer accommodations. If you reserve through a toll-free number, consider also calling the hotel's local number to confirm the information from the central reservations office. Get confirmation in writing when you can.

## SIGHTS & ATTRACTIONS
Tour Guides Ltd. can tailor a tour for you. The London Tourist Board has details of more easily accessible attractions. Suggested sights include London Planetarium, London Zoo, National Portrait Gallery, and Natural History Museum.

## TRANSPORTATION
London cabs have spacious interiors for wheelchair users. Many London buses have kneeling mechanisms and are wheelchair accessible.

◪ Complaints **Aviation Consumer Protection Division** (⇨ Air Travel) for airline-related problems. **Departmental Office of Civil Rights** ✉ For general inquiries, U.S. Department of Transportation, S-30, 400 7th St. SW, Room 10215, Washington, DC 20590 ☎ 202/366-4648 ☎ 202/366-9371 ⊕ www.dot.gov/ost/docr/index.htm. **Disability Rights Section** ✉ NYAV, U.S. Department of Justice, Civil Rights Division, 950 Pennsylvania Ave. NW, Washington, DC 20530 ☎ 202/514-0301 ADA information line, 800/514-0301, 202/514-0383 TTY, 800/514-0383 TTY ⊕ www.ada.gov. **U.S. Department of Transportation Hotline** ☎ 800/778-4838 for disability-related air-travel problems, 800/455-9880 TTY.

## TRAVEL AGENCIES
In the United States, the Americans with Disabilities Act requires that travel firms serve the needs of all travelers. Some agencies specialize in working with people with disabilities.

◪ Travelers with Mobility Problems **Access Adventures/B. Roberts Travel** ✉ 206 Chestnut Ridge Rd., Scottsville, NY 14624 ☎ 585/889-9096 ⊕ www.brobertstravel.com ✉ dltravel@prodigy.net, run by a former physical-rehabilitation counselor. **CareVacations** ✉ No. 5, 5110-50 Ave., Leduc, Alberta, Canada, T9E 6V4 ☎ 780/986-6404 or 877/478-7827 ☎ 780/986-8332 ⊕ www.carevacations.com, for group tours and cruise vacations. **Flying Wheels Travel** ✉ 143 W. Bridge St., Box 382, Owatonna, MN 55060 ☎ 507/451-5005 ☎ 507/451-1685 ⊕ www.flyingwheelstravel.com.

## DISCOUNTS & DEALS
Be a smart shopper and compare all your options before making decisions. A plane ticket bought with a promotional coupon from travel clubs, coupon books, and direct-mail offers or purchased on the Internet may not be cheaper than the least expensive fare from a discount ticket agency. And always keep in mind that what you get is just as important as what you save.

## DISCOUNT RESERVATIONS
To save money, look into discount reservations services with Web sites and toll-free numbers, which use their buying power to get a better price on hotels, airline tickets (⇨ Air Travel), even car rentals. When booking a room, always **call the hotel's local toll-free number** (if one is available) rather than the central reservations number—you'll often get a better price. Always ask about special packages or corporate rates.

When shopping for the best deal on hotels and car rentals, look for guaranteed exchange rates, which protect you against a falling dollar. With your rate locked in, you won't pay more, even if the price goes up in the local currency.

**🎫 Airline Tickets Air 4 Less** ☎ 800/AIR4LESS, low-fare specialist.

**🎫 Hotel Rooms Accommodations Express** ☎ 800/444-7666 or 800/277-1064 ⊕ www.acex. net. **Hotels.com** ☎ 800/246-8357 ⊕ www.hotels. com. **LondonTown.com** ☎ 020/7437-4370 ⊕ www. londontown.com. **Steigenberger Reservation Service** ☎ 800/223-5652 ⊕ www.srs-worldhotels. com. **Turbotrip.com** ☎ 800/473-7829 ⊕ www. turbotrip.com.

## PACKAGE DEALS

Don't confuse packages and guided tours. When you buy a package, you travel on your own, just as though you had planned the trip yourself. Fly–drive packages, which combine airfare and car rental, are often a good deal. In cities, ask the local visitor's bureau about hotel and local transportation packages that include tickets to major museum exhibits or other special events. Discount passes, such as London Pass, are available from the Britain and London Visitor Centre and Tourist Information Centre branches; many offer local transportation, entrance to museums, movie theaters, and galleries, and tours at considerable savings.

If you **buy a rail–drive pass,** you may save on train tickets and car rentals. All Eurail-pass holders get a discount on Eurostar fares through the Channel Tunnel and often receive reduced rates for buses, hotels, ferries, sightseeing cruises, and car rentals.

## ELECTRICITY

To use electric-powered equipment purchased in the United States or Canada, **bring a converter and adapter.** The electrical current in London is 220–240 volts (coming into line with the rest of Europe at 230 volts), 50 cycles alternating current (AC); wall outlets take three-pin plugs, and shaver sockets take two round, over-size prongs.

If your appliances are dual-voltage, you'll need only an adapter. Don't use 110-volt

outlets marked FOR SHAVERS ONLY for high-wattage appliances such as blow-dryers. Most laptops operate equally well on 110 and 220 volts and so require only an adapter. For converters, adapters, and advice, stop in one of the many STA Travel shops around London or at Nomad Travel.

**🎫 Nomad Travel** ✉ 40 Bernard St. ☎ 020/7833-4114 ✉ 52 Grosvenor Gardens ☎ 020/7823-5823. **STA Travel** ⊕ www.statravel.co.uk.

## EMBASSIES

**🎫 Australia Australia House** ✉ Strand, WC2 ☎ 020/7379-4334 ⊕ www.australia.org.uk.
**🎫 Canada MacDonald House** ✉ 1 Grosvenor Sq., W1 ☎ 020/7258-6600 ⊕ www.canada.org.uk.
**🎫 New Zealand New Zealand House** ✉ 80 Haymarket, SW1 ☎ 020/7930-8422.
**🎫 United States U.S. Embassy** ✉ 24 Grosvenor Sq., W1 ☎ 020/7499-9000. For passports, go to the **U.S. Passport Unit** ✉ 55 Upper Brook St., W1 ☎ 020/7499-9000 ⊕ www.usembassy.org.uk.

## EMERGENCIES

If you need to report a theft or an attack (London is a relatively safe city) go to the nearest police station (listed in the Yellow Pages or the local directory). For severe emergencies, dial 999 for police, fire, or ambulance (be prepared to give the telephone number you're calling from). National Health Service hospitals give free, 24-hour treatment in Accident and Emergency sections, where delays can be an hour or more. Prescriptions are valid only if made out by doctors registered in the United Kingdom.

**🎫 Doctors & Dentists Dental Emergency Care Service** ☎ 020/7955-2186. **Doctor's Call** ☎ 020/8900-1000. **Eastman Dental Hospital** ✉ 256 Gray's Inn Rd., WC1 ☎ 020/7915-1000. **Medical Express** ✉ 117A Harley St., W1 ☎ 020/7499-1991.
**🎫 Hospitals Charing Cross Hospital** ✉ Fulham Palace Rd., W6 ☎ 020/8846-1234. **Royal Free Hospital** ✉ Pond St., Hampstead, NW3 ☎ 020/7794-0500. **St. Thomas' Hospital** ✉ Lambeth Palace Rd., SE1 ☎ 020/7928-9292. **University College Hospital** ✉ Grafton Way, WC1 ☎ 020/7387-9300.
**🎫 Hotlines Samaritans** ☎ 020/7734-2800. **Victim Support** ☎ 020/7735-9166, 020/7582-5712 after office hours.

**Late-Night Pharmacies Bliss the Chemist**
✉ 5 Marble Arch, W1 ☎ 020/7723-6116.

## ETIQUETTE & BEHAVIOR

The British stiff upper lip is more relaxed, but on social occasions the rule is to observe and then go with the flow. If you're visiting a family home, a gift of flowers is welcome. If it's for a meal, then take a bottle of wine perhaps, and maybe some candy for the children—but not necessarily all three. Kissing on greeting is still too forward and Continental for most Brits. A warm handshake is just fine. For good-byes, if the atmosphere warrants, a quick one-cheek kiss is appropriate. The British can never say please, thank you, or sorry too often; to thank your host, a phone call or thank-you card does nicely.

### BUSINESS ETIQUETTE

In business, punctuality is of prime importance, so if you anticipate a late arrival, call ahead. On dinners: it is not assumed that spouses will attend unless pre-arranged, and if you proffered the invitation it is usually assumed that you will pick up the tab. If you are the visitor, however, it's good form for the host to do the taking. Alternatively, play it safe and offer to split the check.

### GAY & LESBIAN TRAVEL

The main gay communities are in the center of London (Soho, Old Compton St., and west to Kensington and Earls Court). There's a thriving social scene of clubs and cafés, and the best notice board for gay life and services is Gay's the Word. The *Pink Paper,* available at libraries, large bookstores, and gay cafés, *Gay Times,* and *Time Out* have comprehensive listings. Hotel front desks should serve any couple with courtesy, but using the travel agents listed below should send you in the right direction. The round-the-clock London Lesbian & Gay Switchboard has information on London's gay scene. The British Tourist Authority has a brochure and Web site for gay and lesbian travelers.

**Gay- & Lesbian-Friendly Travel Agencies Different Roads Travel** ✉ 8383 Wilshire Blvd., Suite 520, Beverly Hills, CA 90211 ☎ 323/651-5557 or 800/ 429-8747 (Ext. 14 for both) 🖷 323/651-5454 ✎ lgernert@tzell.com. **Kennedy Travel** ✉ 130 W. 42nd St., Suite 401, New York, NY 10036 ☎ 212/840-8659 or 800/237-7433 🖷 212/730-2269 ⊕ www. kennedytravel.com. **Now, Voyager** ✉ 4406 18th St., San Francisco, CA 94114 ☎ 415/626-1169 or 800/ 255-6951 🖷 415/626-8626 ⊕ www.nowvoyager. com. **Skylink Travel and Tour/Flying Dutchmen Travel** ✉ 1455 N. Dutton Ave., Suite A, Santa Rosa, CA 95401 ☎ 707/546-9888 or 800/225-5759 🖷 707/636-0951, serving lesbian travelers.

**Contacts in London Gay Times** ⊕ www. gaytimes.co.uk. **Gay's the Word** ✉ 66 Marchmont St., WC1 ☎ 020/7278-7654. **London's Lesbian & Gay Switchboard** ☎ 020/7837-7324 ⊕ www.llgs. org.uk.

## HEALTH

Great Britain has been plagued in recent years by concern about Bovine Spongiform Encephalopathy (BSE), commonly known as "mad cow" disease. Although the chance of catching the disease is extremely small, you may wish to avoid eating beef or choose beef or beef products, such as solid pieces of muscle meat (as opposed to burgers or sausages), which might have a reduced opportunity for contamination with tissues that could harbor the BSE agent.

Foot-and-mouth disease, which affects animals, spread in parts of the British countryside in 2001, but is now under control. The disease is very rare in humans and is harmless to them. For the latest information, contact the Centers for Disease Control and Prevention.

## HOLIDAYS

Standard holidays include: New Year's Day, Good Friday, Easter Monday, May Day (first Monday in May), spring and summer bank holidays (last Monday in May and August, respectively), Christmas, and Boxing Day (day after Christmas). On Christmas Eve and New Year's Eve some shops, restaurants, and businesses close early. Some museums and tourist attractions are also closed then. If you want to book a hotel room during this period, make sure you do it well in advance, and check to see whether the hotel restaurant will be open.

## INSURANCE

The most useful travel-insurance plan is a comprehensive policy that includes coverage for trip cancellation and interruption, default, trip delay, and medical expenses (with a waiver for preexisting conditions).

Without insurance you'll lose all or most of your money if you cancel your trip, regardless of the reason. Default insurance covers you if your tour operator, airline, or cruise line goes out of business—the chances of which have been increasing. Trip-delay covers expenses that arise because of bad weather or mechanical delays. Study the fine print when comparing policies.

If you're traveling internationally, a key component of travel insurance is coverage for medical bills incurred if you get sick on the road. Such expenses aren't generally covered by Medicare or private policies. Australian citizens need extra medical coverage when traveling abroad.

Always **buy travel policies directly from the insurance company;** if you buy them from a cruise line, airline, or tour operator that goes out of business you probably won't be covered for the agency or operator's default, a major risk. Before making any purchase, review your existing health and home-owner's policies to find what they cover away from home.

**Travel Insurers** In the U.S.: **Access America** ✉ 2805 N. Parham Rd., Richmond, VA 23294 ☎ 800/284-8300 📠 804/673-1491 or 800/346-9265 ⊕ www.accessamerica.com. **Travel Guard International** ✉ 1145 Clark St., Stevens Point, WI 54481 ☎ 715/345-0505 or 800/826-1300 📠 800/955-8785 ⊕ www.travelguard.com.

In the U.K.: **Association of British Insurers** ✉ 51 Gresham St., London EC2V 7HQ ☎ 020/7600-3333 📠 020/7696-8999 ⊕ www.abi.org.uk. In Canada: **RBC Insurance** ✉ 6880 Financial Dr., Mississauga, Ontario L5N 7Y5 ☎ 800/668-4342 or 905/816-2400 📠 905/813-4704 ⊕ www.rbcinsurance.com. In Australia: **Insurance Council of Australia** ✉ Insurance Enquiries and Complaints, Level 12, Box 561, Collins St. W, Melbourne, VIC 8007 ☎ 1300/780808 or 03/9629-4109 📠 03/9621-2060 ⊕ www.iecltd.com.au. In New Zealand: **Insurance Council of New Zealand** ✉ Level 7, 111-115 Customhouse Quay, Box 474, Wellington ☎ 04/472-5230 📠 04/473-3011 ⊕ www.icnz.org.nz.

## MAIL & SHIPPING

Stamps may be bought from post offices (open weekdays 9–5:30, Saturday 9–noon), from stamp machines outside post offices, and from newsagents' stores and newsstands. Mailboxes are known as post or letter boxes and are painted bright red; large tubular ones are set on the edge of sidewalks, while smaller boxes are set into post-office walls. Allow seven days for a letter to reach the United States. Check the Yellow Pages for a complete list of branches.

**Post Offices** ✉ 17 Euston Rd., NW1 ✉ 125-131 Westminster Bridge Rd., SW1 ✉ 110 Victoria St., SW1 ✉ 15 Broadwick St., W1 ✉ 54 Great Portland St., W1 ✉ 43 Seymour St., Marble Arch, W1 ✉ The Science Museum, SW7 ✉ 24 William IV St., Trafalgar Sq., WC2.

### OVERNIGHT SERVICES

**Major Services DHL** ☎ 0845/710-0300. **Federal Express** ☎ 0800/123800. **Parcelforce** ☎ 0800/224466.

### POSTAL RATES

Airmail letters up to 10 grams (0.35 ounce) to North America, Australia, and New Zealand cost 45p; postcards, 40p. Letters within Britain are 27p for first-class, 19p for second-class (these rates are subject to change).

### RECEIVING MAIL

If you're uncertain where you'll be staying, you can have mail sent to you at the London Main Post Office, c/o Poste Restante. The post office will hold international mail for one month.

**London Main Post Office** ✉ 24-28 William IV St., WC2N 4DL.

### SHIPPING PARCELS

Most department stores and retail outlets can ship your goods home. You should check your insurance for coverage of possible damage.

## MEDIA

### NEWSPAPERS & MAGAZINES

For the latest information about shops, restaurants, and art events, peruse Britain's glossy monthly magazines—*Tatler, Harpers & Queen, Vogue, Wallpaper, House &*

*Garden,* the *Face,* and *Time Out.* The *London Times,* the *Evening Standard,* the *Independent,* and the *Guardian* have comprehensive arts sections including reviews and advance news of future events. In addition, these newspapers have Web sites full of tips on what's hot and happening.

## RADIO & TELEVISION

The main channels are BBC1 and BBC2 from the British Broadcasting Corporation. BBC2 is considered the more eclectic and artsy, with a higher proportion of alternative humor, drama, and documentaries. The independent channels are ITV (Independent Television). There are big-budget highbrow productions occasionally, but there are more mainstream soaps, both homegrown—*Brookside* and *Coronation Street* (which the Queen is rumored to watch)—and international (the Australian *Neighbors* and some U.S. daytime shows such as *Dr. Phil*). There are general-interest shows as well. Channel 4 is a mixture of mainstream and off-the-wall, while Channel 5 has a higher proportion of sports, U.S. cop shows, and films. Satellite and cable channels (many of which are beamed into hotel rooms) have increased the daily diet now available round the clock.

Radio has seen a similar explosion, from 24-hour classics on Classic FM (100–102 mhz), and rock on Virgin (105.8 mhz), or nostalgic on Heart (106.2 mhz), or talk-talk on Talk Radio (MW1053 khz)—and that's just a sample of the independents. The BBC's Radio 1 (FM97.6) is for the young and hip; 2 (FM88) for middle-of-the-roadsters; 3 (FM90.2) for classics, jazz, and arts; 4 (FM92.4) for news, current affairs, drama, and documentary; and 5 Live (MW693 khz) for sports and news with phone-ins.

## MONEY MATTERS

A movie in the West End costs £6–£12 (at some cinemas less on Monday and at matinees); a theater seat, from £8.50 to about £35, more for hit shows; admission to a museum or gallery, around £5 (though some are free and others request a "voluntary contribution"); coffee, £1–£3;

a pint of light (lager) beer in a pub, £2 and more; whiskey, gin, vodka, and so forth, by the glass in a pub, £2.50 and up (the measure is smaller than in the United States); house wine by the glass in a pub or wine bar, around £2, in a restaurant £3.50 or more; a Coke, around £1; a ham sandwich from a sandwich bar in the West End, £2; a 1-mi taxi ride, £4; an average Underground ride, £1.60, a longer one £2.80. For standby theater tickets, many at half-price, go to the SOLT (Society of London Theaters) booth in Leicester Square for that day's shows; it's open Monday–Saturday, 10–7, Sunday noon–3:30. There's a service charge of £2.50, and most tickets are half-price, but a few are only at a 25% discount.

Prices throughout this guide are given for adults. Substantially reduced fees—generally referred to as "concessions" throughout Great Britain—are almost always available for children, students, and senior citizens. For information on taxes, *see* Taxes.

## ATMS

Credit cards or debit cards (also known as check cards) will get you cash advances at ATMs worldwide, but to make sure that your Cirrus or Plus card (to cite just two of the leading names) works in European ATMs, have your bank reset it to use a four-digit PIN number before your departure.

## CREDIT CARDS

Credit cards are accepted virtually everywhere in London.

Throughout this guide, the following abbreviations are used: **AE,** American Express; **DC,** Diners Club; **MC,** MasterCard; and **V,** Visa.

🗐 Reporting Lost Cards **American Express** ☎ 01273/696933. **Diners Club** ☎ 0800/460800. **MasterCard** ☎ 0800/964767. **Visa** ☎ 0800/891725.

## CURRENCY

The units of currency in Great Britain are the pound sterling (£) and pence (p): £50, £20, £10, and £5 bills (called notes); £2, £1 (100p), 50p, 20p, 10p, 5p, 2p, and 1p coins. At press time, the exchange rate was about Australian $2.42, Canadian $2.43, New Zealand $2.81, and U.S. $1.81 to the pound (also known as quid).

## CURRENCY EXCHANGE

For the most favorable rates, **change money through banks.** Although ATM transaction fees may be higher abroad than at home, ATM rates are excellent because they're based on wholesale rates offered only by major banks. You won't do as well at exchange booths in airports or rail and bus stations, in hotels, in restaurants, or in stores. To avoid lines at airport exchange booths, get a bit of local currency before you leave home.

**7 Exchange Services** International Currency Express ⊠ 427 N. Camden Dr., Suite F, Beverly Hills, CA 90210 🖷 888/278-6628 orders 🖷 310/278-6410 ⊕ www.foreignmoney.com. Travel Ex Currency Services 🖷 800/287-7362 orders and retail locations ⊕ www.travelex.com.

## TRAVELER'S CHECKS

Do you need traveler's checks? It depends on where you're headed. If you're going to rural areas and small towns, go with cash; traveler's checks are best used in cities. Lost or stolen checks can usually be replaced within 24 hours. To ensure a speedy refund, buy your own traveler's checks—don't let someone else pay for them: irregularities like this can cause delays. The person who bought the checks should make the call to request a refund.

## PACKING

London can be cool, damp, and overcast, even in summer. You'll need a heavy coat for winter and a lightweight coat or warm jacket for summer. **Always bring an umbrella and, if possible, a raincoat.** Pack as you would for an American city: jackets and ties for expensive restaurants and nightspots, casual clothes elsewhere. Jeans are popular in London and are perfectly acceptable for sightseeing and informal dining. Blazers and sport jackets are popular here with men. For women, ordinary street dress is acceptable everywhere. If you plan to stay in budget hotels, take your own soap.

In your carry-on luggage, pack an extra pair of eyeglasses or contact lenses and enough of any medication you take to last a few days longer than the entire trip. You may also ask your doctor to write a spare prescription using the drug's generic name, as brand names may vary from country to country. In luggage to be checked, **never pack prescription drugs, valuables, or undeveloped film.** And don't forget to carry with you the addresses of offices that handle refunds of lost traveler's checks. Check *Fodor's How to Pack* (available at online retailers and bookstores everywhere) for more tips.

To avoid customs and security delays, carry medications in their original packaging. Don't pack any sharp objects in your carry-on luggage, including knives of any size or material, scissors, nail clippers, and corkscrews, or anything else that might arouse suspicion.

To avoid having your checked luggage chosen for hand inspection, don't cram bags full. The U.S. Transportation Security Administration suggests packing shoes on top and placing personal items you don't want touched in clear plastic bags.

## CHECKING LUGGAGE

You're allowed to carry aboard one bag and one personal article, such as a purse or a laptop computer. Make sure what you carry on fits under your seat or in the overhead bin. Get to the gate early, so you can board as soon as possible, before the overhead bins fill up.

Baggage allowances vary by carrier, destination, and ticket class. On international flights, you're usually allowed to check two bags weighing up to 70 pounds (32 kilograms) each, although a few airlines allow checked bags of up to 88 pounds (40 kilograms) in first class. Some international carriers don't allow more than 66 pounds (30 kilograms) per bag in business class and 44 pounds (20 kilograms) in economy. On domestic flights, the limit is usually 50 to 70 pounds (23 to 32 kilograms) per bag. In general, carry-on bags shouldn't exceed 40 pounds (18 kilograms). Most airlines won't accept bags that weigh more than 100 pounds (45 kilograms) on domestic or international flights. Expect to pay a fee for baggage that exceeds weight limits. Check baggage restrictions with your carrier before you pack.

Airline liability for baggage is limited to $2,500 per person on flights within the United States. On international flights it amounts to $9.07 per pound or $20 per kilogram for checked baggage (roughly $640 per 70-pound bag), with a maximum of $634.90 per piece, and $400 per passenger for unchecked baggage. You can buy additional coverage at check-in for about $10 per $1,000 of coverage, but it often excludes a rather extensive list of items, shown on your airline ticket.

Before departure, itemize your bags' contents and their worth, and label the bags with your name, address, and phone number. (If you use your home address, cover it so potential thieves can't see it readily.) Include a label inside each bag and **pack a copy of your itinerary.** At check-in, make sure each bag is correctly tagged with the destination airport's three-letter code. Because some checked bags will be opened for hand inspection, the U.S. Transportation Security Administration recommends that you leave luggage unlocked or use the plastic locks offered at check-in. TSA screeners place an inspection notice inside searched bags, which are resealed with a special lock.

If your bag has been searched and contents are missing or damaged, file a claim with the TSA Consumer Response Center as soon as possible. If your bags arrive damaged or fail to arrive at all, file a written report with the airline before leaving the airport.

🗐 Complaints U.S. Transportation Security Administration Contact Center ☎ 866/289-9673 ⊕ www.tsa.gov.

## PASSPORTS & VISAS
When traveling internationally, carry your passport even if you don't need one (it's always the best form of ID) and **make two photocopies of the data page** (one for someone at home and another for you, carried separately from your passport). If you lose your passport, promptly call the nearest embassy or consulate and the local police.

U.S. passport applications for children under age 14 require consent from both parents or legal guardians; both parents must appear together to sign the application. If only one parent appears, he or she must submit a written statement from the other parent authorizing passport issuance for the child. A parent with sole authority must present evidence of it when applying; acceptable documentation includes the child's certified birth certificate listing only the applying parent, a court order specifically permitting this parent's travel with the child, or a death certificate for the nonapplying parent. Application forms and instructions are available on the Web site of the U.S. State Department's Bureau of Consular Affairs (⊕ travel.state.gov).

### ENTERING GREAT BRITAIN
U.S. and Canadian citizens need only a valid passport to enter Great Britain for stays of up to 90 days.

### PASSPORT OFFICES
The best time to apply for a passport or to renew is in fall and winter. Before any trip, check your passport's expiration date, and, if necessary, renew it as soon as possible.

🗐 Australian Citizens Passports Australia Australian Department of Foreign Affairs and Trade ☎ 131-232 ⊕ www.passports.gov.au. 🗐 Canadian Citizens Passport Office ⊠ To mail in applications: 200 Promenade du Portage, Hull, Québec J8X 4B7 ☎ 819/994-3500 or 800/567-6868 ⊕ www.ppt.gc.ca. 🗐 New Zealand Citizens New Zealand Passports Office ☎ 0800/22-5050 or 04/474-8100 ⊕ www.passports.govt.nz. 🗐 U.S. Citizens National Passport Information Center ☎ 877/487-2778, 888/874-7793 TDD, TTY ⊕ travel.state.gov.

### SAFETY
Don't wear a money belt or a waist pack, both of which peg you as a tourist. Distribute your cash and any valuables (including your credit cards and passport) between a deep front pocket, an inside jacket or vest pocket, and a hidden money pouch. Do not reach for the money pouch once you're in public.

## SENIOR-CITIZEN TRAVEL

To qualify for age-related discounts, mention your senior-citizen status up front when booking hotel reservations (not when checking out) and before you're seated in restaurants (not when paying the bill). Be sure to have identification on hand. When renting a car, ask about promotional car-rental discounts, which can be cheaper than senior-citizen rates.

**7** Educational Programs **Elderhostel** ✉ 11 Ave. de Lafayette, Boston, MA 02111-1746 ☎ 877/426-8056, 978/323-4141 international callers, 877/426-2167 TTY 🖶 877/426-2166 🌐 www.elderhostel.org. **Interhostel** ✉ University of New Hampshire, 6 Garrison Ave., Durham, NH 03824 ☎ 603/862-1147 or 800/733-9753 🖶 603/862-1113 🌐 www.learn.unh.edu.

## SIGHTSEEING TOURS

### BUS TOURS

Guided sightseeing tours from the top of a double-decker bus, which are open-top in summer, are a good introduction to the city, as they cover all the main central sights. There's a choice of companies, each providing daily tours departing (between 8:30 and 9 AM) from central points. You may board or alight at any of the numerous stops to view the sights, and reboard on the next bus. Tickets are bought from the driver and are good all day. Prices vary according to the type of tour, although £12 is the benchmark.

**7** Tour Operators **Big Bus Company** ☎ 020/7233-9533. **Big Value Tours** ☎ 020/77233-7797. **Black Taxi Tour of London** ☎ 020/7289-4371. **Evan Evans** ☎ 020/7950-1777. **Golden Tours** ☎ 020/77233-7030. **Humdinger Bike Tours** ☎ 01689/827371. **London Bicycle Tour** ☎ 020/7928-6838. **London Pride** ☎ 020/7520-2050. **London Spy Tours** ☎ 0870/060-0100. **Original London Sightseeing Tour** ☎ 020/8877-1722. **Premium Tours** ☎ 020/7278-5300.

### CANAL TOURS

The tranquil side of London is to be found on narrow boats that cruise London's two canals, the Grand Union and Regent's Canal; most vessels operate on the latter, which runs between Little Venice in the west (nearest Tube: Warwick Avenue on the Bakerloo Line) and Camden Lock (about 200 yards north of Camden Town Tube station). Fares are about £5 for 1½-hour cruises.

**7** Cruise Operators **Canal Cruises** ☎ 020/8440-8962. **Jason's Trip** ☎ 020/7286-3428. **London Waterbus Company** ☎ 020/7482-2660.

### WALKING TOURS

One of the best ways to get to know London is on foot, and there are many guided and themed walking tours from which to choose. If you wish to tailor your own tour, you might consider hiring a Blue Badge accredited guide or using Great London Treasure Hunt self-guided tours.

**7** Tour Operators **Blue Badge** ☎ 020/7495-5504. **Blood and Tears Walk** ☎ 020/8348-9022. **Citisights** ☎ 020/8806-4325. **Great London Treasure Hunt** ☎ 020/7928-2627. **Historical Walks** ☎ 020/8668-4019. **Shakespeare City Walk** ☎ 080/8348-9022. **Jack the Ripper Mystery Walks** ☎ 020/8558-9446. **Original London Walks** ☎ 020/7624-3978.

### BOAT TOURS

All year round, but more frequently from April to October, boats cruise the Thames, offering a different view of the London skyline. Most leave from Westminster Pier, Charing Cross Pier, and Tower Pier. Downstream routes go to the Tower of London, Greenwich, and the Thames Barrier via Canary Wharf. Upstream destinations include Kew, Richmond, and Hampton Court (mainly in summer). Most of the launches seat between 100 and 250 passengers, have a public-address system, and provide a running commentary on passing points of interest. Depending upon the destination, river trips may last from one to four hours. Capital Frog Tours uses amphibious vehicles to tour around and in the Thames.

A Sail and Rail ticket combines the modern wonders of Canary Wharf by Docklands Light Railway with a trip on the river. Tickets are available year-round from Westminster Pier or DLR stations; ticket holders also get discounted tickets to the London Aquarium in Westminster and the National Maritime Museum in Greenwich.

Details on all river cruise operators are available from London River Services.

🚢 River Cruise Operators **Catamaran Cruisers** ☎ 020/7987-1185. **London Duck Tours** ☎ 020/7928-3132. **London River Services** ☎ 020/7941-2400. **Sail and Rail** ☎ 020/7363-9700. **Thames Cruises** ☎ 020/7930-4097. **Westminster Passenger Boat Services** ☎ 020/7930-4097.

## EXCURSIONS

London Regional Transport, Green Line, Evan Evans, National Express, and Frames Rickards all offer day excursions by bus to places within easy reach of London, such as Hampton Court, Oxford, Stratford, and Bath.

## STUDENTS IN LONDON

🚢 IDs & Services **STA Travel** ✉ 10 Downing St., New York, NY 10014 ☎ 212/627-3111, 800/777-0112 24-hr service center 🖨 212/627-3387 ⊕ www.sta.com. **Travel Cuts** ✉ 187 College St., Toronto, Ontario M5T 1P7, Canada ☎ 800/592-2887 in the U.S., 416/979-2406 or 866/246-9762 in Canada 🖨 416/979-8167 ⊕ www.travelcuts.com.

## TAXES

An airport departure tax of £20 (£10 for within U.K. and other EU countries) per person is payable and may be subject to more government tax increases, although it's included in the price of your ticket.

### VALUE-ADDED TAX

The British sales tax (V.A.T., Value Added Tax) is 17½%. The tax is almost always included in quoted prices in shops, hotels, and restaurants.

Most travelers can **get a V.A.T. refund** by either the Retail Export or the more cumbersome Direct Export method. Many large stores provide these services, but only if you request them; they will handle the paperwork. For the Retail Export method, you must ask the store for Form VAT 407 (you must have identification—passports are best), to be given to customs at your last port of departure. (Lines at major airports can be long, so allow plenty of time.) The refund will be forwarded to you in about eight weeks, minus a small service charge, either in the form of a credit to your charge card or as a British check, which American banks usually

charge you to convert. With the Direct Export method, the goods go directly to your home; you must have a Form VAT 407 certified by customs, police, or a notary public when you get home and then sent back to the store, which will refund your money. For inquiries, call the local Customs & Excise office listed in the London telephone directory.

When making a purchase, **ask for a V.A.T. refund form** and find out whether the merchant gives refunds—not all stores do, nor are they required to. Have the form stamped like any customs form by customs officials when you leave the country or, if you're visiting several European Union countries, when you leave the EU. Be ready to show customs officials what you've bought (pack purchases together, in your carry-on luggage); budget extra time for this. After you're through passport control, take the form to a refund-service counter for an on-the-spot refund, or mail it to the address on the form (or the envelope with it) after you arrive home.

A service processes refunds for most shops. You receive the total refund stated on the form. Global Refund is a Europe-wide service with 210,000 affiliated stores and more than 700 refund counters—located at major airports and border crossings. Its refund form is called a Tax Free Check. The service issues refunds in the form of cash, check, or credit-card adjustment. If you don't have time to wait at the refund counter, you can mail in the form instead.

🚢 V.A.T. Refunds **Global Refund** ✉ 99 Main St., Suite 307, Nyack, NY 10960 ☎ 800/566-9828 🖨 845/348-1549 ⊕ www.globalrefund.com.

## TAXIS

Those big black taxicabs are as much a part of the London streetscape as the red double-decker buses, yet many have been replaced by the new boxy, sharp-edge model, and the beauty of others is marred by the advertising they carry on their sides. Hotels and main tourist areas have cab stands (just take the first in line), but you can also flag one down from the roadside. If the yellow FOR HIRE sign on the top is lit, the taxi is available. Cab drivers often cruise at night with their signs unlit so that they can choose their passengers and avoid those they think might cause trouble. If you see an unlit, passengerless cab, hail it: you might be lucky.

Fares start at £2 and increase by about £1.80 for every mile or £.30 per minute. Surcharges are a tricky extra, ranging from 40p for additional passengers or bulky luggage to £2 for ordering by phone. Evenings 8 PM–midnight, and until 6 AM on weekends and public holidays the meters tick over faster—and at Christmas and New Year the surcharge is £3. Fares are occasionally raised from year to year. Tip taxi drivers 10%–15% of the tab.

## TELEPHONES

### AREA & COUNTRY CODES

The country code for Great Britain is 44. When dialing from abroad, drop the initial "0" from the local area code. The code for London is 020, followed by a 7 for numbers in central London, or an 8 for numbers in the Greater London area. The whole number is composed of 8 digits. Freephone (toll-free) numbers start with 0800; national information numbers start with 0845.

### DIRECTORY & OPERATOR ASSISTANCE

For information anywhere in Britain, dial 118. For the operator, dial 100. For assistance with international calls, dial 155.

### INTERNATIONAL CALLS

When calling from overseas to access a London telephone number, drop the 0 from the prefix and dial only 20 (or any other British area code) and then the eight-digit phone number. To give one example: Let's say you're calling Buckingham Palace—020/7839–1377 from the United States to inquire about tours and hours. First, dial 011 (the international access code), then 44 (Great Britain's country code), then 20 (London's city center code), then the remainder of the telephone number, 7839–1377.

### LOCAL CALLS

You don't have to dial London's central area code (020) if you are calling inside

London itself—just the eight-digit telephone number.

### LONG-DISTANCE CALLS

For long-distance calls within Britain, dial the area code (which begins with 01), followed by the number. The area-code prefix is only used when you are dialing from outside the city. In provincial areas, the dialing codes for nearby towns are often posted in the booth.

### LONG-DISTANCE SERVICES

AT&T, MCI, and Sprint access codes make calling long-distance relatively convenient, but you may find the local access number blocked in many hotel rooms. First ask the hotel operator to connect you. If the hotel operator balks, ask for an international operator, or dial the international operator yourself. One way to improve your odds of getting connected to your long-distance carrier is to travel with more than one company's calling card (a hotel may block Sprint, for example, but not MCI). If all else fails, call from a pay phone.

You can also pick up one of the many instant international phone cards from newsstands, which can be used from residential, hotel, and public pay phones. With these, you can call the United States for as little as 5p per minute.

🔲 **Access Codes** In the U.K., there are AT&T access numbers to dial the U.S. using three different phone types—**AT&T Direct** ☎ 0500/890011. **MCI World-Phone** ☎ 0800/279–5088 in the U.K., 800/444–4141 for the U.S. via MCI and other areas. In the U.K., there are Sprint access numbers to dial the U.S. using three different phone types—**Sprint International Access** ☎ 0800/890–877.

### PHONE CARDS

Public card phones operate with special cards that you can buy from post offices or newsstands. They are ideal for longer calls; are composed of units of 10p; and come in values of £3, £5, £10, and more. To use a card phone, lift the receiver, insert your card, and dial the number. An indicator panel shows the number of units used. At the end of your call, the card will be returned. Where credit cards are taken, slide the card through, as indicated.

## PUBLIC PHONES

There are three types of phones: those that accept (a) only coins, (b) only British Telecom (BT) phone cards, or (c) BT phone cards and credit cards.

The coin-operated phones are of the push-button variety; the workings of coin-operated telephones vary, but there are usually instructions on each unit. Most take 10p, 20p, 50p, and £1 coins. Insert the coins *before* dialing (minimum charge is 10p). If you hear a repeated single tone after dialing, the line is busy; a continual tone means the number is unobtainable (or that you have dialed the wrong—or no—prefix). The indicator panel shows you how much money is left; add more whenever you like. If there is no answer, replace the receiver and your money will be returned.

All calls are charged according to the time of day. Standard rate is weekdays 8 AM–6 PM; cheap rate is weekdays 6 PM–8 AM and all day on weekends, when it's even cheaper. A local call before 6 PM costs 15p for three minutes; this doubles to 30p for the same from a pay phone. A daytime call to the United States will cost 24p a minute on a regular phone (weekends are cheaper), 80p on a pay phone.

## TIME

London is five hours ahead of New York City. In other words, when it's 3 PM in New York (or noon in Los Angeles) it's 8 PM in London. Note that London and most European countries also move their clocks ahead for the one-hour differential when daylight savings time goes into effect (although they make the changeover several days after the United States).

## TIPPING

Many restaurants and large hotels (particularly those belonging to chains) will automatically add a 10%–15% service charge to your bill, so **always check if tipping is necessary** before you hand out any extra money.

Do not tip movie or theater ushers, elevator operators, or bar staff in pubs—although you can always offer to buy them a drink. Washroom attendants may display

a saucer, in which it's reasonable to leave 20p or so.

Here's a guide for other tipping situations. Restaurants: 10%–20% of the check for full meals if service is not already included (if paying by credit card, check that a tip has not already been included before you fill in the total on your credit slip), a small token if you're just having coffee or tea. Taxis: 10%–15%, or perhaps a little more for a short ride. Porters: 50p–£1 per bag. Doormen: £1 for hailing taxis or for carrying bags to check-in desk. Bellhops: £1 for carrying bags, £1 for room service. Hairdressers: 10%–15% of the bill, plus £1–£2 for the hair washer.

## TOURS & PACKAGES

Because everything is prearranged on a prepackaged tour or independent vacation, you spend less time planning—and often get it all at a good price.

### BOOKING WITH AN AGENT

Travel agents are excellent resources. But it's a good idea to collect brochures from several agencies, as some agents' suggestions may be influenced by relationships with tour and package firms that reward them for volume sales. If you have a special interest, find an agent with expertise in that area; the American Society of Travel Agents (ASTA; ⇨ Travel Agencies) has a database of specialists worldwide. You can log on to the group's Web site to find an ASTA travel agent in your neighborhood.

Make sure your travel agent knows the accommodations and other services of the place being recommended. Ask about the hotel's location, room size, beds, and whether it has a pool, room service, or programs for children, if you care about these. Has your agent been there in person or sent others whom you can contact?

Do some homework on your own, too: local tourism boards can provide information about lesser-known and small-niche operators, some of which may sell only direct.

### BUYER BEWARE

Each year consumers are stranded or lose their money when tour operators—even large ones with excellent reputations—go out of business. So check out the operator. Ask several travel agents about its reputation, and try to **book with a company that has a consumer-protection program.** (Look for information in the company's brochure.) In the United States, members of the United States Tour Operators Association are required to set aside funds ($1 million) to help eligible customers cover payments and travel arrangements in the event that the company defaults. It's also a good idea to choose a company that participates in the American Society of Travel Agents' Tour Operator Program; ASTA will act as mediator in any disputes between you and your tour operator.

Remember that the more your package or tour includes, the better you can predict the ultimate cost of your vacation. Make sure you know exactly what is covered, and beware of hidden costs. Are taxes, tips, and transfers included? Entertainment and excursions? These can add up.

🎲 Tour-Operator Recommendations **American Society of Travel Agents** ( ⇨ Travel Agencies). **National Tour Association** (NTA) ✉ 546 E. Main St., Lexington, KY 40508 ☎ 859/226-4444 or 800/682-8886 🖷 859/226-4404 ⊕ www.ntaonline.com. **United States Tour Operators Association** (USTOA) ✉ 275 Madison Ave., Suite 2014, New York, NY 10016 ☎ 212/599-6599 🖷 212/599-6744 ⊕ www. ustoa.com.

## TRAIN TRAVEL

London has eight major train stations that serve as arteries to the rest of the country (and to Europe). All are served by the Underground. As a general rule of thumb, the stations' location in the city matches the part of the country they serve. Charing Cross serves southeast England, including Canterbury and Dover/Folkestone for Europe. Euston serves the Midlands, north Wales, northwest England, and western Scotland. King's Cross marks the end of the Great Northern Line, serving northeast England and Scotland. Liverpool Street serves East Anglia, including Cambridge and Norwich. Paddington mainly serves south Wales and the West Country, as well as Reading, Oxford, and Bristol. St. Pancras serves Leicester, Nottingham, and

Sheffield in south Yorkshire. Victoria serves southern England, including Brighton, Dover/Folkestone, and the south coast. Waterloo serves southeastern destinations, including Portsmouth and Southampton. The Eurostar service to France and Belgium departs from Waterloo International, within Waterloo station.

Some trains have refreshment carriages, called buffet cars. Smoking is forbidden in rail carriages.

### CLASSES
Some trains have first-class and reserved seats (for which there is a small charge, depending on the rail company). Check with National Rail Enquiries for details.

### CUTTING COSTS
To save money, **look into rail passes.** But be aware that if you don't plan to cover many miles, you may come out ahead by buying individual tickets.

Apex tickets, bought seven days in advance, provide savings. Many discount passes are also available, such as the Young Person's Railcard (for which you must be under 26 and provide two passport-size photos) and the Family Travelcard, which can be bought from most mainline stations. But if you intend to make several long-distance rail journeys, it's far better to invest in a BritRail Pass (if you're leaving from the United States).

### FARES & SCHEDULES
Delays are often a national joking matter, particularly since a renovation of rails and rolling stock. National Rail Enquiries provides an up-to-date state-of-the-railways schedule. Rail travel is expensive: for instance, a round-trip ticket to Bath can cost around £60 per person at peak times. The fee reduces to around £30 at other times, so it's best to travel before or after the frantic business commuter rush (before 4:30 PM and after 9:30 AM). Credit cards are accepted for train fares paid both in person and by phone.

🎲 Train Information **BritRail Travel** ☎ 877/677-1066 in the U.S. **Eurostar** ☎ 0990/186186. **National Rail Enquiries** ☎ 0845/748-4950, 0161/236-3522 outside the U.K. **Rail Europe** ☎ 0870/584-8848.

## TRANSPORTATION AROUND LONDON

By far the easiest and most practical way to get around is on the Underground or "Tube." This underground train system runs daily from early morning to night and provides a comprehensive service throughout the center with lines out to the suburbs. Tube fares can work out to be higher than bus fares, but if you're traveling a lot around town, then you should investigate buying a Travelcard pass, which gives you discounted flexible travel on the Tube, plus bus and some overground rail travel (⇨ Underground Tube Travel).

The overground rail system is a network that connects outlying districts and suburbs to the center. Prices are comparable to the Underground, and you can easily transfer between the Underground and other connecting rail lines at many Tube stations. Some passes are good for both the Underground and the rail system, so check at the point of purchase.

If you want to see the city, buses crisscross all over town. Their routes are more complicated than the Tube, but by reading the route posted on the main bus stop and watching the route on the front of the bus, you won't go far wrong. Bus travel prices are cheaper than the Tube the farther you travel, but be prepared to get stuck in traffic, even though designated lanes for buses and taxis should speed up the journey. Services are frequent, but if you become frustrated and flag down a taxi, the fare can clock up to three times the price of a similar bus fare for the same distance. If you're traveling with several people, however, riding in a taxi is relatively inexpensive and is more comfortable and convenient.

## TRAVEL AGENCIES

A good travel agent puts your needs first. Look for an agency that has been in business at least five years, emphasizes customer service, and has someone on staff who specializes in your destination. In addition, **make sure the agency belongs to a professional trade organization.** The American Society of Travel Agents (ASTA)—the largest and most influential in the field with more than 20,000 members

in some 140 countries—maintains and enforces a strict code of ethics and will step in to help mediate any agent-client disputes involving ASTA members if necessary. ASTA (whose motto is "Without a travel agent, you're on your own") also maintains a Web site that includes a directory of agents. (If a travel agency is also acting as your tour operator, *see* Buyer Beware *in* Tours & Packages.)

**⊞ Local Agent Referrals American Society of Travel Agents (ASTA)** ✉ 1101 King St., Suite 200, Alexandria, VA 22314 ☎ 703/739-2782, 800/965-2782 24-hr hotline 🖶 703/684-8319 ⊕ www. astanet.com. **Association of British Travel Agents** ✉ 68-71 Newman St., London W1T 3AH ☎ 020/7637-2444 🖶 020/7637-0713 ⊕ www.abta.com. **Association of Canadian Travel Agencies** ✉ 130 Albert St., Suite 1705, Ottawa, Ontario K1P 5G4 ☎ 613/237-3657 🖶 613/237-7052 ⊕ www.acta.ca. **Australian Federation of Travel Agents** ✉ Level 3, 309 Pitt St., Sydney, NSW 2000 ☎ 02/9264-3299 or 1300/363-416 🖶 02/9264-1085 ⊕ www.afta.com. au. **Travel Agents' Association of New Zealand** ✉ Level 5, Tourism and Travel House, 79 Boulcott St., Box 1888, Wellington 6001 ☎ 04/499-0104 🖶 04/499-0786 ⊕ www.taanz.org.nz.

## UNDERGROUND TUBE TRAVEL

London's extensive Underground train (Tube) system has color-coded routes, clear signage, and extensive connections. Trains run out into the suburbs, and all stations are marked with the London Underground circular symbol. (In Britain, the word "subway" means "pedestrian underpass.") Trains are all one class; smoking is *not* allowed on board or in the stations.

Some lines have branches (Central, District, Northern, Metropolitan, and Piccadilly), so **be sure to note which branch is needed for your particular destination.** Electronic platform signs tell you the final stop and route of the next train and how many minutes you'll have to wait for the train to arrive. The zippy Docklands Light Railway runs through the modern Docklands with an extension to the *Cutty Sark* and maritime Greenwich.

## FARES & SCHEDULES

London is divided into six concentric zones (ask at Underground ticket booths for a map and booklet, which give details of the ticket options), so make sure to buy a ticket for the correct zone or you may be liable for an on-the-spot fine (£10 at press time).

You can buy a single or return ticket, the equivalent of a one-way and a round-trip, for travel anytime on the day of issue. Singles vary in price from £1.60 to £3.70. If you are planning several trips in one day then consider a Travelcard, which is good for unrestricted travel on both Tube and bus and some overground railways; these are valid weekdays after 9:30 AM, weekends, and on all public holidays, but cannot be used on airbuses, Night Buses, or for certain special services. Other options are: One Day Travelcard (£4.10–£7); Seven-Day Travelcard (£17 for Zone 1); Weekend Travelcards, for the two days of the weekend and on any two consecutive days during public holidays (£6.10–£7.60); Family Travelcards, which are one-day tickets for one or two adults with one to four children (£3–£3.40 with one child, additional children cost 80p each); or the Carnet, a book of 10 single tickets valid for central Zone 1 (£11.50) to use anytime over a year. The Visitor's Travelcard may be bought in the United States and Canada. Three ticket types for periods of two to seven days exist for zones 1–6, zones 1 and 2 or a round-trip Heathrow Express ticket. Prices start at about $20 for a zone 1 and 2 ticket valid for 3 days and go up to about $60 for a zone 1–6 ticket valid for one week. Apply to travel agents or, in the United States, to BritRail Travel.

Trains begin running just after 5 AM Monday–Saturday; the last services leave central London between midnight and 12:30 AM. On Sunday, trains start two hours later and finish about an hour earlier. Frequency of trains depends on the route and the time of day, but normally you should not have to wait more than 10 minutes in central areas.

There are TfL Travel Information Centres at the following Tube stations: Euston, Liverpool Street, Piccadilly Circus, and Victoria, open 7:15 AM–10 PM; and at Heathrow Airport (in Terminals 1, 2, and 4), open 6 AM–3 PM. For travelers with disabilities, get the free leaflet, "Access to the Underground."

🚇 **Underground Information** "Access to the Underground" ☎ 020/7941-4600. **BritRail Travel** ☎ 877/677-1066. **Transport for London** ☎ 020/7222-1234 ⊕ www.tfl.gov.uk.

## VISITOR INFORMATION

Learn more about foreign destinations by checking government-issued travel advisories and country information. For a broader picture, consider information from more than one country.

When you arrive in London, you can go in person to the London Visitor Centre at Waterloo International Terminal arrivals hall for general information (daily 8:30 AM–10:30 PM) or to the Britain and London Visitor Centre for travel, hotel, and entertainment information. It's open June–October, weekdays 9:30–6:30, Saturday 9–5, Sunday 10–4; and November–May, weekdays 9:30–6:30, weekends 10–4). The London Tourist Information Centre also has branches in Greenwich and in Southwark.

The official Web site of VisitBritain, the British Tourist Authority is ⊕ www.visitbritain.com. Its "gateway" Web site, ⊕ www.usagateway.visitbritain.com, provides information most helpful to Britain-bound U.S. travelers.

🚩 **In the U.S. VisitBritain** (BTA) ✉ 551 5th Ave., 7th fl., New York, NY 10176 ☎ 212/986-2200 or 800/462-2748.

🚩 **In Canada VisitBritain** ✉ 5915 Airport Rd., Suite 120, Mississauga, Ontario L4V 1T1 ☎ 905/405-1840 or 800/847-4885.

🚩 **In the U.K. VisitBritain** ✉ Thames Tower, Black's Rd., London W6 9EL ☎ 020/8846-9000.

🚩 **In London Britain and London Visitor Centre** ✉ 1 Regent St., Piccadilly Circus, SW1Y 4NX. **London Tourist Information Centre** ✉ Pepys House, 2 Cutty Sark Gardens, Greenwich SE10 9LW ☎ 0870/608-2000 ✉ Vinopolis, 1 Bank End, Southwark SE1 9BU ☎ 020/7357-9168. **Londonline** ☎ 09068/663344.

🚩 **Government Advisories U.S. Department of State** ✉ Overseas Citizens Services Office, 2100 Pennsylvania Ave. NW, 4th fl., Washington, DC 20520 ☎ 202/647-5225 interactive hotline or 888/407-4747 ⊕ www.travel.state.gov. **Consular Affairs**

**Bureau of Canada** ☎ 800/267–6788 or 613/944–6788 ⊕ www.voyage.gc.ca. **Australian Department of Foreign Affairs and Trade** ☎ 300/139–281 travel advice, 02/6261-1299 Consular Travel Advice Faxback Service ⊕ www.dfat.gov.au. **New Zealand Ministry of Foreign Affairs and Trade** ☎ 04/439–8000 ⊕ www.mft.govt.nz.

## WEB SITES

Do check out the World Wide Web when planning your trip. You'll find everything from weather forecasts to virtual tours of famous cities. Be sure to visit Fodors.com (⊕ www.fodors.com), a complete travel-planning site. You can research prices and book plane tickets, hotel rooms, rental cars, vacation packages, and more. In addition, you can post your pressing questions in the Travel Talk section. Other planning tools include a currency converter and weather reports, and there are loads of links to travel resources.

For more information specifically on London, visit one of the following:

The official London Web site is ⊕ www. visitlondon.com, which supplies event information, accommodation booking, and helpful links to other Web sites. Other sites of interest include ⊕ www.londontown. com and the Evening Standard's Online ⊕ www.thisislondon.com, Transport for London ⊕ www.tfl.gov.uk, The Palace, No. 10 Downing Street, U.K. Weather, and the BBC. For travel around the U.K. by bus, check out ⊕ www.gobycoach.com.

For London events and news months in advance, visit the following culture and entertainment Web sites: ⊕ www.timeout. co.uk, ⊕ www.officiallondontheatre.co. uk, ⊕ www.kidslovelondon.com, and ⊕ www.ukcalling.co.uk.royal-albert. For the hotel scene in London, visit ⊕ www. demon.co.uk/hotel-uk. For the full array of walking tours offered by the excellent Original London Walks, try ⊕ www. walks.com. For walks in and around the city, with maps to download, head to ⊕ www.londonwalking.com.

# EXPLORING
# LONDON

Updated by
Jacqueline
Brown

**IF LONDON CONTAINED ONLY ITS LANDMARKS**—Buckingham Palace, Big Ben, the Tower of London—it would still rank as one of the world's top destinations. But England's capital is much more. It's a bevy of British bobbies, an ocean of black umbrellas, and an unconquered continuance of more than 2,000 years of history. A city that loves to be explored, London beckons with great museums, royal pageantry, and quirky historical hideaways.

London is an ancient city whose history greets you at every turn. To gain a sense of its continuity, stand on Waterloo Bridge at the hour of sunset. To the east, the great globe of St. Paul's Cathedral glows golden in the fading sunlight as it has since the 17th century, still majestic amid the towers of glass and steel that hem it in. To the west stand the mock-medieval ramparts of Westminster—here you'll find the "Mother of Parliaments," which has met here or hereabouts since the 1250s. Past them both snakes the swift, dark Thames, as it flowed past the first Roman settlement here, circa AD 50.

For much of its history, innumerable epigrams and observations have been coined about London by both her enthusiasts and detractors. The great 18th-century writer and wit Samuel Johnson said that a man who is tired of London is tired of life. Oliver Wendell Holmes said, "No person can be said to know London. The most that anyone can claim is that he knows something of it." Simply stated, London is one of the most interesting places on earth. There is no other place like it in its agglomeration of architectural sins and sudden intervention of almost rural sights, in its medley of styles, in its mixture of the green loveliness of parks and the modern gleam of neon. Thankfully, the old London of Queen Anne and Georgian architecture can still be discovered under the hasty routine of later additions.

Discovering it takes a bit of work, however. Modern-day London still largely reflects its medieval layout, a willfully difficult tangle of streets. Even Londoners, most of whom own a copy of the indispensable A–Z street finder (they come under different names), get lost in their own city. But London's bewildering street pattern will be a plus if you want to experience its indefinable historic environment. London is a walker's city and will repay every moment you spend exploring on foot. The undaunted visitor who wants to penetrate beyond the city's crust is well advised to not only visit St. Paul's Cathedral and the Tower but also to set aside some time for random wandering. Walk in the back streets and mews around Park Lane and Kensington. Pass up Buckingham Palace for Hampton Court, beautifully situated by the Thames and a perfect place to spend a summer day. Take in the National Gallery, but don't forget London's "time machine" museums, such as the 19th-century homes of Linley Sambourne and Sir John Soane. For out-and-out glamour, pay a call on the palatial Wallace Collection and Apsley House, the historic residence of the Duke of Wellington. Go beyond the city's standard-issue chain stores to discover unique shopping emporiums, such as the gentlemen's outfitters of St. James's. Getting off the beaten track will help you visualize the shape, or rather the various shapes, of Old London, a curious city that engulfed its own past for the sake of modernity but still lives and breathes the air of history.

Today, that sense of modernity can be seen and sensed all around. No wonder, then, that London remains a major cultural hot spot, with its art, style, and fashions making headlines around the world. London's chefs have transformed the city's restaurants and are widely regarded as superstars; its fashion designers—John Galliano, Julien Macdonald, Stella McCartney, and Alexander McQueen—have conquered Paris; avant-garde artists regularly cause controversy in the media; the vibrant, raging after-hours scene is packed with music mavens ready to catch the next big thing; and the theater, from grand stage to fringe, includes radical productions, while bringing an incisive, witty edge to the classic repertoire.

On the other hand, although the outward shapes may be altered and the inner spirit more diverse and cosmopolitan than in years past, the bedrock of London's character and tradition remains the same. The British bobby is alive and well, although more often to be seen in flashing cars than on the beat, walking the streets. The tall, red, double-decker buses still lumber from stop to stop, though their aesthetic match at street level, the glossy red telephone booth, has almost disappeared in favor of U.S.-style open glass cabinets. And a proper English tea can be found, if you search hard enough, with scones, jam, and clotted cream. Then, of course, there's that greatest living link with the past—the Royal Family. Don't let the tag "typical tourist" stop you from enjoying the pageantry of the Windsors, one of the greatest free shows in the world. Line up for the Changing of the Guard and poke into the Royal Mews for a look at the golden, fairy-tale Coronation Coach. Pomp reaches its zenith in mid-June when the queen celebrates her official birthday with a parade called Trooping the Colour. Royalty-watching is by no means restricted to fascinated foreigners. You only have to open the national newspapers to read reports of the latest rumors.

In the end, the London you'll discover will surely include some of our enthusiastic recommendations, but be prepared to be taken by surprise as well. The best that a great city has to offer often comes in unexpected ways. Armed with energy and curiosity, and the practical information and helpful hints in the following pages, you can be sure of one thing: to quote Dr. Johnson again, you'll be able to find "in London all that life can afford."

# WESTMINSTER & ROYAL LONDON

This tour might be called "London for Beginners." If you went no farther than these few acres, you would see many of the most famous sights, from the Houses of Parliament, Big Ben, Westminster Abbey, and Buckingham Palace to two of the world's greatest art collections, housed in the National and Tate Britain galleries. You can truly call this area Royal London, as it is neatly bounded by the triangle of streets that make up the route that the queen usually takes when journeying from Buckingham Palace to the Abbey or to the Houses of Parliament on state oc-

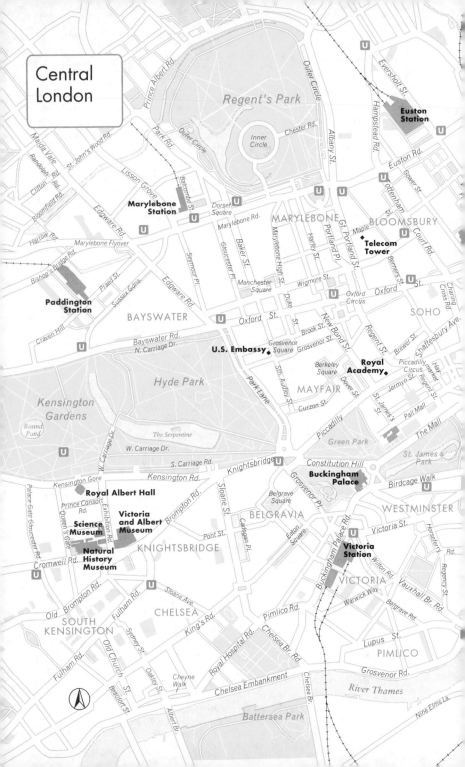

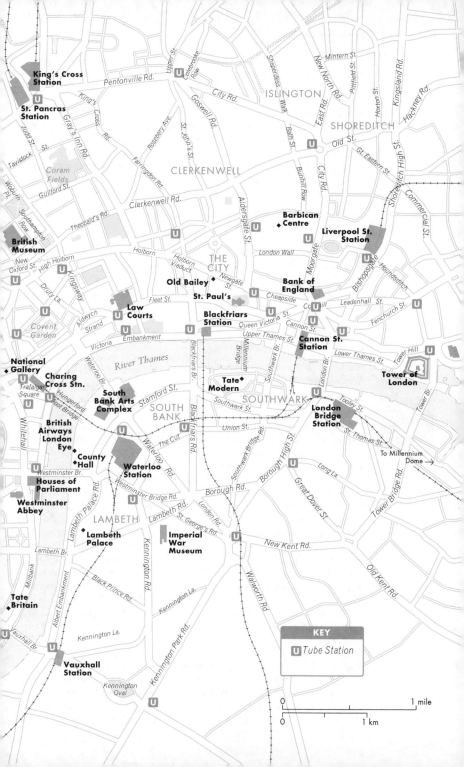

casions. The three points on this royal triangle are Trafalgar Square, Westminster, and Buckingham Palace. If you have time to visit only one part of London, undoubtedly this should be it. There is as much history in these few acres as in many entire cities, as the statues of kings, queens, soldiers, and statesmen that stand guard at every corner attest—this is concentrated sightseeing, so pace yourself. The main drawback to sightseeing here is that half the world is doing it at the same time. So, even if you're tired after a long day on your feet, try to come back in the evening, after the crowds have dispersed, to drink in the serenity and grandeur at your leisure. Not only does it make for a calmer experience, you can also enjoy the floodlit beauty of many of these places by night.

Westminster is by far the younger of the capital's two centers, postdating the City by some 1,000 years. Edward the Confessor put it on the map when he packed up his court from its cramped City quarters and moved it west a couple of miles, founding the abbey church of Westminster—the minster west of the City—in 1050. Subsequent kings continued to hold court here until Henry VIII decamped to Whitehall Palace in 1512, leaving Westminster to the politicians. And here they are still, not in the palace, which burned almost to the ground in 1834, but in the Victorian mock-Gothic Houses of Parliament, whose 320-foot-high Clock Tower (Big Ben) is as much a symbol of London as the Eiffel Tower is of Paris.

*Numbers in the text correspond to numbers in the margin and on the Westminster & Royal London map.*

**a good walk**

**Trafalgar Square** ❶ ☞ is the obvious place to start for several reasons. It is the geographical core of London and a gathering point for many political demonstrations (made easier now that the square has been pedestrianized), a raucous New Year's Eve party, and the highest concentration of bus stops in the capital. After taking in the instantly identifiable **Nelson's Column** ❷ in the center (read about the area on a plaque marking its 150th anniversary), head for the **National Gallery** ❸, on the north side—this is Britain's greatest trove of masterpieces. Detour around the corner to see the **National Portrait Gallery** ❹, a parade of the famous that can be very rewarding to anyone interested in what makes the British tick. East of the National Gallery, still on Trafalgar Square, see the much-loved church **St. Martin-in-the-Fields** ❺; then, stepping through grand **Admiralty Arch** ❻ down on the southwest corner, enter the royal pink road, the **Mall,** with St. James's Park on your left. On your right is the **Institute of Contemporary Arts** ❼, known as the ICA and housed in the great Regency architect John Nash's **Carlton House Terrace** ❽. At the foot of the Mall is one of London's most famous sights, **Buckingham Palace** ❾, home, of course, to the monarch of the land and punctuated by the ornate, white-marble **Queen Victoria Memorial** ❿. Turning right and right again, almost doubling back, follow the southern perimeter of St. James's Park around Birdcage Walk (the **Queen's Gallery** ⓫, with masterpieces from Her Majesty's vast art collection, is a few steps to the right at the side of the palace), passing **Wellington Barracks** ⓬, headquarters of the queen's guards, and, in turn, the hulking Home Office and **Queen Anne's Gate** ⓭. Cross Horse Guards Road at the eastern edge of the park and walk down Great George Street, with **St. Margaret's Church** 🔟 on your right. Continue across Parliament Square to come to another of the great sights of London, the **Houses of Parliament** 🔟, with Big Ben. A clockwise turn around the square brings you to yet another major landmark, breathtaking **Westminster Abbey** 🔟. Complete the circuit and head north up Whitehall, passing the **Cabinet War Rooms** 🔟, where you'll see a simple monolith in the middle of the street—the Cenotaph designed by Edwin Lutyens in 1920 in commemoration of the 1918 armistice. The gated alley on your left is **Downing Street** 🔟, where England's modest "White House" stands at No. 10. Soon after that, you pass **Horse Guards Parade** 🔟, the place where the queen's birthday is celebrated, in a parade called Trooping the Colour, with the classical Inigo Jones **Banqueting House** 🔟, scene of Charles I's execution, opposite. It's well worth it to backtrack a little ways down Whitehall and Abingdon Street to leafy Smith Square, off to your right, with the baroque **St. John's** 🔟 church in its center. Then, continue down Millbank to **Tate Britain** 🔟, the collection of British art.

TIMING  You could complete this walk of roughly 3 mi in just over an hour, but you could just as easily spend a week's vacation on this route alone. Allow as much time as you can for the two great museums—the National Gallery requires at *least* two hours; the National Portrait Gallery can be whizzed round in about one. Westminster Abbey can take half a day—especially in summer, when lines are long—both to get into and to tour around the abbey. In summer you can get inside Buckingham Palace, too, a half-day's operation increased to a whole day if you see the Royal Mews and the Queen's Gallery or the Guards Museum. If the Changing of the Guard is a priority, make sure you time this walk correctly.

HOW TO GET  This is an easy neighborhood to access, especially if you start at Trafal-
THERE  gar Square, where many buses stop. The central neighborhood Tube stop, Charing Cross (on the Jubilee, Northern, and Bakerloo lines), exits at the beginning of Northumberland Avenue, on the southeast corner. Practically all buses stop around here, including Buses 3, 9, 11, 12, 16, 24, 29, 53, 88, 139, and 159. Just to the north of Trafalgar Square on Charing Cross Road is the Leicester Square Tube stop (on the Northern and Piccadilly lines), which is just behind the galleries. Alternative Tube stations on the south side are St. James's Park (on the District and Circle lines), which is the best for Buckingham Palace, or the next stop, Westminster, which deposits you right by the bridge, in the shadow of Big Ben.

## What to See

❻ **Admiralty Arch.** Gateway to the Mall—no, not an indoor shopping center but one of the very grand avenues of London—this is one of London's stateliest urban set pieces. Situated on the southwest corner of Trafalgar Square, the arch, which was named after the adjacent Royal Navy headquarters, was designed in 1910 by Sir Aston Webb as part of a ceremonial route to Buckingham Palace. As you pass under the enormous triple archway—though not through the central arch, opened only for state occasions—the environment changes along with the color of the road, for you are exiting frenetic Trafalgar Square and entering

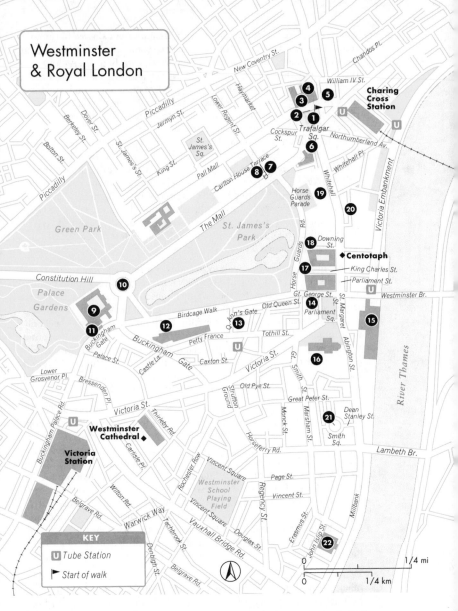

# Westminster & Royal London

New Coventry St.

Chandos Pl.

William IV St.

Haymarket

**Charing Cross Station**

Piccadilly

Jermyn St.

Lower Regent St.

**4**

**3**

**5**

Dover St.

Berkeley St.

St. James's St.

King St.

St. James's Sq.

Pall Mall

Carlton House Terrace

**2**

**1**

Trafalgar Sq.

Cockspur St.

Northumberland Av.

Bolton St.

Piccadilly

**6**

**8**

**7**

Whitehall Pl.

Victoria Embankment

Horse Guards Parade

**19**

Whitehall

**20**

The Mall

St. James's Park

Green Park

**18**

Downing St.

◆ **Centotaph**

Horse Guards Rd.

**17**

King Charles St.

Parliament St.

Constitution Hill

**10**

Palace Gardens

**9**

Birdcage Walk

Ann's Gate

Old Queen St.

**14**

Gt. George St.

St. Margaret St.

Parliament Sq.

Westminster Br.

**11**

Buckingham Gate

**12**

Petty France

**13**

Tothill St.

**15**

River Thames

Palace St.

Castle La.

Caxton St.

Victoria St.

**16**

Abingdon St.

Lower Grosvenor Pl.

Bressenden Pl.

Victoria St.

Strutton Ground

Old Pye St.

Gt. Smith St.

Great Peter St.

Monck St.

Marsham St.

Dean Stanley St.

Lambeth Br.

Buckingham Palace Rd.

**U**

**Westminster Cathedral** ◆

Thirleby Rd.

**Victoria Station**

Carlisle Pl.

Hoseferry Rd.

Smith Sq.

**21**

Belgrave Rd.

Wilton Rd.

Rochester Row

Vincent Square

Vincent Square

**Westminster School Playing Field**

Page St.

Vincent St.

Regency St.

Warwick Way

Tachbrook St.

Vincent Square

Douglas St.

Vauxhall Bridge Rd.

Erasmus St.

John Islip St.

Millbank

**22**

Denbigh St.

Belgrave Rd.

## KEY

**U** Tube Station

▶ Start of walk

0        1/4 mi

0        1/4 km

the Mall (rhymes with shall)—the elegant avenue that leads directly to the palace. ⊠ *The Mall, Cockspur St., Trafalgar Sq., Westminster SW1* Ⓤ *Charing Cross.*

**⑳ Banqueting House.** This is all that remains today of the Tudor Palace of Whitehall, which was (according to one foreign visitor) "ill-built, and nothing but a heap of houses." James I commissioned Inigo Jones (1573–1652), one of England's great architects, to do a grand remodeling. Influenced during a sojourn in Tuscany by Andrea Palladio's work, Jones brought Palladian sophistication and purity back to London with him. The resulting graceful and disciplined classical style of Banqueting House must have stunned its early occupants. In the quiet vaults beneath, James would escape the stresses of being a sovereign with a glass or two. His son, Charles I, enhanced the interior by employing the Flemish painter Peter Paul Rubens to glorify his father all over the ceiling. As it turned out, these allegorical paintings, depicting a wise monarch being received into heaven, were the last thing Charles saw before he was beheaded by Cromwell's Parliamentarians in 1649. But his son, Charles II, was able to celebrate the restoration of the monarchy in this same place 20 years later. The old palace is also the setting for lunchtime concerts, held 1–2 PM. Call or check the Web site for details. ⊠ *Whitehall, Westminster SW1* ☎ *020/7930–4179, recorded information 0870/ 751–5178, 0870/751–5187 concert tickets* ⊕ *www.hrp.org.uk* 🎫 *£4, includes free audio guide* ⊙ *Mon.–Sat. 10–5* ⊙ *Closed Christmas wk* Ⓤ *Charing Cross, Embankment, or Westminster.*

**❾ Buckingham Palace.** Supreme among the symbols of London, indeed of Britain generally and of the Royal Family, Buckingham Palace tops many must-see lists—although the building itself is no masterpiece and has housed the monarch only since Victoria (1819–1901) moved here from Kensington Palace on her accession in 1837. Its great gray bulk sums up the imperious splendor of so much of the city: stately, magnificent, and ponderous. When Victoria moved in, the place was a mess. George IV, on his accession in 1820, had fancied the idea of moving to Buckingham House, his parents' former home, and had employed John Nash, as usual, to remodel it. The government authorized only "repair and improvement"; Nash, that tireless spendthrift, overspent his budget by about half a million pounds. George died, Nash was dismissed, and Edward Blore finished the building, adding the now familiar east front (facing the Mall). Victoria arrived to faulty drains and sticky doors and windows, but that did not mar her affection for the place, nor that of her son, Edward VII. The Portland stone facade dates only from 1913 (the same stone used for the Victoria Memorial outside the Palace and Admiralty Arch at the foot of the Mall), and the interior was renovated and redecorated only after it sustained World War II bomb damage. Indeed, compared to other great London residences, this is a much later affair.

The palace contains 19 state rooms, 52 royal and guest bedrooms, 188 staff bedrooms, 92 offices, and 78 bathrooms—a prerequisite for the 450 people who work there, and the mere 50,000 who are entertained during the year. The state rooms are where much of the business of royalty is played out—investitures, state banquets, and receptions for the great and good. The royal apartments are in the north wing; when the queen is in residence, the royal standard is raised. The state rooms are on show from August to early October, a period when the Royal Family is away. A visit to the palace's west wing is a fascinating glimpse into another world: the fabulously gilt interiors are not merely museum pieces but pomp and pageantry at work. A tour starts from the Ambassadors' Court entrance, through to the **Entrée,** where portraits of past kings look down. The classical tone is set with Ionic columns in honeyed Bath stone, marble pillars in cool Carrara white, fine French and English furniture, and Chinese vases. Once through the **Grand Hall,** the **Grand Staircase,** and **Guard Room** (too small for the royal bodyguards— Yeoman of the Guard and Gentlemen-at-Arms in their traditional red-and-gold uniforms), the superlatives for the richness and elegance before your eyes could begin to wane. Prepare to be completely and utterly gilded out as Nash's ornate designs unfold through the numerous drawing rooms—each more jaw-dropping and neck-craning than the last—decorated with elaborate ceilings and chandeliers, and magnificent objects brought from the Prince Regent's original palatial home, Carlton House. (Some of the most precious Sèvres porcelain in the world found its way here after the French Revolution.) The **Throne Room,** in opulent baroque style, has the original 1953 coronation throne chairs. Queen Victoria used to hold balls here, but today it is the backdrop for royal wedding photographs and presentations. By now, when eyes are becoming glazed, the **Picture Gallery** is a restful feast of renowned art. The collection was begun by Charles I, and the works are periodically rearranged. Highlights among the many masterpieces are works by Rubens, Vermeer, Van Dyck, Cuyp, and Canaletto. The state rooms are graced with some of Her Majesty's most famous old master paintings, but other artwork is on view in the **Queen's Gallery,** near the south side of the palace. The palace tour continues through more galleries and drawing rooms filled with exquisite paintings and tapestries, culminating with the **State Dining Room** and its overly elaborate Blore ceiling. The table is sadly not set for a banquet with its usual crystal, gold, and silverware, but a solitary pair of ewers stands at attention.

From the State Dining Room there are views across the sweeping gardens, and unless you have an invitation to one of the queen's summer garden parties, the most you'll see of the magnificent 45-acre grounds is a walk along the south side of the palace garden. This addition to the tour gives views of the Garden (west) front of the palace and the 19th-century lake. The walled oasis has plenty of wildlife—it contains more than 350 types of wildflowers. Behind the front palace gates, the **Changing of the Guard,** with all the ceremony monarchists and children adore, remains one of London's best free shows and culminates in front of the palace. Marching to live music, the guards proceed up the Mall from St. James's Palace to Buckingham Palace. Shortly afterward, the replacement guard approaches from Wellington Barracks via Birdcage Walk. Then within the forecourt, the old guard symbolically hands over the keys to the palace to the replacement guard. The ceremony usually takes place on schedule, but the guards sometimes cancel because of bad

FodorśChoice
★

# ROYAL ATTRACTIONS

THE QUEEN AND THE ROYAL FAMILY attend approximately 400 functions a year, and if you want to know what they are doing on any given date, turn to the Court Circular, printed in the major London dailies. Trooping the Colour is usually held on the second Saturday in June, to celebrate the queen's official birthday. This spectacular parade begins when she leaves Buckingham Palace in her carriage and rides down the Mall to arrive at Horse Guards Parade at 11 exactly. To watch, just line up along the Mall with your binoculars!

Another time you can catch the queen in all her regalia is when she and the Duke of Edinburgh ride in state to Westminster to open the Houses of Parliament. The famous gilded coach, such an icon of fairy-tale glamour, parades from Buckingham Palace, escorted by the brilliantly uniformed Household Cavalry—on a clear day, it is to be hoped, for this ceremony takes place in late October or early November, depending on the exigencies of Parliament.

But perhaps the nicest time to see the queen is during Royal Ascot, held at the racetrack near Windsor Castle—just a short train ride out of London—usually during the third week of June (Tuesday–Friday). After several races, the queen invariably walks down to the paddock on a special path, greeting race goers as she proceeds. Americans wishing to reserve a seat in the Royal Enclosure should apply to the **American Embassy** (⌧ 24 Grosvenor Sq., Mayfair London W1) before the end of March. But remember: you must be sponsored by two guests who have attended Ascot at least seven times before!

weather; check the signs in the forecourt or phone. Get there by 10:30 AM to grab a spot in the best viewing section at the gate facing the palace, since most of the hoopla takes place behind the railings in the forecourt. Be sure to prebook tour reservations of the palace with a credit card by phone. ⌧ *Buckingham Palace Rd., St. James's SW1* ☎ *020/7839–1377, 020/7799–2331 24-hr information, 020/7321–2233 credit-card reservations, subject to 50p booking charge* ⊕ *www.royal.gov.uk* ⊠ *£12.95, prices change annually* ☉ *Early Aug.–early Oct., daily 9:30–4:15; confirm dates, which are subject to queen's mandate. Changing of the Guard Apr.–July, daily 11:30 AM; Aug.–Mar., alternating days only 11:30 AM* ⊟ *AE, MC, V* Ⓤ *Victoria or St. James's Park.*

☾ ⓱ **Cabinet War Rooms.** It was from this small maze of bomb-proof underground rooms—in the back of the hulking Foreign Office—that Britain's World War II fortunes were directed. The rooms have been preserved exactly as they were when the last light was turned off at the end of the war. During air raids, the Cabinet met here—the Cabinet Room is still arranged as if a meeting were about to convene; in the Map Room, the Allied campaign is charted; the Prime Minister's Room holds the desk from which Winston Churchill (1874–1965) made his morale-boosting broadcasts; and the Telephone Room has his hotline to FDR. Churchill slept here only on a few occasions; he preferred the comfort of Downing Street. The Churchill Museum is set to open here in early 2005. ✉ *Clive Steps, King Charles St., Westminster SW1* ☎ *020/7930-6961* ⊕ *www.iwm.org.uk* 🗾 *£7* ⊘ *Apr.–Sept., daily 9:30–5:15; Oct.–Mar., daily 10–5:15* Ⓤ *Westminster.*

**8 Carlton House Terrace.** This is a glorious example of Regency architect John Nash's genius. Between 1812 and 1830, under the patronage of George IV (Prince Regent until George III's death in 1820), Nash was the architect for the grand scheme of Regent Street and the sweep of neoclassical houses encircling Regent's Park. The Prince Regent, who lived at Carlton House, had plans to build a country villa at Primrose Hill (to the north of the park), connected by a grand road—hence Regent Street. Even though it was considered a most extravagant building for its time, Carlton House was demolished after the prince's accession to the throne. Nash's Carlton House Terrace, no less imposing, with white-stucco facades and massive Corinthian columns, was built in its place. It was a smart address and one that Prime Ministers Gladstone (1856) and Palmerston (1857–75) enjoyed. Today Carlton House Terrace houses the Royal College of Pathologists (No. 2), the Royal Society (No. 6, whose members included Isaac Newton and Charles Darwin), the Turf Club (No. 5), and, at No. 12, the **Institute of Contemporary Arts,** better known as the ICA. ✉ *The Mall, St. James's W1* Ⓤ *Charing Cross.*

**18 Downing Street.** Looking like an unassuming alley but barred by iron gates at both its Whitehall and Horse Guards Road approaches, this is the location of the famous **No. 10,** London's modest version of the White House. Only three houses remain of the terrace built circa 1680 by Sir George Downing, who spent enough of his youth in America to graduate from Harvard—the second man ever to do so. **No. 11** is traditionally the residence of the chancellor of the exchequer (secretary of the treasury), and **No. 12** is the party whips' office. No. 10 has officially housed the prime minister since 1732. (The gates were former prime minister Margaret Thatcher's brainstorm.) Just south of Downing Street, in the middle of Whitehall, you'll see the **Cenotaph,** a stark white monolith designed in 1920 by Edwin Lutyens to commemorate the 1918 armistice. On Remembrance Day (the Sunday nearest November 11, Armistice Day) it is strewn with red poppies to honor the dead of both world wars and all British and Commonwealth soldiers killed in action since; the first wreath is laid by the queen and there's a march past by war veterans. ✉ *Whitehall, Westminster SW1* Ⓤ *Westminster.*

**19 Horse Guards Parade.** Once the tiltyard of Whitehall Palace, where jousting tournaments were held, the Horse Guards Parade is now notable mainly for the annual Trooping the Colour ceremony, in which the queen takes the Royal Salute, her official birthday gift, on the second Saturday in June. (Like Paddington Bear, the queen has two birthdays; her real one is on April 21.) There is pageantry galore, with marching bands—the occasional guardsman fainting clean away from the heat building up under his weighty busby—and throngs of onlookers. Covering the vast expanse of the square that faces Horse Guards Road, opposite St. James's Park at one end and Whitehall at the other, the ceremony is televised. At the Whitehall facade of Horse Guards, the changing of two mounted sentries known as the **mounted guard** provides what may be London's most frequently exercised photo opportunity.  ⊠ *Whitehall, Westminster SW1* ☉ *Queen's mounted guard ceremony Mon.–Sat. 11 AM, Sun. 10 AM* Ⓤ *Westminster.*

**need a break?**

The **Wesley Café** (⊠ Storey's Gate, Westminster SW1 ☎ 020/7222–8010) is a popular budget haunt for office workers around Westminster. It's almost opposite Westminster Abbey, in the crypt of Central Hall, a former Methodist church. A meal costs around £5.

**⑮** **Houses of Parliament.** Overlooking the Thames, the Houses of Parliament are, arguably, the city's most famous and photogenic sight, with the Clock Tower—which everyone calls Big Ben—keeping watch on the corner and Westminster Abbey ahead of you across Parliament Square. The most romantic view of the complex is from the opposite (south) side of the river, a vista especially dramatic at night when the storybook spires, pinnacles, and towers of the great building are floodlit green and gold—a fairy-tale vision only missing the presence of Peter Pan and Wendy on their way to Never-Never Land.

Fodor'sChoice ★

The Palace of Westminster, as the complex is still properly called, was established by Edward the Confessor in the 11th century, when he moved his court here from the City. It has served as the seat of English administrative power, on and off, ever since. In 1512, Henry VIII (1491–1547) abandoned it for Whitehall, and it ceased to be an official royal residence after 1547. At the Reformation, the Royal Chapel was secularized and became the first meeting place of the Commons. The Lords settled in the White Chamber. These, along with everything but the **Jewel Tower** and **Westminster Hall,** were destroyed in 1834 when "the sticks"—the arcane elmwood "tally" sticks notched for loans paid out and paid back, kept beneath the Lords' Chamber, on which the court had kept its accounts until 1826—were incinerated, and the fire got out of hand. Westminster Hall, with its remarkable hammer-beam roof, was the work of William the Conqueror's son, William Rufus. It is one of the largest remaining Norman halls in Europe, and its dramatic interior was the scene of the trial of Charles I.

After the 1834 fire, architects were invited to submit plans for new Parliament buildings in the grandiose "Gothic or Elizabethan style." Charles Barry's were selected from among 97 entries, partly because Barry had invited the architect and designer Augustus Pugin to add the requisite neo-Gothic curlicues to his own Renaissance-influenced style. As you can see, it was a happy collaboration, with Barry's classical proportions offset by Pugin's ornamental flourishes—although the latter were toned down by Gilbert Scott when he rebuilt the bomb-damaged House of Commons after World War II. The two towers were Pugin's work. The **Clock Tower,** now virtually the symbol of London, was completed in 1858 after long delays due to bickering over the clock's design. (Barry designed the faces himself in the end.) It contains the 13-ton bell known as Big Ben, which chimes the hour (and the quarters). Some say Ben was

# LONDON ARCHITECTURE

GREAT ARCHITECTURAL ACHIEVEMENTS in London have often been motivated by disasters and misfortunes. Like a phoenix, London rose from the ashes in a frenzy of rebuilding after the Great Fire of 1666 had destroyed four-fifths of the city. Three centuries later, more fire, caused by the German air raids in the Second World War, flattened huge chunks of London. Gray civic buildings and tower blocks rose from the rubble. As a result of these intense civic reconstructions, a few individuals had the opportunity to leave significant marks on the city.

Inigo Jones (1573–1652), one of England's first great architects, was almost single-handedly responsible for the resurgence of classical styles of architecture in the early 17th century. Often directly modeling his work after that of Italian architect Andrea Palladio, Jones was highly influential during his time, as the Palladian style quickly spread throughout England. His most famous works include St. Paul's Church at Covent Garden and the magnificent Banqueting House on Whitehall.

Sir Christopher Wren (1632–1723) was given the Herculean task of overseeing the rebuilding of London following the Great Fire. His ambitious plans for a complete redesign of the formerly medieval city, drawn up within a week after the fire, were shot down by landowners, businesspeople, and private citizens intent on a quicker reconstruction. It remains a mystery what effect Wren's membership in the secretive Masonic Lodge had on his efforts. Nevertheless, Wren was responsible for 51 new churches (all in the City) and the amazing St. Paul's Cathedral. Only 23 of the City churches still survive, the finest of which are St. Bride's (Fleet Street), St. Mary Abchurch

(Abchurch Yard), and St. Stephen's Walbrook (Walbrook Street). A wander through the deserted streets of the City past the churches is a rewarding way to spend a weekend afternoon.

John Nash (1752–1835) completely redesigned a large section of the city stretching from the Mall northward to Regent's Park and also remodeled Buckingham Palace. He is largely responsible for the look of much of central London; it was his idea to clear Trafalgar Square of its royal stables to make room for the public space as it exists today. For an insight into Nash's vision for London, walk from Buckingham Palace along the Mall, past his white stucco Carlton House Terrace to your left. Walk across Trafalgar Square to Haymarket, where Nash built the Haymarket Theater. Then walk the length of Regent Street, passing on the way All Souls Church, Langham Place, and Park Crescent, which leads into Regent's Park from its southern end.

"Big Ben" Caunt, heavyweight champ; others, Sir Benjamin Hall, the far-from-slim Westminster building works commissioner. At the southwest end of the main Parliament building is the 336-foot-high **Victoria Tower.**

The building itself, which covers 8 acres, is a series of chambers, lobbies, and offices joined by more than 2 mi of passages. There are two Houses, Lords and Commons. The former has been downsized and reformed by Mr. Blair's Labour party. More than 100 hereditary peers (earls, lords, viscounts, and other aristocrats) failed to win the right to continue to be elected to their seats in the House of Lords. The House of Commons is made up of 659 elected Members of Parliament (MPs). The party with the most MPs forms the government, its leader becoming prime minister; other parties form the Opposition. Since 1642, when Charles I tried to have five MPs arrested, no monarch has been allowed into the House of Commons. The state opening of Parliament in November consequently takes place in the House of Lords. Visitors aren't allowed many places in the Houses of Parliament, though the Visitors' Galleries of the House of Commons do afford a view of one of the best free shows in London, staged in the world's most renowned ego chamber. The opposing banks of green leather benches seat only 437 MPs—not that this is much of a problem, since absentees far outnumber the diligent. When MPs vote, they exit by the "Aye" or the "No" corridor, thus being counted by the party whips. When they speak, it is not directly to each other but through the Speaker, who also decides who will get the floor each day. Elaborate procedures notwithstanding, debate is often drowned out by raucous jeers and insults.

Other public areas of the 1,100-room labyrinth are rather magnificently got up in high neo-Gothic style and punctuated with stirring frescoes commissioned by Prince Albert. You pass these on your way to the Visitors' Galleries—if, that is, you are patient enough to wait in line for hours (the Lords line is shorter) or have applied in advance for the special "line of route" tour for overseas visitors during the summer opening (late July–August and mid-September–early October). Tickets can be prebooked by phone or on the Web site; alternatively you can take a chance and buy same-day tickets from the ticket office opposite the Houses of Parliament. The tour takes you through the Queen's Robing Room, Royal Gallery, House of Lords, Central Hall (where MPs meet their constituents—the lucky ones get to accompany their MP to a prestigious tea on the terrace), House of Commons, and out into the spectacular Westminster Hall. Watch for the "VR" (Victoria Regina) monograms in the carpets and carving belying the "medieval" detailing as 19th-century work. The time to catch the action is Question Time—when the prime minister defends himself against the attacks of his "right honorable friends" on Wednesday between noon and 2:30 PM (it's also live on BBC2). Overseas visitors should check tour dates and details on the Parliament's Web site. The next best time to visit is either chamber's regular Question Time, held on Monday, Tuesday, and Thursday from noon to 2:30 PM. The easiest time to get into the Commons is during an evening session—Parliament is still sitting if the top of the Clock Tower is illuminated.

For a special exhibition devoted to the "History of Parliament: Past and Present," head to the **Jewel Tower,** across the street from Victoria Tower, on Abingdon Street (also called Old Palace Yard), south of Parliament Square. Not to be confused with the other famed jewel tower at the Tower of London, this was the stronghold for Edward III's treasure in 1366. It's also one of the original parts of the old Palace of Westminster and still retains some original beams; part of the moat and medieval quay still remain. (The tower is run by English Heritage, with a small charge for entry.) Be sure to have your name placed in advance on the waiting list for the twice-weekly tours of the **Lord Chancellor's Residence,** a popular attraction since its spectacular renovation. ⊠ *St. Stephen's Entrance, St. Margaret St., Westminster SW1* ☎ *020/ 7219–4272 Commons information, 020/7219–3107 Lords information, 020/7222–2219 Jewel Tower, 020/7219–2184 Lord Chancellor's Residence, 0870/906–3773 summer tours* ⊕ *www.parliament.uk* ✉ *Free, £7 summer tours* ⊘ *Commons Mon.–Thurs. 2:30–10, Fri. 9:30–3, although not every Fri.; Lords Mon.–Thurs. 2:30–10; Lord Chancellor's Residence Tues. and Thurs. 10:30–12:30* ⊘ *Closed Easter wk, late July–early Sept., 3 wks for party conference recess mid-Sept.–early Oct., and 3 wks at Christmas* Ⓤ *Westminster.*

**❼ Institute of Contemporary Arts (ICA).** Behind its incongruous white-stucco facade, at No. 12 Carlton House Terrace, the ICA has provided a stage for the avant-garde in performance, theater, dance, visual art, and music since it was established in 1947. There are two cinemas; a library of video artists' works; a bookshop; a café; a lively, hip bar; and a team of adventurous curators. ⊠ *The Mall, St. James's W1* ☎ *020/7930–3647* ⊕ *www.ica.org.uk* ✉ *1-day, weekday membership £1.50; weekends, £2.50; additional charge for cinema screenings* ⊘ *Daily noon–7:30, later for some events* Ⓤ *Charing Cross or Piccadilly Circus.*

> **need a break?**
>
> The **ICAfé** is windowless but brightly lit, with a self-service counter full of good hot dishes, salads, quiches, and desserts. The bar upstairs has lighter food and windows overlooking the Mall. Both are subject to the £1.50 one-day membership fee.

**The Mall.** This street was laid out around 1660 for the game of *paille-maille* (a type of croquet crossed with golf), which also gave Pall Mall its name, and it quickly became the place to be seen. Samuel Pepys, Jonathan Swift, and Alexander Pope all wrote about it, and it continued as the beau monde's social playground into the early 19th century, long after the game it was built for had gone out of vogue. Something of the former style survives on those summer days when the queen is throwing a Buckingham Palace garden party: hundreds of her subjects throng the Mall, from the grand and titled to the humble and hardworking, all of whom have donned hat and frock to take afternoon tea with the monarch—or somewhere near her—on the lawns of Buck House. The old Mall still runs alongside the graceful, pink, 115-foot-wide avenue that replaced it in 1904 for just such occasions. ⊠ *The Mall, St. James's SW1* Ⓤ *Charing Cross or Green Park.*

**3** **National Gallery.** Should you be lucky enough to have the time to pe-
FodorśChoice ruse, there are more than 2,000 paintings here to enjoy for free—many
★ of them instantly recognizable and among the most treasured works of
art anywhere. The museum's low, gray, colonnaded neoclassic facade
fills the north side of Trafalgar Square, which has now been redesigned
exclusively for pedestrians, as if the whole square is the grand and spacious entrance to the gallery. The institution was founded in 1824,
when George IV and a connoisseur named Sir George Beaumont per-
suaded a reluctant government to spend £57,000 to acquire part of the
philanthropist John Julius Angerstein's collection. These 38 paintings,
including works by Raphael, Rembrandt, Titian, and Rubens, were
augmented by 16 of Sir George's own and exhibited in Angerstein's Pall
Mall residence until 1838, when William Wilkins's building was completed. By the end of the century, enthusiastic directors and generous
patrons had turned the National Gallery into one of the world's foremost collections, with works from painters of the Italian Renaissance
and earlier, from the Flemish and Dutch masters, the Spanish school,
and of course the English tradition, including Hogarth, Gainsborough,
Stubbs, and Constable.

The modern extension of the gallery, the Sainsbury Wing, designed by
American architect Robert Venturi, houses the early Renaissance collection, and hosts excellent in-depth exhibitions, on themes or individual artists. Following the pedestrianization of Trafalgar Square, and in
anticipation of increasing visitors, the main building is being modernized. Phase one, due to open in fall 2004, includes a new entrance that
will provide street-level disabled access, a museum store, and café. Architect Sir Jeremy Dixon (who renovated the Royal Opera House), is
also reinventing the somber internal courtyard as a bright, modern
atrium. In phase two of the renovation, the museum's Victorian central
hall is to be modernized.

The gallery is really too overwhelming to absorb in a single viewing. It
is wise to plot a route with the aid of a map from the information desk.
Worthy of a look are the exhibitions in the Sunley Room and Room 1,
where works are organized along a theme, such as Bosch and Breugel,
or focus on an artist, such as El Greco. Alternatively you could start at
the **Micro Gallery,** in the Sainsbury Wing, which gives you access to in-
depth information on all of the museum's holdings; you can choose your
favorites, and print out a free personal tour map.

The following is a list of 10 of the most familiar works, to jog your memory, whet your appetite, and offer a starting point for your own exploration. The first five are in the Sainsbury Wing. In chronological order:
(1) **Van Eyck** (circa 1395–1441), *The Arnolfini Portrait.* A solemn couple holds hands, the fish-eye mirror behind them mysteriously illuminating
what can't be seen from the front view. (2) **Uccello** (1397–1475), *The
Battle of San Romano.* In a work commissioned by the Medici family,
the Florentine commander on a rearing white warhorse leads armored
knights into battle against the Sienese. (3) **Bellini** (circa 1430–1516), *The
Doge Leonardo Loredan.* The artist captured the Venetian doge's beatific
expression (and snail-shell "buttons") at the beginning of his 20 years

in office. (4) **Botticelli** (1445–1510), *Venus and Mars*. Mars sleeps, exhausted by the love goddess, oblivious to the lance wielded by mischievous putti and the buzzing of wasps. (5) **Leonardo da Vinci** (1452–1519), *The Virgin and Child*. This haunting black chalk cartoon is partly famous for having been attacked at gunpoint, and it now gets extra protection behind glass and screens. (6) **Caravaggio** (1573–1610), *The Supper at Emmaus*. A cinematically lighted, freshly resurrected Christ blesses bread in an astonishingly domestic vision from the master of chiaroscuro. (7) **Velázquez** (1599–1660), *The Toilet of Venus*. "The Rokeby Venus," named for its previous home in Yorkshire, has the most famously beautiful back in any gallery. She's the only surviving female nude by Velázquez. (8) **Constable** (1776–1837), *The Hay Wain*. Rendered overfamiliar by too many greeting cards, this is the definitive image of golden-age rural England. (9) **Turner** (1775–1851), *The Fighting Téméraire*. Most of the collection's other Turners were moved to the Tate Britain; the final voyage of the great French battleship into a livid, hazy sunset stayed here. (10) **Seurat** (1859–91), *Bathers at Asnières*. This static summer day's idyll is one of the pointillist extraordinaire's best-known works.

Glaring omissions from the above include some of the most popular pictures in the gallery, by Piero della Francesca, Titian, Holbein, Bosch, Brueghel, Rembrandt, Vermeer, Canaletto, Claude, Tiepolo, Gainsborough, Ingres, Monet, Renoir, and van Gogh. You can't miss the two most spectacular works on view—due to their mammoth size—Sebastiano del Piombo's *Sermon on the Mount* and Stubbs's stunning *Whistlejacket*. These great paintings aren't the only thing glowing in the rooms of the National Gallery—thanks to government patronage and lottery monies, salons here now gleam with stunning brocades and opulent silks. Rubens's *Samson and Delilah* has never looked better.

The collection of Dutch 17th-century paintings is one of the greatest in the world, and pieces by Hals, Hooch, Ruisdel, Hobbema, and Cuyp are shown in renewed natural light and gracious surroundings. If you visit during the school vacations, there are special programs and trails for children that are not to be missed. Neither are the free weekday lunchtime lectures and Ten Minute Talks, which illuminate the story behind a key work of art. Check the information desk, or Web site, for details. ✉ *Trafalgar Sq., Westminster WC2* ☎ *020/7747–2885* ⊕ *www.nationalgallery. org.uk* 🎫 *Free, charge for special exhibitions* ☉ *Daily 10–6, Wed. until 9; 1-hr free guided tour starts at Sainsbury Wing daily at 11:30 and 2:30, and additionally 6:30 Wed.* Ⓤ *Charing Cross or Leicester Sq.*

**need a break?** The muraled **Crivelli's Garden** in the Sainsbury Wing of the National Gallery serves a fashionable lunch—mussels, gravlax, charcuterie, and salads, and has the added perk of huge windows overlooking Trafalgar Square. The self-service café in the basement of the main building has a good range of faster snacks and drinks.

★ 🕐 **❹** **National Portrait Gallery.** An idiosyncratic collection that presents a potted history of Britain through its people, past and present, this museum is an essential stop for all history and literature buffs, where you can choose to take in a little, or a lot. The spacious, bright galleries are accessible via a state-of-the-art escalator, which lets you view the paintings as you ascend to a skylit space displaying the oldest works in the Tudor Gallery. At the summit, a sleek restaurant, open beyond gallery hours, will satiate skyline droolers. Here you'll see one of the best landscapes for real: a panoramic view of Nelson's Column and the backdrop along Whitehall to the Houses of Parliament. Back in the basement are a lecture theater, computer gallery, bookshop, and café.

Walking through the Photography Gallery is like looking at an upmarket celebrity or society magazine. In the Tudor Gallery—a modern update on a Tudor long hall—is a Holbein cartoon of Henry VIII; Stubbs's self-portrait hangs in the refurbished 17th-century rooms; and Hockney's appears in the modern Balcony Gallery, mixed up with photographs, busts, caricatures, and paintings. (The miniature of Jane Austen by her sister Cassandra, for instance, is the only likeness that exists of the great novelist.) Many of the faces are obscure and will be just as unknown to you if you're English, because the portraits outlasted their sitters' fame—not so surprising when the portraitists are such greats as Reynolds, Gainsborough, Lawrence, and Romney. But the annotation is comprehensive, the layout is easy to negotiate—chronological, with the oldest at the top—and there's a separate research center for those who get hooked on particular personages. Don't miss the absorbing mini-exhibitions in the Studio and Balcony Galleries; and there are temporary exhibitions in the Wolfson Gallery, on subjects as diverse as 'Below Stairs–400 Years of Servants' Portraits', to contemporary fashion photography from Terry O'Neill to Mario Testino. ⊠ *St. Martin's Pl., Covent Garden WC2* ☎ *020/7312–2463 recorded information* ⊕ *www.npg.org.uk* ✉ *Free* ☽ *Mon.–Wed., weekends 10–6, Thurs. and Fri. 10–9* Ⓤ *Charing Cross or Leicester Sq.*

❷ **Nelson's Column.** Trafalgar Square takes its name from the Battle of Trafalgar, Admiral Lord Horatio Nelson's great naval victory over the French, in 1805. Appropriately, the dominant landmark here is this famous column, a 145-foot-high granite perch from which E. H. Baily's 1843 statue of Nelson (1758–1805), one of England's favorite heroes, keeps watch; three bas-reliefs depicting his victories at Cape St. Vincent, the Battle of the Nile, and Copenhagen (and a fourth, his death at Trafalgar itself in 1805) sit around the base. All four bas-reliefs were cast from cannons he captured. The four majestic lions, designed by the Victorian painter Sir Edwin Landseer, were added in 1867. ⊠ *Trafalgar Sq., Covent Garden WC2* Ⓤ *Charing Cross or Leicester Sq.*

⓭ **Queen Anne's Gate.** Standing south of Birdcage Walk, by St. James's Park, are these two pretty 18th-century closes, once separate but now linked by a statue of the last Stuart monarch. (Another statue of Anne, beside St. Paul's, inspired the doggerel "Brandy Nan, Brandy Nan, you're left in the lurch, your face to the gin shop, your back to the church"— proving that her attempts to disguise her habitual tipple in a teapot fooled nobody.) ⊠ *Queen Anne's Gate, Westminster SW1* Ⓤ *St. James's Park.*

**⑩ Queen Victoria Memorial.** You can't overlook this monument if you're near Buckingham Palace, which it faces from the traffic island at the west end of the Mall. The monument was conceived by Sir Aston Webb as the nucleus of his ceremonial route down the Mall to the Palace, and it was executed by the sculptor Thomas Brock, who was knighted on the spot when the memorial was revealed to the world in 1911. Many wonder why he was given that honor, since the thing is Victoriana incarnate: the frumpy queen glares down the Mall, with golden-winged Victory overhead and her siblings Truth, Justice, and Charity, plus Manufacture, Progress-and-Peace, War-and-Shipbuilding, and so on—in Osbert Sitwell's words, "tons of allegorical females . . . with whole litters of their cretinous children"—surrounding her. ⊠ *The Mall and Spur Rd., St. James's* Ⓤ *Victoria or St. James's Park.*

**⑪ The Queen's Gallery.** The former chapel at the south side of Buckingham

Fodor'sChoice Palace is now a temple for Her Majesty's collection of art, comprised of

★ acquisitions made by the monarchy over the years. A splendid portico (designed by John Simpson) sets the scene for spacious galleries whose walls are hung with some of the greatest works in the country. The Pennethorne Gallery is dominated by the larger-than-life portrait by Van Dyck of Charles I, in magisterial equestrian mode, presiding over works by other masters such as Holbein, Hals, Vermeer and Rubens. These contrast starkly with the very frank (and some might say unflattering) portrait of the present queen Elizabeth by Lucian Freud in the Nash Gallery. Also in the galleries are some of the Queen's decorative art objects, including cabinets, tables with precious inlays, vases, silver, as well as the finest porcelain from Delft and Sèvres.The E-gallery provides an interactive electronic version of the Royal Treasures catalog and reveals hidden details of some of the works of art on show, allowing the user to open lockets, remove a sword from its scabbard, or take apart the tulip vases. It's probably the closest you could get to eyeing practically every diamond in the sovereign's glittering diadem. ⊠ *Buckingham Palace, Buckingham Palace Rd., St. James's SW1* ☎ *020/7766–7301* ⊕ *www.royal.gov.uk* 🎫 *£7.50* ⊙ *Daily 10–5:30; last admission 4:30* Ⓤ *Victoria or St. James's Park.*

**Ⓒ Royal Mews.** Unmissable children's entertainment, this museum is the home of Her Majesty's Coronation Coach. Standing nearly next door to the Queen's Gallery, the Royal Mews were designed by famed Regency-era architect John Nash. Mews were originally falcons' quarters (the name comes from their "mewing," or feather shedding), but horses gradually eclipsed birds of prey. Now some of the magnificent royal beasts live here alongside the fabulous bejeweled glass-and-golden coaches they draw on state occasions. ⊠ *Buckingham Palace Rd., St. James's SW1* ☎ *020/7766–7302* ⊕ *www.royal.gov.uk* 🎫 *£5.50 Apr.–Jul. and Oct., Sat.–Thurs. 11–4; Aug. and Sept., daily 10–5; last admission 45 mins before closing.* Ⓤ *Victoria or St. James's Park.*

**Ⓒ St. James's Park.** With three palaces at its borders (the ancient Palace of

Fodor'sChoice Westminster, now the Houses of Parliament; the Tudor **St. James's**

★ **Palace**; and Buckingham Palace), St. James's Park is acclaimed as the most royal of the royal parks. It's also London's smallest, most ornamental park, as well as the oldest; it was acquired by Henry VIII in 1532 for a deer park. The land was marshy and took its name from the lepers' hospital dedicated to St. James. Henry VIII built the palace next to the park, which was used for hunting only—dueling and sword fights were forbidden. James I improved the land and installed an aviary and zoo (complete with crocodiles). Charles II (after his exile in France and because of his admiration for Louis XIV's formal Versailles Palace landscapes) had formal gardens laid out, with avenues, fruit orchards, and a canal. Lawns were grazed by goats, sheep, and deer. The Mall, alongside, was also used for the French croquet-type game of *paille-maille,* or pell mell. Its present shape more or less reflects what John Nash designed under George IV, turning the canal into a graceful lake (which was cemented in at a depth of 4 feet in 1855, so don't even think of swimming) and generally naturalizing the gardens. St. James's Park makes a spectacular frame for the towers of Westminster and Victoria—especially at night, when the illuminated fountains play and the skyline beyond the trees looks like a floating fairyland.

About 17 species of birds—including pelicans, geese, ducks, and swans (which belong to the queen)—now breed on and around Duck Island at the east end of the lake, attracting ornithologists at dawn. Later on summer days the deck chairs (which you must pay to use) are crammed with office workers lunching while being serenaded by music from the bandstands. One of the best times to stroll the leafy walkways is after dark, with Westminster Abbey and the Houses of Parliament rising above the floodlit lake. ⊠ *The Mall or Horse Guards approach, or Birdcage Walk, St. James's SW1* Ⓤ *St. James's Park or Westminster.*

㉑ **St. John's, Smith Square.** Completed around 1720, St. John's charmingly dominates Smith Square, an elegant enclave of perfectly preserved early 18th-century town houses that still looks like the London of Dr. Johnson. The Smith Square address is much sought after by MPs, especially of the Tory persuasion; No. 32 is the Conservative Party Headquarters. The baroque church is well known to Londoners as a chamber-music venue; its popular lunchtime concerts are often broadcast on the radio. ⊠ *North of Horseferry Rd., end of John Islip St., Westminster SW1* ☎ *020/7222–1061* ⊕ *www.sjss.org.uk* ☾ *Weekdays 10–5, may be closed during concert rehearsals; Sat. for concerts only* Ⓤ *Westminster.*

**need a break?**

In the Crypt of St. John's, Smith Square, the **Footstool** has varied, simply prepared snacks and meals for lunch and pre- and post-concert dinners. Open weekdays 11:30 AM–2:45 PM and 5:30 PM–10 PM. On Saturday, times vary according to the concert program.

⓮ **St. Margaret's Church.** Dwarfed by its neighbor, Westminster Abbey, St. Margaret's was founded in the 12th century and rebuilt between 1486 and 1523. As the parish church of the Houses of Parliament it's much sought after for weddings: Samuel Pepys married here in 1655, Winston Churchill in 1908. The east Crucifixion window celebrates another union, the marriage of Prince Arthur and Catherine of Aragon. Unfortunately, it arrived so late that Arthur was dead and Catherine had married his brother, Henry VIII. Sir Walter Raleigh is among the notables buried here, only without his head, which had been removed at Old Palace Yard, Westminster, and kept by his wife, who was said to be fond of asking visitors, "Have you met Sir Walter?" as she produced it from a velvet bag. ⊠ *Parliament Sq., Westminster SW1* ⓤ *Westminster.*

❺ **St. Martin-in-the-Fields.** The small medieval chapel that once stood here, probably used by the monks of Westminster Abbey, was indeed surrounded by fields. These gave way to a grand rebuilding, completed in 1726, and St. Martin's grew to become one of Britain's best-loved churches. James Gibbs's classical temple-with-spire design became a familiar pattern for churches in early Colonial America. Though it seems dwarfed by the surrounding structures of Trafalgar Square, the spire is actually slightly taller than Nelson's Column, which it overlooks. It's a welcome sight for the homeless, who have sought soup and shelter here since 1914. The church is also a haven for music lovers; the internationally known Academy of St. Martin-in-the-Fields was founded here, and a popular program of lunchtime (free) and evening concerts continues today (tickets are available from the box office in the crypt). The church's musty interior is a wonderful place for music making— but the wooden benches can make it hard to give your undivided attention to the music. St. Martin's is often called the royal parish church, partly because Charles II was christened here. The crypt is a hive of lively activity, with a café, bookshop, plus the **London Brass-Rubbing Centre,** where you can make your own souvenir knight, lady, or monarch from replica tomb brasses, with metallic waxes, paper, and instructions provided for about £5; and the **Gallery in the Crypt,** showing contemporary work. ⊠ *Trafalgar Sq., Covent Garden WC2* ☎ *020/ 7766–1100, 020/7839–8362 evening-concert credit-card bookings* ⊕ *www.stmartin-in-the-fields.org* ☉ *Church daily 8–8; crypt Mon.–Sat. 10–8 (brass-rubbing centre until 6), Sun. noon–6; box office Mon.–Sat. 10–5* ⓤ *Charing Cross or Leicester Sq.*

**need a break?** St. Martin's **Café in the Crypt,** with its high-arched brick vault, serves full meals, sandwiches, snacks, traditional tea, and wine. The choice here, which includes vegetarian dishes, is one of the best available for such a central location.

☺ ㉒ **Tate Britain.** The gallery, which first opened in 1897, funded by the sugar
Fodor'sChoice magnate Sir Henry Tate, is the older sister of Tate Modern, on the south
★ bank of the Thames. As the name proclaims, great British artists from the 16th century to the present day are the focus. The Linbury Galleries on the lower floors stage temporary exhibitions. Galleries on the upper floors are reached by a wide, sweeping staircase, and house the Tate's permanent collection, much of which was brought out of storage after the opening of Tate Modern. The different rooms cover a massive range, some 500 years of art from the Tudor age to the up-to-the-minute Turner prize offerings. Each room has a theme and includes key works by major British artists: Van Dyck, Hogarth, and Reynolds rub shoulders with Rossetti, Sickert, Hockney, and Bacon, for example. Not to be missed is the generous selection of Constable landscapes.

The Turner Bequest consists of J. M. W. Turner's personal collection; he left it to the nation on condition that the works be displayed together. The James Stirling–designed Clore Gallery (to the right of the main gallery) opened in 1987 to fulfill his wish, and it should not be missed. The annual Turner Prize gets artists and nonartists into a frenzy about what art has come to—or where it's going.

You can rent a "Tateinform," a handheld audio guide, with commentaries by curators, experts, and some of the artists themselves. About a 20-minute walk south of the Houses of Parliament, the Tate is also accessible if you tube it to the Pimlico stop, then take a five-minute, signposted walk. A shuttle bus and boat service link Tate Britain with Tate Modern at Bankside across the river.

Rather than walk back to Pimlico or Victoria, there are two eateries to tempt you right here. The Café Espresso Bar has hot and cold drinks, sandwiches, and cakes; the Tate Restaurant is almost a destination in itself, with its celebrated Rex Whistler murals, and a daily fixed-price three-course lunch menu (around £15) and à la carte choices. Ingredients celebrate British produce, such as Cornish crab, Welsh lamb, organic smoked salmon, Stilton cheese, and seasonal vegetables. Vegetarian meals and children's-size portions are available. It's open Monday through Saturday noon to 3 and Sunday noon to 4. ✉ *Millbank, Westminster SW1* ☎ *020/7887–800, 020/7887–8008 recorded information* ⊕ *www.tate.org.uk* ✑ *Free, exhibitions £3–£10* ☉ *Daily 10–5:50* Ⓤ *Pimlico.*

▶ ❶ **Trafalgar Square.** This is the center of London, by dint of a plaque on the corner of the Strand and Charing Cross Road from which distances on U.K. signposts are measured. It's the home of the **National Gallery** and of one of London's most distinctive landmarks, **Nelson's Column.** Permanently thronged with people—Londoners and tourists alike—it remains London's "living room." Great events, such as the Christmas Tree lighting ceremony, New Year's Eve, royal weddings, political protests, and sporting triumphs will always see the crowds gathering in the city's most famous square.

The square is a commanding open space, built on the grand scale demanded by its central position in the capital of an empire that once reached to the farthest corners of the globe. The site once housed the Royal Mews, where Edward I (1239–1307) kept his royal hawks and lodged his falconers (not the numberless Edward the Confessor of Westminster Abbey fame, who died in 1066; this one, known as "Longshanks," died of dysentery in 1307). Later, all the kings' horses were stabled here, in increasingly smart quarters, until 1830, when John Nash had the buildings torn down as part of his Charing Cross Improvement Scheme. Nash exploited the square's natural incline—it slopes down from north to south—making it a succession of high points from which to look down the imposing carriageways that run dramatically away from it toward the Thames, the Houses of Parliament, and Buckingham Palace. Upon Nash's death, the design baton was passed to Sir Charles Barry and then to Sir Edwin Lutyens.

There's a pathetic history attached to the **equestrian statue of Charles I,** which stands near Whitehall on the southern slope of the square (on a pedestal *possibly* designed by Sir Christopher Wren and *possibly* carved by Grinling Gibbons). After Charles's High Treasurer ordered it (from Hubert le Sueur), the Puritan Oliver Cromwell tumbled Charles from the throne and commissioned a scrap dealer with the appropriate name of Rivett to melt the king down. Rivett apparently buried the statue in his garden and made a fortune peddling knickknacks wrought, he claimed, from its metal, only to produce the statue miraculously unscathed after the restoration of the monarchy—and to make more cash reselling it to the authorities. In 1767 Charles II had it placed where it stands today, near the spot where his father was executed in 1649. Each year, on January 30, the day of the king's death, the Royal Stuart Society lays a wreath at the foot of the statue. ⊠ *Trafalgar Sq., Westminster SW1* Ⓤ *Charing Cross.*

**⓬ Wellington Barracks.** These are the headquarters of the Guards Division, the queen's five regiments of elite foot guards (Grenadier, Coldstream, Scots, Irish, and Welsh) who protect the sovereign and patrol her palace dressed in tunics of gold-purled scarlet and tall fur "busby" helmets of Canadian brown bearskin. If you want to learn more about the guards, or view every kind of toy model soldier, visit the **Guards Museum;** the entrance is next to the Guards Chapel. ⊠ *Wellington Barracks, Birdcage Walk, Westminster SW1* ☎ *020/7414–3428* ⊡ *£2* ☉ *Daily 10–4* Ⓤ *St. James's Park.*

**⓲ Westminster Abbey.** Marked by the teeming human contents of tour buses, off the south side of Parliament Square, this is where nearly all of England's monarchs have been crowned amid great heraldic splendor; many are buried here, too. The main nave, often crowded, is packed with memories, as it has witnessed many splendid royal ceremonies. As the most ancient of London's great churches, the place is crammed with spectacular medieval architecture. Other than the mysterious gloom of the vast interior, the first thing to strike most people is the fantastic proliferation of statues, tombs, and commemorative tablets: in parts, the building seems more like a stonemason's yard than a place of worship. But it's in its latter capacity that this landmark truly comes into its own. Although attending a service is not something to undertake purely for sightseeing reasons, it provides a glimpse of the abbey in its full majesty, accompanied by music from the Westminster choristers and the organ that Henry Purcell once played. During a service, you won't be bothered by the frequent and jarring loudspeaker announcements made during peak hours, requesting "a minute of silence" from the noisy masses.

The origins of Westminster Abbey are uncertain. The first church on the site may have been built as early as the 7th century by the Saxon king Sebert (who may be buried here, alongside his queen and sister); a Benedictine abbey was established in the 10th century. There were certainly preexisting foundations when Edward the Confessor was crowned in 1040, moved his palace to Westminster, and began building a church. Only traces have been found of that incarnation, which was consecrated eight days before Edward's death in 1066. (It appears in the Bayeaux

FodorsChoice
★

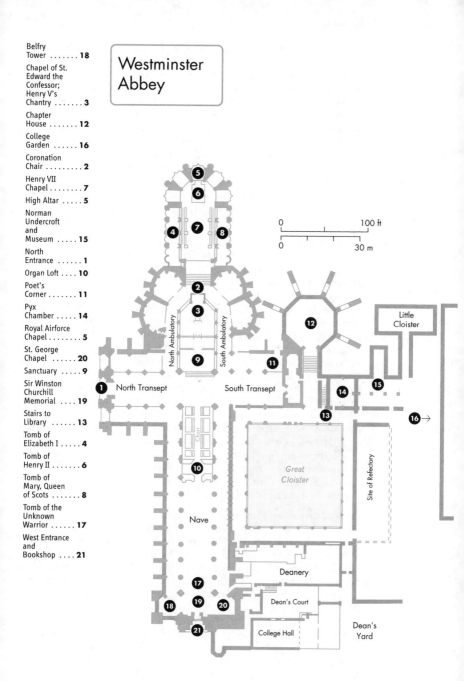

Westminster Abbey

0                    100 ft

0                    30 m

North Ambulatory

South Ambulatory

Little Cloister

North Transept

South Transept

Choir

Great Cloister

Site of Refectory

Nave

Deanery

Dean's Court

Dean's Yard

College Hall

Tapestry.) Edward's canonization in 1139 gave a succession of kings added incentive to shower the abbey with attention and improvements. Henry III, full of ideas from his travels in France, pulled it down and started again with Amiens and Rheims in mind. In fact, it was the master mason Henry de Reyns ("of Rheims") who, between 1245 and 1254, put up the transepts, north front, and rose windows, as well as part of the cloisters and chapter house; and it was his master plan that, funded by Richard II, was resumed 100 years later. Henry V (reigned 1413–22) and Henry VII (1485–1509) were the chief succeeding benefactors. The abbey was eventually completed in 1532. After that, Sir Christopher Wren had a hand in shaping the place; his west towers were completed in 1745, 22 years after his death, by Nicholas Hawksmoor. The most riotous elements of the interior were, similarly, much later affairs.

There's only one way around the abbey, and as there will almost certainly be a long stream of shuffling tourists at your heels, you'll need to be alert to catch the highlights. Entering by the north door, the first thing you see on your left are the overbearing and extravagant 18th-century monuments of statesmen in the north transept and north-transept chapels. Look up to your right to see the painted-glass rose window, the largest of its kind. At many points the view of the abbey is crowded by the many statues and screens; to your right is the 19th-century (and part 13th-century) choir screen, to the left is the sacrarium, containing the medieval kings' tombs, which screen the **Chapel of St. Edward the Confessor.** Due to its great age, the shrine to the pre-Norman king known as Edward the Confessor is closed off (unless via a tour with the verger; details are available at the admission desk and there is a small extra charge), but continuing to the foot of the Henry VII Chapel steps you can still see the hot seat of power, the **Coronation Chair,** which has been briefly graced by nearly every regal posterior. Edward I ordered it around 1300; it used to shelter the Stone of Scone (pronounced "Skoon"), upon which Scottish kings had been crowned since time began, but this precious relic was returned to Scotland's Edinburgh Castle. The stone is to be returned to England, however, for the duration of future coronations.

Proceed up the steps into one of the architectural glories of Britain, the **Henry VII Chapel,** passing the huge white-marble tomb of Elizabeth I, buried with her half sister, "Bloody" Mary I; then the tomb of Henry VII with his queen, Elizabeth of York, by the Renaissance master Torrigiano (otherwise known for having been banished from Florence after breaking Michelangelo's nose). Close by are monuments to the young daughters of James I; Sophia, who only lived for three days, is remembered by a single alabaster candle. An urn holds the purported remains of the so-called Princes in the Tower—Edward V and Richard. All around are magnificent sculptures of saints, philosophers, and kings, with wild mermaids and monsters carved on the choir-stall misericords (undersides) and with exquisite fan vaulting above—one of the miracles of Western architecture. (Keep an eye open for St. Wilgefort, who was so concerned to protect her chastity that she prayed to God for help and woke up one morning with a full growth of beard.)

The tombs and monuments with which Westminster Abbey is packed (some would say stuffed) began to appear at an accelerated rate starting in the 18th century (newest additions are 10 20th-century figures, including Martin Luther King, over the west door of the nave). One earlier occupant, though, was Geoffrey Chaucer, who in 1400 became the first poet to be buried in **Poets' Corner.** Most of the other honored writers have only their memorials here, not their bones: William Shakespeare and William Blake (who both had a long wait before the dean deemed them holy enough to be here at all), John Milton, Jane Austen, Samuel Taylor Coleridge, and William Wordsworth. Charles Dickens is both celebrated and buried in this crowded corner.

After the elbow battle you are guaranteed in Poets' Corner, you exit the main body of the abbey by a door from the south transept and south choir aisle to the comparative calm of the **cloisters,** where monks once strolled in contemplation and you may do the same. Go nearly all the way round and an archway leads to the quiet green **Dean's Yard,** where you can catch a fine view of the massive flying buttresses above. Also here is the entrance to Westminster School, formerly a monastic college, now one of Britain's finest public (which means the exact opposite to Americans) schools; Christopher Wren and Ben Jonson number among the old boys. Return to the cloisters and the abbey rooms used by monarchs of the Middle Ages. The **Chapter House,** a stunning octagonal room supported by a central column and adorned with 14th-century frescoes, is where the King's Council and, after that, an early version of the Commons, met between 1257 and 1547. Underfoot is one of the finest surviving tiled floors in the country. The **Abbey Museum** is in the undercroft, which survives from Edward the Confessor's original church, and includes a collection of deliciously macabre effigies made from the death masks and actual clothing of Charles II and Admiral Lord Nelson (complete with eye patch) and the battle kit of shield, saddle, and helmet of Henry V at Agincourt, among other fascinating relics. Adjoining these rooms, the Little Cloister is a quiet haven, and just beyond, the **College Garden** has been tended by monks for more than 900 years; it's like a secret garden, planted with medicinal herbs.

Returning to the abbey and the nave, look to the foot of the wall in the north aisle opposite the organ loft. All of Ben Jonson is buried here—upright in accord with his modest demand for a 2-by-2-foot grave site (only his memorial is in Poets' Corner). ("O rare Ben Jonson," reads his epitaph, in a modest pun on the Latin *orare,* "to pray for.") James Watt and Michael Faraday are among the scientists with memorials; Sir Isaac Newton has both grave and memorial. There's only one painter: Godfrey Kneller, whose dying words were "By God, I will not be buried in Westminster."

The **Tomb of the Unknown Warrior,** in memory of the soldiers who lost their lives in both world wars, is near the exit. Nearby is one of the very few tributes to a foreigner, a plaque to Franklin D. Roosevelt. Note that photography is not permitted anywhere in the abbey. ⊠ *Broad Sanctuary, Westminster SW1* ☏ *020/7222–5152* ⊕ *www.westminster-abbey. org* ⌨ *Abbey and museum £6* ⊘ *Abbey weekdays 9:30–3:45, Wed. until*

6, Sat. 9–1:45, closes 1 hr after last admission. Museum daily 10–4 Ⓤ Westminster.

**Westminster Cathedral.** This massive cathedral is hard to miss—once you are almost upon it, that is. It is the seat of the Cardinal of Westminster, head of the Roman Catholic Church in Britain, and is consequently London's principal Roman Catholic church. The asymmetrical redbrick Byzantine hulk, dating only from 1903, is banded with stripes of Portland stone and abutted by a 273-foot-high campanile at the northwest corner, which you can scale by elevator. Faced with the daunting proximity of Westminster Abbey, the architect, John Francis Bentley, flew in the face of fashion by rejecting neo-Gothic in favor of the Byzantine idiom, which still provides maximum contrast today—not only with the great church but with just about all of London. The interior is still incomplete, but worth seeing for its brooding mystery, its rich and colorful marble-work, and its noted Eric Gill reliefs depicting the Stations of the Cross (a "station" is a stopping point for prayer or contemplation). The nave is the widest in the country and is constructed in green marble which has a Byzantine connection—it was cut from the same place as the 6th-century St. Sophia's in Istanbul, and was almost confiscated by warring Turks as it traveled across the country. Just inside the main entrance is the tomb of Cardinal Basil Hume, who held the seat for more than 25 years. ⊠ Ashley Pl., Westminster ☎ 020/7798–9055 ⊕ www.westminstercathedral.org.uk ☜ Tower £2 ⊙ Cathedral daily 7–7. Tower Apr.–Sept., daily 9–5; Oct.–Mar., Thurs.–Sun. 9–5 Ⓤ Victoria.

# ST. JAMES'S & MAYFAIR

St. James's and Mayfair form the very core of London's West End, the city's smartest central area. No textbook sights here; rather, these neighborhoods epitomize much of the flavor that is peculiarly London's—the sense of being in a great, rich, (once) powerful city is almost palpable as you wander along its posh and polished streets. Here is the highest concentration of grand hotels, department stores, exclusive shops, glamorous restaurants, commercial art galleries, auction houses, swanky offices—all accoutrements that give this area an unmistakable air of wealth and leisure, even on busy days.

A late-17th-century ghost in the streets of contemporary St. James's would not need to bother walking through walls because practically none have moved since he knew them. Its boundaries, clockwise from the north, are Piccadilly, Haymarket, the Mall, and Green Park: a neat rectangle, with a protruding spur satisfyingly located at Cockspur Street. The rectangle used to describe "gentlemen's London," where Sir was outfitted head and foot (but not in between, since the tailors were, and still are, north of Piccadilly in Savile Row) before repairing to his club. This has been a fashionable part of town from the first, largely by dint of the eponymous palace, St. James's, which was a royal residence—if not *the* palace—from the time of Henry VIII until the Victorian era, and this is the home of Prince Charles.

Mayfair, like St. James's, is precisely delineated—a trapezoid contained by, respectively, Oxford Street and Piccadilly on the north and south, Regent Street and Park Lane on the east and west. Within its boundaries are streets both broad and narrow, but mostly unusually straight and gridlike for London, making it fairly easy to negotiate.

*Numbers in the text correspond to numbers in the margin and on the St. James's & Mayfair map.*

a good walk

Starting in Trafalgar Square, you'll find Cockspur Street off the southwest corner; follow it to the foot of **Haymarket.** On your right is London's oldest shopping arcade, the splendid Regency Royal Opera Arcade, which John Nash finished in 1818. Now you come to **Pall Mall ❶** ▶, a showcase of 18th- and 19th-century patrician architecture; it also houses such famous gentlemen's retreats as the Reform Club, halfway along on the right (from which Phileas Fogg set out to go around the world). At the end of Pall Mall, you collide with the small, Tudor brick **St. James's Palace ❷**. Continue along Cleveland Row by the side of the palace to spy on York House, home of the Duke and Duchess of Kent; then turn left into Stable Yard Road to Lancaster House, built for the Duke of York in the 1820s but more notable as the venue for the 1978 conference that led to the end of white rule in Rhodesia (now Zimbabwe); and **Clarence House ❸**, designed by John Nash and built in 1825 for the Duke of Clarence (who became William IV) and, after the death of the Queen Mother, is now the home of the Prince of Wales. Now, head north up along St. James's Street to St. James's Place, where, if you turn left, you can spot, at No. 27, one of London's most spectacular 18th-century mansions, **Spencer House ❹**, home of ancestors of the late Princess Diana of Wales.

Cross back over St. James's Street to King Street—No. 8 is Christie's, the fine art auctioneers; Duke Street on the left harbors further exclusive little art salons—but straight ahead is **St. James's Square ❺**, one of London's oldest squares and home of the London Library. Leave the square by Duke of York Street to the north, and turn left on **Jermyn Street ❻**, the world center of gentlemen's paraphernalia shops. Set back from the street is the lovely **St. James's Church ❼**. A right on Duke Street brings you to Piccadilly. Turn right again, and you'll pass the exclusive department store that supplies the queen's groceries, Fortnum & Mason, on the right, and the **Royal Academy of Arts ❽**, opposite, with famous **Piccadilly Circus ❾** ahead. Turn around—Wellington Arch and **Apsley House (Wellington Museum) ❿**, the gloriously opulent mansion the Duke of Wellington once called home, are ahead in the distance. Cross the street and head north up the shopping hub **Bond Street ⓫**, with **Burlington Arcade ⓬** to the right. You could detour by turning right before you reach Oxford Street into Brook Street (the composer Handel lived at No. 25, the **Handel House Museum ⓭**), which leads to Hanover Square. Turning right down St. George Street brings you to the porticoes of St. George's Church, where Percy Bysshe Shelley and George Eliot, among others, had their weddings. A right turn after the church down Mill Street brings you into Savile Row, the fashionable center for custommade suits and coats since the mid-19th century. No. 3 is a draw for

Beatlemaniacs: the former headquarters of Apple Records and the site of John, Paul, George, and Ringo's legendary rooftop concert (the building is not open to the public). Continuing from Savile Row to behind the Royal Academy is Albany Street, one of the smartest addresses since the turn of the 19th century. You can peer through the railings at the posh Henry Holland apartments built for fashionable bachelors, who included Byron, Prime Ministers Gladstone and Heath, Graham Greene, and recently actor Terence Stamp. From Savile Row, head west on Grosvenor Street to Duke Street: slightly to the south you'll find a couple of Mayfair's beauty spots—Carlos Place (site of the Connaught) and neighboring Mount Row, both adorned with some beautifully elegant residences. Here, too, is Mount Street, a pedigree-proud shopping avenue; take South Audley Street one block south to discover St. George's Gardens, a fine place for a picnic. Head over to Hyde Park to take in **Speakers' Corner** ⑭ and **Marble Arch** ⑮. Shop-'til-you-droppers can then explore Oxford Street (**Selfridges** ⑯ and Marks & Spencer are here); art lovers might want to continue north to Manchester Square for the magnificent **Wallace Collection** ⑰.

TIMING　Although this walk doesn't cover an enormous distance, you'll probably do a lot of doubling back and detouring down beckoning alleys—and into interesting shops. If you want to do more than window-shop, do a weekday jaunt, starting in the morning, so you get time for visits to the Royal Academy and the Wallace Collection or perhaps some of the commercial art galleries in and around Cork Street. The walk alone should take less than two hours. Add at least an hour for Apsley House, and another two for the Wallace Collection. Any of those could easily consume an afternoon, if you have one to spare (Clarence House is open only during summer). Shopping could take all week.

HOW TO GET THERE　You could start walking around this area from Trafalgar Square, or get the Piccadilly or Bakerloo Line to the Piccadilly Circus Tube stop, the Piccadilly to the Hyde Park Corner stop, or the Central Line to any of the stops along Oxford Street—Marble Arch, Bond Street (also Jubilee Line), Oxford Circus (also Victoria and Bakerloo lines), or Tottenham Court Road (also Northern Line). The Green Park stop on the Piccadilly, Victoria, or Jubilee Line is also central to many of this neighborhood's sights. The best buses are 8, 9, 14, 19, 22, and 38 along Piccadilly, especially the 8, which loops around via New Bond Street to Oxford Street and skims the eastern border of Green Park down Grosvenor Place.

## What to See

⑩ **Apsley House (Wellington Museum).** For Hyde Park Corner read "heroes corner"; even in the subway, beneath the turmoil of traffic, the Duke of Wellington's heroic exploits are retold in murals. The years of war against the French, and the subsequent final defeat of Napoléon at the Battle of Waterloo in 1815 made Wellington—Arthur Wellesley—the greatest soldier and statesman in the land. The house is flanked by imposing statues: opposite is the 1825 John Nash **Wellington Arch** with the four-horse chariot of peace as its pinnacle (open to the public as an exhibition area and viewing platform). Just behind Wellington Arch, and cast from captured French guns, the legendary **Achilles** statue points the way

Fodor'sChoice
★

with thrusting shield to the ducal mansion from the tip of Hyde Park. Next to Apsley House is the 1828 Decimus Burton gateway to the park.

Once known, quite simply, as No. 1, London, this was long celebrated as the best address in town. Built by Robert Adam and later refaced and extended, this housed the Duke of Wellington from 1817 until his death in 1852. As the Wellington Museum, it has been kept as the "Iron Duke" liked it—even the railings outside are painted pale green as the duke once had them—his uniforms and weapons, his porcelain and plate, and his extensive art collection are displayed heroically. Unmissable, in every sense (and considered rather too athletic for the time), is the gigantic Canova statue of a nude (but fig-leafed) Napoléon Bonaparte, Wellington's archenemy, which presides over the grand staircase that leads to the many elegant reception rooms. The most stunning is the Waterloo Gallery, where the annual banquet for officers who fought beside Wellington was held. With its heavily sculpted and gilded ceiling, its feast of old master paintings on red damask walls, and commanding gray candelabra, it's a veritable orgy of opulence. Apsley House installed iron shutters in 1830 after rioters, protesting the duke's opposition (he was briefly prime minister) to the Reform Bill, broke the windows. Yes, the British loved him for defeating Napoléon, but mocked him with the name Iron Duke—referring not only to his military prowess but to his indomitable will. There are commemorative weekends on either side of Waterloo Day, and the day itself when entry to the house is free, with special events and costumed guides. Telephone or check the Web site for details. ⊠ *Hyde Park Corner* ☎ *020/7499–5676* ⊕ *www.english-heritage.org.uk* ⊙ *Tues.–Sun. 11–5* ⌐ *£4.50* Ⓤ *Hyde Park Corner.*

**Berkeley Square.** As anyone who's heard the old song knows, the name rhymes with "starkly." Not many of its original mid-18th-century houses are left, but look at Nos. 42–46 (especially No. 44, which the architectural historian Sir Nikolaus Pevsner thought London's finest terraced house) and Nos. 49–52 to get some idea of why it was once London's top address—not that it's in the least humble now. Snob nightclub Annabels is one current resident. ⊠ *Berkeley Sq., Mayfair W1* Ⓤ *Green Park.*

**⓫ Bond Street.** This world-class shopping haunt is divided into northern "New" (1710) and southern "Old" (1690) halves. On New Bond Street you'll find **Sotheby's,** the world-famous auction house, at No. 35. But there are other ways to flirt with financial ruin on Old Bond Street: the mirror-lined Chanel store, the vainglorious marble acres of Gianni Versace, and the boutique of the more sophisticated Gucci, plus Tiffany's British outpost and art dealers Colnaghi, Léger, Thos. Agnew, and Marlborough Fine Arts. **Cork Street,** which parallels the top half of Old Bond Street, is where London's top dealers in contemporary art have their galleries—where you're welcome to browse. Ⓤ *Bond Street or Green Park.*

**⓬ Burlington Arcade.** Perhaps the finest of Mayfair's enchanting covered shopping alleys is the second oldest in London, built in 1819 for Lord Cavendish, to stop the hoi polloi from throwing rubbish into his garden at Burlington House, which is behind the arcade. It's still patrolled by top-hatted officials, who preserve decorum by preventing you from

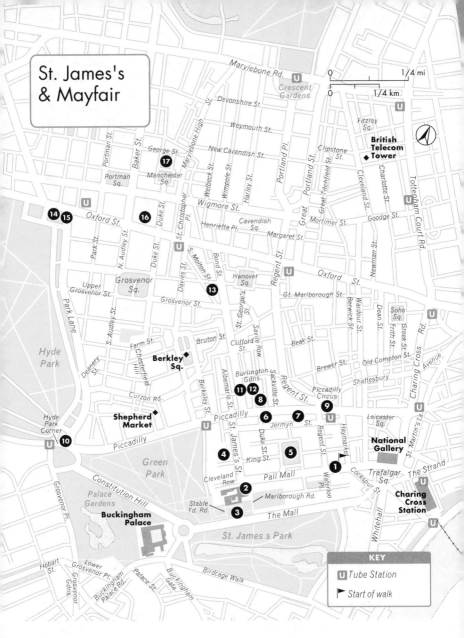

# St. James's & Mayfair

KEY

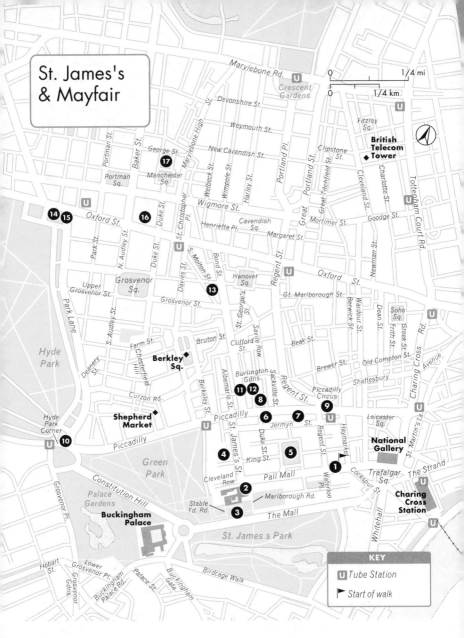 Tube Station

► Start of walk

singing, running, or carrying open umbrellas. The arcade is also the main link between the Royal Academy of Arts and its extended galleries at 6 Burlington Gardens. ⊠ *Piccadilly, Mayfair W1* Ⓤ *Green Park or Piccadilly Circus.*

**❸ Clarence House.** The London home of Queen Elizabeth the Queen Mother for nearly 50 years, Clarence House is now the Prince of Wales's residence. The Regency mansion was built by John Nash for the Duke of Clarence, who found living in St. James's Palace quite unsuitable. Since then it has remained a royal home for princesses, dukes and duchesses, including the present monarch, Queen Elizabeth, after her marriage. The rooms have been sensitively preserved as the Queen Mother chose, with the addition of many works of art from the Royal Collection. You'll find it less palace, and more home (for the Prince and his sons William and Harry) with informal family pictures and comfortable sofas. The tour (by timed ticket entry only) is of the ground floor rooms and includes the Lancaster Room, so called because of the marble chimneypiece presented by Lancaster county to the newly married Princess Elizabeth and the Duke of Edinburgh. Like Buckingham Palace, Clarence House is open only during the summer and tickets must be booked in advance. ⊠ *The Mall, St. James's SW1* ☎ *020/7766–7303* ⊕ *www.royal.gov.uk or www.princeofwales.gov.uk* 🎟 *£5* ⊗ *Aug.–mid-Oct.* Ⓤ *Green Park.*

**Faraday Museum, Royal Institution.** Although there's no plaque outside indicating that the museum is situated here, the front reception desk will point you toward the basement, where you'll find a reconstruction of the laboratory where the physicist Michael Faraday discovered electromagnetic induction in 1831—with echoes of Frankenstein. ⊠ *21 Albermarle St., Mayfair W1* ☎ *020/7409–2992* ⊕ *www.ri.ac.uk* 🎟 *£1* ⊗ *Weekdays 10–5* Ⓤ *Green Park.*

**⓭ Handel House Museum.** The former home of the composer, where he lived for more than 30 years until his death in 1759, is a celebration of his genius. It's the first museum in London solely dedicated to one composer, and that is made much of with room settings in the contemporary fine Georgian style. You can linger over original manuscripts (there are more to be seen in the British Library) and gaze at portraits, accompanied by live music—if the adjoining music rooms are being used by musicians in rehearsal. Some of the composer's most famous pieces were created here, including *Messiah* and *Music for the Royal Fireworks*. The museum occupies both No. 25 and the adjoining house, where life in Georgian London is displayed in exhibit space (another musical star, Jimi Hendrix, lived here for a brief time in the 1960s, although all that remains of his presence is a blue plaque outside the house). ⊠ *25 Brook St., Mayfair W1* ☎ *020/7495–1685* ⊕ *www.handelhouse.org* 🎟 *£4.50* ⊗ *Tues.–Sat. 10–6, Thurs. 10–8, Sun. noon–6* Ⓤ *Bond St.*

**Grosvenor Square.** This square (pronounced "*Grove*-na") was laid out in 1725–31 and is as desirable an address today as it was then. Americans certainly thought so—from John Adams, the second president, who as ambassador lived at No. 38, to Dwight D. Eisenhower, whose wartime headquarters was at No. 20. Now the ugly '50s block of the U.S. Embassy occupies the entire west side, and a British memorial to Franklin D. Roosevelt stands in the center. The little brick chapel used by Eisenhower's men during World War II, the 1730 Grosvenor Chapel, stands a couple of blocks south of the square on South Audley Street, with the entrance to pretty **St. George's Gardens** to its left. Across the gardens is the headquarters of the English Jesuits as well as the society-wedding favorite, the mid-19th-century Church of the Immaculate Conception, known as Farm Street because that is the name of the street on which it stands. ☒ *Mayfair W1* Ⓤ *Bond St.*

❻ **Jermyn Street.** This is where the gentleman purchases his traditional fashion accessories. He buys his shaving sundries and hip flask from Geo. F. Trumper; briar pipe from Astley's; scent from Floris (for women, too—both the Prince of Wales and his mother are Floris customers), whose interiors are exceedingly historic and beautiful, or Czech & Speake; shirts from Turnbull & Asser; and deerstalkers and panamas from Bates the Hatter. Don't forget the regal cheeses from Paxton & Whitfield (founded in 1740 and a legend among dairies). Shop your way east along Jermyn Street, and you're practically in Piccadilly Circus. ☒ *St. James's SW1* Ⓤ *Piccadilly Circus.*

⓯ **Marble Arch.** The name denotes both the traffic whirlpool where Bayswater Road segues into Oxford Street and John Nash's 1827 arch, which moved here from Buckingham Palace in 1851. Search the sidewalk on the traffic island opposite the cinema to find the stone plaque that marks (roughly) the place where the Tyburn Tree stood for four centuries, until 1783. This was London's central gallows, a huge wooden structure with hanging accommodations for 21. Hanging days were holidays, the spectacle supposedly functioning as a crime deterrent. Oranges, gingerbread, and gin were sold, alongside "personal favors," to vast, rowdy crowds, and the condemned, dressed in finery for his special moment, was treated more as hero than as villain. Cross over (or under—there are signs to help in the labyrinth) to the northeastern corner of Hyde Park to Speakers' Corner. ☒ *Park La., Mayfair W1* Ⓤ *Marble Arch.*

> **need a break?** **Sotheby's Café** (☒ 34–35 New Bond St., Mayfair W1) is a cut above the usual street café, as you would expect of this classy auction house on Bond Street. The lobster club sandwich is delicious, although not cheap.

▶ ❶ **Pall Mall.** Like its near-namesake, *the* Mall, Pall Mall rhymes with "shall" and derives its name from the cross between croquet and golf that the Italians, who invented it, called *pallo a maglio* and the French, who made it chic, called *paille-maille.* In England it was taken up with enthusiasm by James I, who called it "pell mell" and passed it down the royal line, until Charles II turned the dusty alley into a proper road so the ball could be seen clearly. Catherine Street, as Pall Mall was officially named (after Charles's queen, Catherine of Braganza), was *very* fashionable. No. 79 must have been one of its livelier addresses, since Charles's gregarious mistress, Nell Gwyn, lived there. The king gave her

# CloseUp

## SIGHTSEEING ON THE CHEAP

*If you want a motorized overview of London without the droning commentary, save some cash by joining London's commuters on a standard double-decker bus. You can use your Zones 1 and 2 Travelcard on the following routes:*

**Bus 11:** *King's Road, Sloane Square, Victoria Station, Westminster Abbey, Houses of Parliament and Big Ben, Whitehall, Trafalgar Square, The Strand, Fleet Street, and St. Paul's Cathedral.*

**Bus 12:** *Bayswater, Marble Arch, Oxford Street, Piccadilly Circus, Trafalgar Square,* *Horse Guards, Whitehall, Houses of Parliament and Big Ben, Westminster Bridge.*

**Bus 19:** *Sloane Square, Knightsbridge, Hyde Park Corner, Green Park, Piccadilly Circus, Shaftsbury Avenue, Oxford Street, Bloomsbury, Islington.*

**Bus 88:** *Oxford Circus, Piccadilly Circus, Trafalgar Square, Whitehall, Houses of Parliament and Big Ben, Westminster Abbey, Tate Britain.*

the house when she complained about being a mere leaseholder, protesting that she had "always conveyed free under the Crown" (as it were); it remains, to this day, the only privately owned bit of Pall Mall's south side. Stroll slowly, the better to appreciate the creamy facades and perfect proportions along this showcase of 18th- and 19th-century British architecture.

Notable examples are two James Barry–designed buildings, the **Travellers' Club** and the **Reform Club,** both representatives of the upper-class gentleman's retreat that made St. James's the club land of London. The Reform is the most famous club of all, thanks partly to Jules Verne's Phileas Fogg, who accepted the around-the-world-in-80-days bet in its smoking room and was thus soon qualified to join the Travellers'. And—hallelujah—women can join the Reform. The RAC Club (for Royal Automobile Club, but it's never known as that), with its marble swimming pool, and the Oxford and Cambridge Club complete the Pall Mall quota; there are other, even older establishments—Brooks's, the Carlton, Boodles, and White's (founded in 1736, the oldest of all)—in St. James's Street around the corner, alongside *the* gentleman's bespoke (custom) shoemaker, Lobb's, and, at No. 6, *the* hatter, James Lock, which has one of the most historic store facades in the city—you half expect Lord Byron or Anthony Trollope to walk out the door. Waterloo Place, around the corner, is a continuation of this gentleman's quarter. ⊠ *St. James's SW1* Ⓤ *Piccadilly Circus.*

❾ **Piccadilly Circus.** New York has its Times Square, in Venice it's Piazza San Marco, and London has Piccadilly Circus. As natives say, if you stand here long enough, you will meet everyone you know. The name came into use during the early 17th century, when a humble tailor on the Strand named Robert Baker sold an awful lot of picadils—a collar ruff all the rage in courtly circles—and built a house with the proceeds. Snobs dubbed his new-money mansion Piccadilly Hall, and the name stuck.

As for "Circus," that refers not to the menagerie of backpackers and camera-clickers clustered around the steps of **Eros** but to the circular junction of five major roads.

Eros, London's favorite statue and symbol of the *Evening Standard* newspaper, is not in fact the Greek god of erotic love at all, but the angel of Christian charity, commissioned in 1893 from the young sculptor Alfred Gilbert as a memorial to the philanthropic Earl of Shaftesbury (the angel's bow and arrow are a sweet allusion to the earl's name). It cost Gilbert £7,000 to cast the statue he called his "missile of kindness" in the novel medium of aluminum, and because he was paid only £3,000, he promptly went bankrupt and fled the country. (Not to worry—he was knighted in the end.) Around Eros, London roars on—this hub includes a very large branch of Tower Records, the tawdry Trocadero Centre (video arcades, food courts, chain stores), and a perpetual traffic jam. Beneath the blight, however, is beauty: just behind the modern bank of neon advertisements are some of the most elegant Edwardian-era buildings in town. ⊠ *St. James's W1* Ⓤ *Piccadilly Circus.*

**Portland Place.** The elegant throughway to Regent's Park was London's widest street in the 1780s, when brothers Robert and James Adam designed it. The first sight to greet you here, drawing the eye around the awkward corner, is the curvaceous portico and pointy Gothic spire of **All Souls Church,** one part of Nash's Regent Street plan that remains. It's now the venue for innumerable concerts and Anglican services broadcast to the nation by the British Broadcasting Corporation. The 1931 block of Broadcasting House next door is where you'll find the BBC's five radio stations. It curves, too, if less beautifully; you'll see an Eric Gill sculpture of Shakespeare's Ariel (aerial—get it?) over the entrance, from which the playful sculptor was obliged to excise a portion of phallus lest it offend public decency—which the modified model did anyway. At No. 66, opposite the Chinese Embassy, the Royal Institute of British Architects has a small exhibitions gallery devoted to shows from its esteemed members. If you need a break, there's a tasteful café here with black leather sofas arranged around architectural models. ⊠ *Marylebone W1* Ⓤ *Oxford Circus or Great Portland St.*

**Regent Street.** This curvaceous thoroughfare was conceived by John Nash and his patron, the Prince Regent—the future George IV—as a kind of ultracatwalk from the Prince's palace, Carlton House, to Regent's Park (then called Marylebone Park). The section between Piccadilly and Oxford Street was to be called the Quadrant and lined with colonnaded shops purveying "articles of fashion and taste," in a big PR exercise to improve London's image as the provincial cousin of smarter European capitals. The scheme was never fully implemented, and what there was fell into such disrepair that, early this century, Aston Webb (of the Mall route) collaborated on the redesign you see today. It's still a major shopping street. Hamleys, the gigantic toy emporium, is fun; and since 1875 there has been Liberty, which originally imported silks from the East then diversified to other Asian goods, and is now best known for its "Liberty print" cottons, its jewelry department, and—still—its high-class Asian imports. The mock-Tudor interior, with stained glass and beams taken from battleships, is worth a look. ✉ *Mayfair W1* Ⓤ *Piccadilly Circus or Oxford Circus.*

❽ **Royal Academy of Arts.** Burlington House was built in the Palladian style for the Earl of Burlington around 1720, and it's one of the few surviving mansions from that period. The chief occupant today is the Royal Academy of Arts (RA), and a statue of one of its famed members, Sir Joshua Reynolds, with artist's palette in hand, is prominent in the piazza of light stone and fountains by Michael Hopkins. It's a tranquil, elegant space for sculpture exhibits, and has a café with outdoor tables in summer. Further exhibition space has been afforded with the opening of 6 Burlington Gardens, the old Museum of Mankind, reached through the elegant walkway of Burlington Arcade. An Armani retrospective proved an equally stylish choice for the opening exhibition in autumn 2003. The collection of works by Academicians past and present as well as its most prized piece, the *Taddeo Tondo* (a sculpted disk) by Michelangelo of the Madonna and Child, on display in the Sackler Wing. The RA has an active program of temporary exhibitions; hugely successful exhibitions here have included Sensation (1997), Monet in the 20th Century (1999), Van Dyck (1999), and the Genius of Rome (2001). Every June, the RA puts on the **Summer Exhibition,** a huge and always surprising collection of sculpture and painting by Royal Academicians and a plethora of other artists working today. ✉ *Burlington House, Piccadilly, Mayfair W1* ☏ *020/7300–8000, 020/7300–5760 recorded information* ⊕ *www.royalacademy.org.uk* ✉ *Admission varies according to exhibition* ⊙ *Sat.–Thurs. 10–6, Fri. 10–10* Ⓤ *Piccadilly Circus or Green Park.*

> **need a break?**
>
> The **Royal Academy Restaurant** has hot dishes at lunchtime, very good vegetarian options, and an extensive salad selection that is inexpensive for such a posh location. It's open weekdays 10–5:30, with a dinner menu on Friday from 6:15–10:30.

❼ **St. James's Church.** Recessed from the street behind a courtyard, the church is filled most days with an antiques and crafts market. Completed in 1684, this was the last of Sir Christopher Wren's London churches and his own favorite. It contains one of Grinling Gibbons's finest works, an ornate limewood reredos (the screen behind the altar). The organ is a survivor of Whitehall Palace and was brought here in 1691. A 1940 bomb scored a direct hit here, but the church has been completely restored, albeit with a fiberglass spire. It's a lively place, offering all manner of lectures and concerts. The courtyard hosts different markets: on Tuesday, antiques and small collectibles; Wednesday to Saturday, arts and crafts. ✉ *Piccadilly, St. James's W1* ☏ *020/7381–0441 for concert program and tickets* ⊕ *www. st-james-piccadilly.org* Ⓤ *Piccadilly Circus or Green Park.*

❷ **St. James's Palace.** With its solitary sentry posted at the gate, this surprisingly small palace of Tudor brick was once a home for many British sovereigns, including the first Elizabeth and Charles I, who spent his last night here before his execution. Today it's the working office of another Charles—the Prince of Wales. The front door actually debouches right onto the street, but he always uses a back entrance. Royals who live within the palace are Princess Alexandra and her husband, Sir Angus Ogilvy. Matters to ponder as you look (you can't go in): the palace was named after a hospital for women lepers, which stood here during the 11th century; Henry VIII had it built; foreign ambassadors to Britain are still accredited to the Court of St. James's even though it has rarely been a primary royal residence; and the present queen made her first speech here. Friary Court out front is a splendid setting for Trooping the Colour, part of the Queen's official birthday celebrations. Everyone loves to take a snap of the scarlet-coated guardsman standing sentinel outside the imposing Tudor gateway. ⊠ *Friary Court, St. James's SW1* ⊕ *www.royal. gov.uk* ⓤ *Green Park.*

❺ **St. James's Square.** One of London's oldest and leafiest squares was also the most snobbish address of all when it was laid out around 1670, with 14 resident dukes and earls installed by 1720. Since 1841, No. 14—one of the several 18th-century residences spared by World War II bombs—has housed the **London Library,** founded by Thomas Carlyle, and which, with its million or so volumes, is considered the best private humanities library in the land. You can go in and read the famous authors' complaints in the comments book—but not the famous authors' books, unless you become a member. ⊠ *St. James's SW1* ⊕ *www.londonlibrary.co. uk* ⓤ *Piccadilly Circus.*

⑯ **Selfridges.** With its row of massive Ionic columns, this huge store was opened three years after Harry Gordon Selfridge came to London from Chicago in 1906. Now British-run, Selfridges rivals Harrods in size and stock, and it's finally rivaling its glamour, too, since investing in major face-lift operations. ⊠ *400 Oxford St., Mayfair W1* ☎ *020/7629–1234* ⊕ *www.selfridges.co.uk* ⊙ *Weekdays 10–8, Sat. 9:30–8, Sun. 11:30–6* ⓤ *Marble Arch or Bond St.*

**Shepherd Market.** Though it looks like a quaint and villagelike tangle of small streets, this was anything *but* quaint when Edward Shepherd laid it out in 1735 on the site of the orgiastic, two-week-long May Fair (which gave the whole district its name). Now there are sandwich bars, pubs and restaurants, boutiques, and nightclubs, and a (fading) red-light reputation in the narrow lanes. ⊠ *Curzon and Shepherd Sts., Mayfair W1* ⓤ *Green Park.*

★ ⑭ **Speakers' Corner.** This corner harbors one of London's most public spectacles. Here, on Sunday afternoons, anyone is welcome to mount a soapbox and declaim upon any topic. It's an irresistible showcase of eccentricity, one such being the (deceased) "Protein Man," who, wearing his publicity board, proclaimed the eating of meat, cheese, and peanuts led to uncontrollable acts of passion that would destroy Western civilization. The pamphlets he sold for four decades the length and breadth of Oxford Street are now collector's items. ⊠ *Cumberland Gate, Park La., Mayfair W1* ⓤ *Marble Arch.*

★ ❹ **Spencer House.** Ancestral abode of the Spencers—Diana, Princess of Wales's family—this great mansion is perhaps the finest example of 18th-century elegance, on a domestic scale, extant in London. Superlatively restored by Lord Rothschild, the house was built in 1766 for the first Earl Spencer, heir to the first Duchess of Marlborough. The gorgeous Doric facade, its pediment adorned with classical statues, makes immediately clear Earl Spencer's passion for the Grand Tour and the classical antiquities of the past. Inside, James "Athenian" Stuart decorated the gilded State Rooms, including the Painted Room, the first completely Neoclassic room in Europe. The most ostentatious part of the house (and the Spencers did not shrink from ostentation—witness the £40,000 diamond shoe buckles the first countess proudly wore) is the florid bow window of the Palm Room: covered with stucco palm trees, it conjures up both ancient Palmyra and modern Miami Beach. ⊠ *27 St. James's Pl., St. James's SW1* ☎ *020/7499–8620* ⊕ *www.spencerhouse.co.uk* ☞ *£6* ☉ *Sept.–Dec. and Feb.–July, Sun. 10:45–4:45; guided tour leaves approx. every 25 mins; tickets on sale Sun. at 10:30* Ⓤ *Green Park.*

★ ☕ ⑰ **Wallace Collection.** Assembled by four generations of Marquesses of Hertford and given to the nation by the widow of Sir Richard Wallace, illegitimate son of the fourth, this collection of art and artifacts is important, exciting, undervisited—and free. As at the Frick Collection in New York, Hertford House itself is part of the show: the fine late-18th-century mansion, built for the Duke of Manchester, contains a basement floor with educational activities, several galleries, and a courtyard, covered by a glass roof, with exhibit space and an upscale restaurant.

The first marquess was a patron of Sir Joshua Reynolds, the second bought Hertford House, the third—a flamboyant socialite—favored Sèvres porcelain and 17th-century Dutch painting; but it was the eccentric fourth marquess who, from his self-imposed exile in Paris, really built the collection, snapping up Bouchers, Fragonards, Watteaus, and Lancrets for a song (the French Revolution having rendered them dangerously unfashionable), augmenting these with furniture and sculpture and sending his son Richard out to do the deals. With 30 years of practice behind him, Richard Wallace continued acquiring treasures after his father's death, scouring Italy for majolica and Renaissance gold, then moving most of it to London. Look for Rembrandt's portrait of his son, the Rubens landscape, Gainsborough and Romney portraits, the Van Dycks and Canalettos, the French rooms, and of course the porcelain. The highlight is Fragonard's *The Swing,* which conjures up the 18th-century's let-them-eat-cake frivolity better than any other painting around. Don't forget to smile back at Frans Hals's *Laughing Cavalier* in the Big Gallery or pay your respects to Thomas Sully's enchanting *Queen Victoria,* which resides in a rouge-pink salon (just to the right of the main entrance). There is a fine collection of armor (which you can try on for size) and weaponry in the basement as a break from all the upstairs gentility. ⊠ *Hertford House, Manchester Sq., Mayfair W1* ☎ *020/7563–9500* ⊕ *www.wallacecollection.org* ☞ *Free* ☉ *Mon.–Sat. 10–5, Sun. noon–5* Ⓤ *Bond St.*

**Waterloo Place.** This is a long rectangle off Pall Mall, punctuated by the Duke of York Memorial Column atop the Duke of York Steps and littered with statues, among them Florence Nightingale, the "Lady with the Lamp" nurse-heroine of the Crimean War; Captain Robert F. Scott, who led a disastrous Antarctic expedition in 1911–12 and is here portrayed in a bronze by his wife; Edward VII, mounted; George VI; and, as usual, Victoria, here in terra-cotta. Flanking Waterloo Place and looking onto Pall Mall are two of the gentlemen's clubs for which St. James's came to be known as Clubland: the **Athenaeum** and the former United Service Club, a favorite haunt of the Duke of Wellington, now the **Institute of Directors.** The latter was built by John Nash in 1827–28 but was given a face-lift by Decimus Burton 30 years later to match it up with the Athenaeum across the way, which he had designed. It's fitting that you gaze on the Athenaeum first, since it was—and is—the most elite of all the societies. (It called itself "the Society" until 1830 just to rub it in.) Most prime ministers and cabinet ministers, archbishops, and bishops have belonged; the founder, John Wilson Croker (the first to call the British right-wingers "Conservatives"), decreed it the club for artists and writers, and so literary types (Sir Arthur Conan Doyle, Rudyard Kipling, J. M. Barrie—the posh ones) have graced its lists, too. Women are barred. Most clubs allow female guests these days, but few admit women members, and anyway it's almost impossible to become a member unless you have the connections—which, of course, is the whole point. ⊠ *Regent St., Pall Mall, St. James's SW1* Ⓤ *Piccadilly Circus.*

# SOHO & COVENT GARDEN

An area delineated by Regent Street, Coventry and Cranbourn streets, Charing Cross Road, and the eastern half of Oxford Street encloses Soho, the most fun part of the West End. This appellation, unlike the New York neighborhood's similar one, is not an elision of anything but a blast from the past—derived (supposedly) from the shouts of "Soho!" that royal huntsmen in Whitehall Palace's parklands were once heard to cry. One of Charles II's illegitimate sons, the Duke of Monmouth, was an early resident, his dubious pedigree setting the tone for the future: for many years, Soho was London's center of strip shows, peep shows, clip joints, sex shops, and brothels. The mid-'80s brought legislation that granted expensive licenses to a few such establishments and closed down the rest; most prostitution had already been ousted by the 1959 Street Offences Act. Only a cosmetic smear of red-light activity remains now, plus one or two purveyors of fetish wear for trendy club goers.

These clubs, which cluster around the Soho grid, are the diametric opposite of the St. James's gentlemen's museums—they cater to youth, and post tyrannical fashion police at the door. Another breed of Soho club is the strictly members-only media haunts (the Groucho, Soho House, Fred's, Black's), salons for carefully segregated strata of high-income hipsters. The same crowd populates the astonishing selection of restaurants, but then so do the rest of London and all its visitors.

It was after the First World War, when London households relinquished their resident cooks en masse, that Soho's gastronomic reputation was established. It had been a cosmopolitan area since the first immigrant wave of French Huguenots arrived in the 1680s. More French came fleeing the revolution during the late 18th century, then the Paris Commune of 1870, followed by Germans, Russians, Poles, Greeks, and (especially) Italians, and, much later, Chinese. Pedestrianized Gerrard Street, south of Shaftesbury Avenue, is the hub of London's compact Chinatown, with restaurants, dim sum houses, Chinese supermarkets, and Chinese New Year's celebrations, plus a brace of scarlet pagoda-style archways and a pair of phone booths with pictogram dialing instructions.

The former Covent Garden Market became the Covent Garden Piazza, with the Central Market in the middle, in 1980, and it still functions as the center of a neighborhood—one that has always been alluded to as "colorful." It was originally the "convent garden" belonging to the Abbey of St. Peter at Westminster (later Westminster Abbey). The land was given to the first Earl of Bedford by the Crown after the Dissolution of the Monasteries in 1536. The earls—later promoted to dukes—of Bedford held on to the place right up until 1918, when the 11th duke managed to off-load what had by then become a liability. In between, the area enclosed by Long Acre, St. Martin's Lane, Drury Lane, and assorted streets north of the Strand had gone from the height of fashion (until the snobs moved west to brand-new St. James's) to a period of arty-literary bohemia during the 18th century. This period was followed by an era of vice and mayhem, once more to become vegetable provisioner to London when the market building went up in the 1830s, followed by the Flower Market in 1870 (Eliza Dolittle's haunt in Shaw's *Pygmalion* and Lerner and Loewe's musical version, *My Fair Lady*).

Still, it was no Mayfair, what with 1,000-odd market porters spending their 40 shillings a week in the alehouses, brothels, and gambling dens that had never quite disappeared. By the time the Covent Garden Estate Company took over the running of the market from the 11th duke, it seemed as if seediness had set in for good, and when the fruit-and-veg trade moved out to the bigger, better Nine Elms Market in Vauxhall in 1974, it left behind a decrepit wasteland. But this is one of London's success stories: the glass-covered market hall for shops and crafts in the midst of a piazza surrounded by retail and eateries, throngs with life seven days a week.

*Numbers in the text below correspond to numbers in the margin and on the Soho and Covent Garden map.*

a good
walk

Soho, being small, is easy to explore, though it's also easy to mistake one narrow, crowded street for another, and even Londoners go astray here. Enter from the northwest corner, Oxford Circus, and head south for about 200 yards down Regent Street, turn left onto Great Marlborough Street, and head to the top of **Carnaby Street** ❶ ☞. Turn right off Broadwick Street into Berwick (pronounced "Berrick") Street, famed as central London's best fruit-and-vegetable market. Then step through tiny Walker's Court (a hookers' haunt); cross Brewer Street, named for two extinct 18th-century breweries; and you'll have arrived at Soho's hip (and very gay) hangout, Old Compton Street. From here, Wardour, Dean, Frith, and Greek streets lead north, all of them bursting with restaurants and clubs. Either of the last two leads north to **Soho Square ❷**, but head one block south instead, to Shaftesbury Avenue, heart of theater-land, across which you'll find Chinatown's main drag, Gerrard Street. Below Gerrard Street is **Leicester Square ❸**, and running along its west side is Charing Cross Road, the bibliophile's dream. You'll find some of the best of the specialist bookshops in little Cecil Court, running east just before Trafalgar Square.

The easiest way to find the **Covent Garden Piazza ❹** and market building is to walk down Cranbourn Street, next to the Leicester Square Tube, then down Long Acre, and turn right at James Street. Around here are **St. Paul's Church ❺**—the actors' church—the **London's Transport Museum ❻**, and the **Theatre Museum ❼**, as well as plenty of shops and cafés. (If your aim is to shop, Neal Street, Floral Street, the streets around Seven Dials, and the Thomas Neal's mall all reward exploration.) From Seven Dials, veer 45 degrees south onto Mercer Street, turning right on Long Acre, then left onto Garrick Street, past the **Garrick Club ❽**, left onto Rose Street, and right onto Floral Street. At the other end you'll emerge onto Bow Street, right next to the **Royal Opera House ❾** and the **Bow Street Magistrates' Court ❿**. Continuing on and turning left onto Russell Street, you reach Drury Lane and the **Theatre Royal, Drury Lane ⓫**.

At the end of Drury Lane is the Aldwych, a great big croissant of a potential traffic accident, with a central island on which stand three hulking monoliths: India House, Melbourne House, and the handsome 1935 Neoclassic Bush House, headquarters of the BBC World Service. Stranded on traffic islands to the west is St. Mary-le-Strand, James Gibbs's (of St. Martin-in-the-Fields fame) first public building, inspired by the Baroque churches of Rome; and Wren's St. Clement Danes (with a tower appended by Gibbs), whose 10 bells peal the tune of the nursery rhyme "Oranges and lemons, Say the bells of St. Clements . . ." even though the bells in the rhyme belong to the St. Clements in Eastcheap. Inside is a book listing 1,900 American airmen who were killed during World War II. Heading west, perhaps stopping at **Somerset House ⓬** and the **Courtauld Institute Gallery** within, walk the ¾-mi traffic-clogged Strand to the southern end, where you take Villiers Street down to the Thames. See the historic York Watergate, once the gateway leading from the Duke of Buckingham's garden to the river steps, and **Cleopatra's Needle ⓭** by Victoria Embankment Gardens; cross the gardens northwest to the **Adelphi ⓮**, circumnavigating the Strand by sticking to the embankment walk, and you'll soon reach Waterloo Bridge, where (weather permitting) you can catch some of London's most glamorous views, toward both the City and Westminster around the Thames bend.

TIMING    The distance covered here is around 5 mi if you include the lengthy walk down the Strand and riverside stroll back. Skip that and it's barely a couple of miles, but you will almost certainly get lost, because the streets in both Covent Garden and Soho are winding, chaotic, and not logically disposed. Although getting lost is half the fun, it does make it hard to predict how long this walk will take. You can whiz round both neighborhoods in an hour, but if the area appeals at all, you'll want all day—

for shopping, lunch, the Theatre and Transport museums, and the Courtauld Galleries. One way to do it is to start at Leicester Square when the Half Price Theatre Booth opens (called TKTS, it opens at 10 AM from Monday to Saturday, and from noon on Sunday); pick up tickets for later, and then walk, shop, and eat in between.

HOW TO GET THERE A popular way to get to Soho is to hop on the Northern Line to Tottenham Court Road and walk south down Charing Cross Road, then west along Old Compton Street into the district proper, or eastward, by turning left at Shaftesbury Avenue, over to the Covent Garden area. The Covent Garden Tube stop is on the Piccadilly Line; Leicester Square—the nearest Tube to Soho—is on the Northern and Piccadilly lines. The best Soho buses are Buses 3, 6, 8, 10, 12, 13, 15, 23, 38, 73, 139, 159, and 176 to Charing Cross Road and Shaftesbury Avenue; for Covent Garden, get those listed above or the ones that stop along the Strand: Buses 9, 11, 13, 15, and 23.

## What to See

⓮ **Adelphi.** This regal riverfront row of houses was the work of London's Scottish architects—all four of them. John, Robert, James, and William Adam, being brothers, gave rise to the name, from the Greek *adelphoi,* meaning brothers. All the late-18th-century design stars were roped in to beautify the interiors, but the grandeur gradually eroded, and today very few of the 24 houses remain; Nos. 1–4 Robert Street, and No. 7 Adam Street are the best. At the **Royal Society of Arts** (⊠ 8 John Adam St. ☎ 020/7930–5115 ⊕ www.rsa.org.uk ⊠ Free ☉ 1st Sun. of month, 10–1), you can see a suite of Adam rooms; no booking is required. ⊠ *The Strand, Covent Garden WC2* Ⓤ *Charing Cross or Temple.*

⓾ **Bow Street Magistrates' Court.** This was where the prototype of the modern police force first operated. Known as the Bow Street Runners (because they chased thieves on foot), they were the brainchild of the second Bow Street magistrate—none other than Henry Fielding, the author of *Tom Jones* and *Joseph Andrews.* The late-19th-century edifice on the site went up during one of the Covent Garden market improvement drives. ⊠ *Bow St., Covent Garden WC2* Ⓤ *Covent Garden.*

▶ ❶ **Carnaby Street.** The '60s synonym for swinging London fell into a postparty depression, reemerging sometime during the 1980s as the main drag of a public-relations invention called West Soho. Blank stares would greet anyone asking directions to such a place, but it is geographically logical, and the tangle of streets—Foubert's Place, Broadwick Street, Marshall Street—do cohere, at least in type of merchandise (youth accessories, mostly, with a smattering of up-and-coming, happening designer boutiques and fashionable restaurants). Broadwick Street is also notable as the birthplace, at No. 74, in 1758, of the great visionary poet and painter William Blake. At age 26 he relocated back to this house for a year to sell prints next door, at No. 72 (now an ugly tower block), and then remained a Soho resident on Poland Street. ⊠ *Soho W1* Ⓤ *Oxford Circus.*

⓭ **Cleopatra's Needle.** Off the triangular-handkerchief Victoria Embankment Gardens is London's *very oldest thing,* predating its arbi-

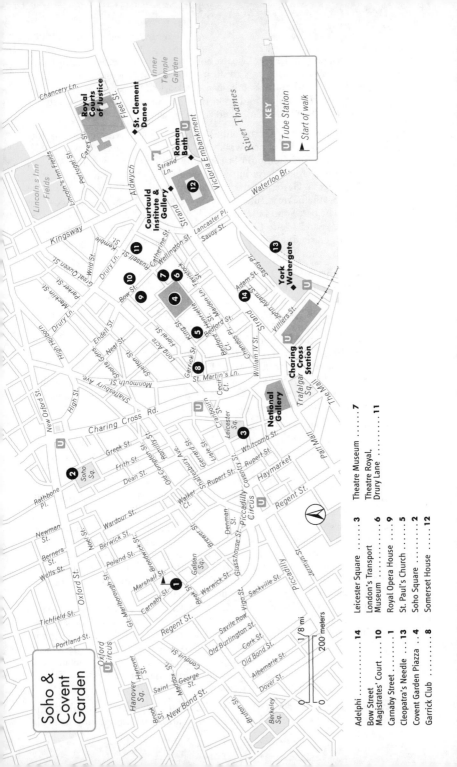

## Soho & Covent Garden

**KEY**
- U Tube Station
- ▲ Start of walk

River Thames

Inner Temple Garden

**Royal Courts of Justice**

◆ St. Clement Danes

◆ Roman Bath

Lincoln's Inn Fields

**Courtauld Institute & Gallery**

12

13

**York Watergate** ◆

14

**Charing Cross Station**

7 · 6
10 · 11
9 · 4
5
8

3

**National Gallery**

Soho Sq.

2

1

Piccadilly Circus

Trafalgar Sq.

The Mall

Hanover Sq.

Berkeley Sq.

0    1/8 mi
0    200 meters

trary namesake, and London itself, by centuries. The 60-foot pink granite obelisk was erected at Heliopolis, in lower Egypt, in about 1475 BC, then moved to Alexandria, where in 1819 Mohammed Ali, the Turkish viceroy of Egypt, presented it to the British. The British, though grateful, had not the faintest idea how to get the 186-ton gift home, so they left it there for years until an expatriate English engineer contrived an iron pontoon to float it to London via Spain. The sphinxes are a later, British addition. Future archaeologists will find an 1878 time capsule underneath, containing the morning papers, several Bibles, a railway timetable, some pins, a razor, and a dozen photos of Victorian pinup girls. ✉ *Embankment, Covent Garden WC2* Ⓤ *Charing Cross or Embankment.*

☘ **Courtauld Institute Gallery.** One of London's most beloved art collections, the Courtauld is set in the grounds of the renovated, grand 18th-century classical **Somerset House.** Founded in 1931 by the textile magnate Samuel Courtauld, this is London's finest impressionist and Postimpressionist collection, ranging from Bonnard to van Gogh (Manet's *Bar at the Folies-Bergère* is the star), with bonus post-Renaissance works thrown in. Botticelli, Brueghel, Tiepolo, and Rubens are also represented, thanks to the exquisite bequest of Count Antoine Seilern's Princes Gate collection. James Cuno, Harvard professor, has taken up the post of director, and remarks that the Fogg Art Museum at Harvard was the model for the founding of the Courtauld. The collection has been expanded with key works by Modernist painters, such as Matisse, Vlaminck, and Dufy, who were much influenced by these earlier artists. There are also some bold and bright Fauvist paintings. ✉ *The Strand, Covent Garden WC2* ☎ *020/7848–2526* ⊕ *www.courtauld.ac.uk* 🎫 *£5, free Mon. 10–2, except bank holidays* ☉ *Sept.–mid-July, daily 10–6, last admission 5:15; late July–Aug., Sat.–Thu. 10–6, Fri. 10–9* Ⓤ *Covent Garden, Holborn, or Temple.*

❹ **Covent Garden Piazza.** The restored 1840 market building around which Covent Garden pivots is known as the Piazza. Inside, the shops are mostly higher-class clothing chains, plus a couple of cafés and some knickknack stores that are good for gifts. There's the superior **Apple Market** for crafts on most days, too. If you turn right, you'll reach the indoor **Jubilee Market,** with stalls selling clothing, army surplus gear, and more crafts and knickknacks. At yet another market off to the left (on the way back to the Tube), the leather goods, antiques, and secondhand clothing stalls are a little more exciting. In summer it may seem that everyone you see around the Piazza (and the crowds are legion) is a fellow tourist, but there's still plenty of office life in the area, and Londoners continue to flock here. By the church in the square, street performers—from global musicians to jugglers and mimes—play to the crowds. ✉ *Covent Garden WC2* Ⓤ *Covent Garden.*

❽ **Garrick Club.** Named for the 18th-century actor and theater manager David Garrick, this club is, because of its literary-theatrical bent, more louche than its St. James's brothers, and famous actors, from Sir Laurence Olivier down, have always been proud to join—along with Dickens, Thackeray, and Trollope, in their time. Find the **Lamb & Flag** down teeny Rose Street to the left. Dickens drank in this pub, better known in its 17th-century youth as the Bucket of Blood, owing to the bare-knuckle boxing matches held upstairs. (You'll find that many London pubs claim Dickens as a habitué, and it's unclear whether they exaggerate or the author was the city's premier sot.) ✉ *15 Garrick St., Covent Garden WC2* Ⓤ *Leicester Sq. or Covent Garden.*

❸ **Leicester Square.** This square (pronounced "Lester") is showing no sign of its great age. Looking at the neon of the major movie houses, the fast-food outlets (plus a useful Häagen-Dazs café), and the disco entrances, you'd never guess it was laid out around 1630. By the 19th century it was already bustling and disreputable, and now it's usually one of the only places crowded after midnight—with suburban teenagers, backpackers, and London's swelling ranks of the homeless. That said, it's not a threatening place, and the liveliness can be quite cheering. In the middle is a statue of a sulking Shakespeare, clearly wishing he were somewhere else and perhaps remembering the days when the cinemas were live theaters—burlesque houses, but live all the same. Here, too, are figures of Hogarth, Reynolds, and Charlie Chaplin, and underneath, but not visible, is a £22 million electrical substation. One landmark certainly worth visiting is the **Society of London Theatre ticket kiosk (TKTS)**, on the southwest corner, which sells half-price tickets for many of that evening's performances. It's open from 10 AM on Monday–Saturday, and from noon on Sunday. On the northeast corner, in Leicester Place, stands the church of **Notre Dame de France**, with a wonderful mural by Jean Cocteau in one of its side chapels. ✉ *Covent Garden WC2* Ⓤ *Covent Garden.*

❻ **London's Transport Museum.** Housed in the old Flower Market at the southeast corner of the Covent Garden Piazza, this museum tells the story of mass transportation in the capital, and it's much better than it sounds. It's particularly child-friendly, with lots of touch-screen interactive material and, best of all, a Tube-driving simulator. There's also a café and a shop selling the wonderful old London Transport posters, plus mugs, socks, bow ties, and so on, printed with that elegant London Tube map, designed by Harry Beck in 1933 and still in use today. ✉ *Piazza, Covent Garden WC2* ☎ *020/7379–6344, 020/7565–7299 recorded info* 🌐 *www.ltmuseum.co.uk* *£5.95* ⏲ *Sat.–Thurs. 10–6, Fri. 11–6; last admission 5:15* Ⓤ *Covent Garden.*

**Neal Street.** One of Covent Garden's most intriguing shopping streets begins north of Long Acre, kitty-corner to the Tube station, and is closed to traffic halfway down. Here you can buy everything you never knew you needed—apricot tea, sitars, vintage aviators' jackets, silk kimonos, Alvar Aalto vases, halogen desk lamps, shoes with heel lower than toe, collapsible top hats, and so on. To the left off Neal Street, on Earlham Street, is Thomas Neal's—a new, upmarket, designerish clothing and housewares mall named after the founder (in 1693) of the star-shape cobbled junction of tiny streets just past there, called Seven Dials—a surprisingly residential enclave, with lots going on behind the tenement-style warehouse facades. The small and intimate **Donmar Warehouse** theater is part of the complex. Turning left onto the next street off Neal Street, Shorts Gardens, you come to Neal's Yard (note the comical, water-operated wooden clock), originally just a whole-foods wholesaler and now an entire holistic village, with therapy rooms, an organic bakery and dairy, a great vegetarian café, and a medical herbalist's shop reminiscent of a medieval apothecary. ⊠ *Covent Garden WC2* Ⓤ *Covent Garden.*

**❾ Royal Opera House.** In the past it was Joan Sutherland, Rudolf Nureyev and Margot Fonteyn, and now Pavarotti, Domingo, and Darcey Bussell wow the audience. Tickets are top dollar, but worth it if you love the red-and-gold Victorian surroundings, which always give a very special feel to the performance. London's premier opera and ballet venue was designed in 1858 by E. M. Barry, son of Sir Charles, the House of Commons architect and is the third theater on the site. The first opened in 1732 and burned down in 1808; the second opened a year later, only to succumb to fire in 1856.

The entire building has been overhauled spectacularly while keeping the magic of the grand Victorian theater. Without doubt, the glass-and-steel Floral Hall (so badly damaged by fire in the 1950s it was used only for storing scenery) is the most wonderful feature; you can wander around and drink in (literally, in the foyer café) the interior during the day. The same is true of the Amphitheatre Bar and Piazza concourse, which give a splendid panorama across the city. There are free lunchtime chamber concerts and lectures as part of the policy to dispel the Opera House's elitist tag. ⊠ *Bow St., Covent Garden* ☏ *020/7304–4000* ⊕ *www. royaloperahouse.org* Ⓤ *Covent Garden.*

**❺ St. Paul's Church.** If you want to commune with the spirits of Vivien Leigh, Noël Coward, Edith Evans, and Charlie Chaplin, this might be just the place. Memorials to them and many other theater greats are found in this 1633 work of the renowned Inigo Jones, which has always been known as "the actors' church" thanks to the neighboring theater district and St. Paul's prominent parishioners (well-known actors often read the lessons at services). Fittingly, its portico was where the opening scene for *Pygmalion* was staged. St. Paul's Church (Wren's mammoth St. Paul's cathedral is eastward in the City) is across the Covent Garden Piazza, often picturesquely punctuated with street entertainers—those who have passed auditions for this most coveted of London's street venues. ⊠ *Bedford St., Covent Garden WC2* Ⓤ *Covent Garden.*

**❷ Soho Square.** Laid out about 1680, this square was fashionable during the 18th century. Only two of the original houses still stand, plus the 19th-century central garden. It's now a place of peace and offices (among them Paul McCartney's music publishers and Bloomsbury Publishing). That isn't a Tudor landmark in the center but a Tudor-style thatch-and-daub Victorian gardener's hut—an almost fairy-tale sight to enjoy during a take-out lunch in the park. ⊠ *Soho W1* Ⓤ *Tottenham Court Rd.*

**need a break?**    **Maison Bertaux** (⊠ 28 Greek St., Soho) has been dispensing savory and sweet delights since the end of the 19th century, in surroundings reminiscent of a faded French *salon de thé,* spread over two floors.

⏱ ⑫ **Somerset House.** An old royal palace once stood on the site, but the 18th-
Fodor'sChoice century building that finally replaced it was the work of Sir William Cham-
★ bers (1726–96) during the reign of George III. It was built to house
government offices, principally those of the Navy; for the first time in
more than 100 years these gracious rooms are on view for free, including the Seamen's Waiting Hall and the Nelson Stair. In addition, the Navy
Commissioners' Barge has returned to dry dock at the Water Gate. The
rooms are on the south side of the building, by the river, and the **Courtauld Institute Gallery** occupies most of the north building, facing the
busy Strand. Between is the cobbled Italianate courtyard, where Admiral Nelson used to walk, which is the scene of an ice rink in the winter
holiday season, as well as summer concerts and other cultural events.
Cafés and a restored river terrace adjoin the property, and a stone-and-
glass footbridge leads up to Waterloo Bridge, which you can walk across
to get to the South Bank.

In the vaults of the house is **The Gilbert Collection,** a museum of intricate works of silver, gold snuff boxes, and Italian mosaics. The micro-
mosaics on tables, portrait miniatures, and jewelry are made in such fine
detail that you might think they're painted, so be glad if you're offered
a magnifying glass—it's the best way to fully appreciate the fine detail.
The **Hermitage Rooms** is the showcase for a selection of rotating exhibitions from the collections of the State Museum in St. Petersburg, and
other Hermitage-related activities. The opening show consisted of a selection of jewels, antiquities, portraits, and miniatures amassed by
Catherine the Great, one of the greatest collectors of all time. Subsequent exhibitions have included masterpieces of the Walpole Collection:
Britain's first Prime Minister amassed works by artists such as Rembrandt,
Rubens, Van Dyck, and Poussin, which were then sold to Catherine the
Great. Ironic that these pieces returned to the country for the first time
in more than 200 years. ⊠ *The Strand, Covent Garden WC2* ☎ *020/
7845–4600 information, 020/7485–4630 Hermitage information* ⊕ *www.
somerset-house.org.uk* ⊠ *Somerset House free, Gilbert Collection £5,
Courtauld Institute Gallery £5, Hermitage Rooms £6. Visit two collections, save £1; visit all three, save £2* ⊙ *Daily 10–6; last admission
5:15* Ⓤ *Charing Cross.*

⏱ ⑦ **Theatre Museum.** This mostly below-ground museum aims to re-create
the excitement of theater itself. There are usually programs in progress
allowing children to get in a mess with makeup or have a giant dressing-up session. Permanent exhibits paint a history of the English stage
from the 16th century to Mick Jagger's jumpsuit, with tens of thousands
of theater playbills and sections on such topics as Hamlet through the
ages and pantomime—the peculiar British theatrical tradition whereby
men dress as ugly women (as distinct from RuPaul) and girls wear tights
and play princes. There's a little theater in the bowels of the museum
and a ticket desk for "real" theaters around town, plus an archive holding video recordings and audiotapes of significant British theatrical
productions. ⊠ *7 Russell St., Covent Garden WC2* ☎ *020/7943–4700*
⊕ *www.theatremuseum.org* ⊠ *Free* ⊙ *Tues.–Sun. 10–6; last admission
5:30* Ⓤ *Covent Garden.*

⑪ **Theatre Royal, Drury Lane.** This is London's best-known auditorium and almost its largest. Since World War II, its forte has been musicals (past ones have included *The King and I, My Fair Lady, South Pacific, Hello, Dolly!,* and *A Chorus Line*)—though David Garrick, who managed it from 1747 to 1776, made its name by reviving the works of the by-then-obscure William Shakespeare. It enjoys all the romantic accessories of a London theater—a history of fires (it burned down three times, once in a Wren-built incarnation), riots (in 1737, when a posse of footmen demanded free admission), attempted regicides (George II in 1716 and his grandson George III in 1800), and even sightings of the most famous phantom of theaterland, the Man in Grey (in the Circle, matinees). The entrance is on Catherine Street. ✉ *Catherine St., Covent Garden WC2* Ⓤ *Covent Garden.*

# BLOOMSBURY & LEGAL LONDON

The character of an area of London can change visibly from one street to the next. Nowhere is this so clear as in the contrast between fun-loving Soho and intellectual Bloomsbury, a mere 100 yards to the northeast, or between arty, trendy Covent Garden and—on the other side of Kingsway—sober Holborn. Both Bloomsbury and Holborn are almost purely residential and should be seen by day. The first district is best known for its famous flowering of literary-arty bohemia, personified by the clique known as the Bloomsbury Group during the last century's first three decades, and for the British Museum and the University of London, which dominate it now. The second sounds as exciting as, say, a center for accountants or dentists, but don't be put off—filled with magnificently ancient buildings, it's more interesting and beautiful than you might suppose.

The elite core of writers and artists who made this quarter famous have no single museum celebrating their existence and achievements, but their works pervade many museums and galleries in the capital. You will, however, find blue oval commemorative plaques adorning the facades of the former residences of the Bloomsbury set: Virginia Woolf (at 50 Gordon Sq.), E. M. Forster, Vanessa and Clive Bell, Duncan Grant, Dora Carrington, Roger Fry, John Maynard Keynes (46 Gordon Sq.), and Lytton Strachey (51 Gordon Sq.). Satellites of the Bloomsburies included the poet Rupert Brooke and writer Christopher Isherwood. They agreed with G. E. Moore's philosophical notion that "the pleasures of human intercourse and the enjoyment of beautiful objects . . . form the rational ultimate end of social progress." True to their beliefs, when they weren't producing art and academia, the friends enjoyed much human intercourse, as has been exhaustively documented, not least in Virginia Woolf's own diaries, on film in *Carrington,* and *The Hours* based on the novel by Michael Cunningham.

More clearly visible than those literary salons is the time-warp territory of interlocking alleys, gardens and cobbled courts, and town houses and halls where London's legal profession grew up. The Great Fire of 1666 razed most of the city but spared the buildings of legal London, and the whole neighborhood oozes history. What is best about the area is that it lacks the commercial veneer of other historic sites, mostly because it still is very much the center of London's legal profession. Barristers, be-robed and bewigged, may add an anachronistic frisson to your sight-seeing, but they're only on their way to work.

They are headed for one of the four Inns of Court: Gray's Inn, Lincoln's Inn, Middle Temple, and Inner Temple. Those arcane names are simply explained. The inns were just that: lodging houses for the lawyers who, back in the 14th century, clustered together here so everyone knew where to find them and ultimately took over the running of the inns them-selves. The temples were built on land owned by the Knights Templar, a chivalric order founded during the First Crusade in the 11th century; their 12th-century Temple Church still stands here. Few barristers (British for trial lawyers) still live in the inns, but nearly all keep cham-bers (British for barristers' offices) here, and all are still obliged to eat a requisite number of meals in the hall of "their" inn during training—no dinner, no career. They take exams, too.

*Numbers in the text correspond to numbers in the margin and on the Bloomsbury and Legal London map.*

a good
walk

From Russell Square Tube stop, walk south down Southampton Row and west on Great Russell Street, passing **Bloomsbury Square** ☞ on the left, en route to London's biggest and most important collection of an-tiquities, the **British Museum** ❶. Leaving this via the north back exit leads you to Montague Place, which you should cross to Malet Street, which leads to Malet Place, to **University College** ❷. For a delightful de-tour, head west over to Scala Street (one block west from the Goodge Street Tube stop, then one block north on Charlotte Street) to find the charming Victorian-era wonders of **Pollock's Toy Museum** ❸. The streets around here and Fitzroy Square, built by the Adam brothers, are known as Fitzrovia, so named by literary soaks who drank at the Fitzroy Tav-ern on Charlotte Street. Back around the university, head over to Gor-don Street to reach Gordon Square. For the prettiest little street with picturesque 19th-century shop fronts, divert to Woburn Walk (Irish poet Yeats lived at No. 5). If you're interested in Asian art, stop in at the **Percival David Foundation of Chinese Art** ❹; if you want to check out the spectacular **British Library** ❺, head north up to Euston Road; and if you're a Harry Potter fan, turn left along Euston Road from the library to **King's Cross Station** ❻, to see the Hogwart's Express platform. Other-wise, continue south down busy Woburn Place, veering left down Guil-ford Street to reach Coram's Fields, home of Thomas Coram's Foundling Hospital, which has been restored as the **Foundling Museum** ❼; then turn left south of there on Guilford Place, then right to Doughty Street and the **Dickens House Museum** ❽. Two streets west, parallel to Doughty Street, is Lamb's Conduit Street (whose pretty pub, the Lamb, Dickens inevitably frequented).

At the bottom of Lamb's Conduit Street you reach Theobalds Road, where you enter the first of the Inns of Court, **Gray's Inn** ❾. From here, emerge onto High Holborn (pronounced "Hoe-bun"); heavy with traffic, it's the main route from the City to the West End and Westminster and the center of London's diamond and jewelry trade around the Hatton Garden road area. Pass **Staple Inn** ⑩, a ghost of the former wool trade, and turn left down tiny Great Turnstile Row to reach **Lincoln's Inn** ⑪, where you pass the Hall and continue around the west side of New Square to Carey Street, which leads you round into Portugal Street. Here you'll find the Old Curiosity Shop, probably one of the rare places in London Dickens did *not* frequent. Recross to the north side of Lincoln's Inn Fields to **Sir John Soane's Museum** ⑫ or walk the other way on Carey Street to reach the **Royal Courts of Justice** ⑬, which run through to the Strand. Off to the left is Fleet Street and the 1610 **Prince Henry's Room** ⑭. Cross the Strand to **Temple** ⑮, and pass through the elaborate stone arch to Middle Temple Lane, which you follow past **Temple Church** ⑯ to the Thames.

TIMING   This is a substantial walk of 3 to 4 mi, and it has two distinct halves. The first half, around Bloomsbury, is not so interesting on the surface, but it includes a major highlight of London, the British Museum, where you could easily add 1 mi to your total and certainly at least two hours. The Dickens House is also worth a stop. The second half, legal London, is a real walker's walk, with most of the highlights in the building architecture and surroundings. The exception is Sir John Soane's Museum, which will absorb an extra hour. The walk alone can be done comfortably in two hours and is best on a sunny day.

HOW TO GET   The best Tube stops for the Inns of Court are Holborn on the Central
THERE   and Piccadilly lines (surface and walk east up High Holborn, then south), or Chancery Lane on the Central Line. For the British Museum, Tottenham Court Road (Northern and Central lines) and Russell Square (Piccadilly Line) are equidistant. Bus 7 is the best bus for the BM; for the Inns of Court, get Bus 8, 17, 25, 45, 46, or 242 to High Holborn or Bus 17, 19, 38, 45, 46, 55, or 243 to Theobalds Road.

## What to See

▶ **Bloomsbury Square.** This was laid out in 1660, making it the earliest of the Bloomsbury squares, although none of the original houses remain; what is most remarkable about it now is that you can always find a parking spot in the huge underground garage. You'll find it by exiting the Tube at Tottenham Court Road—a bustling street where Londoners buy their electronic goods at the ugly Oxford Street end, and their furniture at Heal's and Habitat on the north end—and taking Great Russell Street east. Bloomsbury is dotted with squares—Gordon, Tavistock, Bedford, and Brunswick are some of the more picturesque ones. ✉ *Bloomsbury WC1* Ⓤ *Tottenham Court Rd.*

🐾 ❺ **British Library.** Since 1759, the British Library had been housed in the British Museum on Gordon Square. But space ran out long ago. The collection of around 18 million volumes now has a home in state-of-the-art surroundings, and if you are a researcher, it's a wonderful place to work (special passes are required). The library's treasures are on view to the general public: Magna Carta, a Gutenberg Bible, Jane Austen's writings, Shakespeare's First Folio, and musical manuscripts by Handel and Sir Paul McCartney are on show in the John Ritblat Gallery. Also in the gallery are headphones—you can listen to some of the most interesting snippets in a small showcase of the **National Sound Archive** stored here (it's the world's largest collection, but is not on view), such as the voice of Florence Nightingale, and an extract from the Beatles' last tour interview. The Workshop of Words, Sound & Images explores the vitality of the living word, and on weekends and during school vacations there are hands-on demonstrations of how a book comes together. Feast your eyes also on the six-story glass tower that holds the 65,000-volume collection of George III, plus a permanent exhibition of rare stamps. And if all that wordiness is just too much, you can relax in the library's piazza or restaurant, or take in one of the occasional free concerts in the amphitheater. ⊠ *96 Euston Rd., Bloomsbury NW1* ☏ *020/ 7412–7332* ⊕ *www.bl.uk* ✉ *Free, charge for special exhibitions* ⊙ *Mon. and Wed.–Fri. 9:30–6, Tues. 9:30–8, Sat. 9:30–5; Sun. 11–5* Ⓤ *Euston or King's Cross.*

🕙 ❶ **British Museum.** With a facade like a great temple, this celebrated trea-
Fodor'sChoice sure house—filled with plunder of incalculable value and beauty from
★ around the globe—is housed in a ponderously dignified Greco-Victorian building that makes for a suitably grand impression. Inside you'll find some of the greatest relics of humankind: the Elgin Marbles, the Rosetta Stone, the Sutton Hoo Treasure—everything, it seems, but the Ark of the Covenant. Now 250 years old, the museum has undergone great changes to modernize and update many of the galleries. The focal point is the unmissable Great Court, a massive glass-roofed space, which highlights and reveals the museum's best-kept secret—an inner courtyard, which, for more than 150 years had been used for storage. The tranquil Reading Room, after many years of closure, is a wonderful sight with its restored blue-and-gold dome, and ancient tomes lining the walls, contrasted with banks of computer screens. The museum space is vast, split into nearly 100 galleries—if you want to orient yourself comprehensively, buy a Visit Guide for £2.50, directly as you go in, or keep asking one of the museum staff if you want to avoid having a search party sent out to rescue you.

The collection began in 1753, when Sir Hans Sloane, physician to Queen Anne and George II, bequeathed his personal collection of curiosities and antiquities to the nation. It then quickly grew, thanks to enthusiastic kleptomaniacs after the Napoleonic Wars—most notoriously the seventh Earl of Elgin, who acquired the marbles from the Parthenon and Erechtheum during his term as British Ambassador in Constantinople in the days when Greece was part of the Turkish Empire.

The enormous building, with its classical Greek-style facade featuring figures representing the Progress of Civilization, was finished in 1847, the work of Sir Robert Smirke. Wherever you go, there are marvels, but certain objects and collections are more important, rarer, older, or downright unique, and because you may wish to include these in your wanderings, here follows a highly edited overview (in order of encounter) of the BM's greatest hits:

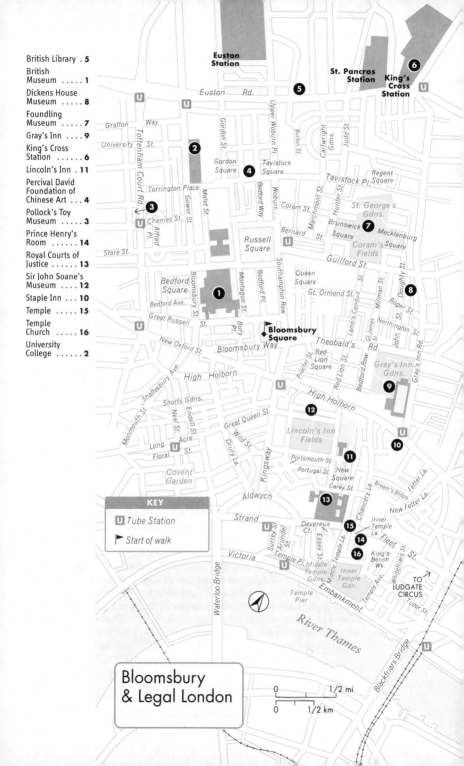

**KEY**

U  *Tube Station*

▶  *Start of walk*

Bloomsbury
& Legal London

0 _____ 1/2 mi

0 _____ 1/2 km

Close to the entrance, in Room 4, is the **Rosetta Stone,** found in 1799 and carved in 196 BC with a decree of Ptolemy V in Egyptian hieroglyphics, demotic, and Greek. It was this multilingual inscription that provided the French Egyptologist Jean-François Champollion with the key to deciphering hieroglyphics.

Perhaps the **Elgin Marbles** ought not to be here, but since they are you can find them in Room 18 in the Parthenon Galleries. Carved around 440 BC, these beautiful, graceful decorations are displayed along with an in-depth, high-tech exhibit of the Acropolis, and bring to the fore the rumbling debate on whether the Greeks should reclaim their spectacular sculptural heritage (the handless, footless Dionysus who used to recline along its east pediment is especially well known). While you're in the west wing, you can see one of the Seven Wonders of the Ancient World—in fragment form, unfortunately—in Room 21: the **Mausoleum of Halikarnassos.** This 4th-century tomb of Mausolus, King of Caria, was the original "mausoleum."

Upstairs are some of the most popular galleries, especially beloved by children: Rooms 62–63, where the **Egyptian mummies** live. The Roxie Walker Galleries have a fascinating collection of relics from the Egyptian realm of the dead—in addition to real corpses, wrapped mummies, and mummy cases, there's a menagerie of animal companions and curious items which were buried alongside them.

Proceeding clockwise, you'll come to Room 49, where the **Mildenhall Treasure** glitters in the refurbished Weston Gallery of Roman Britain. This haul of 4th-century Roman silver tableware was found beneath the sod of a Suffolk field in 1942. Next door, in Room 41, is the equally splendid **Sutton Hoo Treasure,** including brooches, swords and helmets, encrusted with jewels—which was buried at sea with (it is thought) Redwald, one of the first English kings, in the 7th century and excavated from a Suffolk field in 1938–39. The area still holds ancient warrior graves, as excavations in 2001 revealed: some of the discoveries, such as a chieftain's shield, are on display at the museum.

In Room 50 lies Pete Marsh, so named by the archaeologists who unearthed the **Lindow Man** from a Cheshire peat marsh. He was ritually slain, probably as a human sacrifice, in the 1st century and lay perfectly pickled in his bog until 1984. In the upper level of the museum is the Money Gallery, which holds ancient coins and medals. Back on the ground floor, in Room 26, the **JP Morgan Chase North American Gallery** has one of the largest collections of native culture outside the North American continent, going back to the earliest hunters 10,000 years ago. Also worth a look: The Korea Foundation Gallery (Room 67) delves into the art and archaeology of the country, including precious porcelain (much admired by today's artist potters), and colorful, intricately worked screens; and the **Sainsbury African Galleries,** which present a staggering 200,000 objects, including intricate pieces of old ivory, gold, and wooden masks and carvings—highlighting such ancient kingdoms as the Benin and Asante. Make sure to join at least one of the free "Eyeopener" 50-minute tours by museum guides (details at the information desk)—they do just what they say.

✉ *Great Russell St., Bloomsbury WC1* ☎ *020/7636–1555* ⊕ *www. thebritishmuseum.ac.uk* 💲 *Free, suggested donation of £2* ☉ *Museum Sat.–Wed. 10–5:30, Thurs. and Fri. 10–8:30. Great Court Sun.–Wed. 9–6, Thurs.–Sat. 9–11* Ⓤ *Tottenham Court Rd., Holborn, or Russell Sq.*

> **need a break?**
>
> The British Museum's self-service **Gallery Café** gets very crowded, but serves a reasonably tasty menu beneath a plaster cast of a part of the Parthenon frieze that Lord Elgin didn't remove. It's open daily. The café in the Great Court keeps longer hours and is a great place to people-watch and admire the spectacular glass roof, while you eat your salads and sandwiches.

☾ ❽ **Dickens House Museum.** This is the only one of the many London houses Charles Dickens (1812–70) inhabited that's still standing, and it would have had a real claim to his fame in any case because he wrote *Oliver Twist* and *Nicholas Nickleby* and finished *Pickwick Papers* here between 1837 and 1839. The house looks exactly as it would have in Dickens's day, complete with first editions, letters, and a tall clerk's desk (where the master wrote standing up, often while chatting with visiting friends and relatives). "By Dickens!" (a previous generation's exclamation of surprise for "you don't say")–if it is "by him" or anything to do with him, then you can find it here, as this museum is a world authority on the great man. There's a treat for Lionel Bart fans—his score of *Oliver!* Down in the basement is a replica of the Dingley Dell kitchen from *Pickwick Papers*. A program of changing special exhibitions gives insight into the Dickens family and the author's works, with sessions where, for instance, you can try your own hand with a quill pen. Christmas is a memorable time to visit, as the rooms are decorated in traditional style: better than any televised costume drama, this is the real thing. ✉ *48 Doughty St., Bloomsbury WC1* ☎ *020/7405–2127* ⊕ *www. dickensmuseum.com* 💲 *£4* ☉ *Mon.–Sat. 10–5, Sun. 11–5; last admission 4:30* Ⓤ *Chancery La. or Russell Sq.*

☾ ❼ **Foundling Museum.** Captain Thomas Coram devoted half his life to setting up a sanctuary and hospital, which he called the Foundling Hospital, for London's street orphans. He was a remarkable man, a master mariner and shipbuilder who, having played a major role in the colonization of Massachusetts, returned to London in 1732 to encounter sights he could not endure—babies and children "left to die on dung hills." Petitioning the lords of his day and their lunching ladies, he raised the necessary funds to set up what became the most celebrated good cause around, thanks partly to the sparkling benefactors he attracted. The old hospital was also the home of the Foundling Hospital Art Collection, whose artists, including William Hogarth, donated their work so that it would be an inspiration for social charity toward children (children's art activities will also be a focus). Other artists' work, by Gainsborough and Reynolds, is also on show in some superbly decorated rooms. At the time of this writing, the museum was closed for renovations. It's scheduled to reopen in fall 2004; phone for admission price and opening times. ✉ *40 Brunswick Sq., Bloomsbury WC2* ☎ *020/7841–3600* ⊕ *www.coram.org.uk/heritage* Ⓤ *Russell Sq.*

**9  Gray's Inn.** Although the least architecturally interesting of the four Inns of Court and the one most damaged by German bombs in the 1940s, this still has its romantic associations. In 1594, Shakespeare's *Comedy of Errors* was performed for the first time in its hall—which was lovingly restored after World War II and has a fine Elizabethan screen of carved oak. You must make advance arrangements to view the Tudor-style Gray's Inn's Hall (apply in writing, in advance, to the administrator, the Under Treasurer), but you can stroll around the secluded and spacious gardens, first planted by Francis Bacon in 1606. ⊠ *Gray's Inn Rd., Holborn, Bloomsbury WC1* ☎ *020/7458–7800* ⊙ *Weekdays noon–2:30* Ⓤ *Holborn or Temple.*

**6  King's Cross Station.** Known for its 120-foot-tall clock tower, this yellow brick, Italianate building with large, arched windows was constructed in 1851–52 as the London terminus for the Great Northern Railway and routes to the Midlands, the north of England, and Scotland. Harry Potter and fellow aspiring wizards took the Hogwarts Express to school from the imaginary platform 9¾ (platforms 4 and 5 were the actual shooting site) in the movies based on J. K. Rowling's popular novels. The station has put up a sign for platform 9¾ if you want to take a picture there. ⊠ *Euston Rd. and York Way, Euston NW1* ☎ *0845/748–4950* Ⓤ *King's Cross.*

**★ ⓫  Lincoln's Inn.** There's plenty to see at one of the oldest, best-preserved, and most comely of the Inns of Court—from the Chancery Lane Tudor brick gatehouse to the wide-open, tree-lined, atmospheric Lincoln's Inn Fields and the 15th-century chapel remodeled by Inigo Jones in 1620. The wisteria-clad New Square, London's only complete 17th-century square, is not the newest part of the complex; in fact, the oldest-looking buildings are the 1845 Hall and Library, which you must obtain the porter's permission to enter. ⊠ *Chancery La., Bloomsbury WC2* ☎ *020/7405–1393* ⊙ *Gardens weekdays 7–7, chapel weekdays noon–2:30; public may also attend Sun. service in chapel at 11:30 during legal terms* Ⓤ *Chancery La.*

**4  Percival David Foundation of Chinese Art.** This collection, belonging to the University of London, is dominated by ceramics from the Sung to Qing dynasties—from the 10th to the 19th century, in other words. It's on **Gordon Square**, which Virginia Woolf, the Bells, John Maynard Keynes (all at No. 46), and Lytton Strachey (at No. 51) called home for a while. ⊠ *53 Gordon Sq., Bloomsbury WC1* ☎ *020/7387–3909* ⊕ *www.pdfmuseum.org.uk* ⊡ *Free* ⊙ *Weekdays 10:30–5* Ⓤ *Russell Sq.*

**3  Pollock's Toy Museum.** For some, this will merit a visit whether they have children or not. A charmingly small museum in a warren of rooms in an 18th-century town house, Pollock's is crammed with antique dolls, dollhouses, and teddy bears. Best of all are the fabulous little toy theaters that Pollock made famous during the Victorian era—more than a few of England's most famous actors grew up playing with these cardboard delights. Even better: you can still buy reproductions of these cut-and-paste theater kits in the toy store on the premises. At this writing renovation plans were being discussed, so call before you visit. ⊠ *1 Scala*

*St., Bloomsbury W1* ☎ *020/7636–3452* 🎫 *£3* ⊘ *Mon.–Sat. 10–5; last admission 4:30* Ⓤ *Goode St.*

**⑭ Prince Henry's Room.** This is the Jacobean half-timber house built in 1610 to celebrate the investiture of Henry, James I's eldest son, as Prince of Wales; it's marked with his coat of arms and a PH on the ceiling. It's an entrance to the lawyers' sanctum, Temple, where the Strand becomes Fleet Street, and you can go in to visit the small Samuel Pepys exhibition. ⊠ *17 Fleet St., Bloomsbury EC4* ☎ *020/7936–2710* ⊕ *www. cityoflondon.gov.uk* 🎫 *Free* ⊘ *Mon.–Sat. 11–2* Ⓤ *Temple.*

**⑬ Royal Courts of Justice.** Here is the vast Victorian Gothic pile containing the nation's principal law courts, with 1,000-odd rooms running off 3½ mi of corridor. And here are heard the most important civil law cases—that's everything from divorce to fraud, with libel in between—and you can sit in the viewing gallery to watch any trial you like, for a live version of *Court TV.* The more dramatic criminal cases are heard at the Old Bailey. Other sights are the 238-foot-long main hall and the compact exhibition of judges' robes. Check out the gift shop also, where useful items (such as umbrellas) are emblazoned with the royal courts' crest. ⊠ *The Strand, Bloomsbury WC2* ☎ *020/7947–6000* ⊕ *www.open. gov.uk* 🎫 *Free* ⊘ *Weekdays 9:30–4:30; during Aug. there are no sittings and public areas close at 2:30* Ⓤ *Temple.*

**★ ⑫ Sir John Soane's Museum.** Guaranteed to raise a smile from the most blasé and footsore tourist, this museum hardly deserves the burden of its dry name. Sir John (1753–1837), architect of the Bank of England, bequeathed his house to the nation on condition that nothing be changed. (Sir John owned Nos. 12, 13, and 14, Lincoln's Inn Fields, and recently No. 14 was added to the museum space.) He obviously had enormous fun with his home, having had the means to finance great experiments in perspective and scale and to fill the space with some wonderful pieces. There are also different exhibitions on subjects as broad and as varied as Sir John's interests: from early architecture to more modern art. In the Picture Room, for instance, two of Hogarth's *Rake's Progress* series are among the paintings on panels that swing away to reveal secret gallery pockets with more paintings. Everywhere mirrors and colors play tricks with light and space, and split-level floors worthy of a fairground fun house disorient you. In a basement chamber sits the vast 1300 BC sarcophagus of Seti I, lighted by a domed skylight two stories above. When Sir John acquired this priceless object for £2,000, he celebrated with a three-day party. The elegant, tranquil courtyard gardens with statuary and plants are now open to the public, and there's a below street-level passage, which joins two of the courtyards to the museum. ⊠ *13 Lincoln's Inn Fields, Bloomsbury WC2* ☎ *020/7405–2107* ⊕ *www.soane.org* 🎫 *Free* ⊘ *Tues.–Sat. 10–5; also 6–9 on 1st Tues. every month* Ⓤ *Holborn.*

**⑩ Staple Inn.** Despite its name, this is not an inn of court but the former wool staple, where wool was weighed and traded and its merchants were lodged. It's central London's oldest surviving Elizabethan half-timber building and, thanks to extensive restoration, with its overhanging upper stories, oriel windows, and black gables striping the white walls,

# CloseUp

# HISTORIC PLAQUE HUNT

**A** S YOU WANDER AROUND LONDON, you'll see lots of small, blue, oval-shape plaques on the sides and facades of buildings, describing which famous, semifamous, or obscure but brilliant person once lived there. The first was placed outside Lord Byron's birthplace (now no more) by the Royal Society of Arts. There are around 700 blue plaques, erected by different bodies—you may even find some green ones which originated from Westminster City Council—but English Heritage now maintains the responsibility, and if you want to find out the latest, check the Web site www. english-heritage.org.uk. Below are some of the highlights:

James Barrie (100 Bayswater Rd., Hyde Park, W2); Hector Berlioz (58 Queen Anne St., Marylebone, W1); Elizabeth Barrett Browning (50 Wimpole St., Marylebone, W1); Robert Browning (17 Warwick Crescent, Hyde Park, W2);

Frederic Chopin (4 St. James's Place, St. James's, W1); Captain James Cook (88 Mile End Rd., Mile End, E1); Sir Winston Churchill (28 Hyde Park Gate, Kensington, SW7); T. S. Eliot (3 Kensington Court Gardens, Kensington); Mahatma Gandhi (20 Baron's Court Rd., West Kensington, W14); George Frederic Handel (25 Brook St., Mayfair, W1); Karl Marx (28 Dean St., Soho, W1); Wolfgang Amadeus Mozart (180 Ebury St., Belgravia, SW1); Sir Isaac Newton (87 Jermyn St., St. James's, SW1); Florence Nightingale (10 South St., Mayfair, W1); George Bernard Shaw (29 Fitzroy Sq., Bloomsbury, W1); Percy Bysshe Shelley (15 Poland St., Soho, W1); Mark Twain (23 Tedworth Sq., Chelsea, SW3); Oscar Wilde (34 Tite St., Chelsea, SW3); William Butler Yeats (23 Fitzroy Rd., Camden, NW1).

looks the same as it must have in 1586 when it was brand new. ✉ *Holborn, Bloomsbury WC1* ✆ *Courtyard weekdays 9–5* Ⓤ *Chancery La.*

**⑮ Temple.** The entrance to Temple—the collective name for **Inner Temple** and **Middle Temple,** and the exact point of entry into the City—is marked by a young bronze griffin, the **Temple Bar Memorial** (1880). He is the symbol of the City, having replaced (sadly) a Wren gateway (though you can't deny he makes a splendidly heraldic snapshot). In the buildings opposite is an elaborate stone arch through which you pass into Middle Temple Lane, past a row of 17th-century timber-frame houses, and on into Fountain Court. This lane runs all the way to the Thames, more or less separating the two Temples, past the sloping lawns of Middle Temple Gardens, on the east border of which is the Elizabethan **Middle Temple Hall.** If it's open, don't miss that hammer-beam roof, among the finest in the land. ✉ *Middle Temple La., Bloomsbury* ☎ *020/7427–4800* ✆ *Weekdays 10–11 and, when not in use, 2–4* Ⓤ *Temple.*

**⑯ Temple Church.** Featuring "the Round"—a rare circular nave—this church was built by the Knights Templar in the 12th century. The Red Knights (so called after the red crosses they wore—you can see them in effigy around the nave) held their secret initiation rites in the crypt here. Having started poor, holy, and dedicated to the protection of pilgrims, they grew rich from showers of royal gifts, until in the 14th century they were charged with heresy, blasphemy, and sodomy, thrown into the Tower, and stripped of their wealth. You might suppose the church to be thickly atmospheric, but Victorian and postwar restorers have tamed its air of antique mystery. Still, it's a very fine Gothic-Romanesque church, whose 1240 chancel ("the Oblong") has been accused of perfection. ⊠ *The Temple, Bloomsbury EC4* ☎ *020/7353–3470* ⊙ *Wed.–Sat. 11–4, Sun. 1–4, and closures for special services* Ⓤ *Temple.*

❷ **University College.** The college was founded in 1826 and set in a satisfyingly classical edifice designed by the architect of the National Gallery, William Wilkins. In 1907 it became part of the University of London, providing higher education without religious exclusion. The college has within its portals the **Slade School of Fine Art,** which did for many of Britain's artists what the nearby Royal Academy of Dramatic Art (on Gower Street) did for its actors. On view inside is a fine collection of sculpture by an alumnus, John Flaxman. You can also see more Egyptian artifacts, if you didn't get enough at the neighboring British Museum, in the **Petrie Museum** (☎ 020/7679–2884 ⊕ www.petrie.ucl.ac.uk), accessed from Malet Place, on the first floor of the DMS Watson building. It houses an outstanding, huge collection of fascinating objects of Egyptian archaeology—jewelry, toys, papyri, and some of the world's oldest garments. It has proved so popular with schoolchildren that it's now open Saturday 10–1 in addition to Tuesday–Friday 1–5. The South Cloisters contain one of London's weirder treasures: the clothed skeleton of one of the university's founders, Jeremy Bentham, who bequeathed himself to the college. ⊠ *Gower St., Bloomsbury WC1* Ⓤ *Euston Sq. or Goodge St.*

**Wig and Pen Club.** The club—another of those St. James's–style affairs, this time for "men of justice, journalists, and businessmen of the City" (plus former U.S. presidents Nixon and Reagan)—has its home in the only Strand building to have survived the Great Fire of 1666. ⊠ *229–230 The Strand, Bloomsbury WC2* Ⓤ *Aldwych or Temple.*

# THE CITY

You may have assumed you had entered the City of London when your plane touched down at Heathrow, but note that capital letter: the City of London is not the same as the city of London. The "capital-C" City is an autonomous district, separately governed since William the Conqueror's time, and despite its compact size (it's known as the Square Mile), it remains the financial engine of Britain and one of the world's leading centers of trade. The City, however, is more than just London's Wall Street: it's also the neighborhood where you'll find two of London's most notable sights, the Tower of London and St. Paul's, one of the world's greatest cathedrals—truly a case of the money changers' encompassing the temple! Temple Bar marks the western edge of the district, which does cover 677 acres, though not in a remotely straight-sided fashion.

The curvy shape described by its boundaries—Smithfield in the north, Aldgate and Tower Hill in the east, and the Thames in the south—resembles nothing so much as an armadillo, with Temple Bar at snout level.

The City is London's most ancient part, although there's little remaining to remind you of that beyond a scattering of Roman stones. It was Aulus Plautius, a Roman commander under Claudius, who built the first London bridge and thereby established the Romans' first stronghold on the Thames halfway through the 1st century AD. The name "Londinium," though, probably derives from the Celtic *Lyn-dun,* meaning "fortified town on the lake," which suggests far earlier settlement. It was really only after Edward the Confessor moved his court to Westminster in 1060 that the City gathered momentum. As Westminster took over the administrative role, the City was free to develop the commercial heart that still beats strong. There's no greater sign of this than the distinctive modern buildings that now nudge St. Paul's Cathedral: Tower 42, and 30 St. Mary Axe, nicknamed 'The Gherkin', are two of the most modern and spectacular.

The Romans had already found Londinium's position handy for trade—the river being navigable yet far enough inland to allow for its defense—but it was the establishment of crafts guilds in the Middle Ages that nurtured the growth of commerce. The core dozen livery companies swelled to dozens more, but only two of the original buildings were rebuilt after the Fire of London and survive today: The Apothecaries' Hall in Blackfriars Lane and the Vintners' Company in Upper Thames Street. The liveries or guilds were followed in Tudor and Stuart times by the proliferation of great trading companies (the Honourable East India Company, founded in 1600, was the star); then the cash really started to flow.

Three times the City has faced devastation: the Great Fire of 1666 spared but few of the cramped, labyrinthine streets, where the Great Plague of the previous year had already wiped out a huge portion of the population and left houses much degraded. With the wind in the west, they said, you could smell London from Tilbury. The fire necessitated a renaissance for London; Sir Christopher Wren had a big hand in the rebuilding, contributing not only his masterpiece, St. Paul's Cathedral, but 49 parish churches as well. A third wave of destruction, the Blitz, was dealt by German bombers during WWII. The ruins were rebuilt, but slowly and with no overall plan, creating an awkward patchwork of old and new, interesting and flagrantly awful. The City's colorful past can be hard to visualize in the midst of today's gray reality, but there are clues. Wander through its maze of streets and you will come across ancient coats of arms and street names redolent of life in the Middle Ages: Ropemaker Street, Pudding Lane, Jewry Street, and Fish Street. On weekdays, the place is bursting with people and activity, but come the weekend, most restaurants and shops in the center are closed. Yet, with the new developments around Bishopsgate on the City's fringe, this near total silence is beginning to be eroded. The City's age-old tradition of pageantry, however, is still in swing. Where else does the Lord Mayor, clad in ceremonial robes and chain of office, ride in an 18th-century coach—on the Lord Mayor's Show day in November, a celebration of the annually elected office—past buildings in which satellite communications have long since become routine?

*Numbers in the text correspond to numbers in the margin and on the City map.*

Begin (literally) at the gateway to the City. Until the 18th century there were eight such gates, of which only one survives; the others exist in name only (Cripplegate, Ludgate, Bishopsgate, Moorgate, and so on). The surviving one is Temple Bar, a bronze griffin on the Strand opposite the Royal Courts of Justice, at which the sovereign has to ask permission to enter the City from the Lord Mayor. Walk east to **Fleet Street** ⌐ and turn left on Bolt Court to Gough Square and **Dr. Johnson's House** ①, passing **Ye Olde Cheshire Cheese** ② on Wine Office Court en route back to Fleet Street and the journalists' church, **St. Bride's** ③. The end of Fleet Street is marked by the messy traffic intersection called Ludgate Circus, which you should cross to Ludgate Hill to reach **Old Bailey** ④ and the Central Criminal Courts.

Continuing along Ludgate Hill, you come to **St. Paul's Cathedral** ⑤, Wren's masterpiece. A pedestrian-only suspension bridge by Norman Foster, the **Millennium Bridge** ⑥, is in clear view from St. Paul's Churchyard. Then retrace your steps to Newgate Street, to the road called Little Britain, where you'll see the archway to **St. Bartholomew the Great** ⑦ on the left and come to London's meat market, Smithfield, at the end. Cross Aldersgate Street and take the right fork to London Wall, named for the Roman rampart that stood along it. It's a dismal street, now dominated by postmodern architect Terry Farrell's late-'80s follies, but about halfway along you can see a section of 2nd- to 4th-century wall at St. Alphege Garden. There's another bit in an appropriate spot back at the start of London Wall, outside the **Museum of London** ⑧; and behind that are the **Barbican Centre** ⑨, an important arts center of gray concrete, and **St. Giles Without Cripplegate** ⑩. You can walk all around here without touching the ground (well, ground level).

Back on London Wall, turn south into Coleman Street, then right onto Masons Avenue to reach Basinghall Street and the **Guildhall** ⑪; then follow Milk Street south to Cheapside ("cheap" derives from the Old English via Middle English *chep,* for trade); it was on this street that the bakers of Bread Street, the cobblers of Cordwainer Street, the goldsmiths of Goldsmiths Row, and all their brothers gathered to sell their wares. Here is another symbolic center of London, the church of **St. Mary-le-Bow** ⑫. Walk to the east end of Cheapside, where seven roads meet, and you will be facing the **Bank of England** ⑬. Turn your back on the bank, and there's the Lord Mayor's Palladian-style residence, **Mansion House** ⑭. Wren's **St. Stephen Walbrook** ⑮ rises behind it and the **Royal Exchange** ⑯ stands between Threadneedle Street and Cornhill. Farther down Cornhill to Lime Street is **Lloyd's of London** ⑰.

Now head down Queen Victoria Street, where you'll pass the remains of the Roman **Temple of Mithras** ⑱; then, after a sharp left turn onto Cannon Street, you'll come upon the **Monument** ⑲, Wren's memorial to the Great Fire of London. Just south of there is **London Bridge** ⑳. Turn left onto Lower Thames Street, for just under a mile's walk—passing Billings-gate, London's principal fish market for 900 years (until 1982), and the Custom House, built early in the last century—to the **Tower of London ㉑**, which may be the single most unmissable of London's sights. **Tower Bridge ㉒**, just outside it, isn't bad either.

TIMING    This is a marathon. Unless you want to be walking all day without a chance to do justice to London's most famous sights, the Tower of London and St. Paul's Cathedral—not to mention the Museum of London, Tower Bridge, and the Barbican Centre—you should consider splitting the walk into segments. Conversely, if you're not planning to go inside, this walk makes for a great day out, with lots of surprising vistas, river views, and history. The City is a wasteland on weekends and after dark, so choose your time. There's a certain romantic charm to the streets when they're deserted, but it's hard to find lunch.

HOW TO GET    This is a big and confusing area, with, however, several Tube stops that
THERE    will deposit you within walking distance of most sights. They are the following: on the Central Line, the Bank and St. Paul's stops; on the District and Circle lines, the Monument, Cannon Street, and Mansion House stops (plus Blackfriars, which is a little off-center). The Moorgate and Barbican stops (Circle, Metropolitan, Hammersmith, and City lines) are the nearest to the theaters of the Barbican Centre, and the next stop west, Farringdon, is best for exploring Clerkenwell. Finally, the only sensible way to get to the Tower of London is via the District and Circle lines to the Tower Hill stop. As for buses, Nos. 4, 11, 15, 17, 23, 26, and 76 deposit you centrally, by St. Paul's. For the Barbican Centre, Buses 4, 15, and 76 to Silk Street or Moorgate are best.

## What to See

☾ ⓭ **Bank of England.** Known familiarly for the past couple of centuries as "the Old Lady of Threadneedle Street," after someone's parliamentary quip, the bank, which has been central to the British economy since 1694, manages the national debt and the foreign exchange reserves, issues bank-notes, sets interest rates, looks after England's gold, and regulates the country's banking system. Sir John Soane designed the neoclassic hulk in 1788, wrapping it in windowless walls, which are all that survives of his building. It's ironic that an executive of so sober an institution should have been Kenneth Grahame, author of *The Wind in the Willows*. This and other facets of the bank's history are traced in the Bank of England Museum. ⊠ *Bartholomew La., The City EC4* ☎ *020/ 7601–5545* ⊕ *www.bankofengland.co.uk* 🎫 *Free* ⊙ *Weekdays and Lord Mayor's Show day (2nd Sat. in Nov.) 10–5* Ⓤ *Bank or Monument.*

⓽ **Barbican Centre.** With two theaters; the London Symphony Orchestra and its auditorium; the Guildhall School of Music and Drama; a major art gallery for touring and its own special exhibitions; two cinemas; a convention center; an upscale restaurant, cafés, and literary bookshops; and apartments for a hapless two-thirds of the City's residents (most part-time), the Barbican is an enormous concrete maze Londoners love to hate. The name comes from a defensive fortification of the City, and defensive is what Barbican apologists (including architects Chamberlain,

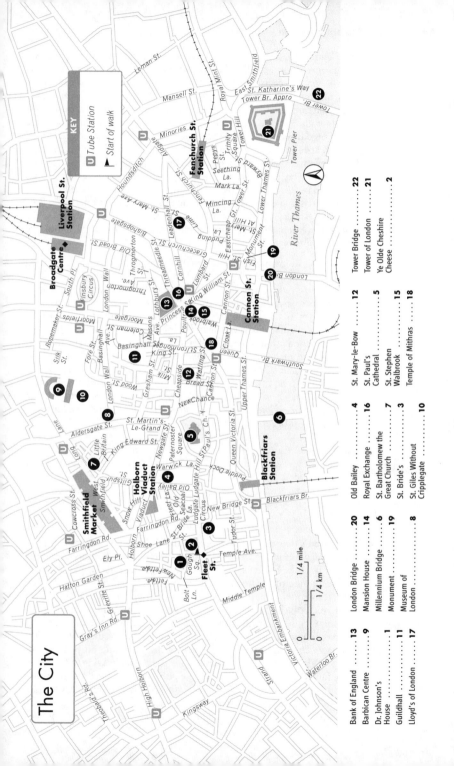

# The City

KEY

U Tube Station

▲ Start of walk

Powell, and Bon) became when the complex was finally revealed in 1982. Navigation around the buildings from the different gates into the Barbican is via the yellow lines, Oz-like, on the floors, plus signs on the walls, although it's still easy to get lost. Londoners accept the place, because of its imaginative contents. Actors rate the theater acoustics especially high, and the steep rake of the seating makes for a good stage view. The dance, music, and theater programs have been transformed into a year-long fest named BITE, which stands for Barbican International Theatre Events, and encompasses dance, puppetry, and music. Contemporary is the buzzword, with the emphasis on presenting tomorrow's artists today, although there are performances by established companies and artists, such as Merce Cunningham. The exhibitions in the **Barbican Art Gallery** showcase modern, popular topics ranging from the Shaker movement to contemporary photography. Also worth a look are the free displays in the Concourse Gallery.

Negotiating the winding walkways of the residential section, spotting stray sculptures and water gardens, then descending to the lower depths of the Centre (where you find the studio auditorium, aptly named the Pit), all has its charm. Secreted on an upper floor is an enormous, lush conservatory in a towering glass palace, and although not open to the public on a regular basis, you may be able to get into a tour. These are conducted for a minimum of 10 people and must be booked in advance. The Museum of London is also part of the complex. ⊠ *Silk St., The City EC2* ☎ *020/7638–8891 box office* ⊕ *www.barbican.org.uk* ✉ *Barbican Centre free, art gallery £3–£5* ⊘ *Barbican Centre Mon.–Sat. 9 AM–11 PM, Sun. noon–11 PM; gallery Mon.–Sat. 10–7:30, Sun. noon–7:30; conservatory weekends noon–5:30 when not in use for private function; call first* Ⓤ *Moorgate or Barbican.*

---

**need a break?**

The Barbican Centre's **Waterside Café** has salads, sandwiches, and pastries; they're unremarkable but are served in a tranquil, enclosed concrete (naturally) terrace with fountains and ponds, and the occasional duck. Sometimes customers are serenaded by practice sessions of the Guildhall School of Music and Drama's orchestra next door.

---

❶ **Dr. Johnson's House.** This is where Samuel Johnson lived between 1746 and 1759, while in the worst of health, compiling his famous dictionary in the attic. Like Dickens, he lived all over town, and as Dickens House is the only one of his houses still extant, this is the only one of Johnson's residences remaining today. It's an appropriately 17th-century house, exactly the kind of place you would expect the Great Bear, as Johnson was nicknamed, to live. It's a shrine to a most literary man who was passionate about London, and it includes a first edition of his *Dictionary of the English Language* among the Johnson and Boswell mementos. When you're done, repair around the corner in Wine Office Court to the famed Ye Olde Cheshire Cheese pub, once Johnson and Boswell's favorite watering hole. ⊠ *17 Gough Sq., The City EC4* ☎ *020/ 7353–3745* ⊕ *www.drjohnsonshouse.org* ✉ *£4* ⊘ *May–Sept., Mon.–Sat. 11–5:30; Oct.–Apr., Mon.–Sat. 11–5* Ⓤ *Blackfriars or Chancery La.*

☛ **Fleet Street.** This famous street follows the course of, and is named after, one of London's ghost rivers. The Fleet, so called by the Anglo-Saxons, spent most of its centuries above ground as an open sewer, offending local nostrils until it was banished below in 1766. It still flows under-foot, now a sanctioned section of London's sewer system. The street's sometime nickname, "Street of Shame," has nothing to do with the stench. It refers to the trade that made it famous: the press. Since the end of the 15th century, when Wynkyn de Worde set up England's first printing press here, and especially after 1702, when the first newspaper, the *Daily Courant,* moved in, followed by (literally) all the rest, "Fleet Street" has been synonymous with newspaper journalism. The papers themselves all moved out during the 1980s, but the British press is still collectively known as "Fleet Street." To find a relic from the old days, check out the black-glass-and-chrome art deco building that was once the hub for the *Daily Express*—the paper has since relocated to south of the river. ⊠ *The City EC4* Ⓤ *Blackfriars or St. Paul's.*

⓫ **Guildhall.** In the symbolic nerve center of the City, the Corporation of London ceremonially elects and installs its Lord Mayor as it has for 800 years. The Guildhall was built in 1411, and though it failed to avoid ei-ther the 1666 or 1940 flames, its core survived. Since then, the exterior has had embellishments added during the '70s. The fabulous hall is a psychedelic patchwork of coats of arms and banners of the City Livery Companies, which inherited the mantle of the medieval trade guilds, to which history owes the invention of the City in the first place. Actually, this honor belongs to two giants, Gog and Magog, the pair of mythical beings who founded ancient Albion and the city of New Troy, upon which London was said to be built, and who glower upon the incoming lord mayor's inaugural November banquet from their west-gallery grandstand in 9-foot-high painted lime-wood form. The Great Hall was also the site of famous trials, including that of Lady Jane Grey in 1553, before her execution at the Tower of London.

To the right of Guildhall Yard is the **Guildhall Art Gallery,** the corpo-ration's collection. It includes portraits from the 16th century (royals and statesmen) and the present, and a fair sprinkling of weighty bat-tlescapes from the 18th century for good measure. London landscapes give a picture of the old City in days gone by, and there are a couple of surprises in the form of pre-Raphaelite beauties. The construction of the art gallery led to the exciting discovery of London's only **Roman am-phitheater,** which had lain underneath Guildhall Yard undisturbed for more than 1,800 years. It was excavated and is preserved in situ, sus-pended between two floors of the building, so that visitors can walk among the remains. More of the relics found during the dig can be seen at the Museum of London, through which guided tours can be booked. Entry to the amphitheater is part of the admission to the art gallery.

The 1970s west wing houses the **Guildhall Library**; it has mainly City-related books and documents, plus a collection belonging to one of the city livery companies, the Worshipful Company of Clockmakers, in the **Clockmakers' Company Museum,** with more than 600 timepieces on show, including a skull-faced watch that belonged to Mary, Queen of

Scots. It's one of the most important horological collections in the country. ⊠ *Gresham St., The City EC2* ☎ *020/7606–3030, 020/7332–1632 gallery, 020/7332–3700 recorded information* ⊕ *www.cityoflondon. gov.uk, www.guildhall-art-gallery.org.uk* ⊠ *Free; gallery and amphitheater £2.50, free Lord Mayor's Show, 2nd Nov., Fri., and after 3:30* PM ⊙ *Mon.–Sat. 9:30–5; clockmakers' museum weekdays 9:30–4:45; gallery Mon.–Sat. 10–5, Sun. noon–4* Ⓤ *St. Paul's, Moorgate, Bank, or Mansion House.*

**⑰ Lloyd's of London.** Richard Rogers' fantastical steel-and-glass medium-rise of six towers around a vast atrium, with his trademark inside-out ventilation shafts, stairwells, and gantries, is one of the city's most exciting structures. The building is best seen at night, when cobalt and lime spotlights make it leap out of the deeply boring gray skyline as though it were Carmen Miranda at a wake. The institution that commissioned this fabulous £163 million fun house has been trading in insurance for two centuries and is famous the world over for several reasons: (1) having started in a coffeehouse; (2) insuring Betty Grable's legs; (3) accepting no corporate responsibility for losses, which are carried by its investors; (4) having its "Names"—the rich people who underwrite Lloyd's losses; (5) seeming unassailable for a very long time . . . ; (6) losing £2.9 billion in 1990; (7) causing, with its losses, the financial ruination, and worse, of many famous names. ⊠ *1 Lime St., The City EC3* Ⓤ *Bank, Monument, Liverpool St., or Aldgate.*

**⑳ London Bridge.** Dating from only 1972, this bridge replaced the 1831 Sir John Rennie number that now graces Lake Havasu City, Arizona, the impulse purchase of someone at the McCulloch Oil Corporation, who (rumor has it) was under the impression that he'd bought the far more picturesque Tower Bridge. The version before that one, the first in stone and the most renowned of all, stood for 600 years after it was built in 1176, the focus of many a gathering thanks to the shops and houses crammed along its length, not to mention the boiled and tar-dipped heads of traitors that decorated its gatehouse after being removed in the Tower of London. Before *that* the Saxons had put up a wooden bridge; it collapsed in 1014 under siege from King Olaf of Norway—there have been finds of axes and swords around the old foundations—which was probably the origin of the refrain "London Bridge is falling down." The earlier Roman version around whose focus London grew was probably very close (near the foot of Pudding Lane) to the 100-foot-wide, three-span cantilever one that you see today. ⊠ *The City EC3, SE1* Ⓤ *London Bridge or Monument.*

**⑭ Mansion House.** The name is entirely appropriate, since this is where the Lord Mayor of the City of London (not to be confused with the Mayor of London, who works from City Hall on the South Bank) lives and entertains in traditonally lavish style. The building was begun in 1739, designed by George Dance the Elder in grand Palladian style. Together with its neighbors, the imposing Royal Exchange, and the Bank of England opposite, it makes up a powerful architectural triumvirate. Behind the colonnaded entrance of Mansion House are some stunning rooms, including the Egyptian Hall, which are only open by written appointment to small groups of visitors. You will catch sight of the Lord Mayor—him or herself—on one of the ceremonial parades that begin at Mansion House, such as opening the sessions of the Old Bailey three times a year; the Lord Mayor's Show on the second Saturday in November when the City celebrates with a parade; and the installation of the incoming lord mayor the day before the show weekend, with a procession to the Guildhall, accompanied by the bells of the City churches. ⊠ *Queen Victoria St., The City EC1* ☎ *020/7606–3030 Guildhall* ⊕ *www.cityoflondon.gov.uk* Ⓤ *Bank, Mansion House.*

★ ❻ **Millennium Bridge.** This is not just another bridge, but the first pedestrian-only bridge to open in central London in more than a century, the last being Tower Bridge in 1894. Designed by Norman Foster and sculptor Anthony Caro, the so-called "blaze of light" is built of aluminum and steel. Thousands lined up to enjoy its opening day. This unique bridge has only one moving part—it pivots upward when it opens for ships passing below. A stabilization problem led to the closing of the bridge, but reparation work opened it in time for the queen's Golden Jubilee celebrations in 2002. The bridge connects the old City—St. Paul's Cathedral area—with the Tate Modern art gallery. On its south side, the bridge marks the middle of the Millennium Mile walkway, which goes past a clutch of popular sights. The views are breathtaking: from the bridge, you can look downriver to the Tower of London, Tower Bridge, and beyond, and up to Somerset House, with the London Eye and Big Ben rising above the river's bend. You'll also have perhaps the best possible view of St. Paul's Cathedral. ⊠ *Peters Hill, to Bankside, The City to the South Bank, EC4, SE1* Ⓤ *Mansion House, Blackfriars, or Southwark.*

🖑 ❿ **Monument.** Commemorating the "dreadful visitation" of the Great Fire of 1666, this is the world's tallest isolated stone column. It is the work of Wren, who was asked to erect it "On or as neere unto the place where the said Fire soe unhappily began as conveniently may be." And so here it is—at 202 feet, exactly as tall as the distance it stands from Farriner's baking house in Pudding Lane, where the fire started. Above the viewing gallery (311 steps up—a better workout than any StairMaster) is a flaming bronze urn with a cage around it to prevent suicidal jumps, which were a trend for a while in the 19th century. ⊠ *Monument St., The City EC3* ☎ *020/7626–2717* ⊕ *www.cityoflondon.gov.uk* 🎫 *£1.50; combination ticket gives £1 discount off entry to Tower Bridge* ⊘ *Daily 10–5:40; hrs subject to change, phone before visiting* Ⓤ *Monument.*

🖑 ❽ **Museum of London.** If there's one place to get the history of London sorted out, it's here—although there's a great deal to sort out: Oliver Cromwell's death mask, Queen Victoria's crinolined gowns, Selfridges's art deco elevators, and the Lord Mayor's coach are just some of the goodies. There are also frequent temporary exhibitions on aspects of London's history. The museum appropriately shelters a section of the 2nd- to 4th-century London wall, which you can view from a window inside, near the Roman monumental arch the museum's archaeologists reconstructed a mere two decades ago. Anyone with an interest in how this city evolved will adore this museum, with its reconstructions and the dioramas—like one of the Great Fire, a 1940s air-raid shelter, a Georgian prison cell, a Roman living room, and a Victorian street complete with fully stocked shops—as well as the Catwalk, which guides you interactively through the ages. The archaeologists and curators at the museum regularly leap from AD to BC, as fresh building work in the city uncovers more treasures. None, though, have been as exciting as the ongoing project of preserving and displaying the Roman amphitheater at the Guildhall, and you can see the rewards here. ⊠ *London Wall, The City EC2* 🕾 *020/7600–0807* ⊕ *www.museumoflondon.org.uk* 🖃 *Free* ⊗ *Mon.–Sat. 10–5:50, Sun. noon–5:50* Ⓤ *Barbican.*

**❹ Old Bailey.** This, the present-day **Central Criminal Court,** is where Newgate Prison stood from the 12th century right until the beginning of the 20th century. Few survived for long in the version pulled down in 1770. Those who didn't starve were hanged, or pressed to death in the Press Yard, or they succumbed to the virulent gaol (the archaic British spelling of "jail") fever—any of which must have been preferable to a life in the stinking, subterranean, lightless Stone Hold or to the robberies, beatings, and general victimization endemic in what the novelist Henry Fielding called the "prototype of hell." The next model lasted only a couple of years before being torn down by raving mobs during the anti-Catholic Gordon Riots of 1780, to be replaced by the Newgate that Dickens described in several novels. Fagin, in *Oliver Twist,* would have been taken from here to the public scaffold that replaced the Tyburn Tree, and stood outside the prison until 1868. The Central Criminal Court replaced Newgate in 1907. The most famous and most interesting feature of the solid Edwardian building is the gilded statue of blind Justice perched on top, scales in her left hand, sword in her right; she was intended to mirror the dome of St Paul's. The day's hearings are posted on the sign outside, but before you venture in, just remember that the proceedings can be ghoulish—Crippen and Christie, England's most notorious wife-murderers, were both tried here. There are also security restrictions, and children under 14 are not allowed in; call the information line first. ⊠ *Newgate St., The City EC4* 🕾 *020/7248–3277 information* ⊕ *www.cityoflondon.gov.uk* ⊗ *Public Gallery weekdays 10:30–1 and 2–4:30; line forms at Newgate St. entrance* Ⓤ *St. Paul's.*

**⓰ Royal Exchange.** Inhabiting the isosceles triangle between Threadneedle Street and Cornhill, this massive templelike building was designed by Sir William Tite. Its pediment has 17 limestone figures (Commerce, plus merchants) supported by eight sizable Corinthian columns—to house the then-thriving futures market. The market has now moved on, leaving the Royal Exchange, which you may no longer enter, as a monument to money. ⊠ *Cornhill and Threadneedle St., The City EC3* Ⓤ *Bank.*

**❼ St. Bartholomew the Great.** Reached via a perfect half-timber gatehouse atop a 13th-century stone archway, this is one of London's oldest churches. Along with its namesake on the other side of the road, St. Bartholomew's Hospital, the Norman church was founded by Rahere, Henry I's court jester. At the Dissolution of the Monasteries, Henry VIII had most of it torn down; the Romanesque choir loft is all that survives from the 12th century. ✉ *Cloth Fair, West Smithfield, The City EC1* ☎ *020/7606–5171* ⊕ *www.greatstbarts.com* ⊗ *Weekdays 8:30–4:30, Sat. 10–3:30, Sun. 11–2 for services only; Crypt closed Sun.* Ⓤ *Barbican.*

**❸ St. Bride's.** From afar, study the extraordinary steeple of this church—its uniquely tiered shape gave rise, legend has it, to the traditional wedding cake. This, the first of Wren's city churches, did not escape wartime bomb damage and was reconsecrated only in 1960 after a 17-year-long restoration. As St. Paul's (in Covent Garden) is the actors' church, so St. Bride's belongs to journalists, many of whom have been buried or memorialized here, as reading the wall plaques will tell you. Even before the press moved in, it was a popular place to take the final rest. By 1664 the crypts were so crowded that diarist Samuel Pepys had to bribe the grave digger to "justle together" some bodies to make room for his deceased brother. Now the crypts house a museum of the church's rich history, and a bit of Roman sidewalk. ✉ *Fleet St., The City EC4* ☎ *020/ 7427–0133* ⊕ *www.stbrides.com* ✆ *Free* ⊗ *Weekdays 8–4:30, Sat. 9–5, Sun. for services only 11–2; crypt closed Sun.* Ⓤ *Chancery La.*

**❿ St. Giles Without Cripplegate.** Standing south of the Barbican complex, this is one of the only City churches to have withstood the Great Fire, only to succumb to the Blitz bombs three centuries later. The tower and a few walls survived; the rest was rebuilt to the 16th-century plan during the 1950s, and now the little church struggles hopelessly for attention among the Barbican towers, whose parishioners it tends. Past parishioners include Oliver Cromwell, married here in 1620, and John Milton, buried here in 1674. St. Giles was the patron saint for cripples, hence Cripplegate. ✉ *Fore St., The City EC2* ☎ *020/7638–1997* ⊕ *www.stgilescripplegate.com* ⊗ *Weekdays 11–4, Sun. 8–5:30 for services only; check on the door* Ⓤ *Barbican or Moorgate.*

**⓬ St. Mary-le-Bow.** Wren's 1673 church has one of the most famous sets of bells around—a Londoner must be born within the sound of Bow Bells to be a true cockney. The origin of that idea was probably the curfew rung on the Bow Bells during the 14th century, even though "cockney" only came to mean Londoner three centuries later, and then it was an insult. The Bow takes its name from the bow-shape arches in the Norman crypt. ✉ *Cheapside, The City EC2* ☎ *020/7248–5139* ⊕ *www. stmarylebow.co.uk* ⊗ *Mon.–Thurs. 6:30–5:45, Fri. 6:30–4* Ⓤ *Mansion House.*

> **need a break?**
>
> The **Place Below** (☎ 020/7329–0789), in St. Mary-le-Bow's crypt, is packed with City workers weekdays at lunchtime—the self-service vegetarian menu includes soup and quiche, which are particularly good. Lunches are served from 10:30 until 2:30, weekdays only. It's also open for breakfast.

**☝ ❺ ★ St. Paul's Cathedral.** The symbolic heart of London, St. Paul's will take your breath away. In fact, its dome—the world's third largest—will already be familiar, since you see it peeping through on the skyline from many an angle, riding high (although now nudged by skyscrapers) over

# St. Paul's Cathedral

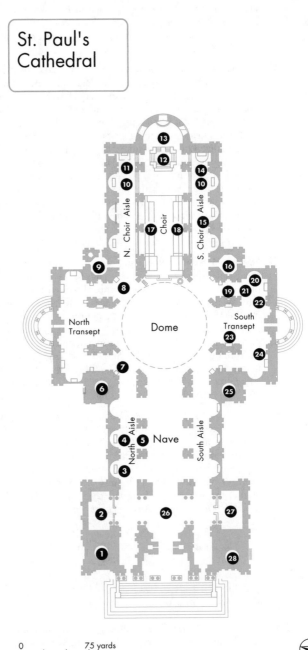

N. Choir Aisle

Choir

S. Choir Aisle

Dome

North
Transept

South
Transept

North Aisle

Nave

South Aisle

0     75 yards

0     75 meters

the rooftops of the City, just as it does in Canaletto's 18th-century views of the Thames. The cathedral is, of course, the masterpiece of Sir Christopher Wren (1632–1723), completed in 1710 after 35 years of building and much argument with the Royal Commission, then, much later, miraculously (mostly) spared by the World War II bombs. Wren had originally been commissioned to restore Old St. Paul's, the Norman cathedral that had replaced, in its turn, three earlier versions, but the Great Fire left so little of it standing that a new cathedral was deemed necessary.

Wren's first plan, known as the "New Model," did not make it past the drawing board; the second, known as the "Great Model," got as far as the 20-foot oak rendering you can see here today before it, too, was rejected, whereupon Wren is said to have burst into tears. The third, however, known as the Warrant Design (because it received the royal warrant), was accepted, with the fortunate coda that the architect be allowed to make changes as he saw fit. Without that, there would be no dome, because the approved design had featured a steeple. Parliament felt that building was proceeding too slowly (in fact, 35 years is lightning speed, as cathedrals go) and withheld half of Wren's pay for the last 13 years of work. He was pushing 80 when Queen Anne finally coughed up the arrears.

When you enter and see the dome from the inside, you may find that it seems smaller than you expected. You aren't imagining things—it *is* smaller, and 60 feet lower than the lead-covered outer dome. Between the inner and outer domes is a brick cone, which supports the familiar 850-ton lantern, surmounted by its golden ball and cross. Nobody can resist making a beeline for the dome, so we'll start beneath it, standing dead center, on the beautiful sunburst floor, Wren's focal mirror of the magnificent design above.

Now climb the 259 spiral steps to the **Whispering Gallery.** This is the part of the cathedral with which you bribe children, who are fascinated by the acoustic phenomenon: whisper something to the wall on one side, and a second later it transmits clearly to the other side, 107 feet away. The only problem is identifying "your" whisper from the cacophony of everyone else's. Look down onto the nave from here, and up to the frescoes of St. Paul by Sir James Thornhill (who nearly fell off while painting them), before ascending farther to the Stone Gallery, which encircles the outside of the dome. Up again (careful—you will have tackled 627 steps altogether), and you reach the Golden Gallery, from which you can view the lantern through a circular opening called the oculus and walk outside the roof.

Back downstairs there are the inevitable monuments and memorials to see, though fewer than one might expect because Wren didn't want his masterpiece cluttered up. The poet John Donne, who had been Dean of St. Paul's for his final 10 years (he died in 1631), lies in the south choir aisle; his is the only monument remaining from Old St. Paul's. There is Wren's own memorial, with an epitaph by his son (who also worked on the building) that reads succinctly: LECTOR, SI MONUMENTUM RE-

QUIRIS, CIRCUMSPICE (READER, IF YOU SEEK HIS MONUMENT, LOOK AROUND YOU). The vivacious choir-stall carvings nearby are the work of Grinling Gibbons, as is the organ, which Wren designed and Handel played. The painters Sir Joshua Reynolds and J. M. W. Turner are commemorated, as is George Washington. The American connection continues behind the high altar in the **American Memorial Chapel,** dedicated in 1958 to the 28,000 GIs stationed here who lost their lives in World War II.

A visit to the **crypt** brings you to Wren's tomb (also with his son's epitaph), the black marble sarcophagus containing Admiral Nelson (who was pickled in alcohol for his final voyage here from Trafalgar), and an equestrian statue of the Duke of Wellington on top of his grandiose tomb. A café and gift shop are also in the crypt. Finally, to catch Wren's facade and dome at its most splendid, remember to make a return trip to see St. Paul's at night. ⊠ *St. Paul's Churchyard, Ludgate Hill, The City EC4* ☎ *020/7236–4128* ⊕ *www.stpauls.co.uk* ⊠ *Cathedral, crypt, ambulatory, and gallery £6* ⊙ *Cathedral Mon.–Sat. 8:30–4, closed occasionally for special services; ambulatory, crypt, and gallery Mon.–Sat. 9–5:15. Shop and Crypt Café also Sun. 10:30–5* Ⓤ *St. Paul's.*

**⑮ St. Stephen Walbrook.** This is the parish church many think is Wren's best, by virtue of its practice dome, which predates the big one at St. Paul's by some 30 years. Two inside sights warrant investigation: Henry Moore's 1987 central stone altar, which sits beneath the dome ("like a lump of Camembert," say critics), and, well, a telephone—an eloquent tribute to that genuine savior of souls, Rector Chad Varah, who founded the Samaritans, givers of phone aid to the suicidal, here in 1953. ⊠ *Walbrook St., The City EC4* ☎ *020/7626–8242* ⊙ *Mon.–Thurs. 10–4, Fri. 10–3* Ⓤ *Bank or Cannon St.*

**⑱ Temple of Mithras.** This minor place of pilgrimage in the Roman City was unearthed on a building site in 1954 and was taken, at first, for an early Christian church. In fact, worshipers here favored Christ's chief rival during the 3rd and 4th centuries: Mithras, the Persian god of light. Mithraists aimed for all the big virtues but still were not appreciated by early Christians, from whom their sculptures and treasures had to be concealed. These devotional objects form the largest display of Roman objects at the Museum of London. While here, you can see the foundations of the temple itself. ⊠ *Temple Court, Queen Victoria St., The City EC4* Ⓤ *Bank.*

☾ **㉒ Tower Bridge.** Despite its venerable, nay, medieval, appearance, this is a
FodorśChoice Victorian youngster. Constructed of steel, then clothed in Portland
★ stone, it was deliberately styled in the Gothic persuasion to complement the Tower next door, and it's famous for its enormous bascules—the "arms," which open to allow large ships through. Nowadays this rarely happens, but when river traffic was dense, the bascules were raised about five times a day.

The exhibition, **Tower Bridge Experience,** is a fun tour inside the building to discover how one of the world's most famous bridges actually works, and to see the fantastic views on the outside. First, take in the romance of the panoramas from the east and west walkways between those grand turrets. On the east, the modern super structures and ships of Docklands, and west, the best look at the steel and glass "futuristic mushroom" that is Greater London Assembly's City Hall, the Tower of London, St. Paul's, and the Monument. Then back down to the nitty gritty of the inner workings, which you learn about through hands-on displays and films. ☎ 020/7403–3761 ⊕ *www.towerbridge.org.uk* ✏ £4:50; joint ticket available for the Monument ⊘ Daily 9:30–5:30; last entry at 5 Ⓤ *Tower Hill.*

★ ⓒ ㉑ **Tower of London.** This has top billing on many tourist itineraries for good reason. Nowhere else does London's history come to life so vividly as in this minicity of 20 melodramatic towers stuffed to bursting with heraldry and treasure, the intimate details of lords and dukes and princes and sovereigns etched in the walls (literally in some places, as you'll see), and quite a few pints of royal blood spilled on the stones. The visitor center, opened in 2004, provides an introduction to the Tower. Systems ensure that lines are minimal, so you can put in place all those grisly torture scenes you saw in the film *Elizabeth*. The prize exhibit, the Crown Jewels, can be seen in glass cabinets on both sides, where moving walkways hasten progress at the busiest times.

The reason the Tower holds the royal gems is that it's still one of the royal palaces, although no monarch since Henry VII has called it home. It has also housed the Royal Mint, the Public Records, the Royal Menagerie (which formed the basis of London Zoo), and the Royal Observatory, although its most renowned and titillating function has been, of course, as a jail and place of torture and execution.

A person was mighty privileged to be beheaded in the peace and seclusion of **Tower Green** instead of before the mob at Tower Hill. In fact, only seven people were ever important enough—among them Anne Boleyn and Catherine Howard, wives two and five, respectively, of Henry VIII's six; Elizabeth I's friend Robert Devereux, the Earl of Essex; and the nine-day queen, Lady Jane Grey, aged 17. Tower Green's other function was as a corpse dumping ground when the chapel just got too full. The executioner's block—with its bathetic forehead-size dent—and his axe, along with the equally famous rack and the more obscure "scavenger's daughter" (which pressed a body nearly to death), plus assorted thumbscrews, "iron maidens," and so forth, have moved to the Royal Armouries in Leeds, Yorkshire. (Fans of this horrifying niche of heavy metal might also want to pay a call on the London Dungeon attraction, just across the Thames.) You should know about the excellent free and fact-packed tours that depart every half hour or so from the Middle Tower. They are conducted by the 39 Yeoman Warders, better known as Beefeaters—ex-servicemen dressed in resplendent navy-and-red (scarlet-and-gold on special occasions) Tudor outfits. Beefeaters have been guarding the tower since Henry VII appointed them in 1485. One of them, the Yeoman Ravenmaster, is responsible for making life comfortable for Hardey, George, Hugine, Mumin, Cedric, Odin, Thor (who talks), and Gwylem—the Tower Ravens. This used to be a delicate duty, because if they were to desert the tower (goes the legend), the kingdom would fall. Today, the tower takes no chances: the ravens' wings are clipped.

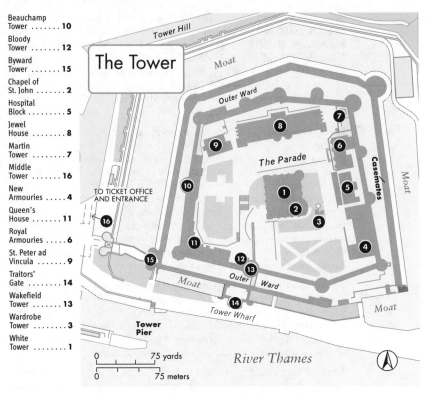

In prime position stands the oldest part of the Tower and the most conspicuous of its buildings, the **White Tower.** This central keep was begun in 1078 by William the Conqueror; by the time it was completed, in 1097, it was the tallest building in London, underlining the might of those victorious Normans. Henry III (1207–72) had it whitewashed, which is where the name comes from, then used it as a barracks and as housing for his menagerie, including the first elephant ever seen in the land.

The spiral staircase—winding clockwise to help the right-handed swordsman defend it—is the only way up, and here you'll find the **Royal Armouries,** Britain's national museum of arms and armor, with about 40,000 pieces on display. One of the tower's original functions was as an arsenal, supplying armor and weapons to the kings and their armies. Henry VIII started the collection in earnest, founding a workshop at Greenwich as a kind of bespoke tailor of armor to the gentry, but the public didn't get to see it until the second half of the 17th century, during Charles II's reign—which makes the Tower Armouries Britain's oldest public museum.

Here you can see weapons and armor from Britain and the Continent, dating from Saxon and Viking times right up to our own. Among the highlights are four suits of armor Henry VIII commissioned to fit his ever-increasing bulk, plus one for his horse. The medieval warhorse was nothing without his *shaffron,* or head protector, and here you'll find a 500-year-old example, one of the oldest pieces of horse armor in the world. Don't miss the tiny armors on the third floor—one belonging to Henry's son (who survived in it to become Edward VI) and another just a bit more than 3 feet tall. The impressive, carved Line of Kings is not to be missed. The **New Armouries** have been renovated into a restaurant.

Most of the interior of the White Tower has been much altered over the centuries, but the **Chapel of St. John the Evangelist**, downstairs from the armories, is a pure example of 11th-century Norman—very rare, very simple, and very beautiful. The other fortifications and buildings surrounding the White Tower date from the 11th to 19th centuries. Starting from the main entrance, you can't miss the **moat**. Until the Duke of Wellington had it drained in 1843, this was a stinking, stagnant mush, obstinately resisting all attempts to flush it with water from the Thames. Now there's a little raven graveyard in the grassed-over channel, with touching memorials to some of the old birds (who are not known for their kind natures, by the way, and you risk a savage pecking if you try to befriend them).

Across the moat, the **Middle Tower** and the **Byward Tower** form the principal landward entrance, with **Traitors' Gate** a little farther on to the right. This is the London equivalent of Venice's Bridge of Sighs, which led to the cells in the Doge's Palace. Unlike the Venetian monument, Traitors' Gate is not architecturally beautiful but was the last walkway of daylight before condemned prisoners were doomed to darkness and death in the dungeons. During the period when the Thames was London's chief thoroughfare, this was the main entrance to the Tower.

Immediately opposite Traitors' Gate is the former Garden Tower, better known since about 1570 as the **Bloody Tower**. Its name comes from one of the most famous unsolved murders in history, the saga of the "little princes in the Tower." In 1483 the uncrowned boy king Edward V and his brother Richard were left here by their uncle, Richard of Gloucester, after the death of their father, Edward IV. They were never seen again, Gloucester was crowned Richard III, and in 1674 two little skeletons were found under the stairs to the White Tower. The obvious conclusions have always been drawn—and were, in fact, even before the skeletons were discovered.

Another famous inmate was Sir Walter Raleigh, who was kept here from 1603 to 1616. It wasn't such an ordeal, as you'll see when you visit his spacious rooms, where he kept two servants, had his wife and two sons live with him (the younger boy was christened in the Tower chapel), and amused himself by writing his *History of the World*. Unfortunately, he was less lucky on his second visit in 1618, which terminated in his execution at Whitehall.

Next to the Bloody Tower is the circular **Wakefield Tower**, which dates from the 13th century and once contained the king's private apartments. It was the scene of another royal murder in 1471, when Henry VI was killed in mid-prayer. Henry founded Eton College and King's

College, Cambridge, and they haven't forgotten: every May 21, envoys from both institutions mark the anniversary of his murder by laying white lilies on the site.

The most dazzling and most famous exhibits in the Tower are, of course, the **Crown Jewels,** housed in the **Jewel House, Waterloo Block.** You get so close to the fabled gems, you feel you could polish them (if it weren't for the wafers of bulletproof glass). Before you meet them in person, you are given a high-definition-film preview, with scenes from Elizabeth's 1953 coronation.

It's commonplace to call these baubles priceless, but it's impossible not to drop your jaw at the notion of their worth. They were, in fact, stolen once—by Col. Thomas Blood, in 1671—though taken only as far as a nearby wharf. The colonel was given a royal pension instead of a beating, fueling speculation that Charles II, short of ready cash as usual, had had his hand in the escapade somewhere. These days security is as fiendish as you'd expect, with the jewels encased behind secure double doors of incredible thickness.

A brief résumé of the top jewels: finest of all is the **Royal Sceptre,** containing the earth's largest cut diamond, the 530-carat Star of Africa. This is also known as Cullinan I, having been cut from the South African Cullinan, which weighed 20 ounces when dug up from a De Beers mine at the beginning of the century. Another chip off the block, Cullinan II, lives on the **Imperial State Crown,** made for Queen Victoria's coronation in 1838, and also worn by Queen Elizabeth II at her coronation, and annually for the State Opening of Parliament. Aside from its 2,800 diamonds, you'll find the Black Prince's ruby, which Henry V was supposed to have worn at Agincourt and which is actually an imposter—it's no ruby but, rather, a semiprecious spinel. The other most famous gem is the Koh-i-noor, or "Mountain of Light," which adorns the late **Queen Mother's crown.** When Victoria was presented with this gift horse in 1850, she looked it in the mouth, found it lacking in glitter, and had it chopped down to almost half its weight.

The **Martin Tower** was known as the Jewel Tower when the Crown Jewels were kept there from 1669 to 1841. These days it has a permanent exhibition entitled "Crowns & Diamonds: the Making of the Crown Jewels." See naked crown frames—the coronation crown of George IV, George I's Imperial State Crown, Victoria's State Crown—surrounded by 12,500 loose diamonds on permanent loan from De Beers. It's a graphic illustration of how the Royals once had to rent the stones that would adorn their headpiece on the big day.

The little chapel of **St. Peter ad Vincula** is the second church on the site, and conceals the remains of some 2,000 people executed at the Tower, Anne Boleyn and Catherine Howard among them. Being traitors, they were not so much buried as dumped under the flagstones, but the genteel Victorians had the courtesy to rebury their bones during renovations.

One of the more evocative towers is **Beauchamp Tower,** built west of Tower Green by Edward I (1272–1307). It was soon designated as a jail for the higher class of miscreant, including Lady Jane Grey, who is thought to have added her Latin graffiti to the many inscriptions here.

Just south of the Beauchamp Tower is an L-shape row of half-timber Tudor houses, with the **Queen's House** at the center. Built for the governor of the Tower in 1530, this place saw the interrogation or incarceration of several celebrated prisoners, including Anne Boleyn and the Gunpowder Plot conspirators. The Queen's House also played host to the Tower's last-ever prisoner, Rudolf Hess, the Nazi who dropped in on Scotland on a propaganda peace initiative and was taken prisoner here.

Allow at least three hours to explore, and arrive early in summer to beat the huge crowds. You can buy your ticket on the Web site, by phone, or at any Tube station. Don't forget to stroll along the battlements before you leave; from them, you get a wonderful overview of the whole Tower of London. For tickets to Ceremony of the Keys (locking of main gates, nightly 9:30–10), write well in advance (to the Queen's House, address below). Give your name, the dates you wish to attend (including alternate dates), and number of people (up to seven) in your party, and enclose a self-addressed, stamped envelope. Yeoman Warder guides leave daily from Middle Tower, subject to weather and availability, at no charge, about every 30 minutes until 3:30 in summer, 2:30 in winter. ⊠ *H. M. Tower of London, Tower Hill, The City, EC3* ☎ *0870/ 756–6060 recorded information and advance ticket booking* ⊕ *www. hrp.org.uk* ✎ *£13.50; joint tickets available with Kensington Palace and Hampton Court Palace* ⊘ *Mar.–Oct., Mon.–Sat. 9–5, Sun. 10–5; Nov.–Feb., Tues.–Sat. 9–4, Sun. and Mon. 10–4; the Tower closes 1 hr after last admission time and all internal buildings close 30 mins after last admission* Ⓤ *Tower Hill.*

❷ **Ye Olde Cheshire Cheese.** This is one of the many places in which that acerbic compiler of the first dictionary, Dr. Johnson, drank (like Dickens, he is claimed by many a pub). This was, in fact, his "local," around the corner from his house. It retains a venerable open-fires-in-tiny-rooms charm when not too packed with tourists. Writers who followed Johnson's footsteps to the bar here were Mark Twain and Charles Dickens. ⊠ *145 Fleet St., The City EC4* ☎ *020/7373–6170* ⊘ *Mon.–Sat. 11–11, Sun. noon–3 and 6–10* Ⓤ *Blackfriars.*

## THE EAST END

Made famous by Dickens and infamous by Jack the Ripper, the East End remains one of London's most hauntingly evocative neighborhoods. There's a good argument for considering it the real London, since East Enders are born "within the sound of Bow Bells" and are therefore cockneys through and through (not to mention models for the characters of England's favorite soap opera, *EastEnders*). The district began as separate villages—Whitechapel and Spitalfields, Shoreditch, Mile End, and Bethnal Green—melding together during the population boom of the 19th century, a boom that was shaped by French Huguenot and Jewish refugees, and by poverty. The East End now houses a large Bengali

# CloseUp

# THE DOCKLANDS RENAISSANCE

BUT FOR THE RIVER, ROMAN LONDINIUM, with its sea link to the rest of the world, would not have grown into a world power. Trade and people came and went on the water from the port, or Pool of London (some of the early American settlers to Virginia set sail from Blackwall, one of the numerous wharves and quaysides along the river). Life was played out by the riverside; palaces redolent of Venice—such as Lambeth, Greenwich, Somerset House, Westminster, and Whitehall—were built. Henry VIII erected dockyards at Woolwich and Deptford to relieve congestion at Billingsgate (fish market). Dock warehouses sprang up during the 18th century from the trade with the Indies for tea and coffee, spices, and silks (some now converted into museums and malls, such as Hay's and Butler's wharves). Along with others, West India and East India Docks were built in the 19th century, extending London's port some miles east, to Millwall and the Isle of Dogs.

Trade took a gradual downturn after World War II, leading to the docks' degeneration when larger vessels pushed trade farther downriver to Tilbury. It took a driverless railway and Britain's tallest building to start a renaissance. Now, what was once a desolate and dirty quarter of the East End is a modern piece of real estate, a peninsula of waterways with cutting-edge architecture, offices, water-based leisure and cultural activities, restaurants, and bars.

The best way to explore is on the Docklands Light Railway, whose elevated track appears to skim over the water past the swanky glass buildings where the railway is reflected in the windows. By foot, however, the Thames Path has helpful plaques along the way, with nuggets of historical information. Canary Wharf, 1 Canada Square (not open to the public),

embodies the bold architecture of the Docklands, but a visit to one of the original dockside warehouses at West India Quay, to the Museum in Docklands (☎ 020/7001–9800), tells the story of days when boats and sailors, rather than blue-chip outfits, were all around here. Everything you could want to know about this fascinating place can be discovered in a series of displays and interactive zones: the water zone, dockwork, building, and early years. Some exhibits are scary—one, for example, reveals the grisly tortures meted out to pirates.

Farther along the river, approached from the south side, and also covering the life cycle of the river in a hands-on exhibition, is the Thames Barrier Visitor Centre (☎ 020/8305–4188, Charlton station). The views of the monster steel flood-restraining shells stretching across the river, with the Millennium Dome in the background, are quite surreal.

If you have time to travel farther downstream to the old Royal Dockyard at Woolwich, you'll find, adjacent to it, a brilliant exhibition of the Royal Artillery, Firepower! (☎ 020/8855–7755, www.firepower.org.uk, Woolwich Arsenal station). Complete with smoke and sound effects, it explores the role of the gunner in film, from the discovery of gunpowder to the Gulf War. Also on show are tanks and guns—some complete with battle scars, and most with individual investigative touch-screen storyboards. Housed in the old regal buildings of the Royal Arsenal leading down to the river shore, there's a powerful sense of the Thames and its lingering effect on the capital's history.

community, and some more recent immigrants from other parts of the world, including China and Africa. You will still find some of the poorest communities in London here, and the gang culture of Eastenders such as the Kray twins in the '60s is still emulated by youths in this area—so beware. Within the shadow of the City walls is London's oldest synagogue, the Bevis Marks, a testament to the huge numbers of Jews who used to live here. Whitechapel is where the Salvation Army was founded and the original Liberty Bell was forged, but, of course, what everyone remembers about it is that its Victorian slum streets were stalked by the most infamous serial killer of all, Jack the Ripper. Many companies offer walking tours of "Jack's London," which certainly evoke a creepy sense of place through the narrow streets, which in that time were often shrouded in thick smog (polluted fog) and only wavering gas lights, if lit at all. Jack the Ripper's identity never has been discovered, although theories abound, which, among others, include a cover-up of a prominent member of the British aristocracy, the artist Walter Sickert, and Francis Twomblety, an American quack doctor. Two centuries earlier, neighboring Spitalfields provided sanctuary for the French Huguenots. They had fled here to escape persecution in Catholic France around 1685, and found work in the nascent silk industry, many of them becoming prosperous master weavers. Today, Spitalfields is one of London's bohemian—but not glamorous—neighborhoods, together with Hoxton, just north of here. There are stylish boutiques and cafés, artists' studios and galleries, thanks to the plentiful old, derelict industrial spaces that were bought up cheaply and have been imaginatively remodeled. All in all, prosperous is not really the word for the East End of today (except the Docklands commercial district, which is of a completely different financial and physical complexion), but what the area lacks in traditional tourist attractions it makes up for in history, burgeoning youth culture, and an urban romantic spirit.

*Numbers in the text correspond to numbers in the margin and on the East End map.*

**a good walk**

The easiest way to reach Whitechapel High Street is via the District Line to Aldgate East Tube stop. Turn right out of the station toward the City. Behind Houndsditch is the **Bevis Marks Spanish and Portuguese Synagogue,** ❶ ☞ London's oldest synagogue, named after the street on which it stands. Back to the Tube where you started, and continuing east on Whitechapel High Street, behind No. 90 once stood George Yard Buildings, where Jack the Ripper's first victim, Martha Turner, was discovered in August 1888. Nowadays you'll come across the **Whitechapel Art Gallery** ❷ instead. Continue east until you reach Fieldgate Street on the right, where you'll find the **Whitechapel Bell Foundry** ❸; then, retracing your steps, turn right onto Osborn Street, which soon becomes **Brick Lane** ❹.

Brick Lane and the narrow streets running off it offer a paradigm of the East End's development. Its population has always been in flux, with some moving in to find refuge here as others were escaping its poverty. Just before the start of Brick Lane you can take a short detour (turn left, then right) to see the birthplace of one who did just that. Flower and Dean streets, past the ugly 1970s housing project on Thrawl Street and once the most disreputable street in London, was where Abe Sapperstein, founder of the Harlem Globetrotters, was born in 1908. On the west end of **Fournier Street** ❺, see Nicholas Hawksmoor's masterpiece, **Christ Church, Spitalfields** ❻, and some fine early Georgian houses; then follow Wilkes Street north of the church, where you'll find more 1720s Huguenot houses, and turn right onto Princelet Street, once important to the Jewish settlers. Where No. 6 stands now, the first of several thriving Yiddish theaters opened in 1886, playing to packed houses until the following year, when a false fire alarm, rung during a January performance, ended with 17 people being crushed to death and so demoralized the theater's actor-founder, Jacob Adler, that he moved his troupe to New York. Adler played a major role in founding that city's great Yiddish theater tradition—which, in turn, had a significant effect on Hollywood. The Spitalfields Centre occupies and is raising funds to restore and open to the public the house at No. 19 Princelet Street, which harbored French Huguenots (the upper windows are wider than usual so the Huguenot silk weavers had light to work) and, later, Polish Jews (behind its elegant Georgian door, Jacob Davidson, a shoe warehouseman, formed the Loyal United Friendly Society and a tiny synagogue). Spitalfields' grand Georgian houses were crammed with lodgings and workshops for the poor and persecuted. As you walk these quiet streets now, where many of the doors and window shutters have fresh, gleaming paint, there's an air of intellectual restoration and concealed charm.

Now you reach Brick Lane again and the **Old Truman Brewery** ❼. Turn left at Hanbury Street, where, in 1888, behind a seedy lodging house at No. 29, Jack the Ripper left his third mutilated victim, "Dark" Annie Chapman. A double murder followed, and then, after a month's lull, came the death on this street of Marie Kelly, the Ripper's last victim and his most revolting murder of all. He had been able to work indoors this time, and Kelly, a young widow, was found strewn all over the room, charred remains of her clothing in the fire grate.

Turn onto Lamb Street and the two northern entrances to **Spitalfields Market** ❽, or turn left on Commercial Street to Folgate Street and **Dennis Severs's House** ❾. Elder Street, just off Folgate, is another gem of original 18th-century houses. On the south and east side of Spitalfields Market are yet more time-warp streets that are worth a wander, such as Gun Street, where artist Mark Gertler (1891–1939) lived at No. 32. If you have kids, they might have fun going to **Spitalfields City Farm** ❿ a few blocks away. Go back west through Folgate Street to reach Shoreditch High Street, where you can catch Bus 149 or 242 north to Kingsland Road, or get there across Bethnal Green Road, left, then right onto Club Row, to **Arnold Circus** ⓫ and then two streets north, to **Columbia Road** ⓬. Cross Hackney Road and slip up Waterson Street—that's about a ½-mi walk. On Kingsland Road, you'll come to the row of early 18th-century almshouses that are the **Geffrye Museum** ⓭. Going farther east along Hackney Road, and then south on Cambridge Heath Road you come almost to Bethnal Green Tube, for the **Bethnal Green Museum of**

**Childhood** ⓮. Alternatively—and we're talking alternative—if you're looking for modern culture, divert west across Shoreditch High Street to Hoxton Square and the **White Cube** ⓯ gallery.

From the Museum of Childhood, you can either catch Bus 253 or walk south about ½ mi down Cambridge Heath Road as far as the Mile End Road. Turning left, you'll pass several historic landmarks. On the north side of the street are the former **Trinity Almshouses** ⓰, with the statue of William Booth on the very spot where the first Salvation Army meetings were held. Behind you, on the northwest corner of Cambridge Heath Road, is the **Blind Beggar** ⓱ pub, with the **Royal London Hospital** ⓲ a few yards to the left and its Archives behind. If you have the time and energy to continue, or if you want to take another option, head toward the Docklands area, using the Docklands Light Railway (DLR). The **Ragged School Museum** ⓳ is off the East End map, but easily walked from Mile End Tube stop skirting south and west by the park; by Docklands Railway Limehouse stop, the museum is north by the canal path. Return to the river to Limehouse and take the Thames Path to Canary Wharf at the West India Docks, for the **Museum in Docklands** ⓴.

TIMING This is a long walk, and not for everyone. The East End isn't picturesque, and the sights are anything but world famous. However, those who get pleasure from discovery and an adventurous route will enjoy these hidden corners. If you visit on a Sunday morning, the East End has a festive air: about half the neighborhood sprouts hundreds of market stalls (especially in and around Middlesex Street, Brick Lane, and Columbia Road). After shopping, you could go on to take brunch among cows and sheep on a farm, then play at being Georgians in a restored, candlelit 18th-century town house. A focus for your jaunt might be the Whitechapel Gallery, Geffrye Museum, or the Bethnal Green Museum of Childhood, any of which will take an hour or two. Aside from visits, the walk alone is a three-hour marathon, (depending on what option you choose), when done at a brisk pace. The suggested bus links might be appealing, since the in-between parts aren't going to win tourism awards.

HOW TO GET THERE The best Tube stop to start from is Whitechapel or Aldgate East on the District–Hammersmith and City lines or Aldgate on the Metropolitan and Circle lines. For Ragged School and Docklands Museums, use the DLR network. Buses 8, 25, 26, and 48 are useful from the west end for the Shoreditch and Spitalfields area. For the Geffrye Museum and Hoxton, get the 67 from Aldgate; 149 and 242 from Bishopsgate; the 243 runs weekdays from Waterloo, weekends from Old Street. The 253 runs from Euston, but goes north before the museum and the Whitechapel Bell Foundry. For Columbia Road market and Museum of Childhood, take the 55 from Old Street Tube. For Docklands take 15 from Aldgate.

## What to See

⓫ **Arnold Circus.** A perfect circle of Arts and Crafts–style houses around a central raised bandstand, this is the core of the Boundary Estate— "model" housing built by Victorian philanthropists for the slum-dwelling locals and completed as the 20th century began. ⊠ *East End E2* Ⓤ *Liverpool St. or Old St.*

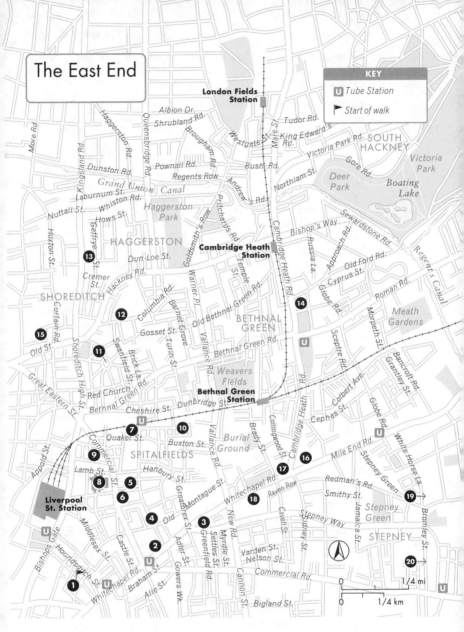

# The East End

**KEY**

U Tube Station

▶ Start of walk

London Fields Station

Albion Dr.
Shrubland Rd.
Pownall Rd.
Regents Row
Haggerston Rd.
Queensbridge Rd.
Brougham Rd.
Westgate St.
Mare St.
Tudor Rd.
King Edward's Rd.
Victoria Park Rd.
SOUTH HACKNEY
Victoria Park
Gore Rd.
Deer Park
Boating Lake

Dunston Rd.
Kingsland Rd.
Laburnum St.
Whiston Rd.
Nuttall St.
Hoxton St.
Geffrye St.
Hows St.
Cremer St.
Hackney Rd.

Grand Union Canal
Haggerston Park
Bush Rd.
Andrew's Rd.
Northiam St.
Pritchards Rd.
Cambridge Heath Rd.
Bishop's Way
Russia La.
Sewardstone Rd.
Approach Rd.
Old Ford Rd.
Cyprus St.
Roman Rd.

HAGGERSTON

Dun-Loe St.

SHOREDITCH

Cambridge Heath Station

Columbia Rd.
Gosset St.
Warner Pl.
Barnet Grove
Turin St.
Old Bethnal Green Rd.
Temple St.
Vallance Rd.
BETHNAL GREEN
Globe Rd.
Sceptre Rd.
Meath Gardens
Morpeth St.
Bancroft Rd.
Grantley Rd.

Curtain Rd.
Old St.
Shoreditch High St.
Swanfield St.
Brick La.
Red Church St.
Bethnal Green Rd.
Cheshire St.
Dunbridge St.

Great Eastern St.
Commercial St.
Quaker St.
Buxton St.
Hanbury St.
Lamb St.
Middlesex St.
Castle St.
Braham St.
Alie St.
Gowers Wk.
Old Montague St.
Greatorex St.
Adler St.
Settles St.
Greenfield Rd.
Myrdle St.
New Rd.
Cannon St.
Varden St.
Nelson St.
Bigland St.

Bethnal Green Station
Weavers Fields
Vallance Rd.
Burial Ground
Brady St.
Collingwood St.
Cambridge Heath Rd.
Cephas St.
Colbert Ave.
Mile End Rd.
Redman's Rd.
Smithy St.
Stepney Green
White Horse La.
Bromley St.
Jamaica St.
STEPNEY
Stepney Way

SPITALFIELDS
Whitechapel Rd.
Raven Row
Cavell St.
Sidney St.

Liverpool St. Station

Bishops Gate
Houndsditch
Whitechapel Rd.
Appold St.

Commercial Rd.

⑬ ⑫ ⑮ ⑪ ⑭
⑦ ⑩ ⑯ ⑰
⑨ ⑧ ⑤ ⑥ ⑱ ⑲
④ ③ ⑳
② ①

0         1/4 mi
0         1/4 km

**Bethnal Green Museum of Childhood.** This is the East End outpost of the Victoria & Albert Museum—in fact, this entire iron, glass, and brown-brick building was transported here from South Kensington in 1875. Since then, believe it or not, its contents have grown into the biggest toy collection in the world. The central hall is a bit like the Geffrye Museum zapped into miniature: here are dollhouses (some royal) of every period. Each genre of plaything has its own enclosure, so if teddy bears are your weakness, you need waste no time with the train sets. The museum's title is justified upstairs, in the fascinating—and possibly unique—galleries on the social history of childhood from baby dolls to Beanie Babies. Free art "carts" of goodies are available Saturday and Sunday for children over the age of 3 with a ticket from the admission desk. There's also a soft-play area for little kids so the "big" ones can gaze longer at the museum's collection, a daily dressing-up area with old-fashioned clothes, and floor-size board games such as Snakes and Ladders—guaranteed to send parents into a world of nostalgia, and children to a tranquil land before techno took its hold. ⊠ *Cambridge Heath Rd., East End E2* ☎ *020/8983–5200, 020/8980–2415 recorded information* ⊕ *www.museumofchildhood.org.uk* 🖂 *Free* ⊙ *Sat.–Thurs. 10–5:50; art workshop weekends 11, noon, 2, and 3* Ⓤ *Bethnal Green.*

**need a break?** If you're in the East End, eat like the locals at **Kelly's,** a pie-and-mash caff, at 414 Bethnal Green Road. There are meat or veggie options, with crisp pastry crust, to eat with mash (mashed potatoes). (For the original old shop, which serves traditional Cockney eel pies, walk farther east toward Roman Road market.) No frills, just food at budget prices with a good local buzz. It's open Monday–Thursday 10–2.30 PM, Friday 10–6.30, and Saturday 10–4. No credit cards.

**Bevis Marks Spanish and Portuguese Synagogue.** Named after the street on which it stands, this is London's oldest and most splendid synagogue. Embellished with rich woodwork for the benches and galleries, marble columns, and many plunging brass chandeliers, it is beautiful simplicity. The wooden ark resembles a Wren-style screen, and contains the sacred scrolls of the five books of Moses. When Cromwell allowed the Jews to return to England in 1655 (they had been expelled in 1290), there was no Jewish community, and certainly no place to worship openly. The site chosen to build a new synagogue in 1701 already had religious connections, as the house which stood here before, Burics Marks, was owned by the Abbot of Bury St. Edmunds; over the years the name re-evolved. ⊠ *Bevis Marks, East End EC1* ☎ *020/7626–1274* ⊙ *Sun.–Fri. 11:30–1* Ⓤ *Aldgate East or Liverpool St.*

**The Blind Beggar.** This is the Victorian den of iniquity where Salvation Army founder William Booth preached his first sermon. Also, on the south side of the street stands a stone inscribed HERE WILLIAM BOOTH COMMENCED THE WORK OF THE SALVATION ARMY, JULY 1865, marking the position of the first Sally Army platform; back by the pub a statue of William Booth stands where the first meetings were held. Booth didn't supply the pub's main claim to fame, though. The Blind Beggar's real notoriety dates only from March 1966, when Ronnie Kray—one of the

Kray twins, the former gangster kings of London's East End underworld—shot dead rival "godfather" George Cornell in the saloon bar. The original Albion Brewery, celebrated home to the first bottled brown ale, was next door. ⊠ *337 Whitechapel Rd., East End E1* Ⓤ *Whitechapel.*

**❹ Brick Lane.** This street has seen the manufacture of bricks (during the 16th century), beer, and bagels, but nowadays it's becoming the hub of artistic bohemia, especially at the Old Truman Brewery with its calendar of diverse cultural activities. Yet it still has some of the best Bengali food in town, along with Indian video shops, colorful saris, and stacks of sticky sweets. On Sunday morning the entire street is packed with stalls in a companion market to the nearby Petticoat Lane. ⊠ *Brick La., East End E1* Ⓤ *Aldgate East or Shoreditch.*

> ( **need a break?** ) The 24-hour **Beigel Bake,** at 159 Brick Lane, has the longest queues in the small hours of the morning, and at Sunday morning market time. The bagels are freshly made in a variety of fillings and flavors. Here's a snack that won't break the bank, but will certainly bust your hunger.

**❻ Christ Church, Spitalfields.** This is the 1729 masterpiece of Wren's associate, Nicholas Hawksmoor. Hawksmoor built only six London churches; this one was commissioned as part of Parliament's 1711 "Fifty New Churches Act." The idea was to score points for the Church of England against such nonconformists as the Protestant Huguenots. (It must have worked; in the churchyard, you can still see some of their gravestones, with epitaphs in French.) As the local silk industry declined, the church fell into disrepair and by 1958 the structure was crumbling and had to be closed. The structure is now completely restored—there's always a fine view of the colonnaded portico and tall spire from Brushfield Street to the west—although the interior work continues and the church is closed for the duration until summer 2004. ⊠ *Commercial St., East End E1* ☎ *020/7247–7202* Ⓤ *Aldgate East.*

**⓬ Columbia Road.** On Sunday this narrow street gets buried under forests of shrubs and blooms of all shapes and sizes during London's main plant and flower market. Prices are ultralow, and lots of the Victorian shop windows around the stalls are filled with horticultural wares, accessories, and antiques. ☉ *Sun. 7–2* Ⓤ *Old St., then Bus 55.*

**★ ❾ Dennis Severs's House.** Enter this extraordinary time machine of a house with your imagination primed to take part in the plot. The Georgian terraced house belonged to the eponymous performer-designer-scholar from Escondido, California, who dedicated his life not only to restoring his house but also to raising the ghosts of a fictitious Jervis family who might have inhabited it over the course of two centuries. Dennis Severs created a replica of Georgian life, without electricity but with a butler in full 18th-century livery to light the candles and lay the fires—for the Jervises. The rooms are shadowy set pieces of rose-laden Victorian wallpapers, Jacobean paneling, Georgian wing chairs, baroque carved ornaments, "Protestant" colors (upstairs), and "Catholic" shades (downstairs). The "Silent Night" candlelit evenings, each Monday, are the most theatrical and memorable way to "feel" the house. Private visits by special arrangement are possible. ⊠ *18 Folgate St., East End E1* ☎ *020/7247–4013* ⊕ *www.dennissevershouse.co.uk* ✉ *£8 for Sun., £5 for Mon. open house; £12 for candlelit Mon. evenings* ⊘ *1st and 3rd Sun. of month 2–5, 1st and 3rd Mon. noon–2. Call for hrs for "Silent Night" Mon., reservations essential* Ⓤ *Liverpool St.*

**❺ Fournier Street.** This contains fine examples of the neighborhood's characteristic Georgian terraced houses, many of them built by the richest of the early-18th-century Huguenot silk weavers (see the enlarged windows on the upper floors). Most of those along the north side of Fournier Street have now been restored by conservationists; others still contain textile sweatshops—only now the workers are Bengali. On the Brick Lane corner is the **Jamme mosque.** The inscription above the entrance reads in Latin: UMBRA SUMMUS (WE ARE SHADOWS), which aptly describes the building's previous incarnations as a Huguenot church, Methodist chapel, and synagogue. ⊠ *East End E1* Ⓤ *Liverpool St.*

**★ ⓭ Geffrye Museum.** An antidote to the grand, high-society town house interiors of the rich royal boroughs in the center of town, here's where you can discover what life was like for the general masses. It's a small museum where you can walk through a series of room sets that re-create everyday domestic interiors from the Elizabethan period through postwar '50s utility. Originally, the museum was a row of almshouses for the poor, built in 1716 by Sir Robert Geffrye, former Lord Mayor of London, which provided shelter for 50 pensioners over the course of 200 years. The houses were rescued from closure by keen petitioners (and the inhabitants were relocated to a healthier part of town), and were transformed into the Geffrye Museum in 1914. The former almshouses were restored to their original condition, with most of the internal woodwork intact, including the staircase, upper floors, closets, and paneling. There are also displays on the almshouses' history and on the kinds of people who lived there. For the present, visits are restricted to prebooked tours on weekdays, and one Saturday a month without booking. Call ahead for details. To discover more, you can attend a regular "bring a room to life" talk. ⊠ *Kingsland Rd., East End E2* ☎ *020/7739–9893* ⊕ *www.geffrye-museum.org.uk* ✉ *Free* ⊘ *Tues.–Sat. 10–5* Ⓤ *Old St., then Bus 243; Liverpool St., then Bus 149 or 242.*

**★ ⓒ ⓴ Museum in Docklands.** On a quaint cobbled quayside, beside the tower of Canary Wharf, this warehouse building alone is museum quality, quite apart from its interesting contents. With uneven wood floors, beams, and pillars, the museum used to be a storehouse for coffee, tea, sugar, or rum from the West Indies—hence the name Docklands. The fascinating story of the old port and the river is told using films, together with interactive displays and reconstructions. Roaming visitor assistants are also on hand to help with further explanation and interesting anecdotes. You can follow the Docklands story through the ages right up to the Docklands at War exhibition detailing the devastation of the Blitz, and the very latest developments with the arrival of newspaper headquarters (the *Times*) and financial institutions. To get a feel of how much the area is on the move—skyward as well as along the waterfront—journey here on the Docklands Light Railway, or by boat (pick up a leaflet of timetables and quays from Tube stations). ⊠ *No. 1 Warehouse, West India Quay, Hertsmere Rd., East End E14* ☎ *0870/444–3855* ⊕ *www. museumindocklands.org.uk* ⊠ *£5; tickets valid for 1 yr* ☉ *Daily 10–6* Ⓤ *Canary Wharf or West India Quay DLR.*

❼ **Old Truman Brewery.** This is the only one of the former East End breweries still standing. It's a handsome example of Georgian and 19th-century industrial architecture, and in 1873 was the largest brewery in the world. The buildings, which straddle Brick Lane, are a conglomeration of art, craft, and photo studios, which are rapidly becoming the heart of cool London. The Atlantis Gallery, host of the sell-out Body Worlds exhibition in 2002, is a major focus—visitors were crammed inside to watch a live autopsy as part of the exhibition. Less controversial events include fashion showcases for young, upcoming designers, and the OTB is becoming a hot choice for London Fashion Week fringe events. The center of cool is at the Vibe Bar, where rock celebs and hip plebs chill out behind a traditional Georgian facade. ⊠ *91 Brick La., East End E1* ⊕ *www.trumanbrewery.com* Ⓤ *Aldgate East or Shoreditch.*

🐣 ⓵⓽ **Ragged School Museum.** In its time, this was the largest school in London and a place where impoverished children could escape their deprived homes to get free education and a good meal. The museum re-creates the children's experiences with a time-capsule classroom, dating from the 1880s. Even after their short school career, the students were helped to find their first jobs and a way out of their poverty. At home, they were probably living in one room with the rest of their usually large family, eking out a sad life with little future prospect of improvement. The school was their passport to a better life.

It's an eye-opener for adults, and a fun time-travel experience for kids who get the chance to work with such materials as scratchy slates and chalks—just like Victorian kids did more than 100 years ago—in one of the many organized workshops. There are guided tours, an exhibit on the history of the area, a bookshop, and a café overlooking the Regent's Canal—which connects with Limehouse Basin by the river Thames—where you can take stock of the facilities young students have at their disposal today. ⊠ *46–50 Copperfield Rd., East End EC3* ☎ *020/ 8980–6405* ⊕ *www.raggedschoolmuseum.org.uk* ⊠ *Free* ☉ *Wed.–Thurs. 10–5, 1st Sun. of month 2–5* Ⓤ *Mile End or Limehouse DLR.*

⓵⓼ **Royal London Hospital.** Founded in 1740, the Royal London was once as nasty as its then-neighborhood near the Tower of London. Waste was carried out in buckets and dumped in the street; bedbugs and alcoholic nurses were problems; but according to hospital records patients didn't die—they were "relieved." In 1757, the hospital moved to its present site, the building of which is the core of the one you see today. By then it had become one of the best hospitals in London, and it was enhanced further by the addition of a small medical school in 1785, and again, 70 years later, an entire state-of-the-art medical col-

# HIP IN HOXTON

THE SEAL OF BOHO APPROVAL came when Damien Hirst's agent and the most important modern art dealer in town, Jay Jopling, set up the White Cube gallery at 48 Hoxton Square. Impoverished artists, however, are not newcomers to the area—in the 1960s, Bridget Riley set up an outfit here to find affordable studio space for British artists—but the latest wave has changed the face of Hoxton. From the Barbican in the City to Whitechapel in the East End, as many as 30 art galleries have opened, showing the latest works of the YBAs (Young British Artists). Boutiques, bars, clubs, and restaurants have followed in their wake and the neighborhood is unapologetically hip and brimming with energy.

**The Bluu Bar** (1 Hoxton Square, N1, ☎ 020–7613/5566) has been established for years; music celeb Jarvis Cocker has been known to tuck into noodles at the **Viet Hoa** (70–72 Kingsland Road, E2, ☎ 020–729–8293); and **The Real Greek** restaurant (15 Hoxton Market, N1, ☎ 020–7739–8212) is one of the rare authentic Greek places in town. **Lux** (2–4 Hoxton Sq. N1, ☎ 020 7684–0201), an arthouse movie theater, specializes in foreign films. New, affluent Hoxton residents prefer trendy loft conversions, a far cry from the cheap spaces Ms. Riley first sought for her colleagues. And here's the lowdown: although real estate agents and the fashion pack may call the quarter their own, there are still the less-than-glam apartment blocks that stood here decades before, and whose inhabitants won't be buying the latest art. The old East End is evident on Brick Lane, by Shoreditch Tube station, with its many curry houses and lively weekend market.

lege. Thomas John Barnado, who went on to found the famous Dr. Barnado's Homes for Orphans, came to train here in 1866. Ten years later, the hospital grew to become the largest in the United Kingdom, and now, though mostly rebuilt since World War II, it remains one of London's most capacious. To get an idea of the huge medical leaps forward, walk through the main entrance and garden to the crypt of St. Augustine with St. Philip's Church (alternatively, go direct two blocks south to the entrance on Newark Street), to the **Royal London Hospital Archives** (🕐 Weekdays 10–4:30), where displays of medical paraphernalia, objects, and documentation illustrate the 250-year history of this East London institution. ✉ *Whitechapel Rd., East End E1* ☎ 020/7377–7608 ⊕ *www.rlhleagueofnurses.org.uk* 💰 *Free* 🕐 *Hospital and garden daily 9–6* Ⓤ *Whitechapel.*

🕐 ❿ **Spitalfields City Farm.** This little farm, squashed into an urban landscape, raises a selection of farm animals, including some rare breeds, to help educate city kids in country matters. A tiny farm shop sells freshly laid eggs and organic seasonal produce. ✉ *Weaver St., off Pedley St., East End E1* ☎020/7247–8762 💰*Free* 🕐*Tues.–Sun. 10:30–5* Ⓤ*Aldgate East, Shoreditch, or Liverpool St.*

**8** **Spitalfields Market.** There's been a market here since the mid-17th century, but the current version is overflowing with crafts and design shops and stalls, a sports hall, restaurants and bars (with a pan-world palette, from tapas to Thai), and different-purpose markets every day of the week. The nearer the weekend, the busier it all gets, culminating in the Sunday arts-and-crafts and green market—the best day to go. There's also a burgeoning events program with arts and concerts. ☒ *65 Brushfield St., East End E1* ☎ *020/7247–8556* ⊕ *www.oldspitalfieldsmarket.com* ☜ *Free* ⊙ *Daily 10–7; market stalls weekdays 10–3, Sun. 9:30–5* Ⓤ *Liverpool St.*

**need a break?** In the heart of the market at Spitalfields, you can pick up takeout, from Eastern dishes to Western, but if you want to sit and enjoy the scene with friendly waiters scurrying about on a busy Sunday market day, then **Meson los Barriles** (☒ 8A Lamb St., E1) is the place to munch on tapas and sip Spanish beer. It's also great for kids, as there are a variety of dishes to suit every appetite. Reservations are not taken, so get here early to avoid a long wait.

**off the beaten path** **SUTTON HOUSE** – Homerton (part of Hackney, east of London) hasn't much to recommend it, but Sutton House has survived the inroads of modern block estates. When it was built in 1535, it was surrounded by fields and a country village. Now run by the National Trust, the mansion was first owned by Ralph Sadleir, an important courtier to Henry VIII. The Tudor linen-fold paneling in the parlor is some of the finest in London and can only be seen elsewhere in Hampton Court; the carved stone fireplaces are also original. The painted stairwell with its wall friezes has been carefully preserved. The kitchen, which has fascinating cooking implements of the time, leads onto a cobbled Italianate courtyard—you could be a thousand miles from deepest Hackney. There's a café, a gift shop, and exhibitions—including a computer on which you can read a copy of a local Victorian child's diary. It's a special place that transports you light-years away from the thronging traffic and ugly apartment blocks just outside. ☒ *2 Homerton High St., East End E9* ☎ *020/ 8986–2264* ⊕ *www.nationaltrust.org.uk* ☜ *£2.20* ⊙ *House: Fri. and Sat. 1–5:30; Sun. 11:30–5:30; last admission 5. Café and shop: Wed., Sun. 11:30–5* Ⓤ *Highbury and Islington, then Bus 377 or 30, or overground Silverlink train line to Hackney Central; Bethnal Green, then Bus 253.*

**16** **Trinity Almshouses.** This square row of cottages with a chapel, around a grass lawn called Trinity Green, was built (possibly with Wren's help) in 1695 for "28 decayed Masters and Commanders of Ships or ye widows of such," bombed during World War II, and restored by the London County Council. Along the noisy, scruffy Mile End Road, this place looks like a timeless oasis of calm. Between the almshouses and the Stepney Green Tube station is the well-concealed, oldest Jewish cemetery in Britain (known as the Velho, which means old) founded by the Sephardic community in 1657 after Cromwell allowed Jews to resettle in the country. If you would like to view the cemetery, call the **Bevis Marks Spanish and Portuguese Synagogue** for an appointment. ☎ *020/7289–2573.* ✉ *Mile End Rd., East End E1* Ⓤ *Whitechapel or Stepney Green.*

⑮ **White Cube.** The neighborhood of Hoxton has become a full-fledged bohemia, with hipsters and artists flocking to its bars, cafés, and residential lofts. This new popularity is due in part to the White Cube art gallery, a magnet for artists and culture-seekers. The original White Cube had cramped quarters in genteel St. James's—it was lured away by the massive open spaces of the East End's former industrial units. Damien Hirst, Tracey Emin, Gilbert and George, Sam Taylor-Wood, and other trailblazers have shown here, and gone on to become internationally renowned. The building looks, appropriately enough, like a white cube—it has a glassed-in upper level called "Inside the White Cube," where international guest curators are invited to show their projects. ✉ *48 Hoxton Sq., Hoxton N1* ☎ *020/7930–5373* ⊕ *www.whitecube. com.* ▣ *Free* ◷ *Tues.–Sat. 10–6* Ⓤ *Old St.*

> **need a break?** You can rub shoulders with the hip residents of Hoxton at **The Furnace** (✉ Rufus St., N1 ☎ 020/7613–0598). It's also a hot spot for pizzas.

❷ **Whitechapel Art Gallery.** Housed in a spacious 1901 art nouveau building, this has an international reputation for its shows, which are often on the cutting edge of contemporary art. The American painter Jackson Pollock exhibited here in the 1950s, as did pop artist Robert Rauschenberg in the '60s, and David Hockney had his first solo show here in the '70s. Other exhibitions highlight the local community and culture, and there are programs of lectures, too. The Whitechapel Café serves remarkably inexpensive, home-cooked, whole-food hot meals, soups, and cakes. ✉ *Whitechapel High St., East End E1* ☎ *020/ 7522–7888* ⊕*www.whitechapel.org.* ▣*£6, free Tues.* ◷ *Tues.–Fri. 11–5, Thurs. 11–9, weekends 11–6* Ⓤ *Aldgate East.*

❸ **Whitechapel Bell Foundry.** It may be off the beaten track, but this working foundry was responsible for some of the world's better-known chimes. Before moving to this site in 1738, the foundry cast Westminster Abbey's bells (in the 1580s), but its biggest work, in every sense, was the 13-ton Big Ben, cast in 1858 by George Mears and requiring 16 horses to transport it from here to Westminster. The foundry's other important work was casting the original Liberty Bell (now in Philadelphia) in 1752, and both it and Big Ben can be seen in pictures, along with exhibits about bell making, in a little museum in the shop. Note: the actual foundry is off-limits, for health and safety reasons, but in the small front shop you can buy bell paraphernalia and browse through the historic photos. There are guided tours of the foundry on Saturday morning only, but bookings are usually made months in advance for larger groups. If you're going alone or with another person, you might be able to join a group (call for information and fees). ✉ *34 Whitechapel Rd., East End E1* ☎ *020/7247–2599* ⊕ *www.whitechapelbellfoundry.co.uk* ▣ *Free* ◷ *Weekdays 9–5* Ⓤ *Aldgate East.*

off the
beaten
path

**WILLIAM MORRIS GALLERY** – An 18th-century house in northeast London where the artistic polymath William Morris (1834–96)—craftsman, painter, and writer—lived for eight years, this gallery contains many examples of his work and that of his fellow artisans in the Arts and Crafts movement. The shop sells Morris prints on stationery and other artsy gifts. ⊠ *Water House, Lloyd Park, Forest Rd., Walthamstow E17* ☎ *020/8527–3782* ⊕ *www.lbwf.gov.uk/ wmg* ⊘ *Tues.–Sat. and 1st Sun. of month 10–1 and 2–5* Ⓤ *Blackhorse Road, then Bus 123 to Lloyd Park stops outside the gallery.*

# THE SOUTH BANK

That old, snide North London quip about needing a passport to cross the Thames is no longer heard, as a host of attractions is drawing even the most ardent northerners across the great divide. Previously, the South Bank Centre was the biggest cultural draw, but the undoubted largest attraction, in every sense is the London Eye (known officially as the British Airways London Eye), the world's largest observation wheel. Hanging over the Thames, it gives a 25-minute ride with views over the rooftops of the capital. With steel tubes and glass, the Hungerford Bridge has been rebuilt as a futuristic covered walkway for pedestrians to get across the river from Charing Cross. The Millennium Bridge, running from St. Paul's to Tate Modern, no longer wobbles. Tate Modern's forbidding exterior is a foil for the inspiration and creativity within, and you can take the Tate shuttle boat between the two Tate museums along the river. Developers and local authorities have expanded the South Bank's potential farther east with an explosion of attractions that have turned this once-neglected district into a vibrant neighborhood. The 1980s brought renovations and innovations such as Gabriel's Wharf, London Bridge City, Hay's Galleria, and Butler's Wharf; the '90s arrived, and so did such headline-making sights as the spectacular reconstruction of Shakespeare's Globe—the most famous theater in the world—the OXO Tower, and the London Aquarium at County Hall. The South Bank has since become a dazzling perch for culture vultures.

It's fitting that so much of London's artistic life should once again be centered here on the South Bank—back in the days of Ye Olde London Towne, **Southwark** was the city's oldest "suburb": though just across London Bridge, it was conveniently outside the City walls and laws and therefore the ideal location for the theaters, taverns, and cock-fighting arenas that served as after-hours entertainment in the Middle Ages. The Globe Theatre, in which Shakespeare acted and held shares, was one of several established here after theaters were banished from the City in 1574 for encouraging truancy in young apprentices and for being generally rowdy. In truth, the Globe was as likely to stage a few bouts of bearbaiting as the latest interpretations of Shakespeare. Today, at the reconstructed "Wooden O," of course, you can just see the latter.

*Numbers in the text correspond to numbers in the margin and on the South Bank map.*

a good
walk

Start in chronological order at **Lambeth Palace** ❶ ⌐, which stands by Lambeth Bridge, with the **Museum of Garden History** ❷ in St. Mary's church next door. A little farther east along Lambeth Road you reach the **Imperial War Museum** ❸. Track back to the river along Westminster Bridge Road, or walk along the embankment between Lambeth and Westminster Bridges, taking in the best view of the Houses of Parliament. Just before Westminster Bridge you can visit the **Florence Nightingale Museum** ❹ with its entrance on Lambeth Palace Road, behind the embankment. Walk down the steps from Westminster Bridge to get back on the embankment, and stroll along to the former County Hall, which houses the **London Aquarium** ❺, the surrealist museum **Dalí Universe** ❻, and the latest occupant, the **Saatchi Gallery** ❼. Looming over this is the magnificent **British Airways London Eye** ❽. As you carry on along the curve of the river, you'll pass the restored **Hungerford Bridge** ❾ running parallel to the Charing Cross rail line. It deposits you at the South Bank Centre, with the **Royal Festival Hall** ❿ concert hall, the **Hayward Gallery** ⓫, the National Film Theatre, and the **Royal National Theatre** ⓬. You can find many distractions as you cover this part of the walk, especially in summer—secondhand-book stalls, entertainers, and a series of plaques annotating the buildings opposite. A little farther along you'll find yourself on Upper Ground, where you might want to spend some time in the Coin Street Community neighborhood. Here is the famous **OXO Tower** ⓭ and Gabriel's Wharf, a marketplace of shops and cafés. Now you reach your fifth bridge on this walk, Blackfriars Bridge, which you pass beneath to reach **Tate Modern** ⓮ and **Bankside Gallery** ⓯. Stretching from the Tate back across the river to the St. Paul's Cathedral steps in the City is the pedestrian Millennium Bridge. At the next little alley, New Globe Walk, you can see the reconstructed Jacobean **Shakespeare's Globe Theatre** ⓰. Just below on the right is the 17th-century Cardinal's Wharf, where, as a plaque explains, Wren lived while St. Paul's Cathedral was being built. Back to the well-signposted Thames Path downriver is **Vinopolis** ⓱, the world's first leisure complex celebrating wine. This stands at the entrance to a dark little cobbled alley, an appropriate route to the dismal **Clink** ⓲ jail. Continue to the end of Clink Street past the ruins of Winchester House, the palace of the Bishops of Winchester until 1626. You can see the west wall, with a rose-window outline. Continuing on, you can take a tour of the little *Golden Hinde* ⓳ in the dry St. Mary Overie Dock. On your right is the organic Borough Market, held every Saturday, just before you reach **Southwark Cathedral** ⓴. Turn right onto Joiner Street underneath the arches of London's first (1836) railway, then left onto St. Thomas Street, where you'll find the **Old Operating Theatre Museum** ㉑. Follow Tooley Street, with the **London Dungeon** ㉒ on your right, and toward the river, **Hay's Galleria** ㉓. Take either the left turn at Morgan's Lane to **HMS Belfast** ㉔ or continue to the south end of Tower Bridge, finding the steps on the east (left) side, which descend to the start of a pedestrians-only street, Shad Thames. Just before the bridge, you can't have failed to notice the massive glass, mushroomlike building–City Hall–which houses the London Assembly. It's the latest innovatory design by Sir Norman Foster. Now turn your back on the bridge and follow this quaint path between cliffs of the good-as-new warehouses, which are now **Butler's**

**Wharf**  but were once the seedy, dingy, dangerous shadow lands where Dickens killed off Bill Sikes in *Oliver Twist*. See the foodies' center, the Gastrodrome, and the **Design Museum** ㉖, taking in a long lasting view of the Thames and Tower Bridge.

TIMING    On a fine day, this 2- to 3-mi walk makes a very scenic wander, since you're following the south bank of the great Thames nearly all the way. Fabulous views across to the north bank take you past St. Paul's and the Houses of Parliament, and you pass—under, over, or around—no fewer than nine bridges, from the Tower to Lambeth. It's bound to take far longer than a couple of hours because there's so much to see. The Tate Modern, the Imperial War Museum, Shakespeare's Globe, the Hayward Gallery, the Design Museum, and the London Aquarium could each take a good deal more than an hour (depending on your interests), although the London Dungeon doesn't take long unless you have kids in tow—which is why you'd go in at all. The other places on this route—the Clink, Rose Theatre, Dalí Universe, Garden History, Old Operating Theatre, Florence Nightingale, the South Bank Centre foyers, and the Bankside Gallery—are compact enough to squeeze together, or you can pick out whichever you prefer. You can finish this walk with a flourish by going to one of three theaters—the Lyttelton, the Cottesloe, or the Olivier—at the National Theatre complex, to the National Film Theatre, or to Shakespeare's Globe, but remember that the theaters stay dark on Sunday. Dinner or a riverside drink at the OXO Tower Brasserie, the Gastrodrome restaurants, or the People's Palace is another idea for a big finish.

HOW TO GET THERE    The Tube stop to use is Westminster station on the Jubilee or Northern line, from where you can walk across Westminster Bridge to the start of the walk; another, slightly easier alternative is to get off at Vauxhall station on the Victoria line and walk right, along the river, to Lambeth Bridge. At the end of the walk you'll end up at Tower Bridge with Tower Hill underground on the District Line, or Tower Gateway on the DLR (Docklands Light Railway). Alternatively you could retrace your steps to London Bridge on the Northern and Jubilee Lines. Buses that take you across Westminster Bridge toward the Imperial War Museum include 12, 159 from Oxford Circus; 77 from Aldwych to Lambeth Palace. For buses behind the South Bank Centre: 1 from Aldwych and Waterloo to the Imperial War Museum, 68 from Euston and Holborn, 76 from St. Paul's and Moorgate, 168 from Euston and Holborn, 171 from Holborn, 176 from Oxford Circus, and 188 from Russell Square. For farther downstream, near Shakespeare's Globe, get the 381 from Waterloo to Tooley Street, or get the Tube to Blackfriars and walk across that bridge (offering a particularly scenic walk) to the latest addition to the Jubilee Line, Southwark station, or to Mansion House and walk across Southwark Bridge. The latter is the best way to the OXO Tower. For a beautiful view, commuter river services are a more leisurely way to go: the route runs from Savoy Pier to Greenland, and for the South Bank hop off at Bankside or London Bridge City.

## What to See

**⓯ Bankside Gallery.** Two artistic societies—the Royal Society of Painter-Printmakers and the Royal Watercolour Society—have their headquar-

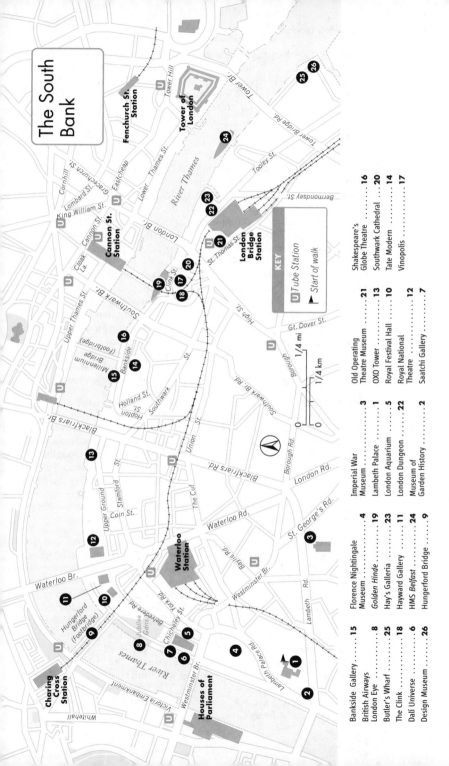

# The South Bank

**KEY**

🇺 *Tube Station*

▲ *Start of walk*

| | | | |
|---|---|---|---|
| Bankside Gallery ...... **15** | Florence Nightingale Museum ...... **4** | Imperial War Museum ...... **3** | Old Operating Theatre Museum ...... **21** | Shakespeare's Globe Theatre ...... **16** |
| British Airways London Eye ...... **8** | *Golden Hinde* ...... **19** | Lambeth Palace ...... **1** | OXO Tower ...... **13** | Southwark Cathedral ... **20** |
| Butler's Wharf ...... **25** | Hay's Galleria ...... **23** | London Aquarium ...... **5** | Royal Festival Hall ...... **10** | Tate Modern ...... **14** |
| The Clink ...... **18** | Hayward Gallery ...... **11** | London Dungeon ...... **24** | Royal National Theatre ...... **12** | Vinopolis ...... **17** |
| Dalí Universe ...... **6** | *HMS Belfast* ...... **24** | Museum of Garden History ...... **2** | Saatchi Gallery ...... **7** | |
| Design Museum ...... **26** | Hungerford Bridge ...... **9** | | | |

ters here. Together they mount exhibitions of current members' work, usually for sale, alongside artists' materials and books—a great place for finding that exclusive, not too expensive gift. There are also themed exhibitions, such as the Winter Festival. For the Society's 200th anniversary, entry is free for 2004; please call for details for 2005. ⌂ *48 Hopton St., South Bank SE1* ☎ *020/7928–7521* ⊕ *www.banksidegallery. com* ⊠ *Free* ☉ *Tues. 10–8, Wed.–Fri. 10–5, weekends 11–5* Ⓤ *Blackfriars or Southwark.*

☾ ❽ **British Airways London Eye.** If you long to see London from a different perspective, look no further. To mark the start of the new millennium, architects David Marks and Julia Barfield conceived an entirely new vision: a beautiful and celebratory structure, which would allow people to see this great city from a completely new perspective—on a giant wheel. As well as representing the turning of the century, a wheel was seen as a symbol of regeneration and the passing of time. The London Eye is the largest observation wheel ever built, and in the top 10 tallest structures in London. From design to construction it took seven years to complete. The 25-minute slow-motion ride is so smooth, you'd hardly know you were suspended over the Thames, moving slowly round. On a clear day you can take in a range of up to 25 mi, viewing London's most famous landmarks from a fascinating angle. If you're looking for a special place to celebrate, champagne and canapés can be arranged ahead; check the Web site for details. ⌂ *Jubilee Gardens, South Bank SE1* ☎ *0870/500– 0600* ⊕ *www.ba-londoneye.com* ⊠ *£11.50* ☉ *Mon.–Thurs. 9:30–8; Fri.–Sun. 9:30–9; hrs subject to change, so call ahead* Ⓤ *Waterloo.*

㉕ **Butler's Wharf.** An '80s development that is maturing gracefully, this wharf is full of deluxe loft-style warehouse conversions and swanky buildings housing restaurants and galleries. People flock here thanks partly to London's saint of the stomach, Sir Terence Conran (also responsible for high-profile central London restaurants Bibendum, Mezzo, and Quaglino's). He has given it his "Gastrodrome" of four restaurants (including the fabulous Pont de la Tour), a vintner's, a deli, and a bakery. Try the Chop House bar for a great view of Tower Bridge and budget-price favorite British dishes, from beef to salmon. ⌂ *South Bank SE1* Ⓤ *London Bridge or Tower Hill, then walk across river.*

⓲ **The Clink.** Giving rise to the term "clink," which still means jail, this institution was originally the prison attached to Winchester House, palace of the Bishops of Winchester until 1626. One of five Southwark prisons, it was the first to detain women, most of whom were called "Winchester geese"—another euphemism meaning prostitutes. The world's oldest profession was endemic in Southwark, especially around the bishops' area of jurisdiction, which was known as "the Liberty of the Clink." Their graces' sensible solution was to license prostitution rather than ban it, but a Winchester goose who flouted the rules ended up in the Clink. Now there's a museum tracing the history of prostitution in "the Liberty" and showing what the Clink was like during its 16th-century prime. ⌂ *1 Clink St., South Bank SE1* ☎ *020/ 7403–0900* ⊕ *www.clink.co.uk* ⊠ *£4* ☉ *Daily 10–6; last admission 5:30* Ⓤ *London Bridge.*

❻ **Dalí Universe.** Here is Europe's most comprehensively arranged collection by master surrealist Salvador Dalí. The many exhibits—from art, to sculpture, to furniture, to jewelry—are organized in themes (Sensuality and Femininity, Religion and Mythology, and Dreams and Fantasy), and thus the museum tries to give visitors a reflection of how Dalí thought out his work. There are more than 500 pieces on show, but highlights undoubtedly include the *Mae West Lips Sofa*, the *Lobster Telephone*, and *Spellbound* for the Hitchcock movie. ✉ *County Hall, Riverside Bldg., Westminster Bridge Rd., South Bank SE1* ☎ *020/ 7620–2720* ⊕ *www.daliuniverse.com* ✆ *£8.50* ✆ *Daily 10–5:30* Ⓤ *Waterloo or Westminster.*

🕐 ❷⑥ **Design Museum.** This was the first museum in the world to elevate everyday design and design classics to the status of art by placing them in their social and cultural context. Fashion, creative technology, and architecture are explored with thematic displays from the museum's permanent collection of design classics, and temporary exhibitions provide an in-depth focus on subjects, including retrospectives on the work of great designers such as Charles Eames and Isamu Noguchi, or thematic shows on the Bauhaus or erotic design. The museum looks forward, too, by showcasing innovative contemporary designs and technologies, an area that kids find absorbing (there are free activity packs to spark their interest further). All of this is supplemented by a busy program of lectures, events, and talks, including a workshop for kids. If you're in need of sustenance, there's the trendsetting Blueprint Café (designed by who else but Terence Conran), with its river terrace and superb views. For quicker snacks at a lower price, the museum's own café is on the ground floor beside the Thames footpath. The museum store sells good quality, high-design products. Entry to both cafés and the store is free. ✉ *28 Shad Thames, South Bank SE1* ☎ *0870/909– 9009 weekdays 9–5, 0870/833–9955 recorded information* ⊕ *www. designmuseum.org* ✆ *£6* ✆ *Sat.–Thurs. 10–5:45, Fri. 10–9; last admission 30 mins. before closing* Ⓤ *London Bridge or DLR: Tower Gateway.*

**off the beaten path**

**DULWICH PICTURE GALLERY** – A highly distinguished small gallery, the Dulwich has impressive works by Rembrandt, Van Dyck, Rubens, Poussin, and Gainsborough, among others, with three critically acclaimed international loan exhibitions each year. Anyone who fell in love with Sir John Soane's house may wish to make the short overground train journey (12 minutes from London Bridge or Victoria) here, since this gallery was also designed by the visionary architect. The Gallery has recently undergone extensive refurbishment and new building, with improved customer facilities, including the Picture Gallery Café. You'll also enjoy wandering around Dulwich Village, with its handsome 18th-century houses strung out along its main street. Most of the land around here belongs to the famous local school, the Dulwich College Estate, founded in the early 17th century by the actor Edward Alleyn, and this keeps strict control of modern development. Opposite the gallery, Dulwich Park is a well-kept municipal park with a particularly fine display of rhododendrons in late May. ✉ *College Rd., Dulwich Village, Southwark SE21* ☎ *020/*

*8693–5254 ⊕ www.dulwichpicturegallery.org.uk ☞ £4, free on Fri. ⊙ Tues.–Fri. 10–5, weekends 11–5 Ⓤ National Rail: West Dulwich from Victoria or North Dulwich from London Bridge.*

**❹ Florence Nightingale Museum.** Here you can learn all about the founder of the first school of nursing, that most famous of health-care reformers, "the Lady with the Lamp." See the reconstruction of the barracks ward at Scutari, Turkey, where she tended soldiers during the Crimean War (1854–56) and earned her nickname. Here you also find a Victorian East End slum cottage showing what she did to improve living conditions among the poor—and the famous lamp. The museum is in **St. Thomas's Hospital,** which was built in 1868 to the specifications of Florence Nightingale. Most of it was bombed to bits in the Blitz, then rebuilt to become one of London's teaching hospitals. ⊠ *2 Lambeth Palace Rd., South Bank SE1* ☎ *020/7620–0374* ⊕ *www.florence-nightingale.co.uk* ☞ *£5.80* ⊙ *Weekdays 10–5, last admission 4, weekends 10–4:30, last admission 3:30* Ⓤ *Waterloo or Westminster, then walk over bridge.*

**🐾 ⑲ *Golden Hinde.*** Sir Francis Drake circumnavigated the globe in this little galleon, or one just like it. This exact replica made a 23-year round-the-world voyage—much of it spent along U.S. coasts, both Pacific and Atlantic—and has settled here to continue its educational purpose. If you want information along with your visit, book a tour in advance. ⊠ *St. Mary Overie Dock, Cathedral St., South Bank SE1* ☎ *020/7403–0123* ⊕ *www.goldenhinde.co.uk* ☞ *£3.50, £4 for prebooked guided tour* ⊙ *Apr.–Oct., daily 9:30–5:30; Nov.–Mar. daily 9:30–5; last admission 30 mins before closing* Ⓤ *London Bridge or Mansion House.*

**㉓ Hay's Galleria.** Hay's Wharf was built by Thomas Cubitt in 1857 on the spot where the port of London's oldest wharf had stood since 1651. It was once known as "London's larder" because of the quantity of edibles that landed here. It then wound down gradually and closed in 1970. In 1987 it was reborn as this Covent Garden–like parade of bars and restaurants, offices, shops and craft stalls, all weatherproofed by an arched glass atrium roof supported by tall iron columns. The centerpiece is a fanciful kinetic sculpture by David Kemp, *The Navigators,* which looks like the skeleton of a pirate schooner crossed with a dragon and spouts water from various orifices. Jugglers, string quartets, and crafts stalls abound. This courtyard hub of the developing London Bridge City needed all the help it could get in its early days, but it has settled in nicely now with its captive crowd of office workers from the adjacent developments. ⊠ *2 Battle Bridge La., South Bank SE1* ☎ *020/7940–7770* ⊕ *www.haysgalleria.co.uk* Ⓤ *London Bridge.*

**⑪ Hayward Gallery.** This is the one gallery you can't miss, literally, due to the multicolor neon tube sculpture atop the building, which blinks away through the night on the South Bank skyline. The gray, windowless bunker tucked behind the South Bank Centre concert halls has had to bear the brunt of architectural criticism over the years, but that's changed with a foyer extension that gives more daylight, more space for exhibits, a café, and better access. The highlight of the project is an elliptical mirrored glass Pavilion by New York–based artist Dan Graham. The gallery encompasses a range of art media, crossing history and cultures, bridging the experimental and established. It's consistently on the cutting edge of new developments in art and critical theory, finding new ways to present the well-known, from Picasso to Lichtenstein, and as a prominent platform for up-and-coming artists. ⊠ *South Bank Complex, South Bank SE1* ☎ *020/7960–5226* ⊕ *www.hayward.org.uk* 🎫 *£9* ☻ *Thurs.–Mon. 10–6, Tues. and Wed. 10–8* Ⓤ *Waterloo.*

☼ ㉔ **HMS Belfast.** At 656 feet, this is one of the largest and most powerful cruisers the Royal Navy has ever had. It played an important role in the D-Day landings off Normandy, left for the Far East after the war, and has been becalmed here since 1971. On board there's an outpost of the **Imperial War Museum,** which tells the Royal Navy's story from 1914 to the present and shows you about life on a World War II battleship (with interactive push button games and quizzes), from mess decks and bakery to punishment cells and from operations room to engine room and armaments. ⊠ *Morgan's La., Tooley St., South Bank SE1* ☎ *020/ 7940–6300* ⊕ *www.hmsbelfast.org.uk* 🎫 *£7* ☻ *Mid-Mar.–Oct., daily 10–6; Nov.–mid-Mar., daily 10–5; last admission 45 mins before closing* Ⓤ *London Bridge.*

off the
beaten
path

**HORNIMAN MUSEUM –** This educational museum of anthropology, which also manages to be fun, is set in 16 acres of gardens in South London with well-displayed ethnographic and natural history collections. Recent additions include an aquarium stocked with endangered species and the African Worlds section. Extended gallery space has been built to include galleries for world cultures and temporary exhibitions; the Centre for Understanding, with hands-on displays for younger visitors; and a café and shop. ⊠ *100 London Rd., Forest Hill SE23* ☎ *020/8699–1872* ⊕ *www.horniman.ac.uk* 🎫 *Free* ☻ *Mon.–Sat. 10:30–5:30, Sun. 2–5:30* Ⓤ *National Rail: Forest Hill, from London Bridge or Victoria.*

❾ **Hungerford Bridge.** These two pedestrian bridges, one on either side of Charing Cross railway bridge, are a stunning suspension update on the previous footbridge here, and provide a convenient crossing from Charing Cross to Jubilee Gardens and South Bank sights. The name comes from a grand 17th-century marketplace built in the gardens of Edward Hungerford's old mansion. ⊠ *Jubilee Gardens, South Bank SE1.*

★ ☼ ❸ **Imperial War Museum.** Despite its title, this museum of 20th-century warfare does not glorify bloodshed but attempts to evoke what it was like to live through the two world wars. There's hardware and interactive material for martial-minded children—a Battle of Britain Spitfire, a German V2 rocket, tanks, guns, submarines—but there's an equal amount of war art (David Bomberg, Henry Moore, John Singer Sargent, Graham Sutherland, to name a few), poetry, photography, and documentary film footage. One very affecting exhibit is *The Blitz Experience,* which is just what it sounds like—a 10-minute taste of an air raid in a street of acrid smoke with sirens blaring and searchlights glaring.

There's also a permanent Holocaust exhibition, and a Crimes Against Humanity exhibition, funded from a generous lottery grant. More recent wars attended by British forces are commemorated, too.

The museum is housed in an elegant domed and colonnaded building, erected in the early 19th century to house the Bethlehem Hospital for the Insane, better known as the infamous Bedlam. By 1816, when the patients were moved here, they were no longer kept in cages to be taunted by tourists (see the final scene of Hogarth's *Rake's Progress* at Sir John Soane's Museum for some sense of how horrific it was), since reformers—and George III's madness—had effected more humane standards of confinement. Bedlam moved to Surrey in 1930. ⊠ *Lambeth Rd., South Bank SE1* ☎ *020/7416–5320* ⊕ *www.iwm.org.uk* ⊠ *Free* ☉ *Daily 10–6* Ⓤ *Lambeth North.*

▶ ❶ **Lambeth Palace.** For 800 years this has been the London base of the Archbishop of Canterbury, head of the Church of England. Much of the palace is hidden behind great walls, and even the Tudor gatehouse, visible from the street, is closed to the public, but you can stand here and absorb the historical vibrations echoing from momentous events. These include the 1381 storming of the palace during the Peasants' Revolt against the poll tax and the 1534 clash of wills when Thomas More refused to sign the Oath of Supremacy claiming Henry VIII (and not the pope) as leader of the English Church, for which he was sent to the Tower and executed for treason the following year. Adjacent to this house is the Museum of Garden History. ⊠ *Lambeth Palace Rd., South Bank SE1* ⊕ *www. archbishopofcanterbury.org* Ⓤ *Waterloo.*

☾ ❺ **London Aquarium.** This curved, colonnaded, neoclassic hulk once housed London's local government administration, the Greater London Council, which was abolished (it's now been reinstated as the London Assembly, and moved to the futuristic City Hall building further downriver by Tower Bridge). Here is a dark and thrilling glimpse into the waters of the world, focused around a superb three-level aquarium full of sharks and stingrays, among other common and more rare breeds. There are also educational exhibits, hands-on displays, feeding displays, and piscine sights previously unseen on these shores. It's not the biggest aquarium you've ever seen—especially if you've been to Sea-World—but the exhibit is well arranged on several subterranean levels, with areas for different oceans, water environments, and climate zones, including a stunning coral reef, and the highlight: the rain forest, which is almost like the real thing. The aquarium also runs a conservation breeding scheme, so look out for new additions to the tanks. ⊠ *County Hall, Riverside Bldg., Westminster Bridge Rd., South Bank SE1,* ☎ *020/ 7967–8000* ⊕ *www.londonaquarium.co.uk* ⊠ *£9.75* ☉ *Daily 10–6, last admission 5* Ⓤ *Westminster or Waterloo.*

☾ ㉒ **London Dungeon.** Here's the goriest, grisliest, gruesomest attraction in town, where realistic waxwork people are subjected in graphic detail to all the historical horrors the Tower of London merely tells you about. Tableaux depict famous bloody moments—like Anne Boleyn's decapitation and the martyrdom of St. George—alongside the torture, murder, and ritual slaughter of lesser-known victims, all to a sound track of screaming, wailing, and agonized moaning. There are displays on the Great Fire of London and Jack the Ripper, and to add to the fear and fun, costumed characters leap out of the gloom to bring the exhibits to life. Naturally, children absolutely adore this place, but be warned—nervous kiddies may find it too truly frightening. Expect long lines. ⊠ *28–34 Tooley St., South Bank SE1* ☎ *020/7403–7221* ⊕ *www.thedungeons. com* ☜ *£14.50* ☉ *Mid-Apr.–mid-July, daily 10–5:30; mid-July–Sept., daily 10–7.30; Sept.–Nov., daily 10–5.30; Nov.–mid-Apr. daily 10:30–5; phone to confirm dates* Ⓤ *London Bridge.*

**❷ Museum of Garden History.** The first of its kind in the world, the museum is set in St. Mary's Church, next to Lambeth Palace. Founded in 1977, the museum has built up one of the largest collections of historic garden tools, artifacts, and curiosities, as well as an expanding library. Alongside the museum is a replica 17th-century knot garden, a peaceful haven of plants that can be traced back to that period. The garden also contains the tombs of the John Tradescants (the elder and younger), enthusiastic collectors of curiosities and adventurous plant hunters—who introduced many familiar blooms, such as lilac, to these shores—and memorials to William Bligh, captain of the *Bounty,* and the Sealy family of Coade stone fame. The shop has gifts in the plant vein, and a café. ⊠ *Lambeth Palace Rd., South Bank SE1* ☎ *020/7401–8865* ⊕ *www. museumgardenhistory.org* ☜ *Suggested donation £2.50* ☉ *Daily 10:30–5; closed mid-Dec.–early Feb.* Ⓤ *Waterloo, then bus 507.*

**♻ National Film Theatre (NFT).** The NFT has easily the best repertory programming in London, favoring obscure, foreign, silent, forgotten, classic, noir, and short films over blockbusters. It's also home to the British Film Institute, and numerous international film festivals, such as the London Film Festival in November, the Gay and Lesbian Film Festival in April, and a Crime Thriller Festival. The Web site and phone lines give latest details of events. ⊠ *South Bank Centre, South Bank SE1* ☎ *020/ 7928–3232* ⊕ *www.bfi.org.uk* ☜ *£7.20* ☉ *Daily 11:30 AM–8:30 PM* Ⓤ *Waterloo.*

> **need a break?**
>
> **Gabriel's Wharf** has a wide choice of cafés and restaurants, from crêpes to burgers, and pizzas at the Gourmet Pizza Company (☎ 020/7928–3188). In summer the restaurants have outdoor seating, amid the cute stores selling crafts and jewelry.

**♻ ㉑ Old Operating Theatre Museum.** All that remains of one of England's oldest hospitals, which stood here from the 12th century until the railway forced it to move in 1862, is the room where women went under the knife. The theater was bricked up and forgotten for a century but has now been restored into an exhibition of early-19th-century medical practices: the operating table onto which the gagged and blindfolded patients were roped; the box of sawdust underneath for catching their blood; the knives, pliers, and handsaws the surgeons wielded; and—this was a theater in the round—the spectators' seats. So authentic are the surroundings that they were used in the film *The Madness of King*

*George.* Next door is a sweeter show: the **Herb Garret,** with displays of medicinal herbs used during the same period. ⊠ *9A St. Thomas St., South Bank SE1* ☎ *020/7955–4791* ⊕ *www.thegarret.org.uk* ⊠ *£4.25* ⊘ *Daily 10:30–5; closed Dec. 15–Jan. 5* Ⓤ *London Bridge.*

⓭ **OXO Tower.** This might very well turn out to be the 21st-century version of Big Ben—a wonderfully renovated art deco–era tower filled with designers' workshops overlooking the Thames. Long a London landmark to the cognoscenti, the OXO has graduated from its former incarnations as a power-generating station and warehouse into a vibrant community of artists' and designers' workshops, a pair of restaurants, as well as five floors of community homes. There's an observation deck for a super river vista (St. Paul's to the east, and Somerset House to the west), and a performance area on the first floor, which comes alive all summer long—as does the entire surrounding neighborhood. All the designers and artisans have been selected by totally nondemocratic methods, meaning the work is of incredibly high standard. They all rely on you to disturb them whenever they're open. Don't be shy—they really mean it; you will be most welcome, whether buying, commissioning, or just browsing. The biggest draw remains the OXO Tower Restaurant extravaganza for a meal or a martini. ⊠ *Barge House St., South Bank SE1* ☎ *020/7401–3610* ⊠ *Free* ⊘ *Studios and shops Tues.–Sun. 11–6* Ⓤ *Blackfriars or Waterloo.*

⓾ **Royal Festival Hall.** This is the largest auditorium of the South Bank Centre, with superb acoustics and a 3,000-plus capacity. It's the oldest of the riverside blocks, raised as the centerpiece of the 1951 Festival of Britain, a postwar morale-boosting exercise. The London Philharmonic resides here; symphony orchestras from the world over like to visit; and choral works, ballet, serious jazz and pop, and even films with live accompaniment are staged. Also featured are a multiplicity of foyers with free rotating exhibitions; a good, independently run restaurant, the People's Palace; free jazz in the main foyer on Sunday; and a very fine bookstore. The next building you come to also contains concert halls, one medium and one small, the **Queen Elizabeth Hall** and the **Purcell Room,** respectively. Both offer predominantly classical recitals of international caliber, with due respect paid to 20th-century composers and established jazz and vocal artists. ⊠ *South Bank Centre, South Bank SE1* ☎ *020/ 7960–4242* ⊕ *www.rfh.org.uk* Ⓤ *Waterloo.*

⓬ **Royal National Theatre.** When this theater opened in 1976 Londoners generally felt the same way about this low-slung, multilayered "brutalist" block the color of heavy storm clouds and designed by Sir Denys Lasdun that they would feel a decade later about the Barbican Centre. But whatever its merits or demerits as a landscape feature, the Royal National Theatre has wonderful insides.

Three auditoriums occupy the complex. The biggest one, the **Olivier,** is named after Sir Laurence, chairman of the first building commission and first artistic director of the National Theatre Company, formed in 1962. (In between the first proposal of a national theater for Britain and the 1949 formation of that building commission, an entire century had passed.) The **Lyttelton** theater has a traditional proscenium arch, and the little **Cottesloe** mounts studio productions and new work in the round. Interspersed with the theaters is a multilayered foyer with exhibitions, bars, and restaurants, and free entertainment. The whole place is lively six days a week. The Royal National Theatre Company does not rest on its laurels: its productions list many of the nation's top actors (Anthony Hopkins, Vanessa Redgrave, Ian McKellen, Judi Dench, and more) in addition to launching future stars. Because it's a repertory company, you'll have several plays from which to choose even if your London sojourn is short; but, tickets or not, wander around and catch the buzz. And on a backstage tour, you may even bump into a star. ⊠ *South Bank SE1* ☎ *020/7452–3000 box office, 020/7452–3400 for tour* 🎫 *Tour £5* 🕐 *Foyer Mon.–Sat. 10 AM–11 PM; 1-hr tour of theater backstage Mon.–Sat. 10:15, 12:30, and 5:30* ⊕ *www.nationaltheatre. org.uk* Ⓤ *Waterloo.*

**❼ Saatchi Gallery.** The Saatchi contemporary art collection moved to the South Bank in 2003, where it rubs shoulders with Tate Modern and the Hayward Gallery. Charles Saatchi is no stranger to newspaper headlines, right from the days when his successful advertising empire "rebranded" Margaret Thatcher's Conservative Party. An astute art collector, he has made acquisitions that sometimes create news and controversy. Paula Rego, Damien Hirst, Rachel Whiteread, Janine Antoni, and Tracey Emin—who is now showing a softer side—are exhibited here. ⊠ *County Hall, Riverside Bldg., Westminster Bridge Rd., South Bank SE1* ☎ *020/ 7823–2363* ⊕ *www.saatchi-gallery.co.uk* 🎫 *£8* 🕐 *Sun.–Thurs. 10–8, Fri. and Sat. 10–10* Ⓤ *Waterloo or Westminster.*

★ ♺ **⓰ Shakespeare's Globe Theatre.** Three decades ago, Sam Wanamaker—then an aspiring actor—pulled up in Southwark in a cab and was amazed to find that the fabled Shakespeare's Globe Playhouse didn't actually exist. Worse, a tiny plaque was the only sign on the former site of the world's most legendary theater. So appalled was he that London lacked a center for the study and worship of the Bard of Bards, Wanamaker worked ceaselessly, until his death, to raise funds for his dream— a full-scale reconstruction of the theater. The dream was realized when an exact replica of Shakespeare's open-roof Globe Playhouse (built in 1599; incinerated in 1613) was created, using authentic Elizabethan materials and craft techniques—green oak timbers joined only with wooden pegs and mortise and tenon joints; plaster made of lime, sand, and goat's hair; and the first thatched roof in London since the Great Fire. In addition, a second, indoor theater has been added, built to a design of the 17th-century architect Inigo Jones. The whole complex stands 200 yards from the original Globe on the appropriate site of the 17th-century Davies Amphitheatre, admittedly more a bullbaiting, prizefighting sort of venue than a temple to the legitimate stage, but at least Samuel Pepys immortalized it in his diaries.

The Globe is a celebration of the great Bard's life (1564–1616) and work, an actual rebirth of his "wooden O" (see *Henry V*), where his plays are presented in natural light (and sometimes rain) to 1,000 people on wooden benches in the "bays," plus 500 "groundlings," who stand on a carpet of filbert shells and clinker, just as they did nearly four centuries ago. For any theater buff, this stunning project is unmissable. Although the open-air Globe Theatre offers performances only during the summer season (generally mid-May to mid-September), it can be viewed year-round if you take the helpful tour offered by the **Shakespeare's Globe Exhibition,** a comprehensive display housed in the adjacent UnderGlobe, which provides fascinating background material on the Elizabethan theater and the construction of the modern-day Globe; it has occasional displays and workshops, some aimed at children. If you're thrilled by the reconstruction of Shakespeare's Globe, you might want to get the complete picture by visiting an exhibition of its near neighbor, the **Rose Theatre,** at 56 Park St., which was built even earlier, in 1587. ✉ *New Globe Walk, Bankside, South Bank SE1* ☎ *020/7401–9919 box office, 020/7902–1500 New Shakespeare's Globe Exhibition* ⊕ *www.shakespeares-globe. org* 🎫 *£8, joint ticket available to Rose Theatre exhibition* ☉ *Exhibition daily 10–5, plays May–Sept., call for performance schedule* Ⓤ *Southwark, then walk to Blackfriars Bridge and descend the steps; Mansion House, then walk across Southwark Bridge; or Blackfriars, then walk across Blackfriars Bridge.*

**⓴ Southwark Cathedral.** Pronounced "Suth-uck," this is the second-oldest Gothic church in London, after Westminster Abbey, with parts dating back to the 12th century. Although it houses some remarkable memorials, not to mention a program of lunchtime concerts, it's seldom visited. It was promoted to cathedral status only in 1905; before that it was the priory church of St. Mary Overy (as in "over the water"—on the South Bank). Look for the gaudily renovated 1408 tomb of the poet John Gower, friend of Chaucer, and for the Harvard Chapel. Another notable buried here is Edmund Shakespeare, brother of William. ✉ *Montague Close, South Bank SE1* ☎ *020/7367–6700* ⊕ *www.dswark.org* 🎫 *Free, suggested donation £4* ☉ *Daily 8–6* Ⓤ *London Bridge.*

**★ ⓒ ⓮ Tate Modern.** This ex-power station was built in the 1930s, and after a dazzling renovation by Herzog & de Meuron, provides a magnificent space for a massive collection of international modern art. The vast Turbine Hall is a dramatic entrance point to the museum. On permanent display in the galleries are classic works from 1900 to the present day, by Matisse, Picasso, Dalí, Moore, Bacon, Warhol, and the most-talked-about British upstarts. The works are not grouped by artist but are arranged in themes that mix the historic with the contemporary—Landscape, Still Life, and the Nude—on different levels, reached by a moving staircase, which is a feature in itself. You could spend a visit merely exploring one floor, but that would be cowardly, as there's usually one major barnstorming exhibition to see (for which there is a charge, and often very long lines waiting to get in), which is always the talking point of Londoners who have their fingers on the pulse. ✉ *Bankside, South Bank SE1* ☎ *020/7887–8000* ⊕ *www.tate. org.uk* 🎫 *Free* ☉ *Sun.–Thurs. 10–6, Fri. and Sat. 10–10* Ⓤ *Blackfriars or Southwark.*

**⑰ Vinopolis.** The Brits are perhaps not the first nation you would expect to erect a monument to wine, but here it is—Vinopolis, City of Wine. Spread over 2 acres between the Globe Theatre and London Bridge, its arched vaults promise multimedia tours of the world's wine cultures, tastings, retail shops, an art gallery, restaurants, and a wine school. You can learn about wine production and history, and then have a chance to put your newfound knowledge to the test in the Tasting Halls. The four restaurants claim to offer more wines by the glass than anywhere else in the city, and you can, of course, buy. Keep in mind that the last entry is two hours before the scheduled closing time, and you should allow at least two hours for a tour. ✉ *1 Bank End St., South Bank SE1* ☎ *0870/444–4777* ⊕ *www.vinopolis.co.uk* ✐ *£11.50* ☉ *Mon. and Sat. noon–9, Tues.–Fri. and Sun. noon–6* Ⓤ *London Bridge.*

# CHELSEA & BELGRAVIA

Chelsea is where J. M. W. Turner painted his sunsets and John Singer Sargent his society portraits, where Oscar Wilde wrote *The Importance of Being Earnest,* and where Mary Quant cut her first miniskirt. Today, Chelsea is a neighborhood as handsome as its real estate is costly. Strolling its streets, you will often notice gigantic windows adorning otherwise ordinary houses. They are remnants of Chelsea's 19th-century bohemian days, when they served to bring light into artists' studios; now they are mostly used to hike property values a few notches higher. This is the place—the King's Road in particular—that gave birth to Swinging '60s London, then to '70s punk youth culture. The millennial version of this colorful thoroughfare is not really the center of anything, but it's hard not to like wandering down it.

Chelsea's next-door neighborhood is aristocratic Belgravia, with the King's Road and Knightsbridge as its respective southern and northern borders, Sloane Street and Grosvenor Place its western and eastern ones, and vast Belgrave Square—where many embassies are located—in the middle. Diagonally across the square, Belgrave Place will lead past grand mansions (all painted Wedgwood-white to denote that they, like every other house in this district, are the property of England's richest landowners, the Dukes of Westminster) through to Eaton Square, the aptly chosen locale for the TV series *Upstairs, Downstairs.* It's no accident that this whole neighborhood of wealth and splendor is grouped around the back of Buckingham Palace—many titled peers wished to live adjacent to the Court. Belgravia is relatively young: it was built between the 1820s and the 1850s by the builder-developer-entrepreneur Thomas Cubitt (who had as great an influence on the look of London in his day as Wren and Nash had in theirs), under the patronage of Lord Grosvenor, and was intended to rival Mayfair for spectacular snob value and expense. Today it still does.

*Numbers in the text correspond to numbers in the margin and on the Chelsea and Belgravia map.*

a good
walk

Start at **Cheyne Walk** ❶ ⬏, stretching in both directions from Albert Bridge, going all the way west to see the statue of Thomas More, then doubling back for a left turn into Cheyne Row to reach **Carlyle's House** ❷. Where the east end of Cheyne Walk runs into Royal Hospital Road, you'll find the **Chelsea Physic Garden** ❸; a right after the garden on Royal Hospital Road brings you to the **National Army Museum** ❹. Royal Hospital Road takes its name from the institution next door to the museum, the magnificent **Royal Hospital** ❺. A left turn from here up Franklin's Row and Cheltenham Terrace brings you to famous **King's Road** ❻, which you could follow east until you reach the beginning of Belgravia: Sloane Square, named after Sir Hans Sloane, whose collection founded the British Museum and who bought the manor of Chelsea in 1712. Cross the square more or less in a straight line, and follow Cliveden Place for a taste of Belgravia. The grand, white-stucco houses have changed not at all since the mid-19th century, and Eaton Square, which you'll soon come upon, remains such a desirable address that the rare event of one of its houses' coming on the market makes all the property pages. Its most famous residents were fictional, of course, as the enduringly popular period soap *Upstairs, Downstairs* was set here. A left turn on **Belgrave Place** ❼ brings you to Belgrave Square, dense with embassies, but the best thing to do around here is follow your nose. Other than Palladian-perfect mansions, chic alleys, and magnificent Georgian squares—in addition to Belgrave and Eaton, the smaller Lowndes, Cadogan, Trevor, Brompton, and Montpelier—there are no particular Belgravia sights. After taking in Belgrave Place and the picturesque mews next to Eaton Place, however, you might continue eastward on Belgrave Place, walk south several blocks on Eaton Place, and head for the lovely warren of streets and alleys around Chester Row and Minerva Mews.

TIMING     This may read like a short hop, but the walk above covers a good 2 to 3 mi. If you explore side streets, you could double the figure—and exploring these streets is the best aspect of these neighborhoods, which are primarily residential and expensive. The houses along the way will detain you, and the shops will for longer; even though King's Road isn't what it used to be, it's still fruitful. In summer you'll want to spend time in the Physic Garden or around the Royal Hospital, so make sure you're heading out on one of the opening days. If you're dead set on the Physic Garden, that means Wednesday or Sunday afternoon from April to October.

HOW TO GET THERE     Chelsea is notoriously ill-served by Tube stops. To start the walk at Cheyne Walk, take the Tube to Earl's Court on the District Line then take Bus 328 on Earl's Court Road to its terminus at World's End on King's Road. From there walk away from the bus on King's Road and take a right on Glebe Place to reach Cheyne Row and Carlyle's House. Alternatively, if you're more interested in shopping than sightseeing, you can take the District and Circle lines to Sloane Square, then strike out by foot along King's Road. Or catch a bus from Sloane Square: 11, 19, 22, 137, 211, and 328 cover the area to World's End. For farther to Fulham, take the 11, 22, 211, or 328. The edge of Belgravia farthest from Chelsea is accessible from Hyde Park Corner on the Piccadilly Line. From Hyde Park

Corner and going on to Belgravia–Victoria are Buses 2 (from Marble Arch), 8 (from Oxford Circus), 14 (from Tottenham Court Road to Fulham via Knightsbridge), 16 (from Marble Arch to Belgravia), 36 (from Marble Arch), 38 (from Bloomsbury and Piccadilly), 52 (from Kensington), 73 (from Tottenham Court Road), 82 (from Baker Street), and 137 (from Oxford Circus). Choose a bus that appears on both lists for travel between the two neighborhoods.

## What to See

**7 Belgrave Place.** One of the main arteries of Belgravia—London's swankiest neighborhood—Belgrave Place is lined with grand, imposing Regency-era mansions (now mostly embassies). Walk down this street toward Eaton Place to pass two of Belgravia's most beautiful mews—Eaton Mews North and Eccleston Mews, both fronted by grand Westminster-white rusticated entrances right out of a 19th-century engraving: there are few other places where London is both so picturesque and elegant.

**2 Carlyle's House.** This house hosted a thriving salon of 19th-century authors, attracted by the fame of Thomas Carlyle (1795–1881)—author of a blockbuster history of the French Revolution that is now almost forgotten and the amusing *Sartor Resartus*—and by the wit of his wife, Jane Carlyle. Dickens, Thackeray, Tennyson, and Browning were regular visitors, and you can see the second-floor drawing room where they met just as they saw it, complete with leather armchair, decoupage screen, fireplace, and oil lamps, all in ruddy Victorian hues. ✉ *24 Cheyne Row, Chelsea SW3* ☎ *020/7352-7087* ⊕ *www.nationaltrust.org.uk* ✉ *£3.80* ⊙ *Apr.–Oct., Wed.–Sun. 11–4:30* Ⓤ *Sloane Sq., then walk down King's Rd. or take Bus 11, 19, 22, 49, or 211 to Chelsea Old Town Hall.*

**3 Chelsea Physic Garden.** First planted by the Society of Apothecaries in 1673 for the study of medicinal plants, these gardens are still in use for the same purpose today. The herbs and shrubs and flowers, planted to a strict plan but tumbling over the paths nevertheless, are interspersed with woodland areas, England's first rock garden, and ancient trees, some of which were tragically uprooted in a 1987 storm. In the middle stands a statue of Sir Hans Sloane, physician to Queen Anne and George II, whose collection formed the basis of the British Museum and who saved the garden from closing in 1722, making sure nobody would ever be allowed to build over it. ✉ *Swan Walk, 66 Royal Hospital Rd., Chelsea SW3* ☎ *020/7352-5646* ⊕ *www.cpgarden.demon.co.uk* ✉ *£5* ⊙ *Apr.–Oct., Wed. noon–5 and Sun. 2–6; daily noon–5 during Chelsea Flower Show 3rd wk of May* Ⓤ *Sloane Sq., then walk down King's Rd., or take Bus 11, 19, 22, 319, or 211 (to Chelsea Old Town Hall), or 239 from Victoria Station.*

▶ **1 Cheyne Walk.** Its name rhymes with "rainy." Expect to find some beautiful Queen Anne houses (particularly Norman Shaw's ornamental 1876 Cheyne House, to the right off Albert Bridge) and a storm of blue plaques marking famous ex-residents' homes. George Eliot died at No. 4 in 1880; Dante Gabriel Rossetti annoyed the neighbors of No. 16 with his peacock collection (there's still a clause in the lease banning the birds);

Henry James died at Carlyle Mansions (after a night at the King's Head and Eight Bells pub), and later residents were T. S. Eliot and Ian Fleming. The western reaches were painters' territory, most notably of James McNeill Whistler, who lived at No. 96 and then No. 101, and J. M. W. Turner, who used No. 119 as a retreat, shielding his identity behind the name Adm. "Puggy" Booth. Also toward the western end, outside the Church of All Saints, is a golden-faced statue of **Thomas More** (who wouldn't sign the Oath of Supremacy at Lambeth Palace in 1534 and was executed as a traitor), looking pensive and beatific on a throne facing the river, a 1969 addition to the Walk.

**❻ King's Road.** This was where the miniskirt first strutted its stuff in the '60s and where Vivienne Westwood and Malcolm McLaren clothed the Sex Pistols in bondage trousers from their shop, "Sex," in 1975, thus spawning punk rock. Westwood, one of Britain's most innovative fashion stars, still runs her shop at No. 430, where the road, fittingly, kinks. Both boutique and neighborhood are called **World's End**, possibly because Chelsea-ites believe that's what happens here. The Fulham district begins around this stretch, full of yuppie singles and places to shop. The other end of King's Road, leading into Sloane Square, has various fashion stores (no longer style-setters, on the whole) and some rather good antiques shops and markets along the way. The **Pheasantry**, at No. 152, is recognizable by some over-the-top Grecian statuary in a fancy portico. Named in its mid-19th-century pheasant-breeding days, it had a phase from 1916 to 1934 as a ballet school where Margot Fonteyn and Alicia Markova learned first position. Now it's a branch of the ubiquitous Pizza Express. The Peter Jones department store marks the exit from the north of Chelsea and the beginning of Belgravia: Sloane Square. Conran's trendy restaurant **Bluebird**, at No. 352, is a great place to stop for lunch.

**❹ National Army Museum.** From the first professional army—the Yeoman of the Guard—to the sophisticated British land forces of today, the story of the army is chronicled through paintings, photographs, uniforms, and equipment. A tour of the gallery begins with the Redcoats, from Henry V (1413–22) and the historic Battle of Agincourt in France, to the army of George III (1760–1820), which occupied America. To put you in the picture of some of the key campaigns of British history (which involved many far corners of the globe), there are ancient cannon, arms and armor, and life-size models in uniform. There's an opportunity to try on some of the old cumbersome helmets and handle extremely heavy cannon balls. Proceeding toward the modern army, there are action videos, computer games, and scenic effects, which give a glimpse of the experience of battle strategy and tactics. The social side of the effects of war on civilians (particularly the wives and families) is also covered, so it's not all *Band of Brothers*; and not to be forgotten, women also played a vital role in the World Wars. ✉ *Royal Hospital Rd., Chelsea SW3* ☎ *020/7730–0717, 020/7730–0717 special events* 🌐 *www.national-army-museum.ac.uk* 🎫 *Free* 🕐 *Daily 10–5:30* Ⓤ *Sloane Sq.*

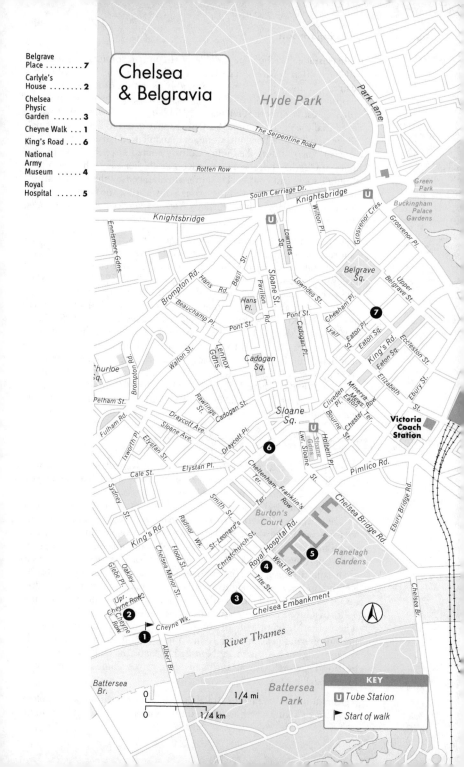

# Chelsea & Belgravia

*Hyde Park*

*Park Lane*

*The Serpentine Road*

*Rotten Row*

*South Carriage Dr.*

Knightsbridge

*Wilton Pl.*

*Grosvenor Cres.*

*Green Park*

*Buckingham Palace Gardens*

*Grosvenor Pl.*

Knightsbridge

*Lowndes Sq.*

*Lowndes St.*

*Belgrave Sq.*

*Upper Belgrave St.*

*Ennismore Gdns.*

*Brompton Rd.*

*Hans Rd.*

*Basil St.*

*Pavilion Rd.*

*Sloane St.*

*Hans Pl.*

*Chesham Pl.*

*Eaton Pl.*

**7**

*Eaton Sq.*

*King's Rd.*

*Eaton Sq.*

*Eccleston St.*

*Beauchamp Pl.*

*Pont St.*

*Pont St.*

*Cadogan Pl.*

*Lyall St.*

*Elizabeth St.*

*Ebury St.*

*Thurloe Sq.*

*Pelham St.*

*Walton St.*

*Lennox Gdns.*

*Cadogan Sq.*

*Brompton Rd.*

*Cliveden Pl.*

*Minerva Mews Row*

*Eaton Ter.*

*Chester Ter.*

**Victoria Coach Station**

*Fulham Rd.*

*Ixworth Pl.*

*Elystan St.*

*Rawlings St.*

*Cadogan St.*

*Draycott Ave.*

*Sloane Ave.*

*Draycott Pl.*

*Sloane Sq.*

*Bourne St.*

*Sidney St.*

*Cale St.*

*Elystan Pl.*

**6**

*Cheltenham Ter.*

*Sloane Gdns.*

*Lwr. Sloane St.*

*Holbein Pl.*

*Pimlico Rd.*

*King's Rd.*

*Redburn Wk.*

*Smith St.*

*St. Leonard's Ter.*

*Christchurch St.*

*Franklin's Row*

**Burton's Court**

*Royal Hospital Rd.*

*Chelsea Bridge Rd.*

*Ebury Bridge Rd.*

*Oakley St.*

*Glebe Pl.*

*Upr. Cheyne Row*

**2**

*Cheyne Row*

*Flood St.*

*Chelsea Manor St.*

**3**

**4**

*Tite St.*

*West Rd.*

**5**

*Ranelagh Gardens*

*Chelsea Embankment*

*Chelsea Br.*

**1**

▶ *Cheyne Wk.*

*Albert Br.*

*River Thames*

*Battersea Br.*

*Battersea Park*

| KEY | |
|---|---|
| 🚇 | *Tube Station* |
| ▶ | *Start of walk* |

0   1/4 mi

0   1/4 km

**❺ Royal Hospital.** The hospice for elderly and infirm soldiers was founded by Charles II in 1682—some say after a badgering from his soft-hearted mistress, Nell Gwyn, but more probably as an act of expedience. His troops had hitherto enjoyed not so much as a meager pension and were growing restive after the civil wars of 1642–46 and 1648. Charles wisely appointed the great architect Sir Christopher Wren to design this small village of brick and Portland stone set in manicured gardens (which you can visit) surrounding the Figure Court—named after the 1692 bronze figure of Charles II dressed up as a Roman soldier—and the Great Hall (dining room) and chapel. The latter is enhanced by the choir stalls of Grinling Gibbons (who did the bronze of Charles, too), the former by a vast oil of Charles on horseback by Antonio Verrio, and both are open to inspection.

In summer, and for special occasions, the "Chelsea Pensioners" can be seen resplendent in their traditional scarlet frock coats with gold buttons, medals, and tricorne hats. In winter the same coats are worn in dark blue. One such important occasion is on May 29, Oak Apple Day, when the pensioners celebrate Charles II's birthday by draping oak leaves on his statue and parading around it in memory of a hollow oak tree that expedited the king's miraculous escape from the 1651 Battle of Worcester. Also in May, and usually the third week, the Chelsea Flower Show, the year's highlight for thousands of garden-obsessed Brits, is also held here. Run by the Royal Horticultural Society, the mammoth event takes up vast acreage here, and the surrounding streets throng with visitors. ✉ *Royal Hospital Rd., Chelsea SW3* ☎ *020/7730–0161* ⊕ *www.chelseapensioners.org.uk* 🎟 *Free* ⊙ *Weekdays 10–noon and 2–4, weekends 10–noon* Ⓤ *Sloane Sq.*

# KNIGHTSBRIDGE & KENSINGTON

The top-notch area of the Royal Borough of Kensington is lined with splendid houses with pillared porches, but there are other fetching attractions here as well. You'll find some of the most fascinating museums in London, stylish squares, elegant antiques shops, and Kensington Palace (formerly the home of Diana, Princess of Wales, and of Queen Victoria when she was a girl). South and west of this historic edifice, you'll find the stomping grounds of the Sloane Rangers—a quintessentially London type of gilded youth whose upper-class accents make English sound like a foreign language. They tend to haunt salubrious Knightsbridge, east of Belgravia and north of Chelsea, offering as it does about equal doses of elite residential streets and ultrashopping venues. To its east is one of the highest concentrations of important artifacts anywhere, the Museum Mile of South Kensington, with the rest of Kensington offering peaceful strolls and a noisy main street. Bordering the western edge of Kensington at Notting Hill Gate, the Holland Park neighborhood is worth visiting for its big, fancy, tree-shaded houses and its lovely park.

Kensington first became the Royal Borough of Kensington (and Chelsea) by virtue of a king's asthma. William III, who suffered terribly from the

Thames mists over Whitehall, decided in 1689 to buy Nottingham House in the rural village of Kensington so that he could breathe more easily. Courtiers and functionaries and society folk soon followed where the crowns led, and by the time Queen Anne was on the throne (1702–14), Kensington was overflowing. In a way, it still is, because most of its grand houses, and the Victorian ones of Holland Park, have been divided into apartments or else are serving as foreign embassies.

*Numbers in the text correspond to numbers in the margin and on the Knightsbridge & Kensington map.*

a good walk

This is an all-weather walk—museums and shops for rainy days, grass and strolls for sunshine. When you surface from the Knightsbridge Tube station you are immediately engulfed by the manic drivers, professional shoppers, and ladies-who-lunch. If you're in a shopping mood, start with Harvey Nichols—right at the Tube—and its six floors of total fashion. Sloane Street, leading south, is strung with the boutiques of big-name designers, **Harrods** ❶ ► is found to the west down Brompton Road; continue west down this road, pausing at Beauchamp (pronounced "Bee-chum") Place and Walton Street if shopping is your intention. At the junction of Brompton and Cromwell roads, you'll come to the pale, Italianate **Brompton Oratory** ❷, which marks the beginning of museum territory, with the vast **Victoria & Albert Museum** ❸, the **Natural History Museum** ❹, and **Science Museum** ❺ behind it. (The neighborhood's three large museums, incidentally, can also be reached via a long underground passage from the South Kensington Tube station.) Turn left to continue north up Exhibition Road, a kind of unfinished cultural main drag that was Prince Albert's conception, toward the road after which British moviemakers named their fake blood, Kensington Gore, to reach the giant, round Wedgwood china–box of the **Royal Albert Hall** ❻, the glittering **Albert Memorial** ❼ opposite, and the **Royal College of Art** ❽ next door.

Now follow Kensington Gardens (which is what this western neighbor of Hyde Park is called) west to its end, and a little farther, perhaps detouring into the park to see **Kensington Palace** ❾ and, behind it, one of London's rare, private "Millionaires' Row" sanctuaries, **Kensington Palace Gardens** ❿. Turn off Kensington High Street down little Derry Street, with the offices of London's local paper, the *Evening Standard,* on the left. Take a turn around peaceful **Kensington Square** ⓫; then, returning to High Street, either follow Kensington Church Street up to Notting Hill Gate—with the little 1870 St. Mary Abbots Church on its southwest corner and a cornucopia of expensive antiques in its shops all along the way—or take the longer, scenic route.

To do this, turn left off Kensington Church Street onto Holland Street, admiring the sweet 18th-century houses (Nos. 10, 12–13, and 18–26 remain). As you cross Hornton Street you'll see to your left an orange-brick 1970s building, the Kensington Civic Centre (donor of parking permits, home of the local council); Holland Street becomes the leafy Duchess of Bedford's Walk, with Queen Elizabeth College, part of London University, on the right. Turn left before Holland Park into Phillimore

Gardens (perhaps detouring east into Phillimore Place to see No. 44, where Kenneth Grahame, author of *The Wind in the Willows,* lived from 1901 to 1908), then left again into Stafford Terrace to reach the home of the cartoonist, **Linley Sambourne House** ⑫. Step back to High Street and turn right. For a tranquil time-out, head past the gates into **Holland Park** ⑬. Exit the park at the gate by the tennis courts (near the Orangery) onto Ilchester Place, follow Melbury Road a few yards, and turn right onto Holland Park Road to reach **Leighton House** ⑭, home of the artist, Frederic Leighton. Late in the 19th century, Melbury Road was a veritable colony of artists, with perhaps the most well remembered now being Dickens's illustrator, Marcus Stone, who had No. 8 built in 1876. From here you could turn right onto Addison Road to see the Technicolor tiles rioting over Sir Ernest Debenham's Peacock House at No. 8 (he founded the eponymous Oxford Street department store). If you continue north, you reach plane tree–lined Holland Park Avenue, main thoroughfare of an expensive residential neighborhood that provides more pleasant strolling territory, if you feel you haven't walked enough.

TIMING   This walk is at least 4 mi long and is almost impossible to achieve without venturing inside somewhere. The best way to approach these neighborhoods is to treat Knightsbridge shopping and the South Kensington museums at one go. The rest of the tour works as a scenic walk on a fine day, because places to see—such as Leighton House and Kensington Palace—are less time-consuming than the V&A, Natural History, and Science museums. The parks are best in the growing seasons—early spring for crocuses and daffodils, late spring for azaleas and rhododendrons, and summer for roses—and in fall, when the foliage show easily rivals New England's. Kensington Gardens closes its gates at sundown, though you can get into Holland Park later in summer, thanks to the restaurant and the Open Air Theatre.

HOW TO GET THERE   There are many Tubes here, but which you choose will depend on which part you want. Knightsbridge on the Piccadilly Line, Kensington High Street on the District and Circle, and Holland Park on the Central Line are the best ones. The best buses between Kensington High Street and Knightsbridge are Buses 9, 10, and 52. From Kensington to Holland Park, get the 9, 27, or 28.

## What to See

❼ **Albert Memorial.** The Victorian era is epitomized in this neo-Gothic shrine to Prince Albert. The 14-foot bronze statue looks as if it were created yesterday, thanks to a brilliant restoration by English Heritage. During the war, the statue was deliberately blackened to avoid attracting Zeppelins to Kensington Palace, then the natural elements caused much damage. It took 1,000 20-page books of gold leaf to bring it to its present glory. Albert's grieving widow, Queen Victoria, had this elaborate confection erected on the spot where his Great Exhibition had stood a mere decade before his early death from typhoid fever in 1861. ✉ *Kensington Gore, opposite Royal Albert Hall, Hyde Park, Kensington SW7* Ⓤ *Knightsbridge.*

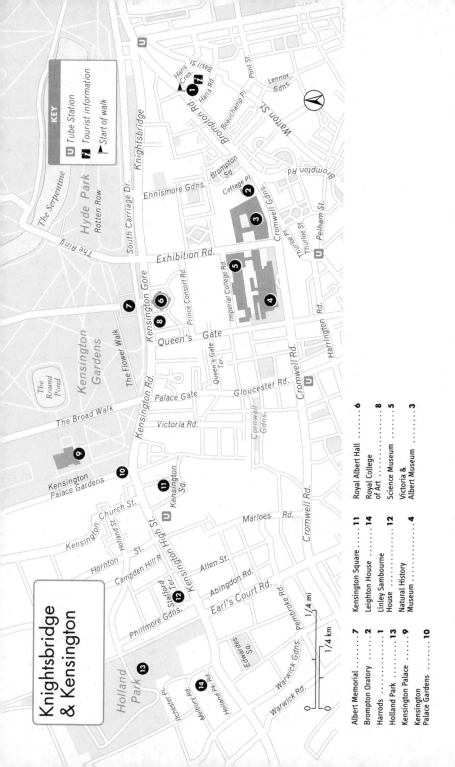

# Knightsbridge & Kensington

## KEY

- 🚇 Tube Station
- 🛈 Tourist information
- ▲ Start of walk

Albert Memorial ........ **7**
Brompton Oratory ...... **2**
Harrods ................ **1**
Holland Park .......... **13**
Kensington Palace ...... **9**
Kensington
Palace Gardens ...... **10**

Kensington Square ..... **11**
Leighton House ....... **14**
Linley Sambourne
House ............... **12**
Natural History
Museum ............. **4**

Royal Albert Hall ...... **6**
Royal College
of Art ............... **8**
Science Museum ...... **5**
Victoria &
Albert Museum ...... **3**

**❷ Brompton Oratory.** This is a late product of the mid-19th-century English Roman Catholic revival led by John Henry Cardinal Newman (1801–90), who established the oratory in 1884 and whose statue you see outside. Architect Herbert Gribble, a previously unknown 29-year-old, won the competition to design the place, an honor that you may conclude went to his head when you see the vast, incredibly ornate interior. It's punctuated by treasures far older than the church itself, like the giant *Twelve Apostles* in the nave, carved from Carrara marble by Giuseppe Mazzuoli in the 1680s and brought here from Siena's cathedral. ⊠ *Brompton Rd., Kensington SW7* ☎ *020/7808–0900* ⌨ *Free* ☉ *6:30 AM–8 PM. Services weekdays 7, 8, 10, 12:30, and 6; Sat. 7, 8, 10, and 6; Sun. 7, 8:30, 11, 12:30, 4:30, and 7* Ⓤ *S. Kensington.*

🖐 ▶ **❶ Harrods.** Just in case you don't notice it, this well-known shopping destination frames its domed terra-cotta Edwardian outline in thousands of white lights each night. The 15-acre Egyptian-owned store's sales weeks are world class, and inside it's as frenetic as a stock market floor. Its motto, *Omnia, omnibus, ubique* (Everything, for everyone, everywhere) is not too far from the truth. Visit the pet department, a highlight for children, and don't miss the extravagant Food Hall, with its stunning art nouveau tiling in the neighborhood of meat and poultry and continuing on in the fishmongers' territory, where its glory is rivaled by displays of the sea produce itself. This is the place to acquire your green-and-gold souvenir Harrods bag, as food prices are surprisingly competitive. ⊠ *87–135 Brompton Rd., Knightsbridge SW1* ☎*020/7730–1234* ⊕ *www.harrods.com* ☉ *Mon.–Sat. 10–7* Ⓤ *Knightsbridge.*

> **need a break?**
>
> **Pâtisserie Valerie** (⊠ 215 Brompton Rd., Knightsbridge SW3 ☎ 020/7832–9971), just down the road from Harrods, keeps in tune with your posh day out offering light café meals and splendid pastries and coffee.

🖐 **⓭ Holland Park.** The former grounds of the Jacobean Holland House opened to the public only in 1952. It was originally owned by Sir Walter Cope, the wealthy Chancellor of James I, and many treats are to be found within its 60 acres. Holland House itself was nearly flattened by World War II bombs, but the east wing remains, now incorporated into a youth hostel and providing a fantastical stage for the April–September **Open Air Theatre** (☎ 020/7602–7856 box office ⊕ www.operahollandpark.com). The glass-wall Orangery also survived to host art exhibitions and wedding receptions. Next door the former Garden Ballroom has become the upmarket Belvedere restaurant; nearby is a lovely café. From the Belvedere's terrace you see the formal Dutch Garden, planted by Lady Holland in the 1790s with the first English dahlias. North of that are woodland walks; lawns populated by peacocks, guinea fowl, and the odd, awkward emu; a fragrant rose garden; great banks of rhododendrons and azaleas, which bloom profusely in May; a well-supervised children's Adventure Playground; and even a Japanese water garden, legacy of the London Festival of Japan. If that's not enough, you can watch cricket on the Cricket Lawn on the south side or tennis on the several courts. ☉ *Daily dawn–dusk* Ⓤ *Holland Park or High St. Kensington.*

off the
beaten
path

**KENSAL GREEN CEMETERY** – Heralding itself as "London's first necropolis," this West London cemetery was established in 1832 and beats the more famous Highgate for atmosphere, if only because it's less populated by the living. Within its 77 acres are more freestanding mausoleums than in any other cemetery in Britain, some of them almost the size of small churches and most of them constructed while their future occupants were still alive. Those who balked at burial but couldn't afford a mausoleum of their own could opt for a spot in the catacombs, and these, with their stacks of moldering caskets, are a definite highlight for seekers of the macabre, though they can only be seen as part of a tour. In the cemetery you'll find the final resting places of the novelists Trollope, Thackeray, and Wilkie Collins; of the great 19th-century engineer Isambard Kingdom Brunel; and of Decimus Burton, Victorian architect of the Wellington Arch and the Kew Gardens greenhouses. ✉ *Harrow Rd., Kensal Green W10* ☎ *020/8969–0152, 020/7402–2749 tours* 🎫 *£5* ⊙ *Mon.–Sat. 9–4:30, Sun. 10–5; tours Sun. 2 PM, including catacombs on 1st and 3rd Sun. of month* Ⓤ *Kensal Green.*

★ ❾ **Kensington Palace.** The long history of this palace has been eclipsed in the last few years by—some might say its most famous inhabitant—the late Princess Diana. Still, royals have lived here in grand style for more than 300 years, and a walk through the palace's Royal Ceremonial Dress Collection and State Apartments (with an excellent audio-guide device as your companion) puts in perspective the protocol- and ceremony-filled royal lifestyle of the past. When King William III decided in the 17th century to make his palace at Kensington, 12 years of renovation to the original building, Nottingham House, were needed by Wren and Hawksmoor before the king and Queen Mary could move in. The palace continued to undergo ambitious refurbishment during the succeeding three reigns. By coincidence, these monarchs suffered rather ignominious deaths. William III fell off his horse when it stumbled on a molehill, and succumbed to pleurisy in 1702. Then, in 1714, Queen Anne suffered an apoplectic fit thought to have been brought on by overeating. Next, George I had a stroke, said to have been caused by "a surfeit of melons"—although en route to Hanover in 1727. Worst of all, in 1760, poor George II burst a blood vessel while on the toilet.

But the royal curtain here always rang up on a remarkable changing cast of characters, no more so than when the 18-year-old Princess Victoria of Kent was called from her bed in June 1837 by the Archbishop of Canterbury and the Lord Chamberlain. She was told that her uncle, William IV, was dead, and she was to be queen. The state rooms where Victoria had her ultrastrict upbringing (originally part of the King's Apartments) have been restored with items that belonged to Victoria and Prince Albert. The rooms seem pleasantly domestic compared with the formality of other palace rooms.

The State Apartments, especially the King's Apartments, reminded visitors none too subtly of the king's power. The King's Grand Staircase (the original entryway; plans are under way to make it the starting point of a visit to the rooms) is impressive, with superb trompe l'oeil paintings by William Kent that show courtiers looking down. As you progress from the Presence Chamber to the Privy Chamber (with its glorious Mortlake tapestries commissioned by Charles I) to the lavish Cupola Room, keep in mind that being admitted beyond the Presence Room was a mark of status. The Cupola Room, the glittering main state room, evokes Roman—and, by extension, Hanoverian—authority; the ceiling appears to be domed but is actually as flat as a pancake. These rooms lack chairs because only the monarch would have been seated. Elsewhere, look out for Tintorettos and Van Dycks among the canvases in the 96-foot-long King's Gallery, with its red damsk walls.

This palace is an essential stop for royalty vultures because it's the only one where you may actually catch a glimpse of the real thing. The Duke and Duchess of Gloucester and Prince and Princess Michael of Kent all have apartments here, as did the late Princess Margaret (at the time of this writing, plans called for her apartments to open for public view before 2005). In the palace's elegant Orangery, a tall-windowed brick building built for Queen Anne, you can buy an expensive cup of tea and relax in the festive hall where many Windsor birthday parties and weddings were held.

With garments dating to the 18th century, the **Royal Ceremonial Dress Collection** (viewed before the State Apartments) showcases a selection of state and occasional dresses, hats, and shoes worn by Britain's Royal Family. On permanent exhibition are 14 of Princess Diana's dazzling evening gowns. Other displays interpret the symbolism of ceremonial court dress and also show the labor that went into producing this attire. Some dazzlers of note are the coronation robes of Queen Mary and George V and a regal mantua—a 6-foot-wide court dress that recalls the truth that part of the aristocratic game was to impress your fellow courtiers with your clothes. ⊠ *The Broad Walk, Kensington Gardens, Kensington W8* ☎ *0870/751–5180 advance booking and information* ⊕ *www.hrp.org.uk* ⊠ *£10.80; joint tickets available with Hampton Court Palace and the Tower of London* ☉ *Mar.–Oct., daily 10–6; Nov.–Feb., daily 10–5; last admission 1 hr before closing* Ⓤ *High St. Kensington.*

⓾ **Kensington Palace Gardens.** Starting behind Kensington Palace, this is one of London's rare private roads, guarded and gated both here and at the Notting Hill Gate end. If you walk it, you can see why it earned the nickname "Millionaires' Row"—it's lined with palatial white-stucco houses designed by a selection of the best architects of the mid-19th century. The novelist William Makepeace Thackeray, author of *Vanity Fair,* died in 1863 at No. 2—which now houses the Israeli embassy. ⊠ *Kensington W8.*

⓫ **Kensington Square.** Laid out around the time William moved to Kensington Palace up the road, this is one of London's most venerable squares. A few early-18th-century houses remain, with Nos. 11 and 12 the oldest. ⊠ *Kensington W8.*

**need a break?** A separate building from the rest of Kensington Palace, the **Orangery** was built for Queen Anne. What could be a more perfect setting to take tea, beneath the bright white-and-gold sweeping arches and among the statuary, with the famous round boating pond close by? Light lunches, coffee, and kids' menus are also served daily 10–6. The Orangery is approached from the Broad Walk, Kensington Gardens. ✉ *Kensington Palace, Kensington W8* ☎ *020/7376–0239.*

**⑭ Leighton House.** This was the home of Frederic Lord Leighton (1830–96)— painter, sculptor, and president of the Royal Academy. After a complete refurbishment, the prize room here is the incredible Arab Hall. George Aitchison designed this Moorish fantasy in 1879 to show off Leighton's valuable 13th- to 17th-century Islamic tile collection, and, adorned with marble columns, dome, and fountain, it's exotic beyond belief. The rest of the rooms are more conventionally, stuffily Victorian, but they are sumptuous nonetheless and contain many paintings by Leighton, plus those of Edward Burne-Jones, John Millais, and other leading Pre-Raphaelites. ✉ *12 Holland Park Rd., Kensington W14* ☎ *020/7602–3316* ⊕ *www.rbkc.gov.uk* 🎟 *£3* ⊙ *Wed.–Mon. 11–5:30* Ⓤ *High St. Kensington.*

**⑫ Linley Sambourne House.** Filled with delightful Victorian and Edwardian antiques, fabrics, and paintings, the home of *Punch* cartoonist Edward Linley Sambourne in the 1870s is one of the most charming 19th-century London houses extant—small wonder that it was used in Merchant and Ivory's *A Room with a View.* An Italianate house, it was the scene for society parties when Anne Messel was in residence in the 1940s. Being Kensington, there's a royal connection, too: her son, Antony Armstrong-Jones, married the late Princess Margaret, and their son has preserved the connection by taking the name Viscount Linley. Admission is by guided tours, given by costumed actors. There are set tour times on weekends, and you can call in advance for a tour appointment on other days. ✉ *18 Stafford Terr., Kensington W8* ☎ *020/7602–3316* ⊕ *www.rbkc.gov.uk* 🎟 *£6* ⊙ *Guided tours weekends 10, 11:15, 1, 2:15, 3:30* Ⓤ *High St. Kensington.*

**④ Natural History Museum.** Architect Alfred Waterhouse had relief panels scattered across the outrageously ornate French Romanesque–style terra-cotta facade of this museum, depicting extant creatures to the left of the entrance, extinct ones to the right. The museum was in danger of becoming crusty itself and has invested millions in a superb modernization program, with more of the wow-power and interactives necessary to secure interest from younger visitors. The Darwin Centre takes you behind the scenes of the museum's collection. It showcases all the museum's creatures, great and small (all 22 million), in their pickling jars and vats, from a tiny Seychellian frog to the giant Komodo dragon lizard. It's a unique opportunity to see these wonders close up and witness the workings of a celebrated scientific research institution. There are 14 daily Explore tours from the main information desk.

You'll find, in the Creepy Crawlies Gallery, a super-enlarged scorpion so nightmarish that it makes tarantulas seem cute (8 out of 10 animal species, one learns here, are arthropods). Other wonderful bits include the Human

Biology Hall, which you arrive at through a birth-simulation chamber; the full-size blue whale; and the moving dinosaur diorama. The Earth Galleries are also unmissable, with ambitious exhibits about the structure of the planet: The Power Within, with an earthquake simulation, Restless Surface, and Visions of the Earth. In the basement, quieter, more absorbing hands-on activities are offered in the Investigate section, which allows you to do just that with actual objects, from old bones to bugs. ⊠ *Cromwell Rd., South Kensington SW7* ☎ *020/7942–5000* ⊕ *www.nhm.ac.uk* ⊠ *Free* ☉ *Mon.–Sat. 10–5:50, Sun. 11–5:50* Ⓤ *S. Kensington.*

**❻ Royal Albert Hall.** This domed, circular 8,000-seat auditorium (as well as the Albert Memorial, opposite) was made possible by the Victorian public, who donated funds for it. More money was raised, however, by selling 1,300 future seats at £100 apiece—not for the first night but for every night for 999 years. (Some descendants of purchasers still use the seats.) The Albert Hall is best known for its annual July–September Henry Wood Promenade Concerts (the "Proms"), with bargain-price standing (or promenading, or sitting-on-the-floor) tickets sold on the night of concert. ⊠ *Kensington Gore, Kensington SW7* ☎ *020/7589–8212* ⊕ *www. royalalberthall.co.uk* ⊠ *Prices vary with event* Ⓤ *S. Kensington.*

**❽ Royal College of Art.** Housed in a glass-dominated building designed by Sir Hugh Casson in 1973, the RCA provides great contrast with the Victoriana surrounding it, including the Albert Hall next door. Famous in the 1950s and 1960s for having David Hockney, Peter Blake, and Eduardo Paolozzi as students, the college is still one of the country's foremost art and design schools, and there's usually an exhibition, lecture, or event going on here that's open to the public. ⊠ *Kensington Gore, Kensington SW7* ☎ *020/7590–4125* ⊕ *www.rca.ac.uk* ⊠ *Free* ☉ *Weekdays 10–6; call to check times* Ⓤ *S. Kensington.*

Ⓒ **❺ Science Museum.** This, the third of the great South Kensington museums,
Fodor'sChoice stands behind the Natural History Museum in a far plainer building. It
★ has loads of hands-on exhibits, with entire schools of children apparently decanted inside to interact with them; but it is, after all, painlessly educational. Highlights include the Launch Pad gallery, which demonstrates basic scientific principles (try the plasma ball, where your hands attract "lightning"—if you can get them on it); *Puffing Billy,* the oldest steam locomotive in the world; and the actual *Apollo 10* capsule. But don't be mistaken in thinking this is kids'-only territory—there's plenty here for all ages. The latest and best offering for that is the Wellcome Wing, a space-age addition devoted to contemporary science, medicine, and technology, which also includes a 450-seat IMAX cinema. Note that there's a special charge for the cinema shows, and for the special exhibitions. ⊠ *Exhibition Rd., South Kensington SW7* ☎ *020/7942–4000* ⊕ *www. sciencemuseum.org.uk* ⊠ *Free* ☉ *Daily 10–6* Ⓤ *S. Kensington.*

★ Ⓒ **❸ Victoria & Albert Museum.** Recognizable by the copy of Victoria's imperial crown on the lantern above the central cupola, this institution is always referred to as the V&A. It's a huge museum, showcasing the applied arts of all disciplines, all periods, all nationalities, and all tastes, and it's a wonderful, generous place to get lost in, full of innovation and completely devoid of pretension. Prince Albert, Victoria's adored consort, was responsible for the genesis of this permanent version of the 1851 Great Exhibition, and his queen laid its foundation stone in her final public London appearance, in 1899. From the start, the V&A had an important role as a research institution, and that role continues today.

There are many beautiful diversions: one minute you're gazing on the Jacobean oak four-poster Great Bed of Ware (one of the V&A's most prized possessions, given that Shakespeare immortalized it in *Twelfth Night*) and the next you're in the celebrated Dress Collection, coveting a Jean Muir frock. As a whirlwind introduction, you could take a free, one-hour daily tour, or a 30-minute version on Wednesday evening. Otherwise, follow your own whims around the enormous space, but updated areas of the museum are worthy destinations. The British Galleries are an ambitious addition that heralds British art and design from 1500 to 1900. Here you'll see such major pieces as George Gilbert Scott's model of the Albert Memorial, and the first-ever English fork made in 1632, but you'll also discover fascinating facts behind the designs, such as the construction of a 16th-century bed and the best way for women in cumbersome hooped skirts to negotiate getting in and out of carriages. Throughout the galleries are interactive corners for all ages, where you can discover, design and build—from your own family emblem to period chairs. Free tours of the British Galleries depart daily from the rear of the Cromwell Road entrance at 12:30 and 2:30 and last one hour. The silver is amassed in the Whiteley Silver Galleries, opened in October 2002, which bring more than 500 shining examples together. From ancient medieval reliquaries to the Napoleonic period, to contemporary pieces, it's a stunning collection, and the largest in the United Kingdom.

Unchanged, but still spectacular, is the Glass Gallery, where a collection spanning four millennia is reflected between room-size mirrors under designer Danny Lane's breathtaking glass balustrade. Don't miss the pure art, too: the Raphael Galleries house seven massive cartoons the painter completed in 1516 for his Sistine Chapel tapestries (now in the Pinoteca of the Vatican Museums in Rome). The shop is the museum in microcosm, and quite the best place to buy art nouveau or arts-and-crafts gifts. ⊠ *Cromwell Rd., South Kensington SW7* ☏ *020/7942-2000* ⊕ *www. vam.ac.uk* ⊠ *Free* ☉ *Thurs.–Tues. 10–5:45; Wed. 10–10; tours daily at 10:30, 11:30, 1:30, 3:30 and Wed. at 7:30 PM* Ⓤ *S. Kensington.*

---

**need a break?** Candlelit dinners on Wednesday nights, traditional roasts on Sunday, occasional live music accompaniments, daily brunch, breakfast and lunch—the **New Restaurant at the V&A** (⊠ Cromwell Rd., Kensington SW7 ☏ 020/7581–2159) serves good value food. And if the weather's fine, you can take a picnic into the Italian Pirelli Gardens.

---

## HYDE PARK TO NOTTING HILL

The royal parks of Hyde Park and Kensington Gardens are among London's unique features: great swaths of green in the middle of the city, where it really is possible to escape from London's fast pace. Although some of this territory was covered in the Knightsbridge, Kensington, and Holland Park tour, this is another option for visiting the royal parks (without the museums) that also takes in Portobello Road and Notting Hill, and for seeing Londoners relax. Although it's probably been centuries since any major royal had a casual stroll here, these parks remain the property of the Crown, and it was the Crown that saved them from being devoured by the city's late-18th-century growth spurt. North of the pair of parks—which are separate entities, although the boundary is virtually invisible—lies Bayswater. Farther northwest lies Notting Hill, a trendsetting square mile of multiethnicity, music, and markets, with lots of restaurants to see and be seen in and younger, more egalitarian, and adventurous modern-art galleries. The style-watching media has dubbed the local residents Notting Hillbillies. The whole area has mushroomed around one of the world's great antiques markets, Portobello Road.

**a good walk**

Where else would you enter **Hyde Park** but at **Hyde Park Corner** ▶ ? The most impressive of the many entrances is the Hyde Park Screen by Apsley House, usually called Decimus Burton's Gateway because it was he who designed this triple-arch monument in 1828. The next gate along to the north, a gaudy unicorns-and-lions-rampant number, was a 90th-birthday gift to Elizabeth the Queen Mother and is therefore the Queen Mother's Gate. Follow the southern perimeter along the sand track called Rotten Row, used by the Household Cavalry, which lives at the Knightsbridge Barracks to the left.

Follow Rotten Row west to the Serpentine. Just by the Lido is the Princess Diana Memorial Fountain. When you pass its Bridge you leave Hyde Park and enter **Kensington Gardens** and its **Serpentine Gallery.** En route to the formal garden at the end of the Long Water, the Fountains, you pass statues of Peter Pan and the horse and rider called "Physical Energy." Continuing westward, you reach Round Pond and Kensington Palace. Follow the Broad Walk north past the playground (where the Princess Diana Memorial Playground is located) on the left and leave the park by Black Lion Gate; you are almost opposite Queensway, a rather peculiar, cosmopolitan street of ethnic confusion, late-night cafés and restaurants, a skating rink, and the Whiteleys shopping-and-movie mall. Turn left at the end into Westbourne Grove, however, and you've entered **Notting Hill**; you'll reach the famous **Portobello Road** after a few blocks. Turn left for the Saturday antiques market and shops, right to reach the Westway and the flea market. For Notting Hill's grandest houses, stroll over to Lansdowne Road, Lansdowne Crescent, and Lansdowne Square—two blocks west of Kensington Park Row.

TIMING    This is a route that changes vastly on weekends. Saturday is Portobello Road's most fun day, so you may prefer to start at the end and work backward, using the parks for relaxation after your shopping exertions. Do the same on Friday if you're a flea-market fan. Sunday, the Hyde Park and Kensington Gardens railings all along Bayswater Road are hung with very bad art, which may slow your progress; this is also prime perambulation day for locals. Whatever your priorities, this is a long walk if you explore every corner, with the perimeter of the two parks alone covering a good 4 mi and about half as far again around the remainder

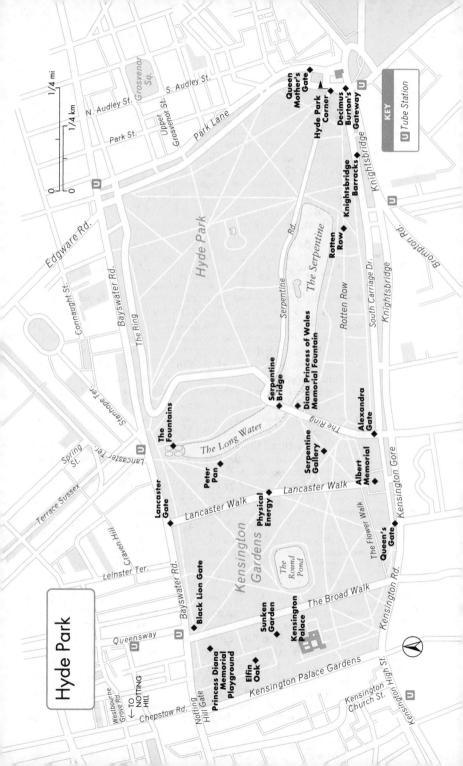

# Hyde Park

**KEY**

Ⓤ *Tube Station*

1/4 mi

1/4 km

Grosvenor Sq.

N. Audley St.
S. Audley St.
Upper St.
Park St.
Park Lane

Edgware Rd.
Bayswater Rd.
Connaught St.
The Ring

Hyde Park

Queen Mother's Gate
Hyde Park Corner
Decimus Burton's Gateway

Knightsbridge Barracks
Knightsbridge
Brompton Rd.

Rotten Row
The Serpentine
Serpentine Rd.
Rotten Row
South Carriage Dr.
Knightsbridge

Stanhope Ter.

Serpentine Bridge
Diana Princess of Wales Memorial Fountain

Alexandra Gate

The Fountains
The Long Water

Spring St.
Lancaster Ter.

Peter Pan
Serpentine Gallery

Albert Memorial
Kensington Gore

The Ring

Terrace Sussex

Lancaster Gate
Lancaster Walk
Lancaster Walk
Lancaster Walk

Physical Energy
The Flower Walk
Queen's Gate

Leinster Ter.

Kensington Gardens

The Round Pond

Kensington Rd.

Bayswater Rd.
Black Lion Gate

The Broad Walk

Queensway
Sunken Garden
Kensington Palace

Princess Diana Memorial Playground
Elfin Oak
Kensington Palace Gardens

Westbourne Grove Rd.
TO NOTTING HILL
Chepstow Rd.
Notting Hill Gate
Kensington Church St.
Kensington High St.

of the route. You could cut out a lot of park without missing out on essential sights and walk the whole thing in a brisk three hours.

HOW TO GET THERE For Hyde Park and Kensington Gardens, get off the Central Line at Queensway or Lancaster Gate, or enter the park from Hyde Park Corner on the Piccadilly Line. If you want Portobello Market and environs, the best Tube stop is Ladbroke Grove or Westbourne Park (Hammersmith and City lines), and then ask directions; the Notting Hill stop on the District, Circle, and Central lines is also an option. Buses for the area include Buses 12 from Oxford Circus, 70 from South Kensington, and 94 from Piccadilly Circus for seeing anything off Bayswater Road or Buses 27 from Paddington and Kensington High Street, 28 from Kensington High Street, and 52 from Victoria and Knightsbridge for penetrating the depths of Notting Hill.

## What to See

★ ☺ ☞ **Hyde Park.** Along with the smaller St. James's and Green parks to the east, Hyde Park started as Henry VIII's hunting grounds. He more or less stole the land for his own personal pleasure from the monks at Westminster in the 1536 Dissolution of the Monasteries. James I was more generous and allowed the public in at the beginning of the 17th century, as long as they were "respectably dressed." Nowadays, as you can see if you're here in summer, you may wear whatever you like—a bathing suit will do, particularly if you want to swim at the Lido. Along its south side runs **Rotten Row.** It was Henry VIII's royal path to the hunt—hence the name, a corruption of *route du roi.* It's still used by the Household Cavalry, who live at the **Knightsbridge Barracks**—a high-rise and a long, low, ugly red block—to the left. This is the brigade that mounts the guard at Buckingham Palace, and you can see them leave to perform this duty in full regalia, plumed helmet and all, at around 10:30, or await the return of the ex-guard about noon. On the south side of the Serpentine, by the Lido, is the site of the **Diana Princess of Wales Memorial Fountain.** Of oval stone with both calm and turbulent cascading water features, it has been designed by Kathryn Gustafason to reflect the moods of a modern princess. Its proposed completion is summer 2004. Sunday's

Fodor'sChoice **Speaker's Corner** in the park near Marble Arch is an unmissable spectacle of vehement, sometimes comical, and always entertaining orators. From June to August, Hyde Park is the venue for the Royal Parks Summer Festival with live jazz evenings, opera, and plays all over the park. ☎ 020/7298–2100 ⊕ *www.royalparks.gov.uk* ☼ *Daily 5 AM–midnight* Ⓤ *Hyde Park Corner, Lancaster Gate, Marble Arch, or Knightsbridge.*

☺ **Kensington Gardens.** More formal than neighboring Hyde Park, Kensington Fodor'sChoice Gardens was first laid out as palace grounds. The paved Italian garden ★ at the top of the Long Water, the **Fountains,** is a reminder of this, though of course **Kensington Palace** itself is the main clue to the gardens' royal status, with its early-19th-century Sunken Garden north of the palace complex, complete with a living tunnel of lime trees (i.e., linden trees) and golden laburnum. Several landmarks are worth looking out for: George Frampton's 1912 *Peter Pan* is a bronze of the boy who lived on an island in the Serpentine and never grew up and whose creator, J. M. Barrie, lived at 100 Bayswater Road, not 500 yards from here. Southwest of Peter at the intersection of several paths is George Frederick Watts's 1904 bronze of a muscle-bound horse and rider, entitled *Physical Energy*. The **Round Pond** acts as a magnet for model-boat enthusiasts and duck feeders. By the children's playground on the north of the Broad Walk toward Black Lion Gate is the remains of a tree carved with scores of tiny woodland creatures, Ivor Innes's *Elfin Oak*. The **Princess Diana Memorial Playground** is a fabulous enclosed space, which besides the usual play apparatus has specially designed structures and areas on the theme of Barrie's Neverland. Hook's ship, crocodiles, "jungles" of foliage, and islands of sand provide a fantasy land for kids. ⊕ *www.royalparks.gov. uk* ⊙ *Daily dawn–dusk* Ⓤ *Lancaster Gate or Queensway.*

**Notting Hill.** Currently the best place to wear sunglasses, smoke Gauloises, and contemplate the latest issue of *Wallpaper,* "the Hill" is much beloved of London's celebrities and fashion set. Centered on the Portobello Road antiques market, this district is bordered to the west by Lansdowne Crescent—lined by the Hill's poshest 19th-century terraced row houses—and to the east by Chepstow Road, with Notting Hill Gate and Westbourne Grove Road marking south and north boundaries. In between, Rastafarians rub elbows with wealthy young Brits (a.k.a. "Trustafarians," urban hippies living off trust funds), and residents like fashion designer Rifat Ozbek, CNN's Christiane Amanpour, and historian Lady Antonia Fraser can be spotted at the chic shops on Westbourne Grove and in the lively bars and cafés on Kensington Park Road. There are no historic sites here, so explore just to savor the flavor. Ⓤ *Notting Hill Gate or Ladbroke Grove.*

**Portobello Road.** Tempted by tassels, looking for a 19th-century snuff spoon, an ancient print of North Africa, or a dashingly deco frock (just don't believe the dealer when he says the Vionnet label just fell off), or hunting for a gracefully Georgian silhouette of the Earl of Chesterfield? Head to Portobello Road, world famous for its Saturday antiques market (arrive before 9 AM to find the real treasures-in-the-trash; after 10, the crowds pack in wall to wall). Actually, the Portobello Market is three markets: antiques, "fruit and veg," and a flea market. The street begins at Notting Hill Gate, though the antiques stalls start a couple of blocks north, around Chepstow Villas. Lining the sloping street are also dozens of antiques shops and indoor markets, open most days—in fact, serious collectors will want to do Portobello on a weekday, when they can explore the 90-some antiques and art stores in relative peace. Where the road levels off, around Elgin Crescent, youth culture and a vibrant neighborhood life kick in, with all manner of interesting small stores and restaurants interspersed with the fruit and vegetable market. This continues to the Westway overpass ("flyover" in British), where London's best flea market (high-class, vintage, antique, and secondhand clothing; jewelry; and junk) happens Friday and Saturday, then on up to Golborne Road. There's a strong West Indian flavor to Notting Hill, with a Trinidad-style Carnival centered along Portobello Road on the August bank-holiday weekend. Ⓤ *Notting Hill Gate or Ladbroke Grove.*

**Serpentine Gallery.** Influential on the trendy art circuit, this gallery hangs several exhibitions of modern work a year, often very avant-garde and always worth a look. It overlooks the west bank of the **Serpentine**, a beloved lake, much frequented in summer, when the south-shore Lido resembles a beach and the water is dotted with hired rowboats. Walk the bank, and you will soon reach the picturesque, stone **Serpentine Bridge**, built in 1826 by George Rennie, which marks the boundary between Hyde Park and Kensington Gardens. ⊠ *Kensington Gardens, Kensington W2* ☎ *020/7402–6075* ⊕ *www.serpentinegallery.org* 🎫 *Free* ☉ *Daily 10–6; call to check if open* Ⓤ *Lancaster Gate.*

# REGENT'S PARK & HAMPSTEAD

Regent's Park and Hampstead in North London contain some of the prettiest and most rural parts of the city, as well as some of the most aristocratic architecture in the world (thanks to the terraces and town houses of John Nash, 19th-century design whiz) and some important historical sights. For the sheer pleasure of idle exploring, these city districts are hard to beat. All told, this section covers a large area. It starts from the Georgian houses superimposed on medieval Maryburne (Marylebone); continues around John Nash's Regency facades and his park; stretches on into North London's canal-side youth center; climbs up the hill to the city's chic, expensive "village"; and finishes, fittingly, at its most famous cemetery in yet another old village.

Marylebone Road (pronounced "Marra-le-bun" after Queen Mary *le bon*) these days is remarkable mostly for its permanent traffic jam, some of it heading to Madame Tussaud's. At the east end is the first part of John Nash's impressive Regent's Park scheme, the elegantly curvaceous Park Crescent (1812–18), which Nash planned as a full circus at the northern end of his ceremonial route from St. James's. Like most of the other Nash houses around the park, it was wrecked during World War II, reconstructed, and rebuilt behind the repaired facade in the 1960s. Northeast of the park, Camden Town is a lively neighborhood whose activity centers around the canalside locks and nearby shops, drawing a large number of teens and twenties.

The cliché about Hampstead is that it is just like a pretty little village—albeit one with designer shops, expensive French delicatessens, restaurants, cafés, cinemas, and so on. In fact, like so many other London neighborhoods, Hampstead did start as a separate village, when plague-bedeviled medieval Londoners fled the city to this clean hilltop 4 mi away. By the 18th century, its reputation for cleanliness had spread so far that its water was being bottled and sold to the hoi polloi down the hill as the Perrier of its day. That was the beginning of Hampstead's heyday as an artistic and literary retreat attracting many famous writers, painters, and musicians to its leafy lanes—as it still does. Just strolling around here is rewarding: not only are the streets incredibly picturesque, they also offer some of London's best Georgian buildings.

*Numbers in the text correspond to numbers in the margin and on the Regent's Park & Hampstead map.*

a good
walk

Begin at the Tube station whose name will thrill the Sherlock Holmes fan: Baker Street—the **Sherlock Holmes Museum** ❶ ⌐ is at No. 221B, of course. Turn left and follow the line of tour buses past **Madame Tussaud's** ❷ and the **London Planetarium**; then go to the end of Harley Street—an English synonym for private (as opposed to state-funded) medicine because it's lined with the consulting rooms of the country's top specialist doctors—to Park Crescent and, across the street, **Regent's Park** ❸. Enter along the Outer Circle and turn left on Chester Road. Straight ahead are Queen Mary's Gardens, the lake, and the **Regent's Park Open-Air Theatre** ❹.

If you want to take a look at the most elegant street in London, head straight ahead up Chester Road to **Cumberland Terrace** (1827), the porticoed white-stucco structure that overlooks the eastern edge of the park like a Grecian temple. This is one of architect Joseph Nash's most famous Regency-era creations. His most elegant urban stage set, however, is reached by continuing two blocks south, where **Chester Place** (1825) debouches into a cream-color, magnificent triumphal arch, with its name emblazoned across the top of the arch. Nash aficionados will want to continue eight blocks to the north to see Park Village East and West, two streets that are lined with enchanting "villas" in the 19th-century mode.

If you haven't made this architectural detour outside the park to see Nash's buildings, continue within the park from Regent's Park Open-Air Theatre along Chester Road until the Broad Walk, and then make a left. Look west past the mock-Tudor prefab tearoom for one of London's rare, uninterrupted open vistas toward the London Central Mosque, and then continue on to the **London Zoo** ❺. From here, you can take a round-trip detour on the water bus and spy on the back gardens along the **Grand Union Canal** (which everyone calls the Regent's Canal) to Little Venice. This canal is flanked with enormous white wedding-cake houses, separated from the banks with willow trees and long gardens, making it a beautiful strolling location. Alternatively you can walk along the whole canal, past the animals in the zoo down to Camden Lock, a vibrant market and café quarter.

North of the zoo, cross Prince Albert Road to the man-made Primrose Hill, a high point (literally, at 206 feet) with a brilliant panoramic view of London, day or night. Heading east from here (the easiest route is Regent's Park Road, then left down Parkway, past the **Jewish Museum** ❻) brings you to the center of Camden Town. Turn left at the foot of Parkway, and battle your way north along Camden High Street (actually, the crowds are unbearably dense only on the weekend) to **Camden Lock** ❼. From here you can keep going east—if you take the canal towpath it's more scenic—to King's Cross, and the **London Canal Museum** ❽.

Back at the Lock, you could walk up Haverstock Hill or travel three stops on the Northern Line from Camden Town Tube station (make sure you take the Edgware branch) to Hampstead. Cross High Street to Heath Street and turn right to Church Row, said to be London's most complete Georgian street. At the west end is the 1745 church of St. John's, where the painter John Constable is buried. Just south of the Tube station, Flask Walk is another beautiful street, narrow and shop-lined at the High Street end, then widening after you pass the Flask—the pub it is named for. This place has a pretty courtyard and was described by Samuel Richardson in his 18th-century novel *Clarissa* as "a place where second-rate persons are to be found, often in a swinish condition." Nearby Well Walk was where a spring surfaced, its place now marked by a dried-up fountain. John Constable lived here, as well as John Keats (in, of course, **Keats House** ⑨) and, later, D. H. Lawrence. Head some blocks north to regal **Fenton House,** a National Trust property with some lovely gardens; then amble around the corner and alongside Fenton House to reach Admiral's Walk, where you may gaze at the house with a roof that echoes the quarterdeck of a ship immortalized in *Mary Poppins.* About 15-minutes' walk farther along East Heath Road you'll find the Gothic manse that inspired Hell Hall in *One Hundred and One Dalmatians.* You now have two choices: if you've had enough fresh air, walk all the way down Fitzjohn's Avenue and visit the **Freud Museum** ⑩, where Sigmund Freud lived and worked; Beatles aficionados will head posthaste, instead, to the fabled **Abbey Road Studios** ⑪. If you've been blessed with a clear London day, take advantage and follow the long walk northeast up Spaniards Road, traversing **Hampstead Heath** to Hampstead Lane, to the bucolic oasis of **Kenwood House** ⑫, well worth a visit for its setting alone. To the east of Hampstead, and also topping a hill, is the former village of Highgate, which has some fine houses, especially along its Georgian High Street, and retains its peaceful period surroundings. But it's most famous for **Highgate Cemetery** ⑬. Cricketing fans might want to pass up the Heath in favor of the gentleman's game—cricket—at the celebrated **Lord's Cricket Ground & Museum** ⑭.

TIMING   You may well want to divide this tour into segments, using the Northern Line of the Tube to jump between the Regent's Park and Hampstead neighborhoods. It will take you at least three or even four hours to cover the full length of this walk on foot.

There are several approaches. In summer, with children, you might consider a North London jaunt in Regent's Park, the zoo, Camden Lock, and a canal trip, a day's worth of sightseeing. If you wanted to add Madame Tussaud's and the planetarium, you'd have a frenetic day, especially in summer, because you might be in line for over an hour. You could start a summer's day without children at the other end, with Hampstead Heath, Kenwood House, a stroll around Hampstead, and a pub or two on the agenda. Teenagers and youth might want to spend all day shopping in Camden Town. Both Camden and Hampstead are usually fairly busy during the week as well, for in addition to being shopping havens they are residential neighborhoods. Bear in mind that much of this itinerary may be washed out by rain.

HOW TO GET   For Regent's Park, go to Regent's Park Tube station (on the Bakerloo
THERE   Line), though Camden Town on the Northern Line, with a walk up Parkway, is almost as close. Hampstead is best reached from the Hampstead Tube stop. Make sure you get on the right branch of the Northern Line— you want the Edgware branch. Buses for Regent's Park include Buses 27 from Paddington, and 30 from Marble Arch along the Marylebone

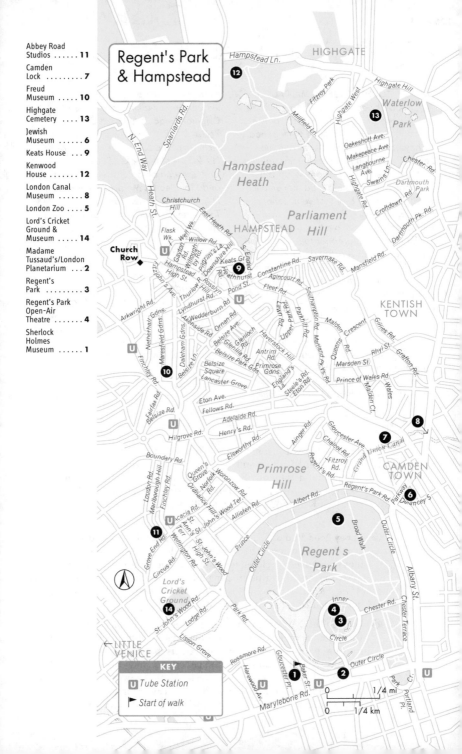

# Regent's Park & Hampstead

HIGHGATE

Hampstead Ln.

Fitzroy Park

Highgate Hill

Highgate West

Waterlow Park

Spaniards Rd.

Millfield Ln.

Oakeshott Ave.

Makepeace Ave.

Langbourne Ave.

Chester Rd.

Dartmouth Rd.

Swains Ln.

Highgate Rd.

Croftdown Rd.

Dartmouth Pk. Rd.

Hampstead Heath

Parliament Hill

KENTISH TOWN

N. End Way

Heath St.

Christchurch Hill

East Heath Rd.

HAMPSTEAD

Flask Wk.

Well Wk.

Willow Rd.

Church Row

Keats Gr.

Constantine Rd.

Savernake Rd.

Mansfield Rd.

Garton Wk.

Downshire Hill

S. End

Mansfield Rd.

Fitzjohn's Ave.

Hampstead High St.

Willoughby Rd.

Pilgrim's La.

Rosslyn Hill

Pond St.

Parkhurst

Fleet Rd.

Agincourt Rd.

Southampton Rd.

Gilles Rd.

Rhyl St.

Grafton Rd.

Arkwright Rd.

Netherhall Gdns.

Thurlow Rd.

Lyndhurst Rd.

Wedderburn Rd.

Ornan Rd.

Haverstock Hill

Upper Park Rd.

Malden Crescent

Queens Crescent

Maresfield Gdns.

Daleham Gdns.

Akenside Rd.

Belsize Ave.

Glenloch

Glenilla Rd.

Belsize Park Gdns.

Antrim Rd.

Primrose Gdns.

England's La.

Steele's Rd.

Eton Rd.

Marsden St.

Prince of Wales Rd.

Malden Cr.

Finchley Rd.

Belsize Ln.

Belsize Square

Lancaster Grove

Eton Ave.

Fellows Rd.

Adelaide Rd.

Henry's Rd.

Ainger Rd.

CAMDEN TOWN

Grand Union Canal

Fairfax Rd.

Belsize Rd.

Hilgrove Rd.

Gloucester Ave.

Chalcot Rd.

Fitzroy Rd.

Regent's Rd.

Regent's Park Rd.

Parkway

Delancey St.

Boundary Rd.

Queen's Grove

Norfolk Rd.

Ordnance Hill

Wood Ter.

Alliston Rd.

Albert Rd.

Primrose Hill

Outer Circle

Broad Walk

Outer Circle

Albany St.

Chester Terrace

Loudon Rd.

Marlborough Hill

Finchley Rd.

Acacia Rd.

St. Ann's

St. John's High St.

Wellington Rd.

Grove End Rd.

Circus Rd.

St. John's Wood Rd.

Prince

Albert Rd.

Regent's Park

Inner Circle

Chester Rd.

Lord's Cricket Ground

Lodge Rd.

Park Rd.

Lisson Grove

Outer Circle

Portland Pl.

Rossmore Rd.

Gloucester Pl.

Baker St.

LITTLE VENICE

Harewood Ave.

Marylebone Rd.

### KEY

Ⓤ *Tube Station*

▶ *Start of walk*

0 — 1/4 mi

0 — 1/4 km

# CloseUp

## A TRIP TO ABBEY ROAD

FOR COUNTLESS BEATLEMANIACS *and baby boomers, No. 3 Abbey Road is one of the most beloved spots in London. Here, outside the legendary Abbey Road Studios, is the most famous zebra crossing in the world, immortalized on the Beatles' 1969 Abbey Road album. This footpath became a mod monument when, on August 8 of that year, John, Paul, George, and Ringo posed—walking symbolically away from the recording facility—for photographer Iain Macmillan for the famous cover shot. In fact, the recording facility's Studio 2 is where the Beatles recorded their entire output, from "Love Me Do" onward, including Sgt. Pepper's Lonely Hearts Club Band (early 1967).*

*Today, tourists like to Beatle-ize themselves by taking the same sort of photo, but be careful: rushing cars make Abbey Road a dangerous intersection. One of the best— and safer—ways Beatle-lovers can enjoy*

*the history of the group is to take one of the smashing walking tours offered by the* **Original London Walks** *(☎ 020/ 7624–3978 ⊕ www.walks.com), including* **"The Beatles In-My-Life Walk"** *(11:20 AM at the Baker Street Underground on Saturday and Tuesday) and* **"The Beatles Magical Mystery Tour"** *(10:55 AM at Underground Exit 3, Tottenham Court Road, on Sunday and Thursday), which cover nostalgic landmark Beatles spots in the city.*

*Abbey Road is in the elegant neighborhood of St. John's Wood, a 10-minute ride on the Tube from central London. Take the Jubilee line to the St. John's Wood Tube stop, head southwest three blocks down Grove End Road, and be prepared for a heart-stopping vista right out of Memory Lane.*

Road or Buses 13 from Oxford Circus, 82 from Victoria, 113 and 139 from Oxford Circus, and 274 from Marble Arch to Lord's Cricket Ground, and the zoo. For Hampstead, catch the 168 from Russell Square or Euston. The 210 bus runs between Hampstead Heath, north end, past Kenwood to Highgate village.

### What to See

⓫ **Abbey Road Studios.** The most famous Beatles site in London, this is the fabled studio where the Fab Four recorded their entire output. The studios themselves are closed to the public, but many travelers journey here to see the famous traffic crossing used by the group on the cover of their *Abbey Road* album. ⊠ *3 Abbey Rd., Hampstead NW8* ⊕ *www. abbeyroad.co.uk* Ⓤ *St. John's Wood.*

🐾 ❼ **Camden Lock.** What was once just a pair of locks on the Grand Union Canal has now developed into London's third-most-visited tourist attraction. It's a vast honeycomb of markets that sell just about everything, but mostly crafts, clothing (vintage, ethnic, and young designer), and antiques. Here, especially on a weekend, the crowds are dense, young, and relentless. You may tire of the identical T-shirts, pants, boots, vintage wear, and cheap leather on their backs and in the shops. Camden does have its charms, though. Gentrification has layered over a once over-whelmingly Irish neighborhood, vestiges of which coexist with the youth culture. Charm is evident in sections of the market itself as well as in other markets, including the bustling fruit-and-vegetable market on Inverness Street. Along the canal are some stylish examples of Nicholas Grimshaw architecture (architect of Waterloo Station), as well as the MTV offices with their designer graffiti. ⊠ *Camden Lock, Camden High St., Camden Town NW1* ⊕ *www.camdenlock.net* ☉ *Weekends* Ⓤ *Camden Town or Chalk Farm.*

**need a break?**

You will not go hungry in Camden Town. Among the countless cafés, bars, pubs, and restaurants, the following stand out for good value and good food: Within the market at Camden Lock there are various stalls selling the usual hot dogs, but you can also find good Chinese takeout, and other ethnic food if you don't mind standing as you eat outdoors, or finding a canalside bench. Alternatively, **Marine Ices** (⊠ 8 Haverstock Hill, Camden Town NW3 ☎ 020/7482–9003) has a window dispensing ice cream to strollers, and pasta, pizza, and sundaes inside. **Bar Gansa** (⊠ 2 Inverness St., Camden Town NW1 ☎ 020/7267–8909) offers tapas—small dishes for sharing among other larger Spanish favorites, such as paella. **Wagamama** (⊠ 3 Jamestown Rd., Camden Town NW1 ☎ 020/7428–0751) has long bench tables with high stools, where you can eat utilitarian bowls of noodles of every description. It's great, filling food that pleases kids, too.

**Fenton House.** This is Hampstead's oldest surviving house. Now a National Trust property, it has an interesting collection of antiques and period interiors, along with some 17th-century–style gardens. Baroque enthusiasts can join a tour of the large collection of keyboard instruments, given by the curator, and there's a summer series of concerts on these very same instruments on Thursday evenings. Call ahead for details. ⊠ *Hampstead Grove, Hampstead NW3* ☎ *020/7435–3471* ⊕ *www.nationaltrust.org.uk* 🎫 *£4.60, joint ticket with 2 Willow Road £6.40* ☉ *Mar., weekends 2–5; Apr.–Oct., Wed.–Fri. 2–5, weekends 11–5* Ⓤ *Hampstead.*

❿ **Freud Museum.** The father of psychoanalysis lived here for a year, between his escape from Nazi persecution in his native Vienna in 1938 and his death in 1939. Many of his possessions emigrated with him and were set up by his daughter, Anna (herself a pioneer of child psychoanalysis), as a shrine to her father's life and work. Four years after Anna's death in 1982 the house was opened as a museum. It replicates Freud's famous consulting rooms, particularly through the presence of *the couch.* You'll find Freud-related books, lectures, and study groups here, too. ⊠ *20 Maresfield Gardens, Hampstead NW3* ☎ *020/7435–2002* ⊕ *www.freud.org. uk* 🎫 *£5* ☉ *Wed.–Sun. noon–5* Ⓤ *Swiss Cottage or Finchley Rd.*

☾ **Hampstead Heath.** For an escape from the ordered prettiness of Hampstead, head to the heath—a wild park, where wolves once roamed and washerwomen laundered clothes for aristocrats—which spreads for

FodorśChoice
★

miles to the north. From its top, at Spaniards Road, there are stunning views for miles to the city. There are signposted paths, but these can be confusing. Maps are available from Hampstead newsagents and book-shops, or the information center at the Gospel Oak entrance, Gordon House Road, where you can also get details about the history of the Heath, and the flora and fauna growing there. Close by here, walking east along the same road, a historic pub stands at the northwest edge, at the toll-house between Spaniards Road and Hampstead Lane. The **Spaniards Inn** (✉ Spaniards Rd., Hampstead NW3 ☎ 020/8731–6571) is little changed since the early 18th century, when (they say) the notorious high-wayman Dick Turpin hung out here. Keats also drank here, as did Shel-ley and Byron. ✉ *Hampstead NW3 ☎ 020/7482–7073 Heath Information Centre ⊕ www.cityoflondon.gov.uk Ⓤ Gospel Oak or Hampstead Heath Silverlink line from Highbury & Islington underground for south of the Heath; Hampstead underground, then walk through Flask Walk, Well Walk for east of the Heath; Golders Green underground, then bus 210, 268 to Whitestone Pond for north and west of the Heath.*

★ ☕ ⓭ **Highgate Cemetery.** Not the oldest cemetery in London, but certainly this is the most celebrated. Such was its popularity that the acreage in-creased across the other side of the road, and this additional east side contains probably the most visited grave, of Karl Marx, where you also find George Eliot, among other famous names. The older west side was once part of a mansion owned by Sir William Ashurst, Lord Mayor of London in 1693. When the cemetery was consecrated in 1839, Victo-rians came from miles around to enjoy the architecture and the view. Both are impressive, from the moment you enter the grand wrought-iron gateway into a sweeping courtyard for horses and carriages. The highlight of the 20-acre site is the colonnaded Egyptian Avenue leading to the Circle of Lebanon, built around an ancient cypress tree—a legacy of Ashurst's garden—with catacombs skirting the edges. By the 1970s, it was unkempt and neglected until a group of volunteers, the Friends of Highgate Cemetery, undertook the huge upkeep. Tours are arranged by the Friends, and among the numerous beautiful stone angels and beloved animals—memorials once hidden by wild brambles—they will show you the most notable graves, which include Michael Faraday and Christina Rossetti, each with their own, sometimes quirky, history. Chil-dren under eight are not admitted; nor are cell phones and video cam-eras. ✉ *Swains La., Highgate N6 ☎ 020/8340–1834 ⊕ www.highgate-cemetery.org 🎫 Prices on request ☉ Call for opening times and visitor information; hrs vary according to whether a funeral service is scheduled Ⓤ Archway, then bus 210 to Highgate Village.*

❻ **Jewish Museum.** This museum tells a comprehensive history of the Jews in London from Norman times, though the bulk of the exhibits date from the end of the 17th century (when Cromwell repealed the laws against Jewish settlement) and later. The Ceremonial Art Gallery holds a col-lection of rare pieces, and the Audio Visual Gallery follows London Jew-ish life from cradle to grave. The museum's branch at the Sternberg Centre in Finchley covers social history, with changing exhibitions, and permanent exhibits and tape archives on the Holocaust, in the words of survivors.

✉ *Raymond Burton House, 129 Albert St., Camden Town NW1* ☎ *020/ 7284–1997* ⊕ *www.jewishmuseum.org.uk* 🖃 *£3.50* ☉ *Sun. 10–5, Mon.–Thurs. 10–4* Ⓤ *Camden Town* ✉ *Sternberg Centre, 80 East End Rd., Finchley N3* ☎ *020/8349–1143* 🖃 *£2* ☉ *Sun. 10:30–4:30, Mon.–Thurs. 10:30–5* Ⓤ *Finchley Central.*

**❾ Keats House.** Here you can see the plum tree under which the young Romantic poet composed "Ode to a Nightingale," many of his original manuscripts, his library, and other possessions he managed to acquire in his short life. It was in February 1820 that Keats coughed blood up into his handkerchief and exclaimed, "I know the color of that blood; it is arterial blood. I cannot be deceived in that color. That drop of blood is my death warrant. I must die." He left this house in September, moved to Rome, and died of consumption there, in early 1821, at age 25. ✉ *Keats House, Wentworth Pl., Keats Grove, Hampstead NW3* ☎ *020/ 7435–2062* ⊕ *www.keatshouse.org.uk* 🖃 *£3, valid for 1 yr* ☉ *Apr.–Oct., Tues.–Sun. noon–5; Nov.–Mar., Tues.–Sun. noon–4* Ⓤ *Hampstead or overground Silverlink Hampstead Heath from Highbury and Islington.*

> **need a break?** Hampstead is full of restaurants, including a few that have been here forever. Try the **Coffee Cup** (✉ 74 Hampstead High St., Hampstead NW3 ☎ 020/7435–7565), which has been serving English breakfasts all day to a hip crowd of locals since the 1950s, from 8 'til late (and you can get steak sandwiches and pasta, too). The **Hampstead Tea Rooms** (✉ 9 South End Rd., Hampstead NW3 ☎ 020/7435–9563) has been run by the same owners for more than 30 years, selling sandwiches, pies, pastries, and cream cakes, on drool view in the window. For a more substantial but still speedy meal on the hoof, stop at the **Hampstead Creperie** (✉ 77 Hampstead High St., Hampstead NW3 ☎ 020/7372–0081), which serves authentic sweet and savory French crêpes from a little cart on the street. The most quaint pub in Hampstead, complete with fireplace and timber frame, is the **Hollybush** (✉ 22 Holly Mount, Hampstead NW3 ☎ 020/ 7435–2892), which dates back to 1807. Tucked away on a side street, it's open until 11 each night and serves traditional English lunches and dinners, often to the accompaniment of live Irish music.

**★ ☺ ⓬ Kenwood House.** Perfectly and properly Palladian, this mansion was first built in 1616 and remodeled by Robert Adam in 1764. Adam refaced most of the exterior and added the gaudy library, which, with its curved painted ceiling, rather garish coloring, and gilded detailing, is the sole highlight of the house for decorative arts and interior buffs. What is unmissable here is the **Iveagh Bequest,** a collection of paintings that the Earl of Iveagh gave the nation in 1927, starring a wonderful Rembrandt self-portrait and works by Reynolds, Van Dyck, Hals, Gainsborough, and Turner. Top billing goes to Vermeer's *Guitar Player,* one of the most beautiful paintings in the world. In front of the house, a graceful lawn slopes down to a little lake crossed by a trompe-l'oeil bridge—all in perfect 18th-century upper-class taste. The rest of the grounds are skirted by Hampstead Heath. Nowadays the lake is dominated by its concert bowl, which stages a summer series of orchestral concerts, including an annual performance of Handel's *Music for the Royal Fireworks*, complete with fireworks. A popular café, the Brew House, is part of the old coach house, and has outdoor tables in the courtyard and terraced garden. ⊠ *Hampstead La., Hampstead NW3* ☎ *020/ 8348–1286* ⊕ *www.english-heritage.org.uk* ☜ *Free* ☉ *House: Easter–Aug., Sat.–Tues. and Thurs. 10–6, Wed. and Fri. 10:30–6; Sept.–Easter, Sat.–Tues. and Thurs. 10–4, Wed. and Fri. 10:30–4. Gardens: daily dawn–dusk* Ⓤ *Golders Green, then Bus 210.*

🐾 ❽ **London Canal Museum.** Here, in a former ice-storage house, you can learn about the rise and fall of London's once extensive canal network. Outside, on the Battlebridge Basin, float the gaily painted narrow boats of modern canal dwellers—a few steps and a world away from King's Cross, which remains one of London's least salubrious neighborhoods. The quirky little museum is accessible from Camden Lock if you take the towpath. ⊠ *12–13 New Wharf Rd., Camden Town N1* ☎ *020/ 7713–0836* ⊕ *www.canalmuseum.org.uk* ☜ *£2.50* ☉ *Tues.–Sun. 10–4; last admission 3:45* Ⓤ *King's Cross.*

🐾 ❺ **London Zoo.** The zoo opened in 1828 and peaked in popularity during the 1950s, when more than 3 million people passed through its turnstiles every year. A modernization program focusing on conservation and education is underway. A great example of this is one of the zoo's highlights, a huge glass pavilion—the Web of Life—which puts these aims into action. Many traditional cages remain, so, in order that they can live in more natural space, the Asian elephants were moved to the zoo's Whipsnade Wild Animal Park in 2002 as part of the breeding program. At the park they have joined the resident breeding herd with bull elephant, Emmett, in state-of-the art facilities with large grass and sand paddocks.

Zoo highlights (unchanged over the years, due to English Heritage conservation listing) include the Casson Pavilion (which closely resembles the South Bank Arts Complex); the graceful Snowdon Aviary, spacious enough to allow its tenants free flight; and the 1936 Penguin Pool, where feeding time sends small children into raptures. The reptile house is a special draw for Harry Potter fans—it's where Harry first talks to snakes, to alarming effect on his horrible cousin. New thrills include a desert swarming with locusts, meerkats perching on termite mounds, bats and hummingbirds, and a new otter exhibit (which opened Easter 2003) with underwater viewing. London zoo is owned by the Zoological Society of London (a charity), and much work is done here in wildlife conservation, education, and the breeding of endangered species. For animal encounter sessions with keepers, and feeding times, check the information board at admission. ⊠ *Regent's Park NW1* ☎ *020/ 7722–3333* ⊕ *www.zsl.org* ☜ *£13* ☉ *Mar.–Oct., daily 10–5:30; Nov.–Feb., daily 10–4; last admission 1 hr before closing* Ⓤ *Camden Town, then Bus 274.*

❶❹ **Lord's Cricket Ground & Museum.** If you can't manage to lay your hands on tickets for a cricket match, the next best thing is to take a tour of the spiritual home of this most British of games. Founded by Thomas

Lord, the headquarters of the MCC (Marylebone Cricket Club) opens its "behind the scenes" areas to visitors. You can see the Long Room with cricketing art on display; the players' Dressing Rooms; and the world's oldest sporting museum, where the progress from gentlemanly village green game to world-class sport over 400 years is charted. Don't miss the prize exhibit: the urn containing the Ashes (the remains of a cricket ball burned by Australia fans mourning their defeat at the hands of the MCC in 1883), and even smaller, the poor sparrow that met its death by a bowled ball. More up-to-date is the eye-catching Media Centre building, which achieved high scores in the architectural league. The tour is not available during matches, but the museum remains open. ⊠ *St. John's Wood Rd., St. John's Wood NW8* ☎ *020/7616–8595* ⊕ *www.lords.org* 🎫 *£7, £2.50 museum only* ⊙ *Apr.–Sept., daily 10–2, not during major matches. Oct.–Mar. noon–2* Ⓤ *St. John's Wood.*

🐾 ❷ **Madame Tussaud's & London Planetarium.** One of London's busiest sights, this is nothing more and nothing less than the world's premier exhibition of lifelike waxwork models of celebrities. Madame T. learned her craft while making death masks of French Revolution victims, and in 1835 set up her first show of the famous ones near this spot. Nowadays, Superstars of Entertainment, in their own hall of the same name, outrank any aristocrat in popularity, along with a segment called the Spirit of London, and a Time Taxi Ride that visits every notable Londoner from Shakespeare to Benny Hill. But top billing still goes to the murderers in the Chamber of Horrors, who stare glassy-eyed at visitors— one from an electric chair, one sitting next to the tin bath where he dissolved several wives in quicklime. What, aside from ghoulish prurience, makes people stand in line to invest in London's most expensive museum ticket? It is the thrill of rubbing shoulders with Shakespeare, Martin Luther King Jr., the queen, and the Beatles—most of them dressed in their very own outfits—in a single day.

The domed London Planetarium building stands right next to Madame Tussaud's, but it could hardly provide greater contrast with the waxworks. Inside the dome, exact simulations of the night sky are projected by the Digistar Mark 2 and accompanied by wow-imagine-that narration. The shows, which change daily, are good enough to get kids addicted to astronomy. There are also regular laser shows and rock music extravaganzas. Beat the crowds by calling in advance for timed entry tickets to both Madame Tussaud's and the Planetarium. ⊠ *Marylebone Rd., Regent's Park NW1* ☎ *0870/400–3000 for timed entry tickets* ⊕ *www.madame-tussauds.com* 🎫 *From £14.99, combined ticket with planetarium £16.99; prices vary according to day and season, call for details, or check the Web site* ⊙ *Sept.–June, weekdays 10–5:30, weekends 9:30–5:30; July–Aug., daily 9:30–5:30; planetarium show every 30 mins; last show 5. Call for showtime details* Ⓤ *Baker St.*

★ 🐾 ❸ **Regent's Park.** The youngest of London's great parks, Regent's Park was laid out in 1812 by John Nash, who worked for his patron, the Prince Regent (hence the name), who was crowned George IV in 1820. The idea was to re-create the feel of a grand country residence close to the center of town, with all those magnificent white-stucco terraces facing in on the park. As you walk the Outer Circle, you'll see how successfully Nash's plans were carried out, although the focus of it all—a palace for the prince—was never actually built (George was too busy fiddling with the one he already had, Buckingham Palace). The most famous and impressive of Nash's terraces would have been in the prince's line of vision from the planned palace. **Cumberland Terrace** has a central block of Ionic columns surmounted by a triangular Wedgwood-blue pediment that's like a giant cameo. Snow-white statuary personifying Britannia and her empire (the work of the on-site architect, James Thomson) single it out from the pack. The noted architectural historian Sir John Summerson described it thus: "the backcloth as it were to Act III, and easily the most breathtaking architectural panorama in London."

As in all London parks, planting here is planned with the aim of having something in bloom in all seasons, but if you hit the park in May, June, or July, head first to the Inner Circle. Your nostrils should lead you to **Queen Mary's Gardens,** a fragrant 17-acre circle that riots with roses in summer and heather, azaleas, and evergreens in other seasons. The **Broad Walk** is a good vantage point from which to glimpse the minaret and golden dome of the **London Central Mosque** on the far west side of the park. If it's a summer evening or a Sunday afternoon, witness a remarkable phenomenon. Wherever you look, the sport being enthusiastically played is not cricket but softball, now Britain's fastest-growing participant sport (bring your mitt). You're likely to see cricket, too, plus a lot of dog walkers—not for nothing did Dodie Smith set her novel *A Hundred and One Dalmatians* in an Outer Circle house. ☎ *020/ 7486–7905* ⊕ *www.royalparks.gov.uk* Ⓤ *Baker St. or Regent's Park.*

❹ **Regent's Park Open-Air Theatre.** The company has mounted Shakespeare productions here every summer since 1932; everyone from Vivien Leigh to Jeremy Irons has performed here. *A Midsummer Night's Dream* is the one to catch—never is that enchanted Greek wood more lifelike than it is here, augmented by genuine bird squawks and a rising moon. The park can get chilly, so bring a blanket; rain stops the play only when heavy. ⊠ *Open-Air Theatre, Regent's Park NW1* ☎ *020/7486–2431* ⊕ *www.open-air-theatre.org.uk* ☉ *June–Aug., evening performances 7:30, matinees 2:30* Ⓤ *Baker St. or Regent's Park.*

▶ ❶ **Sherlock Holmes Museum.** Outside Baker Street station, by the Marylebone Rd. exit, is a 9-foot-high bronze statue of the celebrated detective. Keep your eyes peeled, for close by his image, "Holmes" himself, in his familiar deerstalker hat, will escort you to his abode at 221B Baker Street, the address of Arthur Conan Doyle's fictional detective. Inside, "Holmes's housekeeper" conducts you into a series of Victorian rooms full of Sherlockabilia. It's all so realistic, you may actually begin to believe in Holmes's existence. ⊠ *221B Baker St., Regent's Park NW1* ☎ *020/7935–8866* ⊕ *www.sherlock-homes.co.uk* ⊠ *£6* ☉ *Daily 9:30–6* Ⓤ *Baker St.*

**2 Willow Road.** Modern movement master Ernö Goldfinger put this house up in the 1930s, and the National Trust has now kindly restored it and filled it with important (and currently very trendy) modernist furniture and art. Note that there are limited visitor hours with timed tickets because the house is small. ✉ *2 Willow Rd., Hampstead NW1* ☎ *020/7435–6166* ⊕ *www.nationaltrust.org.uk* 💷 *£4.60, joint ticket with Fenton House £6.40* ◷ *Mar. and Nov., Sat. noon–5; Apr.–Oct., Thurs.–Sat. noon–5* Ⓤ *Hampstead or overground Silverlink Hampstead Heath, from Highbury and Islington.*

# GREENWICH

About 8 mi downstream from central London—which means seaward, to the east—lies a self-contained village with elegant, perfectly proportioned buildings and tall ships anchored at the riverbank. Greenwich was catapulted up the tourist itinerary in 2000, when with the construction of the Millennium Dome it became the focal point for celebrations. The dome is closed to the public (and is likely to become a sporting and events arena), but remains an unforgettable landmark on the riverside. Post-millennium, Greenwich remains a prime destination, with modern transport links.

Greenwich has many attractions. Spreading both grandly and elegantly beside the river are the colonnades and pediments of Sir Christopher Wren's Royal Naval College and Inigo Jones's Queen's House, both of which seem to be part of a complex of Grecian temples transported to the Thames. The structures have been designated a World Heritage Site by UNESCO. Here, too, is the Old Royal Observatory, which measures time for the entire planet, and the Greenwich Meridian, which divides the world in two—you can stand astride it with one foot in either hemisphere. The National Maritime Museum and the proud clipper ship *Cutty Sark* thrill seafaring types, and landlubbers can stroll the green acres of parkland that surround the buildings, the 19th-century houses, and the weekend crafts and antiques markets.

*Numbers in the text correspond to numbers in the margin and on the Greenwich map.*

**a good walk**

To start your walk, begin with the *Cutty Sark* ❶ ⌐. Follow King William Walk and then take a right on College Approach toward Wren's majestic **Royal Naval College** ❷. The **Queen's House** ❸, followed by the **National Maritime Museum** ❹, sit just down King William Walk on Romney Road. Now head up the hill in Greenwich Park, overlooking the Naval College and Maritime Museum, to the **Old Royal Observatory** ❺ and the **Ranger's House** ❻. Walking back through the park toward the river, you'll enter the pretty streets of Greenwich Village to the west. There are plenty of bookstores and antiques shops for browsing and, at the foot of Crooms Hill, the modern Greenwich Theatre—a West End theater, despite its location, that mounts well-regarded, often star-spangled productions—and the **Fan Museum** ❼ opposite. Finish up at the excellent **Village Market** ❽ and the Victorian **Greenwich Market** ❾ by the *Cutty Sark*, on College Approach. If you've still energy and time, a visit to the Thames Barrier Visitors' Centre is a fun way to explore the banks of the Thames.

TIMING  The boat trip takes about an hour from Westminster Pier (next to Big Ben), or 25 minutes from the Tower of London, so figure in enough time for the round-trip. There are such riches here, especially if the maritime theme is your thing, that whatever time you allow will seem halved. If the weather's good, you'll be tempted to stroll aimlessly around the quaint village streets, too, and maybe take a turn in the park. If you want to take in the markets, you'll need to come on a weekend.

HOW TO GET THERE    Take the Jubilee Line through Docklands from Canary Wharf (an architectural award winner), or the zippy "driverless" Docklands Light Railway to Cutty Sark station for a direct route. Alternatively, the old Victorian Foot Tunnel used by dockworkers to go back and forth under the river from Island Gardens station contrasts new and old. The river connections to Greenwich mean that the journey is fun in itself, for you will then get the best possible vista of the Royal Naval College, with the Queen's House behind. One of the most chilling sights is Traitor's Gate, as that's the route the condemned would take. **Ferries** (☎ 020/7222–1234 ⊕ www.transportforlondon.gov.uk) from central London to Greenwich take 30–55 minutes and leave from various piers with various operators. Call London Travel Information for details on all of the following, but it can be hard to get through. From Westminster to Greenwich operated by **City Cruises** (☎ 020/7930–9033 ⊕ www.citycruises.com); Westminster to Barrier Gardens (Thames Barrier) via Greenwich operated by **Westminster Passenger Services** (☎ 020/7930–4097); Embankment to Greenwich via Tower–St. Katharine's operated by **Catamaran Cruisers** (☎ 020/7987–1185 ⊕ www.catamarancruisers.co.uk); From Greenwich to Barrier Gardens operated by **Campion Launches** (☎ 020/8305–0300)..

## What to See

🐾 ► ❶   **Cutty Sark.** This romantic clipper was built in 1869, one of fleets and fleets of similar wooden tall-masted clippers that plied the seven seas in the 19th century, trading in exotic commodities—tea, in this case. The *Cutty Sark,* the last to survive, was also the fastest, sailing the China–London route in 1871 in only 107 days. Now the photogenic vessel lies in dry dock, a museum of one kind of seafaring life—and not a comfortable kind for the 28-strong crew, as you'll see. The collection of figureheads is amusing, too. ⊠ *King William Walk, Greenwich SE10* ☎ *020/8858–3445* ⊕ *www.cuttysark.org.uk* ☑ *£4.25* ⊙ *Daily 10–5; last admission 4:30* Ⓤ *DLR: Cutty Sark.*

❼   **Fan Museum.** In two newly restored houses dating from the 1820s, opposite the Greenwich Theatre, is this highly unusual museum. The 2,000 fans here, which date from the 17th century onward, compose the world's only such collection, and the history and purpose of these often exquisitely crafted objects are satisfyingly explained. It was the personal vision—and fan collection—of Helene Alexander that brought it into being, and the workshop and conservation and study center that she has also set up ensure that this anachronistic art has a future. ⊠ *12 Croom's Hill, Greenwich SE10* ☎ *020/8305–1441* ⊕ *www.fan-museum.org* ☑ *£3.50* ⊙ *Tues.–Sat. 11–5, Sun. noon–5* Ⓤ *DLR: Greenwich.*

❾   **Greenwich Market.** You'll find this Victorian covered crafts market by the *Cutty Sark,* on College Approach. Established as a fruit-and-veg-

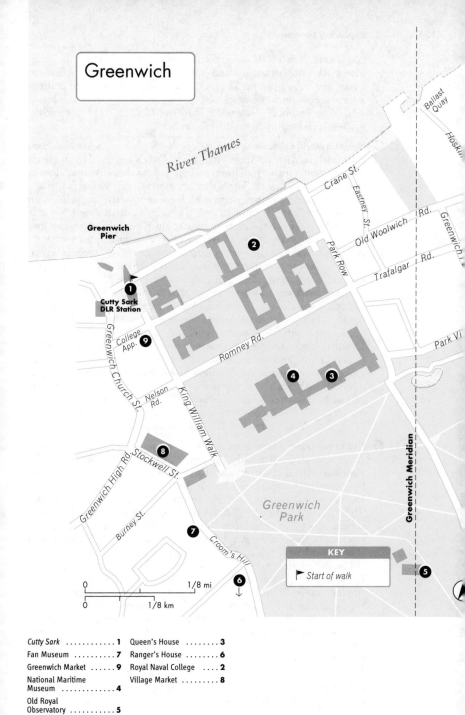

# Greenwich

River Thames

Greenwich Pier

Cutty Sark DLR Station

Crane St.

Eastney St.

Old Woolwich Rd.

Park Row

Trafalgar Rd.

Greenwich

Ballast Quay

Hoskin

Park Vi

Park Vi

Romney Rd.

College App.

Greenwich Church St.

Nelson Rd.

King William Walk

Greenwich High Rd.

Stockwell St.

Burney St.

Croom's Hill

Greenwich Park

Greenwich Meridian

| KEY |
| --- |
| ▶ Start of walk |

0        1/8 mi

0        1/8 km

etable market in 1700, and granted a royal charter in 1849, the glass-roof market now offers arts and crafts Friday through Sunday, and antiques and collectibles on Thursday and Friday. Shopping for crafts is a pleasure, as in most cases you're buying directly from the artist. ⊠ *College Approach, Greenwich SE10* ☎ *020/7515–7153* ⏱ *Fri.–Sun. 9:30–5:30, Thurs. 9–5* Ⓤ *DLR: Cutty Sark.*

★ ☙ ➍ **National Maritime Museum.** One of Greenwich's star attractions has been completely updated to appeal to all. The Queen reopened the museum in 1999 after a major face-lift in preparation for the millennium tourist onslaught at Greenwich. The beautifully grand stone building is all glass, light, and modern within, dominated by huge revolving propeller from a powerful frigate on show in a glass-covered courtyard. Sea power is one of the areas covered in the museum, which has been segregated into themes. Besides containing everything to do with the sea, from seascape paintings to scientific instruments, there are the compelling stories of heroes. There's a whole gallery, for instance, devoted to Nelson (including his uniform, complete with bloodstain, worn at his death at the Battle of Trafalgar). Explorers such as Captain Cook, and Scott of the Antarctic, are celebrated, as is the valuable research they gleaned from their grueling voyages. Environmental issues are not forgotten, either, and the importance of the water cycle is illustrated with audio-visual lighting effects. Opportunities to grapple hands-on with ropes, weights, rowing, and steering are throughout the museum, but energetically so at the All Hands gallery. You'd be well advised to allow at least two hours in this absorbing, adventurous place and if you're in need of refreshment there's a good café with views over Greenwich Park. ⊠ *Romney Rd., Greenwich SE10* ☎ *020/8858–4422* ⊕ *www.nmm.ac.uk* 🎫 *Free* ⏱ *Apr.–Sept., daily 10–6; Oct.–Mar., daily 10–5* Ⓤ *DLR: Greenwich.*

★ ☙ ➎ **Old Royal Observatory.** Founded in 1675 by Charles II, this imposing institution was designed the same year by Christopher Wren for John Flamsteed, the first Astronomer Royal. The red ball you see on its roof has been there only since 1833. It drops every day at 1 PM, and you can set your watch by it, as the sailors on the Thames always have. This Greenwich Timeball, along with the Gate Clock inside the observatory, is the most visible manifestation of Greenwich Mean Time— since 1884, the ultimate standard for time around the world. Greenwich is on the **prime meridian** at 0° longitude. A brass line laid among the cobblestones here marks the meridian, one side being the eastern, one the western hemisphere. In 1948 the Old Royal Observatory lost its official status: London's glow had grown too intense, and the astronomers moved to Sussex, while the Astronomer Royal decamped to Cambridge, leaving various telescopes, chronometers, and clocks for you to view. An excellent exhibition on the solution to the problem of measuring longitude includes John Harrison's famous clocks, H1–H4, now in working order. ⊠ *Greenwich Park, Greenwich SE10* ☎ *020/8312–6565* ⊕ *www.rog.nmm.ac.uk* 🎫 *Free* ⏱ *Apr.–Sept., daily 10–6; Oct.–Mar. daily 10–5; last admission 30 mins before closing* Ⓤ *DLR: Greenwich.*

★ ❸ **Queen's House.** The queen for whom Inigo Jones began designing the house in 1616 was James I's Anne of Denmark, but she died three years later, and it was Charles I's French wife, Henrietta Maria, who inherited the building when it was completed in 1635. It's no less than Britain's first classical building—the first, that is, to use the lessons of Italian Renaissance architecture—and is therefore of enormous importance in the history of English architecture. Inside, the Tulip Stair, named for the fleur-de-lis–style pattern on the balustrade, is especially fine, spiraling up without a central support to the Great Hall. The Great Hall itself is a perfect cube, exactly 40 feet in all three directions, decorated with paintings of the Muses, the Virtues, and the Liberal Arts. ✉ *Romney Rd., Greenwich SE10* ☎ *020/8293–9618* ⊕ *www.nmm.ac.uk* ⌨ *Free* ⊘ *Weekends 10–5, weekdays guided visits only, departing on the hr 11–4* Ⓤ *DLR: Greenwich.*

**need a break?**

After a long walk, the historic **Trafalgar Tavern** (✉ Park Row, Greenwich SE10 ☎ 020/8858–2437), with excellent views of the Thames, is a grand place to have a pint and some upmarket pub grub. In warm weather the riverside terrace offers outdoor seating overlooking the Millennium Dome. At **Goddard's Pie House** (✉ 45 Greenwich Church St., Greenwich SE10 ☎ 020/8293–9313) the flavors include beef, chicken, and cheese, with fruit pies or crumbles for afterward, should you have the space.

❻ **Ranger's House.** This handsome, early-18th-century villa, which was the Greenwich Park Ranger's official residence during the 19th century, is hung with Stuart and Jacobean portraits. But the most interesting diversion is the Wernher Collection, more than 650 works of art with a north European flavor, amassed by millionaire Julius Wernher at the turn of the 20th century. After making his money in diamond mining, he chose to buy eclectic objects, sometimes beautiful, often downright quirky, like the silver coconut cup. Sèvres porcelain and Limoges enamels, the largest jewelry collection in the country, and some particularly bizarre reliquaries, are part of the fascinating items on view. His American wife, Birdie, was a strong influence and quite a personality during this belle epoque, which is easy to imagine from her striking portrait by Sargent. The house also makes a superb setting for concerts, which are regularly scheduled here. It stands just outside the park boundaries, on the southwest side of **Greenwich Park,** one of London's oldest royal parks. It had been in existence for more than 200 years before Charles II commissioned the French landscape artist Le Nôtre (who was responsible for Versailles and for St. James's Park) to redesign it in what was, in the 1660s, the latest French fashion. Look also for Queen Elizabeth's Oak on the east side, around which Henry VIII and his second queen, Anne Boleyn, Elizabeth I's mother, are said to have danced. ✉ *Chesterfield Walk, Blackheath, Greenwich SE10* ☎ *020/8853–0035* ⊕ *www.english-heritage.org.uk* ⌨ *£5* ⊘ *Apr.–Sept., Wed.–Sun. 10–6; Oct., Wed.–Sun. 10–5; Nov.–Mar., Wed.–Sun. 10–4* Ⓤ *DLR: Greenwich; no direct bus access, only to Vanbrugh Hill (east) and Blackheath Hill (west).*

★ ❷  **Royal Naval College.** Begun by Christopher Wren in 1694 as a home, or hospital for ancient mariners, it became instead a school for young ones in 1873. Today the University of Greenwich has classes here. You'll notice how the structures part to reveal the Queen's House across the central lawns. Wren, with the help of his assistant, Nicholas Hawksmoor, was at pains to preserve the river vista from the house, and there are few more majestic views in London than the awe-inspiring symmetry he achieved. Behind the college are two buildings you can visit. The **Painted Hall,** the college's dining hall, derives its name from the baroque murals of William and Mary (reigned 1689–95; William alone 1695–1702) and assorted allegorical figures, the whole supported by trompe-l'oeil pillars that Sir James Thornhill (who decorated the inside of St. Paul's dome, too) painted between 1707 and 1717. In the opposite building stands the **College Chapel,** which was rebuilt after a fire in 1779 and is altogether lighter, in a more restrained, neo-Grecian style. At Christmas 1805, Admiral Nelson's body was brought from the Battle of Trafalgar to lie in state here. ⊠ *Royal Naval College, King William Walk, Greenwich SE10* ☎ *0800/389–3341 recorded information* ⊕ *www.greenwichfoundation.org.uk* ⊠ *Free, guided tours £5* ⊙ *Painted Hall and Chapel Mon.–Sat. 10–5, Sun. 12:30–5, last admission 4:15; grounds 8–6* Ⓤ *DLR: Greenwich.*

❽  **Village Market.** If you're visiting on the weekend, this market on Stockwell Street near the Fan Museum and Greenwich Theatre is open for business. It has a lot of bric-a-brac and books, too, and it's well known among the cognoscenti as a good source for vintage clothing. On the opposite block to the Village Market, more vintage shopping can be found in the weekend **Antiques Market,** on Greenwich High Road, where you can browse among the "small collectibles." It's a weekenders' market haven, where you can find some original and inspired gifts. To make sure you don't miss a bargaining opportunity, get a visitor map from the tourist information center by the *Cutty Sark* to orient your way around the profusion of markets. ⊠ *Stockwell St., Greenwich SE10* ☎ *020/ 8858–0808* ⊙ *Weekends 9–5* Ⓤ *DLR: Cutty Sark.*

off the beaten path

**THAMES BARRIER VISITORS' CENTRE –** Learn what comes between London and its famous river—a futuristic-looking metal barrier that has been described as the eighth wonder of the world. Multimedia presentations, a film on the Thames' history, working models, and views of the barrier itself put the importance of the relationship between London and its river in perspective. ⊠ *Unity Way, Eastmoor St., Woolwich, SE18* ☎ *020/8305–4188* ⊕ *www.environment-agency.gov.uk* ⊠ *£1* ⊙ *Apr.–Sept., daily 10:30–4:30; Oct.–Mar., daily 11–3:30* Ⓤ *National Rail: Charlton (from London Bridge), North Greenwich (Jubilee Line), then bus 161 or 472.*

# UPSTREAM FROM LONDON

The Thames is Britain's longest river. It winds its way through the Cotswolds, beyond Oxford and past majestic Windsor Castle—here far more the lazy, leafy country river than the dark-gray urban waterway you see in London. Once you leave the city center, going west, or upstream, you reach a series of former villages—Chiswick, Kew, Richmond, Putney—that, apart from the roar of aircraft coming in to land at Heathrow a few miles farther west, are still peaceful, almost rural, especially in places where parkland rolls down to the riverbank. In fact it was really only at the beginning of the 20th century that London proper expanded to encompass these villages. The royal palaces and grand houses that dot the area were built as country residences with easy access to London by river.

TIMING  Each of the places listed here could easily absorb a whole day of your time, and Hampton Court is especially huge.

HOW TO GET   Access is fairly easy: the District Line of the underground runs out to
THERE   Kew and Richmond, as does National Rail, South West line, from Waterloo, which also serves Twickenham and Hampton Court. For Chiswick House or Hogarth's House, take National Rail, South West, to Chiswick station or take the District Line to Turnham Green. Both options require walking to reach the destination, but Chiswick station is a bit closer to the houses. National Rail, South West, also runs trains to Kew Bridge, which is convenient to Strand-on-the-Green. For Kew Gardens, take the District Line heading toward Richmond and get off at Kew Gardens. National Rail, Silverlink-North London line, also stops nearby; from the station it's a pleasant walk down a tree-lined residential avenue to the gardens.

A pleasant if slow way to go is by river. Boats depart from **Westminster Pier** (☎ 020/7930–4097), just by Big Ben, for Kew (1½ hours), Richmond (2–3 hours), and Hampton Court (4 hours) several times a day in summer, less frequently from October through March. As you can tell from those sailing times, the boat trip is worth taking only if you make it an integral part of your day out, and even then, be aware that it can get very breezy on the water and that the scenery going upstream is by no means constantly fascinating.

## Chiswick & Kew

Chiswick is the nearest Thames-side destination to London, with Kew just a mile or so beyond it. Much of Chiswick, developed at the beginning of the 20th century, is today a nondescript suburb. Incongruously stranded among the terraced houses, however, a number of fine 18th-century houses and a charming little village survive. The village atmosphere of Kew is still distinct, making this one of the most desirable areas of outer London. What makes Kew famous, though, are the Royal Botanic Gardens.

a good
walk

Start your walk at the Italianate **Chiswick House** ► on Burlington Lane. Then follow Burlington Lane and take a left onto Hogarth Lane, which is anything but a lane, to reach **Hogarth's House.** Chiswick's Church Street (reached by an underpass from Hogarth's House) is the nearest thing to a sleepy country village street in all of London, despite its proximity to the Great West Road. Follow it down to the Thames and turn left at its foot to reach the sturdy 18th-century riverfront houses of

Chiswick Mall. The ½-mi walk along here takes you far away from mainstream London and into a world of elegance and calm. You will pass several riverside pubs as you head along this stretch of the Thames toward Hammersmith Bridge. The Dove is the prettiest, if the most crowded, with its terrace hanging over the water. The food is good at the Blue Anchor, which you'll reach first.

There's a similarly peaceful walk about 1 mi to the west along the 18th-century river frontage of Strand-on-the-Green, whose houses look over the narrow towpath to the river, their tidy brick facades covered with wisteria and roses in summer. Right before you reach Kew Bridge, you may be ready for a break at the Bell & Crown, where crowds congregate on summer days to watch the Thames roll by. Strand-on-the-Green ends at Kew Bridge, opposite which is Kew Green, where local teams play cricket on summer Sundays. All around it are fine 18th-century houses and, in the center, a church in which the painters Thomas Gainsborough and John Zoffany (1733–1810) are buried. **Kew Gardens** and **Kew Palace** are just a short walk away over the Kew Bridge.

## What to See

▶ **Chiswick House.** Built circa 1725 by the Earl of Burlington (the Lord Burlington of Burlington House, Piccadilly, home of the Royal Academy, and, of course, the Burlington Arcade) as a country residence in which to entertain friends, and as a kind of temple to the arts, this is the very model of a Palladian villa, inspired by the Villa Capra near Vicenza in northeastern Italy. The house fans out from a central octagonal room in perfect symmetry, guarded by statues of Burlington's heroes, Palladio himself and his disciple Inigo Jones. Burlington's friends—Pope, Swift, Gay, and Handel among them—were well qualified to adorn a temple to the arts. Burlington was a great connoisseur and an important patron of the arts, but he was also an accomplished architect in his own right, fascinated by— obsessed with, even—the architecture and art of the Italian Renaissance and ancient Rome, with which he'd fallen in love during his Italian grand tour. Along with William Kent (1685–1748), who designed the interiors and the rambling gardens here, Burlington did a great deal toward the dissemination of Palladian ideals around Britain: Chiswick House sparked enormous interest, and you'll see these forms reflected in hundreds of later English stately homes both small and large. Arguably one of the most glorious examples of 18th-century British architecture, Chiswick House was designed by Lord Burlington to emulate the style and elegance of ancient Rome. Sitting in acres of spectacular Italianate gardens filled with classical temples, statues and obelisks, it's home to the sumptuous interiors of William Kent, including the Blue Velvet Room with its gilded decoration and intricate ceiling paintings. It also houses a fabulous collection of paintings and furniture. ✉ *Burlington La., Chiswick W4* ☎ *020/8995–0508* ⊕ *www.english-heritage.org.uk* ✍ *£3.50* ⊙ *Apr.–Sept., Wed.–Sun. 10–6; Oct., 10–5; closed some Sat. afternoons* Ⓤ *Turnham Green.*

**Hogarth's House.** This is where the painter lived from 1749 until his death in 1764. Unprotected from the six-lane Great West Road, which remains a main route to the West Country, the poor house is besieged by the surrounding traffic, but it's worth visiting for its little museum consisting mostly of the amusingly moralistic engravings for which Hogarth is best known, including the most famous of all, the *Rake's Progress* series of 1735. ✉ *Hogarth La., Chiswick W4* ☎ *020/8994–6757* 🎫 *Free* ☉ *Apr.–Sept., Tues.–Fri. 1–5, weekends 1–6; Oct.–Mar., Tues.–Fri. 1–4, weekends 1–5* Ⓤ *Turnham Green.*

> **need a break?**
>
> Pubs are the name of the game here at Chiswick's portion of the Thames. Many pubs sit on the bank of the river, offering watery vistas to accompany stout pints of brew. The **Bell & Crown** (✉ 72 Strand-on-the-Green, Chiswick W4 ☎ 020/8994–4164) is the first pub on the riverside path from Kew Bridge, with a riverside conservatory to check those breezes. The **Blue Anchor** (✉ 13 Lower Mall, Hammersmith W6 ☎ 020/8748–5774) is a cozy 18th-century watering hole, with rowing memorabilia lining the walls. The **Dove** (✉ 19 Upper Mall, Hammersmith W6 ☎ 020/8748–5405) retains the charm of its 300-year plus heritage. If you can find a spot on the tiny terrace it's a tranquil place to watch the energetic oarsmen.

★ ☾ **Kew Gardens.** The Royal Botanic Gardens at Kew are a spectacular 300 acres of public gardens, containing more than 30,000 species of plants. In addition, this is the country's leading botanical institute, and has been named a World Heritage Site by UNESCO. There are also strong royal associations. Until 1840, when Kew Gardens was handed over to the nation, it had been the grounds of two royal residences: the White House (formerly Kew House) and Richmond Lodge. George II and Queen Caroline lived at Richmond Lodge in the 1720s, while their eldest son, Frederick, Prince of Wales, and his wife, Princess Augusta, came to the White House during the 1730s. The royal wives were keen gardeners. Queen Caroline got to work on her grounds, while next door Frederick's pleasure garden was developed as a botanical garden by his widow after his death. She introduced all kinds of "exotics," foreign plants brought back to England by botanists. Caroline was aided by a skilled head gardener and by the architect Sir William Chambers, who built a series of temples and follies, of which the crazy 50-story **Pagoda** (1762), visible for miles around, is the star turn. The celebrated botanist Sir Joseph Banks (1743–1820) then took charge of Kew, which developed rapidly in both its roles—as a landscaped garden and as a center of study and research.

The highlights of a visit to Kew are the two great 19th-century greenhouses filled with tropical plants, many of which have been there as long as their housing. Both the **Palm House** and the **Temperate House** were designed by Sir Decimus Burton, the first opening in 1848, the second in 1899; the latter was the biggest greenhouse in the world, and today contains the largest greenhouse plant in the world, a Chilean wine palm rooted in 1846. You can climb the spiral staircase almost to the roof and look down on this and the dense tropical profusion from the walkway. The **Princess of Wales Conservatory,** the latest and the largest plant house at Kew, was opened in 1987 by Princess Diana. Under its bold glass roofs, designed to maximize energy conservation, there are no fewer than 10 climatic zones.

Plants may be beautiful to look at, and they have many medicinal uses, but how many plants are used in making fabrics, paper, and many more items? In **Museum No. 1,** situated near the Palm House, an interesting exhibition of the economic botany collections shows which plants ". . . help the merchant, physician, chemist, dyer, carpenter and artisans to find raw materials of their profession correctly named." It's free, but opening hours are seasonal, so check beforehand. The plant houses make Kew worth visiting even in the depths of winter, but in spring and summer the gardens come into their own. In late spring the woodland nature reserve of Queen Charlotte's Cottage Gardens is carpeted in bluebells; a little later, the Rhododendron Dell and the Azalea Garden become swathed in brilliant color. High summer brings glorious displays of roses and water lilies, and fall is the time to see the heather garden, near the pagoda. Whatever time of year you visit, something is in bloom, and your journey is never wasted. The main entrance is between Richmond Circus and the traffic circle at Mortlake Road. ⊠ *Kew Rd., Kew* ☎ *020/8332–5655* ⊕ *www.kew.org* ✉ *£8.50* ☽ *Gardens Apr.–Oct., weekdays 9:30–6:30, weekends 9:30–7:30; Nov.–Mar., daily 9:30–4:30* Ⓤ *Kew Gardens.*

**Kew Palace and Queen Charlotte's Cottage.** To this day quietly domestic Kew Palace remains the smallest royal palace in the land. The house and gardens offer a glimpse into the 17th century. Originally known as the Dutch House, it was bought by King George II to provide more room in addition to the White House (another royal residence that used to exist on the grounds) for the extended Royal Family. Currently undergoing careful renovation, the house is likely to reopen to the public in 2005. The grounds and cottage, however, can be visited, and in spring there's a romantic haze of bluebells. ⊠ *Kew Gardens, Kew* ⊕ *www.hrp.org.uk.*

**need a break?**

Maids of Honour (⊠ 288 Kew Rd., Kew ☎ 020/8940–2752), the most traditional of Old English tearooms, is named for the famous tarts invented here and still baked by hand on the premises. Tea is served in the afternoon, Tuesday–Saturday 2:30–5:30. If you can't wait for tea, and want to take some of the lovely cakes and pastries to eat at Kew Gardens or on Kew Green, the shop is open Tuesday–Saturday 9:30–6 and on Monday until 1 PM.

# Richmond

Named after the palace Henry VII built here in 1500, Richmond is still a welcoming and extremely pretty riverside "village," with many handsome (and expensive) houses, antiques shops, a Victorian theater, London's grandest stately home, and, best of all, the largest of London's royal parks.

## What to See

★ **Ham House.** To the west of Richmond Park, overlooking the Thames and nearly opposite the oddly named Eel Pie Island, the house was built in 1610 by Sir Thomas Vavasour, knight marshal to James I, then refurbished later the same century by the Duke and Duchess of Lauderdale, who, although not particularly nice (a contemporary called the duchess "the coldest friend and the most violent enemy that ever was known"), managed to produce one of the finest houses in Britain at the time. It's unique in Europe as the most complete example of a lavish Restoration period house, with a restored formal garden, which has become an influential source for other European palaces and grand villas. Produce from the garden can be enjoyed in the café in the Orangery. After considerable restoration, the library has been filled with 17th- and 18th-century volumes; the original decorations in the Great Hall, Round Gallery, and Great Staircase have been replicated; and all the furniture and fittings, on permanent loan from the V&A, have been cleaned and restored. The gardens and outhouses (Ice House, and Still House) are worth a visit in their own right, and are more conveniently open year-round. A tranquil and scenic way to reach the house is on foot, which takes around 30 minutes, along the eastern riverbank south from Richmond Bridge. ⊠ *Ham St., Richmond* ☎ *020/8940–1950* ⊕ *www. nationaltrust.org.uk* ✉ *House, gardens, and outhouses £6, gardens and outhouses £2* ⊘ *House late Mar.–early Nov., Sat.–Wed. 1–5; gardens all year, Sat.–Wed., 11–dusk* Ⓤ *Richmond, then Bus 65 or 371.*

**Marble Hill House.** On the northern bank of the Thames, almost opposite Ham House, stands another mansion, this one a near-perfect example of a Palladian villa. Set in 66 acres of parkland, Marble Hill House was built in the 1720s by George II for his mistress, the "exceedingly respectable and respected" Henrietta Howard. Later the house was occupied by Mrs. Fitzherbert, who was secretly married to the Prince Regent (later George IV) in 1785. Marble Hill House was restored in 1901 and opened to the public two years later, looking very much like it did in Georgian times, with extravagant gilded rooms in which Ms. Howard entertained famous poets and wits of the age, including Pope, Gay, and Swift. A ferry service operates during the summer from Ham House across the river; access by foot is a half-hour walk south along the west bank from Richmond Bridge. Group tours can be arranged. ⊠ *Richmond Rd., Twickenham, Richmond* ☎ *020/8892–5115* ⊕ *www.english-heritage.org.uk* ✉ *£3.50* ⊘ *Apr.–Sept., Wed.–Sun. and bank holidays 10–6; Oct., Wed.–Sun. 10–5* Ⓤ *Richmond.*

Ⓒ **Richmond Park.** Charles I enclosed this one in 1637 for hunting purposes, as with practically all the other parks. Unlike the others, however, Richmond Park still has wild red and fallow deer roaming its 2,470 acres of grassland and heath and the oldest oaks you're likely to see—vestiges of the forests that encroached on London from all sides in medieval times. White Lodge, inside the park, was built for George II in 1729. Edward VIII was born here; now it houses the Royal Ballet School. You can walk from the park past the fine 18th-century houses in and around Richmond Hill to the river, admiring first the view from the top. At the Thames, you may notice Quinlan Terry's Richmond Riverside development, which met with the approval of England's architectural adviser, Prince Charles, for its classical facades and was vilified by many others for playing it safe. Ⓤ *Richmond.*

The **Cricketers** (⊠ Maids of Honour Row, Richmond Green, Richmond ☎ 020/8940–4372) serves a good pub lunch. The modern, partially glass-roof **Caffé Mamma** (⊠ 24 Hill St., Richmond ☎ 020/8940–1625) is a good spot for inexpensive Italian food.

★ ♻ **Syon House and Park.** The residence of Their Graces the Duke and Duchess of Northumberland, this is one of England's most sumptuous stately homes, and certainly the only one that's near a Tube station. Set in a 55-acre park landscaped by Capability Brown, the core of the house is Tudor—two of Henry VIII's queens, Catherine Howard and Lady Jane Grey, made pit stops here before they were sent to the Tower—but it was redone in the Georgian style in 1761 by famed decorator Robert Adam. He had just returned from studying the sites of classical antiquity in Italy and created two rooms here worthy of any Caesar: the entryway is an amazing study in black and white, pairing neoclassic marbles with antique bronzes, and the Ante-Room contains 12 enormous verdantique columns surmounted by statues of gold—this, no less, was meant to be a waiting room for the duke's servants and retainers. The Red Drawing Room is covered with crimson Spitalfields silk and the Long Gallery is one of Adam's noblest creations (it was used by Cary Grant and Robert Mitchum for a duel in the 1958 film *The Grass Is Greener*). Elsewhere on the beautiful, rolling parkland is a Victorian glass conservatory that's famous among connoisseurs for its charm, not surprising as the designer, Fowler, was also responsible for the grand Covent Garden Flower Market. Also within the grounds, but not part of the Syon enterprise, is a nature center and butterfly house (with separate charges). ⊠ *Syon Park, Brentford* ☎ *020/8560–0881* ⊕ *www.syonpark. co.uk* ⊑ *£6.95 for house, gardens, conservatory, and rose garden; £3.50 gardens and conservatory* ☉ *House early Apr.–early Nov., Wed.–Thurs., Sun., and bank holidays 11–5; gardens daily 10–dusk* Ⓤ *Gunnersbury, then take Bus 237 or 267 to Brentlea stop.*

## Hampton Court Palace

★ Some 20 mi from central London, on a loop of the Thames upstream from Richmond, stands one of London's oldest royal palaces, more like a small town in size and requiring a day of your time to do it justice. It's actually two palaces in one—a Tudor residence and a late-17th-century baroque one—as well as a renowned garden. The magnificent Tudor brick house was begun in 1514 by Cardinal Wolsey, the ambitious and worldly lord chancellor (roughly, prime minister) of England and archbishop of York. He wanted it to be the absolute best palace in the land, and in this he succeeded so effectively that Henry VIII grew deeply envious, whereupon Wolsey felt obliged to give Hampton Court to the king. Henry took charge in 1525, adding a great hall and chapel, and proceeded to live much of his rambunctious life here. James I made further improvements at the beginning of the 17th century, but by the end of the century the palace was getting rather run-down. Plans were drawn up by the joint monarchs William III and Mary II to demolish the building and replace it with a still larger and more splendid structure, in conscious emulation of the great palace of Versailles outside Paris. However, the royal purse

wouldn't stretch quite that far. It was decided to keep the original buildings but add a complex adjoining them at the rear, for which Christopher Wren was commissioned, and his graceful south wing is one of the
highlights of the whole palace. (A serious fire badly damaged some of
Wren's chambers in 1986, but they were restored, with some of the
Tudor features he had covered up uncovered again.) William and, especially, Mary loved Hampton Court and left their mark on the place—see
their fine collections of Delftware and other porcelain.

The palace, steeped in history and hung with priceless paintings, is full
of echoing, cobbled courtyards, not to mention the ghost of Catherine
Howard screaming her innocence of adultery to an unheeding Henry VIII.
Six walking routes—Henry VIII's State Apartments, the Tudor Kitchens,
the Wolsey Rooms and Renaissance Picture Gallery, the King's (William's)
Apartments, the Queen's Apartments, and the Georgian Rooms—help
you organize your time and take in centuries of changing taste in architecture and decoration. Some highlights are Henry's Great Hall and the
Chapel Royal (with its fan vaulting and azure ceiling), and the regal King's
Apartments. Be sure to look outside as you explore the baroque apartments. The gardens were designed to please anyone gazing out the windows, as well as people strolling outside. Throughout the palace, costumed
interpreters and special programs, such as cooking demonstrations in the
cavernous Tudor kitchens, make history fun.

The site beside the slow-moving Thames is idyllic, with 60 acres of fantastic ornamental gardens, lakes, and ponds, including William III's Privy
Garden on the palace's south side. Its parterres, sculpted turf, and
clipped yews and hollies—a hybrid of English and Continental garden-
ing styles—brilliantly set off Wren's addition. Other highlights are
Henry VIII's Pond Garden, the enormous conical yews around the
Fountain Garden, and the daffodil-lined paths of the Wilderness. On
the east side of the house, 544 lime trees were replanted in 2004 along
the Long Water, a canal built during the time of Charles II. The Great
Vine, near the Banqueting House, was planted in 1768 and is still producing black Hamburg grapes. Perhaps best of all are the almost half
mile of paths in the celebrated maze, which you enter to the north of
the palace. It was planted in 1714 and is truly fiendish.

Royalty ceased living here with George III; poor George preferred the
seclusion of Kew, where he was finally confined in his madness. The private apartments that range down one side of the palace are now occupied by pensioners of the Crown. Known as "grace and favor" apartments,
they are among the most coveted homes in the country, with a surfeit
of peace and history on their doorsteps. ⊠ *East Molesey on A308*
☎ *0870/753-7777* ⊕ *www.hrp.org.uk* ⊠ *Palace, gardens, and maze*
*£11.80, gardens £4, maze alone £3.50, park grounds free. Joint tickets*
*available with Kensington Palace and the Tower of London* ⊙ *State apart-*
*ments Apr.–Oct., Tues.–Sun. 9:30–6, Mon. 10:15–6; Nov.–Mar., daily*
*9:30–4:30; grounds daily 7–dusk* Ⓤ *National Rail, South West: Hamp-*
*ton Court Station from Waterloo. Tube: Richmond, then bus R68.*

# WHERE TO EAT

Updated by
Alex Wijeratna

**NO LONGER WOULD SOMERSET MAUGHAM** be justified in warning, "If you want to eat well in England, have breakfast three times a day." England is one of the hottest places around for restaurants of every cultural flavor, with London at its epicenter. As anyone who reads the Sunday papers knows, London has had a restaurant boom or, rather, a restaurant revolution. Nearly everyone in town is passionate about food and will love to tell you where they've eaten recently or where they'd like to go. Nothing seems to slow the onslaught. More than ever, London loves its restaurants—all 6,700 of them—from its "be-there" eateries to its tiny neighborhood joints, from pubs where young foodniks find their feet to swanky trendsetters where celebrity chefs launch their ego flights. You, too, can be smitten, since you can spend, on average, 25% of your travel budget on eating out. After feasting on modern British cuisine, visit one (or two or three) of London's fabulous pubs for a nightcap. Hit the right one on the right night and watch that legendary British reserve melt away.

To appreciate London's culinary rise, it helps to recall that at one time it was understood that the British ate to live while the French lived to eat. Change was slow in coming after the Second World War, when steamed puddings and boiled sprouts were still eaten daily by tweed-and-flannel-wrapped Brits. When people thought of British cuisine, fish-and-chips came to mind, a dish that tasted best wrapped in newspaper (a spoilsport bureaucracy decreed that this wasn't sanitary, so the days of peeping at the latest murder news through a film of oil came to an end). Then there was always shepherd's pie, ubiquitously available in pubs—though not made, according to the song from *Sweeney Todd,* "with real shepherd in it." Visitors used to arrive in London and joke that the reason Britain conquered half the world was that its residents probably wanted some decent food. Didn't Britain invade India for a good curry?

Culinary London has undergone a transformation. New menus evolve constantly as chefs outdo each other, creating hot spots that are all about the buzz of being there. Chefs from continental Europe such as Anton Mosimann, Michel Bourdin, Nico Ladenis, and the Roux brothers showed the way, but it was Sir Terence Conran who brought restaurants to the mass market. He starting the revolution with Quaglino's, in 1993, the first of the city's mega-restaurants. His 480-seat Mezzo was the biggest restaurant in Europe when it opened, and he topped that again with Bluebird, which came complete with grocery store, fishmonger, florist, and food market.

The greatest ambition, though, belongs to superchef-turned-mogul Marco Pierre White. His 11-restaurant empire is everywhere: the Criterion, Mirabelle, and L'Escargot are all under his wing. Gordon Ramsay, his onetime protegé, is making up ground. He bestrides the London culinary scene like a colossus and even has New York in his sights. Happily, though, the vogue has turned against very large restaurants and intimacy is in.

Haute cuisine, too, is in expert hands. Gordon Ramsay powers away at Claridge's, Michel Roux commands at Le Gavroche, and White has led that London institution, L'Escargot, back to the top. There are, of course, many more stars of the celebrity variety (Jamie Oliver—TV's "Naked Chef"—is everywhere); you can read about all of them when you get here by picking up any newspaper. To keep up with the changes (more than 112 restaurants closed down last year) each paper has reviewers aplenty. Read up on the best places in the London *Evening Standard* and *Time Out* or the food pages in the national newspapers, especially in the weekend editions.

London also does a good job of catering to people interested less in following the latest trends than in eating without breaking the bank. We've struck a balance in our listings between these extremes and have included hip, scene restaurants, neighborhood spots, ethnic alternatives, and old favorites. There are about 80 cuisines offered in London, and ethnic restaurants have always been a good bet here, especially the thousands of Indian restaurants, since Londoners see a good curry as their birthright. The range of foreign cuisines has broadened to include Japanese, Malaysian, Thai, Spanish, Turkish, Ethiopian, and North African. With all this going on, traditional British food, when you track it down, appears as just one more exotic cuisine in the pantheon.

Two caveats: first, although there's an all-clear, and the chance of contracting so-called Mad Cow Disease is small, you may wish to avoid eating beef or to select beef with a reduced risk of contamination. Second, beware of Sunday. Many restaurants are closed, especially in the evening; likewise public holidays. Over the Christmas period, London virtually shuts down—only hotels will be prepared to feed you. When in doubt, call ahead. It's a good idea to book a table at all times.

## Bloomsbury

ECLECTIC
**£££**
Fodor'sChoice
★

✕ **Providores.** Kiwi Peter Gordon scores a perfect 10 with his Pacific Rim fusion food at Providores in trendy Marylebone. Have a sophisticated meal in the formal restaurant upstairs, or try out the more relaxed ground-floor Tapa Rooms—on the menu you'll find sweet potato and miso, kangaroo filets, and roast *chioca* (a tuber similar to Jerusalem artichoke). ✉ *109 Marylebone High St., Bloomsbury W1* 🕾 *020/7935–6175* ▭ *AE, MC, V* Ⓤ *Baker St.*

FRENCH
★ **£££–££££**

✕ **Elena's L'Etoile.** London's most popular maitre d' Elena Salvoni presided for years over L'Escargot in Soho, where she made so many friends that she ended up opening her own establishment. This century-old place is one of London's few remaining unreconstructed French bistros. The traditional dishes of confit lamb, salmon cakes, crème brûlée, and apple tart are joined by newer treats, and most diners are guaranteed a warm smile from Elena even if they're not her politician-journalist-actor regulars. ✉ *30 Charlotte St., Bloomsbury W1* 🕾 *020/7636–7189* ▭ *AE, DC, MC, V* ☾ *Closed Sun. No lunch Sat.* Ⓤ *Goodge St.*

**££–££££**

✕ **Villandry.** Heaven for food lovers, Villandry is a posh food hall—with a renowned dining room at the back. This tempting cave of wonders is

## Dining Hours

In London, you could find breakfast all day, and perhaps all night, but it's generally served between 7:30 and 10. Workmen's cafés and sandwich bars for office workers are sometimes open from 7:30, more upscale cafés from 9 to 10:30. Lunch is between noon and 2 and restaurants will be booked then. Tea, often a meal in itself, is taken between 4 and 5:30; dinner or supper between 7:30 and 9:30, sometimes earlier. In London's Theatreland, 6–6:30 is the time for pretheater suppers, and 10 onward for posttheater meals. Many ethnic restaurants, especially Indian, serve food until midnight. Sunday is proper lunch day, and some restaurants will open for lunch only. Unless otherwise noted, the restaurants listed in this guide are open daily for lunch and dinner, but some restaurants do not open on Sunday (or Monday—a fish-and-chip shop worth its salt will not be open on Monday) at all.

## Reservations & Dress

Reservations are always a good idea: we mention them only when they're essential or not accepted. Book as far ahead as you can, and reconfirm as soon as you arrive. We mention dress only when men are required to wear a jacket or a jacket and tie.

## Paying & Tipping

American Express, Diners Club, MasterCard, and Visa are accepted almost everywhere, but a pub, small café, or ethnic restaurant might not take credit cards. Do not tip bar staff in pubs—although you can always offer to buy them a drink. In restaurants, tip 10%–15% of the check for full meals if service is not already included, a small token if you're just having coffee or tea. If paying by credit card, check that a tip has not already been included.

## Prices

The democratization of restaurants in London has not translated into smaller checks, and London is not an inexpensive city. A modest meal for two can cost £35 (about $60). Damage-control strategies include making lunch your main meal—the top places have bargain lunch menus, halving the price of evening à la carte—and ordering a second appetizer instead of an entrée, to which few places object. (Note that an appetizer, usually known as a "starter" or "first course," is sometimes called an "entrée," as it is in France, and an entrée in England is dubbed the "main course" or simply "mains.") Seek out fixed-price menus, and watch for hidden extras on the check: cover, bread, or vegetables charged separately, and service. Many restaurants exclude service charges from the menu (which the law obliges them to display outside), then add 10%–15% to the check, or else stamp SERVICE NOT INCLUDED along the bottom, in which case you should add the 10%–15% yourself. Don't pay twice for service.

| WHAT IT COSTS In pounds | | | | |
| --- | --- | --- | --- | --- |
| | £££££ | ££££ | £££ | ££ | £ |
| AT DINNER | over £22 | £19–£22 | £13–£18 | £7–£12 | under £7 |

Prices are per person for a main course, excluding drinks, service, and V.A.T.

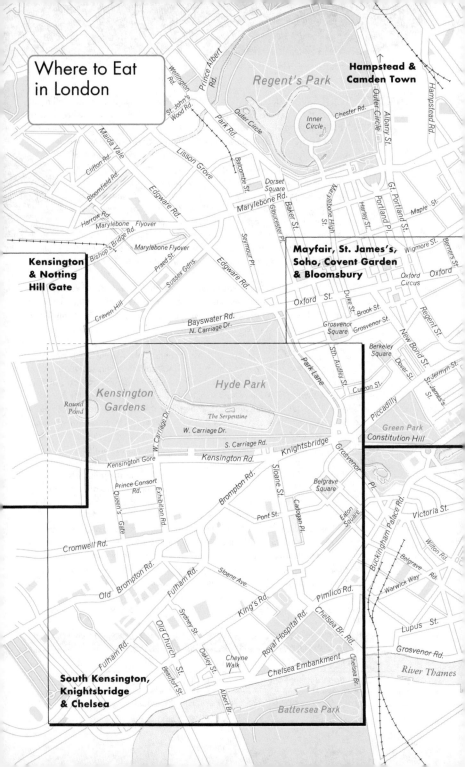

# Where to Eat in London

Regent's Park

Hampstead &
Camden Town

Hampstead Rd.

Wellington Rd.
St. John's Wood Rd.
Prince Albert Rd.
Outer Circle
Inner Circle
Chester Rd.
Outer Circle
Albany St.
Gt. Portland St.
Portland Pl.
Maple St.

Clifton Rd.
Maida Vale
Bloomfield Rd.
Harrow Rd.
Marylebone Flyover
Bishop's Bridge Rd.
Edgware Rd.
Lisson Grove
Park Rd.
Balcombe St.
Dorset Square
Marylebone Rd.
Baker St.
Marylebone High St.
Gloucester Pl.
Harley St.

Marylebone Flyover
Praed St.
Sussex Gdns.
Craven Hill
Seymour Pl.
Edgware Rd.

## Kensington
## & Notting
## Hill Gate

## Mayfair, St. James's,
## Soho, Covent Garden
## & Bloomsbury

Wigmore St.
Berners St.
Oxford Circus
Oxford St.
Oxford St.
Oxford St.
Duke St.
Brook St.
Regent St.
Grosvenor Square
Grosvenor St.
New Bond St.
Berkeley Square
Dover St.
St. Jermyn St.
St. James's St.

Bayswater Rd.
N. Carriage Dr.

Kensington
Gardens
Round Pond
Hyde Park
The Serpentine
W. Carriage Dr.
W. Carriage Dr.
S. Carriage Rd.
Kensington Rd.
Kensington Gore
Knightsbridge
Grosvenor
Sth. Audley St.
Curzon St.

Piccadilly
Green Park
Constitution Hill

Prince Consort Rd.
Queen's Gate
Exhibition Rd.
Brompton Rd.
Sloane St.
Belgrave Square
Eaton Square
Cadogan Pl.
Buckingham Palace Rd.
Victoria St.
Wilton Rd.

Cromwell Rd.
Old Brompton Rd.
Pont St.
Belgrave Rd.
Warwick Way

Fulham Rd.
Sloane Ave.
Lupus St.
Grosvenor Rd.

Fulham Rd.
Old Church St.
Sydney St.
Oakley St.
King's Rd.
Royal Hospital Rd.
Pimlico Rd.
Chelsea Br. Rd.
Chelsea Br.

Beaufort St.
Cheyne Walk
Albert Br.
Chelsea Embankment

River Thames

## South Kensington,
## Knightsbridge
## & Chelsea

Battersea Park

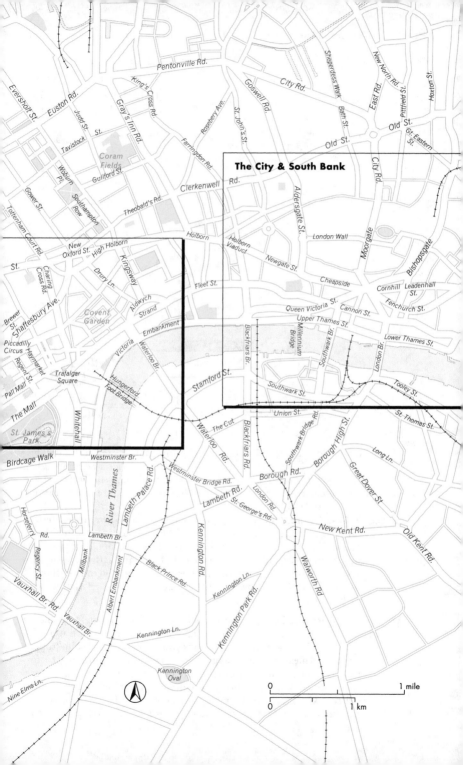

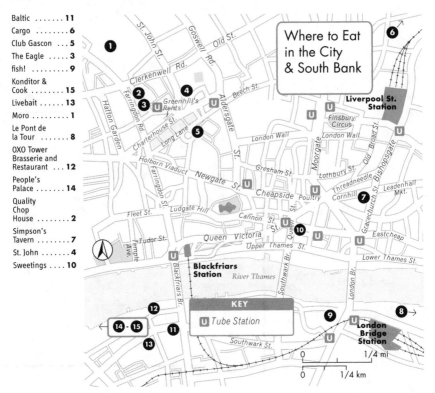

crammed with fancy French pâtés, Continental cheeses, fruit tarts, biscuits, organic vegetables, and breads galore. There's a tearoom, a bar, charcuterie counter, and a fashionable dining room. Breakfast, lunch, and dinner are served daily. ⊠ *170 Great Portland St., Bloomsbury W1* ☎ *020/7631–3131* ➡ *AE, DC, MC, V* Ⓤ *Great Portland St.*

**££–£££** ✗ **Chez Gérard.** One of an excellent chain of steak-*frites* (fries) restaurants (there are eight across London), this one has widened the choice on the Gallic menu to include more for those who don't eat red meat; for example, Icelandic cod with mussels, leeks, and saffron. Steak with shoestring fries and béarnaise sauce remains the reason to visit, though. ⊠ *8 Charlotte St., Bloomsbury W1* ☎ *020/7636–4975* ➡ *AE, DC, MC, V* Ⓤ *Tottenham Court Rd.*

JAPANESE ✗ **Wagamama.** Londoners drain endless bowls of Japanese noodles in
**£–££** this big basement. It's high-tech, high-volume, and high-turnover, with a fast-moving line at the door. Choose ramen in or out of soup (topped with sliced meat) or "raw energy" vegetarian dishes and juices. This formula is so successful that the restaurant now has a clothing line, so grateful diners can *wear* Wagamama. London has 16 branches; call or check out the Web site, www.wagamama.com, for details. ⊠ *4A Streatham St., Bloomsbury WC1* ☎ *020/7323–9223* ⓐ *Reservations not accepted*

≡ *AE, DC, MC, V* Ⓤ *Tottenham Court Rd.* ✉ *10A Lexington St., near Piccadilly Circus* ☎ *020/7292–0990* Ⓤ *Piccadilly Circus* ✉ *101A Wigmore St.* ☎ *020/7409–0111* Ⓤ *Bond St.*

SEAFOOD ✕ **North Sea Fish Restaurant.** Come here and nowhere else for the na-
★ **££–£££** tional British dish of fish-and-chips—battered cod and deep-fried white-fish and thick fries with salt and vinegar and mushy peas. It's tricky to find—three blocks south of St. Pancras station, down Judd Street. They serve only freshly caught fish, which you can order grilled—though that's missing the purpose. You can take out or eat in. ✉ *7–8 Leigh St., Bloomsbury WC1* ☎ *020/7387–5892* ≡ *AE, DC, MC, V* ⊘ *Closed Sun.* Ⓤ *Russell Sq.*

TURKISH ✕ **Gallipoli II.** It's a noisy neighborhood restaurant with loads of style.
**£–££** Crammed full of tables, there's always room for one more. The *meze* (a spread of small dishes) is the best first act: it's full of flavor and color (the falafel and the *kisir,* crushed wheat with walnut and onion, are particularly good). With hot breads fresh from the oven, you won't need more. The bone-of-lamb *incik* (boiled with red, green, and white peppers) is tender, and the baklava is worth the indulgence. ✉ *120 Upper St., Islington N1* ☎ *020/7359–1578* ⚖ *Reservations essential* ≡ *MC, V.*

## Camden Town & Hampstead

CAFÉS ✕ **Coffee Cup.** A Hampstead landmark for as long as anyone can remember,
**£** this smoky, dingy, uncomfortable café is lovable and cheap, and always
**Fodor's**Choice packed. You can get grills, sandwiches, cakes, fry-ups, plus anything
★ (beans, eggs, kippers, mushrooms) on toast—nothing whatsoever healthy or fashionable. The Coffee Cup has no liquor license, but has the added bonus of outdoor seating in summer. ✉ *74 Hampstead High St., Hampstead NW3* ☎ *020/7435–7565* ⚖ *Reservations not accepted* ≡ *No credit cards* Ⓤ *Hampstead.*

GREEK ✕ **Lemonia.** A superior version of London Greek near Regent's Park, Lemo-
★ **££–£££** nia is large and light, friendly, and packed every evening. Besides the usual *mezedes* (appetizers), *souvlaki* (kebabs), and *stifado* (beef stewed in wine), there are interesting specials: quail, perhaps, or *gemista* (stuffed vegetables). ✉ *89 Regent's Park Rd., Euston NW1* ☎ *020/7586–7454* ⚖ *Reservations essential* ≡ *MC, V* ⊘ *No lunch Sat. or dinner Sun.* Ⓤ *Chalk Farm.*

## Chelsea

AMERICAN/ ✕ **PJ's Grill.** Enter PJ's and you've adopted the Polo Joe lifestyle—
CASUAL wooden floors and stained glass, a slowly revolving propeller from a
**££–££££** 1911 Vickers Vimy flying boat, and polo memorabilia. The place is relaxed, friendly, and efficient, and the menu, which includes all-American staples like steaks, salads, and brownies, is likely to please everyone except vegetarians. PJ's stays open late, and the bartenders can mix anything. Weekend brunch is popular. ✉ *52 Fulham Rd., Chelsea SW3* ☎ *020/7581–0025* ≡ *AE, DC, MC, V* Ⓤ *S. Kensington.*

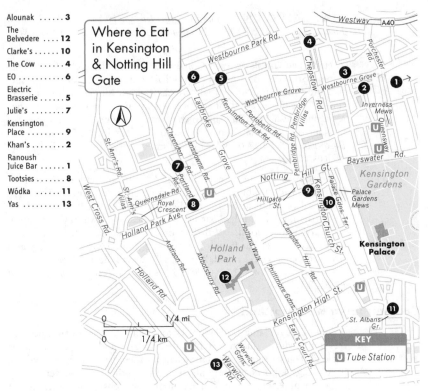

Where to Eat in Kensington & Notting Hill Gate

**£–££**   ✕ **Chelsea Bun Diner.** Get heaps of food for little money at this hybrid
**Fodor's**Choice   of an American diner and an English "greasy spoon." Expect a huge
★   menu with huge portions—burgers, salads, potato skins, many breakfasts (New York, San Francisco, Lumberjack, All-Day English Full), pastas, and pies. ⊠ *9A Limerston St., Chelsea SW10* ☎ *020/7352–3635*
☰ *MC, V* Ⓤ *Sloane Sq., then Bus 11, 19, 22.*

CONTEMPORARY   ✕ **Bluebird.** Sir Terence Conran presents a "gastrodome"—an upscale
**£££–£££££**   Sainsbury's food market, a café, and a restaurant. The place is blue and
white, bright, and large, and the food is good but can sometimes be for-
mulaic: suckling pig with ragout, hamhock and foie gras, and for dessert,
sambuca parfait and cherry jelly. Go for the people-watching and visual excitement; Conran's chefs tend to promise more than they deliver.
The café in the courtyard downstairs is a great spot for a break during
your King's Road shopping expedition. ⊠ *350 King's Rd., Chelsea*
*SW3* ☎ *020/7559–1000* ⌕ *Reservations essential* ☰ *AE, DC, MC, V*
Ⓤ *Sloane Sq.*

FRENCH   ✕ **Aubergine.** William Drabble continues to quietly forge his reputation
★ **£££££**   here. His signature dishes are very accomplished, and often gamey—
*boudin* (sausage) of wood pigeon with foie gras, turnip, and truffle; best-
end Cumbria lamb with onions, garlic, and rosemary. The restaurant is

simply alluring, bathed in the hues of impressionist Provence. For a thrifty option, come for lunch. ✉ *11 Park Walk, Chelsea SW10* ☎ *020/ 7352–3449* ⌕ *Reservations essential* ▤ *AE, DC, MC, V* ⊘ *Closed Sun. No lunch Sat.* Ⓤ *S. Kensington.*

★ **£££££** ✕ **Gordon Ramsay.** Ramsay whips up a storm with white beans, foie gras, scallops, and truffles. He's one of Britain's best chefs, and tables are booked months in advance. For £80, splurge on the seven-course option; for £65 wallow in three dinner courses; or go for lunch (£35 for three courses) for a gentler check. ✉ *68–69 Royal Hospital Rd., Chelsea SW3* ☎ *020/ 7352–4441* ⌕ *Reservations essential* ▤ *AE, DC, MC, V* ⊘ *Closed weekends* Ⓤ *Sloane Sq.*

**£££££** ✕ **Tom Aikens.** Best newcomer on the culinary scene, Tom Aikens trained under Joel Rubichon and excelled at the restaurant Pied à Terre. Now relaunched here, he loves fiddly constructions on the plate. You'll be intrigued by the configurations of his pig's head with pork belly, stuffed pig's trotter, and celeriac lasagne. There's a good wine list and a knowledgeable sommelier to help you navigate the list. ✉*43 Elystan St., Knightsbridge SW3* ☎ *020/7584–2003* ⌕ *Reservations essential* ▤ *AE, DC, MC, V* Ⓤ *S. Kensington.*

★ **£££–££££** ✕ **La Poule au Pot.** With bare brick walls, rustic furniture, and potted red roses on the tables, La Poule au Pot is superb for romantic meals. The "Chelsea Set"—and Americans—love this candlelit corner of France in Belgravia. The country cooking is decent but not spectacular. The *poule au pot* (stewed chicken) and *lapin à la moutarde* (rabbit with mustard) are strong and hearty, and there are fine classics, such as beef bourguignonne and French onion soup. Service is cheerful and friendly. ✉ *231 Ebury St., Knightsbridge SW1* ☎ *020/7730–7763* ⌕ *Reservations essential* ▤ *AE, DC, MC, V* Ⓤ *Sloane Sq.*

**££–££££** ✕ **La Brasserie.** This is a convenient choice if you're on South Kensington museum visits. Opening hours are long (8AM–11PM), and you can get everything from fish soup to tarte tatin. There's a good buzz on Sunday mornings, when the entire well-heeled neighborhood sits around reading the papers and sipping cappuccino. You can't hang out at peak dining hours, however. The food's reliable, if a little overpriced. ✉ *272 Brompton Rd., South Kensington SW3* ☎ *020/7584–1668* ▤ *AE, DC, MC, V* Ⓤ *S. Kensington.*

**££–££££** ✕ **Racine.** There's an upscale, buzzy, all-day atmosphere at this excellent FodorśChoice addition to the Brompton Road dining scene. Henry Harris's smart
★ French brasserie packs them in because he does the simple things well—and doesn't charge the earth. Classics like steak au poivre with bearnaise sauce, or chilled cucumber and mint soup, hit the spot. Desserts are £6 and wines by the glass are reasonably priced. ✉ *239 Brompton Rd., Knightsbridge SW3* ☎ *020/7548–4477* ▤ *AE, MC, V* Ⓤ *S. Kensington.*

INDIAN ✕ **Chutney Mary.** London's stalwart Indian restaurant is holding its own
**££–£££££** as a top notch destination. Dishes like the masala lambshank shakuti (with 21 spices) and Goan chicken curry (with mint and coriander) mingle with more familiar North Indian dishes, such as lamb or chicken tikka. Servers are gracious, and desserts are worth leaving room for. The three-course jazz brunch on Sunday is good value at £16.50. ✉ *535 King's*

Where to Eat in Mayfair, St. James's, Soho, Covent Garden & Bloomsbury

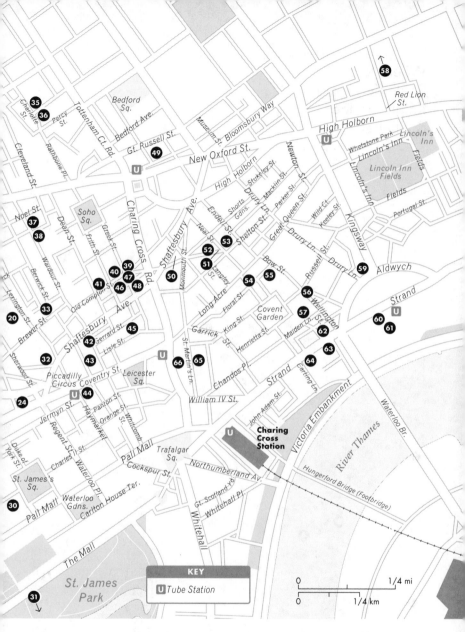

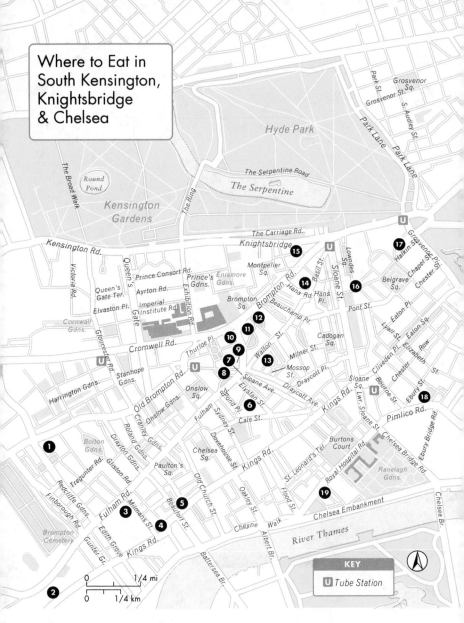

# Where to Eat in South Kensington, Knightsbridge & Chelsea

Hyde Park

The Serpentine Road

The Serpentine

The Broad Walk

Round Pond

Kensington Gardens

The Ring

Grosvenor Sq.

Grosvenor St.

S. Audley St.

Park Lane

Park Lane

The Carriage Rd.

Knightsbridge

Kensington Rd.

Queen's Gate Ter.

Queen's Gate

Prince Consort Rd.

Prince's Gdns.

Ayrton Rd.

Enismore Gdns.

Elvaston Pl.

Imperial Institute Rd.

Exhibition Rd.

Montpelier Sq.

Brompton Rd.

Brompton Sq.

Beauchamp Pl.

Hans Rd.

Hans Pl.

Basil St.

Lowndes Sq.

Sloane St.

Pont St.

**17**

Halkin

Grosvenor Pl.

Belgrave Sq.

Chapel St.

Chester St.

Eaton Pl.

Lyall St.

Eaton Sq.

**16**

Victoria Rd.

Cornwall Gdns.

Gloucester Rd.

Cromwell Rd.

Thurloe Pl.

**15**

**14**

**12**

**10** **11**

**9**

Walton St.

Milner St.

Cadogan Sq.

Cliveden Pl.

Elizabeth St.

Chester Row

Eaton Sq.

**7**

**13**

Mossop St.

Draycott Pl.

**8**

Sloane Ave.

Draycott Ave.

Sloane Sq.

Bourne St.

Ebury St.

**18**

Harrington Gdns.

Stanhope Gdns.

Old Brompton Rd.

Onslow Gdns.

Onslow Sq.

Pond Pl.

Elystan St.

**6**

Cale St.

Kings Rd.

Lwr. Sloane St.

Pimlico Rd.

Chelsea Bridge Rd.

Ebury Bridge Rd.

**1**

Bolton Gdns.

Tregunter Rd.

Redcliffe Gdns.

Finborough Rd.

Gilston Rd.

Fulham Rd.

Drayton Gdns.

Roland Gdns.

Cranley Gdns.

Fulham Rd.

Sydney St.

Milmans St.

Paulton's Sq.

Chelsea Sq.

Dovehouse St.

Beaufort St.

Old Church St.

Kings Rd.

Oakley St.

Flood St.

St. Leonard's Ter.

Burtons Court

Royal Hospital Rd.

Ranelagh Gdns.

Chelsea Br.

**19**

Brompton Cemetery

Edith Grove

Gunter Gr.

Kings Rd.

Cheyne Walk

Albert Br.

Cheyne Walk

Chelsea Embankment

River Thames

Battersea Br.

**3**

**4**

**5**

**2**

0    1/4 mi

0    1/4 km

## KEY

U Tube Station

| | | |
|---|---|---|
| Aubergine . . . . . . . . . . . **3** | Chutney Mary . . . . . . . . **2** | Nahm . . . . . . . . . . . . . . **17** |
| Bibendum . . . . . . . . . . **7** | The Collection . . . . . . . **10** | PJ's Grill . . . . . . . . . . . . **8** |
| Bluebird . . . . . . . . . . . **5** | The Enterprise . . . . . . . **13** | Racine . . . . . . . . . . . . . **12** |
| Brasserie St. Quentin . . . . . . . . **11** | Gordon Ramsay . . . . . . **19** | Tom Aikens . . . . . . . . . **6** |
| The Capital . . . . . . . . **14** | La Brasserie . . . . . . . . . **9** | Zafferano . . . . . . . . . . **16** |
| Chelsea Bun Diner . . . . . . . . . . . . . . **4** | La Poule au Pot . . . . . . **18** | Zuma . . . . . . . . . . . . . . **15** |
| | Lou Pescadou . . . . . . . . . **1** | |

*Rd., Chelsea SW10* ☎ *020/7351–3113* ⌕ *Reservations essential* ▭ *AE, DC, MC, V* Ⓤ *Fulham Broadway.*

## The City & the South Bank

CONTEMPORARY ✕ **OXO Tower Brasserie and Restaurant.** London has a room with a view—
**£££–£££££** and what a view it is. On the eighth floor of the OXO Tower on the South Bank, this elegant restaurant serves Euro-Asian food with the latest trendy ingredients (oxtail with purple broccoli, for instance). The ceiling slats turn from white to blue, but who notices, with St. Paul's Cathedral and the London skyline across the water? The brasserie is cheaper than the restaurant, but both have great river views, especially in summer when there are tables on the terrace. ⊠ *Barge House St., South Bank SE1* ☎ *020/7803–3888* ▭ *AE, DC, MC, V* Ⓤ *Waterloo.*

**£££–£££££** ✕ **St. John.** You either love or hate Fergus Henderson's ultra-British cook-
FodorśChoice ing at this converted smokehouse. His chutzpah is scary: one appetizer
★ is sliced pig spleen, although some of the others (roast bone marrow and parsley salad; smoked eel and horseradish) are less austere. Entrées (venison liver and boiled egg, haddock and fennel) appear stark on the plate but are presented with style. Expect an all-French wine list with affordable bottles, plus malmseys and ports. Try the rice pudding with plums, or the English Eccles cakes and Lancashire cheese. ⊠ *26 St. John St., The City EC1* ☎ *020/7251–0848* ⌕ *Reservations essential* ▭ *AE, DC, MC, V* ☾ *Closed Sun. No lunch Sat.* Ⓤ *Farringdon.*

EASTERN ✕ **Baltic.** To eat well in Southwark, perhaps before a play at the Young
EUROPEAN Vic or a visit to Tate Modern, come to Baltic. Here you'll find a bustling
**££–£££** vodka-party playground—a good spot for drinks at the bar or a decent
FodorśChoice East European meal in a converted former coach house with slick white
★ walls and wooden beams. With the same ownership as Wódka in Kensington, Baltic serves fine blinis—with herring, smoked salmon, or caviar—and great *leniwe* (potato dumplings) and gravlax. The vodkas are fruity and eclectic: Siberian, bison grass, rowanberry, and rye and honey, to name a few. ⊠ *74 Blackfriars Rd., South Bank SE1* ☎ *020/7928–1111* ▭ *AE, MC, V* Ⓤ *Southwark.*

ENGLISH ✕ **Quality Chop House.** Converted from one of the more gorgeous "greasy
★ **££–£££££** spoon caffs" in town, this place retains Victorian fittings (including pew-like bench seats, which you have to share). It's not luxurious, but the grub is superior cafeteria food—bangers and mash turns out to be homemade Toulouse sausage with veal gravy and fluffy potatoes; egg and chips isn't remotely greasy. You'll also find posh dishes, like salmon cakes and rump steak. And there's plenty of seafood on the menu, including lobster, caviar, oysters, clams, and jellied eels. ⊠ *94 Farringdon Rd., The City EC1* ☎ *020/7837–5093* ⌕ *Reservations essential* ▭ *AE, MC, V* ☾ *No lunch Sat.* Ⓤ *Farringdon.*

**£££–££££** ✕ **People's Palace.** Thank goodness for this place—now you can have a civilized meal during your South Bank arts encounter. It's run independently from the Royal Festival Hall, with remarkably low prices considering it commands the greatest river view in town (apart from OXO Tower). There are occasional mistakes here, and generally the more British the dish, the more reliable it proves to be: veal, skate wings, pecan-and-banana

# CloseUp

# WHERE TO REFUEL AROUND TOWN

**W**HEN YOU'RE ON THE GO or don't have time for a leisurely meal, you might want to try a local chain restaurant or sandwich bar where you can stop for a quick bite or get something to take out. Although many of London's chains serve standardized, soulless fare, the ones listed below are fairly priced and committed to quality and use decent, fresh ingredients.

**Carluccio's Caffe:** Affable TV chef Antonio Carluccio's chain of seven all-day traditional Italian cafes/bar/food shops are freshly sourced and make brilliant stops on a shopping spree.

**Ed's Easy Diner:** OD on made-to-order hamburgers, onion rings, and thick milk shakes at this chain of shiny, '50s-theme American diners.

**New Culture Revolution:** There's a lot for vegetarians at these handy north Chinese noodle, soup and dumpling refueling stops. Don't expect much legroom, mind you.

**Pizza Express:** Serving utterly predictable pizzas, Pizza Express seems to be everywhere (there are 95 in London). Soho's branch has a brilliant live jazz program.

**Pret a Manger:** London's take-away (takeout) sandwich shop supremo. There are wraps, noodles, sushi, and tea cakes.

**Strada:** Stop here for great pizzas baked over a wood fire, plus simple pastas and risottos. It's stylish, cheap, packed, and booking-free.

**YO! Sushi:** The Soho one is the best of the seven branches. These futuristic, conveyor-belt sushi outlets have color-coded plates and robotic drink carts.

---

pudding—all these are delicious. Service is flaky, but the soaring space makes up for everything. ⊠ *Royal Festival Hall, Level 3, South Bank SE1* 🕾 *020/7928–9999* ➾ *AE, DC, MC, V* Ⓤ *Waterloo.*

**£–££**
**Fodor'sChoice**
★
✕ **Konditor & Cook.** Very useful for theatrical forays across the river, this cafeteria in the Young Vic theater serves full meals a cut above the tired quiche you might expect. Risotto and pumpkin, potato cakes and smoked salmon, and Toulouse sausages with mash are the kind of dishes to expect, but the pies and cakes—from the bakery around the corner, which supplies half of London—are the standouts. ⊠ *Young Vic Theatre, 66 The Cut, South Bank SE1* 🕾 *020/7620–2700* ➾ *MC, V* ⊗ *Closed Sun.* Ⓤ *Waterloo or Southwark.*

**£–££**
✕ **Simpson's Tavern.** A bastion of English tradition, this back-alley chophouse was founded in 1759 and only started admitting women in 1916. It's popular with stockbrokers, who come for the traditional fare: steak-and-kidney pie, liver and bacon, chops from the grill, Simpson's salmon cakes, or the house specialty, stewed cheese (melted cheddar cheese on toast with béchamel and Worcestershire sauce). The tavern is full at lunch, so wander in early for a taste of the old City of London. ⊠ *38½ Cornhill, at Ball Ct., The City EC3* 🕾 *020/7626–9985* ≼ *Reservations not accepted* ➾ *AE, DC, MC, V* ⊗ *Closed weekends. No dinner* Ⓤ *Bank.*

FRENCH ✕ **Club Gascon.** It's hard to find a sexier scene than this in all London.
**£££–£££££** Maybe it's the restrained, marble and leather-walled interior, the perfect
Fodor'sChoice service, the cut flowers, or the way the tapas-style, new French cuisine
★ is served: on a slab of rock rather than on a plate. Ah, it must be the quality of Club Gascon's lietmotiv: foie gras, which runs through the menu
from start to finish. Feast on foie gras steeped in 10-year-old Maury wine,
and then have it for dessert, with gingerbread and grapes. *Magnifique.*
✉ *57 W. Smithfield The City EC1* ☏ *020/7796–0600* ⌕ *Reservations
essential* ▤ *AE, MC, V* ☉ *Closed Sun. No lunch Sat.* Ⓤ *Barbican.*

★ **££–£££££** ✕ **Le Pont de la Tour.** A perfect spot in summer—the outside tables, just
by Tower Bridge, are heavenly. Inside you'll find a wine merchant, bakery, deli, seafood bar, brasserie, and this diner-style restaurant, smart as
the captain's table. Fish and seafood (lobster salad, Dover sole) and meat
and game (Denham-estate venison and Gressingham duck) are prominent. Prune-and-Armagnac tart is a fine finish to a glamorous meal. ✉ *36D
Shad Thames, Butler's Wharf, South Bank SE1* ☏ *020/7403–8403*
⌕ *Reservations essential* ▤ *AE, DC, MC, V* Ⓤ *Tower Hill.*

**£–££** ✕ **Cargo.** This is possibly London's best venue for a combination of music,
drink, and food. Deep in the trendy east-side Hoxton district, it's a friendly
restaurant—a fave with young urbanites—but also a top late-night bar
with great live acts. The Latin street grub works well for groups—peri
peri chicken, quesadillas—but it's the delicious cocktails, especially
caipirinhas, and the crazy dancing that really make the scene. ✉ *Kingsland Viaduct, 83 Rivington St., Hoxton EC2* ☏ *020/7739–3440* ▤ *AE,
MC, V* Ⓜ *Old St.*

MEDITERRANEAN ✕ **Moro.** Up the road from the City, at the cusp of Clerkenwell and Sadler's
★ **£££–££££** Wells, is Exmouth Market, a cluster of shops, an Italian church, and
more good restaurants like Moro. The menu includes a mélange of
Spanish and North African flavors. Spiced meats, cured Serrano hams,
salt cod, and other delicacies seasoned with herbs are the secret to
Moro's success. The only downside is the persistent noise. But then again,
that's part of the scene. ✉ *34–36 Exmouth Market, The City EC1*
☏ *020/7833–8336* ⌕ *Reservations essential* ▤ *AE, DC, MC, V*
☉ *Closed Sun.* Ⓤ *Farringdon.*

**£–££** ✕ **The Eagle.** It's the gastro-pub of gastro-pubs, and it belongs in the
Fodor'sChoice "Restaurants" section by virtue of the amazingly good-value Portuguese-
★ Spanish food. There are about nine dishes on the menu each day—a pasta,
three vegetarian, and/or risotto always among them. Quite a few places
in London charge three times the price for similar food, but there's a
welcome trend toward pubs serving good meals, a trend that the Eagle
all but started. ✉ *159 Farringdon Rd., The City EC1* ☏ *020/7837–1353*
⌕ *Reservations not accepted* ▤ *DC, MC, V* Ⓤ *Farringdon.*

SEAFOOD ✕ **Livebait.** Although no longer as fantastic as when it was independently
**££–£££££** run, this fish restaurant still packs them in, serving English seafood with
British ales by the pint, home-baked breads (beetroot, garlic, or turmeric),
and all sorts of fish (broiled, baked, stewed, and generally combined in
clever ways). There are branches in Covent Garden, the City, and Southwark. ✉ *41–43 The Cut, South Bank SE1* ☏ *020/7928–7211* ⌕ *Reservations essential* ▤ *AE, DC, MC, V* ☉ *Closed Sun.* Ⓤ *Waterloo.*

**££–££££** ✕ **Sweetings.** Uniquely English, Sweetings (est. 1830) is a time warp from the old City of London. There are many things Sweetings doesn't do: dinner, reservations, weekends, and coffee. It does, however, do seafood. It's not far from St. Paul's Cathedral, and city gents come for "luncheon." They drink tankards of Black Velvet (Guinness and champagne) and eat meals of potted shrimp, whitebait, Welsh rarebit, and roe on toast. The West Mersey oysters are good, and the desserts are English schoolboy favorites—spotted dick (suet pudding with currants) and steamed syrup pudding. ⊠ *39 Queen Victoria St., The City EC4* ☎ *020/7248–3062* ⌂ *Reservations not accepted* ▤ *AE, MC, V* ⊘ *Closed weekends. No dinner* Ⓤ *Mansion House.*

★ **££–£££** ✕ **fish!** A cool diner—sleek and modern—fish! sits in the shadow of Southwark Cathedral, near the excellent Borough Market. The fish here is fresh and organic. The langoustines are creel-caught, the cod is farmed by sustainable methods, and the scallops are landed by divers. There are 12 types of fish on the menu, including swordfish, brill, skate, and turbot. ⊠ *Cathedral St., South Bank SE1* ☎ *020/7407–3803* ▤ *AE, DC, MC, V* Ⓤ *London Bridge.*

# Covent Garden

AMERICAN ✕ **Smollensky's on the Strand.** This American-style bar-restaurant is use-
**££–££££** ful if you have children in tow, especially at lunch on weekends, when the young are fed burgers and "Kids' cocktails" and are taken off your hands by clowns and magicians. The grown-up menu favors red meat, with several cuts of steak, all served with fries and sauces. There are potato skins, salads, and other vegetarian choices, and sandwiches, inspired by cuisines from all over America, from New England to New Mexico. ⊠ *105 The Strand, Covent Garden WC2* ☎ *020/7497–2101* ▤ *AE, DC, MC, V* Ⓤ *Charing Cross.*

★ **££–£££** ✕ **Joe Allen.** Long hours (thespians flock here after curtain fall in Theatreland) and a welcoming interior mean New York Joe's London branch still swings, two decades on. The fun menu helps: roasted poblano peppers and black-bean soup are typical starters; entrées include barbecued ribs and London's only available corn muffins, or monkfish with sun-dried-tomato salsa. There are Yankee desserts, too—such as grilled banana bread with ice cream and hot caramel sauce. Weekend brunch here is a London institution. ⊠ *13 Exeter St., Covent Garden WC2* ☎ *020/7836–0651* ⌂ *Reservations essential* ▤ *AE, MC, V* Ⓤ *Covent Garden.*

**££–£££** ✕ **Maxwell's.** London's first-ever burger joint, dating from the 1970s, cloned itself and then grew up. Here's the result: a happy place under the Royal Opera House serving the kind of food you're homesick for: quesadillas and nachos, buffalo chicken wings, barbecued ribs, chef's salad, and burgers to die for. ⊠ *8–9 James St., Covent Garden WC2* ☎ *020/7836–0303* ▤ *AE, DC, MC, V* Ⓤ *Covent Garden.*

BELGIAN ✕ **Belgo Centraal.** Have mussels and frites in vast quantities, served with
**££–££££** your choice of 101 Belgian beers (Trappist-brewed, white, or light) by waiters dressed as monks, in a hall that could pass for a refectory in a monastery. Also eat *stoemp* (mashed potatoes and cabbage) with steak,

# Read this page.
# And get more out of every other page in this book.

## Save 10% on hotels, car hire and attractions with British Airways Holidays.

Book your holiday and receive great discounts, extraordinary service and our unmatched local expertise.

This offer is available exclusively to Fodor's readers, so book now at ba.com/discount

Chimay-beer sausages, lobster, or roast chicken. The luxury index is low, but it's a satisfying, entertaining meal in the center of town, without breaking the bank. ⊠ *50 Earlham St., Covent Garden WC2* ☎ *020/7813–2233* ⊟ *AE, DC, MC, V* Ⓤ *Covent Garden.*

CONTEMPORARY
**££–£££££**
Fodor's Choice
★

✕ **The Ivy.** It's London's favorite restaurant—and thus hard to get into. In a wood-panel deco room with blinding-white tablecloths and Howard Hodgkins paintings on the walls, the theater set eats Caesar salad, salmon cakes, English school food such as kedgeree and bubble and squeak, and baked Alaska for dessert. For star-trekking ("Don't look now, dear, but there's Ralph Fiennes") this is the prime spot in London. The weekend three-course lunch is a bargain at £19.50. Try walking in off the street for a table on short notice—it's been known to work. ⊠ *1 West St., Covent Garden WC2* ☎ *020/7836–4751* ⌀ *Reservations essential* ⊟ *AE, DC, MC, V* Ⓤ *Covent Garden.*

**££–££££**

✕ **Bank.** Glamorous urbanites flock to this eatery with its spectacular chandelier, open kitchen, and equally dazzling menu. Seared fish and confit of duck, haddock and ricotta tart, mousses, brûlées, and nursery puddings—these are just a few examples of its fast-changing world palette, which has a definitive mod-Brit touch. It's not a steal price-wise, but there's a constant buzz—that's because Bank does breakfast, weekend brunch, and useful pre- and post-theater deals. ⊠ *1 Kingsway, Covent Garden WC2* ☎ *020/7379–9797* ⌀ *Reservations essential* ⊟ *AE, DC, MC, V* Ⓤ *Holborn.*

CONTINENTAL
**£££££**

✕ **Savoy Grill.** Gordon Ramsay's protegé Marus Waring proves triumphant at this bastion of establishment power dining. There's kind lighting, wood paneling, and silver-plated pillars in the classic art-deco interior, and the assembled press barons, corporate executives, and politicians are exceedingly pleased with Waring's menu. On it is pork belly, calves' sweetbreads, omelet "Arnold Bennett" (with smoked haddock and Gruyère béchamel sauce), and chateaubriand beef. And the wines are excellent but pricey. ⊠ *The Strand, Covent Garden WC2* ☎ *020/ 7836–4343* ⌀ *Reservations essential* 🏛 *Jacket and tie* ⊟ *AE, DC, MC, V* Ⓤ *Covent Garden.*

ENGLISH
**£££–££££**

✕ **Rules.** Come, escape from the 21st century. This is probably the single most beautiful dining salon in London. More than 200 years old (it opened in 1798), this gorgeous institution has welcomed everyone from Dickens to the current Prince of Wales. The menu includes fine historic dishes—try the steak-and-kidney pudding for a taste of the 18th century. The decoration is delicious: plush red banquettes and lacquered Regency yellow walls crammed with oil paintings and engravings. For a main dish, try something from the list of daily specials, which will, in season, include game from Rules' Teesdale estate. ⊠ *35 Maiden La., Covent Garden WC2* ☎ *020/7836–5314* ⊟ *AE, DC, MC, V* Ⓤ *Covent Garden.*

FRENCH
**£££££**

✕ **Admiralty.** It's a restaurant worthy of the courtyard setting of Somerset House, just off the Strand. London is rejecting fusion food, and Admiralty does fine French cuisine with simplicity and integrity. The snail ravioli in Chablis with artichokes is a classic starter, and the sea bass and saffron sauce tastes as good as it looks on the plate. Political highflyers flock for the splendid cuisine, and (surely?) their hearts melt when they try the steaming hot chocolate *moelleux* (pudding). There's lots on the menu for vegetarians. ⊠ *Somerset House, Strand, Covent Garden WC2* ☎020/7845–4646 ☰*AE, DC, MC, V* ⊘*No dinner Sun.* Ⓤ*Charing Cross.*

INDIAN ✕ **India Club.** This Indian canteen can be described as "strange to the
£ point of weird," but "idiosyncratic" is probably kinder. You'll find it in the Strand Continental Hotel. It's not pretty—linoleum floors, Formica, and faded photos—but it's a favorite with University of London students, BBC journalists from Bush House next door, and Indian High Commission staff. You need to be a member of the hotel drinking club (£4) to get a beer from the bar (down two flights), so stick with the lassies (yogurt milkshakes) and the *masala dosai* (pancakes stuffed with onion and potato). ⊠ *143 The Strand, Covent Garden WC2* ☎020/7836–0650 ☰ *No credit cards* Ⓤ *Charing Cross.*

ITALIAN ✕ **Bertorelli's.** Across from the stage door of the Royal Opera House,
££–£££ Bertorelli's is quietly chic, the food is tempting, and the menu is just innovative enough: typical dishes include veal Milanese, and monkfish ragout with fennel, wonder beans, and Swiss chard. There's a café-bar below and a restaurant above. There are branches at 19–23 Charlotte Street and 11 Frith Street in Soho. ⊠ *44A Floral St., Covent Garden WC2* ☎ *020/7836–3969* ☰ *AE, DC, MC, V* ⊘ *Closed Sun.* Ⓤ *Covent Garden.*

££–£££ ✕ **Orso.** It shares the same snappy staff and glitzy clientele of showbiz types and hacks as its sister restaurant, Joe Allen. The Tuscan menu changes daily but always includes excellent pizza and pasta dishes plus entrées based, perhaps, on grilled rabbit or roast sea bass and first courses of deep-fried zucchini flowers with ricotta. Food here is never boring, nor is the place itself. Orsino, at 119 Portland Road, W11, is a stylish offshoot, serving much the same food. ⊠ *27 Wellington St., Covent Garden WC2* ☎ *020/7240–5269* ⌔ *Reservations essential* ☰ *AE, MC, V* Ⓤ *Covent Garden.*

PAN-ASIAN ✕ **Asia de Cuba.** A trendy restaurant in a trendy hotel, Asia de Cuba is
£££–£££££ the star attraction at Ian Schrager's St. Martins Lane. Philippe Starck–designed, it's bold and loud—check the dangly light bulbs, Latino music, library books, portable TVs, and satin-clad pillars. The food is Pan-Asian fusion and you're encouraged to share. The palomino of lamb is delicious as is the beef satay with quinoa salad. It isn't cheap, but it's totally disco. ⊠ *45 St. Martin's La., Covent Garden WC2* ☎ *020/ 7300–5588* ☰ *AE, DC, MC, V* Ⓤ *Leicester Sq.*

SEAFOOD ✕ **J Sheekey.** This is where the stars go as an alternative to the Ivy and
££–£££££ Le Caprice. Sleek and discreet, in the heart of Theatreland, the popularity of this seafood haven is evidenced by the photos on the walls—Peter O'Toole, Charlie Chaplin, Noel Coward, and Peter Sellers. And sultry J Sheekey really charms: cracked tiles, lava-rock bar tops, American oak paneling. Sample the wonderful jellied eels, Dover sole, Cornish fish stew, and the famous Sheekey fish pie. To save money, try the weekend fixed-price lunch for £18.50. ⊠ *28–32 St. Martin's Ct., Covent Garden WC2* ☎ *020/7240–2565* ☰ *AE, DC, MC, V* Ⓤ *Leicester Sq.*

**££–£££** ✕**Rock & Sole Plaice.** The appalling pun announces central London's only fish-and-chips joint, complete with inside seating. In addition to salmon, sole, and plaice, there's the usual cod and haddock, battered, deep-fried, and served with fries, ready for the salt and vinegar shakers. ⊠ *47 Endell St., Covent Garden WC2* ☎ *020/7836–3785* ▤ *AE, DC, MC, V* Ⓤ *Covent Garden.*

VEGETARIAN ✕**Food for Thought.** Despite being a simple vegetarian restaurant with **£–££** no liquor license, Food for Thought is extremely popular. You'll almost always find a line of people down the stairs. The menu—stir-fries, casseroles, salads, and desserts—changes daily, and each dish is freshly made. ⊠ *31 Neal St., Covent Garden WC2* ☎ *020/7836–0239* ✍ *Reservations not accepted* ▤ *No credit cards* ☽ *Closed Christmas wk* Ⓤ *Covent Garden.*

# Hammersmith

ITALIAN ✕**River Café.** Touted as serving up some of the best Italian food in Eu- **££££–£££££** rope outside Italy, this superstar restaurant started a trend with its sin- Fodor'sChoice gle-estate olive oils and simple roasts and pastas. Chefs Rose Gray and ★ Ruth Rogers believe in using fresh ingredients, so you get salmon with Sicilian lemons, Tuscan bread soup with *cavolo nero* (black leaf cabbage) and Swiss chard—plus one of London's highest checks. But remember, if you snag a reservation: this is in distant Hammersmith, and you can be stranded if you haven't booked a cab. ⊠ *Thames Wharf Studios, Rainville Rd., Hammersmith W6* ☎ *020/7386–4200* ✍ *Reservations essential* ▤ *AE, DC, MC, V* Ⓤ *Hammersmith.*

# Kensington & Notting Hill Gate

AMERICAN/ ✕**Tootsies.** A superior burger joint, Tootsies is dark but cheerful. Rock CASUAL music plays in the background, usually accompanied by a neighbor- **£–££** hood buzz. Alternatives to the burgers, which come with great fries, are big salads, steaks, BLTs, and chicken divertissements. The usual ice creams and pies will do for dessert. There's a children's meal for £4.95 and branches in Fulham, Chiswick, Ealing, Wimbledon, Kew, South Kensington, Parsons Green, Hampstead, and Richmond. ⊠ *120 Holland Park Ave., Holland Park W11* ☎ *020/7229–8567* ▤ *AE, MC, V* Ⓤ *Holland Park.*

CONTEMPORARY ✕**Clarke's.** Sally Clarke's daily changing four-course set dinners con- **£££££** tain fresh ingredients, plainly but perfectly cooked, and accompanied by home-baked breads. The flower-and-art-speckled room is similarly home-style, if home is one of the £2 million big, white, Kensington town houses with a stucco facade you see around here. ⊠ *124 Kensington Church St., Notting Hill W8* ☎ *020/7221–9225* ✍ *Reservations essential* ▤ *AE, DC, MC, V* ☽ *Closed Sun. and 2 wks in Aug. No lunch Sat.* Ⓤ *Notting Hill Gate.*

**£££–££££** ✕**The Cow.** Not *another* Conran. The Cow belongs to Tom, son of Sir Fodor'sChoice Terence, although it's a million miles from Bluebird. A chic gastro-pub, ★ it comprises a faux-Dublin backroom bar that serves oysters, salmon cakes, and baked brill. Upstairs the chef whips up Anglo-French specialties—

cod and mash is one temptation. Notting Hillbillies love the house special—a half-dozen Irish rock oysters with a pint of Guinness. ✉ *89 Westbourne Park Rd., Notting Hill W2* ☎ *020/7221–0021* ⚐*Reservations essential* ☰ *MC, V* Ⓤ *Westbourne Park.*

★ **£££–££££**   ✕ **Kensington Place.** A favorite among the local glitterati, KP is packed, stylish, and noisy. A huge plate-glass window and mural are backdrops to fashionable food—grilled foie gras with sweet-corn pancake and bitter chocolate mousse are perennials—but it's the buzz that draws the crowds. ✉ *201 Kensington Church St., Notting Hill W8* ☎ *020/ 7727–3184* ☰ *AE, DC, MC, V* Ⓤ *Notting Hill Gate.*

**££–£££**   ✕ **Electric Brasserie.** There's nowhere better than the Electric on market
Fodor'sChoice   day at Portobello. Go for the bustle—the zinc fittings, mirrors, shared
★   tables, and flattering back lighting. And, of course, the great Portobello people-watching. Expect chunky sandwiches, steaks, salads, and seafood platters. Or you can just hang at the bar with a long drink. ✉ *191 Portobello Rd., Notting Hill W11* ☎ *0207/7908–9696* ☰ *AE, DC, V* Ⓤ *Notting Hill.*

CONTINENTAL   ✕ **The Belvedere.** There can be no finer setting for a summer supper or
**£££–£££££**   a Sunday brunch than a table by the window—except, perhaps, one by the balcony if you luck out—at this stunning restaurant in the middle of Holland Park. The menu has good roast venison with raisins and black pepper, and, although things are a little pricey, a meal in the conservatorylike room is thoroughly enjoyable. ✉ *Holland Park off Abbotsbury Rd., Holland Park W8* ☎ *020/7602–1238* ⚐ *Reservations essential* ☰ *AE, DC, MC, V* ☉ *No dinner Sun.* Ⓤ *Holland Park.*

ENGLISH   ✕ **Julie's.** This cute 1960s throwback with a pop-star past has two
**££–££££**   stylish parts: a wine bar and a basement restaurant, both filled with Victoriana and ecclesiastical furniture. Bryan Ferry, Jerry Hall, and Sean Connery came here in the old days (now it's their children who eat here). The cooking is old-fashioned English (pheasant-and-hare terrine, sea bass and parsnips). The Sunday lunches are popular, and in summer there's a garden room for alfresco eating. ✉ *137 Portland Rd., Holland Park W11* ☎ *020/7727–7985* ☰ *AE, MC, V* Ⓤ *Holland Park.*

INDIAN   ✕ **Khan's.** This cheap, 300-seat Queensway stalwart has a permanent
**£**   rush-hour vibe. Go in a group, it's better that way, but remember it's dry: no alcohol at all. Most curries—like madras or vindaloo—are about £3.70, and the rice is £1.75. Khan's is always packed, and if you're not careful you'll have sat, ordered, eaten and settled up before you've taken your hat off. ✉ *13–15 Westbourne Grove, Bayswater W2* ☎ *020/ 7727–5420* ☰ *AE, DC, MC, V* Ⓤ *Queensway.*

MIDDLE EASTERN   ✕ **Yas.** Lavish bread is brought steaming to your table from the oven at
★ **££–£££**   this friendly Persian restaurant. Eat this with *panir o sabzi* (white cheese with herbs), hummus, *borani-e esfenaj* (yogurt and spinach), or any of the dips and salads. Then have a grilled-chicken or lamb dish or the daily specials like Sunday's *baghali polow* (lamb shank, broad beans, dill, and rice). Yas, which is opposite Olympia Exhibition Centre, is open until 5 AM every day. ✉ *7 Hammersmith Rd., Notting Hill W14* ☎ *020/ 7603–9148* ☰ *AE, DC, MC, V* Ⓤ *Olympia.*

**£–££** ✕ **Alounak.** It may have a raffish air, but the Iranian food here is tried and tested. Locals come for the superior hot bread and kebabs that emerge from the clay oven by the door. Try the *joojeh* kebab or the *zereshk polo* (chicken with rice and Iranian forest berries). Take the Iranian black tea and the Persian sweets, but note that the sour yogurt drinks are not to everyone's liking. ⊠ *44 Westbourne Grove, Bayswater W2* ☎ *020/ 7229–0416* ▤ *DC, MC, V* Ⓤ *Queensway.*

**£–££** ✕ **Ranoush Juice Bar.** Succulent, well-spiced shwarmas proliferate at this late-night kebab shop and juice bar (open until 3 AM daily) on Edgware Road, London's main Middle Eastern strip. Forget about the polished brass and the gaudy lighting—concentrate instead on the kebabs and falafal, or vine leaves or tabouleh. The juices, of course, are straight off the press. ⊠ *43 Edgware Rd., Bayswater W2* ☎ *020/7723–5929* ▤ *No credit cards* Ⓤ *Marble Arch.*

PAN-ASIAN ✕ **E&O.** If you like stars, you'll love E&O. It's one of London's most pop-
**££–£££££** ular scene restaurants. E&O stands for Eastern and Oriental, and the
Fodor'sChoice Pan-Asian cuisine also includes many options for vegetarians; it's an in-
★ telligent mix of Chinese, Japanese, Vietnamese, and Thai. Don't skip the Thai rare-beef salad with red *nam jhim* (bean sprouts) or the albacore sashimi. ⊠ *14 Blenheim Crescent, Notting Hill W11* ☎ *020/7229–5454* ⌂ *Reservations essential* ▤ *AE, DC, MC, V* Ⓤ *Ladbroke Grove.*

POLISH ✕ **Wódka.** This smart restaurant serves modern Polish food. It's popu-
★ **££–£££** lar with elegant locals and often seems like it's hosting one big dinner party. Alongside the salmon, herring, caviar, and eggplant blinis, you might find venison or roast duck. Order a carafe of the purest vodka in London; it's encased in ice and is flavored (with bison grass, cherries, and rowanberries) by the owner, a Polish prince. ⊠ *12 St. Alban's Grove, Kensington W8* ☎ *020/7937–6513* ⌂ *Reservations essential* ▤ *AE, DC, MC, V* ⊘ *No lunch weekends* Ⓤ *High St. Kensington.*

# Knightsbridge

CONTEMPORARY ✕ **The Enterprise.** A hot spot for "Sloanes," near Harrods and Bromp-
**££–£££** ton Cross, the Enterprise is filled with decorative types who complement the striped wallpaper, Edwardian side tables covered with baskets, vintage books piled up in the windows, and white linen and fresh flowers on the tables. The menu is fairly subtle—braised lamb shank with rose-
mary and celeriac puree—and the heartiness of the room contributes to a fun experience. ⊠ *35 Walton St., South Kensington SW3* ☎ *020/ 7584–3148* ▤ *AE, MC, V* Ⓤ *S. Kensington.*

FRENCH ✕ **The Capital.** The clublike dining room here has a grown-up atmosphere
**£££££** and the service is formal. Chef Eric Chavot does classic French cook-
ing, and many of his dishes are superb. Try the turbot with creamed baby leeks and mushroom ravioli. Desserts follow the same exciting route. Set-price menus at lunch (£28.50) make it somewhat more affordable than dinner. ⊠ *22–24 Basil St., Knightsbridge SW3* ☎ *020/7589–5171* ⌂ *Reservations essential* ▤ *AE, DC, MC, V* Ⓤ *Knightsbridge.*

**£££–£££££** ✕ **Brasserie St. Quentin.** French expats and locals alike frequent this popular slice of Paris. Every inch of France is explored—queen scallops,

**168** <

CloseUp

# WITH CHILDREN

**T**AKE THE CHILDREN TO *Chinatown: it's welcoming, and a colorful and interesting experience. London's many Italian restaurants and pizzerias are also popular with kids. Unless your children behave impeccably, the key is to avoid the high-class establishments; you won't find a children's menu there, anyway. The Pizza Express chain is family-friendly. At Smollensky's Balloon and Sweeney Todd's, clowns and magicians provide entertainment on the weekends. Hard Rock Cafe and Capital Radio Café have lively, musical atmospheres. The Rainforest Café has waterfalls and thundering jungle fun. There's a colorful interior, a children's menu, and a helpful staff at Giraffe. Belgo Centraal has an under-12 menu that allows children to eat free. At the laid-back Carluccio's Caffe, there are half-portions for kids and scrumptious Italian food for parents. China House serves kids'*

*portions and Chinese arts-and-crafts activities from 1 PM to 4 PM every week. Activities vary but include magicians, caricaturists, and origami experts.*

**Belgo Centraal** (✉ 50 Earlham St., WC2H 9HP ☎ 020/7813–2233). **Capital Radio Café** (✉ Leicester Sq., WC2 ☎ 020/7484–8888). **Carluccio's Caffe** (✉ 28a Neal St., WC2H 9PS ☎ 020/7240–1487). **China House** (✉ 51 Marchmont St., WC1N 1AP ☎ 020/7836–1626). **Giraffe** (✉ 29–31 Essex Rd., N1 ☎ 020/7359–5999). **Hard Rock Cafe** (✉ 150 Old Park La., W1 ☎ 020/7629–0382). **Rainforest Café** (✉ 20 Shaftesbury Ave., W1 ☎ 020/7434–3111). **Smollensky's Balloon** (✉ 1 Dover St., W1 ☎ 020/7491–1199). **Sweeney Todd's** (✉ 3–5 Tooley St., SE1 ☎ 020/7407–5267). **Sticky Fingers** (✉ 1A Phillimore Gardens, W8 ☎ 020/7938–5338).

---

escargots, pheasant, and partridge, fillet of beef brioche, tarte tatin—in the bourgeois provincial comfort that so many London chains (the Dômes, the Cafés Rouges) try for but fail to achieve. ✉ 243 Brompton Rd., Knightsbridge SW3 ☎ 020/7589–8005 ⊟ AE, DC, MC, V Ⓤ S. Kensington.

ITALIAN **££££–£££££** ✕ **Zafferano.** Any number of Cartier–wearing Belgravians flock to Zafferano, one of London's best exponents of *cucina nuova*. The fireworks are in the kitchen, and *what* fireworks: buckwheat pasta with leek and sage, lamb cutlets with hazelnut crust and white truffle polenta. The desserts are *delizioso*, especially the nougat parfait with chestnuts and the poached pears and mascarpone ice cream. ✉ 15 Lowndes St., Knightsbridge SW1 ☎ 020/7235–5800 ⚑ Reservations essential ⊟ AE, DC, MC, V Ⓤ Knightsbridge.

**££–£££££** ✕ **Zuma.** This is a wildly popular, Tokyo–style Japanese restaurant. Superbly lit and designed, with polished granite and blond wood, it includes a great restaurant, bar, and a robata grill and sushi counter, which doesn't accept reservations. Try the fabulous spider rolls, lobster tempura, and wagyu beef. There's also a "sake expert" on hand to help with the 30 hot and cold sakes. ✉ 5 Raphael St., Knightsbridge SW7

☎ *0207/7584–1010* ♨ *Reservations essential* 🖃 *AE, DC, MC, V* Ⓜ *Knightsbridge.*

THAI   ✕ **Nahm.** London's first-class Thai restaurant is manned by an Aussie,
**£££££** David Thompson. All sorts make it into Thompson's dishes: betel leaves, samphire, Chinese chives, and black sticky rice. Don't leave without trying the *yam pak* salad (Thai vegetables, green mango, holly basil, and tamarind sauce); oysters with chilis, ginger, lime, and sorrel; or jungle curry with monkfish, coriander, and shallots. ⊠ *Halkin Hotel, Halkin St., Knightsbridge SW1* ☎ *020/7333–1234* 🖃 *AE, DC, MC, V* Ⓤ *Hyde Park Corner.*

## Mayfair

CONTEMPORARY   ✕ **Greenhouse.** Tucked away behind the Mayfair mansions in a cobbled
**£££££** mews is where you'll find this elegant salon for people who like their food big and strong. You sit among extravagant greenery and men in lilac and black (with chauffeurs), and partake of modern European cooking: foie gras, confit duck and cep rissoto. The chocolate fondant with peanut butter ice cream is a treat. ⊠ *27A Hay's Mews, Mayfair W1* ☎ *020/7499–3331* ♨ *Reservations essential* 🖃 *AE, DC, MC, V* ☉ *Closed Sun. No lunch Sat.* Ⓤ *Green Park.*

ENGLISH   ✕ **Browns.** Crowd-pleasing, child-friendly English feeding is performed
**££–£££** well at the former site of bespoke tailors Messrs. Cooling and Wells. The classic Browns steak-and-Guinness pie is on the menu, but king prawns, lamb rumb, roasted peppers, salads, burgers, and pastas predominate. ⊠ *47 Maddox St., Mayfair W1* ☎ *020/7491–4565* 🖃 *AE, DC, MC, V* Ⓤ *Oxford Circus.*

**£**   ✕ **The Social.** The friendliest of the new wave of hip DJ–bars springing up around town, the Social offers great sounds with decent grub. The weekly DJ sessions are a knockout (you'll hear anything from electronica to Latino dub salsa) and the food is English old-school comfort: bangers and mash, steak-and-Guinness pie, fish-finger sandwiches, and even beans on toast. ⊠ *5 Little Portland St., Marylebone W1* ☎ *020/ 7636–4992* 🖃 *AE, MC, V* Ⓤ *Oxford Circus.*

FRENCH   ✕ **Gordon Ramsay at Claridge's.** Sit at the chef's table inside the kitchens,
**£££££** and marvel at the art and intensity. Ramsay is one of Britain's best chefs,
Fodor'sChoice and Claridge's is booked months in advance. It's open for breakfast, bar-
★ gain three-course lunches (£30), and stunning dinners for £55 and £70. Try the eight-hour roast shoulder of lamb, sea trout, or brill in red wine. Book months ahead but arrive early for dinner and have a drink at Claridge's art deco bar, the sassiest cocktail bar in town. ⊠ *Claridge's Hotel, Brook St., Mayfair W1* ☎ *020/7499–0099* ♨ *Reservations essential* 🏛 *Jacket and tie* 🖃 *AE, MC, V* Ⓤ *Bond St.*

★ **£££££**   ✕ **Le Gavroche.** Michel Roux has inherited the family cooking gene and runs one of London's finest restaurants. He's a master of classic French cooking—formal, flowery, decorated. The fixed-price lunch is relatively affordable at £42 (for canapés, three courses, plus mineral water, a half-bottle of wine, coffee, and petits fours). In fact it's by far the most economical way to eat here if you don't have an expense account, which most patrons do. Book at least a week in advance. ✉ *43 Upper Brook St., Mayfair W1* ☎ *020/7408–0881* ♨ *Reservations essential* 🖃 *AE, DC, MC, V* ⊘ *Closed Sun. and 10 days at Christmas. No lunch Sat.* Ⓤ *Marble Arch.*

★ ✕ **The Square.** Philip Howard's sophisticated set menus, in the modern
**££££–£££££** French haute tradition, include dishes such as foie gras with fig and apple or hare with celeriac and pear tart, followed perhaps by macaroni and Alba truffles, or sea bass with thyme butter. All dishes are arranged carefully and symmetrically. The clientele is heavy on businesspeople who appreciate impeccable service, complete with a friendly (and necessary—the wine list has the heft of a novel) sommelier. ✉ *6–10 Bruton St., Mayfair W1* ☎ *020/7495–7100* ♨ *Reservations essential* 🖃 *AE, DC, MC, V* ⊘ *No lunch weekends* Ⓤ *Green Park.*

★ ✕ **The Connaught.** The men's-club atmosphere at the Connaught's famous
**£££–£££££** dining rooms in Mayfair was swept away by Gordon Ramsay's installation of his protégée Angela Hartnett and—gasp!—her all-women management team. The customer age range dropped 20 years, and now it's all modern European cooking (Italy, the Med, Pays Basque, and Spain), rather than carved beef from the trolley or steak-and-kidney pie. Rest assured, though: there are also interpretations of Connaught classics. ✉ *Carlos Pl., Mayfair W1* ☎ *020/7499–7070* ♨ *Reservations essential* 🖃 *AE, DC, MC, V* Ⓤ *Green Park.*

★ ✕ **Mirabelle.** Marco Pierre White does what he does best at Mirabelle—
**£££–£££££** taking over a fading old establishment, licking it into shape, and turning its fortunes around. The interior is lavish and sparkly, and the food is an excellent interpretation of French with a hint of Italian. Expect exceptional seafood (grilled lemon sole with tartar sauce and creamed potatoes), and some good meat creations (steak with snails and roast venison stand out). The fondant chocolate dessert is a gutsy knockout, as is the pineapple tart with fromage blanc and ice cream. ✉ *56 Curzon St., Mayfair W1* ☎ *020/7499–4636* ♨ *Reservations essential* 🖃 *AE, DC, MC, V* Ⓤ *Green Park.*

INDIAN ✕ **Tamarind.** Some say Tamarind serves the best curry in London; ex-
**£££–£££££** pect to see lots of posh Indians here. This luxurious Mayfair basement is a sumptuous place, with golden arches, framed textiles, gilded staircases, and copper plates. It's expensive, but dishes like *jalpari chat* (fresh scallops with lime and pomegranate) and *makhni dhal* (creamy black lentils) are worth the price and are presented with precision. Try the desserts—they're good and sweet. ✉ *20 Queen St., Mayfair W1* ☎ *020/7629–3561* 🖃 *AE, DC, MC, V* Ⓤ *Green Park.*

IRISH ✕ **Mulligans.** Mulligans is straight out of Dublin, right down to the
**££–£££** draught Guinness. Downstairs, in the upscale restaurant, order traditional dishes such as roasted partridge and chestnuts or Irish stew with homey accompaniments like champ and colcannon (buttery mashed potatoes with cabbage), then a big rice pudding brûlée with whiskey-soused prunes and Irish coffee cheesecake. ✉ *13–14 Cork St., Mayfair W1* ☎ *020/7409–1370* 🖃 *AE, DC, MC, V* ⊘ *Closed weekends* Ⓤ *Green Park.*

ITALIAN ✕ **Locanda Locatelli.** The phones are busy at London's top Italian restau-
**££–£££££** rant. Everything chef Giorgio Locatelli touches turns to gold—hence the
Fodor'sChoice waiting list at this elegant David Collins–designed restaurant at the
★ Churchill Inter-Continental, complete with convex mirrors, etched glass,

swivel chairs, and banquettes. The food's incredibly accomplished—superb risottos, handmade pastas, beautiful desserts. Be bold: try the deep fried calves' head or the sweetbread with articoke and marsala sauce, and choose from the all-Italian wine list. ⊠ *8 Seymour St., Mayfair W1* ☎ *020/7935–9088* ⌂ *Reservations essential* ☰ *AE, MC, V* ⊗ *Closed Sun.* Ⓤ *Marble Arch.*

JAPANESE **✕ Nobu.** Nobuyuki Matsuhisa wows with new-style sashimi with a Pe-
££–£££££ ruvian touch—they sell 300 pounds of Alaskan black cod a day. Nobu is in the Metropolitan, a hip hotel, with staff, attitude, clientele, and prices to match. Ubon (that's Nobu backward), a sister restaurant, operates in Canary Wharf. ⊠ *Metropolitan Hotel, 19 Old Park La., Mayfair W1* ☎ *020/7447–4747* ⌂ *Reservations essential* ☰ *AE, DC, MC, V* ⊗ *No lunch weekends* Ⓤ *Hyde Park.*

## St. James's

AUSTRIAN **✕ The Wolseley.** There's a grand mittel-Europe old world elegance at this
££–£££ instant classic run by Messrs. Corbin and King, two of London's top
Fodor'sChoice restaurateurs. Right on Picadilly and framed with black lacquerware,
★ this Viennese-style café serves breakfast from 7AM through lunch, afternoon tea, and dinner, and stays open until midnight. On the menu, there's Nurnberger bratwurst, Wiener schnitzel, Hungarian goulash, and for dessert, apple strudel and *kaiserschmarren* (shredded pancake with stewed fruit); there are also decadently rich pastries to go. There's probably no better place for afternoon tea. ⊠ *160 Piccadilly, St. James's W1* ☎ *020/7499–6996* ☰ *AE, DC, MC, V.*

CONTEMPORARY **✕ Sketch.** Dinner for two for £450? Surely some mistake! It's make or
££££ break for London's most notorious event–dining experience—manned
Fodor'sChoice by Frenchman Pierre Gagnaire. Mourad Mazouz's madcap £12 million
★ emporium comprises the astronomical Lecture Room restaurant, discodining in the much cheaper Gallery, tearoom, art space, bookshop, and two scene bars, East and West. The Lecture Room's loony prices—main courses £40–£70—cause the outcry. Judge for yourself; it's a one-off, and the food can be sublime. ⊠ *9 Conduit St., St. James's W1* ☎ *0870/777–4488* ⌂ *Reservations essential* ☰ *AE, DC, MC, V* ⊗ *Closed Sun.* Ⓤ *Oxford Circus.*

££–££££ **✕ Le Caprice.** Secreted behind the Ritz Hotel, Le Caprice commands the
Fodor'sChoice deepest loyalty of any restaurant in London because it gets everything
★ right: the glossy Eva Jiricna interior; the perfect service; the menu, halfway between Euro-peasant and fashion plate. This food—grilled rabbit with rosemary, San Daniele ham and figs—has no business being so good. Frequented by Joan Collins and David Bowie, Le Caprice has some of the best people-watching in town. ⊠ *Arlington House, Arlington St., St. James's SW1* ☎ *020/7629–2239* ⌂ *Reservations essential* ☰ *AE, DC, MC, V* Ⓤ *Green Park.*

CONTINENTAL **✕ The Ritz.** This palace of marble, gilt, and trompe l'oeil would moisten
£££££ Marie Antoinette's eye. Add the view over Green Park and the Ritz's sunken garden, and it seems beside the point to eat. But the cuisine stands up to the visual onslaught, with super-rich morsels—foie gras,

lobster, truffles, caviar—all served with a flourish. Englishness is wrested from Louis XVI by a daily roast from the trolley. A three-course lunch at £37 and a four-course dinner at £55 make the check more bearable than the £65 you'll pay for the Friday and Saturday dinner-dance (a dying tradition). ⊠ *150 Piccadilly, St. James's W1* ☎ *020/7493–8181* ⌕ *Reservations essential* 🏛 *Jacket and tie* ▭ *AE, DC, MC, V* Ⓤ *Green Park.*

ENGLISH ✕ **The Fountain.** At the back of Fortnum & Mason is the old-fashioned
★ **££–££££** Fountain, as frumpy and popular as a boarding-school matron, serving delicious light meals and ice-cream sodas. During the day go for Welsh rarebit or Fortnum's steak-and-ale pie; in the evening, a no-frills steak is a typical option. It's just the place for afternoon tea after the Royal Academy or Bond Street shopping, and for pretheater meals. ⊠ *181 Piccadilly, St. James's W1* ☎ *020/7734–8040* ▭ *AE, DC, MC, V* 🕓 *Closed Sun.* Ⓤ *Green Park.*

FRENCH ✕ **L'Oranger.** The food here reaches gobsmacking perfection: duck ma-
**££££–£££££** gret with fondant potato and foie gras sauce; scallops with cured Iberico ham; John Dory with crushed cocoa beans; and hazelnut soufflé with praline ice cream. The conservatory is highly romantic, plus there's a little courtyard where the last duel in London was fought. The waiters are French, courteous, and friendly. ⊠ *5 St. James's St., St. James's SW1* ☎ *020/7839–3774* ⌕ *Reservations essential* ▭ *AE, DC, MC, V* 🕓 *Closed Sun. No lunch Sat.* Ⓤ *Green Park.*

**££–£££** ✕ **Criterion.** You'll love the glamour of this spectacular, neo-Byzantine mirrored marble hall, which first opened in 1874. It's heavy on the awe factor, with dishes to match, and Marco Pierre White's team scores highly. You can find some of his well-known dishes on the menu, for instance the ballotine of salmon with herbs and *fromage blanc*, and grilled calves' liver and lyonnaise sauce. The soaring golden ceiling, oil paintings, and attentive Gallic service adds up to a first-rate night out. ⊠ *224 Piccadilly, St. James's W1* ☎ *020/7930–0488* ▭ *AE, DC, MC, V* Ⓤ *Piccadilly Circus.*

INDIAN ✕ **Cinnamon Club.** MPs and spin doctors flock here for posh Indian
**££–££££** food in the converted Old Westminster Library—hence the wooden floors, high ceilings, double doors, and book-lined galleries. It's a block from Westminster Abbey and the House of Commons. The food is tasty and elaborate (Rajasthan red deer and pickling sauce or Goan spiced duck with curry-leaf–flavored semolina), but generally the simpler the dish, the better. ⊠ *Old Westminster Library, Great Smith St., St. James's SW1* ☎ *020/7222–2555* ▭ *AE, MC, V* Ⓤ *St. James's Park.*

LATIN ✕ **Gaucho Grill.** They say Gaucho Grill serves the best steaks in London,
**££–££££** but that's probably overstating it. Nevertheless, this chain of Argentine chophouses (the other locations are South Kensington, Canary Wharf, Hampstead, Chancery Lane, and the City) is reasonably priced and un-reconstructed in its reverence for meat. The steaks are flown vacuum-packed from Buenos Aires, and they're cut to order. There is not much for vegetarians, but it's great for a beef fix. ⊠ *19 Swallow St., St. James's W1* ☎ *020/7734–4040* ▭ *AE, DC, MC, V* Ⓤ *Piccadilly Circus.*

NORTH AFRICAN ✕ **Momo.** It's a hot ticket—so go if you can. Mourad Mazouz—Momo
**££–££££** to friends—storms beau London with his Casbah-like North African
Fodor'sChoice restaurant off Regent Street. The seats are low and close together and
★ there's a resident DJ and often live North African music. Downstairs
is the members-only Kemia Bar, and next door is Mô—a popular Moroccan tearoom, open to all. The menu doesn't match the excitement
of the scene; but the lamb merguez sausages are delicious. Momo CDs
on sale here are pretty funky, too. ⊠ *23–25 Heddon St., St. James's W1*
☎ *020/7434–4040* ⌣ *Reservations essential* ▭ *AE, DC, MC, V* Ⓤ *Piccadilly Circus.*

## Soho

CAFÉS ✕ **Bar Italia.** This well-established Frith Street caffeine-and-stand-up-snack
**£–££** stop is an oasis for photographers, admen, Soho-ites, theatergoers, and
clubbers early and late. Expect chocolate cake, frothy cappuccino, and
strong espresso. The walls are full of nostalgic pictures of Italian singers
and sporting heroes. It's the *primo* place in London to watch Italy play
in soccer's World Cup. ⊠ *22 Frith St., Soho W1* ☎ *020/7437–4520*
▭ *AE, DC, MC, V* Ⓤ *Leicester Sq.*

★ **£–££** ✕ **Maison Bertaux.** On two floors in central Soho, this French patisserie
is not in the least dainty, but it's the kind of place to refuel after a shopping trek, with a savory pastry at lunchtime, a Danish midmorning, or
even an early supper (it closes at 8:30 PM). The ancient rivalry with Valerie, around the corner, continues. ⊠ *28 Greek St., Soho W1* ☎ *020/
7437–6007* ▭ *No credit cards* Ⓤ *Leicester Sq.*

**£–££** ✕ **Patisserie Valerie.** Beloved of film-biz people, students, shoppers, and
just about everyone, this dimly lit pastry shop and café is cherished because nothing has changed here in years. The cakes are wondrous creations: dark *foret noir* (Black Forest gâteau with Morello cherries),
*cortinas* (creamy sponge cakes with rum and white chocolate), or classic almond croissants (£1.30). Drool at the window: it's a chocoholic's
Shangri-la. ⊠ *44 Old Compton St., Soho W1* ☎ *020/7437–3466* ▭ *AE,
DC, MC, V* Ⓤ *Leicester Sq.*

**£** ✕ **New Piccadilly.** London can be an odd place, so the New Piccadilly makes
it in for sheer eccentricity. Just behind Piccadilly Circus, nothing's changed
at this family-run diner since it opened in 1952 (not even the menu). The
waiter wears whites and shouts out orders as they're received. Fifties fans
love the decor—upturned lampshades, Formica tables, bench seats, and
cigarette cards on the wall—and the food's cheap and not bad, either. Steak,
chips and spaghetti is £6.50; a banana split £1.75. It ain't glam, but it's
got nostalgic charm. Note that it closes at 9 PM. ⊠ *8 Denman St., Soho
W1* ☎ *020/7437–8530* ▭ *No credit cards* Ⓤ *Piccadilly Circus.*

**£** ✕ **Mr Jerk.** You'll find all the best Caribbean flavors at this café-style
eaterie—curry goat, ackee and saltfish, roti, rice 'n peas, "hard food"
(yam and dumplings), plus soursap and Irish moss to drink. Oh, and
jerk chicken. It's no frills and you sit at shared tables, but the portions
are big and there's also takeout. The branch at 19 Westbourne Grove,
W2, is bigger and just as good. ⊠ *189 Wardour St., Soho W1* ☎ *0207/
7287–2878* ▭ *AE, MC, V* ☻ *Closed Sun.* Ⓤ *Tottenham Ct. Rd.*

CHINESE ✕ **Fung Shing.** This cool-green restaurant is a cut above the other
★ **££–£££££** Lisle–Wardour Street Chinese restaurants in terms of service and food.
The better Chinatown food choices are supplemented by even more exciting dishes. Especially fine are the crispy baby squid with Chinese sausage and the salt-baked chicken, served on or off the bone with a bowl of broth. Reserve a table in the backroom conservatory. ⊠ *15 Lisle St., Soho WC2* ☎ *020/7437–1539* ▭ *AE, DC, MC, V* Ⓤ *Leicester Sq.*

£ ✕ **Wong Kei.** One of the cheapest Chinese restaurants in Chinatown, with legendary rude waiters. The interior looks better after a makeover, there's free jasmine tea, and it's good for single dining. You'll find it full of London's Chinese residents enjoying tasty food at rock-bottom prices. The all-in-one meals are good, and the soups—like hot-and-sour—are decent pungent broths. ⊠ *41–43 Wardour St., Soho W1* ☎ *020/ 7437–8408* ▭ *No credit cards* Ⓤ *Piccadilly Circus.*

CONTEMPORARY ✕ **Sugar Club.** David Selex's eclectic menu goes down a treat here.
**£££–££££** Among the exotic dishes are kangaroo salad and lime chili and lamb shanks with parsnip puree and *gremolata* (parsley, garlic, and lemon zest). The Black Sea–bream sashimi with Avruga "caviar" (from herring roe) and purple shiso cress is a hit with the restaurant's fans. It's one of those places so loved by London's chattering classes that you have to reserve way ahead—two weeks is recommended. ⊠ *21 Warwick St., Soho W1* ☎ *020/7437–7776* ⌕ *Reservations essential* ▭ *AE, DC, MC, V* Ⓤ *Oxford Circus, Piccadilly Circus.*

CONTINENTAL ✕ **L'Escargot.** It's hard not to feel glamorous at this Soho haunt that serves
**£££** French food in an art deco ground-floor salon and a formal upstairs restaurant called the Picasso Room. The wine goes well with partridge and cèpes, wood-pigeon pithiviers (puff pastries) and chestnuts, simple grilled fish, or calves' liver. Owned by Marco Pierre White, L'Escargot is grown-up, glamorous, relaxed, and reliable. ⊠ *48 Greek St., Soho W1* ☎ *020/ 7437–2679* ▭ *AE, DC, MC, V* ☾ *Closed Sun.* Ⓤ *Leicester Sq.*

ECLECTIC ✕ **Andrew Edmunds.** Good food at realistic prices defines this perpetu-
**££** ally jammed, softly lit restaurant—though you'll wish it were larger and the seats more forgiving. Tucked away behind Oxford and Carnaby streets, it's a favorite with the film and media lunch crowd who like the daily-changing, fixed-price menu. Starters and main courses draw on the taste of Ireland, the Mediterranean, and the Middle East. ⊠ *46 Lexington St., Soho W1* ☎ *020/7437–5708* ▭ *AE, MC, V* Ⓤ *Oxford Circus, Piccadilly Circus.*

FRENCH ✕ **Spoon +.** There's a nightclub vibe at this groovy destination in the
**£££–£££££** Sanderson. Designed by Philippe Starck, French legend Alain Ducasse's London foray is a place to be seen. You can pick and mix the ingredients: ask for help, or try the £25 "Speedy Spoon" option before 7 PM. The soups are delicious—pumpkin or potato-and-truffle—and the meats tender. The 80-foot Long Bar is a bit posy, but dining in the covered garden is sensational. ⊠ *Sanderson Hotel, 50 Berners St., Covent Garden W1* ☎ *020/7300–1444* ⌕ *Reservations essential* ▭ *AE, DC, MC, V* Ⓤ *Oxford Circus.*

INDIAN
£–££ ✕**Masala Zone.** The contemporary canteen approach is applied successfully to Indian cuisine at Masala Zone. Expect shared tables, slick service, and cheap eats—this is a pit-stop place rather than somewhere to linger. The thali option has lots of little portions with rice and daal (lentils), and the "street food" bhajis and samosas are spicy and delicious. ⊠ 9 *Marshall St., Soho W1* ☎ 0207/7287–9966 ⊟ MC, V.

IRISH
★ £££–££££ ✕ **Lindsay House.** Come here for some of the finest dining in London. Richard Corrigan brings his Irish charm to Soho and fills up this 1740s Georgian town house with his large personality. He wraps rabbit and black pudding in Bayonne ham and excels with mash and Irish beef, and his white asparagus and langoustine dish can't be bettered. Petits fours with coffee will send you home oh-so-happy. ⊠ *21 Romilly St., Soho W1* ☎ *020/7439–0450* ⊟ *AE, DC, MC, V* ☯ *Closed Sun.* Ⓤ *Leicester Sq.*

ITALIAN
£ ✕ **Pollo.** A boisterous Italian café that's been around forever and through which all Londoners pass during their student and/or clubbing days, Pollo is good for a quick meal with a bottle of house wine pretheater, or for an afternoon spaghetti carbonara. Beware of the evening crowds, though—it's no fun unless you're 18 and in art school. ⊠ *20 Old Compton St., Soho W1* ☎ *020/7734–5917* ⊟ *No credit cards* Ⓤ *Leicester Sq.*

LATIN
£ ✕ **Market Place.** It's sauna-style blond wood all the way at this central London DJ bar, just off Oxford Street. The trendy new-media crowd—and some after-work suits—jam the popular spot, spread across two floors and a terrace. There's tasty Latin bar food; the roast pumpkin empanadas are especially good. The bar serves exotic beers and the DJs spin the decks every night. ⊠ *11 Market Pl., Soho W1* ☎ *020/7079–2020* ⊟ *AE, MC, V* Ⓤ *Oxford Circus.*

SEAFOOD
££–£££££ ✕ **Randall & Aubin.** Ed Baines's converted French butcher's shop (with meat hooks and marble tabletops) is one of London's buzziest champagne-oyster bars—right in the middle of Soho. Go for the Loch Fyne oysters, crab, or lobster with chips. At peak time you'll spend 15 minutes at the bar waiting for a seat, but it's worth it. Another Randall & Aubin has opened at 329–331 Fulham Road, in Chelsea. ⊠ *16 Brewer St., Soho W1* ☎ *020/7287–4447* ⊿ *Reservations not accepted* ⊟ *AE, DC, MC, V* Ⓤ *Piccadilly Circus.*

££–£££ ✕ **Café Fish.** There's an encyclopedic selection of fish at this cheerful, bustling restaurant—marlin, bream, salmon, and monkfish—which is arranged on the menu according to cooking method (char-grilled, pan-fried). The Mediterranean and Asian accents usually delight. Try the bar and canteen on the ground floor for a cornucopia of shellfish; in the upstairs restaurant you can linger longer over cod, fish pie, and kedgeree. It's a great pretheater spot. ⊠ *36–40 Rupert St., Soho W1* ☎ *020/ 7287–8989* ⊟ *AE, DC, MC, V* Ⓤ *Piccadilly Circus.*

THAI
★ £–££ ✕ **busabe eathai.** One of Londoners' favorite cheap spots in Soho, this superior Thai canteen is fitted with rattans, benches, hardwood tables, and paper lamp shades. It's no less seductive for its communal dining. The menu includes noodles, curries, stir-fries, rice, and sides. Try chicken with butternut squash, cuttlefish curry, or seafood vermicelli (prawns, squid, and scallops). The mantra here is *gan gin gan yuu,* which means

"as you eat, so you are." It's no smoking and there's a great second branch at 22 Store Street, W1. ✉ *106–110 Wardour St., Soho W1* ☎ *020/ 7255–8686* ⌂ *Reservations not accepted* ☰ *AE, MC, V* Ⓤ *Leicester Sq.*

## South Kensington

CONTEMPORARY ✕ **Bibendum.** This converted 1911 Michelin showroom, adorned with
★ art deco prints and stained glass, remains a London showpiece. Chef
**£££–£££££** Matthew Harris cooks with Euro-Brit flair. Try calves' brains, any risotto, or Pyrenean lamb with garlic and gravy. Here, too, you will find tripe as it ought to be cooked. The £25 fixed-price lunch menu is money well spent. ✉ *Michelin House, 81 Fulham Rd., South Kensington SW3* ☎ *020/7581–5817* ⌂ *Reservations essential* ☰ *AE, DC, MC, V* Ⓤ *S. Kensington.*

FRENCH ✕ **Lou Pescadou.** Imagine a slice of the south of France, in sea-theme sur-
★ **£–£££** roundings and with an emphatically French staff. Fish predominates here, and the menu changes often—don't miss the *soupe de poisson* (fish soup) with croutons and *rouille* (rose-color, garlicky mayonnaise). The French-dominated wine list can be pricey. ✉ *241 Old Brompton Rd., South Kensington SW5* ☎ *020/7370–1057* ⌂ *Reservations essential* ☰ *AE, DC, MC, V* Ⓤ *Earl's Court.*

MEDITERRANEAN ✕ **The Collection.** Enter this former Katharine Hamnett shop through the
**££–££££** spotlighted tunnel over a glass drawbridge, make your way past the style police, and you'll find yourself engulfed by a fashionable crowd. The huge warehouse setting, with industrial wood beams and steel cables, a vast bar, and a suspended gallery, makes a great theater for people-watching. Well-dressed wannabes peck at Med food with Japanese and Thai accents. ✉ *264 Brompton Rd., South Kensington SW3* ☎ *020/ 7225–1212* ☰ *AE, DC, MC, V* Ⓤ *S. Kensington.*

## Brunch & Afternoon Tea

*Supposedly,* brunch is catching on among Londoners, while the afternoon ritual often mistakenly referred to as "high tea" is dying out. Tea the drink, however, is so ingrained in the national character that tea the meal will always have a place in the capital, if only as an occasional celebration, a children's treat, or something you do when your American friends are in town. Reserve for all these, unless otherwise noted.

### Brunch
**Butlers Wharf Chop House.** What you'll get here, at £16.95 for three courses, is brunch that's as British as brunch ever gets, with lobster mayonnaise,

# ON THE MENU

**N LONDON, LOCAL COULD MEAN** *any global flavor, but for pure Britishness, roast beef probably tops the list. If you want the best-value traditional Sunday lunch, go to a pub. Gastro-pubs, where Sunday roasts are generally made with top-quality ingredients, are a good bet. The meat is usually served with crisp, roast potatoes and brussels sprouts, and with the traditional Yorkshire pudding, a savory batter baked in the oven until crisp. A rich, dark gravy is poured on top.*

*Other tummy liners include shepherd's pie, made with stewed minced lamb and a mashed potato topping and baked until lightly browned on top; cottage pie is a similar dish, but made with minced beef instead of lamb. Steak-and-kidney pie, with chunks of beef and pig's kidneys braised in a thick gravy and topped with a light puff-pastry crust is a delight when done properly; a good place to try this is*

*at the Green Man pub in Harrods, on the lower ground floor.*

*Fish-and-chips, usually cod or haddock, comes with thick french fries. A ploughman's lunch in a pub is crusty bread, a strong flavored English cheese with bite (cheddar, blue Stilton, crumbly white Cheshire, or smooth red Leicester), and pickles with a side salad garnish. As for puddings, seek out a sweet bread-and-butter pudding, served hot with layers of bread and dried fruit baked in a creamy custard until lightly crisp. And we musn't forget the English cream tea, which consists of scones served with jam and clotted cream, and sandwiches made with wafer-thin slices of cucumber—and of course plenty of tea.*

Stilton and celery soup, and a fabulous Thames-side setting. ⊠ *36E Shad Thames, South Bank SE1* ☎ *020/7403–3403* ⊟ *AE, DC, MC, V* ☺ *Brunch served weekends noon–4* Ⓤ *Tower Hill.*

**Christopher's Grill.** Imagine you're in Manhattan at this superior Covent Garden purveyor of American food. They serve everything from pancakes, steak, eggs, and fries to salmon cakes and Caesar salad. ⊠ *18 Wellington St., Covent Garden WC2* ☎ *020/7240–4222* ⊟ *AE, DC, MC, V* ☺ *Brunch served weekends 11:30–3:30* Ⓤ *Covent Garden.*

★ **Joe Allen.** A hangout famous among theater people, Joe Allen is a place to hide from the lovely British weather and down some Bloody Marys. Supplement that with a grilled-chicken sandwich or a salad of spicy sausage, shrimp, and new potatoes. ⊠ *13 Exeter St., Covent Garden WC2* ☎ *020/7836–0651* ⊟ *AE, MC, V* ☺ *Brunch served weekends 11:30–4* Ⓤ *Covent Garden.*

**Veeraswamy.** It's been here since 1926, but the Chutney Mary group from Chelsea has taken it over and made the mezzanine-level space sleek, chic, and full of color. The brunch menu (£15 for three courses) is a great way to sample authentic regional Indian cuisines. You'll be so taken with the aromatic fish and chicken dishes and mod-Euro–trad-Indian desserts, you'll want to come back for dinner. ✉ *Victory House, 99–101 Regent St., St. James's W1* ☏ *020/7734–1401* ⊟ *AE, DC, MC, V* ⊙ *Brunch served Sun. 12:30–3* Ⓤ *Regent St.*

## Afternoon Tea

Note that Claridge's and the Savoy require jacket and tie.

**Claridge's.** This is the real McCoy, with liveried footmen proffering sandwiches, scones, and superior patisseries (£27, or £35) in the palatial yet genteel foyer, to the sound of the resident "Hungarian orchestra" (actually a string quartet). ✉ *Brook St., Mayfair W1* ☏ *020/ 7629–8860* ⊟ *AE, DC, MC, V* ⊙ *Tea daily 3–5:30* Ⓤ *Bond St.*

**Fortnum & Mason.** Upstairs at the Queen's grocers, three set teas are ceremoniously served: standard afternoon tea (sandwiches, scone, cakes, £18.50), old-fashioned high tea (the traditional nursery meal, adding something more robust and savory, £20.50), and champagne tea (£26.50). ✉ *St. James's Restaurant, 4th floor, 181 Piccadilly, St. James's W1* ☏ *020/ 7734–8040* ⊟ *AE, DC, MC, V* ⊙ *Tea Mon.–Sat. 3–5:45* Ⓤ *Green Park.*

**Harrods.** For sweet-toothed people, the fourth-floor Georgian Restaurant at this ridiculously well-known department store has a high tea that will give you a sugar rush for a week. ✉ *87–135 Brompton Rd., Knightsbridge SW3* ☏ *020/7730–1234* ⊟ *AE, DC, MC, V* ⊙ *Tea weekdays 3:30–5:30, Sat. 4–5:30* Ⓤ *Knightsbridge.*

**The Orangery at Kensington Palace.** This Georgian, gorgeous, sunlight-flooded (assuming the sun is out), yes, orangery is the perfect place for a light lunch or tea. You can get homemade soups and quiche, cakes, shortbread, pastries, and pots of Earl Grey. Go when it's balmy, or you'll freeze. ✉ *Kensington Gardens, Holland Park W8* ☏ *020/7376–0239* ⊟ *AE, MC, V* Ⓤ *High St. Kensington or Queensway.*

**The Ritz.** The Ritz's huge, stagy, sometimes cold and overly formal Palm Court serves tiered cake stands, silver pots, a harpist, and Louis XVI chaises, plus a great deal of rococo gilt and glitz, all for £29. Reserve at least four weeks ahead, more for weekends. ✉ *150 Piccadilly, St. James's W1* ☏ *020/7493–8181* ⊟ *AE, DC, MC, V* ⊙ *Tea daily 1:30–5:30* Ⓤ *Green Park.*

**The Savoy.** The glamorous Thames-side hotel does one of the most pleasant teas (£24 or £27). Its triple-tier cake stands are packed with goodies, and its tailcoated waiters are wonderfully polite. ✉ *The Strand, Covent Garden WC2* ☏ *020/7836–4343* ⊟ *AE, DC, MC, V* ⊙ *Tea daily 2–6* Ⓤ *Charing Cross.*

# Pubs

Even today, when TV keeps so many glued to hearth and home, the pub, or public house, or "local," is still a vital part of British life. It also should be a part of the tourist experience, as there are few better places to meet the natives in their local habitat. There are hundreds of pubs in London, but the best—ever fewer of which still have original Victorian etched glass, Edwardian panels, and art nouveau carvings—are listed below.

Gastro-pub fever is still sweeping London. At many places, char-grills are installed in the kitchen out back, and up front the faded wallpaper is replaced by abstract paintings. Some of the following also serve nouveau pub grub, but whether you have Moroccan chicken or the ploughman's special, you may also want to order a pint. Remember that what Americans call beer, the British call lager. However, the real pub drink is "bitter," usually served at room temperature. There's a movement to bring back the traditionally prepared ale that is much less gassy. There are also plenty of other potations: stouts like Guinness and Murphy's are thick, pitch-black brews you'll either love or hate; ciders, made from apples, are an alcoholic drink in Britain (Bulmer's and Strongbow are the names to remember); shandies are a mix of lager and lemon soda; and black-and-tans are a blend of lager and stout named for the distinctive uniforms worn by early 20th-century British troops. Discuss your choice of drink with the barman, turn to your neighbor, raise the glass, and utter that most pleasant of toasts, "Cheers."

Arcane licensing laws forbid the serving of alcohol after 11 PM (10:30 on Sunday; different rules for restaurants) and have created, some argue, a nation of binge drinkers and alcoholics, driven to down more pints than is decent in a limited time—a circumstance you see in action at 10 minutes to 11, when the "last orders" bell signals a stampede to the bar. That noted, "lock-ins" are an old tradition—pubs that lock the front door after hours and ask remaining customers to leave by the side door—that bobbies tend to overlook. The list below offers a few pubs selected for central location, historical interest, a pleasant garden, music, or good food, but you might just as happily adopt your own temporary local.

**The Albert.** The Albert must have been designed to be *the* complete, authentic London pub, with its burnished wood, walls adorned with Victorian prints about the evils of drinking, and "division bell" (which calls back members of Parliament in time for a vote). The food in the restaurant upstairs is so good that reservations are usually required. ✉ *52 Victoria St., St. James's SW1* ☎ *020/7222–5577* Ⓤ *St. James's Park.*

**Black Friar.** A step from Blackfriars Tube stop, this spectacular pub has an arts-and-crafts interior that is entertainingly, satirically ecclesiastical, with inlaid mother-of-pearl, wood carvings, stained glass, and marble pillars all over the place. In spite of the finely lettered temperance tracts on view just below the reliefs of monks, fairies, and friars, there is, needless to say, a nice group of beers on tap from independent brewers. ✉ *174 Queen Victoria St., The City EC4* ☎ *020/7236–5474* Ⓤ *Blackfriars.*

**Crown and Goose.** This is an art-bedecked Camden Town local, where armchairs augment the tables and coffee and herb tea the beers, and good food (steak in baguettes, smoked chicken salad, baked and stuffed mushrooms) is served to the crowds. ✉ *100 Arlington Rd., Camden Town NW1* ☎ *020/7485–8008* Ⓤ *Camden Town.*

**Dove Inn.** Read the list of famous ex-regulars, from Charles II and Nell Gwyn to Ernest Hemingway, as you wait for a beer at this very popular, very comely 16th-century riverside pub by Hammersmith Bridge. If the

Dove is too full, stroll upstream to the Old Ship or the Blue Anchor. ✉ *19 Upper Mall, Hammersmith* W6 ☎ *020/8748–5405* Ⓤ *Hammersmith.*

**French House.** In the pub where the French Resistance convened during World War II, Soho hipsters and eccentrics rub shoulders now—more than shoulders, actually, because this tiny, tricolor-waving, photograph-lined pub is always packed with theater people and the literati. ✉ *49 Dean St., Soho W1* ☎ *020/7437–2799* Ⓤ *Piccadilly Circus.*

**George Inn.** The inn overlooks a courtyard where Shakespeare's plays were once staged. The present building dates from the late 17th century and is central London's last remaining galleried inn. Dickens was a regular, and the George is featured in *Little Dorrit*. Entertainments include Shakespeare performances, medieval jousts, and morris dancing. ✉ *77 Borough High St., South Bank SE1* ☎ *020/7407–2056* Ⓤ *London Bridge.*

**Island Queen.** This sociable Islington pub has home-cooked food, a busy pool table, and a fab jukebox. Playwright Joe Orton frequented the place; he lived—and died, murdered by his lover—next door. ✉ *87 Noel Rd., Islington N1* ☎ *020/7704–7631* Ⓤ *Angel.*

**The Lamb.** Another of Dickens's locals is now a picturesque place for a pint in summer, when you can drink on the patio. ✉ *94 Lamb's Conduit St., The City WC1* ☎ *020/7405–0713* Ⓤ *Russell Sq.*

**Lamb & Flag.** This 17th-century pub was once known as the Bucket of Blood because the upstairs room was used as a ring for bare-knuckle boxing. Now it's a trendy, friendly, and bloodless pub, serving food (lunchtime only) and real ale. It's on the edge of Covent Garden, off Garrick Street. ✉ *33 Rose St., Covent Garden WC2* ☎ *020/7497–9504* Ⓤ *Covent Garden.*

**Mayflower.** An atmospheric 17th-century riverside inn with exposed beams and a terrace, this is practically the very place from which the Pilgrims set sail for Plymouth Rock. The inn is licensed to sell American postage stamps. ✉ *117 Rotherhithe St., South Bank SE16* ☎ *020/7237–4088* Ⓤ *Rotherhithe.*

**Museum Tavern.** Across the street from the British Museum, this gloriously Victorian pub makes an ideal resting place after the rigors of the culture trail. With lots of fancy glass—etched mirrors and stained-glass panels—gilded pillars, and carvings, the heavily restored hostelry once helped Karl Marx unwind after a hard day in the Library. He could have spent his *Kapital* on any of six beers available on tap. ✉ *49 Great Russell St., Bloomsbury WC1* ☎ *020/7242–8987* Ⓤ *Tottenham Court Rd.*

**Princess Louise.** This fine, popular pub has an over-the-top Victorian interior—glazed terra-cotta, stained and frosted glass, and a glorious painted ceiling. It's not all show, either; the food is a cut above normal pub grub, and there's a good selection of real ales. ✉ *208 High Holborn, Holborn WC1* ☎ *020/7405–8816* Ⓤ *Holborn.*

**Prospect of Whitby.** Named after a ship, this is London's oldest riverside pub, dating from 1520. Once upon a time it was called the Devil's Tavern because of the lowlife criminals—thieves and smugglers—who congregated here. It's ornamented with pewter ware and nautical objects. ✉ *57 Wapping Wall, The City E1* ☎ *020/7481–1095* Ⓤ *Wapping.*

**St. James Tavern.** This pretty pub is steps from Piccadilly Circus and five major West End theaters; another plus is that it stays open until 1 AM Thursday through Saturday. The interior has lovely hand-painted Doulton tiles depicting Shakespearean scenes. The kitchen prides itself on its fish-and-chips. ✉ *45 Great Windmill St., Soho W1* ☎ *020/7437–5009* Ⓤ *Piccadilly Circus.*

**Sherlock Holmes.** This pub used to be known as the Northumberland Arms, and Arthur Conan Doyle popped in regularly for a pint. It figures in *The Hound of the Baskervilles,* and you can see the hound's head and plaster casts of its huge paws among other Holmes memorabilia in the bar. ✉ *10 Northumberland St., Euston WC2* ☎ *020/ 7930–2644* Ⓤ *Charing Cross.*

**Spaniards Inn.** Another historic, oak-beam pub on Hampstead Heath? Yes, but this one has a gorgeous rose garden, scene of the tea party in Dickens's *Pickwick Papers.* Dick Turpin, the highwayman, frequented the inn; you can see his pistols on display. Shelley, Keats, and Byron hung out here, as did Dickens. It's extremely popular, especially on Sunday, when Londoners take to the heath in search of fresh air. ✉ *Spaniards Rd., Hampstead NW3* ☎ *020/8731–6571* Ⓤ *Hampstead.*

**Star Tavern.** In the heart of elegant Belgravia, this pub has a postcard-perfect Georgian-era facade. The inside is charming, too: Victorian furnishings and two roaring fireplaces make this a popular spot. ✉ *6 Belgrave Mews W, Belgravia SW1* ☎ *020/7235–3019* Ⓤ *Knightsbridge.*

**Windsor Castle.** Rest here if you're on a Kensington jaunt, and save your appetite for the food, especially on Sunday, when they do a traditional roast. On other days expect oysters, salads, fish cakes, and steak sandwiches. In winter a fire blazes; in summer an exquisite patio garden awaits. ✉ *114 Campden Hill Rd., Notting Hill W8* ☎ *020/7727–8491* Ⓤ *Notting Hill Gate Park.*

**Ye Grapes.** This 1882 traditional (smoky, noisy, and anti-chic) pub has been popular since Victoria was on the throne. It's in the heart of Shepherd Market, the village-within-Mayfair, and is still home-away-from-home for a full deck of London characters. ✉ *16 Shepherd Market, Mayfair W1* ☎ *020/7499–1563* Ⓤ *Green Park.*

**Ye Olde Cheshire Cheese.** Yes, it's a tourist trap, but it's also the most historic of all London pubs (it dates from 1667), and it deserves a visit for its sawdust-covered floors, low wood-beam ceilings, and the 14th-century crypt of Whitefriars' monastery under the cellar bar. But if you want to see the set of 17th-century pornographic tiles that once adorned the upstairs you'll have to go to Blacks Museum. This was the most regular of Dr. Johnson's and Dickens's *many* locals. ✉ *145 Fleet St., The City EC4* ☎ *020/7353–6170* Ⓤ *Blackfriars.*

# WHERE TO STAY

Updated by
Catherine
Belonogoff

**QUEEN ELIZABETH HASN'T INVITED YOU THIS TIME?** No matter. Staying at one of London's grande-dame hotels is the next best thing to being a guest at the palace—some say even better. Resplendent furnishings, armies of pampering staff—the Windsors should have it so good. Even the more affordable hotels convey an inimitable British style: tea makers and pastel wallpaper, Victorian-style parlors and country-house antiques.

Standing in the parlorlike lobby—burnished oak paneling, time-stained antiques, chintz sofas, the distant tinkle of teacups in the air—a century seems to slip away. The concierge whispers that Queen Victoria used to visit—she, too, probably got willingly lost in the corridors and crannies. In the grand salon sit Chippendale desks that once bore the concentrated energy of the empire's Kiplings and Hardys. Set near a crackling fire, a roomy leather Chesterfield beckons you to approach its quilted field. Yes, Olde London Towne fantasies may be fading fast in the light of Blair's Britain, but when it comes time to rest your head, the old-fashioned continues to entice. Who wouldn't want to lounge in a brocade armchair while a frock-coated retainer serves cream tea? Or enjoy coffee, toast, and croissants in a handmade bed in your powder-blue and white boudoir as the Thames flows lazily past the French windows? Choose one of London's heritage-rich hotels—Claridge's supplies perfect parlors; the Savoy has that river view—and these fantasies can, and always will, be fulfilled.

Still, faster times are bringing more changes to the London hotel scene than there have been in years. Hotels are springing up in places not previously considered tourist spots, meaning your stay need not be confined to the bustle and noise of the West End or the exclusive neighborhoods of Kensington or Knightsbridge. And the variety is not limited to location. Immaculately designed, entirely contemporary hotels now are challenging luxurious, old, chintzy favorites while nationwide budget chains take on the bed-and-breakfast scene, with clean, functional accommodations at friendly prices. Chain hotels with cookie-cutter furnishings and all modern conveniences have moved to the center of town, attracted by Chunnel travelers and other inter-Europe wayfarers. So you no longer need to blow your entire budget on your bed.

If you want to do just that, however, London is the place. Prices can soar into the empyrean here, but many of the best hotels are worth it. Take the Connaught, a landmark whose regulars wouldn't *dream* of staying anywhere else. Its Edwardian lobby, created in 1897, is unadulterated by things modern; grand and faded, it's filled with oil paintings and antiques. In contrast to this dowager-aunt type are hotels such as the Pelham and Covent Garden—most of them renovated town houses, aglitter with sensationally atmospheric Regency-style interiors and richly appointed with stunning furnishings. Designed to be the epitome of English country-housedom, these newer boutique hotels appeal to clientele bent on revisiting the landed gentry culture. Waving the banner SMALL IS BEAUTIFUL, they have stolen a march on the genteel sleeping beauties—the Claridges, the Savoys, and the Dorchesters—who have launched a broad counterattack.

The Sultan of Brunei has lavished tens of millions on refurbishing the Dorchester; a Hunt heiress sponsored a complete makeover of the Lanesborough; and the Connaught, the Savoy, and Claridge's have each been renovated to the tune of a mint. Paying top dollar, of course, does not always mean you'll get stately grandeur—several places have moved away from Regency flounces and Laura Ashley–isms into neo-Bauhaus minimalism. Even Brown's, bastion of tradition, closed in 2004 for an overhaul to streamlined modernism; look for its reopening in spring 2005. The Halkin was the first frill-free grand hotel. Others now include the ultrafashionable Metropolitan, the understated Hempel, and the grand Great Eastern near groovy Spitalfields market and the gray expanse of the City. At the other end of the price scale, things can be almost as trendy. In design-crazy London, even hostels have become stylish—just look at the Generator.

Where you stay can affect your experience significantly. For instance the West End is equivalent to downtown, but it covers a lot of ground. There's a great deal of difference between, say, posh Park Lane and bustling, touristy Leicester Square, yet both are in the West End. Hotels in Mayfair and St. James's are central and yet distant in both mileage and sensibility from funky, youthful neighborhoods like Notting Hill and Camden Town and from major tourist sights like the Tower of London, St. Paul's Cathedral, and the Kensington museums. On the edges of the West End, Soho and Covent Garden are crammed with eateries and entertainment options.

South Kensington, Kensington, Chelsea, and Knightsbridge are all patrician and peaceful, which will give you a more homey feeling than anything in the West End, and Belgravia is super-elegant, geographically and atmospherically about halfway between the extremes. From Bloomsbury it's a short stroll to the shops and restaurants of Covent Garden, to Theatreland, and to the British Museum. From here, it's a short bus ride to Camden and Regent's Park, too, and Hampstead and Islington are close enough to explore easily. Bayswater is a particularly affordable haven. It's barely considered a real neighborhood by Londoners, but everything is accessible from there. Notting Hill and Holland Park are worth considering as bases if you want something more down-home plus the antiques of Portobello Road.

## Bayswater & Notting Hill Gate

£££££ ⊡ **The Hempel.** Anouska Hempel did the lush and lavish Blakes, then did a 180-degree turn into these stunning, crisp, clean, white-on-white-on-white spaces—and no kidding about spaces. There's nothing jarring or extraneous, and no visible means of support beneath the furniture. Naturally, the Hempel appeals greatly to showbizzy style hounds. But beware: the stark, minimalist sensibility is not for everyone. ⊠ *31–35 Craven Hill Gardens, Bayswater W2 3EA* ☎ *020/7298–9000* 🖷 *020/ 7470–4666* ⊕ *www.the-hempel.co.uk* ⟿ *35 rooms, 12 suites* ♿ *Restaurant, room service, in-room data ports, in-room fax, in-room safes, minibars, cable TV with movies, in-room VCRs, 2 bars, lobby lounge, library,*

**3**

## Facilities

The lodgings we list are the cream of the crop in each price category. We always list the facilities that are available, but we don't specify whether they cost extra. When pricing accommodations, always ask what's included and what costs extra. Modern hotels usually have air-conditioning. You should specify if you wish to have a double bed. All hotels listed have private baths unless otherwise noted.

Hotels in England are graded from one to five stars, and guest houses, inns, and B&Bs are graded from one to five diamonds by VisitBritain in assocation with the Automobile Association (AA) and the Royal Automobile Association (RAC). Basically, the more stars or diamonds a property has, the more facilities it has.

## Reservations

Finding budget accommodations in London, especially during July and August, can be difficult; you should try to book well ahead if you are visiting during these months. Many hotels, however, offer special off-season (October–March) rates.

## Cutting Costs

Finding a cheap but tolerable double room in pricey London is a real coup. Your best bet is to look around Bloomsbury, Victoria, and King's Cross stations, Earl's Court, and Notting Hill Gate. Some places may be prepared to drop their rates during the off-season, so try your luck at haggling. Your cheapest options are a B&B or a dorm bed in a hostel. University residence halls offer a clean, cheap alternative to dodgy hotels and to noisy hostels during university vacation periods. Whatever the price, don't expect a room that's large by American standards.

## Prices

The general custom these days in all but the bottom end of the scale is for rates to be quoted for the room alone; breakfast, whether Continental or full English, usually comes at extra cost. We've noted at the end of each review if breakfast is included in the rate (CP for Continental breakfast daily and BP for full breakfast daily). Note: some establishments serve hearty breakfasts, others may have little more than coffee and rolls, so check ahead if breakfast is important to you. All hotels listed here are graded according to their weekday, high-season rates. Remember there may be significant discounts on weekends and in the off-season. British hotels are obliged by law to display a tariff at the reception desk. Study it carefully if you have not booked ahead. And make sure to make reservations well in advance.

| WHAT IT COSTS In pounds | | | | |
| £££££ | ££££ | £££ | ££ | £ |
| --- | --- | --- | --- | --- |
| HOTEL over £250 | £180–£250 | £120–£180 | £70–£120 | under £70 |

Prices are for two people in a standard double room in high season, V.A.T. included.

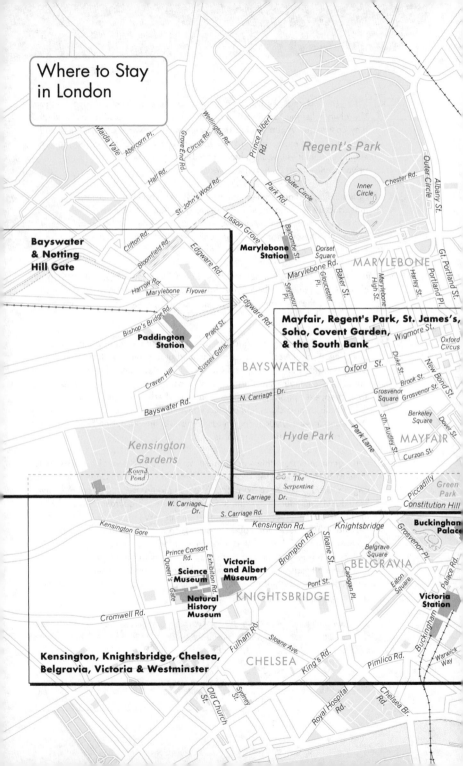

# Where to Stay in London

**Bayswater & Notting Hill Gate**

**Marylebone Station**

MARYLEBONE

**Mayfair, Regent's Park, St. James's, Soho, Covent Garden, & the South Bank**

BAYSWATER

**Paddington Station**

MAYFAIR

*Regent's Park*

*Inner Circle*

*Kensington Gardens*

*Round Pond*

*Hyde Park*

*The Serpentine*

*Green Park*

Constitution Hill

**Buckingham Palace**

BELGRAVIA

*Belgrave Square*

**Victoria Station**

**Science Museum**

**Victoria and Albert Museum**

**Natural History Museum**

KNIGHTSBRIDGE

CHELSEA

**Kensington, Knightsbridge, Chelsea, Belgravia, Victoria & Westminster**

### Street labels
Maida Vale, Abercorn Pl., Grove End Rd., Hall Rd., Circus Rd., Wellington Rd., Prince Albert Rd., Park Rd., Outer Circle, Chester Rd., Albany St., Outer Circle, St. John's Wood Rd., Lisson Grove, Balcombe St., Dorset Square, Marylebone Rd., Gloucester Pl., Baker St., Marylebone High St., Harley St., Gt. Portland St., Portland Pl., Clifton Rd., Bloomfield Rd., Edgware Rd., Harrow Rd., Marylebone Flyover, Bishop's Bridge Rd., Praed St., Sussex Gdns., Craven Hill, Seymour Pl., Wigmore St., Oxford Circus, Oxford St., Duke St., New Bond St., Brook St., Grosvenor Square, Grosvenor St., Berkeley Square, Dover St., Sth. Audley St., Park Lane, Curzon St., Bayswater Rd., N. Carriage Dr., W. Carriage Dr., W. Carriage Dr., S. Carriage Rd., Kensington Gore, Prince Consort Rd., Queen's Gate, Exhibition Rd., Cromwell Rd., Kensington Rd., Brompton Rd., Sloane St., Knightsbridge, Grosvenor Pl., Palace Rd., Cadogan Pl., Pont St., Eaton Square, Buckingham, Fulham Rd., Sloane Ave., King's Rd., Pimlico Rd., Warwick Way, Old Church St., Sydney St., Royal Hospital Rd., Chelsea Br.

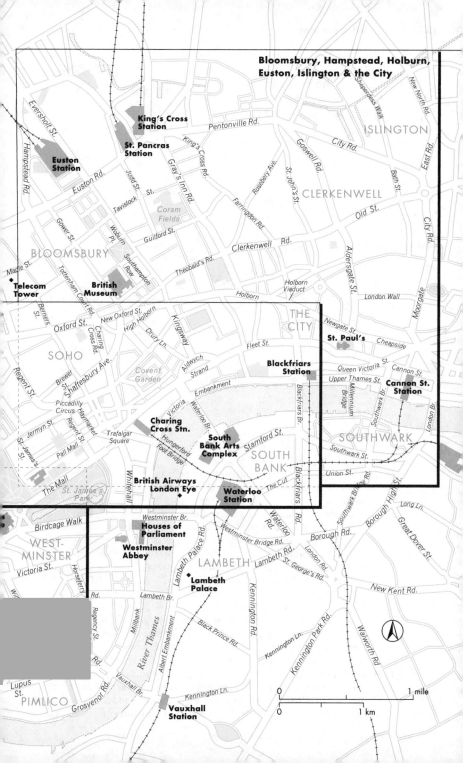

Bloomsbury, Hampstead, Holburn,
Euston, Islington & the City

ISLINGTON

King's Cross
Station

St. Pancras
Station

Euston
Station

CLERKENWELL

Coram
Fields

BLOOMSBURY

Telecom
Tower

British
Museum

THE
CITY

St. Paul's

SOHO

Blackfriars
Station

Cannon St.
Station

Covent
Garden

Charing
Cross Stn.

South
Bank Arts
Complex

SOUTHWARK

SOUTH
BANK

Piccadilly
Circus

Trafalgar
Square

British Airways
London Eye

Waterloo
Station

WEST-
MINSTER

Houses of
Parliament

Westminster
Abbey

LAMBETH

Lambeth
Palace

River Thames

PIMLICO

Vauxhall
Station

0                    1 mile

0                    1 km

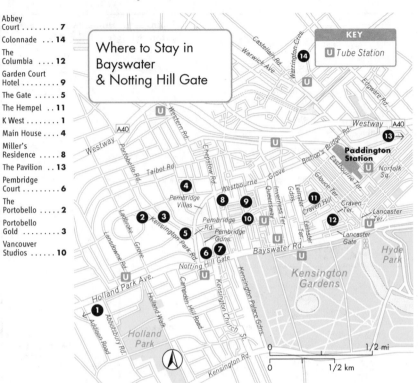

Where to Stay in
Bayswater
& Notting Hill Gate

dry cleaning, laundry service, concierge, meeting rooms, parking (fee)
☐ AE, DC, MC, V Ⓤ Lancaster Gate.

££££ 🏨 **K West.** Just a few minutes by bus or Tube from Notting Hill, K West
is a contemporary, big city hotel in an undistinguished glass-and-steel
building. The busy, all white lobby houses the K Lounge, while upstairs
is the hotel restaurant, Kanteen; the health club, K Spa, is in the basement. The minimalist approach continues in the bedrooms where dark
wood, soft suede, and sleek beige walls and floors create a designer look.
High-grade audio-visual equipment is standard in the rooms as are
tea/coffeemakers. The free Internet computers in the chill-out area come
as a bonus. ⊠ *Richmond Way, Shepherd's Bush W14 OAX* ☎ *020/
7674–1000* 🖷 *020/7674–1050* ⊕ *www.k-west.co.uk* 🛏 *216 rooms, 6
suites* ♧ *Restaurant, room service, in-room data ports, in-room safes,
minibars, cable TV with video games, in-room DVDs, gym, hot tub,
massage, steam room, sauna, spa, bar, dry cleaning, laundry service, Internet, meeting rooms, parking (fee), no-smoking rooms* ☐ *AE, DC, MC,
V* ⏏♦ *CP* Ⓤ *Shepherd's Bush.*

£££–££££ 🏨 **Abbey Court.** A little hotel in a gracious white mansion, in a quiet
street off Notting Hill Gate, Abbey Court is deep in the era of Victoria:
dark-red wallpaper, gilt-frame mirrors, mahogany, and plenty of antiques.
A Continental breakfast buffet is served in the conservatory. Bathrooms

look the part but are entirely modern: gray Italian marble, with brass fittings and whirlpool baths. ⊠ *20 Pembridge Gardens, Notting Hill W2 4DU* ☎ *020/7221–7518* 🖷 *020/7792–0858* ⊕ *www. abbeycourthotel.co.uk* ⇆ *19 rooms, 3 suites ⌂ Restaurant, room service, fans, in-room data ports, in-room safes, in-room hot tubs, cable TV, dry cleaning, laundry service, concierge, Internet, car rental, no-smoking rooms; no a/c* ▤ *AE, DC, MC, V* ⦿I *CP* Ⓤ *Notting Hill Gate.*

**£££–££££** 🏨 **Miller's Residence.** From the moment you ring the bell and are ush-
**Fodor'sChoice** ered up the winding staircase flanked by antiques and curios, you know
★ you've entered another realm where history is paramount. Jacobean, Victorian, Georgian, and Tudor antiques create a rich lesson in bygone days. Run by Martin Miller of famed *Miller's Antique Price Guides,* this town house serves as his home, gallery, and B&B. Sip a complimentary evening cocktail in the long, candlelit drawing room with fireplace while mixing with other guests or the convivial staff. The rooms are named for Romantic poets. ⊠ *111a Westbourne Grove, Notting Hill W2 4UW* ☎ *020/7243–1024* 🖷 *020/7243–1064* ⊕ *www.millersuk.com* ⇆ *6 rooms, 2 suites ⌂ Dining room, fans, in-room data ports, some in-room faxes, lounge, dry cleaning, laundry service, concierge, Internet, meeting room; no a/c* ▤ *AE, DC, MC, V* ⦿I *CP* Ⓤ *Notting Hill Gate.*

**£££–££££** 🏨 **Pembridge Court.** In a colonnaded white-stucco Victorian row house, this sweet, cozy hotel has scatter cushions and books, quirky Victoriana, two resident cats, and framed fans from the neighboring Portobello Market. Bedrooms have a great deal of swagged floral drapery, and each room is individually decorated. ⊠ *34 Pembridge Gardens, Notting Hill W2 4DX* ☎ *020/7229–9977* 🖷 *020/7727–4982* ⊕ *www.pemct.co.uk* ⇆ *20 rooms ⌂ Dining room, room service, in-room data ports, in-room safes, cable TV, in-room VCRs, lobby lounge, dry cleaning, laundry service, Internet, business services, meeting rooms, parking (fee), some pets allowed; no a/c in some rooms* ▤ *AE, DC, MC, V* ⦿I *BP* Ⓤ *Notting Hill Gate.*

**£££–££££** 🏨 **The Portobello.** This small, eccentric place has long been a favorite
**Fodor'sChoice** of high-style mavens in the music and design worlds. The two adjoin-
★ ing Victorian houses back onto a large garden. Cabin Rooms are minute. Many bigger rooms (in the ££££ range) have Victorian clawfoot bathtubs, though the famous round-bed suite has the pièce de résistance of the bath world—a Victorian "bathing machine," all knobs and shiny brass pipes. Most rooms have computers, and some have balconies. Access to a nearby health club with an indoor pool can be arranged. ⊠ *22 Stanley Gardens, Notting Hill W11 2NG* ☎ *020/7727–2777* 🖷 *020/7792–9641* ⊕ *www.portobello-hotel.co.uk* ⇆ *24 rooms ⌂ Restaurant, dining room, room service, fans, in-room data ports, in-room safes, some in-room hot tubs, minibars, cable TV, in-room VCRs, bar, lounge, babysitting, dry cleaning, laundry service, concierge, Internet, business services, car rental, no-smoking rooms; no a/c in some rooms* ⦿I *CP* ▤ *AE, MC, V* ⊘ *Closed 10 days at Christmas* Ⓤ *Notting Hill Gate.*

**£££** 🏨 **Colonnade.** You'll find this lovely town house in quiet, residential Little Venice, near a canal filled with colorful narrow boats. From the Freud suite (Sigmund visited in 1938) to the rooms with four-poster beds or

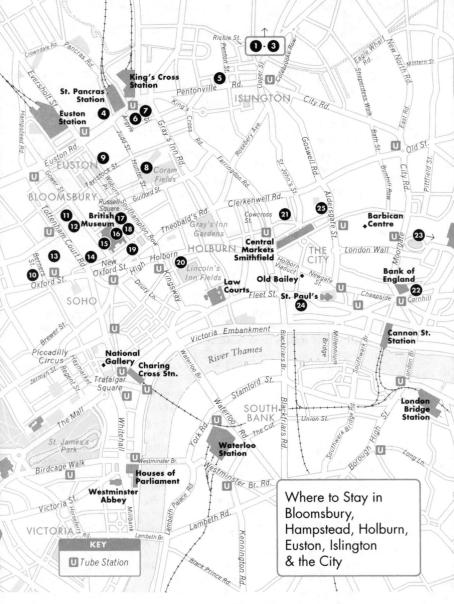

**Where to Stay in Bloomsbury, Hampstead, Holburn, Euston, Islington & the City**

KEY

🚇 Tube Station

balconies, you'll find rich brocades, velvets, and antiques. It's a former home, so each room is different; some are split-level. The 1920s elevator and Wedgwood lobby fireplace add to the historic style of the place. A bathrobe and slippers, a bowl of apples, and a CD player in each room add a touch of luxury. ⊠ *2 Warrington Crescent, Bayswater W9 1ER* ☎ *020/7286–1052* 🖷 *020/7286–1057* ⊕ *www.theetoncollection.com* ⮐ *15 rooms, 28 suites* ⌂ *Restaurant, dining room, room service, in-room data ports, in-room safes, minibars, cable TV, lobby lounge, wine bar, babysitting, dry cleaning, laundry service, business services, parking (fee), some pets allowed, no-smoking rooms* ⊟ *AE, DC, MC, V* Ⓤ *Warwick Av.*

££–£££ 🎫 **Main House.** A brass lion door knocker marks the front door of the unassuming Main House run by Caroline Main. With just four floors and four rooms, it has a simple aim: to provide a good night's sleep in an interesting Victorian house. Furnished with animal hide rugs, antique furniture, Asian objets d'art, and huge beds, the rooms are uncluttered and delightfully spacious. Coffee or tea is brought to your room in the morning, and breakfast is made with organic ingredients. The tiny urban terrace is a great place for stargazing or reading the morning paper. The owner can arrange to have dinner brought to your room. A day rate at the local health club is available, and bicycles can be borrowed, too. ⊠ *6 Colvile Rd., Notting Hill W11 2BP* ☎ *020/7221–9691* ⊕ *www. themainhouse.com* ⮐ *4 rooms* ⌂ *Fans, in-room data ports, in-room VCRs, massage, babysitting, dry cleaning, laundry service, Internet, meeting rooms, airport shuttle, parking (fee); no smoking* ⊟*MC, V* ⍾⃝*CP* Ⓤ *Notting Hill Gate.*

££ 🎫 **The Columbia.** The public rooms in these five adjoining Victorians are as big as museum halls. Some of the clean, high-ceiling bedrooms are very large (three to four beds) and have park views and balconies. The design tends toward teak veneer, khaki-beige-brown color schemes, and avocado bathroom suites, but who would expect Regency Revival at these prices? It's popular with tour groups. ⊠ *95–99 Lancaster Gate, Bayswater W2 3NS* ☎ *020/7402–0021* 🖷 *020/7706–4691* ⊕ *www. columbiahotel.co.uk* ⮐ *103 rooms* ⌂ *Restaurant, in-room safes, bar, lobby lounge, dry cleaning, laundry service, concierge, meeting room; no a/c* ⊟ *AE, MC, V* ⍾⃝ *BP* Ⓤ *Lancaster Gate.*

££ 🎫 **The Gate.** It's an absolutely teeny house on the quiet part of Portobello Road. The plain bedrooms have tea/coffeemakers plus bath (unless you opt for a smaller, £15-cheaper, shower-only room), and Continental breakfast is brought directly to your room. ⊠ *6 Portobello Rd., Notting Hill W11 3DG* ☎ *020/7221–0707* 🖷 *020/7221–9128* ⊕ *www.gatehotel.com* ⮐ *7 rooms* ⌂ *Fans, in-room DVDs, minibars, refrigerators; no a/c* ⊟ *MC, V* ⍾⃝ *CP* Ⓤ *Notting Hill Gate.*

££ 🎫 **The Pavilion.** This eccentric town house is the trendy address in London for fashionistas and musicians. Bedrooms are decorated along different themes, such as "Casablanca Nights," a Moroccan fantasy, or "Enter the Dragon," a quirky mix of East Asian styles. Often used for fashion shoots, the rooms each have their own unique quality. It's a relaxed, laid-back hotel, and the triples and family rooms are ideal for groups looking for lots of space while still in a stylish setting. ⊠ *34–36*

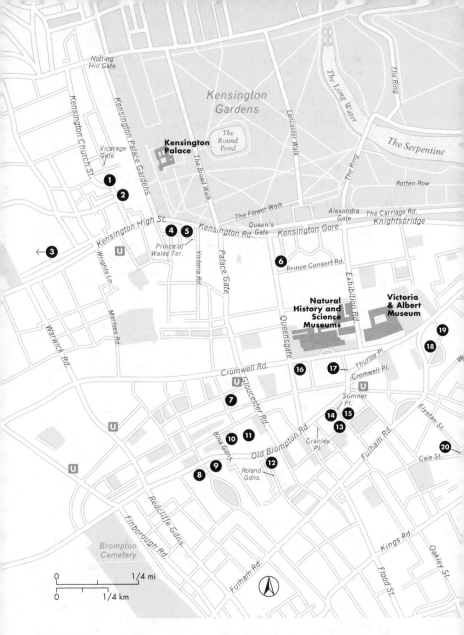

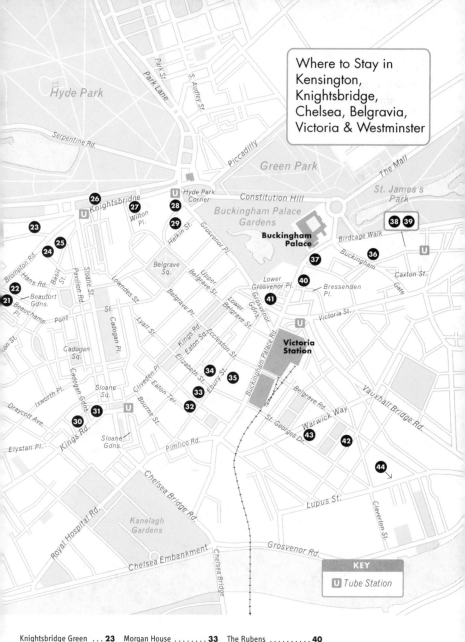

# Where to Stay in Kensington, Knightsbridge, Chelsea, Belgravia, Victoria & Westminster

**KEY**

U Tube Station

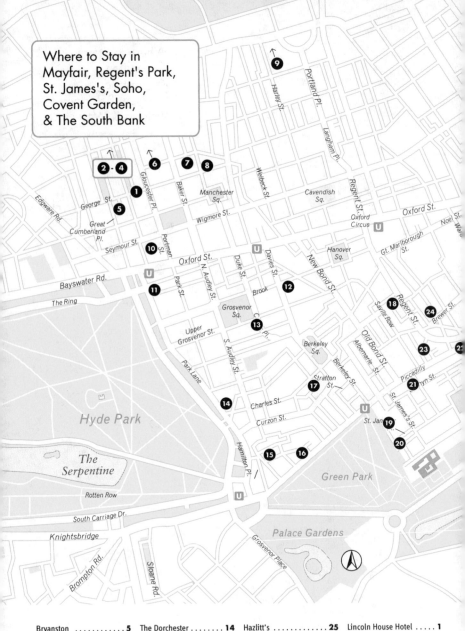

Where to Stay in
Mayfair, Regent's Park,
St. James's, Soho,
Covent Garden,
& The South Bank

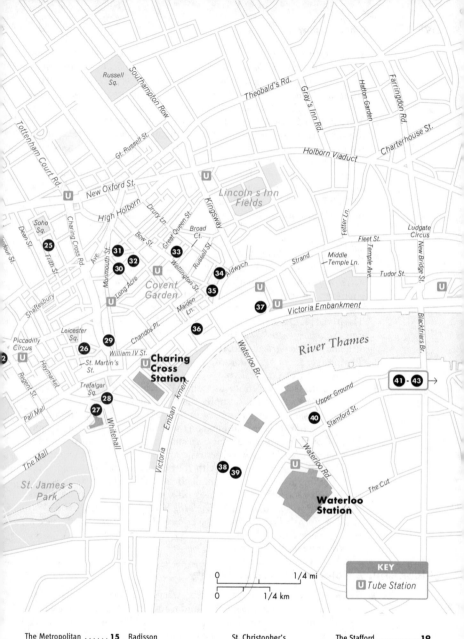

*Sussex Gardens, Bayswater W2 1UL* ☎ *020/7262–0905* 🖷 *020/ 7262–1324* ⊕ *www.pavilionhoteluk.com* ➡ *30 rooms* ⚐ *Room service, fans, in-room data ports, cable TV, some in-room DVDs, lounge, dry cleaning, laundry service, parking (fee), no-smoking rooms; no a/c* ▭ *AE, D, MC, V* ⍾ *CP* Ⓤ *Paddington or Edgware Rd.*

**££** 🏨 **Vancouver Studios.** This little hotel in a Victorian town house is perfect for those wanting a home away from home. Rooms come complete with minikitchens, and you can even pre-order groceries to stock your mini-refrigerator on arrival. Each studio has daily maid service as well as room service. Some rooms have working fireplaces, and one opens onto the leafy, paved garden. ⊠ *30 Prince's Sq., Bayswater W2 4NJ* ☎ *020/7243–1270* 🖷 *020/7221–8678* ⊕ *www.vancouverstudios.co. uk* ➡ *45 studios* ⚐ *Room service, in-room data ports, kitchens, microwaves, refrigerators, dry cleaning, laundry facilities, lounge, parking (fee); no a/c* ▭ *AE, DC, MC, V* Ⓤ *Bayswater or Queensway.*

**£–££** 🏨 **Garden Court Hotel.** Built in 1870, the hotel consists of two 19th-century town houses in a quiet garden square. Each of the rooms has a character of its own, some with original Victorian fittings. Note that some rooms are more recently refurbished than others. Rooms with toilet and shower cost an extra £30, and family-size rooms are in the ££ category. The paved garden is relaxing in good weather. ⊠ *30–31 Kensington Gardens Sq., Bayswater W2 4BL* ☎ *020/7229–2553* 🖷 *020/7727–2749* ⊕ *www.gardencourthotel.co.uk* ➡ *12 rooms, 10 with bath* ⚐ *Fans, cable TV, lounge, some pets allowed, no smoking; no a/c* ▭ *MC, V* ⍾ *BP* Ⓤ *Bayswater or Queensway.*

**£–££** 🏨 **Portobello Gold.** This no-frills, quirky B&B in the heart of the antiques
FodorsChoice area of Portobello Road occupies the floor above the pub and restau-
★ rant of the same name. The beds in the double rooms take up almost the entire room. TVs are mounted on the wall, and the beds convert into desks. Double rooms have their own shower and basin, but share a toilet. The backpackers rooms are basic affairs. The best of the bunch is the split-level apartment (3£) with roof terrace, living room complete with soothing aquarium, and a small kitchen. The restaurant serves modern British food with an emphasis on seafood and vegetarian dishes. ⊠ *95–97 Portobello Rd., Notting Hill W11 2QB* ☎ *020/7460–4910* ⊕ *www.portobellogold.com* ➡ *6 rooms, 1 apartment* ⚐ *Restaurant, room service, cable TV, bar, laundry service, Internet* ▭ *MC, V* ⍾ *CP* Ⓤ *Notting Hill Gate.*

## Bloomsbury, Holborn, Euston & the City

**£££££** 🏨 **Charlotte Street Hotel.** On a quiet street in the media hub of North Soho, this hotel fuses the modern and traditional. Bathrooms are lined with gleaming granite and oak, and there are walk-in showers and deep baths; and, since each bathroom has a mini flat-screen TV, you can catch up on the news while you soak. The restaurant, Oscar, is excellent. There's a public screening room with Ferrari leather chairs, perfect for watching a movie at the Sunday night dinner-and-film club. Or you might just want to read a paper by the fire in the drawing room. ⊠ *15 Charlotte St., Bloomsbury W1P 1HB* ☎ *020/7806–2000, 800/553–6674 in U.S.* 🖷 *020/7806–2002* ⊕ *www.charlottestreethotel.com* ➡ *44 rooms, 8 suites*

&#9978; *Restaurant, room service, in-room data ports, in-room safes, mini-bars, cable TV, in-room VCRs, gym, bar, lobby lounge, cinema, library, dry cleaning, laundry service, concierge, Internet, business services, meeting rooms* &#61441; *AE, DC, MC, V* &#9446; *Goodge St.*

£££££ &#9633; **Great Eastern.** Another style coup for designer and gourmand Sir Terence Conran, the Great Eastern Hotel is a sturdy pillar of the modern establishment. There are five restaurants (serving sushi, fish, brasserie, pub grub, and haute cuisine), two bars, private dining and function rooms, a florist, and a Ren bath-products shop. Some of the rooms look out over Liverpool Street and Bishopsgate. Others look inward to the stained-glass dome of the Aurora restaurant or the Gallery. All rooms have a modern, sleek sense of style. &#9993; *Liverpool St. at Bishopsgate, The City E2M 7QN* &#9742; *020/7618–5010* &#61629; *020/7618–5011* &#9429; *www.great-eastern-hotel.co.uk* &#8618; *246 rooms, 21 suites* &#9978; *5 restaurants, 12 dining rooms, room service, in-room data ports, some in-room faxes, in-room safes, minibars, cable TV with video games, in-room VCRs, gym, spa, bar, pub, library, shop, babysitting, dry cleaning, laundry service, concierge, Internet, business services, meeting rooms, car rental, no-smoking rooms* &#61441; *AE, DC, MC, V* &#9446; *Liverpool St.*

£££££ &#9633; **Renaissance Chancery Court.** This landmark structure, built by the Pearl Assurance Company in 1914, has been transformed into a beautiful hotel. So striking is the architecture that the building was featured in the film *Howard's End.* The spacious bedrooms are popular with business travelers. The spa in the basement is a cocoon of peacefulness. There's marble everywhere, from the floors in public spaces and the massive staircase to the bathrooms. The £30 supplement for the club rooms includes snacks all day, dedicated check-in, and a fruit basket. &#9993; *252 High Holborn, Holborn WC1V 7EN* &#9742; *020/7829–9888* &#61629; *0207/829–9889* &#9429; *www.renaissancehotels.com/loncc* &#8618; *343 rooms, 14 suites* &#9978; *Restaurant, room service, in-room data ports, in-room safes, minibars, cable TV with video games, gym, sauna, spa, steam room, bar, lobby lounge, shop, babysitting, laundry service, concierge, business services, meeting rooms, no-smoking rooms* &#61441; *AE, MC, V* &#9446; *Holborn.*

★ £££££ &#9633; **The Rookery.** An 18th-century hotel in the City, the Rookery is just steps away from the Jerusalem Tavern, from which it's said the Knights of St. John left to fight the Crusades. In the Rook's Nest, the hotel's duplex suite, you can relax in an antique bath in the corner of the bedroom or enjoy a magnificent view of the City's historic buildings. Each beautiful double room has a claw-foot bathtub, antique carved wooden headboard, and period furnishings, including exquisite salvaged pieces. The conservatory, with its small patio garden, is an especially nice place to unwind. &#9993; *12 Peter's La., at Cowcross St., The City EC1M 6DS* &#9742; *020/7336–0931* &#61629; *020/7336–0932* &#9429; *www.rookeryhotel.com* &#8618; *30 rooms, 3 suites* &#9978; *Room service, fans, in-room data ports, in-room safes, minibars, cable TV, bar, lobby lounge, library, babysitting, dry cleaning, laundry service, concierge, meeting rooms, airport shuttle, car rental, parking (fee), no-smoking floors; no a/c* &#61441; *AE, DC, MC, V* &#9446; *Farringdon.*

£££££ &#9633; **Sanderson.** Sister to St. Martins Lane hotel, the Sanderson urban spa sits in the revamped box that was the Sanderson fabrics headquarters. From the serene Japanese garden to the billowy cloth that separates the bathrooms from the bedrooms, this hotel is definitely walking to the beat of its own whimsical drum. The furniture is a mix of French Louis XV and industrial, and bedrooms have sleigh beds. Some might find Agua (the "holistic bath house"), the in-room massage and spa services, and the indoor–outdoor fitness classes just what the doctor ordered. Gourmands can try the popular Spoon+ restaurant. ⊠ *50 Berners St., Bloomsbury W1T 3NG* ☎ *020/7300–1400* 🖷 *020/7300–1401* ⊕ *www. ianschragerhotels.com* ⤴ *150 rooms* ⚫ *Restaurant, room service, in-room data ports, some in-room faxes, in-room safes, minibars, cable TV, in-room VCRs, gym, sauna, spa, billiards, 2 bars, lobby lounge, shop, babysitting, dry cleaning, laundry service, concierge, Internet, business services, meeting room, parking (fee), no-smoking rooms* ▭ *AE, DC, MC, V* Ⓤ *Oxford Circus or Tottenham Court Rd.*

£££££ ▦ **Threadneedles.** Owned by the people who run the Colonnade in Maida Vale, Threadneedles is a first-rate boutique hotel. The building, affectionately called the Old Lady of Threadneedle Street, is a former bank, and the hotel has kept the banking hall and reused the mahogany panels from the original interior in its "heritage wing." If you have business in the City, Threadneedles can't be beat for luxury and contemporary style. Guests are served complimentary fresh fruit, tea, and coffee. ⊠ *5 Threadneedle St., The City EC2R 8AY* ☎ *020/7657–8080* 🖷 *020/ 7657–8100* ⊕ *www.theetoncollection.com* ⤴ *63 rooms, 6 suites* ⚫ *Restaurant, room service, in-room data ports, in-room safes, in-room hot tubs, minibars, refrigerators, cable TV, bar, lounge, dry cleaning, laundry service, concierge, meeting rooms, no-smoking floors* ▭ *AE, DC, MC, V* Ⓤ *Bank.*

£££–£££££ ▦ **Montague on the Gardens.** Converted from a row of 1830s Georgian town houses, the Montague keeps the antique look alive with its period furnishings and collection of objets d'art. Standard double rooms are small, but there are plenty of cozy public areas in which to unwind. The bar hosts jazz evenings, and the sitting room is filled with comfy, flowery furniture. The best views are from the small terrace and conservatories, where you can look out on a stretch of lawn running an entire city block. What the hotel lacks in space, it makes up for in charm with its yards of fabric-cover walls and ceilings. ⊠ *15 Montague St., Bloomsbury WC1B 5BJ* ☎ *020/7637–1001* 🖷 *020/ 7637–2516* ⊕ *www.redcarnationhotels.com* ⤴ *93 rooms, 11 suites* ⚫ *Restaurant, room service, in-room data ports, some in-room faxes, some in-room safes, minibars, cable TV with movies, gym, sauna, steam room, bar, lounge, dry cleaning, laundry service, concierge, Internet, business services, meeting rooms, no-smoking rooms* ▭ *AE, DC, MC, V* Ⓤ *Russell Sq.*

££££ ▦ **Blooms.** This white Georgian town-house hotel is a home away from home. Rooms in the back of the hotel look out onto a leafy green garden, and some have a four-poster bed. The Theatre Royal and the Lords Room work off drama and cricket themes, respectively, and the rest of the rooms, though small, are reasonable, and very close to the British Museum. ⊠ *7 Montague St., Bloomsbury WC1B 5BP* ☎ *020/7323–1717* 🖷 *020/7636–6498* ⊕ *www.bloomshotel.com* ⤴ *26 rooms, 1 suite* ⚫ *Restaurant, room service, cable TV, bar, lounge, babysitting, Inter-*

*net, meeting rooms, some pets allowed; no a/c* ☰ *AE, DC, MC, V* Ⓤ *Russell Sq.*

££££ 🏨 **Jurys Great Russell Street.** Originally designed by architect Sir Edwin Lutyens for the Young Women's Christian Association in the early 1930s, today this neo-Georgian building stands proudly restored as an upscale hotel aimed at corporate travelers during the week and leisure travelers on the weekend when rates drop considerably. Throughout the reception area and lounge, much of the original design, including reproduction furniture, has been retained. Rooms are fairly spacious and have a classy 1930s look to them, though they have all the perks of the 21st century. ⊠ *16–22 Great Russell St., Bloomsbury WC1B 3NN* ☎ *020/7347–1000* 🖷 *020/7347–1001* ⊕ *www.jurysdoyle.com* 🛏 *124 rooms, 6 suites* ⚭ *Restaurant, room service, in-room data ports, minibars, cable TV, lounge, wine bar, library, dry cleaning, concierge, Internet, business services, meeting rooms, no-smoking rooms* ☰ *AE, DC, MC, V* Ⓤ *Tottenham Court Rd.*

££££ 🏨 **Malmaison.** Part of a small chain of U.K. boutique hotels, this Clerkenwell address is very trendy, with contemporary furnishings, clean lines, and black-and-white photographs of London scenes on the walls. Guest rooms have huge beds, CD systems with a library of music on demand, and up-to-the-minute style. The brasserie serves French cuisine and has a long wine menu. ⊠ *Charterhouse Sq., The City EC1M 6AH* ☎ *020/7012–3700* 🖷 *020/7012–3702* ⊕ *www.malmaison.com* 🛏 *95 rooms, 2 suites* ⚭ *Restaurant, room service, in-room data ports, in-room safes, minibars, cable TV, gym, bar, dry cleaning, laundry service, babysitting, concierge, meeting room, no-smoking rooms* ⦿❘ *CP* ☰ *AE, MC, V* Ⓤ *Barbican or Farringdon.*

★ ££££ 🏨 **myhotel bloomsbury.** Before you arrive you'll be asked to fill out a preferences sheet so that your room is just as you like it. If anything should go wrong, no need to call the front desk: just contact your personal assistant for help. Rooms are minimalist, with wooden floors and simple color schemes. Superior doubles are bigger and have separate sitting rooms. For the most space, book one of the two penthouse apartments in "myspace" on the top floor. From the "jinja" spa to the library stocked with CDs, books, and free beverages, myhotel's novel approach succeeds brilliantly. ⊠ *11–13 Bayley St., Bedford Sq., Bloomsbury WC1B 3HD* ☎ *020/7667–6000* 🖷 *020/7667–6001* ⊕ *www.myhotels.com* 🛏 *76 rooms* ⚭ *Restaurant, room service, in-room data ports, in-room safes, cable TV with movies, gym, spa, bar, lounge, library, babysitting, concierge, Internet, business services, no-smoking floors* ☰ *AE, DC, MC, V* Ⓤ *Tottenham Court Rd.*

£££ 🏨 **Novotel Euston.** Handy for the British Library and Bloomsbury, this tower of a hotel is situated between St. Pancras and Euston stations. It's popular with conference groups and business travelers for its stylish, modern rooms and central location. There are often special rates, whereby you might find a double room in the ££ range. Be aware that the busy Euston road in front of the hotel has building works due to the Eurostar extension at Kings Cross. There are, however, some spectacular views of the spires of St. Pancras and the British Library. ⊠ *100–110 Euston Rd., Bloomsbury NW1 2AJ* ☎ *020/7666–9000* 🖷 *020/7666–9100* ⊕ *www.*

*parkplazaeurope.com* 📠 *309 rooms, 3 suites* ⚐ *Restaurant, room service, in-room data ports, in-room safes, minibars, cable TV with movies, gym, massage, sauna, steam room, bar, lobby lounge, theater, dry cleaning, laundry service, concierge, Internet, business services, meeting rooms, no-smoking floors* ⊟ *AE, MC, V* Ⓜ *King's Cross or Euston.*

**££** 🏨 **Arosfa Hotel.** The friendly owners, Mr. and Mrs. Dorta, set this B&B

Fodor'sChoice apart from the Gower Street hotel pack—that, and the fact that this was

★ once the home of Pre-Raphaelite painter Sir John Everett Millais. Rooms are simple and comfortable. Those at the back are far quieter, though the double glazing somewhat tames the din of the students on their way to and from class at University College London. ⊠ *83 Gower St., Bloomsbury WC1E 6HJ* ☎ *020/7636–2115* 🖷 *020/7636–2115* 📠 *16 rooms* ⚐ *Dining room, fans, lounge; no a/c, no smoking* ⊟ *MC, V* ¶⊙¶ *BP* Ⓤ *Goodge St.*

**££** 🏨 **Harlingford Hotel.** The Harlingford is by far the sleekest and most contemporary of the Cartwright Gardens hotels, which includes a bevy of other hotels that aren't nearly as stylish. Bold color schemes and beautifully tiled bathrooms enliven this family-run hotel. The quad rooms are an excellent choice for traveling families. ⊠ *61–63 Cartwright Gardens, Bloomsbury WC1H 9EL* ☎ *020/7387–1551* 🖷 *020/7383–4616* ⊕ *www.harlingfordhotel.com* 📠 *43 rooms* ⚐ *In-room data ports, tennis court, lounge; no a/c* ⊟ *AE, DC, MC, V* ¶⊙¶ *BP* Ⓤ *Russell Sq.*

**££** 🏨 **Morgan Hotel.** This is a Georgian row-house hotel, family-run with charm and panache. Rooms are small and functionally furnished, yet friendly and cheerful. The five apartments (£££) are particularly pleasing: three times the size of normal rooms, complete with kitchens and private phone lines. The tiny, paneled breakfast room is straight out of an 18th-century dollhouse. The back rooms overlook the British Museum. ⊠ *24 Bloomsbury St., Bloomsbury WC1B 3QJ* ☎ *020/7636–3735* 🖷 *020/7636–3045* 📠 *15 rooms, 5 apartments* ⚐ *In-room safes, some refrigerators, cable TV; no a/c* ⊟ *MC, V* ¶⊙¶ *BP* Ⓤ *Tottenham Court Rd. or Russell Sq.*

**££** 🏨 **St. Margaret's.** A popular hotel near the British Museum and on a

Fodor'sChoice street full of budget hotels, St. Margaret's has well-lit rooms with high

★ ceilings in a Georgian-era building. The friendly Italian family that runs the hotel is sure to welcome you by name if you stay long enough. Back rooms have garden views, and each room retains Georgian touches such as a fireplace and beautiful cornice moldings. ⊠ *26 Bedford Pl., Bloomsbury WC1B 5JL* ☎ *020/7636–4277* 🖷 *020/7323–3066* ⊕ *www. stmargaretshotel.co.uk* 📠 *64 rooms, 12 with bath* ⚐ *Dining room, fans, cable TV, lounge, babysitting, laundry service, no-smoking rooms; no a/c* ⊟ *MC, V* ¶⊙¶ *BP* Ⓤ *Russell Sq.*

**£** 🏨 **Alhambra Hotel.** One of the best bargains in Bloomsbury, this fam-

Fodor'sChoice ily-run hotel has singles as low as £32 and doubles as low as £45.

★ Rooms tend to be small and look dated, but they're definitely good value. Some rooms have a shower but no toilet; others have both. The hotel is spread across several properties on the street, some of which are newer than others. ⊠ *17–19 Argyle St., Bloomsbury WC1H 8EJ* ☎ *020/ 7837–9575* 🖷 *020/7916–2476* ⊕ *www.alhambrahotel.com* 📠 *52 rooms* ⚐ *Dining room, concierge, parking (fee), no-smoking rooms; no a/c, no room phones* ⊟ *AE, MC, V* ¶⊙¶ *BP* Ⓤ *King's Cross.*

**£** ▣ **Ashlee House.** This welcoming hostel has singles, twins, and large and small dorm rooms. Prices range from £15 per person for a dorm room to £36 per person for a double. Expect a hospitable staff, but there are few amenities save the lounge with a television and pay phone. Cooks will welcome the chance to use the shared kitchen to save a few more quid on eating out. ⊠ *261 Gray's Inn Rd., Holborn WC1X 8QT* ☎ *020/7833–9400* 🖷 *020/7833–9677* ⊕ *www.ashleehouse.co.uk* 🛏 *26 rooms, 175 beds* ♿ *Dining room, lounge, laundry facilities, Internet, no-smoking rooms; no a/c, no room phones, no room TVs* ▭ *MC, V* ⦿ *CP* Ⓤ *King's Cross.*

**£** ▣ **City of London YHA.** The beautiful oak-panel chapel of this former choir school is now used as a meeting room. Although concessions have been made to the modern hosteler, there are still a few antique touches in the building. On your doorstep are St. Paul's Cathedral and the Millennium Bridge to the Tate Modern. Most of the rooms have four to eight beds, but there are a few singles, doubles, and triples. Cots can be provided for babies. ⊠ *36 Carter La., The City EC4V 5AB* ☎ *0870/770–5764* 🖷 *020/7236–7681* ⊕ *www.yha.org.uk* 🛏 *193 beds* ♿ *Restaurant, lounge, laundry facilities, Internet, meeting room; no a/c, no room phones, no room TVs, no smoking* ▭ *AE, MC, V* ⦿ *BP* Ⓤ *St. Paul's.*

**£** ▣ **The Generator.** Easily the grooviest youth hostel in town, this former police barracks has a friendly, funky, international clientele. The Internet café provides handy maps and leaflets, plus a chance to get online. The Generator Bar has cheap drinks and a rowdy, young clientele, and the Fuel Stop cafeteria provides inexpensive meals. Rooms are designed on a prison-cell theme, complete with bunk beds and dim views. There are singles, twins, and dormitory rooms, each with a washbasin, locker, and free bed linen. Prices run from £23 per person for a double room to £12 per person for a 14-bed dorm room. ⊠ *MacNaghten House, Compton Pl. off 37 Tavistock Pl., Bloomsbury WC1H 9SE* ☎ *020/ 7388–7666* 🖷 *020/7388–7644* ⊕ *www.generatorhostels.com* 🛏 *215 beds* ♿ *Restaurant, fans, lobby lounge, pub, sports bar, recreation room, shop, concierge, Internet, meeting rooms, airport shuttle, travel services, parking (fee), no-smoking floors; no a/c, no room phones, no room TVs* ▭ *MC, V* ⦿ *CP* Ⓤ *Russell Sq.*

**£** ▣ **The Ridgemount.** The kindly British owners, Mr. and Mrs. Rees, make you feel at home. Rooms tend to have a 1970s style, but are great for cheap accommodations in a central neighborhood. The public areas, especially the family-style breakfast room, are cluttered Victorian-style parlors. Some rooms overlook a leafy garden and some have an en-suite bathroom for about £15 extra per night. ⊠ *65 Gower St., Bloomsbury WC1E 6HJ* ☎ *020/7636–1141* 🖷 *0207/636–2558* ⊕ *www. ridgemounthotel.co.uk* 🛏 *32 rooms, 15 with bath* ♿ *No-smoking rooms; no room phones; no a/c* ▭ *MC, V* ⦿ *BP* Ⓤ *Goodge St.*

## Hampstead & Islington

**£££** ▣ **Hilton London Islington.** Next door to the Islington Business Design Centre, this hotel has a modern lobby complete with restaurant and free newspapers, which perfectly complements the media-filled, trendy borough of Islington. The hotel has standard, good-size rooms with tea/coffeemakers, and many have panoramic views. The in-house gym and spa are an added bonus for weary travelers. ⊠ *53 Upper St., Islington N1 0UY* ☎ *020/7354–7700* 📠 *020/7354–7711* ⊕ *www.hilton.com* 🛏 *183 rooms, 6 suites* ♨ *2 restaurants, coffee shop, room service, in-room data ports, in-room safes, cable TV, gym, hot tub, sauna, spa, steam room, bar, lobby lounge, babysitting, Internet, business services, meeting room, no-smoking rooms* ⊟ *AE, DC, MC, V* ⫾◯⫾ *BP* Ⓤ *Angel.*

££ 🏨 **Hampstead Village Guesthouse.** This eccentric Victorian guesthouse
Fodor'sChoice has distinctive, comfortable rooms cluttered with antiques and cu-
★ riosities. The Blue Room has a freestanding tub, and the Yellow Room has a roof terrace and canopy bed. You are encouraged to relax in the garden or play with the resident dog, Marley. Families might appreciate the separate garden studio, which houses up to five people and has its own kitchenette. Book well ahead for this hot property. ⊠ *2 Kemplay Rd., Hampstead NW3 1SY* ☎ *020/7435–8679* 📠 *020/7794–0254* ⊕ *www.hampsteadguesthouse.com* 🛏 *8 rooms* ♨ *Dining room, refrigerators, lounge, parking (fee); no a/c, no smoking* ⊟ *No credit cards* Ⓤ *Hampstead.*

££ 🏨 **Jurys Inn.** Just a 10-minute walk to King's Cross and St. Pancras stations, this nondescript, purpose-built, U.K. chain hotel provides low-price accommodations. Upper Street, with its quiet cafés, lively bars, and international restaurants, is close by. The rooms are standard but spacious and accommodate up to three adults or a family of four. ⊠ *60 Pentonville Rd., Islington N1 9LA* ☎ *020/7282–5500* 📠 *020/ 7282–5511* ⊕ *www.jurysinn.com* 🛏 *229 rooms* ♨ *Restaurant, in-room data ports, cable TV, pub, babysitting, dry cleaning, laundry service, meeting rooms, parking (fee), no-smoking rooms* ⊟ *AE, DC, MC, V* Ⓤ *Angel or King's Cross.*

££ 🏨 **La Gaffe.** A short walk up one of Hampstead's magnificent hills, La Gaffe is run by Italian Lorenzo Stella, who has welcomed people back to these early 18th-century shepherds' cottages for more than 20 years. His restaurant has been going for nearly 40. Make no mistake, rooms are tiny, with showers only, but the popular wine bar and restaurant, which naturally serve Italian food, are yours to enjoy. Between the two wings of the hotel is a raised patio for summer. ⊠ *107–111 Heath St., Hampstead NW3 6SS* ☎ *020/7435–8965* 📠 *020/7794–7592* ⊕ *www. lagaffe.co.uk* 🛏 *15 rooms, 3 suites* ♨ *Restaurant, café, fans, wine bar, laundry facilities, concierge, Internet, free parking; no a/c, no smoking* ⊟ *AE, MC, V* ⫾◯⫾ *CP* Ⓤ *Hampstead.*

## Kensington

£££££ 🏨 **Bentley.** This hotel is a luxurious escape, right in the heart of Kensington. The bedrooms are almost palatial in proportion, and have silk wallpaper, golden furnishings, and fine marble bathrooms. The staff is obliging, and the marble Turkish steam room is a haven from the stresses of the day. ⊠ *27–33 Harrington Gardens, South Kensington SW7 4JK* ☎ *020/7244–5555* 📠 *020/7244–5566* ⊕ *www.thebentley-hotel.com* 🛏 *52 rooms, 12 suites* ♨ *2 restaurants, in-room data ports, in-room fax, in-room safes, some in-room hot tubs, minibars, cable TV with movies* *and video games, in-room DVDs and VCRs, gym, hair salon, spa, Turkish bath, bar, lounge, babysitting, dry cleaning, laundry service, concierge, Internet, business services, meeting rooms, airport shuttle, car rental, parking (fee), some pets allowed, no-smoking rooms* ▤ *AE, D, MC, V* Ⓤ *Gloucester Rd.*

££££ᴸ   ⊞ **Milestone Hotel & Apartments.** An intimate, luxurious hotel experience
Fodor'sChoice   awaits at this gorgeous pair of intricately decorated brick Victorian town
★   houses overlooking Kensington Palace and Gardens. From offering you a welcome drink upon arrival to preparing a post-theater midnight snack in your room, the staff is friendly and efficient. Each sumptuous room is full of antiques; many have canopied beds, and some have balconies. The staff makes a point of getting to know visitors, which makes this place special. ⊠ *1 Kensington Ct., Kensington W8 5DL* ☎ *020/ 7917–1000* 🖷 *020/7917–1010* ⊕ *www.milestonehotel.com* ⇗ *45 rooms, 12 suites, 6 apartments* ⌂ *2 restaurants, room service, in-room fax, in-room safes, some kitchens, minibars, cable TV with movies, in-room VCRs, gym, hot tub, sauna, bar, lounge, babysitting, dry cleaning, laundry service, concierge, Internet, business services, meeting rooms, some pets allowed (fee); no smoking* ▤ *AE, DC, MC, V* Ⓤ *High St. Kensington.*

★   ⊞ **Blakes.** Designed by owner Anouska Hempel, Blakes is another
££££–£££££   world. Each room is a fantasy packed with precious Biedermeier, Murano glass, and modern pieces collected from all over the world. Rooms range from Chinese opium den fantasies to bright spaces with colonial furnishings. The foyer sets the tone with piles of cushions, Phileas Fogg valises and trunks, black walls, rattan, and bamboo. You can get a massage here, and there's a garden as well as a rooftop terrace. ⊠ *33 Roland Gardens, South Kensington SW7 3PF* ☎ *020/7370–6701* 🖷 *020/ 7373–0442* ⊕ *www.blakeshotels.com* ⇗ *38 rooms, 11 suites* ⌂ *Restaurant, room service, in-room data ports, some in-room faxes, in-room safes, minibars, cable TV, in-room VCRs, gym, bar, babysitting, dry cleaning, laundry service, concierge, Internet, business services, meeting rooms, car rental, parking (fee); no a/c in some rooms* ▤ *AE, DC, MC, V* Ⓤ *S. Kensington.*

££££   ⊞ **The Cranley.** This small, Victorian town-house hotel brings together traditional standards of service and style. High ceilings and huge windows make the bedrooms light and bright. The antique desks and four-poster or half-tester beds are in line with the period furnishings. Even the bathrooms have traditional Victorian fittings. Afternoon tea and evening canapés are complimentary. Some rooms are big enough for families. The overall feeling is of old-fashioned British properness. ⊠ *10–12 Bina Gardens, South Kensington SW5 0LA* ☎ *020/7373–0123* 🖷 *020/ 7373–9497* ⊕ *www.thecranley.com* ⇗ *29 rooms, 5 suites, 4 apartments* ⌂ *Room service, in-room data ports, in-room safes, some kitchens, cable TV, in-room VCRs, babysitting, laundry service, concierge, Internet, business services, parking (fee), no-smoking rooms* ▤ *AE, DC, MC, V* Ⓤ *Gloucester Rd.*

££££   ⊞ **The Gore.** Just down the road from the Albert Hall, this friendly hotel, run by the same people who run Hazlitt's and the Rookery, has a similarly eclectic selection of Victoriana, prints, etchings, and antiques: the lobby looks like a set from a Luchino Visconti film, evoking centuries past. Upstairs are spectacular follylike rooms—Room 101 is a Tudor fantasy with minstrel gallery, stained glass, and four-poster bed, and Room 211, done in over-the-top Hollywood style, has a tiled mural of Greek goddesses in its bathroom. As with everything eccentric, this place is not for everyone. ⊠ *189 Queens Gate, Kensington SW7 5EX* ☎ *020/7584–6601* 🖷 *020/7589–8127* ⊕ *www.gorehotel.com* 🛏 *54 rooms* ♨ *Restaurant, room service, fans, in-room data ports, in-room safes, minibars, cable TV, in-room VCRs, bar, lounge, babysitting, dry cleaning, laundry service, concierge, meeting rooms, no-smoking floors; no a/c* ⊟ *AE, DC, MC, V* Ⓤ *Gloucester Rd.*

★ **££££** 🏠 **Number Sixteen.** A luxury B&B close to the South Kensington Tube and three blocks or so from the great museums, Number Sixteen stands in a white-portico row of Victorian houses. There's no uniformity to the bedrooms except for their similar spaciousness and marble and oak-clad bathrooms, but the style is not so much interior-designed as understated—new furniture and modern prints are juxtaposed with yellowed oils and antiques. There's an honor bar, two drawing rooms, and an enticing garden where drinks and snacks are served. ⊠ *16 Sumner Pl., South Kensington SW7 3EG* ☎ *020/7589–5232, 800/553–6674 in U.S.* 🖷 *020/7584–8615* ⊕ *www.firmdale.com* 🛏 *42 rooms* ♨ *Room service, in-room data ports, in-room safes, minibars, cable TV, in-room VCRs, bar, lounge, library, babysitting, dry cleaning, laundry service, concierge; no a/c in some rooms* ⊟ *AE, MC, V* �†Ol *CP* Ⓤ *S. Kensington.*

**£££** 🏠 **Aster House.** Rooms in this delightful guesthouse are country casual. The owners are very friendly, and go out of their way to make you feel at home and answer questions. The conservatory where breakfast is served is an airy, light place, and the small garden at the back has a charming pond. Note that this is a five-story building with no elevator. Rooms have tea/coffeemakers. ⊠ *3 Sumner Pl., South Kensington SW7 3EE* ☎ *020/7581–5888* 🖷 *020/7584–4925* ⊕ *www.welcome2london.com/asterhouse* 🛏 *14 rooms* ♨ *Dining room, in-room safes, cable TV, lounge, Internet; no smoking* ⊟ *MC, V* �†Ol *BP* Ⓤ *S. Kensington.*

**£££** 🏠 **Five Sumner Place.** Once you've checked into this tall Victorian town house on a quiet residential street, you get your own key to the front door. If the weather is pleasant, you can enjoy the small garden. In the morning, take breakfast in the conservatory. Guest rooms are vaguely Victorian, with reproduction furniture. There's an elevator. ⊠ *5 Sumner Pl., South Kensington SW7 3EE* ☎ *020/7584–7586* 🖷 *020/7823–9962* ⊕ *www.sumnerplace.com* 🛏 *17 rooms* ♨ *Room service, in-room data ports, minibars, parking (fee); no smoking, no a/c* ⊟ *AE, MC, V* �†Ol *BP* Ⓤ *S. Kensington.*

**£££** 🏠 **The Gallery.** It's a small, Edwardian world apart from the bustling city. Across the street from its sister property, the Gainsborough hotel, the Gallery has an Arts-and-Crafts–style living room with a piano, lush carpets, cozy fires, and sturdy furniture. You can check your e-mail on the computer in the Morris Room, a sitting area with William Morris furnishings. The bedrooms are a good size for the city, with solid, comfortable beds. The bathrooms have London's ubiquitous polished granite. Included in the price is a full English breakfast, which will make lunch a challenge.

Suites have a roof terrace, hot tubs, and minibars. ⊠ *10 Queensberry Pl., South Kensington SW7 2E8* ☎ *020/7915–0000, 800/270–9206 in U.S.* 🖷 *020/7915–4400* ⊕ *www.eeh.co.uk* ➥ *34 rooms, 2 suites* ⟐ *Room service, in-room data ports, some in-room faxes, in-room safes, some in-room hot tubs, some minibars, cable TV, bar, dry cleaning, laundry service, concierge, Internet, meeting rooms, airport shuttle; no a/c in some rooms* ▭ *AE, DC, MC, V* ¶◯┤ *BP* Ⓤ *S. Kensington.*

£££ 🏨 **Kensington House Hotel.** This refurbished 19th-century town house off Kensington High Street has modern, streamlined rooms with large windows and contemporary furnishings. Rear rooms have views of trees and mews houses, and all rooms have tea/coffeemakers and bathrobes. ⊠ *15–16 Prince of Wales Terr., Kensington W8 5PQ* ☎ *020/7937–2345* 🖷 *020/7368–6700* ⊕ *www.kenhouse.com* ➥ *41 rooms* ⟐ *Restaurant, room service, fans, in-room data ports, in-room safes, cable TV, bar, babysitting, dry cleaning, parking (fee), no-smoking rooms; no a/c* ▭ *AE, DC, MC, V* ¶◯┤ *CP* Ⓤ *High St. Kensington.*

££ 🏨 **Abbey House.** This white-stucco 1860 Victorian town house has an excellent location close to trendy Notting Hill and Kensington High Street's many shops. Rooms have dated decor. The quads are suitable for families and have washbasins, but every room shares a bath with another. There's no elevator. The slightly nicer but still budget Vicarage is next door. ⊠ *11 Vicarage Gate, Notting Hill W8 4AG* ☎ *020/7727–2594* 🖷 *020/7727–1873* ⊕ *www.abbeyhousekensington.com* ➥ *16 rooms without bath* ⟐ *Lounge, concierge; no a/c, no room phones* ▭ *No credit cards* ¶◯┤ *BP* Ⓤ *High St. Kensington.*

££ 🏨 **Hotel 167.** This white-stucco, Victorian corner house is just a two-minute walk from the V&A. The dated rooms are functional, with pine furniture and muted tones. The hallways and stairwells have seen better days, but the breakfast room–lounge has nice wrought-iron furniture and sunny yellow walls. Avoid the dark basement rooms. ⊠ *167 Old Brompton Rd., South Kensington SW5 0AN* ☎ *020/7373–3221* 🖷 *020/7373–3360* ⊕ *www.hotel167.com* ➥ *18 rooms* ⟐ *Dining room, minibars, cable TV; no a/c* ▭ *AE, DC, MC, V* ¶◯┤ *CP* Ⓤ *Gloucester Rd.*

££ 🏨 **Swiss House Hotel.** Around the corner from Hotel 167, this hotel is slightly more modern than its neighbor. Rooms have Scandinavian-style pine furniture, dried flower arrangements, and simple dark-blue rugs. Ask for a back room for a garden view. Some single rooms do not have bathrooms. The triple and quad rooms, with more space and beds, are convenient for families. ⊠ *171 Old Brompton Rd., South Kensington SW5 0AN* ☎ *020/7373–2769* 🖷 *020/7373–4983* ⊕ *www.swiss-hh. demon.co.uk* ➥ *15 rooms, 14 with bath* ⟐ *Dining room, fans, babysitting, parking (fee), no-smoking rooms; no a/c* ▭ *AE, DC, MC, V* ¶◯┤ *CP* Ⓤ *Gloucester Rd.*

££ 🏨 **The Vicarage.** Family-owned and set on a leaf-shaded street just off Kensington Church Street, The Vicarage occupies a large white Victorian house that's full of dark-stained wood furniture, patterned carpets, and dated flowery fabrics, and it's beginning to fray around the edges. All rooms share the bathroom, but a few doubles have their own showers. ⊠ *10 Vicarage Gate, Notting Hill W8 4AG* ☎ *020/7229–4030* 🖷 *020/7792–5989* ⊕ *www.londonvicaragehotel.com* ➥ *14 rooms, 8* *with bath* 🏊 *Dining room, lounge; no a/c, no room TVs* 🖃 *No credit cards* 🍴 *BP* Ⓤ *High St. Kensington.*

£ 🏨 **Holland House YHA.** This is certainly the most historic and pastoral of London's youth hostels. It's part Jacobean mansion and part 1970s addition. Dorm rooms overlook the wooded park, where black bunnies scamper and peacocks strut around the central Kyoto Gardens. The park also has an open-air opera theater in summer and the Orangery Art Gallery year-round. Kensington High Street and civilization are just a few steps away. Inexpensive lunches and dinners are available for purchase, too. ⊠ *Holland Walk, Kensington W8 7QU* ☎ *0870/770–5866* 🖷 *020/7376–0667* ⊕ *www.hollhse.btinternet.co. uk* 🛏 *201 beds* 🏊 *Dining room, 4 tennis courts, lounge, recreation room, laundry facilities, Internet, meeting rooms; no a/c, no room phones, no room TVs, no smoking* 🖃 *AE, MC, V* 🍴 *BP* Ⓤ *High St. Kensington.*

## Knightsbridge, Chelsea, Belgravia, & Westminster

£££££ 🏨 **The Berkeley.** The Berkeley successfully mixes the old and the new— it's a luxurious, air-conditioned, double-glaze, modern building with a splendid penthouse swimming pool. The bedrooms either have swags of William Morris prints or are art deco. All have sitting areas, CD players, and big bathrooms with bidets. There are spectacular penthouse suites with their own conservatory terrace, and others with saunas or balconies. Dining venues include Marus Wareing's high-class Pétrus restaurant, Gordon Ramsay's New York-style Boxwood café, the eclectic and sumptuous Blue Bar, and the whimsical Caramel Room where morning coffee and scrumptious doughnuts are served. ⊠ *Wilton Pl., Belgravia SW1X 7RL* ☎ *020/7235–6000, 800/637–2869 in U.S.* 🖷 *020/7235–4330* ⊕ *www.the-berkeley.com* 🛏 *103 rooms, 55 suites* 🏊 *Restaurant, room service, in-room fax, in-room safes, some kitchens, minibars, cable TV, in-room VCRs, indoor-outdoor pool, gym, hair salon, sauna, spa, Turkish bath, bar, cinema, babysitting, dry cleaning, laundry service, concierge, Internet, business services, meeting rooms, airport shuttle, car rental, parking (fee), no-smoking floors* 🖃 *AE, DC, MC, V* Ⓤ *Knightsbridge.*

£££££ 🏨 **The Capital.** Reserve well ahead if you want a room here—as you must for a table in the hotel's popular, top-quality French restaurant. This grand hotel decanted into a private house is the work of the Levin family, who also own nearby L'Hotel, and it exudes their impeccable taste: fine-grain woods, original prints, and soothing, country-chic furnishings. Ask for a front-facing room to get more space. If you're going for a deluxe double, ask for the L-shape rooms in the atmospheric Edwardian wing, where each room has a desk. The staff is conscientious and friendly. ⊠ *22–24 Basil St., Knightsbridge SW3 1AT* ☎ *020/759–1202, 800/926–3199 in U.S.* 🖷 *020/7225–0011* ⊕ *www.capitalhotel.co.uk* 🛏 *40 rooms, 8 suites* 🏊 *Restaurant, dining room, room service, in-room data ports, in-room safes, minibars, cable TV, bar, lounge, babysitting, dry cleaning, laundry service, concierge, Internet, business services, meeting rooms, car rental, parking (fee), some pets allowed, no-smoking rooms* 🖃 *AE, DC, MC, V* Ⓤ *Knightsbridge.*

££££££ 🖼 **The Goring.** Buckingham Palace is just around the corner, and visiting VIPs use the Goring as a convenient, suitably dignified base for royal occasions. The hotel, built by Mr. Goring in 1910 and now run by third-generation Gorings, retains an Edwardian style. Bathrooms are marble-fitted; bedrooms are opulently decorated, and some have brass bedsteads and original built-in closets. ☒ *15 Beeston Pl., Grosvenor Gardens, Victoria SW1W 0JW* 🕿 *020/7396–9000* 🖷 *020/7834–4393* ⊕ *www.goringhotel.co.uk* ↪ *68 rooms, 6 suites* ♻ *Restaurant, room service, in-room data ports, in-room safes, in-room hot tubs, cable TV with movies, gym, bar, babysitting, dry cleaning, laundry service, concierge, business services, meeting rooms, parking (fee), no-smoking rooms* ▭ *AE, DC, MC, V* Ⓤ *Victoria.*

££££££ 🖼 **The Halkin.** Escape the clutter and floral motifs of other hotels and chill out in the understated design here: the clean-cut, white-marble, lobby bar with its burgundy-leather bucket chairs; the arresting, curved, charcoal-gray-and-chrome corridors; and the muted earth-tone bedrooms with bedside control panels for everything from lights to air-conditioning. It's akin to staying in the Design Museum, except that you have Knightsbridge and Hyde Park practically on your doorstep, and the exceptional Nahm Thai restaurant in your lobby. The Shambhala Health Club at the nearby Metropolitan Hotel is at your disposal. ☒ *5 Halkin St., Belgravia SW1X 7DJ* 🕿 *020/7333–1000* 🖷 *020/7333–1100* ⊕ *www.halkin.co.uk* ↪ *41 rooms* ♻ *Restaurant, in-room data ports, some in-room faxes, in-room safes, cable TV with video games, in-room VCRs, bar, babysitting, dry cleaning, laundry service, concierge, Internet, business services, parking (fee), no-smoking rooms* ▭ *AE, DC, MC, V* Ⓤ *Hyde Park Corner.*

££££££ 🖼 **The Lanesborough.** Royally proportioned public rooms distinguish this
Fodor'sChoice multimillion-pound, American-run conversion of St. George's Hospi-
★ tal. Everything undulates with richness—moiré silks and fleurs-de-lis in the colors of precious stones, magnificent antiques and oil paintings, reproductions of more gilded splendor than the originals, handwoven £250-per-square-yard carpet—as if Liberace and Laura Ashley had collaborated. To check in, sign the visitor's book, then retire to your room, where you are waited on by a personal butler. If you yearn for a bygone age and are very rich, this is certainly for you. ☒ *Hyde Park Corner, Belgravia SW1X 7TA* 🕿 *020/7259–5599, 800/999–1828 in U.S.* 🖷 *020/7259–5606, 800/937–8278 in U.S.* ⊕ *www.lanesborough.com* ↪ *49 rooms, 46 suites* ♻ *2 restaurants, room service, in-room data ports, in-room fax, in-room safes, some in-room hot tubs, some kitchens, minibars, cable TV with movies and video games, exercise equipment, 2 bars, lobby lounge, library, babysitting, dry cleaning, laundry service, concierge, Internet, meeting rooms, car rental, parking (fee), no-smoking rooms* ▭ *AE, DC, MC, V* Ⓤ *Hyde Park Corner.*

££££££ 🖼 **Mandarin Oriental Hyde Park.** Stay here, and the three greats of
Fodor'sChoice Knightsbridge are on your doorstep—Hyde Park, Harrods, and Har-
★ vey Nichols. The Mandarin Oriental, built in 1880, is one of the poshest places to stay in London. Bedrooms are traditional Victorian with hidden high-tech gadgets and luxurious touches—potted orchids, chocolates, and fruit. The service here is legendary and includes butlers on

every floor. Some rooms facing the park have balconies. Shopping, spa, and theater packages are available. ✉ *66 Knightsbridge, Knightsbridge SW1X 7LA* ☎ *020/7235–2000* 🖷 *020/7235–2001* 🌐 *www. mandarinoriental.com* 🖙 *177 rooms, 23 suites* ↻ *2 restaurants, room service, in-room data ports, some in-room faxes, in-room safes, mini-bars, cable TV, in-room VCRs, gym, hot tub, sauna, spa, steam room, bar, babysitting, dry cleaning, laundry service, concierge, Internet, business services, meeting rooms, airport shuttle, car rental, parking (fee), no-smoking rooms* ▭ *AE, DC, MC, V* Ⓤ *Knightsbridge.*

£££££ 🏨 **No. 41.** Everything you might want is included in the rate in this hotel that cocoons and pampers its guests—late-night snacks and drinks, cocktails, wine, Internet, dry cleaning, laundry, and local calls. Rooms, some split-level and some with low ceilings, are filled with high-tech gadgets: printer, scanner, and fax. When you're not working, you can relax on the butter-soft leather sofa in front of the fireplace, recline on the exquisite bed linens and feather duvets, or luxuriate in the marble bath. The "whatever, whenever" button on the telephone connects you with the extremely helpful, amiable staff. ✉ *41 Buckingham Palace Rd., Victoria SW1W 0PS* ☎ *020/7300–0041* 🖷 *020/7300–0141* 🌐 *www.41hotel.com* 🖙 *14 rooms, 4 suites* ↻ *Room service, in-room data ports, in-room fax, in-room safes, some in-room hot tubs, minibars, cable TV with movies and video games, in-room VCRs, lounge, babysitting, dry cleaning, laundry service, concierge, Internet, business services, meeting rooms, car rental, parking (fee), no-smoking rooms* ▭ *AE, DC, MC, V* ⏹❘ *CP* Ⓤ *Victoria.*

£££££ 🏨 **The Rubens at the Palace.** This hotel, which looks out over the Royal Mews of Buckingham Palace, provides the sort of deep comfort needed to soothe away a hard day's sightseeing, with cushy armchairs crying out for you to sink into them with a cup of Earl Grey. With decent-size rooms—not quite furnished like the ones at the palace, it must be said—and a location that couldn't be more central, this hotel is a favorite with tour groups. ✉ *39 Buckingham Palace Rd., Westminster SW1W 0PS* ☎ *020/7834–6600* 🖷 *020/7233–6037* 🌐 *www. rubenshotel.com* 🖙 *160 rooms, 13 suites* ↻ *2 restaurants, room service, in-room data ports, some in-room faxes, in-room safes, some minibars, cable TV with movies, some in-room VCRs, lobby lounge, piano bar, babysitting, dry cleaning, laundry service, concierge, Internet, business services, meeting rooms, parking (fee), no-smoking floors* ▭ *AE, DC, MC, V* Ⓤ *Victoria.*

£££££ 🏨 **The Sloane.** Many hotels use the word *unique* to describe their identical canopied beds or garden views, but the tiny Sloane really *is* unique. You can lie in your canopied bed, pick up the phone, and buy the bed. The covetable Victorian antiques are difficult to resist. Nothing so tacky as a price tag besmirches the gorgeous decor—instead, the staff maintains a price list. The roof terrace, which has upholstered garden furniture and a panoramic view of Chelsea, is a great spot. ✉ *29 Draycott Pl., Chelsea SW3 2SH* ☎ *020/7581–5757* 🖷 *020/7584–1348* 🌐 *www. sloanehotel.com* 🖙 *14 rooms, 8 suites* ↻ *Dining room, in-room data ports, in-room safes, cable TV, in-room VCRs, lobby lounge, dry cleaning, laundry service, concierge, Internet, business services, parking (fee)* ▭ *AE, DC, MC, V* Ⓤ *Sloane Sq.*

**££££–£££££** 🏨 **Eleven Cadogan Gardens.** This aristocratic, late-Victorian, gabled town house has a clubby feel—there's no sign, just a simple 11 above the door. Antiques, landscape paintings and portraits, coupled with some of that solid, no-nonsense furniture that *real* English country houses have in abundance make it seem like you're staying in a family home. The best rooms are at the back, overlooking a private garden. If you want to spare no expense and hire a chauffeur-driven car, there's one standing by. The complimentary freshly baked cake for afternoon tea, and sherry and canapés in the evening are excellent. ⊠ *11 Cadogan Gardens, Sloane Sq., South Kensington SW3 2RJ* 🕿 *020/7730–7000* 🖷 *020/7730–5217* ⊕ *www.number-eleven.co.uk* 🛏 *62 rooms ⚿ Dining room, room service, in-room data ports, in-room safes, cable TV, in-room VCRs, exercise equipment, massage, sauna, bar, dry cleaning, laundry service, concierge, Internet, business services, meeting rooms, airport shuttle, car rental; no a/c in some rooms, no kids* ⊟ *AE, DC, MC, V* Ⓤ *Sloane Sq.*

**££££–£££££** 🏨 **Jolly Hotel St. Ermin's.** The hotel is just a short stroll from Westminster Abbey, Buckingham Palace, and the Houses of Parliament. An Edwardian anomaly in the shadow of modern skyscrapers, the hotel is set on a tiny cul-de-sac courtyard. The lobby is an extravaganza of Victorian baroque—all cake-frosting stucco-work in shades of baby blue and creamy white. The Cloisters restaurant, an ornately carved 19th-century Jacobean-style salon, is one of the most magnificent rooms in which to dine in London. Guest rooms are tastefully decorated; some are quite small. ⊠ *2 Caxton St., Westminster SW1H 0QW* 🕿 *020/7222–7888* 🖷 *020/7222–6914* ⊕ *www.jollyhotels.it* 🛏 *277 rooms, 8 suites ⚿ Restaurant, room service, in-room data ports, some in-room safes, minibars, cable TV with movies, bar, lounge, babysitting, dry cleaning, laundry service, meeting rooms, parking (fee), no-smoking rooms* ⊟ *AE, DC, MC, V* Ⓤ *St. James's Park.*

**££££–£££££** 🏨 **Knightsbridge Hotel.** Just off glamorous Knightsbridge near Harrods and Harvey Nichols in quiet Beaufort Gardens, this chic hotel is well placed for shoppers. The balconied suites and regular rooms benefit from CD players, writing desks, and large granite and oak bathrooms. The fully loaded honor bar in the drawing room is an excellent place to unwind amid African sculptures and modern art. Bedrooms offer marble and oak bathrooms and understated, classic interiors. ⊠ *10 Beaufort Gardens, Knightsbridge SW3 1PT* 🕿 *020/7584–6300, 800/553–6674 in U.S.* 🖷 *020/7584–6355* ⊕ *www.knightsbridgehotel.co.uk* 🛏 *42 rooms, 2 suites ⚿ Room service, in-room data ports, in-room safes, minibars, cable TV, some in-room VCRs, gym, bar, library, babysitting, dry cleaning, laundry service, concierge, Internet, meeting rooms, parking (fee)* ⊟ *AE, MC, V* Ⓤ *Knightsbridge.*

**££££–£££££** 🏨 **myhotel chelsea.** This fashionable town house, which is part of the small myhotel chain that includes myhotel bloomsbury, sends out a pre-arrival form asking guests preferences on smoking, music, and movies; likes and dislikes; and dietary requirements. Quirky services like hot water bottles at bedtime, botox specialists on call, and resident tarot card and palm reader in the bar during cocktail hour, set this place apart. Rooms are equipped with all the super modern amenities like widescreen TVs and are decorated in pinks, grays, and creams. Well placed for high-end shopping, and with an emphasis on well-being, it's very of-the-moment. ⊠ *35 Ixworth Pl., Chelsea SW3 3QZ* ☎ *020/7225–7500* 🖶 *020/7225–7555* ⊕ *www. myhotels.com* ⇆*45 rooms, 9 suites* ♢ *Room service, fans, minibars, in-room safes, in-room data ports, cable TV, in-room DVDs, gym, spa, massage, bar, lounge, babysitting, laundry service, Internet, some pets allowed, no-smoking floors* ⊟ *AE, D, MC, V* Ⓤ *S. Kensington.*

££££–£££££ 🖼 **The Pelham.** Museum lovers flock to this sweet hotel across the street from the South Kensington Tube station. The Natural History, Science, and Victoria & Albert (V&A) museums are all a short stroll away, as is the famous King's Road. At the end of a day's sightseeing, settle down in front of the fireplace in one of the two snug drawing rooms with their honor bars—a truly relaxing proposition. The stylish, contemporary rooms have sash windows and marble bathrooms. Some top-floor rooms have sloping ceilings and casement windows. ⊠ *15 Cromwell Pl., South Kensington SW7 2LA* ☎ *020/7589–8288, 800/553–6674 in U.S.* 🖶 *020/7584–8444* ⊕ *www.firmdale.com* ⇆ *47 rooms, 4 suites* ♢ *Restaurant, bar, room service, in-room data ports, some in-room safes, minibars, cable TV, in-room VCRs with movies, bar, concierge, business services, meeting rooms, parking (fee)* ⊟ *AE, MC, V* Ⓤ *S. Kensington.*

££££ 🖼 **The Beaufort.** This elegant pair of Victorian houses contains a guesthouse where you get a lot for your money. Guests get a front-door key, free run of the drinks cabinet in the drawing room, and an in-room CD player and radio. The high-ceiling, contemporary rooms have muted, sophisticated colors. Rates include flowers, fruit, chocolates, cookies, and water in your room; free e-mail and movies via the TV; cream tea in the drawing room; and membership at a local health club. Junior suites include a free one-way airport transfer. Four of the rooms have pretty wrought-iron balconies. ⊠ *33 Beaufort Gardens, Knightsbridge SW3 1PP* ☎ *020/7584–5252* 🖶 *020/7589–2834, 800/584–7764 in U.S.* ⊕ *www.thebeaufort.co.uk* ⇆ *20 rooms, 7 suites* ♢ *Room service, in-room data ports, in-room safes, cable TV with movies and video games, lobby lounge, babysitting, dry cleaning, laundry service, concierge, Internet, business services, meeting rooms, car rental, no-smoking rooms; no a/c in some rooms* ⊟ *AE, DC, MC, V* 🍴❘ *CP* Ⓤ *Knightsbridge.*

🔥 ££££ 🖼 **City Inn Westminster.** In a rather stark steel and glass building steps from the Tate Britain, this modern hotel, which is part of a small U.K. chain, has some rooms with spectacular views of Big Ben and London Eye. Extras like floor-to-ceiling windows, CD players, and flat-screen TVs complement the sleek, contemporary, monochrome guest rooms. Cots, baby baths, Nickelodeon, special menus, and baby food are all on tap for kids. The restaurant and bar serve modern British cooking. ⊠ *30 John Islip St., Westminster SW1P 4DD* ☎ *020/7630–1000* 🖶 *020/ 7233–7575* ⊕ *www.cityinn.com* ⇆ *444 rooms, 16 suites* ♢ *Restaurant, room service, minibars, in-room data ports, in-room safes, cable TV, in-room DVDs, bar, lobby lounge, gym, babysitting, dry cleaning, laundry service, concierge, Internet, business services, parking (fee), meeting rooms, no-smoking rooms* ⊟ *AE, MC, V* Ⓤ *Pimlico.*

££££ 🖼 **Dolphin Square Hotel.** You can get an entire apartment here, on the outer edge of Westminster near the Thames. The hotel has contemporary, bright, and comfortable one-, two-, and three-bedroom suites, all with kitchens and some with living rooms. You can be totally independent staying here; there is, however, room service if you just can't be bothered. The extensive gardens provide lots of green space. Another perk: celebrity chef Gary Rhodes owns one of the hotel's restaurants, Rhodes in the Square. ⊠ *Dolphin Sq., Chichester St., Westminster SW1V 3LX* ☎ *020/7798–3800* 🖷 *020/7798–8896* ⊕ *www.dolphinsquarehotel.co.uk* ⟳ *2 restaurants, room service, in-room safes, kitchens, microwaves, refrigerators, cable TV with movies, tennis court, indoor pool, fitness classes, gym, hair salon, sauna, spa, steam rooms, croquet, squash, wine bar, shop, babysitting, dry cleaning, laundry service, concierge, Internet, business services, meeting rooms, travel services, parking (fee), no-smoking rooms; no a/c* ▭ *AE, DC, MC, V* Ⓤ *Pimlico.*

££££ 🏨 **Egerton House.** This utterly peaceful, small hotel was the first in the group that includes the Franklin and Dukes hotels. Chintz, floral, or Regency-stripe bedrooms overlook the gorgeous gardens in back or the red-brick facades of the buildings in the area; some have quirky shapes, one has a four-poster bed, still others are bigger with closet space. The two drawing rooms, decorated in high-Victorian style, are good places to write letters or relax with a drink from the honor bar. ⊠ *17–19 Egerton Terr., Knightsbridge SW3 2BX* ☎ *020/7589–2412, 800/473–9492 in U.S.* 🖷 *020/7584–6540* ⊕ *www.egertonhousehotel.co.uk* ⟳ *23 rooms, 6 suites* ⟳ *Dining room, room service, in-room data ports, minibars, cable TV, some in-room VCRs, bar, lounge, dry cleaning, laundry service, concierge, Internet, business services, meeting rooms, car rental, parking (fee), no-smoking rooms* ▭ *AE, DC, MC, V* Ⓤ *Knightsbridge or S. Kensington.*

££££ 🏨 **The Franklin.** It's hard to imagine, while taking tea in this romantic hotel overlooking a quiet garden, that you're an amble away from busy Brompton and Cromwell roads and the splendors of the V&A Museum. A few of the rooms are small, but the marble bathrooms are not, and the large garden rooms and suites are romantic indeed. Some rooms have four-poster beds; all have antique furnishings. Tea is served daily in the lounge, and there's an honor bar, and a free Internet computer. Dukes and the Egerton House are sister properties. ⊠ *28 Egerton Gardens, Knightsbridge SW3 2DB* ☎ *020/7584–5533, 800/473–9487 in U.S.* 🖷 *020/7584–5449, 800/473–9489 in U.S.* ⊕ *www.franklinhotel.co.uk* ⟳ *50 rooms* ⟳ *Dining room, room service, in-room data ports, in-room safes, minibars, cable TV, some in-room VCRs, bar, dry cleaning, laundry service, concierge, Internet, business services, meeting rooms, parking (fee), no-smoking rooms* ▭ *AE, DC, MC, V* Ⓤ *S. Kensington.*

£££–££££ 🏨 **L'Hotel.** Rooms at this upscale B&B have an air of provincial France, with white bedcovers, pine furniture, and beige color schemes. Delicious breakfast croissants and baguettes are served in Le Metro cellar wine bar or brought to your room. It's like staying in a house—you're given your own front-door key, there's no elevator, and the staff leaves in the evening. Ask for a fireplace room: they're the biggest. All rooms have tea/coffeemakers; some rooms have only handheld showerheads. You have access to the restaurant and concierge services of the plush

Capital hotel, run by the same family, a few doors down the street. ⊠ *28 Basil St., Knightsbridge SW3 1AT* ☎ *020/7589–6286* 🖷 *020/7823–7826* ⊕ *www.lhotel.co.uk* 🗗 *11 rooms, 1 suite* ⚲ *Restaurant, fans, in-room data ports, minibars, cable TV, in-room VCRs, bar, babysitting, dry cleaning, laundry service, concierge, Internet, parking (fee); no a/c* ☰ *AE, V* ¶◎¶ *CP* Ⓤ *Knightsbridge.*

**£££** 🏨 **Knightsbridge Green.** Near Harrods and Hyde Park, this modern hotel has affordable triples and quads with sofa beds that are good for families or those wanting extra space. All rooms have trouser presses and tea/coffeemakers. Rooms have double-glaze windows that help muffle the sound of traffic on busy Knightsbridge. Breakfast can be delivered to your room and there are two lounges where you can have tea or coffee for free. Daytime reception only. ⊠ *159 Knightsbridge, Knights-bridge SW1X 7PD* ☎ *020/7584–6274* 🖷 *020/7225–1635* ⊕ *www. thekghotel.co.uk* 🗗 *28 rooms, 12 suites* ⚲ *In-room data ports, in-room safes, cable TV, babysitting, dry cleaning, concierge, Internet; no smoking* ☰ *AE, DC, MC, V* Ⓜ *Knightsbridge.*

**£££** 🏨 **Tophams Belgravia.** The family that runs this hotel extends a warm welcome and has many loyal clients. Family-owned since 1937, the hotel consists of five Georgian houses linked together. Rooms are done in florals or deep greens and reds. There are many different configurations including family rooms and four-poster rooms. Enduring are the staff's friendliness and the good value offered. ⊠ *28 Ebury St., Belgravia SW1W 0LU* ☎ *020/7730–8147* 🖷 *020/7823–5966* ⊕ *www.tophams. co.uk* 🗗 *39 rooms* ⚲ *Restaurant, room service, in-room data ports, cable TV, bar, lobby lounge, babysitting, meeting room, parking (fee)* ¶◎¶ *BP* ☰ *AE, DC, MC, V* Ⓤ *Victoria.*

**££–£££** 🏨 **Astons Budget Studios.** This lodging is made up of three redbrick Victorian town houses on a residential street. The studios and apartments all have concealed kitchenettes, and the apartments (£££) have marble bathrooms, hair dryers, robes, irons, and trouser presses. Rooms tend toward Ikea chic. It's worth paying that little bit extra for the designer rooms because the regular rooms have plastic, prefab bathrooms. ⊠ *31 Rosary Gardens, South Kensington SW7 4NH* ☎ *020/7590–6000, 800/525–2810 in U.S.* 🖷 *020/7590–6060* ⊕ *www.astons-apartments. com* 🗗 *43 rooms, 12 suites* ⚲ *Dining room, fans, in-room data ports, in-room safes, kitchenettes, microwaves, refrigerators, cable TV, concierge, Internet, business services, airport shuttle, car rental, parking (fee), some pets allowed, no-smoking floors; no a/c* ☰ *AE, MC, V* Ⓤ *Gloucester Rd.*

**££–£££** 🏨 **Sanctuary House Hotel.** Stick with tradition, and enjoy this pub hotel in an excellent location minutes from Westminster Abbey and the Houses of Parliament. Renovated by Fuller's brewery, the hotel rooms are on the floors above the Fuller's Ale & Pie House. The pub is Victorian and traditional, but the rooms are more modern. Friday and Saturday night rates are cheapest. ⊠ *33 Tothill St., Westminster SW1H 9LA* ☎ *020/ 7799–4044* 🖷 *020/7799–3657* ⊕ *www.sanctuaryhousehotel.com* 🗗 *33 rooms, 1 suite* ⚲ *Restaurant, room service, cable TV, pub, dry cleaning, laundry service, parking (fee), no-smoking floors* ☰ *AE, DC, MC, V* Ⓤ *St. James's Park.*

**££** 🏠 **James & Cartref House.** These two town houses are run by husband-and-wife team, Derek and Sharon James. All rooms are equipped with washbasins and tea/coffeemakers. Though the rooms are small, they are well taken care of by the extremely pleasant proprietors. Most rooms have en-suite bathrooms, but for the few that haven't there are showers and toilets on the landings right outside of the bedrooms. ⊠ *108 & 129 Ebury St., Victoria SW1W 9QD* ☎ *020/7730–6176* 🖹 *020/7730–7338* ⊕ *www.jamesandcartref.co.uk* 🛏 *19 rooms, 13 rooms with bath* ⚷ *fans; no smoking, no a/c* ⦿| *BP* ⊟ *AE, MC, V* Ⓤ *Victoria.*

**££** 🏠 **Lime Tree Hotel.** On a street filled with budget hotels, the Lime Tree stands out for its gracious proprietors, the Davies family, who endeavor to provide a homey atmosphere as well as act as concierges to their loyal clientele. The rooms have flowery fabrics and are dated, but the place is cared for. Rooms include tea/coffeemakers. The triples and quads are suitable for families, but children under five are not allowed. The simple breakfast room covered with notes and gifts from former guests opens onto a garden. ⊠ *135–137 Ebury St., Victoria SW1W 9RA* ☎ *020/ 7730–8191* 🖹 *020/7730–7865* ⊕ *www.limetreehotel.co.uk* 🛏 *25 rooms* ⚷ *Fans, in-room safes; no children under 5, no a/c* ⦿| *BP* ⊟ *MC, V* Ⓤ *Victoria.*

**££** 🏠 **New England Hotel.** This family-run B&B in a 19th-century town house is an excellent find. The power showers, comfortable beds, and electronic key cards are unexpected in this price category. There's nothing trend-setting about the interior, but the plaid-and-floral motif is welcoming. ⊠ *20 Saint George's Dr., Victoria SW1V 4BN* ☎ *020/7834–8351* 🖹 *020/7834–9000* ⊕ *www.newenglandhotel.com* 🛏 *25 rooms* ⚷ *Fans, in-room data ports, cable TV, meeting room, parking (fee), no-smoking floors; no a/c* ⊟ *AE, DC, MC, V* ⦿| *BP* Ⓤ *Victoria.*

**£–££** 🏠 **Vandon House Hotel.** Popular with students and families on a budget, this welcoming hotel is close to Westminster Abbey and Buckingham Palace. Singles and some twin rooms share facilities, but the rest are en suite with a shower only. The family rooms include a double bed and bunk bed to accommodate four people. Tea/coffeemakers in the rooms, packed lunches, and tour and theater ticket arrangements set this little budget hotel apart. ⊠ *1 Vandon St., Westminster SW1H 0AH* ☎ *020/ 7799–6780* 🖹 *020/7799–1464* ⊕ *www.vandonhouse.com* 🛏 *32 rooms* ⚷ *Lounge, laundry service, Internet, meeting rooms, airport shuttle; no smoking, no a/c* ⦿| *CP* ⊟ *MC, V* Ⓤ *St. James's Park.*

**£–££** 🏠 **Morgan House.** Near Victoria Station in classy Belgravia, this charming Georgian B&B has flowery rooms with orthopedic mattresses, TVs, hair dryers, ornamental fireplaces, and tea/coffeemaking facilities. The house has one family room with bunk beds and a double bed. Ask for a room in the back if you're sensitive to street noise. Neighboring Woodville House at No. 107, with 12 rooms without bath, is under the same ownership and has some rooms with kitchenettes as well as a back patio for enjoying the rare sunny day. ⊠ *120 Ebury St., Belgravia SW1W 9QQ* ☎ *020/7730–2384* 🖹 *020/7730–8442* ⊕ *www. morganhouse.co.uk* 🛏 *11 rooms, 8 without bath* ⚷ *No a/c* ⊟ *No credit cards* ⦿| *BP* Ⓤ *Victoria.*

# LODGING ALTERNATIVES

## Apartment Rentals

*For a home base that's roomy enough for a family and comes with cooking facilities, consider a furnished rental. These can save you money, especially if you're traveling with a group. Home-exchange directories sometimes list rentals as well as exchanges. In Britain, apartments are called flats. If you want to deal directly with local agents in Britain, get a personal recommendation from someone who has used the company; unlike hotels, there's no accredited system for standards. The London Tourist Board also has accommodation lists.*

**International Agents At Home Abroad** ⌂ 163 Third Ave., No. 319, New York, NY 10003 ☎ 212/421–9165 ⛫ 212/533–0095 ⊕ www.athomeabroadinc.com. **Hideaways International** ✉ 767 Islington St., Portsmouth, NH 03801 ☎ 603/430–4433 or 800/843–4433 ⛫ 603/430–4444 ⊕ www.hideaways.com, annual membership $145. **Hometours International** ✉ 1108 Scottie La., Knoxville, TN 37919 ☎ 865/690–8484 or 866/367–4668 ⊕ thor.he.net/~hometour/. **Interhome** ✉ 1990 N.E. 163rd St., Suite 110, North Miami Beach, FL 33162 ☎ 305/940–2299 or 800/882–6864 ⛫ 305/940–2911 ⊕ www.interhome.us. **Vacation Home Rentals Worldwide** ✉ 235 Kensington Ave., Norwood, NJ 07648 ☎ 201/767–9393 or 800/633–3284 ⛫ 201/767–5510 ⊕ www.vhrww.com. **Villanet** ✉ 1251 N. W. 116th St., Seattle, WA 98177 ☎ 206/417–3444 or 800/964–1891 ⛫ 206/417–1832 ⊕ www.rentavilla.com. **Villas and Apartments Abroad** ✉ 183 Madison Ave., Suite 201, New York, NY 10016 ☎ 212/213–6435 or 800/433–3020 ⛫ 212/213–8252 ⊕ www.vaanyc.com. **Villas International** ✉ 4340 Redwood Hwy., Suite D309, San Rafael, CA 94903 ☎ 415/499–9490 or 800/221–2260 ⛫ 415/499–9491 ⊕ www.villasintl.com.

**Local Agents Acorn Apartments** ✉ 103 Great Russell St., WC1B 3LA ☎ 020/7813–3223 ⛫ 020/7813–3270 ⊕ www.acorn-apartments.co.uk, cost from £90. **The Apartment Service** ✉ 5 Francis Grove, Wimbledon SW19 4DT ☎ 020/8944–1444 ⛫ 020/8944–6744 ⊕ www.apartmentservice.com. **The Landmark Trust** ☎ 01628/825925 ⊕ www.landmarktrust.co.uk for London apartments in unusual and historic buildings.

## University Halls of Residence

*University student dorms can be ideal for single travelers as well as those on a tight budget who want to come to London in summer when deals on other lodging are at their most scarce. Walter Sickert Hall has year-round lodging in their "executive rooms" (six single and three twin), and breakfast is even delivered to your room. Beds are usually available for a week around Easter, and from mid-June to mid-September in all of the university accommodations around town. As you might expect, showers and toilets are shared, and there are no bellhops to carry your bags or concierges to answer your questions.*

**Universities City University Hall of Residence: Walter Sickert Hall** (✉ Graham St., N1 8LA ☎ 020/7040–8822 ⛫ 020/7040–8825 ⊕ www.city.ac.uk/ems) costs £60 for a double year-round and includes Continental breakfast. **London School of Economics Vacations** (☎ 020/7955–7575 ⛫ 0207/955–7676 ⊕ www.lsevacations.co.uk) costs £38 for a double without a toilet to £62 for a double with a toilet. You can choose from a variety of rooms in their five halls of residence around London. **University College London** (✉ Residence

Manager, Campbell House, 5-10 Taviton St., WC1H 0BX ☎ 020/7679–1479 🖷 020/7388–0060) costs £35–£40 for a double and is open from mid-June to mid-September.

## Home Exchanges

If you would like to exchange your home for someone else's, join a home-exchange organization, which will send you its updated listings of available exchanges for a year and will include your own listing in at least one of them. It's up to you to make specific arrangements. 🎫 Exchange Clubs **HomeLink International** ⌖ Box 47747, Tampa, FL 33647 ☎ 813/975–9825 or 800/638–3841 🖷 813/910–8144 ⊕ www.homelink.org; $110 yearly for a listing, online access, and catalog; $70 without catalog. **Intervac U.S.** ⌖ 30 Corte San Fernando, Tiburon, CA 94920 ☎ 800/756–4663 🖷 415/435–7440 ⊕ www.intervacus.com; $125 yearly for a listing, online access, and a catalog; $65 without catalog.

## Hostels

No matter what your age, you can save on lodging costs by staying at hostels. In some 4,500 locations in more than 70 countries around the world, Hostelling International (HI), the umbrella group for a number of national youth-hostel associations, offers single-sex, dorm-style beds and, at many hostels, rooms for couples and family accommodations. Membership in any HI national hostel association, open to travelers of all ages, allows you to stay in HI-affiliated hostels at member rates; one-year membership is about $28 for adults (C$35 for a two-year minimum membership in Canada, £14 in the United Kingdom, A$52 in Australia, and NZ$40 in New Zealand); hostels charge about $10–$30 per night. Members have priority if the hostel is full; they're also eligible for discounts around

the world, even on rail and bus travel in some countries.

🎫 Organizations **Hostelling International–USA** ⌖ 8401 Colesville Rd., Suite 600, Silver Spring, MD 20910 ☎ 301/495–1240 🖷 301/495–6697 ⊕ www.hiusa.org. **Hostelling International–Canada** ⌖ 205 Catherine St., Suite 400, Ottawa, Ontario K2P 1C3 ☎ 613/237–7884 or 800/663–5777 🖷 613/237–7868 ⊕ www.hihostels.ca. **YHA England and Wales** ⌖ Trevelyan House, Dimple Rd., Matlock, Derbyshire DE4 3YH, U.K. ☎ 0870/870–8808, 0870/ 770–8868, 0162/959–2600 🖷 0870/770–6127 ⊕ www.yha.org.uk. **YHA Australia** ⌖ 422 Kent St., Sydney, NSW 2001 ☎ 02/9261–1111 🖷 02/9261–1969 ⊕ www.yha.com.au. **YHA New Zealand** ⌖ Level 1, Moorhouse City, 166 Moorhouse Ave., Box 436, Christchurch ☎ 03/379–9970 or 0800/278–299 🖷 03/365–4476 ⊕ www.yha.org.nz.

## Mayfair to Regent's Park

££££   🏨 **Chesterfield Mayfair.** Set deep in the heart of Mayfair, this hotel is the former town house of the Earl of Chesterfield. The welcoming wood-and-leather public rooms match the snug bedrooms, which are done in burgundy and forest green with dark wood furnishings. Double rooms may be on the small side, but the service is warm and the hotel suitably upscale. ✉ *35 Charles St., Mayfair W12 SEB* ☎ *020/ 7491–2622* 🖷 *020/7491–4793* ⊕ *www.redcarnationhotels.com* ⇆ *101 rooms, 9 suites* ♿ *2 restaurants, room service, in-room data ports, in-room fax, some in-room safes, some minibars, cable TV with movies, exercise equipment, bar, library, dry cleaning, laundry service, concierge, Internet, business services, meeting rooms, no-smoking rooms* ▭ *AE, DC, MC, V* Ⓤ *Green Park.*

★ ££££   🏨 **The Connaught.** Make reservations well in advance for this very exclusive small hotel—it's the most understated of any of London's grand hostelries and is the London home-away-from-home for those who have inherited the habit of staying here from their great-grandfathers. The bar and lounges have the air of an ambassadorial residence, an impression reinforced by the imposing oak staircase and dignified staff. Each bedroom has a foyer, antique furniture (if you don't like the desk, they'll change it), and fresh flowers. If you value privacy, discretion, and the kind of luxury that eschews new-money flashiness, this is the place for you. ✉ *Carlos Pl., Mayfair W1K 6AL* ☎ *020/7499–7070* 🖷 *020/ 7495–3262* ⊕ *www.savoy-group.co.uk* ⇆ *75 rooms, 27 suites* ♿ *2 restaurants, room service, in-room data ports, in-room fax, in-room safes, minibars, cable TV, gym, massage, 2 bars, lobby lounge, babysitting, dry cleaning, laundry service, concierge, Internet, business services, meeting rooms, airport shuttle, car rental, travel services, parking (fee), no-smoking rooms* ▭ *AE, DC, MC, V* Ⓤ *Bond St.*

££££   🏨 **The Dorchester.** No other hotel this opulent manages to be quite so
Fodor'sChoice   charming. The glamour level is off the scale: 1,500 square yards of gold
★   leaf and 1,100 square yards of marble. Bedrooms (some not as spacious as you might expect) have Irish-linen sheets on canopied beds, brocades and velvets, and Italian marble and etched-glass bathrooms with Floris toiletries. Furnishings throughout are opulent English country-house style, with more than a hint of art deco, in keeping with the original 1930s building. You can take afternoon tea, drink, lounge, and pose in the catwalk-shape Promenade lounge. ✉ *Park La., Mayfair W1A 2HJ* ☎ *020/ 7629–8888* 🖷 *020/7409–0114* ⊕ *www.dorchesterhotel.com* ⇆ *195 rooms, 55 suites* ♿ *3 restaurants, in-room data ports, in-room safes, minibars, cable TV with movies, in-room VCRs, gym, health club, hair salon, spa, bar, lobby lounge, nightclub, shop, babysitting, dry cleaning, laundry service, concierge, Internet, business services, meeting rooms, car rental, parking (fee), no-smoking rooms* ▭ *AE, DC, MC, V* Ⓤ *Marble Arch or Hyde Park Corner.*

♺ ££££   🏨 **The Landmark.** A palm-filled, eight-story atrium Winter Garden forms the core, and odd-numbered rooms overlook this. If size matters to you, note that even standard rooms here are among the largest in London and have glamorous bathrooms in marble and chrome, outfitted with robes and hair dryers. Despite appearances, this is one of the only London grand hotels that doesn't force you to dress up. ⊠ *222 Marylebone Rd., Marylebone NW1 6JQ* ☎ *020/7631–8000* 🖷 *020/7631–8080* ⊕ *www.landmarklondon.co.uk* ⮑ *252 rooms, 47 suites* ☖ *2 restaurants, in-room data ports, in-room fax, in-room safes, some kitchenettes, minibars, some microwaves, some refrigerators, cable TV with movies and video games, some in-room VCRs, indoor pool, health club, spa, lobby lounge, piano bar, pub, shop, babysitting, dry cleaning, laundry service, concierge, Internet, business services, meeting rooms, no-smoking floors* ☰ *AE, DC, MC, V* Ⓤ *Marylebone.*

££££ 🏨 **Le Meridien Piccadilly.** The massive 1908 building is fin-de-siècle elegant and carefully retains its exquisite architectural features. Guest rooms vary between "traditional" (read: outdated, standard decor) and "executive" (read: stylish, minimalist decor). Bedrooms vary in size; a few on the seventh floor have balconies overlooking Piccadilly. The hotel's Champneys, one of the most exclusive health clubs in London, is luxurious. ⊠ *21 Piccadilly, Mayfair W1J 0BH* ☎ *020/7734–8000* 🖷 *020/7437–3574* ⊕ *www.lemeridien-piccadilly.com* ⮑ *232 rooms, 35 suites* ☖ *2 restaurants, room service, in-room data ports, in-room fax, in-room safes, minibars, cable TV with movies and video games, indoor pool, gym, health club, spa, billiards, squash, 4 bars, lobby lounge, library, babysitting, dry cleaning, laundry service, concierge, Internet, business services, meeting rooms, parking (fee), no-smoking rooms* ☰ *AE, DC, MC, V* Ⓤ *Piccadilly Circus.*

★ ££££ 🏨 **The Metropolitan.** This supertrendy hotel is one of the only addresses for fashion, music, and media folk in London. Its Met bar has an exclusive guest list and is a hotel resident-only bar, and the restaurant is the famed Nobu, leased by Japanese wonder chef Nobu Matsuhisa. The lobby is sleek and postmodern, as are the bedrooms, which have identical minimalist taupe-and-white furnishings. The best rooms overlook Hyde Park, but all have a groovy minibar hiding the latest alcoholic and health-boosting beverages, as well as an emergency kit with aspirin, condoms, and other necessities you'd rather not have to ask for in person. ⊠ *Old Park La., Mayfair W1K 1LB* ☎ *020/7447–1000, 800/337–4685 in U.S.* 🖷 *020/7447–1100* ⊕ *www.metropolitan.co.uk* ⮑ *137 rooms, 18 suites* ☖ *Restaurant, room service, in-room data ports, in-room fax, in-room safes, minibars, cable TV with movies and video games, some in-room VCRs, gym, massage, bar, shop, babysitting, dry cleaning, laundry service, concierge, Internet, business services, meeting room, parking (fee), no-smoking floors* ☰ *AE, DC, MC, V* Ⓤ *Hyde Park Corner.*

££££ 🏨 **No. 5 Maddox Street.** At No. 5 Maddox you'll find suites with everything you need to set up residence. Deluxe suites have balconies and working fireplaces. Room service will cater to your every whim, such as delivering groceries or lending you CDs, videos, or a bicycle. Bedrooms have an understated Asian minimalist aesthetic with white-on-beige-on-brown color schemes and lots of bamboo. The minibars are stocked with everything from sweets to herbal tea. You have access to a nearby health club. ⊠ *5 Maddox St., Mayfair W1R 9LE* ☎ *020/7647–0200* 🖷 *020/7647–0300* ⊕ *www.no5maddoxst.com* ⮑ *12 suites* ☖ *Restaurant,* room service, in-room data ports, in-room fax, in-room safes, kitchens, minibars, microwaves, refrigerators, cable TV, in-room VCRs, massage, babysitting, dry cleaning, laundry service, concierge, business services, parking (fee) ▭ AE, DC, MC, V Ⓤ Oxford Circus.

**£££££** 🏨 **Park Lane Sheraton.** Walking into the Park Lane Hotel via the decadent, Asian-inspired, art deco Palm Court tearoom and bar is worth the price of admission. The choice of doubles here ranges from regular doubles with traditional-style furnishings to "smart" rooms, which include ergonomically designed chairs, extra outlets and lighting, and a combination printer/copier/fax machine. Many executive doubles have stunning views of Green Park, which is just across busy Piccadilly. The ballroom, of *Golden Eye* and *End of the Affair* fame, is exquisite. ✉ *Piccadilly, Mayfair W1J BX* ☎ *020/7499–6321* 🖷 *020/7499–1965* ⊕ *www.sheraton.com* 🛏 *268 rooms, 39 suites* ♿ *3 restaurants, room service, some in-room data ports, some in-room faxes, in-room safes, minibars, cable TV with movies, gym, hair salon, bar, lounge, babysitting, dry cleaning, laundry service, concierge, Internet, business services, meeting rooms, car rental, parking (fee), no-smoking rooms* ▭ AE, DC, MC, V Ⓤ *Hyde Park Corner.*

**££££–£££££** 🏨 **The Leonard.** Its four 18th-century buildings make up a stunning, relaxed, and friendly boutique hotel. Shoppers will appreciate the location, just around the corner from Oxford Street. All suites are remarkably cozy, with sitting and bedroom areas set off by small foyers. Rooms are decorated with a judicious mix of lived-in antiques and comfortable reproductions. For more elbow room, try one of the aptly named grand suites, with their palatial sitting rooms and tall windows. The welcoming lobby area is stocked with complimentary newspapers to read by the fire, and the roof garden is great for warm weather. ✉ *15 Seymour St., Mayfair W1H 5AA* ☎ *020/7935–2010* 🖷 *020/7935–6700* ⊕ *www.theleonard.com* 🛏 *22 rooms, 21 suites* ♿ *Café, dining room, room service, in-room data ports, in-room safes, some kitchens, minibars, cable TV, in-room VCRs, gym, bar, lounge, babysitting, dry cleaning, laundry service, concierge, Internet, business services, meeting rooms, no-smoking rooms* ▭ AE, DC, MC, V Ⓤ *Marble Arch.*

**££££–£££££** 🏨 **Marriott Park Lane.** A very swanky Marriott on posh Park Lane, this large hotel goes for a boutique feel. They even have their own cocktail, Crantini 140 (a heady mix of white cranberries, vodka and Cointreau). Originally an apartment building, the ornate facade and beautiful interior date to 1919 when the place was an apartment building. Today its wonderful location at the Oxford Street end of Park Lane gives access to great shopping on Bond Street and lovely strolls through Hyde Park. Bedrooms are standard Marriott fare, but have the benefit of being quite large. ✉ *140 Park La., Mayfair W1K 7AA* ☎ *020/7493–7000* 🖷 *020/7493–8333* ⊕ *www.marriott.com* 🛏 *148 rooms, 9 suites* ♿ *Restaurant, room service, in-room data ports, in-room fax, in-room safes, minibars, cable TV with movies, gym, spa, indoor pool, dry cleaning, laundry service, babysitting, concierge, Internet, business services, meeting rooms, car rental, no-smoking rooms* ▭ AE, DC, MC, V Ⓤ *Marble Arch.*

**££££** 🏨 **Dorset Square Hotel.** A fine pair of Regency town houses have the English country look with antiques, rich colors, and design ideas *House*

*& Garden* subscribers would love. Each room is different: the first-floor balconied Coronet rooms are the largest. There's a reason for the ubiquitous cricket memorabilia: Dorset Square was the first Lord's grounds. ⊠ *40 Dorset Sq., Marylebone NW1 6QN* ☎ *020/7723–7874, 800/525– 4800 in U.S.* 🖷 *020/7724–3328* 🌐 *www.dorsetsquare.co.uk* ⤳ *35 rooms, 3 suites* ⏥ *Restaurant, room service, in-room data ports, some in-room safes, minibars, cable TV, in-room VCRs, lobby lounge, dry cleaning, laundry service, concierge, business services, parking (fee), some pets allowed, no-smoking rooms; no a/c in some rooms* ▭ *AE, MC, V* Ⓤ *Baker St.*

£££ ▥ **Bryanston.** These three converted Georgian houses are decorated in a style that's traditional English—open fireplaces, comfortable leather armchairs, oil portraits. The bedrooms are small and modern, with pink furnishings, creaky floors, and tiny bathrooms. Rooms at the back are quieter and face east, so they're bright in the morning; Room 77 is as big as a suite, but, typical of rooms in London houses, it's dark. This family-run hotel is an excellent value for the area—a few blocks north of Hyde Park and Park Lane. ⊠ *56–60 Great Cumberland Pl., Mayfair W1H 8DD* ☎ *020/7262–3141* 🖷 *020/7262–7248* 🌐 *www. bryanstonhotel.com* ⤳ *81 rooms, 8 apartments* ⏥ *Dining room, some kitchens, some microwaves, some refrigerators, cable TV, lobby lounge, lounge, pub, dry cleaning, laundry service, concierge, business services, meeting rooms, airport shuttle, parking (fee); no a/c* ▭ *MC, V* ⏁◉⏁ *CP* Ⓤ *Marble Arch.*

£££ ▥ **Durrants.** A hotel since the late 18th century, Durrants occupies a quiet corner almost next to the Wallace Collection, a stone's throw from Oxford Street and the smaller, posher shops of Marylebone High Street. It's a good value for the area, especially if you like the old-English wood-panel, leather-armchair, dark-red pattern carpet style. ⊠ *26–32 George St., Mayfair W1H 5BJ* ☎ *020/7935–8131* 🖷 *020/7487–3510* 🌐 *www.durrantshotel.co.uk* ⤳ *87 rooms, 5 suites* ⏥ *Restaurant, dining room, room service, in-room data ports, cable TV, bar, babysitting, dry cleaning, laundry service, concierge, meeting rooms; no a/c in some rooms* ▭ *AE, MC, V* Ⓤ *Bond St.*

£££ ▥ **10 Manchester Street.** Tucked away on a quiet street between bustling Oxford Street and posh Marylebone High Street, "Number 10" claims to offer no frills, good value, and high quality—and it delivers on the promise. This early-20th-century town house has been refurbished to a high standard. Rooms have CD players with radios, trouser presses, and tea/coffeemakers. The small doubles are indeed small, but for the price and location these no-frills rooms are great. ⊠ *10 Manchester St., Mayfair W1U 5DG* ☎ *020/7486–6669* 🖷 *020/7224–0348* 🌐 *www.10manchesterstreet.com* ⤳ *37 rooms, 9 suites* ⏥ *Dining room, fans, in-room data ports, refrigerators, cable TV, dry cleaning, concierge, Internet, no-smoking rooms; no a/c* ▭ *AE, MC, V* ⏁◉⏁ *CP* Ⓤ *Baker St.*

££ ▥ **Four Seasons Hotel.** This has nothing to do with the Four Seasons opposite Hyde Park; there are no stunning views over the Thames, no soundless elevators here. The hotel has, however, well-presented, Italianate bedrooms in soothing pastel colors, and is close to Regent's Park. The conservatory is a light, airy space for breakfast. ⊠ *173 Gloucester Pl.,*

*Mayfair NW1 6DX* ☎ *020/7724–3461* 🖷 *020/7402–5594* ⊕ *www.4sea-sonshotel.co.uk* 🛏 *28 rooms* ♿ *Room service, fans, in-room data ports, cable TV, babysitting, dry cleaning, laundry service, Internet, business services, car rental, some pets allowed, no-smoking rooms; no a/c* 🖃 *AE, DC, MC, V* 🍴 *CP* Ⓤ *Baker St.*

**££** 🖸 **Lincoln House Hotel.** On a fairly busy street just north of Oxford Street and Marble Arch, this family-run Georgian town house is done up with lots of wood and plaid. The rooms with three or four beds are more spacious and only slightly more expensive. Rooms have a slightly dated look, but are well equipped. Prices decrease the more days you stay. ✉ *33 Gloucester Pl., Mayfair W1U 8HY* ☎ *020/77486–7630* 🖷 *020/77486–0166* ⊕ *www.lincoln-house-hotel.co.uk* 🛏 *24 rooms* ♿ *Cable TV, some refrigerators, lounge, babysitting, dry cleaning, laundry service, parking (fee); no a/c* 🍴 *BP* 🖃 *AE, D, MC, V* Ⓤ *Marble Arch.*

**££** 🖸 **22 York Street.** This Georgian town house has a cozy, family feel with pine floors and plenty of antiques. Pride of place goes to the central, communal dining table where guests enjoy a rather varied Continental breakfast of croissants, fruit, and cereal. A living room with tea/coffeemaker is at guests' disposal as well. The homey bedrooms are individually furnished with quilts and antiques. Triples and family rooms for four are also available. ✉ *22 York St., Mayfair W1U 6PX* ☎ *020/7224–2990* 🖷 *020/7224–1990* ⊕ *www.22yorkstreet.co.uk* 🛏 *10 rooms* ♿ *Cable TV, lounge, no smoking; no a/c* 🖃 *AE, MC, V* 🍴 *CP* Ⓤ *Baker St.*

**£** 🖸 **St. Christopher's Inn Camden.** In bustling, hippie Camden Town just north of the center of London, this branch of St. Christopher's Inn is perfectly situated for wandering around Camden Lock and Camden Market. Unlike most hostels there's no curfew, and you get key-card security and 10% off food and drink in the raucous Belushi's bar on the ground floor. Rooms range from doubles to 10-bed dorms; linen is free. The lounge has cable TV. ✉ *48–50 Camden High St., Camden Town NW1 0JH* ☎ *020/7407–1856* 🖷 *020/7403–7715* ⊕ *www.st-christophers.co.uk* 🛏 *52 beds, some without bath* ♿ *Restaurant, bar, lounge, video game room, laundry facilities, Internet; no a/c, no room phones, no room TVs, no smoking* 🖃 *MC, V* 🍴 *CP* Ⓤ *Camden Town or Mornington Crescent.*

## St. James's

★ **£££££** 🖸 **Claridge's.** Stay here, and you're staying at a hotel legend (founded in 1812), with one of the world's classiest guest lists. The friendly, liveried staff is not in the least condescending, and the rooms are never less than luxurious. Enjoy a cup of tea in the lounge, or retreat to the stylish bar for cocktails—or, better, to Gordon Ramsay's inimitable restaurant. The bathrooms are spacious (with enormous showerheads), as are the bedrooms (Victorian or art deco), with bells to summon maid, waiter, or valet. The grand staircase and magnificent elevator complete with sofa and driver are equally glamorous. ✉ *Brook St., St. James's W1A 2JQ* ☎ *020/7629–8860, 800/637–2869 in U.S.* 🖷 *020/7499–2210* ⊕ *www.claridges.co.uk* 🛏 *203 rooms* ♿ *Restaurant, in-room data ports, in-room fax, in-room safes, some in-room hot tubs, minibars, cable TV with movies, in-room VCRs, gym, hair salon, spa, bar, lobby lounge,* *shop, babysitting, dry cleaning, laundry service, concierge, Internet, business services, meeting rooms, airport shuttle, car rental, parking (fee), no-smoking rooms* ☰ *AE, DC, MC, V* Ⓤ *Bond St.*

££££ ▦ **Dukes.** This small, exclusive, Edwardian-style hotel, with a gas lantern-lit courtyard entrance, is central but still quiet—it's in a discreet cul-de-sac where the Stafford also lies. Overstuffed sofas, oil paintings of assorted dukes, and muted, rich colors create the perfect setting for sipping the finest dry martinis in town. The hotel's trump card is that, for such a central location, it's peaceful and quiet with personal service. Rooms are cozy and covered in floral prints and dark wood. ⊠ *35 St. James's Pl., St. James's SW1A 1NY* ☎ *020/7491–4840, 800/381–4702 in U.S.* 🖷 *020/7493–1264* ⊕ *www.dukeshotel.co.uk* ⥲ *80 rooms, 9 suites* ⌂ *Restaurant, dining room, in-room data ports, some in-room faxes, in-room safes, minibars, cable TV, some in-room VCRs, gym, sauna, spa, steam room, bar, lobby lounge, dry cleaning, laundry service, concierge, business services, meeting rooms, parking (fee)* ☰ *AE, DC, MC, V* Ⓤ *Green Park.*

££££ ▦ **The Ritz.** The name conjures the kind of luxury associated with swagged curtains, handwoven carpets, and the smell of cigars, polish, and fresh lilies; it signifies a magical Edwardian opulence. The only thing that has been lost is a certain vein of moneyed naughtiness that someone like F. Scott Fitzgerald, at least, would have banked on. The bedrooms are bastions of pastel, Louis XVI style with gilded furniture and crystal chandeliers. With a ratio of two staff to every bedroom, you're guaranteed personal service despite the massive size of the hotel. Formal dress is encouraged, and jeans are not allowed in public areas. ⊠ *150 Piccadilly, St. James's W1J 9BR* ☎ *020/7493–8181* 🖷 *020/7493–2687* ⊕ *www.theritzhotel.co.uk* ⥲ *133 rooms* ⌂ *2 restaurants, room service, in-room data ports, some in-room faxes, in-room safes, cable TV, some in-room VCRs, gym, hair salon, bar, babysitting, dry cleaning, laundry service, concierge, Internet, business services, meeting rooms, car rental, parking (fee), no-smoking rooms* ☰ *AE, DC, MC, V* Ⓤ *Piccadilly Circus.*

££££ ▦ **Sofitel St. James London.** The updated art deco style of this renovated Cox's and King's Bank building is sophisticated. Though French-owned, the hotel is a pleasant blend of English roses and afternoon teas, with superb French food and Parisian chic. The rooms tend toward the contemporary with chocolate, black-and-white color schemes and lacquered furniture. Enjoy a cigar and a roaring fire, in the champagne bar or eat at the brasserie under the aegis of French chef Albert Roux of Le Gavroche fame. ⊠ *6 Waterloo Pl. on Pall Mall, Mayfair SW1Y 4AN* ☎ *020/7747–2200* 🖷 *020/7747–2210* ⊕ *www.sofitel.com* ⥲ *166 rooms, 20 suites* ⌂ *Restaurant, room service, in-room data points, in-room safes, some in-room hot tubs, some kitchens, minibars, cable TV, gym, massage, spa, Turkish bath, bar, library, lobby lounge, baby-sitting, dry cleaning, laundry service, concierge, Internet, business services, meeting rooms, parking (fee), no-smoking rooms* ☰ *AE, DC, MC, V* Ⓜ *Charing Cross.*

££££ ▦ **The Stafford.** This hotel is most famous for its utterly amazing American Bar, where a million ties, baseball caps, and toy planes hang from a ceiling modeled, presumably, on New York's "21" Club. But it's also prized for its 13 carriage-house rooms, installed in the 18th-century stable block. Relative bargains, each of these cute, private accommodations has a cobbled mews entrance and gas-log fire, black-stain exposed beams, and CD player. One nice perk is that you get complimentary access to Champney's Piccadilly, one of London's top health clubs. ⊠ *St. James's Pl., St. James's SW1A 1NJ* ☎ *020/7493–0111* 🖷 *020/7493–7121* ⊕ *www.thestaffordhotel.co.uk* ↩ *81 rooms* Ꮚ *Restaurant, dining room, in-room data ports, cable TV, bar* ▤ *AE, DC, MC, V* Ⓤ *Green Park.*

🗘 **££££** 🖂 **22 Jermyn Street.** On a fashionable shopping street near Fortnum & Mason, this guesthouse is run by the Togna family. Flexible configurations in rooms, including sitting rooms that convert to bedrooms, mean families have plenty of space. The hotel welcomes children by providing candies on arrival, nannies, a children's newsletter, kids' bathrobes, kids' movies and popcorn, coloring books and crayons, cribs and playpens, games, high chairs, and strollers. For parents, there's access to a nearby gym, a London newsletter that lists what's new in town, complimentary newspapers, and a shoe shine. ⊠ *22 Jermyn St., St. James's SW1Y 6HL* ☎ *020/7734–2353, 800/682–7808 in U.S.* 🖷 *020/ 7734–0750* ⊕ *www.22jermyn.com* ↩ *5 rooms, 13 suites* Ꮚ *Room service, in-room data ports, in-room safes, minibars, cable TV with movies, in-room VCRs, babysitting, dry cleaning, laundry service, concierge, Internet, business services, airport shuttle, car rental, parking (fee)* ▤ *AE, DC, MC, V* Ⓤ *Piccadilly Circus.*

## Soho & Covent Garden

**£££££** 🖂 **Covent Garden Hotel.** A former 1880s hospital in the midst of artsy, Fodor'sChoice boisterous Covent Garden, this hotel is now the London home-away-from-home for a mélange of off-duty celebrities, actors, and style mavens. ★ The public salons keep even the most picky happy: with painted silks, style *anglais* ottomans, and 19th-century Romantic oils, they're perfect places to decompress over a glass of sherry from the honor bar. Guest rooms are *World of Interiors* stylish, each showcasing matching-but-mixed couture fabrics to stunning effect. For £30 the popular Saturday-night film club includes dinner in the brasserie and a film in the deluxe in-house cinema. ⊠ *10 Monmouth St., Covent Garden WC2H 9HB* ☎ *020/7806–1000, 800/553–6674 in U.S.* 🖷 *020/7806–1100* ⊕ *www. firmdale.com* ↩ *55 rooms, 3 suites* Ꮚ *Restaurant, room service, in-room data ports, some in-room faxes, in-room safes, minibars, cable TV, in-room VCRs, gym, spa, cinema, library, babysitting, dry cleaning, laundry service, concierge, Internet, business services, meeting rooms, car rental* ▤ *AE, MC, V* Ⓤ *Covent Garden.*

**£££££** 🖂 **The Howard Swissotel.** The rather spartan modern shell that encases the Howard Swissotel hides a contemporary, hip interior within. It has a crisp brown color palette, with dark wood furniture, light wood floors, and lots of suede and leather, punctuated with bright white and red. Some rooms have spectacular river views, and all have Lavazza coffee machines. Suites have the option of a riverside balcony. There's al fresco dining in the Asian fusion restaurant, in good weather. ⊠ *Temple Pl., Covent Garden WC2R 2PR* ☎ *020/7836–3555* 🖷 *020/7 379–4547* ⊕ *www.swissotel.com* ↩ *189* *rooms* ♿ *Restaurant, room service, in-room data ports, in-room safes, minibars, cable TV with movies, lobby lounge, bar, dry cleaning, laundry service, concierge, Internet, business services, meeting rooms, parking (fee), no-smoking rooms* ▭ *AE, D, MC, V* Ⓤ *Temple.*

**£££££** ⊡ **Le Meridien Waldorf.** Following a massive overhaul, the Waldorf once synonymous with luscious Edwardiana now sports frosted glass, white marble and understated, modern bedrooms. The "Art + Tech" rooms cater to modern travelers' demands with plasma screen TVs, complimentary fruit, herbal teas and soft drinks, as well as innovative safes with laptop chargers. The "contemporary" rooms have retained period features while incorporating all the new gadgets. The Palm Court was inspired by the ballroom on that famous luxury ship the *Titanic* and even doubled for it in the eponymous Hollywood movie. The weekend tea dances with big band music are still going strong after a century. ⊠ *Aldwych, Covent Garden WC2B 4DD* ☎ *020/7836–2400* ⊟ *020/7836–7244* ⊕ *www.lemeridien-waldorf.com* ⇌ *303 rooms* ♿ *Restaurant, room service, in-room data ports, in-room safes, minibars, cable TV with movies and video games, indoor pool, fitness classes, gym, hair salon, sauna, spa, steam room, bar, babysitting, dry cleaning, laundry service, concierge, Internet, business services, meeting rooms, parking (fee), no-smoking rooms* ▭ *AE, DC, MC, V* Ⓤ *Aldwych.*

**£££££**
Fodor'sChoice
★
⊡ **One Aldwych.** One Aldwych's understated blend of contemporary and classic is pure, modern luxury. This flawlessly designed hotel inside an Edwardian building is coolly eclectic, with an artsy lobby, feather duvets, Italian linen sheets, and quirky touches (a TV in every bathroom, broadband Internet in the bedrooms, and a pool with underwater music). It's the ultimate in 21st-century style. Suites have amenities like a private gym, a kitchen, and a terrace. The toiletries are all natural, and breakfast is made with organic ingredients. ⊠ *1 Aldwych, Covent Garden WC2 4BZ* ☎ *020/7300–1000* ⊟ *020/7300–1001* ⊕ *www. onealdwych.co.uk* ⇌ *93 rooms, 12 suites* ♿ *2 restaurants, room service, in-room data ports, in-room safes, some kitchens, minibars, cable TV with movies, indoor pool, health club, spa, 3 bars, cinema, shop, dry cleaning, laundry service, concierge, business services, meeting rooms, parking (fee), no-smoking floors* ▭ *AE, MC, V* Ⓤ *Charing Cross or Covent Garden.*

**£££££** ⊡ **Radisson Mountbatten.** Named after the late Lord Mountbatten, last viceroy of India and favorite uncle of Prince Charles, the interior reflects Mountbatten's life: photos of the estate where he lived, plus some Indian furnishings and animal prints and figurines. There's a good standard of service; bedrooms come in various shades of beige, with black and white accents; and bathrooms have lashings of Italian marble. Corner suites have the best views of the city. ⊠ *20 Monmouth St., Covent Garden WC2H 9HD* ☎ *020/7836–4300* ⊟ *020/7240–3540* ⊕ *www. radissonedwardian.com* ⇌ *143 rooms, 8 suites* ♿ *Restaurant, bar room service, in-room data ports, some in-room faxes, in-room safes, minibars, cable TV with movies, gym, bar, lobby lounge, babysitting, dry cleaning, laundry service, concierge, Internet, business services, meeting rooms, car rental, parking (fee), some pets allowed (fee), no-smoking floor* ▭ *AE, DC, MC, V* Ⓤ *Covent Garden.*

**£££££** 🏨 **St. Martins Lane.** Designed by Philippe Starck for Ian Schrager, the lobby of this extremely hip hotel is sparsely furnished with big golden molars doubling as tables and some life-size chess pieces. Expect to play your part (along with the staff) as an actor here—on display as you sit at the ice trough in the fish bar, wield your chopsticks in Asia de Cuba, or lounge on leather armchairs in the brasserie. Guest rooms are small, expensive, and homogeneous. Unfortunately, the place is practically all style and barely any substance. ✉ *45 St. Martins La., Covent Garden WC2N 4HX* ☎ *020/7300–5500* 🖷 *020/7300–5501* ⊕ *www.ianschragerhotels.com* ⮐ *204 rooms △ 2 restaurants, café, room service, in-room data ports, in-room safes, minibars, cable TV, in-room VCRs, gym, massage, sauna, 2 bars, lobby lounge, cinema, shop, babysitting, dry cleaning, laundry service, concierge, Internet, business services, meeting room, parking (fee), no-smoking rooms, no-smoking floors* ▭ *AE, MC, V* Ⓤ *Leicester Sq.*

★ **£££££** 🏨 **The Savoy.** This grand hotel hosted Elizabeth Taylor's first honeymoon in one of its famous river-view rooms; and it poured one of Europe's first dry martinis in its equally famous American Bar, which is haunted by Hemingway, Fitzgerald, and Gershwin. Does it measure up to this high profile? Absolutely. The art deco rooms are especially fabulous, but all rooms are impeccably maintained, spacious, elegant, and comfortable. A room facing the Thames costs a fortune and requires an early booking, but it's worth it. Bathrooms have original fittings, with sunflower-size showerheads. Top-floor rooms are newer and less charming. ✉ *Strand, Covent Garden WC2R 0EU* ☎ *020/7836–4343* 🖷 *020/7240–6040* ⊕ *www.savoy-group.com* ⮐ *263 rooms, 19 suites △ 3 restaurants, room service, in-room data ports, in-room fax, in-room safes, minibars, cable TV with movies, in-room VCRs, indoor pool, gym, hair salon, sauna, spa, steam room, 2 bars, lobby lounge, theater, shop, babysitting, dry cleaning, laundry service, concierge, Internet, business services, meeting rooms, parking (fee), no-smoking rooms* ▭ *AE, DC, MC, V* Ⓤ *Aldwych.*

★ **££££** 🏨 **Hazlitt's.** This Soho hotel is in three connected, early-18th-century houses, one of which was the last home of essayist William Hazlitt (1778–1830). It's a disarmingly friendly place, full of personality but devoid of elevators. Robust antiques are everywhere, floors slant and creak, and every room has a Victorian claw-foot tub in its bathroom. There are tiny sitting rooms, wooden staircases, and more restaurants within strolling distance than you could patronize in a year. This is *the* London address of antiques dealers and theater and literary types. ✉ *6 Frith St., Soho W1V 5TZ* ☎ *020/7434–1771* 🖷 *020/7439–1524* ⊕ *www. hazlittshotel.com* ⮐ *20 rooms, 3 suites △ Room service, fans, in-room data ports, minibars, cable TV, in-room VCRs, dry cleaning, laundry service, concierge, Internet, meeting rooms, parking (fee), some pets allowed, no-smoking floors; no a/c in some rooms* ▭ *AE, DC, MC, V* Ⓤ *Tottenham Court Rd.*

**££££** 🏨 **Radisson Hampshire.** Right on Leicester Square and steps from the half-price ticket booth, this hotel is perfectly placed for theatergoers. Bedrooms are old-fashioned with plenty of rose prints, beige carpets and flowery bedspreads, and bathrooms are modern. Public spaces exude plushness with thick carpets, gold chandeliers and sparkling cut glass and mirrors. Ask for a room facing Leicester Square, they have arched windows and interesting views. ⊠ *31-36 Leicester Sq., Covent Garden WC2H 7LH* ☎ *020/7839-9399* 🖷 *020/7930-8122* ⊕ *www. radissonedwardian.com* ↩ *119 rooms, 5 suites* ৬ *Restaurant, room service, in-room data ports, in-room safes, minibars, cable TV with movies, gym, 2 bars, lobby lounge, babysitting, dry cleaning, laundry service, concierge, Internet, business services, meeting rooms, car rental, parking (fee), some pets allowed (fee), no-smoking floor* ⊟ *AE, DC, MC, V* Ⓤ *Leicester Sq.*

££££ 🏨 **Trafalgar Hilton.** This fresh, contemporary hotel defies the Hilton's norm. The rooms here, in either sky-blue or beige color schemes, keep many of the 19th-century office building's original features and some have floor-to-ceiling windows with expansive views of Trafalgar Square. Twenty-one rooms are split-level, with upstairs space for chilling out with a CD or DVD and sleeping space below. Bathrooms take the cake with deep baths, full-size toiletries, eye masks, and mini-TVs. Go up to the roof garden for spectacular views of the Houses of Parliament, Westminster Abbey, and the British Airways London Eye. ⊠ *2 Spring Gardens, Covent Garden SW1A 2TS* ☎ *020/7870-2900* 🖷 *020/ 7870-2911* ⊕ *www.hilton.com* ↩ *127 rooms, 2 suites* ৬ *Restaurant, room service, in-room data ports, in-room safes, minibars, cable TV with movies and video games, bar, dry cleaning, laundry service, concierge, Internet, business services, meeting rooms, parking (fee), no-smoking floors* ⊟ *AE, DC, MC, V* Ⓤ *Charing Cross.*

££ 🏨 **Fielding.** On a quiet pedestrian alley by the world's first police station (now Bow St. Magistrates' Court), this small hotel is popular with budget travelers visiting London to take in an opera—the Royal Opera House Covent Garden is just down the street. For the money, you can get more comfort elsewhere. There are no amenities save for the residents' bar and the tea/coffeemakers in each room. ⊠ *4 Broad Ct., at Bow St., Covent Garden WC2B 5QZ* ☎ *020/7836-8305* 🖷 *020/7497-0064* ⊕ *www.the-fielding-hotel.co.uk* ↩ *24 rooms* ৬ *In-room data ports, bar; no a/c, no smoking* ⊟ *AE, DC, MC, V* Ⓤ *Covent Garden.*

££ 🏨 **Regent Palace Hotel.** If you're on a tight budget, are not too fussy, and need to be in the thick of it, this is the place for you. There are 920 rooms in this warren just off Piccadilly Circus; some have a toilet and shower. The entire place is in need of an overhaul, and the foyer is reminiscent of a small airport terminal; however, the hotel is very central, and the concierge can help with theater tickets and tours. ⊠ *Glass House St., Soho W1A 4BZ* ☎ *0870/400-8703* 🖷 *0870/400-8703* ⊕ *www. regentpalacehotel.co.uk* ↩ *920 rooms, 362 with bath* ৬ *Café, some in-room data ports, lobby lounge, pub, concierge, Internet; no a/c* ⊟ *AE, DC, MC, V* Ⓤ *Piccadilly Circus.*

££ 🏨 **Seven Dials Hotel.** Just across the street from the upscale Covent Garden hotel, the budget Seven Dials might as well be a world away in terms of style, size, and services. The small rooms done in dark floral patterns are, however, a good budget option for the theatergoer looking for a bed. Cheaper rooms share a bathroom. ⊠ *7 Monmouth St., Covent Garden WC2H 9DA* ☎ *020/7681-0791* 🖷 *020/7681-0792* ⊕ *www. smoothhound.co.uk/hotels/sevendials.html* ↩ *10 rooms* ৬ *Dining room, fans; no a/c* ⫧❘ *BP* ⊟ *AE, MC, V* Ⓤ *Covent Garden.*

## The South Bank

**£££££** ⌕ **London Marriott Hotel County Hall.** This exceptionally grand hotel has what many want—a view of the London Eye and the Houses of Parliament across the Thames. It's in the former home of the long-defunct local governing body—a mammoth, spectacular, pedimented, and columned affair—and uses the old Members' entrance, with its bronze doors and marble lobby leading into the former Council Chamber. A Marriott is a reliable thing, and this one has all the expected deluxe accoutrements—from a modern, businesslike style to almost instantly arriving elevators to a fantastic 24-hour health-and-fitness spa. ⌂ *County Hall, South Bank SE1 7PB* ☎ *020/7928–5200* 🖷 *020/7928–5300* ⊕ *www.marriotthotels.com* 🛏 *200 rooms* ♿ *2 restaurants, room service, in-room data ports, in-room safes, minibars, cable TV with movies, indoor pool, health club, hair salon, spa, 2 bars, babysitting, dry cleaning, laundry service, concierge, Internet, business services, meeting rooms, parking (fee)* ▭ *AE, DC, MC, V* Ⓤ *Westminster.*

**££££** ⌕ **London Bridge Hotel.** Just steps away from the London Bridge rail and Tube station, this thoroughly modern, stylish hotel is popular with business travelers. Most of the South Bank's attractions are within walking distance. Each sleek room is decorated in understated, contemporary style. Three spacious two-bedroom apartments in the £££££ range come complete with kitchen, living room, and dining room. Foodies will definitely want to stop in at the delightful Borough Market on Friday and Saturday, just across the street, for some local London color. ⌂ *8–18 London Bridge St., South Bank SE1 9SG* ☎ *020/7855–2200* 🖷 *020/7855–2233* ⊕ *www.london-bridge-hotel.co.uk* 🛏 *138 rooms, 3 apartments* ♿ *Restaurant, room service, in-room data ports, in-room safes, some kitchens, minibars, cable TV with movies, gym, sauna, bar, lobby lounge, dry cleaning, laundry service, concierge, meeting rooms, parking (fee), no-smoking floors* ▭ *AE, DC, MC, V* Ⓤ *London Bridge.*

**££** ⌕ **County Hall Travel Inn Capital.** Don't get too excited—this neighbor
FodorsChoice of the fancy Marriott lacks the river view (it's at the back of the grand
★ former seat of local government). Still you get an incredible value, with the standard facilities of the cookie-cutter rooms of this chain: TV, tea/coffeemaker, en-suite bath–shower, and—best of all for families on a budget—foldout beds that let you accommodate two kids at no extra charge. *That's* a bargain. ⌂ *Belvedere Rd., South Bank SE1 7PB* ☎ *087/0238–3300* 🖷 *020/7902–1619* ⊕ *www.travelinn.co.uk* 🛏 *313 rooms* ♿ *Restaurant, coffee shop, fans, in-room data ports, bar, business services, meeting rooms, parking (fee), no-smoking floors; no a/c* ▭ *AE, DC, MC, V* Ⓤ *Westminster.*

**££** ⌕ **Mad Hatter Hotel.** On a busy thoroughfare just south of the Southbank pedestrian river-walk, this modern hotel is hidden on the top floors of a 19th-century Fuller's Ale & Pie House. Friday and Saturday nights are cheapest and include a full English breakfast in the rate. Rooms are identical but serviceable. ⌂ *3–7 Stamford St., South Bank SE1 9NY* ☎ *020/7401–9222* 🖷 *020/7401–7111* ⊕ *www.madhatterhotel.com* 🛏 *30 rooms* ♿ *Restaurant, cable TV, pub, laundry service, no-smoking floor; no a/c* ▭ *AE, DC, MC, V* Ⓤ *Waterloo.*

**0800 LONDON**®

LONDON'S FREE TELEPHONE BOOKING SERVICE

You can now call **FREE** on **0800 LONDON** for London information and to book discounted rates for London hotels, theatre and sightseeing.

Advisors available every day from 8am to midnight.
From outside the UK dial **+44 800 LONDON**

**0800 LONDON - London's Free Telephone Booking Service**

# London Information Centre™
## LEICESTER SQUARE

## Free information and half price hotels. Every day.

Visit us in person in the centre of Leicester Square or call us on **020 729 22 333.**
From outside the UK call **+44 20 729 22 333**.

London Information Centre, Leicester Square, London
Open every day from 8am to 11pm

.com™

The number one internet site for London offers essential information to help organise the perfect visit to London. Guaranteed lowest rates on London's leading hotels and information on 15,000 reviewed and quality assessed London products and services.

**You can now also book over the phone on 0207 437 4370**
**From outside the UK call +44 207 437 4370**

The **#1 Internet Site** for **London**™

*Over 30 million customers served*

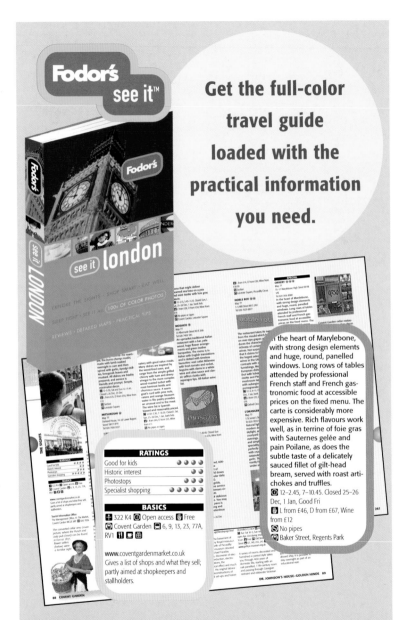

££   🏨 **Premier Lodge Southwark.** Practically riverside, this branch of the Premier Lodge chain has an excellent location across the cobbled road from
Vinopolis. Rooms have desks, tea/coffeemakers, and the chain's signature 6-foot-wide beds (really two zipped together). Family rooms can
accommodate four people. The nautical Anchor restaurant and pub is
adjacent to the hotel. ☒ *34 Park St., South Bank SE1 9EF* ☎ *0870/990–
6402* 🖷 *0870/990–6403* ⊕ *www.premierlodge.co.uk* ↪ *56 rooms*
♿ *In-room data ports, cable TV, parking (fee), no-smoking rooms*
▤ *AE, DC, MC, V* Ⓤ *London Bridge.*

£   🏨 **St. Christopher's Inn Village.** Named for the patron saint of travelers,
St. Christopher's Inn is the headquarters of this small hostel chain.
Rooms are cheerful and have swipe-card access and shared bathrooms.
The hostel's most endearing feature is its rooftop sauna and open-air
hot tub. For entertainment, try the sports bar downstairs. Other hostels in the chain are just down the street–Original at 121 Borough High
Street, SE1 1NP, and Orient Espresso at 59 Borough High Street, SE1
1NE. These hostels are also booked through the Village. ☒ *161–165
Borough High St., South Bank SE1 1HR* ☎ *020/7407–1856* 🖷 *020/
7403–7715* ⊕ *www.st-christophers.co.uk* ↪ *166 beds at Village, 50 beds
at Inn, 36 beds at Orient Espresso; all without bath* ♿ *Restaurant, outdoor hot tub, sauna, pub, laundry facilities, Internet, no-smoking rooms;
no a/c, no room phones, no room TVs* ▤ *MC, V* Ⓤ *London Bridge or
Borough* ⓘ *CP.*

# Bed-and-Breakfast & Apartment Agencies

££–££££   🏨 **Coach House London Vacation Rentals.** Stay in the properties of Londoners who are temporarily away. Apartments and houses are primarily in Notting Hill, Kensington, and Chelsea. The extra touches—airport
pickup, complimentary breakfast provisions, and a welcome drink with
a representative—make this service personal. Homes also come with a
phone number to call for help in planning your stay. ☒ *2 Tunley Rd.,
Balham SW17 7QJ* ☎ *020/8772–1939* 🖷 *0870/1334957* ⊕ *www.
vacrent.cwc.net* ▤ *AE, MC, V* ☞ *Payment by credit card only; 10%
deposit required.*

££   🏨 **Bulldog Club.** It promises luxe, chic, delightful accommodations with
fresh flowers and fruit, robes, use of a sitting room, and a no smoking
policy. A three-year membership is about £25, with most properties available for about £105 per night. A full British breakfast as well as other
goodies are often provided. Accommodations are generally available in
Knightsbridge, Kensington, and Chelsea. ☒ *14 Dewhurst Rd., Kensington
W14 0ET* ☎ *020/7371–3202, 877/727–3004 in U.S.* 🖷 *020/7371–2015*
⊕ *www.bulldogclub.com* ▤ *AE, MC, V.*

££   🏨 **London B&B.** This long-established family-run agency has some truly
spectacular—and some more modest—London homes in practically all
neighborhoods of the city. Check many of them out via its Web site before making a commitment. The staff here is most personable and helpful. ☒ *437 J St., Suite 210, San Diego, CA 92101* ☎ *800/872–2632*
🖷 *619/531–1686* ⊕ *www.londonbandb.com* ☞ *30% deposit required.*

££   🏨 **Primrose Hill B&B.** This is a small, friendly bed-and-breakfast agency
genuinely "committed to the idea that traveling shouldn't be a rip-off."

Expatriate American Gail O'Farrell has family homes (to which you get your own latchkey) in or near village-y Hampstead, all of which are comfortable or more than comfortable. So far this has been one of those word-of-mouth secrets, but now that everyone knows, book well ahead. ⊠ *14 Edis St., Regent's Park NW1 8LG* ☎ *020/7722–6869* ⊟ *No credit cards.*

**££** 🏠 **Uptown Reservations.** As the name implies, this B&B booking service accepts only the more upscale addresses and specializes in finding hosted homes or short-term apartments for Americans, often executives of small corporations. Nearly all of the 85 homes on its register are in Knightsbridge, Belgravia, Kensington, and Chelsea, with a few farther west in Holland Park or to the north in Hampstead. The private homes vary, of course, but all are good-looking and have private bathrooms, plus a full Continental breakfast. ⊠ *41 Paradise Walk, Chelsea SW3 4JL* ☎ *020/7351–3445* 🖨 *020/7351–9383* ⊕ *www.uptownres.co.uk* ⊟ *AE, MC, V* ✆ *Facilities vary. Payment by bank transfer or U.S. check or credit card; 20% deposit required.*

**£–££** 🏠 **At Home in London.** More than 70 private homes in central London locations, including Knightsbridge, Kensington, Mayfair, Chelsea, and West London, are on their books. They're closed on weekends, so make sure to phone between 9:30 and 5:30 on a weekday. Breakfast is included in the rate. ⊠ *70 Black Lion La., Hammersmith W6 9BE* ☎ *020/ 8748–1943* 🖨 *020/8748–2700* ⊕ *www.athomeinlondon.co.uk* ⊟ *MC, V* ✆ *£7.50 per person booking fee.*

**£** 🏠 **Host & Guest Service.** In business for 40 years, this service has a huge selection of B&Bs in London as well as the rest of the United Kingdom. They also book stays on farms in rural Britain and conduct tourist services such as bus tours. ⊠ *103 Dawes Rd., Chelsea SW6 7DU* ☎ *020/ 7385–9922* 🖨 *020/7386–7575* ⊕ *www.host-guest.co.uk* ⊟ *MC, V* ✆ *Full payment in advance.*

# NIGHTLIFE
# & THE ARTS

4

Updated by
Julie Tomasz

**AFTER DARK, LONDON IS A WONDERFUL PLACE TO PLAY.** Shakespearean theater and Handel oratorios, the roof-rattling Proms concerts, Andrew Lloyd Webber–ish extravaganzas, magnificent opera and contemporary dance theater, opulent cocktail lounges, and the latest U.K. garage dance music—if you're into the arts or the glamorous late-night scene, London will definitely fill your fancy.

The arts may still be underfunded but they have at least acquired some shiny new buildings and renovated homes. The Royal Ballet now has a permanent home inside the world-renowned Royal Opera House, and the English National Opera is in the London Coliseum. The Donmar, Almeida, and Royal Court theaters have all been renovated to reveal their stripped-down, essential structures. And saved from Bingo-hall oblivion, the legendary Hackney Empire theater is thriving again after a £15-million refurbishment. And there are new studios and a renovated theater for contemporary dance at The Place. But the biggest story is south of the river. Architects Herzog and de Meuron's magnificent transformation of the Bankside Power Station into the Tate Modern has given London a flagship contemporary art gallery to rival the best in the world. Though some of the more tourist-oriented shows have suffered from a downturn in international visitors, much of London's vibrant cultural scene is in a better position than ever to play on the world stage.

# NIGHTLIFE

London is the party capital of Europe. Discussion of relaxing the draconian liquor laws continues, and though the Tubes inconveniently stop running around midnight there's a good network of night buses. Even with the old licensing laws there's a staggering variety of places with late licenses where you can party after 11 PM when the fuzzy, friendly neighborhood pubs close their doors.

Not everyone likes a loud, smoky bar. Thankfully, nightlife in London is diverse enough that whatever your pleasure, there's always somewhere to go. If you prefer a romantic evening at the opera, wine-soaked experimental jazz, Camden's rough indie guitar sounds, raucous laughter in a comedy club, or a few cocktails in a sexy bar where the clientele look like they've stepped off the catwalk, our listings provide a sampling of the best the capital has to offer. The gay scene is thriving and our listings give you all you need to find it.

In one night, you can circle the West End (or some trendy district like Hoxton), drop into half a dozen bars and in each one find a completely unique world. There's everything from Moulin Rouge–style lounge clubs, velvet-dripping drum 'n' bass clubs, to lavish Asian-theme cocktail bars. Bars go in and out of fashion with incredible speed here. The fashion for minimalist chic design has been replaced with the extravagance and opulence of Asian designs. The phenomenon of absinthe, which has always intrigued drinkers by its high alcohol content, mystique, and ritual pouring, has now been eclipsed by the Russian decadence of vodka bars, which offer flavor-infused varieties, everything from chocolate to chicken tikka.

If you want to savor the high life with the glitterati, you have to pay for the privilege of glamour. The price of a Bellini (with Dom Perignon, of course) in an ultraswank hotel bar will put you back £20. But then, that's London's West End. In trendier-than-thou East London, drinks aren't so expensive. Communities like Clerkenwell, Hoxton, and Shoreditch are hubs for artists, indie musicians, and fashion and media types. The raw culture of racially diverse Brixton, with its heady mix of art, poetry, and music on Coldharbour Lane, is like Harlem in the 1920s, contrasting starkly with the Disney-like attractions of mainstream Leicester Square.

Once 2 AM arrives, much of the bar scene moves on to clubs, where you can dance until 9 AM. Whether you're into twisted disco, bhangra, deep house, jazzy breaks, or hip-hop, the multi-dance-floor clubs will have a room to suit your musical tastes, and whoever is behind the decks will be delivering the most cutting-edge sounds on the planet. The talent pool here is enormous; chances are whatever you're looking for, you'll find it here first.

## Bars

London bar culture is known for its innovative elixirs, its stylishness, and its fashionable people. Bars used to be the place to go post-pub or pre-club, but with the emergence of the "club bar"—essentially a swank bar with DJs spinning the latest sounds, a late license that caters to a clubbing clientele, and sometimes dancing—the boundaries between club and bar are fading, and many people stay until it's over. You can choose from expensive hotel bars (from ultrachic postmodern to stately Victorian), swank cocktail lounges in the West End, pool halls, and chilled hangouts in Hoxton, or up-for-it style clubs in Brixton.

Fodor'sChoice
★
**American Bar.** Festooned with a chin-dropping array of club ties, signed celebrity photographs, sporting mementos, and baseball caps, this sensational cocktail bar has superb martinis. ⊠ *Stafford Hotel, 16–18 St. James's Pl., St. James's SW1A* ☎ *020/7493–0111* ⋔ *Jacket required after 5 PM* ☉ *Weekdays 11:30 AM–11 PM, Sat. noon–3 PM and 5:30–11 PM, Sun. noon–2:30 PM and 6:30–10:30* Ⓤ *Green Park.*

**Atlantic Bar.** A huge marble staircase descends into what feels like a hotel lobby, but just through the main doors is the glamorous art deco ballroom that is the Atlantic Bar. The original furnishings are intact and the impeccable service, fantastic cocktails, and Oliver Peyton's excellent restaurant keep pulling in the crowds. ⊠ *20 Glasshouse St., Soho W1* ☎ *020/7734–4888* ☉ *Mon.–Sat. noon–3 AM* Ⓤ *Piccadilly Circus.*

**Beach Blanket Babylon.** In Notting Hill, close to Portobello Market, this always-packed bar is distinguishable by its eclectic interior of indoor–outdoor spaces filled with Gaudi-esque curves and snuggly corners—like a fairy-tale grotto or a medieval dungeon, visited by the gargoyles of Notre Dame. ⊠ *45 Ledbury Rd., Notting Hill W11* ☎ *020/7229–2907* ☉ *Mon.–Thurs. noon–midnight, Fri. and Sat. noon–1 AM, Sun. noon–10:30 PM* Ⓤ *Notting Hill Gate.*

**Bug Bar.** Inside the crypt of a church, this intimate vaulted bar with Gothic overtones is attached to the tasty Bar Humbug restaurant and the trendy dance club Mass. Brixton hipsters shake it up to top DJs spinning the decks, and knock back "Bugtai" shooters at the bar. ⊠ *Brixton Hill, under St. Matthew's Church, Brixton SW2* ☎ *020/7738–3366* ⊙ *Wed., Thurs., and Sun. 7 PM–2 AM, Fri. and Sat. 8 PM–3 AM* Ⓤ *Brixton.*

**Fodor'sChoice**
★ **Cadogan Hotel Bar.** Once you've done Harrods, Harvey Nichols, Gucci, Chanel, and Armani, stop by this elegant hotel for afternoon tea, or a cocktail, in the bar that exudes comfort and surroundings still characteristic of the late Victorian age when it was built. Oscar Wilde was arrested in room 118. ⊠ *Cadogan Hotel, 75 Sloane St., Knightsbridge SW1* ☎ *020/7235–7141* ⊙ *Daily 11 AM–11 PM* Ⓤ *Sloane Sq.*

**Cafe des Amis.** This relaxed brasserie–wine bar near the Royal Opera House is the perfect pre- or post-theater spot—and a place you can go on your own. More than 30 wines are served by the glass along with a good selection of cheeses. Opera buffs will enjoy the performance and production prints on the walls. ⊠ *11–14 Hanover Pl., Covent Garden WC2* ☎ *020/7379–3444* ⊙ *Mon.–Sat. 11:30 AM–11:30 PM* Ⓤ *Covent Garden.*

**Detroit.** Reminiscent of a sand dune or a Moroccan cave, this subterranean bar has mud-color walls lit in luminous green, blue, and orange. Burrow into your own little nook, sip a Detropolitan, or one of 70 cocktails, including the more daring "overproofs." ⊠ *35 Earlham St., Covent Garden WC2* ☎ *020/7240–2662* ⊙ *Mon.–Sat. 5 PM–midnight* Ⓤ *Covent Garden.*

★ **Dogstar.** This popular South London hangout is frequented by local hipsters and counterculture types. The vibe is unpretentious and hip. Visual projections light up the interior and top-name DJs play cutting-edge sounds free on weekdays. Move on to the nearby dance club, Mass, and your sampling of local Brixton life will be complete. ⊠ *389 Coldharbour La., Brixton SW9* ☎ *020/7733–7515* 🎟 *Free–£5* ⊙ *Mon.–Thurs. noon–2 AM, Fri. and Sat. noon–4 AM* Ⓤ *Brixton.*

**Hackney Central.** A hip newcomer to the East London nightlife scene, this bar and music club is the new incarnation of Hackney's old Victorian railway station. Cutting-edge DJs and live bands perform in the bar upstairs, while food and drink flows in the restaurant and bar downstairs. ⊠ *Amhurst Rd., Hackney E8* ☎ *020/8986–5111* ⊕ *www.hackneycentral.com* ⊙ *Mon.–Thurs. 9 AM–midnight, Fri. and Sat. 9 AM–2 AM, Sun. 10 AM–10:30 PM* Ⓜ *Train: Hackney Central.*

**Hoxton Square Bar & Kitchen.** The rectangular concrete bar, reminiscent of a Swedish airport hangar, has long, comfortable sofas, plate-glass windows at the front and back, and outdoor tables overlooking leafy Hoxton Square. The vibe is less pretentious than neighboring bars, and creative types keep it packed. ⊠ *2–4 Hoxton Sq., Hoxton E1* ☎ *020/7613–0709* ⊙ *Mon.–Sat. 11 AM–midnight, Sun. 11 AM–10:30 PM* Ⓤ *Old St.*

**Fodor'sChoice**
★ **Library Bar.** In this exquisite bar at the luxurious Lanesborough Hotel, bar manager Salvatore Calabrese offers a remarkable collection of vintage cognacs, some of which are more than 200 years old. A shot of liquid history can set you back £700. Enjoy the luxurious surroundings and don't ask for a brandy Alexander. ⊠ *1 Lanesborough Pl., Hyde Park Corner, Knightsbridge SW1* ☎ *020/7259–5599* ⊙ *Mon.–Sat. 11 AM–1 AM, Sun. noon–10:30 PM* Ⓤ *Hyde Park Corner.*

**Opium.** Fashionable young things sip exotic cocktails amid the trappings of the Orient. Amber-color light, delicate wooden carvings, burning incense, and small alcoves dripping in velvet and gold take you back to French Colonial Vietnam. The cocktails are impressive and pricey, as is the nouvelle Vietnamese cuisine. ✉ *1 Dean St., Soho W1* ☎ *020/7287–9608* ⊙ *Weekdays 5 PM–3 AM, Sat. 7:30 PM–3 AM* Ⓤ *Tottenham Court Rd.*

★ **Oxo Bar.** The views of London don't get much better than from this eighth-floor bar near the Tate Modern on the south bank of the Thames. Most people come to eat at the excellent restaurant, one of London's best, but the bar is a wonderful place in its own right, perfect for a pre-dinner drink or a vertiginous nightcap. ✉ *Bargehouse St., South Bank SE1* ☎ *020/7803–3888* ⊙ *Mon.–Sat. 11 AM–11 PM, Sun. noon–10:30 PM* Ⓤ *Waterloo.*

**The Pool.** The glass-front industrial-style bar attracts a hip beer-swilling crowd who play pool on three full-size tables, dance to some of London's most famous DJs, and chill out in the beanbag chairs. There's a modest menu and daily specials. ✉ *104 Curtain Rd., East End EC2* ☎ *020/7739–9608* ⊙ *Mon. and Tues. noon–11 PM, Wed. and Thurs. noon–1 AM, Fri. and Sat. noon–2 AM, Sun. noon–midnight* Ⓤ *Old St.*

★ **Revolution.** Here there's a lively vodka bar with obscure premium vodkas from Russia, Poland, and Finland, plus more than 100 ways to enjoy the clear elixir. Try it blended with melted chocolate, ice cold from the freezer, stirred in a martini, or in a three-pint pitcher for sharing with friends. ✉ *2 St. Anne's Court, Soho W1* ☎ *020/7434–0330* ⊙ *Mon.–Sat. noon–11 PM, Sun. 1 PM–10:30 PM* Ⓤ *Tottenham Court Rd.*

**Smiths of Smithfield.** This loft-style megabar with exposed wood beams, steel columns, and huge windows overlooks the Victorian Smithfield's market. Have a beer in the airy ground-floor pub, a cocktail in the intimate champagne cocktail bar upstairs (open until 1 AM on weekends), or some fine British Modern cuisine in the restaurants. The 7 AM opening hour captures the fallout from nearby superclub Fabric. ✉ *67–77 Charterhouse St., East End EC1N* ☎ *020/7251–7950* ⊙ *Mon.–Wed. 7 AM–11 PM, Thurs. and Fri. 7 AM–midnight, Sat. 11 AM–11 PM, Sun. 11 AM–10:30 PM* Ⓤ *Farringdon.*

**Vibe Bar.** In the Old Truman Brewery, this funky bar caters to an eclectic mix of artists and neighborhood hipsters, plus an after-work crowd. There's free Internet access and entertainment is provided by DJs and live bands. ✉ *91 Brick La., East End E1* ☎ *020/7426–0491* ⊕ *www. vibe-bar.co.uk* Ⓤ *Aldgate E. or Shoreditch.*

## Comedy & Cabaret

**Banana Cabaret.** This pub is one of London's finest comedy venues. Well worth the trek, it's only 100 yards from Balham station and there's a minicab office close by for those tempted to make a long night of it. ✉ *Bedford Pub, 77 Bedford Hill, Balham SW12* ☎ *020/8673–8904* 💷 *£10–£14* ⊙ *Fri. 7:30 PM–2 AM, Sat. 6:30 PM–2 AM* Ⓤ *Balham.*

**Canal Café Theatre.** You'll find famous comics and cabaret performers every night of the week in this intimate, picturesque canal-side venue. The long-running NewsRevue is a topical song and sketch show every night, Thursday–Sunday. ✉ *Bridge House, Delamere Terr., Little Venice W2* ☎ *020/7289–6054* 💷 *£5–£9* ⊙ *Mon.–Sat. 7:30 PM–11 PM, Sun. 7 PM–10:30 PM* Ⓤ *Warwick Ave.*

**Comedy Café.** In addition to lots of stand-up comedy, this popular dive in trendy Hoxton has an open mike on Wednesday and late-night disco on weekends. Tex-Mex cuisine is available and there's a late license. ✉ *66 Rivington St., East End EC2* ☎ *020/7739–5706* 💷 *Free–£14* ⊙ *Wed. and Thurs. 7 PM–midnight, Fri. and Sat. 7 PM–1 AM* Ⓤ *Old St.*

★ **Comedy Store.** Known as the birthplace of alternative comedy, the United Kingdom's funniest stand-ups have cut their teeth here before being launched onto prime-time TV. Comedy Store Players entertain audiences on Wednesday and Sunday; the Cutting Edge team steps in every Tuesday; and weekends have up-and-coming comedians performing on the same stage as established talent. There's a bar with food also available. Tickets can be booked through Ticketmaster (www.ticketmaster.co.uk) or over the phone. Note that children under 18 are not admitted to this venue. ✉ *1A Oxendon St., Soho SW1* ☎ *0870/060–2340* 💷 *£12–£15* ⊙ *Shows Tues.–Thurs. and Sun. 8 PM–10:15 PM, Fri. and Sat. 8 PM–10:15 PM and midnight–2:30 AM* Ⓤ *Piccadilly Circus or Leicester Sq.*

**Jongleurs Camden Lock.** Jongleurs was the first chain of comedy clubs in the country and this flagship venue, housed in an old stable in the Camden Lock, is popular because of its late-night bar and disco. The bill, sometimes featuring North American comics, is strong but not quite as tasty as at the Comedy Store. ✉ *Dingwalls Bldg., 36 Camden Lock Pl., Camden Market, Chalk Farm Rd., Camden Town NW1* ☎ *0870/787–0707* 💷 *£15–£16* ⊙ *Fri. 7:15 PM–2 AM, Sat. 7:15 PM–9:45 PM and 11:30 PM–2 AM* Ⓤ *Camden Town.*

Fodor'sChoice ★ **Soho Theatre.** This innovative theater programs excellent comedy shows by established acts and award-winning new comedians. The bar downstairs stays open until 1 AM. Check local listings or the Web site for what's on and book tickets in advance. ✉ *21 Dean St., Soho W1* ☎ *020/7478–0100* 🌐 *www.sohotheatre.com* 💷 *£5–£15* Ⓤ *Tottenham Court Rd.*

## Casinos

The 1968 Gaming Act states that any person wishing to gamble must make a declaration of intent to gamble at the gaming house in question and must apply for membership in person. Membership takes 24 hours to process and usually requires a driver's license and passport as proof of identification. Some clubs prefer that a member sponsor you as an applicant. Personal guests of existing members are always allowed in.

**Crockford's.** Established almost two centuries ago, this civilized club has none of the jostling for tables that mars many of the flashier clubs. It attracts a large international clientele and offers American roulette, Punto Banco, three-card stud poker, and blackjack. ✉ *30 Curzon St., Mayfair W1* ☎ *020/7493–7771* 🎩 *Jacket required after 8 PM* 💷 *Membership £300 yearly* ⊙ *Weekdays and Sun. noon–6 AM, Sat. noon–4 AM. Gaming daily from 2 PM* Ⓤ *Green Park.*

**50 St. James.** Built in 1828, this magnificent London club in the Regency baroque style combines opulent decor with an intimate environment. Done in crimson, gold, and white, with a grand staircase, domed ceiling, *salles prives* (private rooms), and art deco restaurant, reminiscent of ocean liners, it's the epitome of elegance. Average wager £2,500. ⊠ *50 St. James's St., St. James's SW1* ☎ *020/7491–4678* 🏛 *Jacket required* ⊞ *Annual membership charge £1,000, waived for guests of members* ⊙ *Daily 2 PM–4 AM* Ⓤ *Green Park.*

**Golden Nugget.** This large and friendly casino just off Piccadilly has a fast-moving, exciting pace. It has blackjack, roulette, Punto Banco, slot machines, and new gaming technology. ⊠ *22–32 Shaftesbury Ave., Soho W1* ☎ *020/7439–0099* ⊞ *Life membership £10, free membership via the Internet* ⊙ *Sun.–Fri. 2 PM–6 AM, Sat. 2 PM–4 AM.* Ⓤ *Piccadilly Circus.*

**Palm Beach Casino.** An elegant club with palm trees, chandeliers, and deco styling—it used to be the famous ballroom of the Mayfair Hotel. A cosmopolitan crowd chooses from American roulette, blackjack, casino stub poker, slot machines, and Punto Banco. Average wager is £600. Smart casual dress with jacket is required after 7 PM. ⊠ *30 Berkeley St., Mayfair W1* ☎ *020/7493–6585* 🏛 *Jacket required after 7 PM* ⊞ *No membership fee* ⊙ *Daily 12:30 PM–6 AM, Sat. until 4 AM* Ⓤ *Green Park.*

# Dance Clubs

If you're looking for the latest craze in dance music, you've come to the right place. Britain pioneered rave culture, and for the past decade, London DJs and club owners have been the style-makers of cool. As residents of one of the most ethnically diverse cities in the world, Londoners "mix up" their music to create a fusion of sounds that has revolutionized dance. DJs are the gods of the dance world with a devoted following of punters who flock from club to club to dance to U.K. garage, drum 'n' bass, hip-hop, deep house, Latin house, Japanese bible, London Zok, Oriental eclectica, and the latest decknology. Megaclubs, like **Ministry of Sound** and **Fabric,** housed in multilevel buildings with numerous dance floors, bars, and chill-out rooms—and devastatingly loud state-of-the-art sound systems—accommodate hundreds. But the most cutting-edge sounds are heard in more intimate clubs, like **333** and **The Edge,** or the clubby bars like **Dogstar** in Brixton, where DJs play for free on weeknights.

The club scene is in constant flux, especially the "club nights" that take place at particular clubs on the same night every week, or which shift locations. So keep an eye out for music fliers in the various style bars. Also check the daily listings in *Time Out.* These days security is tight, so don't be put off if you find yourself being frisked at the door.

**Bar Rumba.** Though nothing special to look at, this smallish West End venue has a reputation for good fun. The staff is friendly and the club is almost always heaving with serious clubbers grooving to different styles of music each night. Stop by weekdays for cheap cocktails during happy hour. ⊠ *36 Shaftesbury Ave., Soho W1* ☎ *020/7287–2715* ⊞ *£3–£12* ⊙ *Weekdays 6 PM–3 AM, Sat. 8 PM–3 AM, Sun. 8 PM–1:30 AM* Ⓤ *Piccadilly Circus.*

**Café de Paris.** Open since 1924 and known as the "Bower of Love," this is one of London's most glamour-puss settings. Once a haunt of royals and consorts, the boîte brought in such stars as Noel Coward, Marlene Dietrich, Fred Astaire, and Frank Sinatra. These days, it pays host to the A-list—Kate Moss, Puff Daddy, and Madonna. ⊠ *3–4 Coventry St., Soho W1V 7FL* ☎ *020/7734–7700* 🖷 *020/7434–0347* 🖭 *£15 after 10 PM* ⊗ *Wed.–Sat. 6 PM–4 AM* Ⓤ *Piccadilly Circus.*

**Camden Palace.** Popular with the New Romantics post-punk music style (from Manchester's legendary Hacienda Club) in the 1980s, this Victorian theater with original plasterwork, and five levels of balconies, is one of London's most stunning venues. Excellent lights and the sounds of U.K. garage, live indie-rock, and hard house keeps the big dance floor heaving. ⊠ *1A Camden High St., Camden Town NW1* ☎ *090/6210–0200* 🖭 *£5–£20* ⊗ *Tues.–Thurs. 10 PM–2:30 AM, Fri. and Sat. 10 PM–6 AM* Ⓤ *Mornington Crescent or Camden Town.*

**Elbow Room.** This innovative club designed in '60s pool-hall chic has 11 tables, leather-booth seating, and a neon-lit bar. One of the best deals is the Sunday Marmalade when indie bands play for free from 7 PM. There's also a branch in Shoreditch. ⊠ *89–91 Chapel Market, Islington N1* ☎ *020/7278–3244* 🖭 *Free–£5* ⊗ *Mon. 5 PM–2 AM, Tues.–Thurs. noon–2 AM, Fri. and Sat. noon–3 AM, Sun. noon–midnight* Ⓤ *Angel.*

**The End.** Owned by Mr. C (ex-Shamen MC), this intimate club was designed by clubbers for clubbers. Top-name DJs, state-of-the-art sound system, and minimalist steel-and-glass decor—clubbing doesn't get much better than this. Next door, the AKA Bar (owned by same) is a stylish split-level Manhattan-esque cocktail bar with excellent food. ⊠ *18 West Central St., Holborn WC1* ☎ *020/7419–9199* ⊕ *www.the-end.co.uk* 🖭 *£4–£15* ⊗ *Mon. 10 PM–3 AM, Thurs. 9 PM–4 AM, Fri. 10 PM–5 AM, and Sat. 10 PM–7 AM. Also some Sundays* Ⓤ *Tottenham Court Rd.*

FodorśChoice ★ **Fabric.** This sprawling subterranean club has been *the* place to be for the past few years. *Fabric Live* hosts hip-hop crews and live acts on Friday; international big-name DJs play slow sexy bass lines and cutting-edge music on Saturday. Sunday is "Polysexual Night." The devastating sound system and bodysonic dance floor ensure that bass riffs vibrate through your entire body. Get there early to avoid a lengthy queue, and don't wear a suit. ⊠ *77A Charterhouse St., East End EC1* ☎ *020/ 7336–8898* ⊕ *www.fabriclondon.com* 🖭 *£12–£15* ⊗ *Fri. and Sun. 9:30 PM–5 AM, Sat. 10 PM–7 AM* Ⓤ *Farringdon.*

**Mass.** In what was previously St. Matthew's Church, but is now an atmospheric club with Gothic overtones, winding stone steps lead to the main room where an extended balcony hangs over the dance floor. An unpretentious and friendly crowd dances, on rotating club nights, to hip-hop grooves and jazzy beats. ⊠ *Brixton Hill, St. Matthew's Church, Brixton SW2* ☎ *020/7737–1016* 🖭 *£8–£20* ⊗ *Fri. and Sat., 10 PM–6 AM* Ⓤ *Brixton.*

**Ministry of Sound.** It's more of an industry than a club, with its own record label, online radio station, a magazine, and international DJs. The stripped down warehouse-style club has a super sound system and pulls in the world's most legendary names in dance. There are chill-out rooms, two bars, and three dance floors. ⊠ *103 Gaunt St., South Bank SE1*

☎ *020/7378–6528* ✉ *£10–£15* ⊗ *Fri. 10:30* PM*–5* AM*, Sat. 11* PM*– 7* AM Ⓤ *Elephant and Castle.*

**Notting Hill Arts Club.** Rock stars like Liam Gallagher and Courtney Love have been seen at this small basement club-bar. An alternative crowd swills beer to eclectic music that spans Asian underground, Latin-inspired funk, deep house, and jazzy grooves. What it lacks in looks it makes up for in mood. ✉ *21 Notting Hill Gate, Notting Hill W11* ☎ *020/ 7460–4459* ⊕ *www.nottinghillartsclub.com* ✉ *Free before 8* PM*, then £5–£8* ⊗ *Mon.–Wed. 6* PM*–1* AM*, Thurs. and Fri. 6* PM*–2* AM*, Sat. 4* PM*–2* AM*, Sun. 4* PM*–12:30* AM Ⓤ *Notting Hill Gate.*

**Pacha.** London's version of the Ibizan superclub is in a restored 1920s dancehall next to Victoria bus station. The classic surroundings—all wood and chandeliers—don't stop the sounds being eminently up-to-date. The crowd is slightly older than average and stylish, but not necessarily as monied as you might expect. ✉ *Terminus Pl., Victoria SW1* ☎ *020/7833–3139* ✉ *£20* ⊗ *Fri. and Sat. 10* PM*–6* AM Ⓤ *Victoria.*

**Sound.** One of the best ways to experience this high-tech, futuristic, but cramped West End palace is by listening to Trevor Nelson (R&B's biggest name in Europe) Friday nights. There are gay nights upstairs on Sunday. ✉ *Swiss Center, Leicester Sq., Soho WC2* ☎ *020/7287–1010* ✉ *Free–£12* ⊗ *Sun.–Thurs. 5* PM*–2* AM*, Fri. and Sat. 5* PM*–4* AM Ⓤ *Leicester Sq.*

★ **333.** This is *the* last word in dance music for the trendy Shoreditch crowd. Fashionable bright young things dance to drum 'n' bass, twisted disco, and underground dance genres. Sunday is gay night. There are three floors. You can chill on leather sofas at the relaxed Mother Bar upstairs, open from 8 PM daily, 7:30 PM Sunday, when there's free live music. ✉ *333 Old St., East End EC1* ☎ *020/7739–5949* ⊕ *www.333mother.com* ✉ *£5–£10* ⊗ *Fri. and Sat. 10* PM*–5* AM*, Sun. 10* PM*–4* AM Ⓤ *Old St.*

**Turnmills.** On the scene since the late 1980s, this legendary space in trendy Clerkenwell is still one of the trendiest places to go for big-night clubbing. A typical industrial-look club, here you'll find two dance floors, smoke machines, light effects, and the usual off-limits VIP areas. ✉ *63b Clerkenwell Rd., Clerkenwell EC1M* ☎ *020/7250–3409* ⊕ *www. turnmills.com* ✉ *£3–£15* ⊗ *Thurs. 9* PM*–3* AM*, Fri. 10* PM*–7:30* AM*, Sat. 10* PM*–6* AM*, Sun. 10* PM*–3* AM Ⓤ *Farringdon.*

## Eclectic Music

**The Borderline.** This important small venue has a solid reputation for booking everything from metal to country and beyond. Oasis, Pearl Jam, Blur, Sheryl Crow, PJ Harvey, Ben Harper, Jeff Buckley, and Counting Crows have all played live here. ✉ *Orange Yard off Manette St., Soho W1* ☎ *020/ 7395–0777* ✉ *£6–£15* ⊗ *Mon.–Sat. 7* PM*–3* AM*, Sun. 7* PM*–midnight* Ⓤ *Tottenham Court Rd.*

★ **Brixton Carling Academy.** This legendary Brixton venue has seen it all— mods and rockers, hippies and punks. Despite a capacity of 4,000 people, this refurbished Victorian hall with original art deco fixtures retains a clublike charm; it has plenty of bars and upstairs seating. ✉ *211 Stockwell Rd., Brixton SW9* ☎ *0870/771–2000* ✉ *£10–£30* ⊗ *Opening hrs vary* Ⓤ *Brixton.*

**Lock 17.** This midsize venue (formerly known as Dingwalls) in the Camden Lock warehouses caters to the full spectrum of musical tastes—country, jazz, blues, folk, indie, and world beat. (Note that on Friday and Saturday it becomes a comedy club, Jongleurs.) ☒ *Camden Lock off Camden High St., Camden Town NW1* ☎ *020/7267–1577* ☒ *£8–£20* ☉ *Sun.–Thurs. 7:30 PM–midnight* Ⓤ *Camden Town.*

**Ocean.** Bhangra to blues, classical to country, rock to reggae. This state-of-the-art building sports three venues and bars, an atrium, and a café-bar. There are three rooms of resident DJs on Decks Territory Saturday. ☒ *270 Mare St., East End E8* ☎ *020/8533–0111 or 020/8533–0111* ⊕ *www.ocean.org.uk* ☒ *£6–£25* ☉ *Mon.–Thurs. 10 AM–11 PM, Fri. and Sat. 11 AM–2 AM, Sun. 6 PM–10 PM* Ⓤ *British Rail: Hackney Central.*

**Shepherd's Bush Empire.** Once a grand old theater and former BBC TV studio, this intimate venue with fine balcony views now hosts a great cross section of mid-league U.K. and U.S. bands. ☒ *Shepherd's Bush Green, Shepherd's Bush, W12* ☎ *0870/771–2000* ☒ *£12–£15* Ⓤ *Shepherd's Bush.*

**Spitz.** In charming Spitalfields Market, where the City interfaces with the East End, this two-level venue has eclectic music that includes world-beat, folk, jazz, Americana, and electronic sounds. The downstairs bar and bistro has DJs and live jazz free on Friday nights. ☒ *109 Commercial St., East End E1* ☎ *020/7392–9032* ☒ *£5–£8* ☉ *Mon.–Sat. 11 AM–midnight, Sun. 10 AM–10:30 PM* Ⓤ *Liverpool St.*

**12 Bar Club.** This rough-and-ready acoustic club hosts notable singer-songwriters. Four different acts of new folk and contemporary country perform each night in this intimate venue. There's a good selection of bottled beer and gastro-pub food here. ☒ *22–23 Denmark St., West End WC2* ☎ *020/7916–6989* ☒ *£5–£10* ☉ *Daily 8 PM–1 AM. Café opens at noon* Ⓤ *Tottenham Court Rd.*

**Fodor'sChoice**
★ **Union Chapel.** This beautiful old chapel has excellent acoustics and sublime architecture. The beauty of the space and its impressive multicultural programming has made it one of London's best musical venues. Performers have included Ravi Shankar, Björk, Beck, Beth Orton, and Bob Geldof. ☒ *Compton Terr., Islington N1* ☎ *020/7226–1686 or 0870/1201349* ⊕ *www.unionchapel.org.uk* ☒ *Free–£25* ☉ *Opening hrs vary* Ⓤ *Highbury & Islington.*

## Jazz & Blues

Expect a highly individual scene of British-based musicians supplemented by top-name visiting artists. The city hosts two major festivals: the *Soho Jazz Festival* (October) is traditional jazz and Dixieland, and the *London Jazz Festival* (November) promotes experimental jazz and top world-beat names. These festivals are held at venues throughout the capital.

**Ain't Nothin' but Blues.** The name sums up this bar that whips up a sweaty and smoky environment. Local musicians, as well as some notable names, squeeze onto the tiny stage. There's good bar food of the chili-and-gumbo variety. Most weekday nights there's no cover. ☒ *20*

*Kingly St., Soho W1* ☎ *020/7287–0514* 🖃 *Free–£6* 🕑 *Mon.–Wed. 6 PM–1 AM, Thurs. 6 PM–2 AM, Fri. and Sat. 6 PM–3 AM, Sun. 7:30 PM–midnight* Ⓤ *Oxford Circus.*

★ **Bull's Head.** Its pleasant location, right on the River Thames, and the big-name musicians who jam here regularly, make the excursion to Bull's Head worthwhile. It's open normal pub hours, and jazz-and-blues shows start nightly at 8:30 PM, 2 PM and 8 PM on Sunday. 🖂 *373 Lonsdale Rd., Barnes Bridge, Barnes SW13* ☎ *020/8876–5241* 🖃 *£5–£10* Ⓤ *Hammersmith, then Bus 209 to Barnes Bridge.*

★ **Jazz Café.** A palace of high-tech cool in bohemian Camden—it remains an essential hangout for fans of both the mainstream end of the repertoire and hip-hop, funk, rap, and Latin fusion. Book ahead if you want a prime table overlooking the stage, in the balcony restaurant. 🖂 *5 Parkway, Camden Town NW1* ☎ *020/7916–6060 or 020/7344–0044* 🖃 *£10–£25* 🕑 *Mon.–Thurs. 7 PM–1 AM, Fri. and Sat. 7 PM–2 AM, Sun. 7 PM–midnight* Ⓤ *Camden Town.*

**100 Club.** Since it opened in 1942, all the greats have played here, from Glen Miller and Louis Armstrong on down to the best traditional jazz artists, British and American blues, R&B, and punk. Little has changed in this cool, inexpensive club. You can still take jitterbug and jive lessons from the London Swing Dance Society. 🖂 *100 Oxford St., Soho W1* ☎ *020/7636–0933* ⊕ *www.the100club.co.uk* 🖃 *£6–£12* 🕑 *Mon.–Thurs. 7:30–midnight, Fri. 8:30 PM–2 AM, Sat. 7:30 PM–2 AM, Sun. 7:30 PM–11:30 PM* Ⓤ *Oxford Circus or Tottenham Court Rd.*

**Pizza Express.** The capital's best-loved pizza chain is also a great jazz venue. The darkly lit restaurant hosts top-quality international jazz acts every night except Monday. The Italian-style thin-crust pizzas are good, too, though on the small side. Eight other branches also have live music. 🖂 *10 Dean St., Soho W1* ☎ *020/7439–8722* 🖃 *£12–£20* 🕑 *Daily from 11:30 AM for food; music Mon.–Thurs. and Sun. 9 PM–midnight, Fri. and Sat. 7:30 PM–midnight* Ⓤ *Tottenham Court Rd.*

**Pizza on the Park.** This upscale restaurant across from Hyde Park has a spacious jazz club in the basement that hosts mainstream acts. They also serve excellent pizzas. 🖂 *11 Knightsbridge, Hyde Park Corner, Knightsbridge W1* ☎ *020/7235–5273* 🖃 *£10–£20* 🕑 *Daily from 8:15 AM for food; music nightly 9:15 PM–midnight* Ⓤ *Hyde Park Corner.*

**Roadhouse.** Roadhouse pays homage to the American dream of the open road, with a Harley behind the bar and much memorabilia. The music fits into the feel-good-but-middle-of-the-road end of the R&B-blues-rock-soul spectrum, with live bands every night. 🖂 *Jubilee Hall, 35 The Piazza, Covent Garden WC2* ☎ *020/7240–6001* 🖃 *Free–£10* 🕑 *Mon. 5:30 PM–2:30 AM, Tues.–Sat. 5:30 PM–3 AM, Sun. 5:30 PM–1 AM* Ⓤ *Covent Garden.*

Fodor'sChoice ★ **Ronnie Scott's.** Since the '60s, this legendary jazz club has attracted big names. It's usually crowded and hot, the food isn't great, and service is slow—but the mood can't be beat, even since the sad departure of its eponymous founder and saxophonist. Reservations are recommended. 🖂 *47 Frith St., Soho W1* ☎ *020/7439–0747* 🖃 *£15–£25 nonmembers, £5–£15 members, annual membership £100* 🕑 *Mon.–Sat. 8:30 PM–3 AM, Sun. 7:30 PM–11 PM* Ⓤ *Leicester Sq.*

**606 Club.** Expect a civilized Chelsea club that showcases mainstream and contemporary jazz by well-known British-based musicians. You must eat a meal in order to consume alcohol, so allow for an extra £10–£20. Booking is advisable. ⊠ *90 Lots Rd., Chelsea SW10* ☎ *020/7352–5953* ⊠ *£6–£8 music charge is added to bill* ⊗ *Mon.–Wed. 7:30 PM–1:30 AM, Thurs.–Sat. 8 PM–2 AM, Sun. 8 PM–12:30 AM* Ⓤ *Earl's Court or Fulham Broadway.*

## Rock

Since the '60s, London has had one of the best live music scenes in the world. Everyone of note (except Elvis Presley) has played here, and the city is an essential stop on any band's world tour.

A few years ago, headlining bands would kick off at 9 PM and it would all be over by 11 PM. Now that rock clubs have late licenses it's less likely you'll be thrown out on the street with nowhere to go. Most shows sell out quickly, leaving fans at the mercy of scalpers; it's a good idea to buy tickets in advance. The "Gigs" page at ⊕ www.nme.com, one of the most comprehensive search engines, lets you book tickets online.

**The Astoria.** A balconied theater, the Astoria hosts cutting-edge alternative bands (punk, metal, indie guitar). Shows start early, at 7 PM most nights; the building is often cleared, following gigs, for club events. ⊠ *157 Charing Cross Rd., West End W1* ☎ *020/7434–9592* ⊠ *£8–£25* ⊗ *Weekdays 7 PM–4 AM, Sat. 6 PM–4:30 AM, Sun. 7 PM–midnight* Ⓤ *Tottenham Court Rd.*

★ **Barfly Club.** At one of the finest small clubs in the capital, punk, indie guitar bands, and new metal rock attract a non-mainstream crowd. Weekend club nights upstairs host DJs who rock the decks. ⊠ *49 Chalk Farm Rd., Camden Town NW1* ☎ *020/7691–4244* ⊠ *£5–£8* ⊗ *Mon.–Thurs. 7:30 PM–midnight, Fri. and Sat. 8 PM–2 AM, Sun. 7:30 PM–11 PM* Ⓤ *Camden Town or Chalk Farm.*

**Forum.** The best medium-to-big-name rock performers consistently play at the 2,000-capacity club. It's a converted 1920 art deco cinema, with a balcony overlooking the dance floor. Consult the Web site for current listings. ⊠ *9–17 Highgate Rd., Kentish Town NW5* ☎ *020/7284–1001* ⊕ *www.meanfiddler.com* ⊠ *£12–£25* ⊗ *Opening hrs vary depending on concert schedule* Ⓤ *Kentish Town.*

**The Garage.** Popular with the younger set, this intimate, two-stage club has a solid reputation for programming excellent indie and rock bands, including American bands. Club nights start after the gigs on weekends. ⊠ *20–22 Highbury Corner, Islington N1* ☎ *020/7607–1818* ⊠ *£5–£12* ⊗ *Mon.–Wed. 8 PM–11:30 PM, Thurs. 8 PM–2 AM, Fri. and Sat. 8 PM–3 AM* Ⓤ *Highbury & Islington.*

**Water Rats.** This high-spirited pub hosted Bob Dylan on his 1963 tour, as well as the first Oasis gig. Anything from alt-country, hip-hop, to indie guitar bands thrash it out most nights of the week. ⊠ *328 Gray's Inn Rd., Euston WC1* ☎ *020/7336–7326* ⊠ *£5–£7* ⊗ *Mon.–Sat. 7:30 PM–11:30 PM* Ⓤ *King's Cross.*

## The Gay Scene

London's gay and lesbian scene is diverse and well established. Soho is the heart of gay London. The clubs cater to every taste: besuited boyzy clubs, divey drag, tea dances, lesbian-only strip joints, and late-night queer-core with butch leather, rubber, and uniform fetish nights. Whatever your preference, you can be guaranteed a steamy, cruisey, or sleazy night out in London. Lesbian chic is as trendy in London as it is in New York or Los Angeles, but although a few clubs have opened up in prime Soho spots, the scene is predominantly male.

The big annual outdoor event is *The National Pride Parade/Pride in the Park* in July. The largest pink party of the year starts as a colorful parade that winds through London before ending up in Hyde Park. There the festivities continue as a ticketed party with lots of musical events and performances. Call ☎ 020/7494–2225 or check ⊕ www.londonmardigras.com for details.

Queer theater and other arts take place throughout the year, but there are several gay-oriented annual arts festivals. The National Film Board hosts the Gay and Lesbian film festival in March.

Check the listings in *Time Out, Boyz, Gay Times, Attitude,* or the lesbian monthly, *Diva.* GAY to Z (⊕ www.gaytoz.com) offers a comprehensive online directory. The Web site ⊕ www.rainbownetwork.com has up-to-date listings and reviews of bars, clubs, and events.

### Bars, Cafés & Pubs

Café–bars (café by day, club bar by night) have emerged on the London scene, with DJs and a late license. Unless otherwise stated, hours for pubs and bars are the same as for all London pubs, with drinks available up to 11 PM, 10:30 PM on Sunday.

**Box.** True to its name, this modern, industrial-chic bar is small and square. Though nothing special to look at, it's a staple on the pre-club circuit and gets packed to the hilt with muscular boys. For peckish punters there's food before 5 PM daily. ⊠ *32–34 Monmouth St., Soho WC2* ☎ *020/7240–5828* ⊙ *Mon.–Sat. 11 AM–11 PM, Sun. noon–10:30 PM* Ⓤ *Leicester Sq.*

**Candy Bar.** The United Kingdom's first girls' bar is intimate, chilled, and cruisey, with DJs mixing the latest sounds. Men are welcome as guests. ⊠ *4 Carlisle St., Soho W1* ☎ *020/7494–4041* 🖭 *£5 after 9 PM, Fri. and Sat.* ⊙ *Mon.–Thurs. 5 PM–11:30 PM, Fri. and Sat. 5 PM–2 AM, Sun. 5 PM–10:30 PM* Ⓤ *Tottenham Court Rd.*

**The Edge.** *Poseurs* are welcome at this hip hangout. Straight groovers mingle with gay men over the four jam-packed floors. In summer, sidewalk tables provide an enviable view of Soho's daily street theater. ⊠ *11 Soho Sq., Soho W1* ☎ *020/7439–1313* ⊙ *Mon.–Sat. 11 AM–1 AM, Sun. 11 AM–10:30 PM* Ⓤ *Oxford Circus.*

**Rupert Street.** For smart boyz, this gay chic island among the sleaze has a new loungey feel with brown-leather sofas and floor-to-ceiling windows. It's crowded and cruisey at night with pre-clubbers, civilized and café-like by day, with traditional British food served until 5 PM. ⊠ *50 Rupert St., Soho W1* ☎ *020/7292–7141* ⊘ *Mon.–Sat. noon–11 PM, Sun. noon–10:30 PM* Ⓤ *Leicester Sq. or Piccadilly Circus.*

**Yard.** A lively bar, popular with the after-work and pre-clubbing crowds, Yard has an outdoor courtyard with heater lamps in winter. It gets packed and smoky at night. Upstairs is lower-key, with sofas and a balcony overlooking the courtyard for prime scoping. ⊠ *57 Rupert St., Soho W1* ☎ *020/7437–2652* ⊘ *Mon.–Sat. noon–11 PM, Sun. noon–10:30 PM* Ⓤ *Piccadilly Circus.*

## Clubs

Some of the best gay dance clubs are held once a week in mixed clubs. Gay clubs, like **Heaven,** also offer straight nights. Most clubs are gay friendly, but if that's not your thing you can find ones more targeted to your taste. The following are well established and likely still to be going strong, but given the rate that clubs open and close in London, it's best to call first.

**G.A.Y.** London's largest gay party is at the Astoria on Monday, Thursday, Friday, and Saturday. Saturday night hosts big-name talent; regular guests include Kylie Minogue, Geri Halliwell, and a whole host of B-list TV celebrities. Buy advance tickets to avoid the long Saturday night queue. ⊠ *157 and 165 Charing Cross Rd., Soho WC2* ☎ *020/7434–9592 or 020/7734–6963* 🎟 *£1–£10* ⊘ *Mon. and Thurs. 10:30 PM–4 AM, Fri. 11 PM–4 AM, Sat. 10:30 PM–5 AM* Ⓤ *Tottenham Court Rd.*

★ **Heaven.** With by far the best light show on any London dance floor, Heaven is unpretentious, loud, and huge, with a labyrinth of quiet rooms, bars, and live-music parlors. Friday is predominantly straight. If you go to just one club, Heaven should be it. ⊠ *The Arches, Villiers St., Covent Garden WC2* ☎ *020/7930–2020* ⊕ *www.heaven-london. com* 🎟 *£4–£12* ⊘ *Mon. 10:15 PM–4 AM, Wed. 10:30 PM–3 AM, Fri. 5 PM–3 AM, Sat. 10:30 PM–6 AM* Ⓤ *Charing Cross or Embankment.*

**Original Sunday Tea Dance.** A longtime fave with the girls, this is a very camp and very fun Sunday ballroom, Latin, line-dance, time-warp disco. Tea and biscuits are served up until 7 PM. ⊠ *BJ's White Swan, 556 Commercial Rd., East End E14* ☎ *020/7780–9870* 🎟 *£2* ⊘ *Sun. 5:30–midnight* Ⓤ *Aldgate E.*

**Fodor'sChoice**
★ **Sanctuary.** There's something for everyone at this Soho hotspot. If you're not in the mood to let loose to pumping house music on the dance floor downstairs, you can ascend to the wood-panel upstairs and sip your cocktail on a leather sofa. Then gather 'round the grand piano and sing along to the pianist's favorites—everything from Madonna's "Like a Virgin" to classic show tunes. ⊠ *5 Greek St., Soho W1* ☎ *020/7434–3323* ⊘ *Mon.–Sat. noon–3 AM, Sun. noon–midnight* Ⓤ *Tottenham Court Rd.*

★ **The Shadow Lounge.** This fabulous little lounge and dance club glitters with faux jewels and twinkling fiber-optic lights over its sunken dance floor, which comes complete with pole for those inclined to do their thing around it. It has a serious A-list celebrity factor, with the glamorous London glitterati camping out in the VIP booth. Members are given entrance priority when the place gets full, especially on weekends, so show up early or prepare to queue. ⊠ *5 Brewer St., Soho W1*

☎ 020 /7287–7988 ✉ Free–£10 ✆ Mon.–Wed. 9 PM–3 AM, Thurs.–Sat. 8 PM–3 AM Ⓤ Leicester Sq.

**Trade.** This London institution among the hedonistic muscle boys is now over a decade old, and begins when many clubs are closing. It's on only once or twice a month, so check the Web site for dates. ✉ Turnmills, 63 Clerkenwell Rd., East End EC1 ☎ 020/7250–3409 ⊕ www.tradeuk. net ✉ £15–£25 ✆ Dates vary, 4 AM–1 PM Ⓤ Farringdon.

# THE ARTS

Whether you fancy your art classical or modern, or as a contemporary twist on a time-honored classic, you'll find that London's arts scene pushes the boundaries. Watch a Hollywood star in a West End theater, or a troupe of Latin American acrobats. See a blockbuster contemporary art show at the Tate Modern, or a William Blake retrospective at the Tate Britain. There are international theater festivals, innovative music festivals, and obscure seasons of postmodern dance. Celebrity divas sing original-language librettos at the Royal Opera House; the Almeida Opera is more daring with its radical productions of new opera and music theater. Shakespeare's plays are brought to life at the reconstructed Globe Theatre, and challenging new writing is produced at the Royal Court. Whether you feel like the lighthearted extravagance of a West End musical or the next shark-in-formaldehyde sculpture at the Saatchi Gallery, the choice is yours.

We've attempted a representative selection in the following listings, but to find out what's showing now, the weekly magazine *Time Out* (£2.20, issued every Tuesday) is invaluable. The *Evening Standard* also carries listings, especially in the supplement "Metro Life," which comes with the Thursday edition, as do many Sunday papers and the Saturday *Independent, Guardian,* and *Times.* You'll find leaflets and flyers in most cinema and theater foyers, too, and you can pick up the free fortnightly *London Theatre Guide* leaflet from hotels and tourist information centers.

## Dance

Dance fans in London can enjoy the classicism of the world-renowned Royal Ballet, as well as innovative contemporary dance from several companies—Ballet Rambert, Matthew Bourne's Adventures in Motion Pictures, Random Dance Company, Michael Clark Dance Company, Richard Alston Dance Company, Wade McGregor, Charles Lineham Company, DV8 Physical Theatre, and Akram Khan—and scores of independent choreographers. The English National Ballet and visiting international companies perform at the Coliseum and at Sadler's Wells, which also hosts various other ballet companies and dance troupes. The Royal Festival Hall has a seriously good contemporary dance program that hosts top international companies and important U.K. choreographers, as well as multicultural offerings—from Japanese Butoh and Indian Kathak to hip-hop. The Place is where you'll find the most daring, cutting-edge performances.

The biggest annual event is **Dance Umbrella** (☎ 020/8741–5881 ⊕ www. danceumbrella.co.uk), a six-week season in October–November that hosts international and British-based artists at various venues across the city.

## Dance Box Offices

The following theaters are the key dance venues. Check weekly listings for current performances and fringe venues.

**The London Coliseum.** The English National Ballet (www.ballet.org.uk) and other dance companies often perform in this Edwardian baroque theater (1904) with a magnificent auditorium and an illuminated globe, newly restored and reopened in February, 2004. ✉ *St. Martin's La., Covent Garden WC2N* ☎ *020/7632–8300* Ⓤ *Leicester Sq.*

**Peacock Theatre.** Sadler's Wells' West End annex, this modernist theater near the University of London offers commercial dance as well as ballet. ✉ *Portugal St., Holborn WC2* ☎ *020/7863–8222* Ⓤ *Holborn.*

**The Place.** The Robin Howard Dance Theatre is London's only theater dedicated to contemporary dance. *Resolution!* is the United Kingdom's biggest platform event for new choreographers. ✉ *17 Duke's Rd., Bloomsbury WC1* ☎ *020/7380–1268* ⊕ *www.theplace.org.uk* Ⓤ *Euston.*

**Riverside Studios.** The two performance spaces are noted for postmodern movement styles and performance art. ✉ *Crisp Rd., Hammersmith W6* ☎ *020/8237–1111* ⊕ *www.riversidestudios.co.uk* Ⓤ *Hammersmith.*

**Fodor'sChoice ★** **Royal Opera House.** The renowned Royal Ballet performs classical and contemporary repertoire in this spectacular state-of-the-art Victorian theater. ✉ *Bow St., Covent Garden WC2* ☎ *020/7304–4000* ⊕ *www. royaloperahouse.org* Ⓤ *Covent Garden.*

**Fodor'sChoice ★** **Sadler's Wells.** Ballet Rambert and Random Dance Company have their home in this lovely modern theater, which produces an excellent season of ballet and contemporary dance. ✉ *Rosebery Ave., Islington EC1* ☎ *020/7863–8000* ⊕ *www.sadlers-wells.com* Ⓤ *Angel.*

**South Bank Centre.** A diverse and exciting season of international and British-based contemporary dance companies is presented in the Royal Festival Hall, Queen Elizabeth Hall, and Purcell Room. ✉ *Belvedere Rd., South Bank SE1* ☎ *020/7960–4242* ⊕ *www.sbc.org.uk* Ⓤ *Waterloo or Embankment Station.*

# Classical Music

Whether you want to hear cellist Yo-Yo Ma at the Barbican or a Mozart requiem by candlelight, it's possible to hear first-rate musicians in world-class venues almost every day of the year. The London Symphony Orchestra is in residence at the Barbican Centre, although other top orchestras—including the Philharmonia and the Royal Philharmonic—also perform here. The Barbican also hosts chamber music concerts with such celebrated orchestras as the City of London Sinfonia. Wigmore Hall, a lovely venue for chamber music, is renowned for its song recitals by up-and-coming young instrumentalists. The South Bank Centre has an impressive international music season, held in the Royal Festival Hall (one of the finest concert halls in Europe), the Queen Elizabeth Hall, and the small Purcell Room. Full houses are rare, so even at the biggest concert halls you should be able to get a ticket for £12. If you can't book in advance, arrive at the hall an hour before the performance for a chance at returns.

Lunchtime concerts take place all over the city in smaller concert halls, the big arts-center foyers, and churches; they usually cost less than £5 or are free, and will feature string quartets, singers, jazz ensembles, or gospel choirs. St. John's, Smith Square and St. Martin-in-the-Fields are popular locations. Performances usually begin about 1 PM and last one hour.

Classical music festivals range from the stimulating avant-garde Meltdown (⊕ www.meltdown.co.uk) at the South Bank Centre in June to the more conservative Kenwood Lakeside Concerts (⊕ www. picnicconcerts.com), at which you can listen to classical music outdoors. There are also church hall recitals at Spitalfields Festival (⊕ www. spitalfieldsfestival.org.uk), venues around Covent Garden at the BBC Covent Garden Festival (⊕ www.cgf.co.uk) and in livery stables and churches in and around the city during the month-long City of London Festival (⊕ www.colf.org) in June and July.

A great British tradition since 1895, the Henry Wood Promenade Concerts (more commonly known as the "Proms"; ⊕ www.bbc.co.uk/ proms) lasts eight weeks, from July to September, at the Royal Albert Hall. It's renowned for its last night, a madly jingoistic display of singing "Land of Hope and Glory," Union Jack waving, and general madness. Demand for tickets is so high you must enter a lottery. For regular Proms, tickets run £4–£80, with hundreds of standing tickets for £4, available at the hall on the night of the concert. The last night is broadcast in Hyde Park on a jumbo-screen, but even here a seat on the grass requires a paid ticket that can set you back around £20.

**Barbican Centre.** Home to the London Symphony Orchestra and frequent host of the English Chamber Orchestra and the BBC Symphony Orchestra, the Barbican has an excellent season of big-name virtuosos. ⊠ *Silk St., East End EC2* ☎ *020/7638–8891 box office, 020/7638–4141* ⊕ *www. barbican.org.uk* Ⓤ *Barbican.*

**Kenwood House.** Concerts are held in the grassy amphitheater in front of Kenwood House on Saturday evenings from July to late August. ⊠ *Hampstead Heath, Hampstead* ☎ *0870/333–6206* ⊕ *www. picnicconcerts.com* Ⓤ *Hampstead.*

★ **Royal Albert Hall.** Built in 1871, this splendid iron-and-glass–dome auditorium hosts a varied music program, including Europe's most democratic music festival, the Henry Wood Promenade Concerts—the Proms. ⊠ *Kensington Gore, Kensington SW7* ☎ *020/7589–8212* ⊕ *www. royalalberthall.com* Ⓤ *S. Kensington.*

**St. James's Church.** The organ was brought here in 1691 after fire destroyed its former home, the Palace of Whitehall. St. James's holds regular classical music concerts, including free lunchtime recitals several times a week. ⊠ *197 Piccadilly, St. James's W1* ☎ *020/7381–0441 concert program and tickets* ⊕ *stjamesconcerts.musicwise.net* Ⓤ *Piccadilly Circus or Green Park.*

**St. John's, Smith Square.** This baroque church behind Westminster Abbey offers chamber music and organ recitals as well as orchestral concerts

# THE ARTS FOR FREE

M**ANY OF LONDON'S ARTS** venues are either free or accessible for a nominal fee or donation.

## Museums & Galleries

Perhaps no other city in the world can match up to London's offerings of free art. Most of London's museums and galleries do not charge entrance fees. The National Gallery, Tate Modern, the Photographer's Gallery, the V&A, the White Cube, and the British Museum are just some of the places you can see great arts and antiquities, all without spending a penny.

London's private art galleries around Cork Street in Mayfair and the Hoxton/ Shoreditch/Spitalfields area in the East End are happy for you to visit and wander around. The monthly Galleries magazine, available from galleries themselves or online at www.artefact.co.uk, has listings for all private galleries in the capital.

## Contemporary Music

Brixton's Dogstar pub has an excellent selection of DJs playing for free on weekday evenings. Ain't Nothing But the Blues in Soho has live blues most nights, often without a cover charge. Spitz, in Spitalfields Market, frequently has live music for free. The largest of the music superstores, such as Tower Records Piccadilly and HMV Oxford Street, have occasional live performances of pop and rock bands, often to accompany album or single launches.

## Classical Music & Jazz

The Barbican, the Royal Festival Hall, the Royal National Theatre, and the Royal Opera House often have free music in their foyers or in dedicated spaces, usually of a very high standard. The "Commuter Jazz" series, on Friday evenings around 5 PM in the main foyer of the Royal Festival Hall, is a great way to conclude an afternoon of culture at the South Bank.

Many of London's world-class music colleges give free concerts several times a week. The Royal Academy of Music and the Royal College of Music often have free concerts. St. Martin-in-the-Fields has free lunchtime concerts. Other churches, including Westminster Abbey and Christchurch Spitalfields, also have frequent free music. For the Proms, which run from July to September at the Royal Albert Hall, good seats are expensive, but hundreds of standing tickets are available at £4: not quite free, but a good value.

## Drama & Performance Arts

Look out for occasional festivals where innovative performances take place on the South Bank. Check the newspapers and Time Out for upcoming performances.

## Park Life

London's parks come to life in summer with a wide-ranging program of music, dance, and visual arts. See ⊕ www. royalparks.gov.uk for details or phone ☎ 020/7298–2000 for a free printed program. Radio stations also organize free summer music concerts (generally aimed at the teenybopper set) in London parks, with lots of big-name pop stars, but entry is usually by ticket only and events are often oversubscribed.

## Radio & Television

With so much broadcast material made in London, much of it recorded in front of live audiences, there are often opportunities to watch a free quiz show, current affairs debate, comedy, or even drama. Check the BBC Web site for forthcoming recordings or call **BBC Audience Services** (☎ 020/ 8576–1227 ⊕ www.bbc.co.uk/tickets). **Hat Trick Productions** (☎ 020/7434–2451 ⊕ www.hattrick.co.uk) makes a number of good comedy programs, including the excellent satirical current affairs program Have I Got News For You.

September through July. Free lunchtime recitals are held fortnightly. ✉ *Smith Sq., Westminster W1* ☎ *020/7222–1061* ⊕ *www.sjss.org.uk* Ⓤ *Westminster.*

★ **St. Martin-in-the-Fields.** Popular free lunchtime concerts are held in this lovely 1726 church, as are regular evening concerts. ✉ *Trafalgar Sq., Covent Garden WC2* ☎ *020/7839–8362* ⊕ *www.stmartin-in-the-fields. org* Ⓤ *Charing Cross.*

**South Bank Centre.** Home to both the Philharmonia and the London Philharmonic orchestras, the Royal Festival Hall hosts large-scale choral and orchestral works, the Queen Elizabeth Hall hosts chamber orchestras and A-team soloists, and the intimate Purcell Room has chamber music and solo recitals. ✉ *Belvedere Rd., South Bank, SE1* ☎ *020/7960–4242* ⊕ *www.sbc.org.uk* Ⓤ *Waterloo.*

FodorśChoice **Wigmore Hall.** Hear chamber music and song recitals in this charming ★ hall with near-perfect acoustics. Don't miss the mid-morning Sunday concerts. ✉ *36 Wigmore St., Marylebone W1* ☎ *020/7935–2141* ⊕ *www. wigmore-hall.org.uk* Ⓤ *Bond St.*

## Film

There are many wonderful movie theaters in London and several that are committed to non-mainstream cinema, in particular, the National Film Theatre. Now almost 50 years old, the *London Film Festival* (⊕ www.lff.com) brings hundreds of films made by masters of world cinema to London for 16 days each October into November, accompanied by often-sold-out events.

West End movie theaters continue to do good business. Most of the major houses, such as the Odeon Leicester Square and the UCI Empire, are in the Leicester Square–Piccadilly Circus area, where tickets average £8. Monday and matinees are often cheaper, at around £5, and there are also fewer crowds.

Check out *Time Out* or the Guardian's the *Guide* section (free with the paper on Saturday) for listings.

**Barbican.** In addition to Hollywood films, obscure classics and occasional film festivals with Screen Talks are programmed in the three cinemas here. Saturday Family Film Club often has animation for the entire family. ✉ *Silk St., East End EC2* ☎ *020/7382–7000 information, 020/ 7638–8891 box office* Ⓤ *Barbican.*

**BFI London IMAX Cinema.** The British Film Institute's glazed drum-shape IMAX theater has the largest screen in the United Kingdom (approximately 75 feet wide and the height of five double-decker buses) playing state-of-the-art 2-D and 3-D films. ✉ *1 Charlie Chaplin Walk, South Bank SE1* ☎ *020/7902–1234* Ⓤ *Waterloo.*

★ **Curzon Mayfair.** This very comfortable cinema runs an artsy program of mixed rep and mainstream films. There's also a Soho branch. ✉ *38 Curzon St., Mayfair W1* ☎ *020/7495–0500* Ⓤ *Green Park* ✉ *99 Shaftesbury Ave., Soho W1* ☎ *0871/871–0022* Ⓤ *Piccadilly Circus or Leicester Sq.*

★ **The Electric Cinema.** This refurbished Portobello Road art house screens mainstream and international movies. The emphasis is on comfort, with leather sofas, armchairs, and footstools and mini coffee tables for your popcorn. ⊠ *191 Portobello Rd., Notting Hill W11* ☎ *020/7727–9958 information, 020/7908–9696 box office* Ⓤ *Ladbroke Grove or Notting Hill Gate.*

**Everyman.** London's oldest repertory theater is cozy and shows an excellent selection of classic, foreign, cutting-edge, and almost-new Hollywood titles. ⊠ *5 Hollybush Vale, Hampstead NW3* ☎ *020/7431–1777* Ⓤ *Hampstead.*

**ICA Cinema.** Underground and vintage movies are shown in the avant-garde Institute of Contemporary Arts. ⊠ *The Mall, St. James's SW1* ☎ *020/7930–6393 information, 020/7930–3647 box office* Ⓤ *Piccadilly Circus or Charing Cross.*

**National Film Theatre.** The NFT's three cinemas show more than 1,000 titles each year, including foreign-language films, documentaries, director's seasons, cult Hollywood features, and animation. The *London Film Festival* is based here; throughout the year there are minifestivals, seminars, and guest speakers. Members (£24) get priority on bookings (useful for special events) and get £1 off each screening. ⊠ *Belvedere Rd., South Bank SE1* ☎ *020/7633–0274 information, 020/7928–3232 box office* Ⓤ *Waterloo.*

**Riverside Studios Cinemas.** The selection at this converted movie studio changes almost daily. Admission fees are very reasonable; £5.50 gets you entrance to a double bill. ⊠ *Crisp Rd., Hammersmith W6* ☎ *020/ 8237–1111* Ⓤ *Hammersmith.*

**Tricycle Theatre.** Expect the best of new British, European, and World Cinema, as well as films from the United States. There are annual Irish, Black, and Asian Film Festivals. ⊠ *269 Kilburn High Rd., Kilburn NW6* ☎ *020/ 7328–1900 information, 020/7328–1000 box office* Ⓤ *Kilburn.*

## Opera

The two key players in London's opera scene are the Royal Opera House (which ranks with the Metropolitan Opera House in New York), and the more innovative English National Opera (ENO), which presents English-language productions at the London Coliseum. Only the Theatre Royal, Drury Lane, has a longer theatrical history than the Royal Opera House, and the current theater—the third to be built on the site since 1858—completed a monumental 16-year renovation in 1999.

Despite Björk playing a concert in 2001, the Royal Opera House struggles to shrug off its reputation for elitism. Ticket prices rise to £170. It is, however, more accessible than it used to be—the cheapest tickets are just £6 (for a restricted-view matinee seat). Conditions of purchase vary; call for information. Prices for the ENO are generally lower, ranging from £8 to £80. You can get same-day balcony seats for as little as £5.

Almeida Opera and BAC Opera produce opera festivals that showcase new opera and cutting-edge music theater. In summer Holland Park Opera presents the usual chestnuts in the open-air theater of leafy Holland Park. Bring a picnic and an umbrella. Serious opera fans should not miss the

Glyndebourne Festival. It's the jewel in the crown of the country house opera circuit, and the greatest opera festival in the United Kingdom. Pavarotti made his British debut here.

Opening in 2004, the Savoy Opera promises fresh, provocative stagings of English-language classics; with ticket prices starting at £10, you can afford to see for yourself. International touring companies often perform at Sadler's Wells, Barbican, South Bank Centre, and Wigmore Hall, so check the weekly listings for details.

★ **Almeida Theatre.** The Almeida Opera Festival in July has an adventurous program of new opera and music theater. ☒ *Almeida St., Islington N1* ☎ *020/7359–4404* ⊕ *www.almeida.co.uk* Ⓤ *Angel.*

**BAC Opera.** New opera is presented at the BAC Opera Festival each May. ☒ *Lavender Hill, Battersea SW11* ☎ *020/7223–2223* ⊕ *www.bac.org. uk* Ⓤ *Clapham Junction.*

**English National Opera.** ENO produces innovative opera for lower prices than the Royal Opera House. The company is based at the London Coliseum. ☒ *St. Martin's La., Covent Garden WC2* ☎ *020/7632–8300* ⊕ *www.eno.org* Ⓤ *Leicester Sq.*

★ **Glyndebourne.** Fifty-four miles south of London, Glyndebourne is one of the most famous opera houses in the world. Six operas are presented from mid-May to late-August. The best route by car is the M23 to Brighton, then the A27 toward Lewes. There are regular trains from London (Victoria) to Lewes with coach connections to and from Glyndebourne. ☒ *Lewes, BN8 5UU* ☎ *01273/815–000 information, 01273/ 813–813 box office* ⊕ *www.glyndebourne.com.*

**Holland Park Opera.** In summer new productions and well-loved operas are presented against the remains of Holland House, one of the first great houses built in Kensington. Ticket prices range from £30 to £40. ☒ *Holland Park, Kensington High St., Kensington W8* ☎ *020/7602–7856* Ⓤ *Kensington High St.*

FodorśChoice **Royal Opera House.** Original-language productions are presented in this
★ extravagant theater. If you can't afford £100 for a ticket, consider showing up the morning of (the box office opens at 10 AM, but queues for popular productions can start as early as 7 AM) to purchase a same-day seat, of which a small number are offered for £20 to £50. There are free lunchtime recitals most Mondays in the Linbury Studio Theatre and occasional summer concerts broadcast live to a large screen in Covent Garden Piazza. ☒ *Bow St., Covent Garden WC2* ☎ *020/7304–4000* ⊕ *www.royalopera.org* Ⓤ *Covent Garden.*

**Savoy Opera.** In its inaugural season, the Savoy Opera performs eight times a week in the intimate, art-deco Savoy Theatre. ☒ *The Strand, at Savoy Street, West End, WC2R OET* ☎ *0870/166-7372* ⊕ *www. savoyopera.com* Ⓤ *Embankment or Charing Cross.*

## Theater

London's theatrical past goes back to the streets, marketplaces, and cathedrals. These were a backdrop for the medieval mystery plays—when London, indeed, was a stage. Theaters here, which are some of the finest theatrical gems in the world, embody this history.

The first permanent theater, The Theatre, was built by Richard Burbage in Shoreditch in 1576, and was soon followed by the Swan, Curtain, Rose Fortune, Hope, and Shakespeare's Globe Theatre on the South Bank—where the Bard's plays were staged alongside brothels, bearbaiting, and cock-fighting pits. The Puritans put an end to the fun, and the next dramatic boom didn't happen until after the Restoration of 1660, with the building of the Theatre Royal, Drury Lane (1662), and the Royal Opera House (1732). Most of London's theaters were built toward the end of the Victorian era when Shaftesbury Avenue cut through the Soho slums, and theaters like the Shaftesbury (1886) and Aldwych (1905) became the center of London's theater scene. Covent Garden became host to frothy Edwardian theater facades along St. Martin's Lane and the Strand. The 1930s saw the emergence of jazzy art deco theaters until the outbreak of World War II, and the 1970s saw the first intervention of state funding and the concrete Brutalist-style architecture of the Barbican Centre and National Theatre. In more recent years, lottery funds have subsidized renovations of existing spaces like the Royal Court, as well as new construction, most of which has resulted in unremarkable, modernist structures. Sitting in an exquisite Edwardian theater, soaking up the intricate plasterwork and plush boxes, even ordering a drink at the classy bar during intermission, is a big part of the theater-going experience.

But really, the play is the thing, and chances are good you can see a Sam Mendes Off-West End production, the umpteenth production of *Les Misérables,* a Peter Brook deconstruction of Shakespeare, innovative physical theater from *Le Théatre de Complicité,* the latest offering from *Cirque du Soleil* or Robert Lepage, or even a fringe production above a pub. West End glitz and glamour continues to pull in the audiences, and so do the more innovative players. Only in London will a Tuesday matinee of the Royal Shakespeare Company's *Henry IV* be sold out in a 1,200-seat theater.

In London, the words "radical" and "quality," or "classical" and "experimental," are not mutually exclusive. The Royal Shakespeare Company (⊕ www.rsc.org.uk) and the Royal National Theatre Company often stage contemporary versions of the classics. The Almeida, Battersea Arts Centre (BAC), Donmar Warehouse, Royal Court Theatre, Soho Theatre, the Young Vic, and The Old Vic attract famous actors and have excellent reputations for new writing and innovative theatrical languages. These are the places that shape the theater of the future, the venues where you'll see an original production before it becomes a hit in the West End. (And you'll see them at a fraction of the cost.)

Another great thing about the London theater scene is that it doesn't shut down in summer—it's business as usual for the Royal Shakespeare Company and Royal National Theatre. From mid-May through mid-September, you can see the Bard served up in his most spectacular manifestation—at the open-air reconstruction of Shakespeare's Globe Theatre. In addition, the Open Air Theatre presents a season of Shakespeare-under-the-stars, from the last week in May to the third week in September, in the lovely Regent's Park. **London Mime Festival** (⊕ www.mimefest.co.uk)

happens in January. Some theater festivals take place throughout the year, so unlike other cities, there's always something good to see in London. **L.I.F.T** (⊕ www.liftfest.org), the London International Festival of Theatre, stages productions at venues throughout the city. **B.I.T.E.**, the Barbican International Theater Events, presents top-notch cutting-edge performances. Check *Time Out* for details. The Web sites ⊕ www.whatsonstage. com and ⊕ www.officiallondontheatreguide.co.uk are both good sources of information about performances.

Theater going isn't cheap. Tickets under £10 are a rarity; in the West End you should expect to pay from £15 for a seat in the upper balcony to at least £25 for a good one in the stalls (orchestra) or dress circle (mezzanine). However, as the vast majority of theaters have some tickets (returns and house seats) available on the night of performance, you may find some good deals. Tickets may be booked through ticket agents, at individual theater box offices, or over the phone by credit card; be sure to inquire about any extra fees. All the larger hotels offer theater bookings, but they tack on a hefty service charge.

**Warning:** Be very wary of scalpers and unscrupulous ticket agents outside theaters and working the line at TKTS (a half-price ticket booth)—they try to sell tickets at five times the price of the ticket at legitimate box offices. You might be charged £200 or more for a sought-after ticket (and you'll pay a stiff fine if caught buying a scalped ticket).

**Ticketmaster** (☎ 020/7344–0055,800/775–2525 in U.S. ⊕ www. ticketmaster.com) sells tickets to a number of different theaters, although they charge a booking fee. **First Call** (☎ 020/7420–0000 ⊕ www. firstcalltickets.com) sells theater tickets. You can book tickets in the United States through **Keith Prowse** (✉ 234 W. 44th St., Suite 1000, New York, NY 10036 ☎ 212/398–1430 or 800/669–8687). You can buy tickets at the New York office of **Edwards & Edwards** (✉ 1 Times Sq. Plaza, 12th fl., New York, NY 10036 ☎ 800/223–6108). For discount tickets, **Society of London Theatre** (☎ 020/7557–6700) operates TKTS, the SOLT half-price ticket booth (no phone) on the southwest corner of Leicester Square and sells the best available seats to performances at about 25 theaters. It's open Monday–Saturday 10–7, Sunday noon–3; there's a £2 service charge. Major credit cards are accepted. You might consider using one particular booking line that doubles the price of tickets: **West End Cares** (☎ 020/7833–3939) donates half of what it charges to AIDS charities.

★ **Almeida Theatre.** This Off-West End venue premieres excellent new plays and exciting twists on the classics. Hollywood stars often perform here. ✉ *Almeida St., Islington N1* ☎ *020/7359–4404* ⊕ *www.almeida.co. uk* Ⓤ *Angel, Highbury and Islington.*

**Barbican Centre.** Built in 1982, the Barbican Centre puts on a number of performances by British and international theater companies as part of its year-round **B.I.T.E.** (Barbican International Theatre Events), which also features ground-breaking performance, dance, drama, and music theater. ✉ *Silk St., East End EC2* ☎ *020/7638–8891* ⊕ *www.barbican. org.uk* Ⓤ *Barbican.*

★ **BAC.** Battersea Arts Centre has an excellent reputation for producing innovative new work. Check out Scratch, a night of low-tech cabaret theater by emerging artists, and the BAC Octoberfest of innovative performance. ✉ *176 Lavender Hill, Battersea SW11* ☎ *020/7223–2223* ⊕ *www.bac.org.uk* Ⓤ *British Rail: Clapham Junction.*

Fodor'sChoice **Donmar Warehouse.** Hollywood stars often perform in diverse and daring
★ new works, bold interpretations of the classics, and small-scale musicals. It works both ways, too—former director Sam Mendes went straight from here to directing *American Beauty.* ✉ *41 Earlham St., Covent Garden WC2* ☎ *020/7369–1732* ⊕ *www.donmar-warehouse.com* Ⓤ *Covent Garden.*

★ **Hackney Empire.** The history of this treasure of a theater is drama in its own right. Charlie Chaplin is said to have appeared here during its days as a thriving variety theater and music hall in the early 1900s. Sixty years later its glory had all but completely faded, and it was reduced to operating as a bingo hall. But in 1984 preservationists managed to get the building listed as a grade II historic site and, bingoers evicted, the Empire was resurrected. Badly in need of restoration, once funds were raised it closed in 2001 for a £15-million overhaul and three years later, in January 2004, the curtain went up on the new-old Empire shining again. ✉ *291 Mare St., Hackney E8* ☎ *020/8985–2424* ⊕ *www. hackneyempire.co.uk* Ⓜ *Train: Hackney Central.*

**The Old Vic.** American actor Kevin Spacey is the artistic director of this grand 1818 Victorian theater, one of London's oldest. Legends of the stage have performed here, including John Gielgud, Vivian Leigh, Peter O'Toole, Richard Burton, Judi Dench, and Laurence Olivier, who called it his favorite theater. After decades of financial duress threatening to shut it down, the Old Vic is now safely under the ownership of a dedicated trust and is thriving again. ✉ *The Cut, Southwark SE1* ☎ *020/ 7928–7616* ⊕ *www.oldvictheatre.com* Ⓤ *Waterloo.*

Fodor'sChoice **Open Air Theatre.** On a warm summer evening, classical theater in the
★ pastoral, and royal, Regent's Park is hard to beat for magical adventure. Enjoy a supper before the performance and during the intermission on the picnic lawn, and drinks in the spacious bar. ✉ *Inner Circle, Regent's Park NW1* ☎ *020/7486–2431* ⊕ *www.openairtheatre.org. uk* Ⓤ *Baker St.or Regent's Park.*

**Players' Theatre.** This long-running music hall takes you back to the reign of Queen Victoria. It's quite a hoot—actors in period costume perform bawdy Victorian songs, and the audience joins in the choruses (lyrics are printed in the program). Dinner is served before and after performances in their own restaurant, where you can also have afternoon tea and Sunday lunch; there are also two bars. It's closed Monday. ✉ *The Arches, Villiers St., Strand, Covent Garden WC2* ☎ *020/7839–1134* 🖶 *020/7839–8067* ⊕ *www.theplayerstheatre.co.uk* Ⓤ *Charing Cross or Embankment.*

★ **Royal Court Theatre.** Britain's undisputed epicenter of new writing, the RCT has produced gritty British and international drama since the middle of the 20th century, much of which gets produced in the West End. Don't miss the best deal in town–£7.50 tickets on Monday. ✉ *Sloane Sq., Chelsea SW1* ☎ *020/7565–5000* ⊕ *www.royalcourttheatre.com* Ⓤ *Sloane Sq.*

★ **Royal National Theatre.** Opened in 1976, the RNT has three theaters: the 1,120-seat Olivier, the 890-seat Lyttelton, and the 300-seat Cottesloe. Musicals, classics, and new plays are in repertoire. It's closed Sunday. ⊠ *South Bank Arts Centre, Belvedere Rd., South Bank SE1* ☎ *020/ 7452–3000* ⊕ *www.nt-online.org* Ⓤ *Waterloo.*

Fodor'sChoice **Shakespeare's Globe Theatre.** This faithful reconstruction of the open-
★ air playhouse where Shakespeare worked and wrote many of his great-est plays re-creates the 16th-century theater-going experience. Standing room costs £5. The season runs May through September. ⊠ *New Globe Walk, Bankside, South Bank SE1* ☎ *020/7401–9919* ⊕ *www. shakespeares-globe.org* Ⓤ *Southwark, Mansion House (walk across Southwark Bridge), or Blackfriars (walk across Blackfriars Bridge).*

**Soho Theatre** + Writers' Centre. This sleek theater in the heart of Soho is devoted to fostering new writing and is a prolific presenter of work by emerging writers. ⊠ *21 Dean St., Soho W1* ☎ *020/7478–0100* ⊕ *www. sohotheatre.com* Ⓤ *Tottenham Court Rd.*

**Tricycle Theatre.** The Tricycle is committed to the best in Irish, African-Caribbean, Asian, and political drama, and the promotion of new plays. ⊠ *269 Kilburn High Rd., Kilburn NW6 7JR* ☎ *020/7328–1000* ⊕ *www. tricycle.co.uk* Ⓤ *Kilburn.*

★ **Young Vic.** Big names perform in daring, innovative productions of clas-sic plays. No one sits more than five rows from the stage in this unique theater-in-the-round auditorium. The seats are unreserved; each has a perfect view. ⊠ *66 The Cut, South Bank SE1* ☎ *020/7928–6363* ⊕ *www.youngvic.org* Ⓤ *Waterloo.*

## Contemporary Art

For centuries, Britain has accumulated extraordinary caches of art and housed them in London in national institutions like the National Gallery, the National Portrait Gallery, Tate Britain, and the Victoria and Albert Museum. Include the precious Courtauld and the Wallace Collection and you have an extraordinary treasure trove of Western art.

No less high-profile is London's contemporary art scene, displayed in public-funded exhibition spaces like the Barbican Gallery, Hayward Gallery, Institute of Contemporary Arts, Serpentine Gallery, and Whitechapel Art Gallery. And with the arrival of the Tate Modern, that's even more the case; London now has a flagship modern art gallery on par with Bilbao's Guggenheim and New York's Museum of Mod-ern Art. Since the early 1990s, the contemporary art scene here has ex-ploded, and Young British Artists (YBAs)—Damien Hirst, Tracey Emin, Gary Hume, Rachel Whiteread, Jake and Dinos Chapman, Sarah Lucas, Gavin Turk, Steve McQueen, and others—are firmly planted in the public imagination. This is largely thanks to the annual Turner Prize, which always stirs up controversy in the media during month-long dis-play of the work at Tate Britain.

British artists may complain about how the visual arts here are severely underfunded, and about the rough ride they get in the media, but Damien Hirst is a household name in London, and where else would his 6-meter-high bronze version of an anatomy model fetch £1 million?

Hirst and his Goldsmith's College contemporaries were catapulted to fame in the late 1980s, when they rented an unused Docklands warehouse to put on seminal shows, like *Freeze*. It coincided with a recession that saw West End galleries closing, and a property slump that enabled young artists to open trendy artist-run places in the East End.

West End dealers like Jay Jopling and, in particular, the enigmatic advertising tycoon and art collector Charles Saatchi, championed these Young British Artists. Depending on whom you talk to, the Saatchi Gallery is considered to be either the savior of contemporary art or the wardrobe of the emperor's new clothes. Since 1992, Saatchi has shown several shows of YBA, including the period's most memorable sculptures—Damien Hirst's shark in formaldehyde, *The Impossibility of Death in the Mind of the Living*, and Rachel Whiteread's plaster cast of a room, *Ghost*. The Saatchi Gallery moved into a magnificent new space in County Hall in 2003, joining Tate Modern and the Hayward Gallery on the South Bank, and making it London's premier modern and contemporary art destination.

The South Bank may house the giants of modern art, but the East End is where the real action is. There are dozens of galleries in the fashionable spaces around Old Street. The Whitechapel Art Gallery continues to flourish, exhibiting exciting new British artists. And in 2002, when Jay Jopling moved his influential White Cube gallery into much larger quarters in Hoxton Square, it was widely seen as the final stamp of establishment approval for the East End art scene.

There are hundreds of small private galleries all over London with interesting work by famous and not-yet-famous artists. Check the weekly newspaper and listings for details. The bi-monthly free pamphlet "new exhibitions of contemporary art" ⊕ www.newexhibitions.com, available at most galleries, lists and maps nearly 200 art spaces in London. Expect to pay around £8 for entry into touring exhibitions, but most permanent displays and commercial galleries are free. The **Contemporary Art Society** (☎020/7612–0731 ⊕www.contempart.org.uk), runs bus tours (£20 per person) for serious art enthusiasts the last Saturday of every month (except December), a great opportunity to get the inside scoop on off-the-beaten-track spaces. Book well ahead, as spaces fill up quickly.

**Barbican Centre.** Innovative exhibitions of 20th-century and current art and design are shown in the Barbican Gallery and **The Curve** (☜ Free ☉ Mon.–Sat. 10 AM–7:30 PM). Recent highlights have included the world-renowned photographer David La Chapelle, Grayson Perry's classical yet provocative vases, and architectural designs by Daniel Libeskind, who built the Jewish Museum in Berlin. ⊠ *Silk St., East End EC2* ☎ *020/7638–8891* ⊕ *www.barbican.org.uk* ☜ *£5–£7* ☉ *Mon.–Sat. 10–6, Wed. until 9 PM, Sun. noon–6* Ⓤ *Barbican.*

**The Blue Gallery.** After starting out in posh Chelsea, this slick gallery made the move east to trendy Clerkenwell in 2000. In addition to exhibiting contemporary paintings and photographs, many by award-winning young artists, The Blue Gallery often showcases its own ongoing project (invited by NASA to Washington, D.C. in 1999): striking, large-format photographic images taken from the Hubble space telescope. ⊠ *15 Great Sutton St., Clerkenwell EC1V* ☎ *020/7490–3833* ⊕ *www.thebluegallery.co.uk* ⊠ *Free* ⊙ *Weekdays 10–6, Sat. noon–4* Ⓤ *Farringdon.*

**hammer sidi.** Current and future stars of the contemporary art talent pool are represented at this serious commercial gallery in ultra-hot East London. ⊠ *53 Fashion St., Spitalfields E1* ☎ *020/7377–2137* ⊕ *www.hammersidi.com* ⊠ *Free* ⊙ *Wed.–Sat. noon–6* Ⓤ *Aldgate E.*

★ **Hayward Gallery.** This modern art gallery is a classic example of 1960s Brutalist architecture, part of the South Bank Centre, and is one of London's major venues for important touring exhibitions. ⊠ *Belvedere Rd., South Bank Centre, South Bank SE1* ☎ *020/7960–5226* ⊕ *www.hayward.org.uk* ⊠ *£7* ⊙ *Daily 10–6, Tues. and Wed. until 8* PM Ⓤ *Waterloo.*

**Institute of Contemporary Arts.** Housed in an elegant John Nash–designed Regency terrace, the ICA's three galleries have changing exhibitions of contemporary visual art. The ICA also programs contemporary drama, film, new media, literature, and photography. There's an arts bookstore, cafeteria, and bar. To visit you must be a member of the ICA; a day membership costs £1.50. ⊠ *Nash House, The Mall, St. James's SW1* ☎ *020/7930–3647 or 020/7930–0493* ⊕ *www.ica.org.uk* ⊠ *Weekdays £1.50, weekends £2.50* ⊙ *Daily noon–7:30* Ⓤ *Charing Cross.*

★ **Lisson.** Arguably the most respected gallery in London, owner Nicholas Logsdail represents about 40 blue-chip artists, including minimalist Sol Lewitt and Dan Graham. The gallery is most associated with New Object sculptors like Anish Kapoor and Richard Deacon, many of whom have won the Turner Prize. A new branch down the road at 29 Bell Street features work by younger up-and-coming artists. ⊠ *52–54 Bell St., Marylebone NW1* ☎ *020/7724–2739* ⊕ *www.lisson.co.uk* ⊠ *Free* ⊙ *Weekdays 10–6, Sat. 11–5* Ⓤ *Edgware Rd.*

**Photographer's Gallery.** Britain's first photography gallery brought world-famous photographers like André Kertesz, Jacques-Henri Lartigue, and Irving Penn to the United Kingdom, and continues to program cutting-edge photography. The prestigious annual Citigroup Photography Prize is exhibited and awarded here before going on world tour. There's a print sales room (closed Sunday and Monday), bookstore, and a café. ⊠ *5 & 8 Great Newport St., Covent Garden WC2* ☎ *020/7831–1772* ⊠ *Free* ⊙ *Mon.–Sat. 11–6, Sun. noon–6* Ⓤ *Leicester Sq.*

**Royal Academy.** Housed in an aristocratic mansion and home to Britain's first art school (founded in 1768), the Academy is best known for its blockbuster special exhibitions—like the record-breaking Monet, and the controversial "Sensation" drawn from the Saatchi collection of contemporary British art. The annual Summer Exhibition has been a popular London tradition since 1769. ⊠ *Burlington House, Soho W1* ☎ *020/7300–8000* ⊕ *www.royalacademy.org.uk* ⊠ *£9* ⊙ *Daily 10–6, Fri. until 10* PM Ⓤ *Piccadilly Circus.*

★ **Saatchi Gallery.** Charles Saatchi's ultramodern gallery tends to grab headlines. Even its 2003 relocation to the South Bank was high-profile, the new location seen as provocatively close to Tate Modern. Damien Hirst's notorious shark in formaldehyde is here, as is Tracy Emin's "My Bed" and Chris Ofili's controversial elephant-dung works. ⊠ *County*

*Hall, South Bank SE1* ☎ *020/7823–2363* ⊕ *www.saatchi-gallery.com* ✉ *£8.50* ☺ *Daily 10–8, Fri. and Sat. until 10* PM Ⓤ *Waterloo.*

**Serpentine Gallery.** In a classical 1930 tea pavilion in Kensington Gardens, the Serpentine has an international reputation for exhibitions of modern and contemporary art. Man Ray, Henry Moore, Andy Warhol, Bridget Riley, Damien Hirst, and Rachel Whiteread are a few of the artists who have exhibited here. ✉ *Kensington Gardens, South Kensington W2* ☎ *020/7402–6075* ⊕ *www.serpentinegallery.org* ✉ *Donation* ☺ *Daily 10–6* Ⓤ *S. Kensington.*

Fodor'sChoice ★  **Tate Modern.** This converted power station is the largest modern art gallery in the world: give yourself ample time to take it all in! The permanent collection, which includes work by all the major 20th-century artists, is organized thematically rather than chronologically, and alongside blockbuster touring shows and solo exhibitions of international artists. The café on the top floor has gorgeous views overlooking the Thames and St. Paul's Cathedral. ✉ *Bankside, South Bank SE1* ☎ *020/7887–8008* ⊕ *www.tate.org.uk* ✉ *Free–£8.50* ☺ *Daily 10–6, Fri. and Sat. until 10* PM Ⓤ *Southwark.*

★  **Victoria Miro Gallery.** This important commercial gallery has exhibited some of the biggest names on the British contemporary art scene—Chris Ofili, the Chapman brothers, Peter Doig, to name a few. It also brings in exciting new talent from abroad. ✉ *16 Wharf Rd., Islington N1* ☎ *020/7336–8109* ⊕ *www.victoria-miro.com* ✉ *Free* ☺ *Tues.–Sat. 10–6* Ⓤ *Old Street or Angel.*

★  **Whitechapel Art Gallery.** Established in 1897, this independent East End gallery is one of London's most innovative. Jeff Wall, Bill Viola, Gary Hume, and Janet Cardiff have exhibited here. ✉ *80–82 Whitechapel High St., East End E1* ☎ *020/7522–7888* ⊕ *www.whitechapel.org* ✉ *Free* ☺ *Tues.–Sun. 11–6, Thurs. until 9* PM Ⓤ *Aldgate E.*

★  **White Cube.** Jay Joplin's influential gallery is housed in a 1920s light-industrial building on Hoxton Square. Many of its artists are Turner Prize stars—Hirst, Emin, Hume, et al., and many live in the East End, which supposedly has the highest concentration of artists in Europe. ✉ *48 Hoxton Sq., East End N1* ☎ *020/7930–5357* ⊕ *www.whitecube.com* ✉ *Free* ☺ *Tues.–Sat. 10–6* Ⓤ *Old St.*

# SPORTS & THE OUTDOORS

5

Updated by
Julius Honnor

**THERE ARE THE WIMBLEDON TENNIS CHAMPIONSHIPS,** and there's cricket, and then there's football (soccer), and that's about it for the sports fan in London, right? Wrong. The salaries of professional athletes in the United Kingdom may not be as high as they are in the United States, but don't believe for one second that the British aren't dead serious about sports. When things are going well for an English national team, especially in football, there's a definite "feel-good" factor that envelops the capital.

London is a great city for the weekend player of almost anything. It comes into its own in summer, when the parks sprout nets and goals and painted white lines, outdoor swimming pools open, and a season of spectator events gets under way. If you feel like joining in, the London version of *Time Out* magazine, available in newsstands, is a great resource. On the Web, Sport England (⊕ www.sportengland.org/gateway) has a good database of information on local clubs, facilities, and organizations. The listings below concentrate on facilities available in various sports, and on the more accessible or well-known spectator events. Bring your gear, and branch out from that hotel gym.

## Baseball & Softball

Join in a game on summer afternoons and evenings in Regent's Park or on the south edge of Hyde Park. If you're serious about joining a team contact **BaseballSoftballUK** (☎ 020/7453–7055 ⊕ www.baseballsoftballuk.com).

## Bicycling

London is becoming more cycle-friendly, with special lanes marked for bicycles on some roads, especially in central London, and a growing network of cycle-only lanes, often along canal paths. Remember, though, that it isn't safe to ride without a helmet. If you plan to cycle much in the city, get the excellent London Cycling Campaign maps, with detailed cycling routes through the city. They're available free from bike shops, Tube stations, or by post via the Web site of **London Cycling Campaign** (☎ 020/7928–7220 ⊕ www.lcc.org.uk).

★ **London Bicycle Tour Company,** right beside the Oxo Tower on the South Bank, offers 3½-hour bike tours of the East End, West End, and central London for £14.95. Reserve in advance by phone or on the Internet. You can also go it alone: bikes can be rented for £2.50 an hour or £12 per day (£6 for each subsequent day). Or, if you prefer, there are in-line skates, tandems, and rickshaws for rent. ⊠ *1A Gabriel's Wharf, South Bank SE1* ☎ *020/7928–6838* ⊕ *www.londonbicycle.com* Ⓤ *Waterloo.*

## Boating

**The Serpentine, Hyde Park** (☎ 020/7262–1330) has pedalos (paddleboats), canoes, and rowboats holding up to seven people for £5 per hour, available from February through October, and weekends in November from 10 AM to 7 PM or dusk. You can spend a vigorous afternoon rowing about **Regent's Park Boating Lake** (☎ 020/7724–4069), where rowboats hold up to five adults and cost £5.50 per hour per person, £3.50

FodorśChoice
★

for kids, March through October. Hours vary with daylight and park opening times.

One of London's most beloved sporting events (since 1845) is also the easiest to see, and it's free. The only problem with the late-March **Oxford and Cambridge Boat Race** is securing a good position among the crowds that line the Putney-to-Mortlake route (most gather at pubs along the Hammersmith Lower and Upper Malls, or on Putney Bridge). The Saturday start time varies from year to year according to the tides but is usually around 2:30 PM. The **Head of the River Race** is the professional version, only this time up to 420 crews of eight row the university course in the other direction, setting off at 10-second intervals. It usually happens the Saturday before the university race, beginning at 10 AM; the best view is from above Chiswick Bridge.

## Cricket

Fodor'sChoice ★ **Lord's** has been hallowed turf for worshipers of England's summer game since 1811. Tickets can be hard to procure for the five-day Test Matches (full internationals) and one-day internationals played here: obtain an application form and enter the ballot (lottery) to purchase tickets. Forms are sent out from early December. Standard Test Match tickets cost between £26 and £48. County matches (Middlesex plays here) can usually be seen by lining up on the day. ⊠ *St. John's Wood Rd., St. John's Wood NW8* ☎ *020/7432–1066* ⊕ *www.lords.org* Ⓤ *St. John's Wood.*

★ The **Oval**, home of Surrey County Cricket Club, is an easier place than Lord's to witness the *thwack* of leather on willow, with tickets for internationals sold on a first-come first-served basis from late October. Though slightly less venerated than its illustrious cousin, the standard of cricket here is certainly no lower. ⊠ *Kennington Oval, Kennington SE11* ☎ *020/7582–6660* Ⓤ *Oval.*

## Equestrian Events

RACING ★ The main events of "the Season," as much social as sporting, occur just outside the city. Her Majesty attends **Royal Ascot** (⊠ Grand Stand, Ascot, Berkshire ☎01344/622211 ⊕www.ascot.co.uk) in mid-June, driving from Windsor in an open carriage for a procession before the plebs daily at 2. You'll need to book good seats far in advance for this event, although some tickets—far away from the Royal Enclosure and winning post—can usually be bought on the day of the race for £10–£15. Grandstand tickets, which go on sale on the first working day of the year, cost £52. There are also Ascot Heath tickets available for a mere £3, but these only admit you to a picnic area in the middle of the race course. You'll be able to see the horses, of course, but that's not why people come to Ascot. The real spectacle is the crowd itself: enormous headgear is de rigueur on Ladies Day—the Thursday of the meet—and those who arrive dressed inappropriately (jeans, shorts, sneakers) will be turned away from their grandstand seats.

Fodor'sChoice ★ **Derby Day** (⊠ The Grandstand, Epsom Downs, Surrey ☎ 01372/470047 ⊕ www.epsomderby.co.uk), usually held on the first Saturday in June, is, after Ascot, the second biggest social event of the racing calendar; it's

# A RUNDOWN OF CRICKET RULES

CRICKET IS PLAYED by two 11-member teams on a roughly circular grass pitch about 90 yards in diameter, surrounded by a rope boundary. Most of the action, however, takes place on a central rectangle, 22 yards long. The batting team places two batsmen (batters) at opposite sides of this rectangle; wickets (two bails balanced atop three stumps of wood) stand behind each batsman. The object of the batsman is twofold: to guard the wickets and to score runs. The fielding team's bowler (pitcher) at one end of the rectangle bowls a ball to the batsman at the opposite end, attempting to bowl them out by knocking the bails off the stumps. The ball is bowled overhand with a straight arm (bent elbows count as "throwing," accusations of which are taken very seriously) and is usually bounced off the pitch, which has been hardened by rollers.

The batsman attempts to hit the ball far enough that he and his batting partner can exchange places and score runs. Unlike in baseball, there are no foul lines, so the ball may go in any direction. If the ball crosses the boundary on the ground, the batsman scores four runs; if it crosses the boundary before touching the ground, six runs are scored. The batsman's wicket is taken (he's out) if the bails are knocked off the stumps by the bowler or while the batsmen are changing places, or if his ball is caught on the fly. The LBW (Leg Before Wicket) rule is complex, but essentially means that players can't defend their wickets with their legs or feet. Once a player's wicket is taken, he is replaced by the next batsman.

Unless a batsman is bowled (the bails knocked off his stumps), the fielding team must appeal to the umpire for a decision. This is usually done with an enthusiastically screamed "Howzat?" Increasingly in the modern game, batsmen will wait for the umpire's dreaded raised finger before walking to the pavilion, though it is still considered good sportsmanship to walk immediately if you know you should be out.

An over (six balls) is bowled from one end of the rectangle; then another bowler takes over from the other end and the fielders rotate accordingly. The batting team remains in bat until 10 wickets have been taken (the end of an inning) or until they declare (decide to stop batting and take the field). A team will declare because to win, they must not only score the most runs but also take all of the opposing side's wickets by the scheduled end of the game.

The length of a match varies widely: limited over matches have a set number of overs and are usually one-day events; other county matches last four days, and international test matches last up to five days. A new innovation begun in 2003, and much frowned upon by the old guard, "Twenty20" matches are exciting slogs, where each team has only 20 overs. Rain and bad light frequently stop play, and draws (when time runs out without a result) are common.

also one of the world's greatest races for three-year-olds. Lord Derby and Sir Charles Bunbury, the founders of the mile-and-a-half race, tossed a coin to decide who the race would be named after. It was first run in 1780.

## Football

To refer to the national sport as "soccer" is to blaspheme. It is football, and its importance to the people and the culture of the country seems to grow inexorably. Massive injections of money from television, sponsorship and foreign investors often fail to filter down through the game, leaving some lower division clubs in financial difficulty, but public interest in millionaire players and high-profile foreign stars in the domestic game is immense. The domestic season (August through May) culminates in the FA Cup Final, traditionally the biggest day in the sporting calendar, for which tickets are about as easy to get as they are for the Super Bowl. Increasingly important, the European Champions League, a club competition, brings together many of the world's best players in a quest for Continental glory and riches. The three or four top English clubs are involved. International matches are normally held at Wembley but these games will take place at the country's other top grounds until the rebuilding of the National Stadium is complete in 2006.

For a real sample of this British obsession, nothing beats a match at the home ground of one of the London clubs competing in the Premier League, and a taste of the electric atmosphere only a vast football crowd can generate. Try to book tickets (from about £25 upward) in advance. You might also check out London's lower division games: though the standard of football in Division 3 may not match that of the Premiership, tickets are much cheaper and easier to get hold of, and the environment can be just as fervent. For more information on teams, games, and prices, look in *Time Out* magazine.

PREMIER LEAGUE TEAMS **Arsenal** is historically London's most successful club and, after winning both the premiership and the FA Cup in 2002, threatened to take over from northern giant Manchester United as the team to beat. ⊠ *Highbury, Avenell Rd., Islington N5* ☎ *0870/906–3366* ⊕ *www.arsenal.com* Ⓤ *Arsenal.*

**Charlton Athletic** has more passion than money, and its main goal is to prolong its stay in the top division as long as possible, though they have a habit of outperforming expectations. You can get here by taking British Rail to Charlton. ⊠ *The Valley, Floyd Rd., Greenwich SE7* ☎ *020/8333–4010* ⊕ *www.cafc.co.uk.*

**Chelsea,** adored by a mix of thugs and genteel west Londoners, has long been famous for its showy players and style of play, but also its inconsistent results. This promised to change when the club was bought by one of Russia's richest men in 2003. ⊠ *Stamford Bridge, Fulham Rd., Fulham SW6* ☎ *0870/300–2322* ⊕ *www.chelseafc.co.uk* Ⓤ *Fulham Broadway.*

**Fulham** has relatively little recent experience in the top division, but, with the same owner as Harrods, they certainly possess the money and the self-confidence to stay with the big boys. ⊠ *Craven Cottage, Stevenage Rd., Fulham SW6* ☎ *0870/442–1234* ⊕ *www.fulhamfc.co.uk* Ⓤ *Putney Bridge.*

**Tottenham Hotspur,** or "Spurs," traditionally an exponent of attractive, positive football, has underperformed for many years, and its claim to be London's second team is starting to ring hollow. Take British Rail to White Hart Lane to get here. ⊠ *White Hart La., 748 High Rd., Tottenham N17* ☎ *0870/420–5000* ⊕ *www.spurs.co.uk.*

## Gyms

As you'd expect from the Y, **Central YMCA** has every facility and sport, including a 25-meter pool and a well-equipped gym. Weekly membership is £42.50, a "one-day taster" £15. ⊠ *112 Great Russell St., Bloomsbury WC1* ☎ *020/7343–1700* ⊕ *www.centralymca.org.uk/club/* Ⓤ *Tottenham Court Rd.*

The conveniently central **Oasis** sports center has a gym that costs £5.75 per session. ⊠ *32 Endell St., Covent Garden WC2* ☎ *020/7831–1804* Ⓤ *Covent Garden.*

The day rate is £8 at **The Gym Covent Garden,** a very crowded but happening and super-well-equipped central gym. Many are addicted to the circuit training here, but there are also classes in everything from body sculpting to Pilates, kickboxing to jazz dance. Classes cost £6.50. ⊠ *30 The Piazza, Covent Garden, WC2* ☎ *020/7379–0008* ⊕ *www.jubileehallclubs.co.uk* Ⓤ *Covent Garden.*

**The Peak** is expensive but has top equipment, a pool, great ninth-floor views over Knightsbridge, and a sauna—with TV—in the full beauty spa. A day membership is £40, £35 for just the pool. ⊠ *Hyatt Carlton Tower Hotel, 2 Cadogan Pl., Belgravia SW1* ☎ *020/7858–7008* Ⓤ *Sloane Sq.*

FITNESS CLASSES    **Porchester Centre** has about eight daily classes, from beginner to pro; step, yoga, circuit training, and aquaerobics are included in the mix. All classes cost £4.65 for nonmembers. ⊠ *Porchester Centre, Queensway, Bayswater W2* ☎ *020/7792–2919* Ⓤ *Bayswater.*

**Portobello Green Fitness Club** is under the Westway overpass, and you'll have to battle through flea-market shoppers on weekends to reach these popular classes. Membership is £11 for a day, £30 for a week or £70 for a month, which also gives you access to the squash courts. ⊠ *3–5 Thorpe Close, Notting Hill W10* ☎ *020/8960–2221* Ⓤ *Ladbroke Grove.*

## Horseback Riding

**Hyde Park Riding Stables** keeps horses for hacking the sand tracks. Rates for riding and lessons vary: lessons are £40 per person per hour in a group or £50 privately, £60 on weekends. ⊠ *63 Bathurst Mews, Bayswater W2* ☎ *020/7723–2813* Ⓤ *Lancaster Gate.*

## Ice-Skating

FodorsChoice ★ 🄲 It's hard to beat the skating experience at **Somerset House,** where during December and January a rink is set up in the spectacularly grand courtyard of this central London palace. Adults £9.50–£10.50, children £6. ✉ *The Strand, Covent Garden WC2* ☎ *020/7845–4670* ⊕ *www. somerset-house.org.uk/icerink* Ⓤ *Covent Garden or Charing Cross.*

London's most central year-round ice-skating rink is the **Queens Ice Bowl,** where the per-session cost, including skate rental, is £6, £4 for children and students. ✉ *17 Queensway, Bayswater W2* ☎ *020/7229–0172* Ⓤ *Queensway.*

**Broadgate Ice** is an outdoor rink for skaters of all abilities. It's open between November and April, and costs £7 a session, including skate rental, £4 for children. Call for opening times. ✉ *Broadgate Arena, Eldon St., The City EC2* ☎ *020/7505–4068* Ⓤ *Liverpool St.*

## In-Line Skating

🄲 **Hyde Park** is the place to go for in-line skating at any time, but on Friday keen skaters of all abilities meet for enthusiastic mass skating sessions, complete with music and whistles. If you're a bit unsure on your wheels, arrive half an hour earlier for the free lesson on how to stop. A more laid-back version of the same thing (the Sunday Stroll) runs on Sunday afternoons. *Friday: meet 7 PM, Sunday: meet 2 PM* ✉ *Duke of Wellington Arch, Hyde Park Corner, Hyde Park W2* ⊕ *www.citiskate. com* Ⓤ *Hyde Park Corner.*

## Rugby

An ancestor of American football that's played unpadded, rugby raises the British (especially Welsh) blood pressure enormously. The popularity of the game in the capital is on the up following England's success in the Rugby World Cup in 2003. To find out about top clubs playing Rugby Union in and around the capital during the September to May season, peruse *Time Out* magazine.

★ **Twickenham** hosts the Rugby Union Six–Nations tournament, where relative newcomer Italy joins old-timers England, France, Scotland, Wales, and Ireland. During this competition, held January through March, rugby can rival even football for the nation's sporting attentions, and tickets for these matches are more precious than gold. The domestic Pilkington Cup Final is fought out at Twickenham in early May. Harlequins and London Scottish are club teams that both play their rugby here. To get there, take National Rail to Twickenham station; the stadium is a 10-minute walk away. You can also take the Tube to Richmond and take a bus or walk 15 minutes to the ground. ✉ *Twickenham Rugby Football Ground, Whitton Rd., Twickenham TW2* ☎ *020/ 8892–2000* ⊕ *www.twickenhamstadium.com.*

Rugby League is played almost exclusively in the north of England, but you can catch the one southern Super League team, the London Broncos, at **Griffin Park** (✉ Braemar Rd., Brentford, Twickenham TW8

# CloseUp

## MAKING A BET

Horses, greyhounds, football, and whether it will snow on the roof of the Meteorological Office on Christmas Day are all popular reasons for a "flutter" in all corners of the capital. Now that technology and the abolition of tax on betting has encouraged a massive surge in Internet wagers, you don't even need to leave home to put a pound on just about anything you want, or any combination of likely or unlikely events. If you do, however, you'll find London's ubiquitous bookmakers (Ladbroke and William Hill are the biggest) increasingly comfortable places with live satellite link-ups to sporting events around the world. At both equine and canine racecourses these chains are also represented, but here they struggle to compete for attention with the furious calling and signaling of the traditional bookies.

☎ 0871/222–1132 ⊕ www.londonbroncos.co.uk Ⓤ Gunnersbury or South Ealing; National Rail: Brentford).

### Running

London is a delight for joggers. If you don't mind a crowd, popular spots include Green Park, which gets a stream of runners armed with maps from Piccadilly hotels, and—to a lesser extent—adjacent St. James's Park. Both can get perilous with deck chairs on summer days. You can run a 4-mi perimeter route around Hyde Park and Kensington Gardens or a 2½-mi route in Hyde Park alone if you start at Hyde Park Corner or Marble Arch and encircle the Serpentine. Most Park Lane hotels offer jogging maps for this, their local green space. Regent's Park has the most populated track because it's a sporting kind of place; the Outer Circle loop measures about 2½ mi.

Away from the center, there are longer, scenic runs over more varied terrain at Hampstead Heath: highlights are Kenwood, and Parliament Hill, London's highest point, where you'll get a fabulous panoramic sweep over the entire city. Richmond Park is the biggest green space of all, but watch for deer during rutting season (October and November). Back in town, there's a rather traffic-heavy 1½-mi riverside run along Victoria Embankment from Westminster Bridge to the Embankment at Blackfriars Bridge, or a beautiful mile among the rowing clubs and ducks along the Malls—Upper, Lower, and Chiswick—from Hammersmith Bridge.

If you don't want to run alone, call the **London Hash House Harriers** (☎ 020/8567–5712 ⊕ www.londonhash.org). They organize noncompetitive hour-long hare-and-hound group runs around interesting bits of town, with loops, shortcuts, and pubs built in. Runs start at Tube stations at noon on Saturday or Sunday in winter, and at 7 PM on Monday in summer. The cost is £1.

MARATHON  Starting at 9:30 AM on a Sunday in April, some 30,000 runners in the huge **Flora London Marathon** (☎ 020/7620–4117) race from Greenwich to the Mall. Entry forms for the following year are available between August and October. The Web site (www.london-marathon.co.uk) has details, including pubs and entertainment along the route.

## Spas

★  In the chic Philippe Starck minimalism of **Agua,** the white-drape and high-ceiling rooms are as much a part of the experience as the opulent treatments. Ancient eastern traditions combine with the clean lines of modernity and everything is unfailingly chic. Packages cost from £145 for a combination of three mud, massage, bath or "bed of roses" treatments. ✉ *Sanderson Hotel, 50 Berners St., Fitzrovia W1* ☎ *020/ 7300–1414* Ⓤ *Goodge St.*

An enormous range of facilities and treatments can be found amid the marbled and frescoed elegance of **Champney's Piccadilly,** a health club and spa right in the center of town. Various day packages cost £120–£299 and span the full range of spa treatments from facials to foot massage. ✉ *21A Piccadilly, Mayfair W1* ☎ *020/7255–8000* ⊕ *www. champneyspiccadilly.co.uk* Ⓤ *Piccadilly Circus.*

Fodor'sChoice  One of London's oldest spas, **The Sanctuary** still has the rope swing made
★  famous by a naked Joan Collins in the 1970s movie *The Stud,* and although it lacks some of the modern design aesthetics of others in the city, it retains a slightly dated sense of style. Day membership is £60–£70, or you can soothe away a hard day's shopping with an evening's pampering Wednesday to Friday 5 PM–10 PM for £40. Women only. ✉ *12 Floral St., Covent Garden WC2E* ☎ *0870/770-3350* ⊕ *www. thesanctuary.co.uk* Ⓤ *Covent Garden.*

## Squash

There are four squash courts at **Finsbury Leisure Centre,** a popular sports center in the City frequented by execs who work nearby. You can book by phone without a membership, and you're more likely to get a court if you show up to play during Londoners' regular office hours, or possibly on weekends, when courts are less busy. A court costs £7.40 per 40 minutes for nonmembers (£5 off-peak) and £5.90 for members (£4 off-peak). Annual membership is £36. ✉ *Norman St., Finsbury EC1* ☎ *020/7253-2346* Ⓤ *Old St.*

## Swimming

INDOOR POOLS  **Chelsea Sports Centre,** with a renovated, early 20th century 32- by 12-
ᶜ  meter pool, is just off King's Road, so it's usually busy, especially on weekends when it's packed with kids. Each swim costs £2.80. ✉ *Chelsea Manor St., Chelsea SW3* ☎ *020/7352–6985* Ⓤ *S. Kensington.*

There's a 36- by 14-meter pool for serious lap swimmers at **Porchester Baths,** costing £2.65 a swim, plus a 1920s Turkish bath, sauna, and spa of gorgeous (though slightly faded) grandeur at £18.95. It has separate sessions for men and women. ✉ *Queensway, Bayswater W2* ☏ *020/ 7792–2919* Ⓤ *Queensway.*

INDOOR–OUTDOO R POOLS    **Oasis** has a heated outdoor pool (open year-round) and a 32- by 12-meter pool indoors. Needless to say, both are packed in summer. A swim costs £3.10. ✉ *32 Endell St., Covent Garden WC2* ☏ *020/7831–1804* Ⓤ *Covent Garden.*

PARKS    **Hampstead Ponds,** three Elysian little lakes, are surrounded by grassy lounging areas. Originally the lakes were brick pits, where clay was dug out for making bricks up until the 19th century. The women's one is particularly secluded (though crowded in summer) and is open all year, as is the men's. Opening times vary with sunrise and sunset. The Mixed Pond is open May through September, 7 AM to 7 PM. All have murky-looking but clean, fresh water, and all are free. Less murky is **Hampstead Lido,** open May through September. A swim here is free from 7 AM to 9:30 AM, £3.60 for the day after that. The 1930s Grade II–listed swimming pool is due to start a £2.3 million refurbishment in 2005. ✉ *E. Heath Rd., Hampstead NW3* ☏ *020/7485–4491* Ⓤ *Tube or British Rail: Hampstead Heath.*

☾ **Serpentine Lido** is technically a beach on a lake, but a hot day in Hyde
Fodor'sChoice Park is surreally reminiscent of the seaside. There are changing facili-
★ ties, and the swimming section is chlorinated. There's also a paddling pool, sandpit, and kids' entertainer in the afternoons. It's open daily from June through September 10–5:30; admission costs £3, children £0.60. ✉ *Hyde Park, Kensington W2* ☏ *020/7706–3422* ⊕ *www.serpentinelido. com* Ⓤ *Knightsbridge.*

A Brixton sun trap, **Brockwell Evian Lido,** open May through September, has a younger and more modern feel than its Hyde Park and Hampstead Heath alternatives. Entrance costs £2.50 for a morning, £5 for an afternoon. The easiest way to get here is to take British Rail to Herne Hill. ✉ *Brockwell Park, Brixton SE24* ☏ *020/7274–3088* ⊕ *www. thelido.co.uk* Ⓤ *Brixton.*

## Tennis

★    Many London parks have courts that are often cheap or even free: **Holland Park** is one of the prettiest places to play, with six hard courts available all year. The cost here is £4.80 per game but only borough residents can book in advance. ✉ *Holland Park, W8* ☏ *020/7602–2226* Ⓤ *Holland Park.*

**Islington Tennis Centre** is about the only place where you don't need a membership to play indoors year-round, but you do need to reserve by phone. There are two outdoor courts, too, and coaching is available. Prices range from £16.50 for the indoor courts to £7.40 for outdoors. ✉ *Market Rd., Islington N7* ☏ *020/7700–1370* ⊕ *www.aquaterra. org* Ⓤ *Caledonian Rd.*

A surprisingly large and busy green space, **Paddington Sports Club** has a set of 10 courts. Annual membership at this members-only club is £410 with a £100 joining fee. Use of squash courts and gym is extra. Per-game charges only apply to floodlit games. ✉ *Castellain Rd., Maida Vale W9* ☏ *020/7286–4515* Ⓤ *Maida Vale.*

The **Wimbledon Lawn Tennis Championships** are famous among fans for the green, green grass of Centre Court; for strawberries and cream; and for rain, which always falls, despite the last-week-of-June–first-week-of-July high-summer timing. This event is the most prestigious of the four Grand Slam events of the tennis year. Whether you can get grandstand tickets is literally down to the luck of the draw, because there's a ballot system (lottery) for advance purchase. To apply, send a self-addressed stamped envelope (or an international reply coupon), return the completed application form between August 1 and December 31, and hope for the best.

There are other ways to see the tennis. A block of Centre and Number 1 Court tickets is kept back to sell each day and fanatics line up all night for these, especially in the first week. Each afternoon tickets collected from early-departing spectators are resold (profits go to charity). These can be excellent grandstand seats (with plenty to see—play continues until dusk). You can also buy entry to the grounds to roam matches on the outside courts, where even the top-seeded players compete early in the two-week period. Get to Southfields or Wimbledon Tube station as early as possible and start queuing to be sure of getting one of these. ⊕ *Ticket Office, All England Lawn Tennis & Croquet Club, Box 98, Church Rd., Wimbledon SW19 5AE* ☎ *020/8946–2244* ⊕ *www.wimbledon.org.*

If you don't fancy the crowds and snaking queues of Wimbledon, you can watch many of the top names in men's tennis play in the pre-Wimbledon **Stella Artois Tournament,** though this, too, is usually oversubscribed. Ticketmaster (☎ 020/7413–1414, www.ticketmaster.co.uk) sells tickets. ⊠ *Queen's Club, Palliser Rd., West Kensington W14* ☎ *020/7385–3421* ⊕ *www.queensclub.co.uk* Ⓤ *Barons Court.*

## Walking

There are plenty of possibilities for rambling in the countryside around the city. Generally well-signposted footpaths offer attractive routes through rural southern England. The Chiltern Hills to the northwest, the South Downs to the south, and Kent to the southeast are probably the best areas to try, and are all reasonably well served by local trains. If you want to walk in a group, the Saturday Walkers' Club, based around the *Time Out Book of Country Walks* (£10.99, available from most bookshops), leaves from a London station every Saturday of the year. In the city, attractive routes run alongside Regents Canal and the Thames. To see an alternative London, ⊕ www.londonspy.com details excellent walks, often through distinctly un-touristy parts of the city.

## Yoga

**Life Centre,** London's best yoga school, specializes in the dynamic, energetic Ashtanga Vinyasa technique, though yoga classes also cater to 12 other different types. Beautiful premises enhance the experience. A huge variety of holistic health therapies is available upstairs. Classes cost from £9–£12 and run all day every day. ⊠ *15 Edge St., Kensington W8* ☎ *020/7221–4602* ⊕ *www.thelifecentre.org* Ⓤ *Notting Hill Gate.*

# SHOPPING

Updated by
Jacqueline
Brown

**NAPOLÉON MUST HAVE KNOWN** what he was talking about when he called Britain a nation of shopkeepers. The finest emporiums are in London, still. You can shop like royalty at Her Majesty's jeweler, run down a leather-bound copy of *Wuthering Heights* at a Charing Cross bookseller, find antique Toby jugs on Portobello Road, or drop in on clothier Paul Smith—a fave of Sir Paul McCartney. Whether you're out for fun or for fashion, London can be the most rewarding of hunting grounds.

Shopping in London can be a transforming experience. It's an open secret that Cary Grant was virtually "created" by a bespoke suit from Kilgour, French, Stanbury (the tailors extended the shoulders of his jackets 6½ inches to improve his form and draped the material to slim his hips). Then there was that other fashion plate, the Duchess of Windsor—for at-home style, she couldn't be beat, thanks in part to the soigné accessories she bought at Colefax & Fowler, still purveying the "country-house look" from its shop on Brook Street. Today, London's stores continue to create icons and make styles—as you can see from a visit to Harvey Nichols, shrine of the *Absolutely Fabulous* crowd. While you're seeking the cutting edge, you'll notice that tradition shares the same shelf space. Selfridges, Harvey Nichols, and Harrods, for instance, stock suppliers for the royals, such as Cornelia James, glove maker to HM the Queen. If you have a yen to keep up with the Windsors, look for the BY APPOINTMENT royal coat of arms, which means that this particular emporium supplies Her Majesty the Queen, Prince Philip, or the Prince of Wales—check the small print and the insignia to find out which. More fashionable types will prefer to check out the ever-expanding Browns of South Molton Street (bliss, to label hunters), although the surrounding small stores there and along quaint St. Christopher's Place aren't bad either. The most ardent fashion victims will shoot to Notting Hill, London's prime fashion location and scene of *that* movie. London's emporiums have gifts in every price range. Head to Bond Street or Knightsbridge if you're looking for the sort of thing you would find in every Rockefeller's Christmas stocking; if you're bargain-hunting, try one of the street antiques fairs (it wasn't so long ago that a Wordsworth manuscript was discovered in Brick Lane Market for less than $50).

If you have only limited time, zoom in on one or two of the West End's grand department stores, where you'll find enough booty for your entire gift list. Marks & Spencer is one of Britain's largest, and most beloved, chain stores, legendary primarily for its women's lingerie, its men's knitwear, and its food, good enough to pass off as home-cooked. Selfridges is a splendid pile of '20s architecture that dominates the whole of one block toward Marble Arch and is increasingly fashion-conscious, with independent, hard-to-find labels as well as all the famous names. Liberty is famous for its prints—multitudes of floral designs, which you can buy as fabric or have made into everything from book covers to dresses. It may be hokey, but Harrods is not to be missed; apart from anything else, it's one of the best free shows in the city. And though Harrods trumpets that it can supply anything to anyone anywhere in the world (once, a baby elephant to Ronald Reagan), you can just pick up one of its distinctive green-and-gold-logo totes—a perfect touch of class for your marketing back home.

Apart from bankrupting yourself, the only problem you'll encounter is exhaustion, since London is a town of many far-flung shopping areas. The farthest—in fact on the outskirts of London, at Greenhithe in the county of Kent just by the Thames—is Europe's largest gift to shopaholics, the 240-acre Bluewater. The mega glass-and-steel pleasure palace (with cute Kentish oasthouse roofs) by the water was designed by American architect Eric Kuhne and contains every up-market, high-street, brand-name store, department store, and chain store (more than 320) a shopper could desire. Trains depart frequently from Charing Cross. Shuttle buses go directly to the center from the local rail station.

## Shopping Districts

### Camden Town
Crafts and vintage-clothing markets and shops are clustered in and around picturesque but over-renovated canal-side buildings in Camden Town. They have filled up every available space all the way up to the Roundhouse, Chalk Farm, in this frenetic locale for the world's youth. It's a good place for boots, T-shirts, inexpensive leather jackets, ethnic crafts, antiques, and recycled trendy wear. Things are quieter midweek.

### Chelsea
Chelsea centers on King's Road, which is no longer synonymous with ultra fashion but still harbors some designer boutiques, plus antiques and home-furnishings emporiums. The fashionable section is more off-road Chelsea, toward Belgravia, where you'll find sophisticated artisan fashion in a quiet quarter: bag maker Lulu Guinness (on Ellis Street), hatter Philip Treacy, and artisan perfumerie les Senteurs line up on Elizabeth Street. Farther afield, north of Belgrave Square, is the very eclectic Egg.

### Covent Garden
The restored 19th-century market building—in a something-for-everyone neighborhood named for the market itself—houses mainly high-class clothing chains, plus good-quality crafts stalls. Neal Street and the surrounding alleys offer amazing gifts of every type—bikes, kites, tea, herbs, beads, hats . . . you name it. Floral Street and Long Acre have designer and chain-store fashion in equal measure, and Monmouth Street, Shorts Gardens, and the Thomas Neal's mall on Earlham Street offer trendy clothes for the young street scene. The area is good for people-watching, too.

### Fulham
Divided into two postal districts, SW6 (which is conversely the farthest away from the center) and SW10 (which is the closer, beyond World's End, Chelsea) on the high-fashion King's Road. Quieter than the Chelsea end around Sloane Square, there are many different shops to entice you to spend. Antiques make a presence at Judy Greenwood and Rupert Cavendish, with modern ceramics at Bridgewater and Divertimenti. For cutting-edge style there's Lucy Benzecry's The West Village, Agnés B, and the Conran Shop among many others.

**6**

## Super Shopping Tour

For those who can make their way across the map faster than Napoléon and only have a few hours to spare, here's a suggested plan of action. Just keep in mind that you will return to your hotel room weary and wiped out, and your bathroom scale will show you've become three pounds lighter! Let's start with a great London trademark: **Harrods.** Be there when the doors open—this is one-stop shopping at its best (and one of the city's great sights). If you're chic to the cuticles, then make a beeline for **Harvey Nichols,** just a block away. Harvey Nicks always has the best in modern Brit style, be it couture, menswear, or home furnishings. Want a more traditional gift that would please any Lord and Lady Fitzuppity? Head to the nearby **General Trading Co.** on Sloane Street for that lovely Staffordshire spaniel, or run down to Pimlico to see the objets d'art and furniture of **David Linley,** the most talented royal around. For still more decorative goodies, tube or cab it over to Regent Street—one of London's main consumer hubs—and **Liberty** (which actually helped create the Arts-and-Crafts style of the Edwardian era). High rollers should walk east several blocks to Bond Street, Old and New. Of course, there's nothing like a visit to **Asprey** or the other upper-crust stores here to make you acutely aware of how poor you are. Fashionistas should then stroll up through Mayfair several blocks to the northwest and South Molton Street to find **Browns,** flooded with Kate Moss lookalikes, then head down Davies Street to the couture salon of **Vivienne Westwood.** On Davies Street you'll also find **Grays Antique Market** and **Grays in the Mews**—just the places to find a Charles II silver spoon. For gifts with gentler price tags, tube or cab it south to Piccadilly and **Hatchards**—bookseller to the royals, which still retains a trad atmosphere—or nearby **Fortnum & Mason,** the Queen's grocers, to buy some tea. Speaking of which, head upstairs and collapse for the high tea here, or make a last stop at **Floris,** a few blocks south on Jermyn Street—it's one of London's prettiest perfumeries. Opt for a scent once favored by Queen Victoria or—at almost pocket-money prices—a natural-bristle toothbrush. Oh, yes: if you want to add the very latest stores to this list, check out the suggestions in the monthly glossies, such as the *World of Interiors* "Antennae" section, or the glossy shopping sections in the Sunday newspapers. Whew! As you can see, for out-of-the-ordinary shopping, London can't be beat.

## Antiques

Start early morning around 8 AM (Saturday or Wednesday, when the dealers haggle) and head to **Camden Passage** in Islington, where you can browse through silverware, porcelain, prints, and old books. For under £30 you can often find pretty silver spoons. Take the Tube from Highbury and Islington to Oxford Circus and the **Liberty** Antiques Department, whose top floor has top-scale antiques, the refurbished chairs with the distinctive Liberty print. If you fancy your chances at auction, just a few blocks south is **Sotheby's,** which has some classy pieces, from impressionist paintings to country-house furnishings. You can stop for lunch at the Sotheby's Café, or stride on to **Grays Antiques Market** on Davies Street for smaller, more affordable pieces, such as old jewelry, prints, and ceramics.

Shopping (A):
Mayfair, Soho
& Covent Garden

KEY

U Tube Station

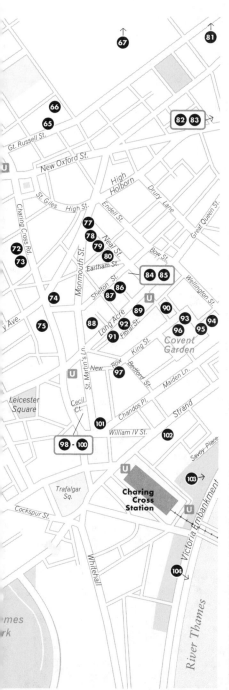

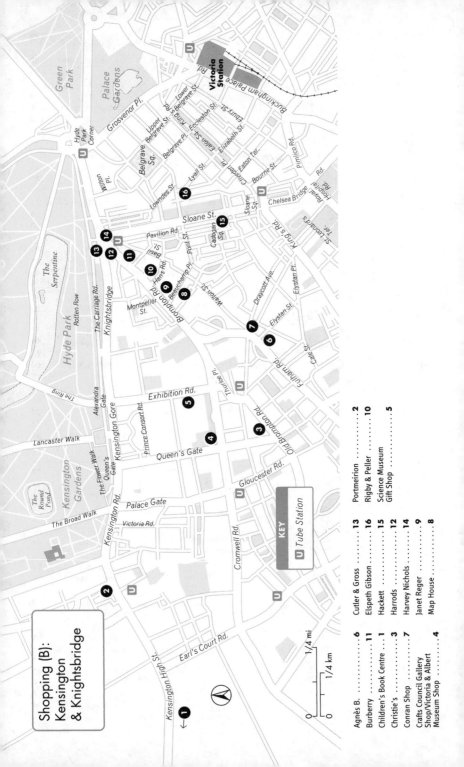

# Shopping (B): Kensington & Knightsbridge

Agnès B. ............ **6**
Burberry ............ **11**
Children's Book Centre ... **1**
Christie's ............ **3**
Conran Shop ......... **7**
Crafts Council Gallery
Shop/Victoria & Albert
Museum Shop ......... **4**

Cutler & Gross ....... **13**
Elspeth Gibson ...... **16**
Hackett ............. **15**
Harrods ............. **12**
Harvey Nichols ...... **14**
Janet Reger ......... **9**
Map House .......... **8**

Portmeirion ......... **2**
Rigby & Peller ...... **10**
Science Museum
Gift Shop ........... **5**

1/4 mi

1/4 km

### Hampstead

For picturesque peace and quiet with your shopping, stroll around here midweek. Upscale clothing stores and representatives of the better chains share the half-dozen streets with cozy boutique-size shops catering to the home and stomach. Little passageways such as Perrin's Walk are great if you're nosing around for antiques.

### Kensington

Kensington Church Street has expensive antiques, plus a little fashion. The main drag, Kensington High Street, is a smaller, less crowded, and classier version of Oxford Street, with a selection of clothing chains and larger stores at the eastern end.

### Knightsbridge

Harrods dominates Brompton Road, but there's plenty more, especially for the well-heeled and fashion-conscious. Harvey Nichols is the top clothes stop, with many expensive designers' showcases along Sloane Street. Walton Street and narrow Beauchamp (pronounced "Beecham") Place offer more of the same, plus home furnishings and knickknacks; and Brompton Cross, at the start of Fulham Road, is the most design-conscious corner of London, with the Conran Shop and Joseph Ettudgui's store leading the field.

### Marylebone

Behind the masses of Oxford Street lies this quiet backwater with Marylebone High Street as its main artery. Restaurants once coexisted peacefully along with delis and practical stores until the arrival of the Conran Shop and Orrery restaurant, which paved the way for a retinue of smart designer furniture stores. Satellite streets now have understated designer women's wear and menswear. Stride along a block or two to Great Portland Street and you'll arrive at the smart Villandry food emporium and the gateway to fashionable Fitzrovia.

### Mayfair

Here is Bond Street, Old and New, with desirable dress designers, jewelers, plus fine art (old and new) on Old Bond Street and Cork Street. South Molton Street has high-priced, high-style fashion—especially at Browns—and the tailors of Savile Row are of worldwide renown.

### Notting Hill

Branching off from the famous Portobello Road market are various enclaves of boutiques selling young designers' wares, antiques, and things for the home—now favored stops for trendsetters. Go westward and explore the Ledbury Road–Westbourne Grove axis, Clarendon Cross, and Kensington Park Road, for an eclectic mix of antiques and up-to-the-minute must-haves for body and lifestyle. Toward the more bohemian foot of Portobello are Ladbroke Grove and Golborne Road, where, in among the various stores, Portuguese cafés, and patisseries, you can bag a bargain. This is a hot treasure-trove area.

### Oxford Street

Overcrowded Oxford Street is past its prime and is lined with tawdry discount shops at the Tottenham Court Road end, but many still flock

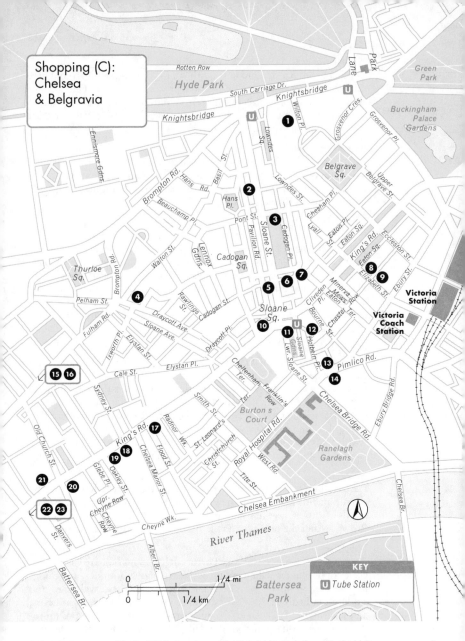

Shopping (C):
Chelsea
& Belgravia

here for some of London's great department stores in the run up to Marble Arch—particularly Selfridges, John Lewis, and Marks & Spencer—and the interesting boutiques secreted in little St. Christopher's Place and Gees Court.

## Piccadilly

The actual number of shops is small for a street of its length (Green Park takes up a lot of space), but Piccadilly fits in several quintessential British emporiums. Fortnum & Mason is the star, and the historic Burlington Arcade is an elegant experience even for shop-phobics.

## Regent Street

At right angles to Oxford Street, this wider, curvier version has several department stores, including the legendary Liberty. Hamleys is the capital's toy center; other shops tend to be stylish men's chain stores or airline offices, though there are also shops selling china and bolts of English tweed. "West Soho," around Carnaby Street, stocks designer youth paraphernalia, which these days is becoming more grown-up and desirable.

## St. James's

Where the English gentleman shops, this district has some of the most elegant emporiums for hats, handmade shirts, shoes, and silver shaving kits and flasks. Doorways often bear royal warrants, and shops along Jermyn Street, like Floris, have museum-quality interiors and facades. Nothing is cheap, in any sense.

# Department Stores

London's department stores range from Harrods—which every tourist is obliged to visit—through many serviceable middle-range stores devoted to the middle-of-the-road tastes of the middle class, to a few cheapjack ones that sell merchandise you would find at a better price back home. Most of the best and biggest department stores are grouped in the West End around Regent Street and Oxford Street, with two notable exceptions out in Knightsbridge.

Fodor'sChoice   **Harrods.** The only English department store classed among monuments ★ and museums on every visitor's list, it hardly needs an introduction. It's swanky and plush and as deep-carpeted as ever; its spectacular food halls are alone worth the trip, and it stands out from the pack for fashion, too. You can forgive the store its immodest motto, *Omnia, omnibus, ubique* ("Everything, for everyone, everywhere"), because there are more than 230 departments, including a pet shop rumored to supply you with anything from aardvarks to zebras on request and a toy department—sorry, "kingdom"—which does the same with plush versions. During the pre-Christmas period and sales—the legendary one is during the last three weeks of January, but another storewide event, usually only one week, is held in mid-July—the entire store is a menagerie. (⇨ Map B) ✉ *87 Brompton Rd., Knightsbridge SW1* ☎ *020/7730–1234*  *Knightsbridge.*

★ **Harvey Nichols.** It's just a block away from Harrods, but it's not competing on the same turf, because its passion is fashion, all the way. There

are nearly six floors of it, including departments for dressing homes and men, but the woman who invests in her wardrobe is the main target. Harvey Nicks is strong on accessories, especially jewelry, handbags, scarves, and makeup. The fourth floor has a chic home-design department, stocking such names as Nina Campbell, Mulberry, Ralph Lauren, and Designers Guild. A reservation at the Fifth Floor restaurant is coveted. (⇨ Map B) ✉ *109 Knightsbridge, Knightsbridge SW1* ☎ *020/7235–5000* Ⓤ *Knightsbridge.*

**John Lewis.** This store's motto is "Never knowingly undersold," and for all kinds of goods at sensible prices, John Lewis is hard to beat. The brother store, Peter Jones, in Sloane Square, has a place in Sloane Ranger history, and you will probably encounter more Barbour jackets, velvet hair bands, and pearls here than anywhere else in town—and that's just on the customers. If you're handy with the needle, John Lewis has a wonderful selection of dress and furnishing fabrics. Many's the American home with John Lewis drapes. (⇨ Map A) ✉ *278 Oxford St., Mayfair W1* ☎ *020/7629–7711* Ⓤ *Oxford Circus.*

Fodor'sChoice   **Liberty.** With a wonderful black-and-white mock-Tudor facade, it's a pea-
★   cock among pigeons in humdrum Regent Street. Inside, it's a labyrinthine building, full of nooks and crannies stuffed with goodies, like a dream of an Eastern bazaar. Famous principally for its fabrics, it also has an Oriental department, rich with color; menswear that tends toward the traditional; and women's wear by the latest names in fashion. It's a hard store to resist, and you may well find an original gift—especially one made from those classic Liberty prints. (⇨ Map A) ✉ *200 Regent St., Mayfair W1* ☎ *020/7734–1234* Ⓤ *Oxford Circus.*

★   **Selfridges.** It's near the Marble Arch end of Oxford Street, where blocks are crowded in the middle of the day and at sale time. This giant, bustling store was started early in the 20th century by an American, though it's now British-owned. If this all-rounder has one outstanding department it has to be its frenetic cosmetics department—one of the largest in Europe—which seems to perfume the air the whole length of Oxford Street. Selfridges has made a specialty of high-profile popular designer fashions. And don't miss the spectacular Food Hall. There's a theater-ticket counter

and British Airways travel shop in the basement. ( ⇨ Map A) ⊠ *400 Ox-*
*ford St., Mayfair W1* ☎ *020/7629–1234* Ⓤ *Bond St.*

## Specialty Stores

### Antiques

Investment quality or lovable junk, London has lots. Try markets first—
even for pedigree silver, the dealers at these places often have the best
wares and the knowledge to match. Camden Passage and Bermondsey
are the best; the Portobello market has become a bit of a tourist trap,
but its side streets are filled with interesting shops that are open outside
market hours (Westbourne Grove is fast becoming the most stylish section of this part of town). Kensington Church Street is *the* antiques-shop-
ping street, with prices and quality both high. If you know your stuff
(and your price limit) head out to Tower Bridge Road, south of the river,
where there are mammoth antiques warehouses, some of which are open
on Sunday. The Furniture Cave, at the corner of Lots Road, Chelsea,
has one of the largest stocks around. Or you could try your luck at auction against the dealers. Summer is usually a quiet period, but at any
other time there are plenty of bargains to be had. Listed here is a selection of the hundreds of stores to whet your appetite. Opening times vary:
many places that are open on Saturday and Sunday will close Monday
or Tuesday.

★ **Alfie's Antique Market.** A huge and exciting labyrinth on several floors,
it has dealers specializing in anything and everything but particularly in
textiles, furniture, and theater memorabilia. You won't be deliberately
stiffed, but it's a caveat emptor kind of place, thanks to the amazing range
of merchandise. ( ⇨ Map A) ⊠ *13–25 Church St., Regent's Park NW8*
☎ *020/7723–6066* ⊘ *Closed Sun. and Mon.* Ⓤ *Edgware Rd.*

**Antiquarius.** At the Sloane Square end of King's Road is an indoor antiques market with more than 200 stalls offering collectibles, including
things that won't bust your baggage allowance: art deco brooches, meer-
schaum pipes, silver salt cellars, and so on. ( ⇨ Map C) ⊠ *131–145 King's*
*Rd., Chelsea SW3* ☎ *020/7351–5353* ⊘ *Closed Sun.* Ⓤ *Sloane Sq.*

**Christopher Gibbs.** This shop attracts leading London tastemakers who
won't make a purchase without Mr. Gibbs's legendary eye. If you're in
the market for large decorative items, such as marble busts, priceless Elizabethan embroidery, and truly one-of-a-kind antiques from all ages, this
is the place to go and dream. ( ⇨ Map C) ⊠ *3 Dove Walk, Pimlico Rd.,*
*Belgravia SW1* ☎ *020/7730–8200* ⊘ *Closed weekends* Ⓤ *Sloane Sq.*

★ **Colefax & Fowler.** The virtual birthplace of the English country-house look,
this is one of the most beautiful interior decorating shops in London.
John Fowler, Lady Colefax, and, most importantly, Virginia-born Nancy
Lancaster together created that cozy yet grand style, and their legacy is
preserved here in wonderful wallpapers, pretty painted-wood flower holders, and assorted antique accents. If you want to make your apartment
back home a mini-Chatsworth, be sure to stop in here, if only to soak
up the style. ( ⇨ Map A) ⊠ *39 Brook St., Mayfair W1* ☎ *020/7493–2231*
⊘ *Closed weekends* Ⓤ *Bond St.*

**Gallery of Antique Costume and Textiles.** Numerous movie directors come here to get the period just right, because everything on the premises, from bedspreads to bloomers, was stitched before 1930—except for the copy-cat brocade vests. Models and Hollywood actors find incredible (and expensive) clothes here, too. It lies off our maps, but it's easily found three blocks north of the Edgware Road Tube stop. ( ⇨ Map A) ⊠ *2 Church St., Lisson Grove, Regent's Park NW8* ☎ *020/7723–9981* ⊘ *Closed Sun.* Ⓤ *Marylebone.*

**Grays Antique Market.** Dealers specializing in everything from Sheffield plates to Chippendale furniture assemble here under one roof. Bargains are not impossible, and proper pedigrees are guaranteed. Also try Grays in the Mews around the corner—it has more inexpensive, downscale merchandise. ( ⇨ Map A) ⊠ *58 Davies St., Mayfair W1* ☎ *020/ 7629–7034* ⊘ *Closed Sun.; closed Sat. during Jan.–Nov.* Ⓤ *Bond St.* ⊠ *1–7 Davies Mews, Mayfair W1* ☎ *020/7629–7034* Ⓤ *Bond St.*

**Hope and Glory.** This is one of the many specialty stores in Kensington with commemorative china and glass from 1887 to the present; there are also affordable lesser pieces. The entrance is on Peel Street. ( ⇨ Map D) ⊠ *131A Kensington Church St., Kensington W8* ☎ *020/7727–8424* ⊘ *Closed Sun.* Ⓤ *Notting Hill Gate.*

**Judy Greenwood Antiques.** It beckons with its glowing red walls and a delightful selection of high-style antiques: Miss Havisham-y settees, vintage fabrics and textiles, gilded mirrors, and side tables. ( ⇨ Map C) ⊠ *657 Fulham Rd., Chelsea SW6* ☎ *020/7736–6037* ⊘ *Closed Sun.* Ⓤ *Fulham Broadway.*

**London Silver Vaults.** A basement conglomeration of around 40 dealers, it's a great place for the average Joe. Some pieces are spectacular, of course, but you can also pick up a set of Victorian cake forks, jugs, cruet sets, candlesticks, and other smaller pieces for lower prices. ( ⇨ Map A) ⊠ *Chancery House, 53–64 Chancery La., Holborn WC2* ☎ *020/ 7242–3844* ⊘ *Closed Sat. after 1, and Sun.* Ⓤ *Chancery La.*

**Rupert Cavendish.** This most elevated of dealers has the Biedermeier market cornered, with Empire and deco bringing up the rear. The shop is a museum experience. ( ⇨ Map C) ⊠ *610 King's Rd., Chelsea SW6* ☎ *020/7731–7041* ⊘ *Closed Sun.* Ⓤ *Sloane Sq.*

## Auction Houses

The pointers on going to auction: you don't need bags of money; the catalog prices aren't written in stone; and if you are sure of what you want when you view the presale, then bid with confidence. Listed below are the main houses, which all deal in fine art and furniture. And if you find these are out of your budget, snoop around Lots Road in Chelsea, where you can find more budget-price contemporary furniture that compares favorably with the price of new.

**Bonhams.** One of the more buyer-friendly places, it has many interesting collections. Along with antiques, Bonhams specializes in 20th-century design. Its merger with the celebrated auction house Phillips, in 2002, has increased the depth and scope of other specialty areas, such as old master painting sales, at the old Phillips's premises in New Bond Street. ( ⇨ Map A) ⊠ *101 New Bond St., Mayfair W1* ☎ *020/7629–6602, 020/*

# FINE FOOD & WINE

**W**HETHER FOR TEMPTING *tidbits for lunch to munch on the move, for picnics in the park, or for gifts, London is a veritable larder with its fine food stores, some of which have been in existence for generations and still retain that sense of old-fashioned personal service.*

**Berry Bros. & Rudd.** *Family run, with casks and carafes galore in the vintage surroundings; to visit is an education. In days gone by, your order would have been preceded by a journey down to the venerable cellars, but now you can choose from the bottles on display. Naturally, the wonderful advice and sampling is accompanied by highly prized—and priced—bottles.* ✉ 3 St. James's St., St. James's SW1 ☎ 020/7396–9600.

**The Vintage House.** *If whiskey is more to your taste, The Vintage House has the country's largest selection of malts, and some are notable by their age.* ✉ 42 Old Compton St., Covent Garden WC2 ☎ 020/7437–2592.

**The Chocolate Society.** *Thank goodness you don't need to be a member to buy some of the irresistible confections on display, from gorgeous handmade chocolates (samples often available), and brownies, which go very well with a cup of coffee here.* ✉ 36 Elizabeth St., Belgravia SW1 ☎ 020/7259–9222.

**Neal's Yard Dairy.** *NYD favors a traditional approach to small independent British cheesemakers. In a cobbled "yard" with neighboring natural and organic shops, you can try a range of produce with names that evoke the countryside, such as Cornish Yarg and Sussex Golden Cross. Good baked breads are also on sale from the Neal's Yard Bakery.* ✉ 17 Shorts Gardens, Covent Garden WC2 ☎ 020/7240–5700.

7393–3900 Ⓤ *Bond St.* ✉ *Chelsea Galleries, 65–69 Lots Rd., Chelsea SW10* ☎ *020/7393–3900* Ⓤ *Fulham Broadway.*

**Christie's.** You'll find some great English country-house furniture in varying states of repair, paintings, prints, carpets, lighting, plus all manner of bona fide treasures. It's amazing what can be classed as infinitely desirable with surprising price tags: the blue door from the film *Notting Hill* and the blue pinafore dress worn by Judy Garland in *Wizard of Oz* went for a record £5,750 and £199,500, respectively. (⇨ Map B) ✉ *85 Old Brompton Rd., Knightsbridge SW7* ☎ *020/7581–7611* Ⓤ *S. Kensington.*

**Sotheby's.** There's a well-publicized calendar of regular auctions for the more well-heeled. But if you just want to look, ponder on possible purchases and break for lunch in the superb café. (⇨ Map A) ✉ *34–35 New Bond St., Mayfair W1* ☎ *020/7293–5000* Ⓤ *Bond St.*

## Books

Charing Cross Road is London's booksville, with a couple dozen stores here or hereabout. The many antiquarian booksellers tend to look daunting (deceptively, as Helene Hanff found by correspondence with No. 84), but there are many mainstream bookshops, too. When the Borders chain burst on to London main streets with its bright lights and coffee, it was a wake-up call for the British Waterstones chain, which is nationwide. Books are big business, and that has been reflected in a welcome number of burgeoning bookstores, both general and specialized, although Foyles is the market leader with its enormous range.

GENERAL
Fodor'sChoice
★

**Foyles.** Only a family-run business could provide so quirky a visit until just recently, but after more than a hundred years in the business, there's a new look to this labyrinthine store. The Foyle brothers began a successful enterprise selling their own secondhand textbooks from the kitchen table, followed that up with a small shop, and the rest is history. Back then, Foyles was *the* best source for textbooks, along with top pop titles and diverse specialist fields—such as illustrated military uniforms through the ages. As befits its century of expertise, the customer list, past and present, is a *Who's Who* of arts and politics. Christina Foyle instituted a literary luncheon, which since 1930 has attracted more than 700 top authors to speak at the ballroom in Grosvenor House; check the Web site or call for details. Since 1999 Foyles has undergone a massive modernization program. Far from catering only to the mass market, as many of the larger chain bookstores have done, the off-mainstream can still be found here. The Silver Moon for women, and Ray's Jazz, are stores within the store. Ensuring refreshment for the body as well as the mind, there's a café.( ⇨ Map A) ✉ *113–119 Charing Cross Rd., Soho WC2* ☎ *020/7437–5660* Ⓤ *Tottenham Court Rd.*

Fodor'sChoice
★

**Hatchards.** This is one of London's well-established bookshops beloved by writers themselves, as it retains a cozy, independent character. You can revel in its old-fashioned charm while perusing the well-stocked shelves lining the winding stairs. The staff has retained old-fashioned helpfulness, too. ( ⇨ Map A) ✉ *187 Piccadilly, St. James's W1* ☎ *020/7439–9921* Ⓤ *Piccadilly Circus.*

**Waterstone's.** For book buying as a hedonistic leisure activity, the monster-size store by Piccadilly Circus caters to all tastes: literally. Previously the fashionable Deco Simpsons store, a sweeping staircase takes you up to the fifth floor Studio Lounge where until 10 PM you can sip a gin and tonic while browsing through a book, admiring the view, or all three. Scholars should head for the Gower Street branch: close to London University, it has a cozy coffee lounge and a comprehensive range of more highbrow books. Waterstone's is the country's leading book chain. ( ⇨ Map A) ✉ *203–206 Piccadilly, St. James's W1* ☎ *020/7851–2400* Ⓤ *Piccadilly Circus.*

SPECIALTY

**Tindley & Chapman.** Previously Bell, Book and Radmall, the range remains the same: it has quality antiquarian volumes and specializes in modern first editions. ( ⇨ Map A) ✉ *4 Cecil Ct., Covent Garden WC2* ☎ *020/7240–2161* Ⓤ *Tottenham Court Rd.*

**Books for Cooks.** With just about every cuisine from around the globe between covers, as well as the complete lineup of celebrity chef editions, it's quite simply the last word in food and cooking. Occasional cookery demonstrations (call for details) offer tempting samples. ( ⇨ Map D) ✉ *4 Blenheim Crescent, Notting Hill W11* ☎ *020/7221–1992* Ⓤ *Notting Hill Gate.*

# YE ODDE SHOPPES

**Anything Left-Handed.** Lefties of the world unite: buy yourself all the elusive equipment you need for kitchen (vegetable peelers, can openers), garden (pitchforks and pruners), and leisure. All these indispensable objects and more are available at the shop for you. ✉ 57 Brewer St., Soho W1 ☎ 020/7437–3910.

**Button Queen.** Much more than your usual display at any department store, this quiet little corner shop (behind busy Oxford Street) has historic buttons from army uniforms as well as sparkly diamanté pieces to parade on party dresses. ✉ 19 Marylebone La., Regent's Park W1 ☎ 020/7935–1505.

**Escapade.** For your alter-ego needs, from Austin Powers to George Washington, you'll find all kinds of wigs, rubber face masks, and costumes galore, supplied by friendly staff who like dressing fancy. Prices start from £30 for costume hire, and you can get wigs and masks for as little as a fiver. ✉ 150 Camden High St., Camden Town NW1 ☎ 020/7485–7384.

**The Kite Store.** Purchase a whimsical kite here and spend a sunny day flying it on Primrose Hill, just north of London Zoo, or better still, Hampstead Heath's "kite hill," or Parliament Hill. There are many different types here to suit different budgets and levels of skill. ✉ 48 Neal St., Covent Garden WC2 ☎ 020/7836–1666.

**Mysteries.** Here you'll find paraphernalia for the upcoming séance, including Ouija boards, magic oils, and how-to books. You can also make an appointment to have your palm read or see your destiny in the Tarot cards. ✉ 9 Monmouth St., Covent Garden WC2 ☎ 020/7240–3688.

**Children's Book Centre.** In addition to children's books, it carries cards and a mass of multimedia. And if that doesn't spark the imagination, there are toys in the basement. (⇨ Map B) ✉ *237 Kensington High St., Kensington W8* ☎ *020/7937–7497* Ⓤ *High St. Kensington.*

**Cinema Bookshop.** It has the subject tapped with a comprehensive selection of old and new books on film from every angle. (⇨ Map A) ✉ *13 Great Russell St., Bloomsbury WC1* ☎ *020/7637–0206* Ⓤ *Tottenham Court Rd.*

**Fisher & Sperr.** If you look hard you could be rewarded with some real finds—secondhand books that time forgot, in an equally historic Georgian high street. The bay shop front displays prints of old London views, and inside is a section devoted to the history of the capital. This store is off our map, 6 ½ mi northeast of Notting Hill. ✉ *46 Highgate High St., Highgate N6* ☎ *020/8340–7244* Ⓤ *Highgate.*

**Forbidden Planet.** Sci-fi, fantasy, horror, and comic books are for sale along with videos, magazines, and models. (⇨ Map A) ✉ *179 Shaftesbury Ave., Bloomsbury WC1* ☎ *020/7420–3666* Ⓤ *Tottenham Court Rd.*

**Gay's the Word.** In the heart of London's gay community is this hot spot for literary and leisure interests, with a good selection of newly published and old books, magazines, and videos. ( ⇨ Map A) ✉ *66 Marchmont St., Bloomsbury WC1* ☎ *020/7278–7654* Ⓤ *Leicester Sq.*

**Marchpane.** It stocks covetable rare and antique illustrated children's books and first editions, from the 18th century to Harry Potter. ( ⇨ Map A) ✉ *16 Cecil Ct., Charing Cross Rd., Covent Garden WC2* ☎ *020/ 7836–8661* Ⓤ *Tottenham Court Rd.*

**Murder One.** This is a must for fans of traditional Agatha Christie novels and techno sci-fi stories; it has everything from crimes of passion to fiendish horror. ( ⇨ Map A) ✉ *71–73 Charing Cross Rd., Soho WC2* ☎ *020/7734–3483* Ⓤ *Tottenham Court Rd.*

**Pleasures of Past Times.** You can indulge your nostalgia for Victoriana here, with a good selection of old and used books. ( ⇨ Map A) ✉ *11 Cecil Ct., Charing Cross Rd., Covent Garden WC2* ☎ *020/7836–1142* Ⓤ *Tottenham Court Rd.*

★ **Silver Moon.** When the shop couldn't pay the rent, the management of Foyles gave it room on the third floor of their building. And it was certainly well rescued, as the largest choice of literature—from politics to romance—for women, by women. ( ⇨ Map A) ✉ *113–119 Charing Cross Rd., Soho WC2* ☎ *020/7437–5660* Ⓤ *Tottenham Court Rd.*

**Sportspages.** It's an excellent place to start your cricket library. ( ⇨ Map A) ✉ *Caxton Walk, 94–96 Charing Cross Rd., Soho WC2* ☎ *020/ 7240–9604* Ⓤ *Tottenham Court Rd.*

**Stanfords.** The shop spread over several floors specializes in travel books and maps. ( ⇨ Map A) ✉ *12 Long Acre, Covent Garden WC2* ☎ *020/ 7836–1321* Ⓤ *Covent Garden.*

**Talking Bookshop.** Just behind Oxford Street, it has the listening scene covered, with a large selection of fiction, autobiography, and famous memoirs—in user-friendly recorded form—in a selection to suit both adults and children. ( ⇨ Map A) ✉ *11 Wigmore St., Regent's Park W1* ☎ *020/ 7491–4117* Ⓤ *Oxford Circus.*

**Travel Bookshop.** A short journey from foodies' paradise (Books for Cooks), this store covers the world on its shelves. It's great for globe-trotters and armchair travelers alike, and was Hugh Grant's bookstore in the movie *Notting Hill.*) ( ⇨ Map D) ✉ *13 Blenheim Crescent, Notting Hill W11* ☎ *020/7229–5260* Ⓤ *Notting Hill Gate.*

**Zwemmer.** There are two locations on Charing Cross Road; at No. 72 you'll find the media specialist, selling books on design and related fields; at No. 80 the range covers cinema and photography. ( ⇨ Map A) ✉ *72 Charing Cross Rd., Covent Garden WC2* ☎ *020/7240–1559* Ⓤ *Tottenham Court Rd.* ✉ *80 Charing Cross Rd., Covent Garden WC2* ☎ *020/ 7240–4157* Ⓤ *Tottenham Court Rd.*

## CDs & Records

The great megastores such as HMV and Richard Branson's Virgin (which began as mail order in the back pages of the music papers) that have taken over the globe started out in London. There are also specialty stores galore for cutting-edge music mixed by club DJs, and for stocking up your own collection of good old-fashioned vinyl records. If, after all this, you need megaselection U.S. style, then Tower Records occupies a prominent position on Piccadilly Circus.

**Black Market.** Indie, house, garage, world—you'll find the hottest club music around. (⇨ Map A) ✉ *25 D'Arblay St., Soho W1* ☏ *020/ 7437–0478* Ⓤ *Tottenham Court Rd.*

**HMV.** Make a special trip to the HMV flagship store for the widest selection at top volume. There are lots of autograph sessions and free shows, too. (⇨ Map A) ✉ *150 Oxford St., Soho W1* ☏ *020/7631–3423* Ⓤ *Oxford Circus.*

**MDC Classic Music.** The helpful staff will guide you without a blink to the best deals, from Callas to Sutherland, and tell you whether the diva was in form. There's some jazz, too. (⇨ Map A) ✉ *437 Strand, Covent Garden WC2* ☏ *020/7240–2157* Ⓤ *Charing Cross.*

**Mr. CD.** This tiny shop stocks a wide selection for all possible tastes. You must delve to find the bargains, but your discovery will likely be worthwhile. (⇨ Map A) ✉ *80 Berwick St., Soho W1* ☏ *020/7439–1097* Ⓤ *Oxford Circus.*

**Music & Video Exchange.** It's fast becoming a destination for seekers of unusual and mainstream chart music. Young aspiring DJs can be seen rifling among the used discs and 12-inch records. (⇨ Map A) ✉ *95 Berwick St., Soho W1* ☏ *020/7434–2939* Ⓤ *Piccadilly Circus.*

★ **Ray's Jazz.** Although Ray used to have his own store, there's no less selection here within the Foyles empire. Not only do you get to buy from a superior selection of jazz and world music, but you can hear live sessions, too, in one of the top jazz spots in the country—all from the comfort of the café. Check the busy events calendar on the Web or by phone. (⇨ Map A) ✉ *Foyles, 113–119 Charing Cross Rd., Soho WC2* ☏ *020/7437–5660* Ⓤ *Tottenham Court Rd.*

**Tower Records.** Despite the fact that it doesn't carry records, its specialty departments are some of the best in London. (⇨ Map A) ✉ *1 Piccadilly Circus, St. James's W1* ☏ *020/7439–2500* Ⓤ *Piccadilly Circus.*

**Virgin Megastore.** This is Richard Branson's pride and joy (though his New York City store is even bigger). It's nice to have it all under one roof, but be prepared for an ear-blasting experience on the massive ground floor, which is stacked with current chart music. Other areas, with jazz and classics, are slightly more relaxed. Computer games are in vast supply. (⇨ Map A) ✉ *14–16 Oxford St., Soho W1* ☏ *020/7631–1234* Ⓤ *Tottenham Court Rd.*

## China & Glass

English Wedgwood and Minton china are as collectible as they ever were, and most large department stores carry a selection, alongside lesser varieties with smaller price tags. Regent Street has several off-price purveyors, and, if you're in search of a bargain, Harrods' sale (usually held during the last three weeks of January) can't be beat—but sharpen your elbows first. And for the latest in sleek Italian, French, and Scandinavian china and glassware, check out the modern kitchenware shops, which stock trendy designers—stores such as Conran shops, Bluebird, Habitat, and Heal's. For handmade, signature glassware, try the London Glassblowing Workshop, which has its own gallery.

**Bridgewater.** This is the home of all those fruit bowls, cream jugs, and cheese platters that grace every country-style designer kitchen in London and the fashionable burbs. In the neighboring Bridgewater Pottery Café, you can create some of your own designs to take home. ( ⇨ Map C) ✉ *739 Fulham Rd., Chelsea SW6* ☎ *020/7371–5264* Ⓤ *Fulham Broadway.*

★ **David Mellor.** It has practical Dartington crystal along with more unusual porcelain and pottery pieces by British craftspeople. ( ⇨ Map C) ✉ *4 Sloane Sq., Chelsea SW1* ☎ *020/7730–4259* Ⓤ *Sloane Sq.*

★ **Divertimenti.** The store sells beautiful kitchenware, unusual culinary gifts—such as spoons made from polished horn—and lovely French pottery from Provence. ( ⇨ Map A) ✉ *33–34 Marylebone High St., Regent's Park W1* ☎ *020/7935–0689* Ⓤ *Oxford Circus* ✉ *139 Fulham Rd., Chelsea SW10* ☎ *020/7581–8065* Ⓤ *South Kensington.*

**Portmeirion.** It's been around for 40 years in its tabletop form (the design inspiration for the signature china is the famed town in North Wales). If you want to delve further into your re-creation of a country kitchen, this is the place. ( ⇨ Map B) ✉ *13 Kensington Church St., Kensington W8* ☎ *020/7938–1891* Ⓤ *Notting Hill Gate.*

**Summerill & Bishop.** A little piece of French country kitchen right down to the ancient black bicycle with basket (which probably contains garlic strings), it supplies French embroidered linen, Portuguese, and Tuscan stoneware, natural candles and soaps, and all manner of authentic designer culinary ware for sleek city kitchens. ( ⇨ Map D) ✉ *100 Portland Rd., Notting Hill W11* ☎ *020/7221–4566* Ⓤ *Notting Hill Gate.*

**Thomas Goode.** One of the world's top shops for formal china and leaded crystal has on display dinner plates designed and made for Dame Nellie Melba, Edward VII, Queen Victoria, and the last viceroy of India. ( ⇨ Map A) ✉ *19 S. Audley St., Mayfair W1* ☎ *020/7499–2823* Ⓤ *Bond St.*

## Clothing

London is one of the world's four fashion capitals (along with Paris, Milan, and New York), and every designer you've ever heard of is sold here somewhere. As well as hosting the top names, though, London retains a reputation for quirky street style, and many an exciting young designer has cut his or her teeth selling early collections at a London street market or on the borders of the central shopping streets—Notting Hill, Islington, East End. Don't just go by the label, and you could be the first to wear clothes by a future star. Traditional British men's outfitters are rather well known. From the Savile Row suit, handmade shirt, and custom shoes to the Harris-tweeds-and-Oxford-brogues English country look that Ralph Lauren purloined, England's indigenous garments make for real investment dressing.

ACCESSORIES **Accessorize.** Shrewd shoppers head here for the latest high-fashion items at low prices. Beady bags, feathery jewels, devoré scarves—clever copies of each season's catwalk versions reach these stores fast. There are branches across town. ( ⇨ Map A) ✉ *Unit 22, The Market, Covent Garden WC2* ☎ *020/7240–2107* Ⓤ *Covent Garden.*

★ **Anya Hindmarch.** Exquisite leather bags and witty, printed canvas totes are what made Hindmarch famous. Her designs are sold at Harrods and Harvey Nichols, but the real pleasure lies in her store where you can see her complete collection of bags, plus her line of shoes, and printed sweaters and tees. ( ⇨ Map C) ⊠ *15–17 Pont St., Belgravia SW1* ☎ *020/ 7838–9177* Ⓤ *Sloane Sq. or Knightsbridge.*

**Connolly.** The leather made by this elite company is the essence of Rolls-Royce elegance and the flash of Ferrari. Drivers leave their vehicles to be made over inside, but you can content yourself with the accessories: a pair of leather driving gloves or a leather driving helmet and goggles. Prices are on a prestige basis—high—although you could settle for a smaller-statement souvenir belt or cuff links. ( ⇨ Map A) ⊠ *41 Conduit St., Mayfair W1* ☎ *020/7439–2510* Ⓤ *Oxford Circus or Bond St.*

Fodor'sChoice **Cutler and Gross.** Couture eyewear that attracts haute celebrities and British ★ aristocrats is the scene here. Optometrists Graham Cutler and Tony Gross carved a niche for themselves in the early 1970s, creating glasses that weren't merely necessities for the short-sighted, but handmade, stylish fashion accessories. They haven't looked back since. Just down the street, at 7 Knightsbridge Green, is Cutler and Gross Vintage, where you'll find Cutler and Gross vintage specs, as well as YSL, Pucci, and others. ( ⇨ Map B) ⊠ *16 Knightsbridge Green, Knightsbridge SW1* ☎ *020/ 7581–2250* Ⓤ *Knightsbridge.*

**Georgina von Etzdorf.** Made with finely woven metallic threads and delicate clusters of trapped fibers, Etzdorf's scarves and stoles give any outfit a million-dollar shimmer through the night. Too way-out? Then drool over sumptuous deep-color devoré velvets and crushed silks (there are irresistible silk ties for men). Phosphorescent designs stretch to bags, shoes, and the most gorgeous jackets. ( ⇨ Map C) ⊠ *4 Ellis St., Chelsea SW1* ☎ *020/7259–9715* Ⓤ *Sloane Sq.*

**Herbert Johnson.** This store is one of a handful of gentlemen's hatters who still know how to construct deerstalkers, bowlers, flat caps, and panamas—all the classic headgear, with some Ascot-worthy hats for women, too. Now part of Swaine, Adeney, Brigg at the same premises, for your complete elegant outfit. ( ⇨ Map A) ⊠ *54 St. James's St., St. James's W1* ☎ *020/7408–1174* Ⓤ *Piccadilly Circus.*

★ **Lulu Guinness.** Bags and shoes of beads, colored silks, and the loveliest designs are the trademark here. Guinness's store is equally girlish and fun (*Vogue* covers adorn a see-through floor), with a downstairs salon where you can take tea while selecting. With boutiques in Hollywood and New York, Ms. Guinness plans to "bag" an increasingly starry clientele—just watch Oscars night. ( ⇨ Map C) ⊠ *3 Ellis St., Chelsea SW1* ☎ *020/7823–4828* Ⓤ *Sloane Sq.*

**Mulberry.** It outdoes Ralph Lauren in packaging the English look. This quintessentially British company makes covetable, top-quality leather bags, belts, wallets, and cases for all sorts of things (even a mobile phone case and a travel case for laptop or computer organizer). Separates in fine wools, fine cotton shirts, and silk scarves and ties have widened the range. Although it's still considered traditional, Mulberry has increasingly been pursuing a quietly modern, international style niche. The boutique-size store remains at St. Christopher's Place; the larger, main store is at New Bond Street. ( ⇨ Map A) ⊠ *11–12 Gees Ct., St. Christopher's Pl., Mayfair W1* ☎ *020/7493–2546* Ⓤ *Bond St.* ⊠ *41–42 New Bond St., Mayfair W1* ☎ *020/7491–3900* Ⓤ *Bond St.*

**Philip Treacy.** This name tops every fashion maven's Santa Claus list. Treacy's magnificent hats regularly grace the pages of *Harper's Bazaar*; one-half Mad Hatter, one-half Cecil Beaton, Treacy's creations always guarantee Making an Entrance. Only the most serious fashion plates need apply, truly: the atelier is open by appointment only. Cheapskates can shoot along to Debenhams department store on Oxford Street, where Treacy has a diffusion line. ( ⇨ Map C) ⊠ *69 Elizabeth St., Belgravia SW1* ☎ *020/7730–3992* Ⓤ *Victoria.*

★ **Swaine, Adeney, Brigg.** It's been selling practical supplies for country pursuits since 1750. Not just for the horsey set, it has golf umbrellas, walking sticks, and hip flasks, all beautifully crafted and ingenious. One shouldn't be without the umbrella, with slim tipple-holder flask secreted inside the stick, on a frosty morning. Herbert Johnson, hatter, is housed downstairs. ( ⇨ Map A) ⊠ *54 St. James's St., St. James's SW1* ☎ *020/7409–7277* Ⓤ *Piccadilly Circus.*

GENERAL   **Aquascutum.** Known for its classic raincoats, it also stocks the garments to wear underneath, for both men and women. Their styles keep up with the times but are firmly on the safe side, making this a good bet for solvent professionals with an anti-fashion-victim attitude. ( ⇨ Map A) ⊠ *100 Regent St., Soho W1* ☎ *020/7675–8200* Ⓤ *Piccadilly Circus.*

**Burberry.** It tries to evoke an English Heritage feeling, with mahogany closets and stacks of neatly folded merchandise adorned with the trademark "Burberry Check" tartan. In addition to being seen on those famous raincoat linings, the tartan graces scarves, umbrellas, and even pots of passion-fruit curd and tins of shortbread. ( ⇨ Map B) ⊠ *2 Brompton Rd., Knightsbridge SW1* ☎ *020/7581–2151* Ⓤ *Knightsbridge* ⊠ *21–23 New Bond St., Mayfair W1* ☎ *020/7839–5222* Ⓤ *Piccadilly Circus.*

**Debenhams.** This is one of the large department stores lining Oxford Street that has moved up the fashion stakes. Years ago it wasn't on the hip shoppers' map, but with the arrival of the pretty, affordable Jasper Conran collection, wise buying gals soon homed in. Other big names to join the store are Ben de Lisi and Lulu Guinness, with Ozwald Boateng for the boys (and other creations, by in-house designers, are desirable, too). ( ⇨ Map A) ⊠ *334–348 Oxford St., Mayfair W1* ☎ *020/ 7580–3000* Ⓤ *Oxford Circus.*

**Favourbrook.** It tailors exquisite handmade vests, jackets, and dresses, all crafted from silks and brocades, velvets and satins, embroidered linens and chenilles. For ties and cummerbunds as well, men should stock up at 19–21 Jermyn Street, but from both branches you can order your own *Four Weddings and a Funeral* outfit. ( ⇨ Map A) ⊠ *18 Piccadilly Arcade, St. James's W1* ☎ *020/7491–2331* Ⓤ *Piccadilly Circus.*

**Holland & Holland.** At this place for the hunting-and-shooting fraternity, bespoke is the byword. It has everything from guns (by appointment to the Duke of Edinburgh and the Prince of Wales) to clothing requirements for hunting, all with the Holland & Holland brand label. Tailor-made travel wear (especially of the adventure variety) is also available. The company has been in business since 1830 (rifles have been made by the same London factory since 1835) but was bought out by Chanel—a reason for the brighter, trendy yet practical separates aimed at the younger country set. "Sloane rangers" have their own branch at 171–172 Sloane

Street. (⇨ Map A) ✉ *31–33 Bruton St., Mayfair W1* ☎ *020/7499–4411* Ⓤ *Bond St.*

**Jigsaw.** It's popular for separates that don't sacrifice quality to fashion and suits women from their twenties to their forties. There's a men's branch on Bruton Street, W1, and other branches are found across town. There's a wonderful vintage line, and kids get in on the act, too, with their own line, Jigsaw Junior. (⇨ Map A) ✉ *126–127 New Bond St., Mayfair W1* ☎ *020/7491–4484* Ⓤ *Bond St.*

★ **Marks & Spencer.** A major chain of stores that's an integral part of the British way of life, it sells sturdy practical clothes, good-quality knitwear, and basic accessories, all at moderate, though not bargain-basement, prices. "Marks and Sparks," as it's popularly known, has never been renowned for its high style, though that's changing as it continues to bring in big-name designers to spice up its lines. Even famous footballer dad David Beckham has made a design contribution to childrenswear. Check out the Autograph line—highly regarded by fashion writers. Whatever the latest moves, it *is* renowned for its underwear; the British all buy theirs here. The Marble Arch branch has the highest stock turnover of any shop in the land. (⇨ Map A) ✉ *458 Oxford St., main store, Mayfair W1* ☎ *020/7935–7954* Ⓤ *Marble Arch.*

**Muji.** This exponent of no-frills lifestyle has functional white cotton T-shirts, simply cut underwear, pants in neutral and plain colors, and navy-and-black sweaters that are all extremely popular. The merchandise is in complete harmony: white earthenware tableware on minimal steel shelving, cream duvets on understated maple beds, gray towels and skin-care products in white recyclable containers—it's a lifestyle dream that defies the cumulative heaps in most mortals' homes. Branches are as follows: 187 Oxford Street, W1; 135 Long Acre, Covent Garden, WC2; 157 Kensington High Street, W8; 77 King's Road, Chelsea, SW3. (⇨ Map A) ✉ *Unit 5, 6–17 Tottenham Court Rd., Bloomsbury W1* ☎ *020/7436–1779* Ⓤ *Tottenham Court Rd.*

**Next.** This consistently popular upmarket fashion chain store is a welcome feature on most high streets throughout the country, and London has its share with branches in most of the main shopping streets and throughout the suburbs. It carries clothing for men, women, and children that gives Gap a run for its money. (⇨ Map A) ✉ *203 Oxford St., Soho W1* ☎ *020/7434–0477* Ⓤ *Oxford Circus.*

★ **Paul Smith.** He's your man if you don't want to look too outlandish but you're bored with plain pants and sober jackets. Smith's well-tailored suits have a subtle quirkiness (like an outrageous, witty flash of colorful lining); his shirts and ties have a sense of humor; and his jeans and sweats are cut well. Customers include Paul McCartney, Harrison Ford, and David Hockney. The boutique itself is worth seeing: it's re-created from a Victorian chemist's shop, and Smith's own collection of toiletries and jewelry (women are also catered to here) adorns the shelves. The sale shop for discontinued lines is at 23 Avery Row (W1), and the minimalist-style women's store is at 84–86 Sloane Avenue (SW3). Westbourne House (122 Kensington Park Road, Notting Hill W11) is Smith's shop in a house designed to feel like an actual London home where women's, men's, and children's clothes and accessories are arranged in homelike settings. ( ⇨ Map A) ✉ *40–44 Floral St., Covent Garden WC2* ☎ *020/ 7379–7133* Ⓤ *Covent Garden.*

★ **River Island.** With branches throughout the land, this chain targets young and dedicated fashion followers. You'll discover clothes that are as hot as those of close competitor Topshop. Prices are low and commitment to fast fashion is high. Along with this new larger store there's another at Marble Arch, and there are branches throughout town. ( ⇨ Map A) ✉ *301–306 Oxford St., Soho W1* Ⓤ *Oxford Circus.*

★ **Topshop.** Here's one of London's niftiest retail fashion operations for girls and women who still think girlie. Topman is the boys and men's store of the chain. Both have a similar fashion philosophy: to copy catwalk trends and translate the buzz from the street into affordable gear that moves in and out of the store fast. Their own trendy label name is Moto, and they use young top designers, such as Clements Ribeiro and Sophie Kokosalak, so the store keeps one step ahead. You'll find accessories galore, and there's a bead bar for your own do-it-yourself design jewelry. ( ⇨ Map A) ✉ *214 Oxford St., Soho W1* ☎ *020/7636–7700* Ⓤ *Oxford Circus.*

**Zara.** It has swept across the world (the price tags carry 25 flags and related prices) and has won a firm position in London. It's not hard to see why. The style is young and snappy; colors are great, with clothes sorted into color groupings for work and play; and the prices are unbelievably low. However, don't expect durability. These are fun, fashion pieces with a few basics. The whole spectrum is covered, including accessories: beady bags, wacky shoes and boots, and jewelry. Menswear and a terrific line for kids each has its own floor. ( ⇨ Map A) ✉ *118 Regent St., Soho W1* ☎ *020/7534–9500* Ⓤ *Piccadilly Circus.*

CHILDREN'S WEAR
Kids are making it big in retail fashion. Although the chain stores, such as Marks & Spencer and Debenhams, produce sensible and fun collections, the fashion chains offer hipper versions and greater selection. Check out H&M at Oxford Street and High Street Kensington, Next, and Zara, which rival Gap for variety and reduced prices. For the mid-price to expensive range, there's Jigsaw Junior at Westbourne Grove and Hampstead. For ultra-expensive label gear, Harrods and Selfridges give plenty of choice. If you're on the lookout for lesser-known kidswear designers, check out one of the growing number of small boutiques especially for kids, such as those below; kids' clothes are increasingly found in shops for mom, too, such as Cath Kidston and The Cross, both in Notting Hill.

**Daisy & Tom.** This shop is for cool kids and smart parents, who know that a happy child is an entertained child. Sadly there's no designer gear for mom to try on while her child is busy on the carousel, cuddling soft toys, or having a haircut. On one dedicated floor there are high-fashion junior clothes (Kenzo, IKKS, and Polo), shoes aplenty (for newborns to 10-year-olds), a bookshop, and a soda fountain–café. What's more, it's all open on Sunday. ( ⇨ Map C) ✉ *181–183 King's Rd., Chelsea SW3* ☎ *020/7352–5000* Ⓤ *Sloane Sq.*

**Humla.** Set in a Georgian cobbled street in pretty Hampstead village, owner Mrs. Harris's colorful taste of Sweden arrived before superstore IKEA steamrolled in further north of London. Beautifully made, quality children's clothes have been her stock in trade for 25 years, and not so long ago she used to make her own stripey handknits at the back of the shop. That originality is there still, although not her own work. There's also a collection of nursery furniture and timeless wooden toys. The store is in Hampstead, in north London. (⇨ Map A) ⊠ *9 Flask Walk, Hampstead NW1* ☎ *020/7794–7877* Ⓤ *Hampstead.*

**Trotters.** This store is the last word in the latest lines for parents who want to dress their darlings in trad styles, and for cool young things who want to look just that. All the trendy labels can be found here, to cater from top to toe (a hairdressing service is offered, plus shoes with good fitting attendants) along with videos to keep tempers cool, toys, and books. Convenient for style-hunters at the Sloane end of King's Road, and open seven days. (⇨ Map C) ⊠ *34 King's Rd., Chelsea SW3* ☎ *020/7259–9620* Ⓤ *Sloane Sq.*

MEN'S WEAR  Most stores listed above under General Clothing stock excellent menswear. Try Aquascutum, Burberry, and Paul Smith. All the large department stores, too, carry men's clothing, Selfridges and Harrods especially. There's a stealthy revolt away from the bastion of traditional made-to-order suits as young careerists break away from fatherly City-gent tailors. Sharp suiters, such as Ozwald Boateng, are noticeably un–Savile Row in style and demeanor. Those with more flash than cash will hotfoot to the trend-setting fashion chains: Topman and Zara.

**Duffer of St. George.** In addition to having fashions by hip designers of street style, it sells its own label of sporty and dress-up lines for clubbing and posing with attitude. No. 34 is a few paces slower with more everyday wear; city slickers should head to the Savile Row branch (of course) for classic looks. (⇨ Map A) ⊠ *29–34 Shorts Gardens, Covent Garden WC2* ☎ *020/7379–4660* Ⓤ *Covent Garden.*

**Hackett.** Started as a posh thrift shop, it once recycled cricket flannels, hunting pinks, Oxford brogues, and similar British wear. Now it makes its own attire, and it has become a genuine—and very good—gentlemen's outfitter, though polo shirts and faux sports gear are a strong theme. (⇨ Map B) ⊠ *137–138 Sloane St., main store, Knightsbridge SW3* ☎ *020/7730–3331* Ⓤ *Sloane Sq.*

**Kilgour, French & Stanbury.** This classic and highly expensive tailor makes custom-cut suits and shirts (but note the cutters all go to lunch between 1:30 and 2:30 every afternoon). The 11th commandment here: you know a man looks like an English gentleman only when you do not notice that he is well dressed. (⇨ Map A) ⊠ *8 Savile Row, Mayfair W1* ☎ *020/7734–6905* Ⓤ *Piccadilly Circus.*

**Mercer.** Before he got the top job, Tony Blair used to shop here. In trendy Marylebone, Mercer is filled with softly constructed menswear (casual weekend wear, trendy business suits, and a hint of formal evening attire) in more unusual fabrics sourced and made in Italy. The soft tones and styles don't scream fashion but show a quiet cut of confidence. The staff is delightfully helpful. (⇨ Map A) ⊠ *13–15 Chiltern St., Regent's Park W1* ☎ *020/7487–4383* Ⓤ *Baker St.*

**Nick Ashley.** This boutique in one of the coolest areas of shops and restaurants in London, just west of Portobello Road, is in the mold of big-outdoors-goes-urban-cool. Ashley calls it performance wear—whether you're streaking about on a motorbike, loafing about looking cool in the city, or just keeping warm in Egyptian cotton vests and thermal long johns. The laid-back formula of chunky boots, polar fleece, and leather lookalike fabrics brings in the pop stars and young politicos. ( ⇨ Map D) ✉ *57 Ledbury Rd., Notting Hill W11* ☎ *020/7221–1221* Ⓤ *Notting Hill Gate.*

★ **Ozwald Boateng.** It's one of the breed of bespoke tailors, not on Savile Row, but on the fringe. Boateng's made-to-measure suits are sought after (by rock luminaries George Michael, Mick Jagger, Bill Wyman, and even Lisa Stansfield) for their exclusive fabrics, fashionable detail, and shock-color lining as well as great classic cut. If custom tailoring is out of financial reach (upward of £2,000), there's a ready-to-wear collection, or the zappiest ties to be had in town (from £60). ( ⇨ Map A) ✉ *9 Vigo St., Mayfair W1* ☎ *020/7437–0620* Ⓤ *Piccadilly Circus.*

★ **Turnbull & Asser.** This is *the* custom shirtmaker, dripping exclusivity from every fiber; and what fibers, the cottons feel as good as silk. Unfortunately for those of average means, the first order must be for a minimum of six shirts, from around £100 each. But you'll find less expensive, though still exquisite, ready-to-wear shirts, too. ( ⇨ Map A) ✉ *71–72 Jermyn St., St. James's W1* ☎ *020/7808–3000* Ⓤ *Piccadilly Circus.*

WOMEN'S WEAR    London does classic women's wear galore: from timeless Aquascutum and Burberry to the high-style department stores, such as Harrods and Harvey Nichols. For fast off-the-catwalk fashion at fast off-the-peg prices you cannot beat H&M, River Island, and Topshop, all covered in the General clothing section. At the lower-price end of the spectrum, H&M resembles a wild jumble sale as customers sift through hangers whose content changes almost weekly. For mid-price clothes, if you're over 30, Next, and Marks & Spencer, and department stores such as Debenhams and John Lewis, are always fruitful hunting grounds. Hot on the heels of the successful Spanish international chain, Zara, is Mango, for top-style fashion at lower prices.

★ **Agnès B.** It has pretty, understated French clothing: many items are timelessly perfect, like fine knitwear and feminine cotton tops. Prices are mid-range and worthy for the quality—Ms. B. has been a stalwart of the fashion press for years. There are branches at 41 Marylebone High Street, Marylebone W1, 58–62 Heath Street, Hampstead NW3, and 35–36 Floral Street, Covent Garden WC2, which has elegant men's suits. ( ⇨ Map B) ✉ *111 Fulham Rd., South Kensington SW3* ☎ *020/ 7225–3477* Ⓤ *S. Kensington.*

**Brora.** You'll find the very latest in cashmere and *those* shawls (pashminas, of course) here. There are prettily dressed-up camisoles, jumpers, and cardigans, practical pants, and noncashmere items as well (picnic blankets and wash bags). Prices are surprisingly mid-range for such high-fashion products. There are branches at 66 Ledbury Road (Notting Hill W11) and 81 Marylebone High Street (Marylebone W1). ( ⇨ Map C) ✉ *344 King's Rd., Chelsea SW3* ☎ *020/7352–3697* Ⓤ *Sloane Sq.*

★ **Browns.** It was the first notable store to populate South Molton Street, and it seems to sprout more offshoots every time you visit it. Well-established, collectible designers (Donna Karan, Romeo Gigli, Jasper

Conran, Jil Sander, Yohji Yamamoto) rub shoulder pads here with younger, funkier names (Dries Van Noten, Clements Ribeiro, Anne Demeulemeester, Hussein Chalayan), and Browns also has its own label. Its July and January sales are famed. Menswear gets a corner, too. Bargain hunters should hotfoot it down to Browns Labels for Less at No. 50. A branch of mainstream Browns is at 6C Sloane Street (Knightsbridge SW1). ( ⇨ Map A) ⊠ *23–27 S. Molton St., Mayfair W1* ☎ *020/ 7491–7833* Ⓤ *Bond St.*

**Cath Kidston.** This store brings charming ginghams and flower-sprig cotton prints to housecoats (with matching bed linens, cushions, wallpaper, and bath wear) and nightshirts. In fact, Kidston has everything you could want for a girl's bedroom in an English country cottage. The sweaters are practical, cozy handknits; the Anonymous line includes skimpy lace-edge vest tops and cardigans, and skirts in flouncy wools. There's a delightful children's wear line in the same nostalgic vein. ( ⇨ Map D) ⊠ *8 Clarendon Cross, Notting Hill W11* ☎ *020/7221–4000* Ⓤ *Notting Hill Gate.*

**Droopy & Browns.** Beautifully constructed, extravagantly theatrical frocks and suits, made up in raw silks, fine linens, brocades, and velvets can be found here. Colors are strong, tailoring is impeccable, and salespeople don't turn up their noses at larger ladies. ( ⇨ Map A) ⊠ *99 St. Martin's La., Covent Garden WC2* ☎ *020/7379–4514* Ⓤ *Leicester Sq.*

**Egg.** The loosely ethnic work wear in limited colors with minimal, almost-no-fashion details is a winner. Maureen Doherty (cofounder) worked for Issey Miyake, so you get the idea. The off-street address and locale add to the shop's interest factor: a former Victorian dairy tucked away in a Knightsbridge mews. ( ⇨ Map C) ⊠ *36 Kinnerton St., Belgravia SW1* ☎ *020/7235–9315* Ⓤ *Knightsbridge.*

**Elspeth Gibson.** It's been building up a steady following as the firm favorite of models and personalities in the glossy mags and Sunday supplements: these clothes are for the flaunty girlie in you. There are delicate beads on soft cardies; swirly, flirty, embroidered Tyrol-type skirts; and simply herds of cashmere. It's so exclusive, you may try on creations by appointment only. ( ⇨ Map B) ⊠ *7 Pont St., Knightsbridge SW1* ☎ *020/ 7235–0601* Ⓤ *Knightsbridge.*

★ **Fenwick.** Around for years in a prime fashion spot, this shop manages to be very competitive. At sale time, it's a bargain one-stop shop, with a vast selection of bags, gloves, scarves, and shoes, and with a good selection of designers on the upper floors: Ben de Lisi, Jean Muir, Christian Lacroix, and Katherine Hamnett to name a few. ( ⇨ Map A) ⊠ *63 New Bond St., Mayfair W1* ☎ *020/7629–9161* Ⓤ *Bond St.*

**Ghost.** This store can be found with regularity in the fashion press. The design team, led by Tania Sarne, has the feel of the moment, producing willowy dresses and skirts in silks, velvets, and the ubiquitous viscose, which sculpts into wonderful crinkly textures. Indispensable little cardigans in silky weaves have been the wardrobe essential for quite some time and show no signs of fading. Pretty puff-sleeve blouses are also a strong feature. It's also at 14 Hinde Street, Marylebone W1. ( ⇨ Map D) ⊠ *36 Ledbury Rd., Notting Hill W1* ☎ *020/7229–1057* Ⓤ *Notting Hill Gate.*

**Janet Reger.** It's queen of the silk teddy, having become synonymous with the ultimate in luxurious negligees and lingerie many years ago. ( ⇨ Map B) ⊠ *2 Beauchamp Pl., Knightsbridge SW3* ☎ *020/7584–9360* Ⓤ *Knightsbridge.*

**Karen Millen.** Striking a clever balance between functional working clothes with subtle fashion detailing (muted pastels and soft colors in separates), fun urban weekend wear (leather biker jackets and black-and-white ponyskin coats), and glam for evenings (little dresses with Japanese almond-sprig detail), Millen appeals to all from grown-up teens through women in their forties. Mid-range prices are also a draw. ( ⇨ Map A) ⊠ *262–264 Regent St., Soho W1* ☎ *020/7287–6158* Ⓤ *Oxford Circus.*

★ **Koh Samui.** It stocks the clothing and accessories—some still steaming off the catwalk—of around 40 young designers, most of them British, some exclusive to this store, and all on the cutting edge. There are small items for under ten pounds (eclectic hair clips by Japanese designer Heesoo) and drop-dead dresses for thousands of pounds (an exquisite hand-beaded dress by Berardi for £4,500). KS is the place to discover the next wave before *Vogue* gets the story. ( ⇨ Map A) ⊠ *65 Monmouth St., Covent Garden WC2* ☎ *020/7240–4280* Ⓤ *Covent Garden.*

**Laura Ashley.** The country dresses, blouses, and skirts, plus wallpapers and fabrics in dateless patterns that rely heavily on flowers, fruit, leaves, or just plain stripes, have captured the nostalgic imagination of the world. ( ⇨ Map A) ⊠ *256–258 Regent St., main store, Soho W1* ☎ *020/ 7437–9760* Ⓤ *Oxford Circus.*

**Margaret Howell.** Along with Paul Smith, Margaret Howell is the top exponent of Britishness in the Far East. Think classic fabrics—wools, silks—and perfect detail. It's the ultimate in investment, one-stop shopping. ( ⇨ Map A) ⊠ *34 Wigmore St., Soho W1* ☎ *020/7009–9009* Ⓤ *Oxford Circus.*

**Nicole Farhi.** This is the place for the career woman who requires quality, cut, *and* style in a suit, plus weekend wear in summer linens and silks, or winter hand-knit woolens. Prices are on the high side, but there's some affordable wear as well, especially the sporty, casual Diversion label. Farhi offers an equally desirable men's line at 11 Floral Street, Covent Garden WC2. Further outlets for women are also at Unit 15, The Piazza, Covent Garden WC2; 193 Sloane Street, Belgravia SW1; and farther afield at 27 Hampstead High Street, Hampstead NW3. The downstairs in-store restaurant, **Nicole's** (☎ 020/7499–8408), is not just somewhere to resuscitate between purchases: Ms. Farhi designed the space and the menu to her own taste, and it's an extension of the fashion statement, a hot spot for lunching fashionistas who like to be seen. It's wise to reserve ahead. ( ⇨ Map A) ⊠ *158 New Bond St., Mayfair W1* ☎ *020/7499–8368* Ⓤ *Bond St.*

**Oasis.** Good interpretations of designer trends are the stock in trade here. The latest colors and fabrics—from neutrals and brights to heavy jacquards and microfibers, whatever's hot on the catwalk—are translated into pared-down versions that suit all pockets. ( ⇨ Map A) ⊠ *13 James St., Covent Garden WC2* ☎ *020/7240–7445* Ⓤ *Covent Garden.*

**Rigby & Peller.** It's for those who love pretty lingerie. Many of the luxurious makes are here: La Perla and Gottex, as well the corsetières' own line. But if the right fit eludes, have one made to measure. Most of the young royal and aristo ladies buy here, not just because the store holds the royal appointment but because the quality and service are excellent, and much friendlier than you might expect. There's also a branch at 22A Conduit Street, off New Bond Street, Mayfair W1. ( ⇨ Map B) ✉ *2 Hans Rd., Knightsbridge SW3* ☎ *020/7589–9293* Ⓤ *Knightsbridge.*

**Shirtsmith.** Custom-made and ready-made shirts, suits, and jackets for women, using fine cottons and Indian silks are the staple here. Some designs are classic and fitted; others are slightly outrageous. ( ⇨ Map D) ✉ *2A Ledbury Mews N, Notting Hill W11* ☎ *020/7229–3090* Ⓤ *Notting Hill Gate.*

**Vivienne Westwood.** If you want to see where it all started, the Pompadour-punk ball gowns, Lady Hamilton vest coats, and foppish landmark getups are the core of Westwood's first boutique at 430 King's Road, Chelsea SW3. The designer still represents the apex of high-style British couture, and the Davies Street boutique sells the Gold Label line of intoxicatingly glamorous creations: ready-to-wear or made-to-measure. At 44 Conduit Street, Mayfair W1, the story is the sharper Red Line: hot, pared-down catwalk versions; menswear is also offered here—the Westwood influence is far-reaching. ( ⇨ Map A) ✉ *6 Davies St., Mayfair W1* ☎ *020/7629–3757* Ⓤ *Bond St.*

**Whistles.** This small chain stocks its own high-fashion, mid-price label, plus several selected eclectic designers. Clothes are hung in color-coordinated groupings in shops that resemble designers' ateliers. Other branches are at: The Market, Covent Garden, WC2, and Heath Street, Hampstead NW3. ( ⇨ Map A) ✉ *12 St. Christopher's Pl., Mayfair W1* ☎ *020/7487–4484* Ⓤ *Bond St.*

## Design

There's been a tremendous resurgence of interest in objects not mass-produced. The burgeoning market areas such as Spitalfields, the state-of-the-art OXO Tower, and Lesley Craze have become the new, eclectic fashion suppliers of jewelry, clothes, and housewares, and often to personal order. These sites are not in a central place. If you can't stretch out to these areas, then a good starting point is the Crafts Council Gallery Shop within the Victoria & Albert Museum. But forget the outmoded word "crafts"—this work is often more modern than modems.

**Contemporary Applied Arts.** Expect to see quite a range of work by designers and craftspeople. Regular shows and exhibitions display anything from glassware and jewelry to furniture and lighting. ( ⇨ Map A) ✉ *2 Percy St., Soho W1* ☎ *020/7436–2344* Ⓤ *Tottenham Court Rd.*

★ **Contemporary Ceramics.** Formed by some of the best British potters as a cooperative venture to market their wares, this modernized store carries a wide spectrum of pottery, from thoroughly practical pitchers, plates, and bowls to ceramic sculptures. It's possibly the best selection of ceramics to be found in central London (just behind Oxford Street), with each piece carrying its own biography. There are lots of books on the art as well. Prices range from the reasonable to way up. ( ⇨ Map A) ✉ *7 Marshall St., Soho W1* ☎ *020/7437–7605* Ⓤ *Oxford Circus.*

**Crafts Council Gallery Shop/Victoria & Albert Museum Shop.** This is where you'll find a microcosmic selection of British craftspeople's work (jewelry, glass, ceramics, toys). Accompanying the exhibitions in the museum are more focused displays, such as the Summer Show showcase. The Crafts Council has a smaller shop at its base in Islington, where you can source information on craftspeople and browse in the showcase gallery. ( ⇨ Map B) ✉ *Cromwell Rd., South Kensington SW7* ☎ *020/7589–5070* Ⓤ *S. Kensington* ✉ *44A Pentonville Rd., Islington N1* ☎ *020/7806–2559* Ⓤ *Angel.*

**David Linley Furniture.** This outpost for Viscount Linley—the only gentleman in the kingdom who can call the queen "Auntie" and, more importantly, one of the finest furniture designers of today—has heirlooms of the future; the desks and chairs have one foot in the 18th century, another in the 21st. The large pieces are suitably expensive, but small desk accessories and objets d'art are also available. ( ⇨ Map C) ✉ *60 Pimlico Rd., Chelsea SW1* ☎ *020/7730–7300* Ⓤ *Sloane Sq.*

**Designers Guild.** Tricia Guild shows her fabrics and accessories of fabulous, saturated colors here. Inspirational, many designers vouch; and she has now incorporated furniture, objets d'art, and linens. ( ⇨ Map C) ✉ *267–271 and 275–277 King's Rd., Chelsea SW3* ☎ *020/7351–5775* Ⓤ *Sloane Sq.*

★ **Lesley Craze Gallery.** This gallery has made quite a name for itself. Craze has cornered a design market in a fashionable corner on the edge of the city. You'll find the most exquisite jewelry to drool over, by some 100 young British designers (fashion editors source upcoming talent here for their glossy spreads). The adjacent Craze Two specializes in nonprecious metals and sumptuous scarves and textiles by design graduates—tomorrow's craze today. ( ⇨ Map A) ✉ *33–35 Clerkenwell Green, East End EC1* ☎ *020/7608–0393* Ⓤ *Farringdon.*

**London Glassblowing Workshop.** Glassblowers and designers make decorative and practical pieces on site. The artists are British-based and display their work in the gallery. If you visit on weekdays, you can see them at work, and buy or commission your own variation. Prices can go into the thousands, but there are Saturday sales in April, July, November, and December, when many pieces go for less than £30. In the Leathermarket, which is off our map, you can find other craftspeople as well, most notably a silversmith and papermaker. ( ⇨ Map A) ✉ *7 The Leathermarket, Weston St., South Bank SE1* ☎ *020/7403–2800* Ⓤ *London Bridge.*

**OXO Tower.** Many and varied artisans have to pass rigorous selection procedures to set up in the prime riverside workshops and make, display, and sell their work. The workshops are glass-walled, and you're invited in, even if you're just browsing. You can commission, too—anything from a cushion cover to custom-made jewelry, furniture, and sculpture. There are 23 studios in all, over two floors. The trendy Oxo Tower Brasserie & Restaurant is on the top floor, with a fantastic view across the river. There's also a public terrace where you can take in the view. You'll find more craftspeople at Gabriel's Wharf, next door. ( ⇨ Map A) ✉ *Bargehouse St., South Bank SE1* ☎ *020/7401–2255* Ⓤ *Southwark.*

**Themes & Variations.** The name encapsulates what you'll encounter here: a selection of styles, ranging from post-war to new-wave, with a permanent selection of Fornasetti furnishings. (⇨ Map D) ⊠ *231 Westbourne Grove, Notting Hill W11* ☏ *020/7727–5531* Ⓤ *Notting Hill Gate.*

**Walter Castellazzo Design.** Castellazzo has been getting lots of notice in the glossy interiors press with his very individual designs of modern-Gothic painted furniture. His signature style is the tall bookcase with its gently curving pointed apex. A similar theme is used for wall and corner cabinets and mirrors. Castellazzo's shelves are filled with other craft designers' work: silk purses, metallic cushions, jewelry. Castellazzo will work on your commissions, from space-capsule bunk beds to whatever a young space cadet could want to hold his stuff. The store is off our map, in the center of Georgian Highgate Village close to the Gothic Highgate Cemetery. ⊠ *84 Highgate High St., Highgate N6* ☏ *020/8340–3001* Ⓤ *Archway or Highgate, then bus.*

## Food Halls & Stores

London excels at posh nosh, and the place with the widest selection of all is Harrods' Food Halls. Even if you don't actually buy one of the beautifully packaged teas, chocolates, or biscuits (though it's hard to resist), you can salivate at the gorgeous displays, from freshly caught fish to furry and feathered game, which are as much akin to art as food. Selfridges is the department store that comes in a close second. It's not as daunting, specializing in more streamlined self-service, with shelves filled with enough goodies to make a five-star dinner party—to which any of the following places would provide a delicious contribution.

Fodor'sChoice ★ **Fortnum & Mason.** Although it's the Queen's grocer, this store is, paradoxically, the most egalitarian of gift shops; it has plenty of irresistibly packaged luxury foods, stamped with the gold BY APPOINTMENT crest, for less than £5. Try the teas, preserves, blocks of chocolate, tins of pâté, or a box of Duchy Originals oatcakes—like Paul Newman, the Prince of Wales has gone into the retail food business. (⇨ Map A) ⊠ *181 Piccadilly, St. James's W1* ☏ *020/7734–8040* Ⓤ *Piccadilly Circus.*

★ **Paxton & Whitfield.** This is the most venerable of London's cheese shops, in business for more than 200 years. The fabulous aromas come from some of the world's greatest cheeses stacked on the shelves—in rounds, in boxes, and on straw, but always ready to be tasted. Whichever cheese is in season and ripe for eating is on display for sampling, and the staff is ready to help you pick the best wine to serve with it. (⇨ Map A) ⊠ *93 Jermyn St., St. James's SW1* ☏ *020/7930–0259* Ⓤ *Piccadilly Circus.*

**Rococo.** It's run by Chantal Coady, who writes, eats, and lives for chocolate. Vegetable fats are forbidden words in this cocoa fantasyland, and there are interesting and offbeat additions to the main chocolate recipe, such as essence of Earl Grey. (⇨ Map C) ⊠ *321 King's Rd., Chelsea SW3* ☏ *020/7352–5857* Ⓤ *Sloane Sq.*

**Thorntons.** It may not be the classiest chocolatier, but that doesn't make one of Britain's most popular chocolate makers any the less desirable. Filled chocolates, chocolate bars, fudge, and toffee are their mainstays, but the truffles are to die for (and there's an extensive selection). Come at Easter-time, and the gift-wrapped eggs are rushing out the door. At

# CloseUp

# WHERE THE ROYALS SHOP

FROM SOFT DRINKS (Coca-Cola) and breakfast cereal (Weetabix) and household cleaning fluid (Jeyes), the royal family chooses the products it likes and hands their makers a warrant, a seal of satisfaction. Warrant holders can then adorn their packaging with a regal coat of arms, as well as the words "By Royal Appointment."

Only three royals can bestow warrants: the Queen, the Duke of Edinburgh, and Prince Charles. The warrants appear proudly on the facades of many an old and established London specialist shop; you'll find the stores are within a short carriage ride from the royal palaces. Fortnum & Mason is the royal grocer, but for British and Continental cheeses, Paxton & Whitfield holds the seal of approval. The glass cases at Floris, which have displayed classic perfumes since 1730, could be out of a Jane Austen novel. Penhaligon's is similarly well perfumed,

and has products for the well-groomed gentleman and lady.

All members of the royal family pursue sports with a passion. The outfitter for bridling is **W& H Gidden** (⊠ 15 Clifford St., Mayfair W1 ☎ 020/7734–0433). **Farlows** (⊠ 9 Pall Mall, St. James's SW1 ☎ 020/7839–2423) tackles other hardware (including fishing rods, reels, and shooting accessories). **Swaine, Adeney, Brigg** (⊠ 54 St. James's St., St. James's SW1 ☎ 020/7409–7277) provides everything from top to toe for country sporting pursuits, including riding whips, saddles, and breeches in the best possible taste. And hatter Herbert Johnson is downstairs, to complete the outfit.

this branch you can enjoy tea, coffee, and pastries—in addition to chocolate, of course. (⇨ Map A) ⊠ 353 Oxford St., Soho W1 ☎ 020/7493–7498 Ⓤ Bond St.

★ **Villandry.** Step inside the characterless building to a Provençal-style food store. Dark-wood shelves from floor to ceiling are laden with French and Belgian pâtés, French and Italian cheeses, pretty colored pastas, jars of fancy sauces, and other goodies galore. Bread baskets filled with rolls and pastries sit on heavy wood trestle tables. Behind the rustic calm of the food store are a café and dining room where you can indulge in some of the products. (⇨ Map A) ⊠ 170 Great Portland St., Regent's Park W1 ☎ 020/7631–3131 Ⓤ Great Portland St.

## Gifts

Of course, virtually anything from any shop in this chapter has gift potential, but these selections lean toward stores with a lot of choice, both in merchandise and price. Chances are you'll be wanting the recipients of your generous bounty to know how far you traveled to procure it for them, so these gift suggestions tend toward identifiable Britishness. You should also investigate the possibilities in the shops attached to the major museums, most of which offer far more than racks of souvenir postcards these days. Some of the best are at the British Museum and the V&A. For specialized gifts, the Royal Academy has great prints and cards and art paraphernalia; the London Transport Museum has transport models; the Natural History Museum has the largest selection of toy dinosaurs and real gemstones; and the London Aquarium is top-scale for all things undersea.

**GENERAL**  **British Museum Company.** Just around the corner from the museum itself, here's where you can find stacks of Egyptiana, particularly cute scarabs in ceramic. You can be an archaeologist for an afternoon and buy your own ancient pottery pieces. The bookshop has a huge selection and is a mine of historical information for adults and children. ( ⇨ Map A) ⊠ *22 Bloomsbury St., Bloomsbury WC1* ☎ *020/7637–9449* Ⓤ *Tottenham Court Rd.*

**Cross.** It's an ultrachic cornucopia with something to suit everyone— even your pet pooch. The idea has been around in other London shops for years, but the Cross succeeds with its selection of hedonistic, beautiful things: silk scarves, brocade bags, embroidered chinoiserie, check housecoats, and fragrant candles and butterflies by Jade Jagger. Finally, the location: the Cross is right in the middle of Portobello–cum–Holland Park, one of London's trendy hot spots. ( ⇨ Map D) ⊠ *141 Portland Rd., Notting Hill W11* ☎ *020/7727–6760* Ⓤ *Notting Hill Gate.*

**General Trading Co.** This place has just about every upper-class wedding gift list but also caters to slimmer pockets with merchandise shipped from farther shores (as the name suggests). ( ⇨ Map C) ⊠ *2 Symons St., Sloane Sq., Chelsea SW3* ☎ *020/7730–0411* Ⓤ *Sloane Sq.*

**Soccerscene.** At this mammoth temple to the world's most popular sport you can grab any replica kit you care to mention. Beware of some high prices. ( ⇨ Map A) ⊠ *56–57 Carnaby St., Soho W1* ☎ *020/7439–0778* Ⓤ *Oxford Circus.*

**Tea House.** It purveys everything to do with the British national drink; you can dispatch your entire gift list here. Alongside the varieties of tea (including strange or rare brews like orchid, banana, Japanese Rice, and Russian Caravan) you'll find teapots in the shape of a British bobby or a London taxi, plus books, and what the shop terms "teaphernalia"— strainers, trivets, and infusers, and some gadgets that need explaining. ( ⇨ Map A) ⊠ *15A Neal St., Covent Garden WC2* ☎ *020/7240–7539* Ⓤ *Covent Garden.*

**PERFUMES &**  **Floris.** One of the most beautiful shops in London, it has gleaming glass
**COSMETICS**  and Spanish mahogany showcases (acquired from the Great Exhibition
**Fodor's**Choice  of 1851). Gift possibilities include swan's-down powder puffs, cut-glass
★  bottles, and the elegant ivory and faux tortoiseshell combs that the shop has sold since the place opened in 1730. Queen Victoria used to daub her favorite Floris fragrance on her lace handkerchief. ( ⇨ Map A) ⊠ *89 Jermyn St., St. James's W1* ☎ *020/7930–2885* Ⓤ *Piccadilly Circus.*

**Les Senteurs.** An intimate, unglossy perfumery run by a French family, it sells some of the lesser-known yet wonderfully timeless fragrances in town. Sample Creed, worn by Eugénie, wife of Emperor Napoléon III. ( ⇨ Map C) ⊠ *71 Elizabeth St., Belgravia SW1* ☎ *020/7730–2322* Ⓤ *Sloane Sq.*

**Lush.** It's crammed with fresh, pure, very wacky, handmade cosmetics, like 13 Rabbit, chocolate and spice soap for the shower. Angels on Bare

Skin is divine lavender cleansing mush; Banana Moon, Dirty Boy, and Pineapple Grunt are soaps sliced off huge slabs like cheese and paper-wrapped as in an old-fashioned grocer's; Bath Bombs fizz furiously, then leave the water scattered with rosebuds or scented with honey and vanilla. (⇨ Map A) ✉ *Unit 11, The Piazza, Covent Garden WC2* ☏ *020/7240–4570* Ⓤ *Covent Garden.*

★ **Neal's Yard Remedies.** This place has exquisitely fragranced bath oils, shampoos, massage lotions, soaps, and so on, plus some of the purest essential oils money can buy, complete with burners for scenting the air back home; all are packaged in the company's distinctive cobalt-blue apothecary bottles. (⇨ Map A) ✉ *15 Neal's Yard, Covent Garden WC2* ☏ *020/7379–7222* Ⓤ *Covent Garden.*

**Penhaligon's.** William Penhaligon, court barber at the end of Queen Victoria's lengthy reign, established this shop. He blended perfumes and toilet waters and often created private blends for such customers as Lord Rothschild and Winston Churchill, using essential oils and natural, sometimes exotic ingredients. You can buy the very same formulations today, along with soaps, talcs, bath oils, and accessories, with the strong whiff of Victoriana both inside and outside the pretty bottles and boxes. Although constructed only a decade ago, the shop is sumptuously outfitted with 19th-century perfumer furnishings. Main branches: (⇨ Map A) ✉ *41 Wellington St., Covent Garden WC2* ☏ *020/7836–2150* Ⓤ *Covent Garden* ✉ *16 Burlington Arcade, Mayfair W1* ☏ *020/7629–1416* Ⓤ *Piccadilly Circus.*

**Pout.** There's nothing to get sulky about here, as the latest exciting brands in makeup, including Pout's own products, will give you plenty to smile about. You can try before you buy, in a fun, girlie boudoir setup, complete with pink walls and loveheart seating. Pretty irresistible. (⇨ Map A) ✉ *32 Shelton St., Covent Garden WC2* ☏ *020/7379–0379* Ⓤ *Covent Garden.*

**Space NK.** This shop is rapidly acquiring cult status as the cutting-edge purveyor of makeup and cosmetics. The makeup lines (Becca, Nars, and Stila) lead the alternative trend to the giant names, and the upcoming niche lines here always have the newest, hottest colors. You'll also find everything else to complete your body pampering. (⇨ Map A) ✉ *37 Earlham St., Covent Garden WC2* ☏ *020/7379–7030* Ⓤ *Covent Garden.*

STATIONERY **Ordning & Reda.** It has the hottest colors of the moment for cool, sleek Swedish stationery and useful pieces to dress up the drabbest of desks. There are high-style rucksacks, too. Also at 186A King's Road, Chelsea SW3. (⇨ Map A) ✉ *21–22 New Row, Covent Garden WC2* ☏ *020/7240–8090* Ⓤ *Covent Garden.*

**Paperchase.** The stationery superstore of London, it sells writing paper in every conceivable shade and in a dozen mediums. There are lovely cards, artists' materials, notebooks, and paperware. The three-floor store has a bookstore and café. (⇨ Map A) ✉ *213 Tottenham Court Rd., Bloomsbury W1* ☏ *020/7467–6200* Ⓤ *Goodge St.*

TOYS & MODELS **Armoury of St. James's.** This shop stocks perfect playthings for kids of all ages in the form of some of the world's finest antique and newly painted lead soldiers (most wars with British involvement can be fought in miniature), plus medals, brass buttons, uniforms, painted drums, and military prints. (⇨ Map A) ✉ *17 Piccadilly Arcade, St. James's SW1* ☎ *020/7493–5082* Ⓤ *Piccadilly Circus.*

★ **Hamleys.** The huge stock, including six floors of toys and games for children and adults, ranges from traditional teddy bears to computer games and all the latest technological gimmickry. Try to avoid it at Christmas, when police have to rope off a section of Regent Street for customers. (⇨ Map A) ✉ *188–196 Regent St., Soho W1* ☎ *0870/333–2455* Ⓤ *Oxford Circus.*

**London Dolls House Company.** A fantastic display of classic English dollhouses and accessories makes this store the leader in its field, but prices are not cheap. The houses themselves might not fit in your hand baggage, but you can still treat yourself to one or two of the exquisite extras. (⇨ Map A) ✉ *29 The Market, Covent Garden WC2* ☎ *020/7240–8681* Ⓤ *Covent Garden.*

**Science Museum Gift Shop.** It's best for imaginative toys and models, such as those darling little balsa-wood planes. The books and puzzles are extensive and will satisfy the most inquiring minds. (⇨ Map B) ✉ *Exhibition Rd., South Kensington SW7* ☎ *020/7942–4499* Ⓤ *S. Kensington.*

## Housewares

London's main department stores, such as John Lewis, Harrods, and Selfridges, have just about everything you would need in a home from day to night, but if you are looking for something that's a little more cutting edge, then stroll along Tottenham Court Road to the grandfather of them all—Heal's—which is now the grandee among a crop of modern imitators and innovators, including the first Terence Conran baby of the '60s, Habitat. Muji takes home style a step further by embracing clothes to match the furnishings. For handmade, eclectic designer pieces, you should explore farther afield to David Mellor, David Linley Furniture in Chelsea, and the wacky Walter Castellazzo Design in Highgate, North London.

**Cargo Homeshop.** It makes a virtue of light, bright, and funky: you'll find functional tables, chairs, and inexpensive sofas in the latest earthy and vibrant shades—many can be made-to-order in tempting fabrics from Italy and Spain. If you want to carry away a little something for under £10, try the colorful Indian rag rugs. There's another branch at 245–249 Brompton Road, SW3. (⇨ Map A) ✉ *209 Tottenham Court Rd., Bloomsbury W1* ☎ *020/7580–2895* Ⓤ *Goodge St.*

★ **Conran Shop.** This is the domain of Sir Terence Conran, who has been informing British middle-class taste since he opened Habitat in the '60s. Home enhancers from furniture to stemware, both handmade and mass-produced, famous-name and young-designer, are displayed in a suitably gorgeous building. The household articles are almost objets d'art in their own right. Bluebird on King's Road and the Conran Shop on Marylebone High Street have similarly beautiful wares. (⇨ Map B) ✉ *Michelin House, 81 Fulham Rd., South Kensington SW3* ☎ *020/7589–7401* Ⓤ *S. Kensington.*

**Habitat.** It has all the cool furnishings from global sources, colorful and shiny kitchen stuff, and linens in the latest ethnic and traditional themes by the store's own designers. Although most items are affordable, the workmanship is such that they may only last until the next decade's trend. The other central branch is at 206 King's Road, Chelsea SW3. (⇨ Map A) ✉ *196 Tottenham Court Rd., Bloomsbury W1* ☎ *020/7631–3880* Ⓤ *Goodge St.*

**Heal's.** The king of the furniture shops lining Tottenham Court Road, it has designs that combine modern style with classicism and are well made, particularly beds and seating. Prices are high, but the store makes for delightful browsing, and the kitchenware and decorative pieces are more affordable while still retaining good looks. At Christmas time, Heal's decorative baubles are gorgeous. There is another store at 234 King's Road, Chelsea SW3. (⇨ Map A) ✉ *196 Tottenham Court Rd., Bloomsbury W1* ☎ *020/7636–1666* Ⓤ *Goodge St.*

**Purves & Purves.** It's a great place whether you've over £500 or only a £5 note to spend. Classic modern furniture and kitchenware designs by Philippe Starck and cool Italian trendsetters are definitely upscale, but almost investment pieces. Inexpensive, colorful, and witty gift items, such as bubbly plastic napkin rings, toothbrushes, or silly soap dishes, abound. The store showcases many British designs. (⇨ Map A) ✉ *220–222 Tottenham Court Rd., Bloomsbury W1* ☎ *020/7580–8223* Ⓤ *Goodge St.*

## Jewelry

Jewelry—precious, semiprecious, and totally fake—can be had by just rubbing an Aladdin's lamp in London's West End. Of the department stores, Liberty and Harvey Nichols are particularly known for their fashion jewelry (drool over David Morris's creations, which have become beloved by celeb royalty, such as the Beckhams). But, in addition to viewing the more traditional baubles, bangles, and beads, check out the exceptionally creative kids on the jewelry block, such as Slim Barrett, whose designs are worn by supermodels, young aristos, and TV personalities. Seek out also the talent in the crafts and jewelry galleries, such as OXO Tower and Lesley Craze.

★ **Asprey.** It offers exquisite jewelry and gifts, both antique and modern, and is among the poshest and most luxurious shops in the world. If you're in the market for a six-branch Georgian candelabrum or a six-carat emerald-and-diamond brooch, you won't be disappointed. (⇨ Map A) ✉ *168–169 New Bond St., Mayfair W1* ☎ *020/7493–6767* Ⓤ *Bond St.*

Fodor'sChoice **Butler & Wilson.** Designed to set off its irresistible costume jewelry to the ★ very best advantage—against a dramatic black background—this shop has some of the best displays in town; it keeps very busy marketing silver, diamanté, French gilt, and pearls by the truckload. You'll also find some vintage gowns that set off the jewelry nicely. There's another branch at 189 Fulham Road, South Kensington SW3. (⇨ Maps A and B) ✉ *20 S. Molton St., Mayfair W1* ☎ *020/7409–2955* Ⓤ *Bond St.*

**Cartier.** It exudes an exclusivity that captures the very essence of Bond Street, combining royal connections—Cartier was granted its first royal warrant in 1902—with the last word in luxurious good taste. The store also sells glassware, leather goods, and stationery. (⇨ Map A) ✉ *175 New Bond St., Mayfair W1* ☎ *020/7408–5700* Ⓤ *Bond St.*

**Dinny Hall.** There's a very simple collection of designs in mainly gold and silver. Pared-down necklaces with a single drop feature, delicate gold spot-diamond earrings, and simple chokers with delicate curls are indicative of the styles offered. There's another branch at 54 Fulham Road, South Kensington SW3. (⇨ Map D) ✉ *200 Westbourne Grove, Notting Hill W11* ☎ *020/7792–3913* Ⓤ *Notting Hill Gate.*

**Garrard.** After sharing premises with Asprey, it has returned to its original site, and to put a little sparkle back into the wares, Jade Jagger is the designer employed by the company to draw in the younger market. Her graffiti collection has oodles of street style. Garrard is the royal jeweler, in charge of the upkeep of the Crown Jewels. (⇨ Map A) ✉ *24 Albemarle St., Mayfair W1* ☎ *020/7758–8520* Ⓤ *Bond St.*

**Steinberg & Tolkien.** This shop has the last word in costume jewelry from the 1920s and onward. Chanel and Schiaparelli are just two of the famous designers that you might leap on here. And if you're lucky, you may find a piece that's been signed by its creator. These pieces are sometimes cheaper than those of the top-notch jewelers, and they may be of extra interest because you know who made them. (⇨ Map C) ✉ *193 King's Rd., Chelsea SW3* ☎ *020/7376–3660* Ⓤ *Sloane Sq.*

## Prints

London harbors loads of prints, and they make great gifts—for yourself, perhaps. You'll find, below, some West End stores, but also try street markets (in particular Camden Passage in Islington) and Cecil Court, just north of Trafalgar Square; the intriguing shops close to the British Museum; and the Royal Academy museum shop, which has a small selection. Tate Modern and Bankside Gallery (on the South Bank) and Tate Britain have a good selection. Browsing around Waterloo Bridge along the Riverside Walk Market, or St. James's Craft Market at St. James's Church, Piccadilly, and at the Apple Market, The Piazza, Covent Garden, could present something tempting. Auction houses, such as Christie's, South Kensington, and Bonhams, New Bond Street, can often prove fun hunting grounds, but the prices can be high. In the bargain range, it's well worth making a date for one of the many art fairs during the year, such as the Affordable Art Fair around March and October at Battersea Park, where you can bag original work from the artists (☎ 020/7371–8787 ⊕ www.affordableartfair.co.uk).

**Curwen Gallery.** You can browse through a wide selection of modern art prints here. (⇨ Map A) ✉ *4 Windmill St., Soho W1* ☎ *020/7636–1459* Ⓤ *Tottenham Court Rd.*

★ **Grosvenor Prints.** Antiquarian prints and 18th- and 19th-century portraits, with an emphasis on views and architecture of London—and dogs—are for sale. It's an eccentric collection, and the prices range widely, but the stock is so odd that you are bound to find something interesting and unusual to meet both your budget and your taste. (⇨ Map A) ✉ *28 Shelton St., Covent Garden WC2* ☎ *020/7836–1979* Ⓤ *Covent Garden.*

**Map House.** It has antique maps (that run from a few pounds to several thousand) and excellent reproductions of maps and prints, especially of botanical subjects, cityscapes, and *Punch* cartoons and prints. (⇨ Map B) ✉ *54 Beauchamp Pl., Knightsbridge SW3* ☎ *020/7589–4325* Ⓤ *Knightsbridge.*

## Shoes

★ **Emma Hope.** This shop with handmade shoes first opened in Amwell Street, Islington—handy if you are mooching around Islington and Camden Passage antiques stalls. But since custom footwear has had a mini-meteoric upturn, and the designer's pretty pumps in brocades and satins have been gliding down the catwalks of Nicole Farhi and Betty Jackson, Hope has opened a more upscale central branch in Sloane Square, and at 207 Westbourne Grove, Notting Hill, W11. ( ⇨ Map C) ⊠ *53 Sloane Sq., Chelsea SW1* ☎ *020/7259–9566* Ⓤ *Sloane Sq.*

**Jimmy Choo.** It's the name on every supermodel's and fashion editor's feet. Choo's exquisite, elegant designs are fantasy itself, and he's become a contender for Manolo Blahnik's crown. Obviously, these designs aren't cheap—nothing under £100—but the workmanship is out of this world. ( ⇨ Map C) ⊠ *169 Draycott Ave., Chelsea SW3* ☎ *020/ 7584–6111* Ⓤ *S. Kensington.*

**John Lobb.** If you're planning to visit for your first pair of handmade shoes (after which your wooden "last," or foot mold, is kept), take note: this shop has a waiting list of six months plus. As well as plenty of time, you will need to have plenty of money: around £1,500. But this buys a world of choice—from finest calf to exotic elk—and they will be your finest pair of shoes ever. ( ⇨ Map A) ⊠ *9 St. James's St., St. James's SW1* ☎ *020/7930–3664* Ⓤ *Piccadilly Circus.*

**L. K. Bennett.** Geared toward London's working women, this chain makes good quality, trendy shoes, from loafers to boots to sexy stilettos. There are many branches all over the city; some carry handbags, too. ( ⇨ Map A) ⊠ *130 Long Acre, Covent Garden WC2* ☎ *020/ 7379–1710* Ⓤ *Covent Garden.*

**Patrick Cox.** The "Wannabe" shoe collection is affordable and irreverant, with retro design and quirky materials and colors. The store also carries clothes and accessories for serious hipsters. The sophisticated Patrick Cox signature collection is very popular among trendy Londoners. ( ⇨ Map C) ⊠ *129 Sloane St., Chelsea SW3* ☎ *020/7730–8886* Ⓤ *Knightsbridge or Sloane Sq.*

**Shellys.** It sells shoes for men and women, from city slickers to shoes for clubbing, at all prices and even at unimaginable platform heights. ( ⇨ Map A) ⊠ *266–270 Regent St., Soho W1* ☎ *020/7287–0939* Ⓤ *Oxford Circus.*

**Swear.** This was the shoemaker for the movie *Star Wars*, which is an indicator of the style you can expect to encounter here: wild and wacky, larger-than-life platforms for daring wearers who have a head for the heights of fashion—around 4 inches and up. There are branches at 22 Carnaby Street, Soho W1, and Stables Market, Camden NW1. ( ⇨ Map A) ⊠ *61 Neal St., Covent Garden WC2* ☎ *020/7240–7673* Ⓤ *Covent Garden.*

# Street Markets

London is as rich in street markets as it is in parks, and they contribute as much to the city's thriving culture. Practically every neighborhood has its own cluster of fruit-and-vegetable stalls, but listed here is the bigger, specialist sort of market, which provides not only a bargain (if you luck out) but also a great day out. A Sunday morning strolling the stalls of Brick Lane and breakfasting on the native bagels (smaller than New York's, but some say just as good) or a Saturday antiquing on Portobello Road is a Londoner's pastime as much as it is a tourist activity, and markets are a great way to see the city from the inside out.

**Bermondsey.** Also known as the New Caledonian Market, it's London's best antiques market, one of the largest, and the one the dealers frequent. The Friday-only market starts at the unearthly hour of 5 AM, and it's then that the really great buys will be snapped up. You should still be able to find a bargain or two if you turn up a bit later. ⊠ *Tower Bridge Rd., South Bank SE1* 🕙 *Fri. 5 AM–noon* 🚌 *Bus 15 or 25 to Aldgate, then Bus 42 over Tower Bridge to Bermondsey Sq.* Ⓤ *London Bridge or Borough.*

**Berwick Street.** It's a relief from the frenzy of Oxford Street and its chain and department stores. The hub of the market is in Berwick Street, but there's an overspill through backstreet Soho, past Raymond's Revue Bar, and onto Rupert Street. Behind the bustling stalls there are pleasures galore: cafés, from greasy spoon to chic bar; fresh meat and game; Camembert on the edge of over-ripeness; giant slabs of chocolate; fresh fruits and vegetables; natty custom tailors; Borovik's fabrics; classy, risqué underwear to be found at Agent Provocateur (from Vivienne Westwood's son)—they all provide a cosmopolitan, lively, delightfully brassy backdrop. ⊠ *Soho W1* 🕙 *Weekdays 8–6, Sat. 9–4* Ⓤ *Oxford Circus or Piccadilly Circus.*

Fodor's Choice ★ **Borough Market.** A foodie's paradise with whole grain, organic everything. The produce is mainly from Britain, but there are some international flavors. ⊠ *Borough High St., South Bank SE1* 🕙 *Fri. noon–6, Sat. 9–4* Ⓤ *London Bridge or Borough.*

**Brick Lane.** Not a showcase but more a collection of bric-a-brac, it's worth a visit for the bagels from the all-night bakery and a host of bargain Bengali curry houses. The Old Truman Brewery has a trendy retail focus, with the Vibe Bar at its hub. Arty types hang out at the Atlantis Art Shop—and Whitechapel Art Gallery is a block away. From here it's a stone's throw to Spitalfields, the Columbia Road flower market, where cheap flowers for window boxes and gardens are a magnet for Londoners. ⊠ *East End E1* 🕙 *Sun. 8–1* 🚌 *Bus 25 to Whitechapel Rd., or Bus 8 to Bethnal Green Rd.* Ⓤ *Aldgate E or Shoreditch.*

**Camden Lock Market.** Actually several markets gathered around a pair of locks in the Regent's Canal, and it was once very pretty. Now that more stalls and a faux warehouse have been inserted into the surrounding brick railway buildings, the haphazard charm of the place is largely lost, although the variety of merchandise is mind-blowing: vintage and new clothes (design stars have been discovered here), antiques and junk, jewelry and scarves, candlesticks, ceramics, mirrors, and toys. Underneath it's really a date spot for hip teens. The neighborhood is bursting with shops, cafés, and other markets, and it's a whole lot calmer, if stall-free, at midweek. ⊠ *Camden Town NW1* 🕙 *Shops Tues.–Sun. 9:30–5:30, stalls weekends 8–6* 🚌 *Bus 24 or 29 to Camden Town* Ⓤ *Camden Town.*

**Camden Passage.** Despite the name, it's not in Camden but a couple of miles away in Islington. Around 350 antiques dealers set up stalls here Saturday and Wednesday, with the surrounding antiques shops open Tuesday to Saturday 10–5 PM; even in the shops you can try your hand at price negotiation, although prices are generally fair. All in all, this remains a fruitful and picturesque hunting ground. ⊠ *Islington N1* ⊙ *Wed. and Sat. 8:30–3* ☞ *Bus 19 or 38 to Angel* Ⓤ *Angel.*

**Covent Garden.** Craft stalls, jewelry designers, clothes makers—particularly of knitwear—potters, and many more artisans congregate in the undercover central area known as The Apple Market. The Jubilee Market, toward Southampton Street, is less classy, with printed T-shirts and the like, but on Monday has a worthwhile selection of vintage collectibles. ⊠ *The Piazza, Covent Garden WC2* ⊙ *Daily 9–5* Ⓤ *Covent Garden.*

**Greenwich Antiques Market.** If you're planning to visit Greenwich, then combine your trip with a wander around this open-air market near St. Alfege Church. You'll find one of the best selections of secondhand and antique clothes in London—quality tweeds and overcoats can be had at amazing prices. ⊠ *Greenwich High Rd., Greenwich SE10* ⊙ *Antiques, crafts, and clothes weekends 9–5; fruit and vegetables weekdays 9–5* Ⓤ *Cutty Sark Docklands Light Railway.*

**Leadenhall Market.** The draw here is not so much what you can buy—plants and posh food, mainly—as the building itself. It's a handsome late-Victorian structure, ornate and elaborate. ⊠ *Whittington Ave., The City EC3* ⊙ *Weekdays 7–4* Ⓤ *Bank or Monument.*

**Petticoat Lane.** Actually, Petticoat Lane doesn't exist; this Sunday clothing and fashion market, one of London's most entertaining diversions, centers on Middlesex Street, then sprawls in several directions, including northeast to Brick Lane and Spitalfields. Between them, the crammed streets turn up items of dubious parentage (CD players, bikes, car radios), alongside clothes (vintage, new, and just plain tired), jewelry, books, underwear, antiques, woodworking tools, bed linens, jars of pickles, and outright junk. ⊠ *Middlesex St., Aldgate E1* ⊙ *Sun. 9–2* Ⓤ *Liverpool St., Aldgate, or Aldgate East.*

Fodor'sChoice  **Portobello Market.** London's most famous market still wins the prize for
★  the all-round best. It sits in a most lively and multicultural part of town; the 1,500-odd antiques dealers don't rip you off (although you should haggle where you can); and it stretches over a mile, changing character completely as it goes. The top end (Notting Hill Gate) is antiquesland and more tourist-bound; the middle is where locals buy fruit and vegetables and hang out in trendy restaurants; the section under the elevated highway called the Westway has the best flea market in town; and then it tails off into a giant rummage sale among record stores, vintage-clothing boutiques, and art galleries. The bargains can be found here in Golborne Road (W10) at the Ladbroke Grove end of Portobello. For original French country furniture and other pretty pieces, the market is hard to beat. For refreshment, pop into one of the many Portuguese patisseries and cafés. The western section of Portobello around the Westbourne Grove end is also worthy of exploration. ⊠ *Portobello Rd., Notting Hill W11* ⊙ *Fruit and vegetables Mon.–Wed. and Fri. 8–5, Thurs. 8–1; antiques Fri. 8–3; both food market and antiques Sat. 6–5* Ⓤ *Bus 52 or Tube to Ladbroke Grove or Notting Hill Gate.*

**Spitalfields.** Around the market area, crafts-and-design shops have sprung up with trendy bars and restaurants. The old 3-acre indoor fruit market, near Petticoat Lane, is reminiscent of a more chic Camden Lock Market, with food, crafts, and clothes stalls. On Sunday the place really comes alive, with stalls selling beautiful paper lamp shades, antique clothing, handmade rugs, soap filled with flowers and fruits, homemade cakes, Portuguese deli foods, and cookware. In the center, racks of easels are filled with the cheapest (around £10) original artwork from the Alternative Art Market. For refreshment it's possible to eat from West to East, with Spanish tapas or Thai among the bars and food stalls. ⊠ *Brushfield St., East End E1* ⊘ *Organic market Fri. and Sun. 10–5; general market weekdays 11–3, Sun. 10–5* Ⓤ *Liverpool St., Aldgate, or Aldgate E.*

# SIDE TRIPS FROM LONDON

7

Updated by
Robert
Andrews,
Catherine
Belonogoff,
and Julius
Honnor

**SOMETIMES YOU JUST NEED TO GET AWAY** from Old Smoke, and even if time is limited, a trip to the countryside is well worth your while. A train ride past hills dotted with sheep, a stroll through a preserved medieval town, or a history lesson at one of England's great castles will make you feel as though you added another week to your vacation.

Londoners are undeniably lucky. Few urban populations enjoy such glorious—and easily accessible—options for day-tripping. England is extremely compact, and absolutely nothing is very far from the capital. Moreover, the train and bus networks, although somewhat inefficient and expensive compared to their European counterparts, are extensive and easy to figure out. By train from London, it takes a mere 55 minutes to reach Oxford, an hour to reach Cambridge, and 90 minutes to reach Bath. Stratford takes a bit more planning, since direct trains from London take 2 hours, 20 minutes.

Although you could tackle any one of the towns in this chapter on a frenzied day trip—heavy summer crowds make it difficult to cover the sights in a relaxed manner—consider staying for a day or two. You'd then have time to explore a very different England, one blessed with quiet country pubs, fluffy sheep, and neatly trimmed farms. No matter where you go, lodging reservations are a good idea from June through September, when foreign visitors saturate the English countryside.

### Where to Eat

When dining outside London, stick to local specialties and produce wherever possible—get seafood in Brighton, for example. Don't forget that one of the best ways to experience any town is to pop into a good old-fashioned pub.

| WHAT IT COSTS In pounds | | | | |
|---|---|---|---|---|
| **£££££** | **££££** | **£££** | **££** | **£** |
| AT DINNER over £22 | £19–£22 | £13–£18 | £7–£12 | under £7 |

Prices are per person for a main course, excluding drinks, service, and V.A.T.

# BATH

"I really believe I shall always be talking of Bath . . . I do like it so very much. Oh! who can ever be tired of Bath," wrote Jane Austen in *Northanger Abbey*. Today, thousands of visitors heartily concur. A remarkably unsullied Georgian city, Bath looks as if John Wood, its chief architect, "Beau" Nash, its principal dandy, and Jane Austen (1775–1817) might still be seen strolling on the promenade. Stepping out of the train station puts you right in the center, and Bath is compact enough to explore on foot. A single day is sufficient for you to take in the glorious yellow-stone buildings, tour the Roman baths, and stop for tea, though it will give only a brief hint of the cultural life that thrives in this vibrant town.

## Exploring Bath

The Romans set about building the **Pump Room and Roman Baths** around the healing spring of the English goddess Aquae Sulis in AD 60, after wars with the Brits had laid the city to waste. The site became famous as a temple to Minerva, the Roman goddess of wisdom. Legend has it the first taker of these sacred waters was King Lear's leprous father, Prince Bladud, in the 9th century BC. (Yes, it's claimed he was cured.) Below the beautifully restored 18th-century Pump Room (oft-described in Austen's works) is a museum of quirky objects found during excavations. Last admission is an hour before closing, but allow at least 90 minutes for the museum. ⊠ *Abbey Churchyard* ☎ *01225/477784* ⊕ *www.romanbaths.co.uk* ✑ *£9; combined ticket with Assembly Rooms £12* ☉ *Mar.–June, Sept. and Oct., daily 9–6; July and Aug., daily 9 AM–10 PM; Nov.–Feb., daily 9:30–5:30.*

**Bath Abbey** was commissioned by God. Really. The design came to Bishop Oliver King in a dream, and was built during the 15th century. In the **Heritage Vaults** is a museum of archaeological finds, with a scale model of 13th-century Bath. Look up at the fan-vaulted ceilings in the nave and the carved angels on the restored West Front. ⊠ *Abbey Churchyard* ☎ *01225/422462* ⊕ *www.bathabbey.org* ✑ *Abbey free, suggested donation £2.50; Heritage Vaults £1* ☉ *Abbey Easter–Oct., Mon.–Sat. 9–6, Sun. 1:15–2:45; Nov.–Easter, Mon.–Sat. 9–4:30, Sun. 1:15–2:45 and 4:45–5:30. Heritage Vaults Mon.–Sat. 10–4.*

need a break? **Sally Lunn's Refreshment House & Museum** (⊠ 4 N. Parade Passage ☎ 01225/461634), in Bath's oldest house (1482), may be the world's only tearoom-museum. It's open 10 to 10 Monday through Saturday and 11 to 10 on Sunday.

One of the most famous landmarks of the city, **Pulteney Bridge** (⊠ Off Bridge St. at the Grand Parade) was the great Georgian architect Robert Adam's sole contribution to Bath and is, in its way, as fine as the only other bridge in the world with shops lining either side: the Ponte Vecchio in Florence.

★ Among Bath's remarkable architectural achievements is **The Circus** (⊠ Intersection of Brock, Gay, and Bennett Sts.), a perfectly circular ring of three-story stone houses designed by John Wood. The painter Thomas Gainsborough lived at No. 17 from 1760 to 1774.

On the east side of Bath's Circus are more thrills for Austen readers: her much-mentioned **Assembly Rooms,** which now contain the **Museum of Costume,** which displays fashions from the 17th through 20th centuries. Last admission is one hour before closing, but allow at least an hour to tour the museum. ⊠ *Bennett St.* ☎ *01225/477789* ⊕ *www. museumofcostume.co.uk* ✑ *£6, combined ticket with Roman Baths £12* ☉ *Mar.–Oct., daily 11–6; Nov.–Feb., daily 11–5.*

The **Royal Crescent** is the most famous site in Bath, and you can't help but see why. Designed by John Wood the Younger, it's perfectly proportioned and beautifully sited, with sweeping views over parkland. A marvelous museum at **Number 1 Royal Crescent** shows life as Beau Nash would have lived it circa 1765. ⊠ *1 Royal Crescent* ☎ *01225/428126* ⊕ *www.bath-preservation-trust.org.uk* ⊠ *£4* ⊘ *Mid-Feb.–Oct., Tues.–Sun. 10:30–5; Nov., Tues.–Sun. 10:30–4; last admission 30 mins before closing.*

### Where to Eat

**£££** ✕ **Number Five.** Just over the Pulteney Bridge from the center of town, this airy bistro, with its plants, framed posters, and cane-back chairs, is an ideal spot for a light lunch. The regularly changing menu includes tasty homemade soups, foie gras served with toasted brioche, and roast loin of lamb with aubergine (eggplant) caviar. ⊠ *5 Argyle St.* ☎ *01225/ 444499* ⊟ *AE, MC, V* ⊘ *Closed Sun.*

# BRIGHTON

Ever since the Prince Regent first visited in 1783, Brighton has been England's most exciting seaside city, and today it's as eccentric and cosmopolitan as ever. With its rich cultural mix—Regency architecture, amusement pier, specialist shops, pavement cafés, lively arts, and, of course, the odd and exotic Royal Pavilion—Brighton is a truly extraordinary city by the sea. For most of the 20th century the city was known for its tarnished allure and faded glamour. Happily, a young, bustling spirit has given a face-lift to this ever-popular resort, which shares its city status with neighboring Hove, as genteel a retreat as Brighton is abuzz.

### Exploring Brighton

FodorśChoice
★

In the 1850s, the county of Sussex featured the first examples of that peculiarly British institution, the amusement pier. The **Brighton Pier** follows the great tradition, with a crowded maze of arcade games, amusement-park rides, and chip shops. The decaying ghost of a Victorian structure down the beach from Brighton Pier is the **West Pier** (☎ 01273/ 321499 ⊕ www.westpier.co.uk). Built in 1866 it was the more upmarket of Brighton's piers and was for many the most recognizable landmark of the city. In 2002, however, storm damage and a partial collapse, followed by two fires in 2003, have left little more than the charred and distorted remnants of the original structure. Opinion in the city is split about a proposed £30 million renovation program. ⊠ *Waterfront along Madeira Dr.* ☎ *01273/609361* ⊕ *www.brightonpier.co.uk* ⊠ *Free, costs of rides vary* ⊘ *June–Aug. daily 9 AM–2 AM; Sept.–May daily 10 AM–midnight.*

The heart of Brighton is the **Steine** (pronounced *steen*), a large open area close to the seafront. This was a river mouth until the Prince of Wales had it drained in 1793.

FodorśChoice
★

The most remarkable building on the Steine, perhaps in all Britain, is unquestionably the extravagant, fairy-tale **Royal Pavilion.** Built by architect Henry Holland in 1787 as a simple seaside villa, the Pavilion was transformed by John Nash between 1815 and 1823 for the Prince Regent (later George IV), who favored an exotic, Eastern design with opulent Chinese interiors. When Queen Victoria came to the throne in 1837, she disapproved of the palace and planned to demolish it. Fortunately, the local council bought it from her, and after a lengthy process of restoration, the Pavilion looks much as it did in its Regency heyday. Take particular note of the spectacular **Music Room,** styled as a Chinese pavilion, and the **Banqueting Room,** with its enormous flying-dragon "gasolier," or gaslight chandelier, a revolutionary invention in the early 19th century. The gardens, too, have been restored to Regency splendor, following John Nash's naturalistic design of 1826. ⊠ *Old Steine* ☎ *01273/290900* ⊕ *www.royalpavilion.org.uk* 🖻 *£5.80* ⊙ *Oct.–Mar., daily 10–5:15; Apr.–Sept., daily 9:30–5:45; last admission 45 mins before closing.*

The grounds of the Royal Pavilion contain the **Brighton Museum and Art Gallery,** whose buildings were designed as a stable block for the Prince Regent's horses. The museum includes especially interesting art nouveau and art deco collections. Look out for Salvador Dalí's famous sofa in the shape of Mae West's lips, and pause at the Balcony Café for its bird's-eye view over the 20th century Art and Design Gallery. ⊠ *Church St.* ☎ *01273/290900* 🖻 *Free* ⊙ *Tues. 10–7, Wed.–Sat. 10–5, Sun. 2–5* ⊙ *Closed Mon. except public holidays.*

**The Lanes** (⊠ Bordered by West, North, East, and Prince Albert Sts.), a maze of alleys and passageways, was once the home of fishermen and their families. Closed to vehicular traffic, the area's cobbled streets are filled with interesting restaurants, boutiques, and antiques shops. Fish and seafood restaurants line the heart of the Lanes, at Market Street and Market Square.

Ⓒ **Volk's Electric Railway,** built by inventor Magnus Volk in 1883, was the first public electric railroad in Britain. In summer you can take the 1¼-mi trip along Marine Parade. ⊠ *Marine Parade* ☎ *01273/292718* 🖻 *£1.20 one-way, £2.20 round-trip* ⊙ *Mid-Apr.–Sept., weekdays 10:30–5, weekends 10:30–6.*

Below the boardwalk near Palace Pier, the enchanting **Mechanical Memories** museum fills a tiny room with Victorian-era nickelodeons and fortune-telling machines. Buy a few Victorian pennies, drop them in the slots, and you'll agree: there's nothing like good old-fashioned fun. ⊠ *250C King's Rd. Arches, Lower Esplanade, opposite the end of East St.* ☎ *01273/608620* 🖻 *Free* ⊙ *Easter–Sept., school holidays and weekends noon–6; fine-weather weekends Oct.–Easter.*

## Where to Eat

££–£££ ✕ **English's of Brighton.** One of the few old-fashioned seafood havens left in England is buried in the Lanes in three fishermen's cottages. It has been a restaurant for more than 150 years and a family business for more than 50. You can eat succulent oysters and other seafood dishes at the counter or take a table in the smart restaurant section. Its popularity means it's usually busy and service can sometimes be slow. ⊠ *29–31 East St.* ☎ *01273/327980* ➡ *AE, DC, MC, V.*

£–£££ ✕ **Havana.** In a mock Cuban building, the high ceilings, dark-wood-and-leather furnishings, and sophisticated food at Havana might make you think you're in London. Don't let that deter you, however—this place is a pleasure. Expect modern twists on British classics: the sautéed sea bream, for example, comes on a bed of braised fennel. The chic bar area is a perfect place to rest your feet at the end of the day. ✉ *32 Duke St.* ☎ *01273/773388* ▤ *AE, MC, V.*

★ ££  ✕ **Terre à Terre.** This inspiring vegetarian restaurant is popular, so come early for a light lunch, or book a table for an evening meal. The Jerusalem artichoke soufflé, sumac-scented almond eggplant, and an eclectic choice of salads should satisfy most palates, and dishes have names to match their culinary inventiveness, such as Colonel Gnocchi Chowder and Jabba Jabba Beefy Tea. ✉ *71 East St.* ☎ *01273/729051* ⌦ *Reservations essential* ▤ *AE, DC, MC, V* ⊘ *No lunch Mon; in winter, closed Mon., no lunch Tues.*

# CAMBRIDGE

Having trouble distinguishing between Oxford and Cambridge? That's not surprising, because in the United Kingdom, the names of these two important educational institutions are often elided into the term "Oxbridge." Their histories, too, are inextricable: Cambridge was founded by Oxford students after a bloody 13th-century clash with Oxford townspeople. Today, a healthy rivalry persists between the two schools.

This university town may be one of the most beautiful cities in Britain, but it's no museum. Even when the students are on vacation, there's a strong cultural and intellectual buzz here. It's a preserved medieval city of some 100,000 souls and growing, dominated culturally and architecturally by its famous university and beautified by parks and gardens and the quietly flowing River Cam. Punting on the Cam (one occupant propels the narrow, square-end, flat-bottom boat with a long pole, while another steers with a small paddle) is a quintessential Cambridge pursuit, followed by a stroll along the Backs, the quaintly named left bank of the Cam fringed by St. John's, Trinity, Clare, King's, and Queens' colleges, and Trinity Hall.

VISITING THE COLLEGES  College visits are certainly a highlight of a Cambridge tour, but remember that the colleges are private homes and workplaces, even when school isn't in session. Each is an independent entity within the university; some are closed to the public, while at others you can see the chapels, dining rooms (called halls), and sometimes the libraries, too. Some colleges charge a small fee for the privilege of nosing around. All are closed during exams, usually from mid-April to late June. For details about visiting specific colleges not listed here, you can contact **Cambridge University** (☎ 01223/337733 ⊕ www.cam.ac.uk).

By far the best way to gain access without annoying anyone is to join a walking tour led by an official Blue Badge guide—in fact, many areas are off-limits unless you do. The two-hour tours leave daily from the **Tourist Information Centre** (✉ The Old Library, Wheeler St. ☎ 0906/5862526 ⊕ www.tourismcambridge.com).

## Exploring Cambridge

**Pembroke College** (1347) has delightful gardens and bowling greens. Its chapel, completed in 1665, was Christopher Wren's first commission.

✉ *Trumpington St.* ☎ *01223/338100* ⊕ *www.pem.cam.ac.uk* 🎟 *Free* ⊘ *Daily 9–dusk.*

**Emmanuel College** (1584) is the alma mater of one John Harvard, who gave his books and his name to the American university. A number of the Pilgrims were Emmanuel alumni; they named Cambridge, Massachusetts, after their alma mater. ✉ *Emmanuel and St. Andrew's Sts.* ☎ *01223/334200* ⊕ *www.emma.cam.ac.uk* 🎟 *Free* ⊘ *Daily 9–6.*

★ East Anglia's finest art gallery, the **Fitzwilliam Museum** houses outstanding collections of art, including several Constable paintings, oil sketches by Rubens, and antiquities from ancient Egypt, Greece, and Rome. ✉ *Trumpington St.* ☎ *01223/332900* ⊕ *www.fitzmuseum.cam.ac.uk* 🎟 *Free* ⊘ *Tues.–Sat. 10–5, Sun. 2:15–5; guided tours Sun. at 2:45.*

**King's College** (1441) is notable as the site of the world-famous Gothic-style **King's College Chapel** (built 1446–1547). Some deem its great fan-vaulted roof, supported by a delicate tracery of columns, the most glorious example of Perpendicular Gothic in Britain. It's the home of the famous choristers, and, to cap it all, Rubens's *Adoration of the Magi* is secreted behind the altar. ✉ *Kings Parade* ☎ *01223/331100 college, 01223/331155 chapel* ⊕ *www.kings.cam.ac.uk* 🎟 *£3.50* ⊘ *Oct.–June, weekdays 9:30–3:30, Sat. 9:30–3:15, Sun. 1:15–2:15; July–Sept., Mon.–Sat. 9:30–4:30, Sun. 1:15–2:15 and 5–5:30; hrs vary with services, call to confirm before visiting.*

FodorsChoice ★

In 1284, the Bishop of Ely founded **Peterhouse College,** Cambridge's smallest and oldest college. Take a tranquil walk through its former deer park, by the riverside of its ivy-clad buildings. ✉ *Trumpington St.* ☎ *01223/338200* ⊕ *www.pet.cam.ac.uk* 🎟 *Free* ⊘ *Daily 9–5.*

★ Reached along the Backs, **Queens' College**—built around 1448, and named after Margaret, queen of Henry VI, and Elizabeth, queen of Edward IV—enjoys a reputation as one of Cambridge's most eye-catching colleges. Enter over the **Mathematical Bridge,** said to have been built by Isaac Newton without any binding save gravity, then dismantled by curious scholars anxious to learn Sir Isaac's secret. The college maintains, however, that the bridge wasn't actually put together until 1749, 22 years after Newton's death, thus debunking the popular myth. ✉ *Queen's La.* ☎ *01223/335511* ⊕ *www.quns.cam.ac.uk* 🎟 *£1* ⊘ *Apr.–Oct., daily 10–4:30; Nov.–Mar., daily 10–4.*

Along King's Parade is **Corpus Christi College.** If you visit only one quadrangle, make it the beautiful, serene, 14th-century Old Court here; it's the longest continuously inhabited college quadrangle in Cambridge. ✉ *King's Parade* ☎ *01223/338000* ⊕ *www.corpus.cam.ac.uk* 🎟 *Free* ⊘ *Daily dawn–dusk.*

**St. John's College** (1511), the university's second largest, has noted alumni (Wordsworth studied here) and two of the finest sights in town: the School of Pythagoras, the oldest house in Cambridge; and the Bridge of Sighs, whose only resemblance to its Venetian counterpart is its covering. (Unlike Venice's bridge, this one does not lead to a prison.) The windowed, covered stone bridge reaches across the Cam to the mock-

Gothic New Court (1825–31). The New Court's cupola's white crenellations have earned it the nickname "the wedding cake." ⊠ *St. John's St.* ☎*01223/338600* ⊕*www.joh.cam.ac.uk* ☜*£1.75* ☉*Apr.–Oct., weekdays 10–5, Sat. 9:30–5.*

FodorśChoice **Trinity College** was founded by Henry VIII in 1546, and has the largest
★ student population of all the colleges. It's also famous for being attended by Herbert, Dryden, Byron, Thackeray, Tennyson, Bertrand Russell, Nabokov, and Nehru, India's first prime minister. Many of Trinity's features reflect its status as the largest college, not least its 17th-century "great court" and the massive gatehouse that houses Great Tom, a giant clock that strikes each hour with high and low notes. Don't miss the wonderful library by Christopher Wren, where you can see a letter written by alumnus Isaac Newton with early notes on gravity, and Milne's handwritten manuscript of *The House at Pooh Corner.* ⊠ *St. John's St.* ☎ *01223/338400* ⊕ *www.trin.cam.ac.uk* ☜ *£2, Mar.–Oct.* ☉ *College Mar.–Oct., daily 10–5, except exam time; library weekdays noon–2, Sat. in term time 10:30–12:30; hall and chapel open to visitors but hrs vary.*

### Where to Eat

★ **£££–££££** ╳ **Midsummer House.** In fine weather, the gray-brick Midsummer House's conservatory, beside the River Cam, makes for a memorable lunchtime jaunt. Choose from a selection of traditional European and Mediterranean dishes. You might get tender local lamb or the best from the daily fish market, adorned with inventively presented vegetables. ⊠*Midsummer Common* ☎ *01223/369299* ♨ *Reservations essential* ▤ *AE, MC, V* ☉ *Closed Mon. No lunch Sat., no dinner Sun.*

£2 ╳ **Vaults.** Stark, whitewashed walls and slate floors lend a sleek, contemporary twist to the otherwise traditional Vaults. The zinc-topped bar with red sofas is the perfect place for lounging with a cocktail. On Sunday there's a brunch with live blues. The menu is full of traditional but imaginatively prepared dishes such as grilled sea bass with salsa, and lamb shank with parsnip broth; for dessert, try the chocolate and star anise mousse cake. ⊠ *14a Trinity St.* ☎ *01223/506090* ♨ *Reservations essential* ▤ *AE, MC, V.*

# CANTERBURY

For many people, Geoffrey Chaucer's *The Canterbury Tales,* about a pilgrimage to Canterbury Cathedral, brings back memories of sleepy high-school English classes. Judging from the tales, however, medieval Canterbury was as much a party for people on horses as it was a spiritual center.

The height of Canterbury's popularity came in the 12th century, when thousands of pilgrims flocked here to see the shrine of the murdered Archbishop St. Thomas à Becket. Buildings that served as pilgrims' inns still dominate the streets of Canterbury's pedestrian center.

Dig a little deeper and there's evidence of prosperous society in the Canterbury area as early as the Bronze Age (around 1000 BC). An important Roman city, an Anglo-Saxon center in the Kingdom of Kent, and currently headquarters of the Anglican Church, Canterbury remains a lively place, a fact that has impressed visitors since 1388, when Chaucer wrote his stories.

You can easily cover Canterbury in a day. The 90-minute journey south from London's Victoria Station leaves plenty of time for a tour of the cathedral, a museum visit or two, and (if the weather's right) a walk around the perimeter of the old walled town. Canterbury is bisected by a road running northwest, along which the major tourist sites cluster. This road begins as St. George's Street, then becomes High Street, and finally turns into St. Peter's Street.

On St. George's Street a lone church tower marks the site of **St. George's Church**—the rest of the building was destroyed in World War II—where playwright Christopher Marlowe was baptized in 1564.

★ The **Canterbury Roman Museum,** including its colorful mosaic Roman pavement, and a hypocaust (the Roman version of central heating), is below ground, at the level of the Roman town. Displays of excavated objects (some of which you can hold in the Touch the Past area) and computer-generated reconstructions of Roman buildings and the marketplace help re-create the past. ⊠ *Butchery La.* ☎ *01227/785575* ⊕ *www.canterbury-museums.co.uk* 🖃 *£2.70* ☉ *June–Oct., Mon.–Sat. 10–5, Sun. 1:30–5; Nov.–May, Mon.–Sat. 10–5; last entry at 4. Closed last wk in Dec.*

Mercery Lane, with its medieval-style cottages and massive, overhanging timber roofs, runs right off High Street and ends in the tiny **Buttermarket,** a market square that was known in the 15th century as the Bullstake: animals were tied here for baiting before slaughter.

The immense **Christchurch Gate,** built in 1517, leads into the cathedral close. As you pass through, look up at the sculpted heads of two young figures: Prince Arthur, elder brother of Henry VIII, and the young Catherine of Aragon, to whom he was betrothed. After Arthur's death, Catherine married Henry. Her failure to produce a male heir after 25 years of marriage led to Henry's decision to divorce her, creating an irrevocable breach with the Roman Catholic Church and altering the course of English history.

Fodor'sChoice **Canterbury Cathedral,** the focal point of the city, was the first of England's
★ great Norman cathedrals. Nucleus of worldwide Anglicanism, the Cathedral Church of Christ Canterbury (its formal name) is a living textbook of medieval architecture.

The cathedral was only a century old, and still relatively small in size, when Thomas à Becket, the Archbishop of Canterbury, was murdered here in 1170. An uncompromising defender of ecclesiastical interests, Becket had angered his friend Henry II, who supposedly exclaimed, "Who will rid me of this troublesome priest?" Thinking they were carrying out the king's wishes, four knights burst in on Becket in one of the side chapels and killed him. Two years later Becket was canonized, and Henry II's subsequent penitence helped establish the cathedral as the undisputed center of English Christianity.

Becket's tomb, destroyed by Henry VIII in 1538 as part of his campaign to reduce the power of the Church and confiscate its treasures, was one of the most extravagant shrines in Christendom. In **Trinity Chapel,** which held the shrine, you can still see a series of 13th-century stained-glass windows illustrating Becket's miracles. The actual site of Becket's murder is down a flight of steps just to the left of the nave.

If time permits, be sure to explore the **Cloisters** and other small monastic buildings north of the cathedral. ⊠ *Cathedral Precincts* ☎ *01227/ 762862* ⊕ *www.canterbury-cathedral.org* ✉ *£4; free for services and for ½ hr before closing* ☉ *Easter–Sept., weekdays 9–6:30, Sun. 12:30–2:30 and 4:30–5:30; Oct.–Easter, weekdays 9–5; Sun. 12:30–2:30 and 4:30–5:30. Restricted access during services.*

To vivify some of Canterbury's history, spend some time at an exhibition called **The Canterbury Tales,** an audio-visual (and occasionally olfactory) dramatization of 14th-century English life. You'll "meet" Chaucer's pilgrims at the Tabard Inn near London and view tableaus illustrating five tales. Don't be surprised if one of the figures comes to life: an actor dressed in period costume often performs a charade as part of the scene. ⊠ *St. Margaret's St.* ☎ *01227/479222* ⊕ *www. canterburytales.org.uk* ✉ *£6.75* ☉ *Nov.–Feb., daily 10–4:30; Mar.–June, Sept., and Oct, daily 10–5; July and Aug., daily 9:30–5.*

★ ❾ The medieval Poor Priests' Hospital is now the site of the **Museum of Canterbury** (previously the Canterbury Heritage Museum). The exhibits provide an excellent overview of the city's history and architecture from Roman times to World War II, as well as special features on Bagpuss, the Blitz, Rupert Bear, and the mysterious death of Marlowe. You can even look at "medieval poo" under a microscope. Visit early in the day to avoid the crowds. ⊠ *20 Stour St.* ☎ *01227/452747* ⊕ *www.canterbury-museum.co.uk* ✉ *£3* ☉ *Jan.–May, Nov., and Dec., Mon.–Sat. 10:30–5; June–Oct., Mon.–Sat. 10:30–5, Sun. 1:30–5; last admission at 4.*

Only one of the city's seven medieval gatehouses survives, complete with ⚬ twin castellated towers; it now contains the **West Gate Museum.** Inside are medieval bric-a-brac and armaments used by the city guard, as well as more contemporary weaponry. The building became a jail in the 14th century and you can view the prison cells. Climb to the roof for a panoramic view of the city spires. ☎ *01227/452747* ⊕ *www.canterbury-museums.co.uk* ✉ *£1* ☉ *Mon.–Sat. 11–12:30 and 1:30–3:30.*

For an essential Canterbury experience, follow the circuit of the mainly 13th- and 14th-century **medieval city walls,** built on the line of the original Roman walls. Those to the east survive intact, towering some 20 feet high and offering a sweeping view of the town. You can access these from a number of places, including Castle and Broad streets.

Augustine, England's first Christian missionary, was buried in 597 at **St. Augustine's Abbey,** one of the oldest monastic sites in the country. When Henry VIII seized the abbey in the 16th century, he destroyed some of the buildings and converted others into a royal manor for his fourth wife,

Anne of Cleves. A free interactive audio tour vividly puts events into context. The abbey is the base for Canterbury's biannual Sculpture Festival (held on odd-number years). Contemporary sculpture is placed on the grounds, and in other locations in the city, May through August. ⊠ *Longport* ☎ *01227/767345* ⊕ *www.english-heritage.org.uk* ✉ *£3* ⊙ *Apr.–Sept., daily 10–6; Oct., daily 10–5; Nov.–Mar., daily 10–4.*

☺ The **Dane John Mound**, just opposite the Canterbury East train station, was originally part of the city defenses. There's a fantastic medieval maze here.

### Where to Eat

★ **£–£££** ✕ **Weavers.** In one of the Weavers' Houses on the River Stour, this popular restaurant in the center of town is an ideal place to revel in the Tudor surroundings and feast on generous portions of British comfort food, such as traditional pies, seafood, and pasta dishes. You'll find a good selection of wines. Ask for a table in the more sedate ground-floor dining area. ⊠ *1 St. Peter's St.* ☎ *01227/464660* ▭ *AE, MC, V.*

**£–££** ✕ **Marlowe's.** For lunch or a late-afternoon snack, lively Marlowe's is a worthwhile alternative to the café franchises that populate Canterbury's pedestrian center. The staff is friendly and welcoming, as is the setting— walls are brightly colored and plastered with posters of old-time movie stars. The menu is eclectic: expect lunchtime standards (soup, sandwiches, baked potatoes), Tex-Mex dishes, and daily specials, such as lemon-dill chicken. ⊠ *55 St. Peter's St.* ☎ *01227/462194* ⊕ *www. marlowesrestaurant.co.uk* ▭ *AE, DC, MC, V.*

# OXFORD

To get Oxford fixed in your mind's eye, say the phrase "Dreaming Spires" over and over—all the tour guides do—and think *Brideshead Revisited*, Sebastian Flyte, and Evelyn Waugh in general. Think Rhodes scholars—former President Clinton was one—and think J. R. R. Tolkien, Percy Bysshe Shelley, Oscar Wilde, W. H. Auden, and C. S. Lewis. Wannabe wizards will want to visit Oxford for yet another reason: many of its most formidable buildings stood in for the Hogwarts School in the Harry Potter films.

Oxford University is older than its sibling to the east, dating from the 12th century, but the city is bigger and more cosmopolitan than Cambridge. Of course, here, too, there's no shortage of hushed quadrangles, chapels, and gardens. Bikes are propped against wrought-iron railings, and punting is popular along the Cherwell (rent a punt yourself, at the foot of Magdalen Bridge), but Oxford is also a major industrial center, with large car and steel plants based in its suburbs.

VISITING THE COLLEGES The same concerns for people's work and privacy hold here as in Cambridge. Guided city walking tours leave the Oxford Information Centre several times a day. If you have limited time, get a detailed map from the tourist office and focus on selected sights. The Oxford University Web site (⊕ www.ox.ac.uk) is a great source of information if you're planning to go it alone.

Note that many of the colleges and university buildings are closed around Christmas (sometimes Easter, too) and on certain days from April to June for exams and degree ceremonies.

## Exploring Oxford

Any Oxford visit should begin at its very center—a pleasant walk of 10 minutes or so east from the train station—with the splendid university church of **University Church of St. Mary the Virgin** (1280). Climb 127 steps to the top of its 14th-century tower for a panoramic view of the city. ⊠ *High St.* ☎ *01865/279111* ⊕ *www.university-church.ox.ac.uk* ☜ *Church free, tower £2* ⊙ *Church and tower Sept.–June, daily 9–5, until 4:30 in winter; July and Aug., daily 9–6.*

Fodor'sChoice ★ Among Oxford's most famous sights, the **Radcliffe Camera** (1737–49) is one of the buildings that house the august **Bodleian Library**. Not many of the 6-million-plus volumes are on view to those who aren't dons, but you can see part of the collection on a tour. (Harry Potter fans should know that the Bodleian Library's other buildings—Duke Humfrey's Library, the Old Schools Quadrangle, and the Clarendon Building—stood in for some of Hogwarts' interiors.) ⊠ *Broad St.* ☎ *01865/277224* ⊕ *www.bodley.ox.ac.uk* ☜ *£3.50, extended tour £7, call to prebook* ⊙ *Bodleian tours Mar.–Oct., weekdays 10:30, 11:30, 2, 3 and Sat. 10:30, 11:30; Nov.–Feb., weekdays 2, 3 and Sat. 10:30, 11:30. Children under 14 not admitted. Divinity School weekdays 9–4:45, Sat. 9–12:30.*

★ The **Sheldonian Theatre**, built between 1664 and 1668, was Sir Christopher Wren's first major work (the chapel at Pembroke College was his first commission). The theater, which he modeled on a Roman amphitheater, made his reputation. It was built as a venue for the University's public ceremonies, and graduations are still held here, entirely in Latin, as befits the building's spirit. Outside is one of Oxford's most striking sights—a metal fence topped with stone busts of 18 Roman emperors (modern reproductions of the originals, which were eaten away by pollution). ⊠ *Broad St.* ☎ *01865/277299* ⊕ *www.sheldon. ox.ac.uk* ☜ *£1.50* ⊙ *Mon.–Sat. 10–12:30 and 2–4:30; mid-Nov.–Feb., closes at 3:30.*

Brush up on local history at the **Oxford Story.** Take your place at a medieval student's desk as it trundles, Disney-style, through 800 years of Oxford history. In 20 minutes you can see Edmund Halley discover his comet, and watch the Scholastica's Day Riot of 1355. There's commentary tailored for kids, too. ⊠ *6 Broad St.* ☎ *01865/728822* ⊕ *www. oxfordstory.co.uk* ☜ *£6.75* ⊙ *July and Aug., daily 9:30–5; Sept.–June, Mon.–Sat. 10–4:30, Sun. 11–4:30.*

Outside the "new" (that is, Victorian) college gates of prestigious **Balliol College** (1263), a cobblestone cross in the sidewalk marks the spot where Archbishop Cranmer and Bishops Latimer and Ridley were burnt in 1555 for their Protestant beliefs. The original college gates (rumored to have existed at the time of the scorching) hang in the library passage, between the inner and outer quadrangles. ⊠*St. Giles St.* ☎*01865/277777* ⊕ *www.balliol.ox.ac.uk* ☜ *£1* ⊙ *Daily 2–5, or dusk if earlier.*

★ The **chapel** of **Trinity College** (1555) is an architectural gem, with some superb wood carvings by Grinling Gibbons, a 17th-century master carver whose work can be seen in Hampton Court Palace and St. Paul's Cathedral, and who inspired Thomas Chippendale. ☒ *Broad St.* ☎ *01865/279900* ⊕ *www.trinity.ox.ac.uk* 🎟 *£2* ⊘ *Daily 10–noon and 2–4, or dusk if earlier.*

**Fodor'sChoice** The **Ashmolean Museum,** founded in 1683, is Britain's oldest public mu-
★ seum. Some of the world's most precious art objects are stashed here—Egyptian, Greek, and Roman artifacts; drawings by Michelangelo and Raphael; European silverware and ceramics; and a world-class numismatic collection. All of the objects are the property of the university. The café upstairs, with delightful sandwiches and tasty cakes, makes a good rest stop. ☒ *Beaumont St.* ☎ *01865/278000* ⊕ *www.ashmol.ox.ac. uk* 🎟 *Free* ⊘ *Tues.–Sat. 10–5, Sun. 2–5.*

**St. John's College,** founded in 1555, is worth a stop for its very lovely gardens and its library, where you can view some of Jane Austen's letters, and the William Caxton's illustrated 1482 edition of *The Canterbury Tales.* ☒ *St. Giles St.* ☎ *01865/277300* ⊕ *www.sjc.ox.ac.uk* 🎟 *Free* ⊘ *Daily 1 PM–dusk.*

**Tom Tower,** designed by Christopher Wren, marks the entrance to the
★ ☉ leading college of the southern half of Oxford: **Christ Church College.** Called "the House" by its modest members, Christ Church has the largest quadrangle in town, named Tom Quad, after the more than six-ton bell in the tower. Christ Church is where Charles Dodgson, better known as Lewis Carroll, was a math don; a shop opposite the meadows in St. Aldate's was the inspiration for the shop in *Through the Looking Glass.* Don't miss the 800-year-old chapel, or the medieval dining hall, with its portraits of former students—John Wesley, William Penn, and 14 prime ministers. The dining hall should look familiar to fans of a certain young wizard: it appeared as the Hogwarts School dining hall in *Harry Potter.* ☒ *St. Aldate's* ☎ *01865/286573* ⊕ *www.chch.ox.ac.uk* 🎟 *£4* ⊘ *Mon.–Sat. 9:30–5:30, Sun. 1–5:30.*

## Where to Eat

★ **£££** ✕ **Le Petit Blanc.** Raymond Blanc's Conran-designed brasserie is sophisticated even by London standards. The top British chef populates his menu with modern European and regional French dishes: you might see a goats' cheese soufflé with hazelnut dressing, or fresh salmon trout with lemon sabayon. At £12.50 for two courses or £15 for three, the prix-fixe lunch is an incredible value, and well worth the short walk north of town. ☒ *71–72 Walton St.* ☎ *01865/510999* ⚒ *Reservations essential* 🖃 *AE, DC, MC, V.*

★ **£** ✕ **Grand Café.** Golden-hue tiles, columns, and antique marble tables mean this café is architecturally impressive as well as being an excellent spot for a light meal or leisurely drink. The tasty menu lists sandwiches, salads, and tarts as well as perfect coffee drinks and desserts. ☒ *84 High St.* ☎ *01865/204463* 🖃 *AE, MC, V.*

# STRATFORD-UPON-AVON

Stratford-upon-Avon has become adept at accommodating the hordes of people who come for a glimpse of William Shakespeare's world. Punctuated with distinctive Tudor half-timber buildings that have survived from its 16th-century heyday as a crafts and trading center, Stratford is a handsome town. But it can feel, at times, like a literary amusement park, so if you're not a fan of Bill, you'd probably do better to explore some other quaint English village.

That said, how best to maximize your immersion in the Bard's works? It's difficult to avoid feeling like a herd animal as you board the Shakespeare bus, but tours like **Stratford and the Shakespeare Story** (⊠ 14 Rother St. ☎ 01789/294466 ⊕ www.city-sightseeing.com ⊠ £8.50), with a hop-on/hop-off route around the five Shakespeare Birthplace Trust properties—two of which are out of town—can make a visit infinitely easier if you don't have a car.

## Exploring Stratford-upon-Avon

Most who visit Stratford start at **Shakespeare's Birthplace Museum.** The half-timber building in which Shakespeare grew up has been a national memorial since 1847, and it's now split in half: one part is a re-creation of a typical home of the time, while the other contains an intelligent biographical exhibit about Shakespeare, and a history of the house itself. ⊠ *Henley St.* ☎ *01789/204016* ⊕ *www.shakespeare.org.uk* ⊠ *£6.50; combined ticket with Shakespeare Birthplace Trust properties (Nash's House; Hall's Croft; Anne Hathaway's Cottage; Mary Arden's House; allow at least 4 hrs, but ticket is valid for 1 yr) £13; 3 in-town properties (not including Anne Hathaway's Cottage and Mary Arden's House) £9 ⊙ Late Mar.–late Oct., Mon.–Sat. 9–5, Sun. 9:30–5; late Oct.–late Mar., Mon.–Sat. 9:30–4, Sun. 10–4.*

**Nash's House,** which belonged to Thomas Nash, first husband of Shakespeare's granddaughter Elizabeth Hall, now houses an exhibit charting the history of Stratford, against a backdrop of period furniture and tapestries. On the grounds of Nash's House is **New Place,** the home where the Bard spent his last years and died in 1616. An Elizabethan knot garden is set around the remaining foundation of the house, which was destroyed in 1759 by its last owner, Reverend Francis Gastrell, in an attempt to stop the tide of visitors. ⊠ *Chapel St.* ☎ *01789/204016* ⊕ *www. shakespeare.org.uk* ⊠ *£3.50; combined ticket with Shakespeare's Birthplace Trust properties £13; 3 in-town properties £9 ⊙ Nov.–Mar., daily 11–4; Apr.–May, Sept., and Oct., daily 11–5; June–Aug., Mon.–Sat. 9:30–5, Sun. 10–5; last entry 30 mins before closing.*

★ **Hall's Croft** is Stratford's most beautiful Tudor town house. This was—almost definitely—the home of Shakespeare's daughter, Susanna, and her husband, Dr. John Hall. It's outfitted with furniture of the period and the doctor's dispensary, and the walled garden is delightful. ⊠ *Old Town St.* ☎ *01789/204016* ⊕ *www.shakespeare.org.uk* ⊠ *£3.50; combined ticket with Shakespeare's Birthplace Trust properties £13;*

*3 in-town properties £9 ☉ Nov.–Mar., daily 11–4; Apr., May, Sept., and Oct., daily 11–5; June–Aug., Mon.–Sat. 9:30–5, Sun. 10–5; last entry 30 mins before closing.*

"Shakespeare's church," the 13th-century **Holy Trinity,** is fronted by a beautiful avenue of lime trees. Shakespeare is buried here, in the chancel. The bust of Shakespeare is thought to be an authentic likeness, executed a few years after his death. ✉ *Trinity St.* ☎ *01789/266316* 🖃 *Church free, chancel £1* ☉ *Mar., Mon.–Sat. 9–5, Sun. 12:30–5; Apr.–Oct., Mon.–Sat. 8:30–6, Sun. 12:30–5; Nov.–Feb., Mon.–Sat. 9–4, Sun. 12:30–5; last admission 20 mins before closing.*

**Fodor's**Choice
★ On the bank of the Avon is the **Royal Shakespeare Theatre,** where the Royal Shakespeare Company performs in Stratford; they mount several productions each season. The design of the smaller **Swan Theatre,** in the same building, is based on the original Elizabethan Globe. It's best to book in advance, but day-of-performance tickets are nearly always available. Backstage tours take place around performances, so call ahead. ✉ *Waterside* ☎ *0870/6091110 ticket hotline, 01789/296655 information, 01789/403405 tours* ⊕ *www.rsc.org.uk* 🖃 *Tours £4* ☉ *Tours weekdays, except matinee days, 1:30 and 5:30; matinee days 5:30 and after show; tours Sun. noon, 1, 2, and 3. No tours when shows are being prepared. Gallery Mon.–Sat. 9:30–6:30, Sun. noon–4:30.*

STRATFORD
ENVIRONS
★ The two remaining stops on the Shakespeare trail are just outside Stratford. **Anne Hathaway's Cottage,** the early home of the playwright's wife, is possibly the most picturesque abode in Britain—a rather substantial thatched cottage, it has been restored to reflect the comfortable middle-class Hathaway life. You can walk—it's just over a mile from downtown Stratford. ✉ *Cottage La., Shottery* ☎ *01789/204016* ⊕ *www.shakespeare.org.uk* 🖃 *£5; Shakespeare Trust joint ticket £13* ☉ *Apr., May, Sept., and Oct., Mon.–Sat. 9:30–5, Sun. 10–5; June–Aug., Mon.–Sat. 9–5, Sun. 9:30–5; Nov.–Mar., Mon.–Sat. 10–4, Sun. 10:30–4; last entry 30 mins before closing.*

☾ The **Shakespeare Countryside Museum,** with displays that illustrate life in the English countryside from Shakespeare's time to the present day, is the main attraction at **Palmer's Farm,** the site of a recent and radical Shakespearean revelation. In late 2000, research findings based on newly discovered real-estate records revealed that the property, which had been referred to since the 18th century as Mary Arden's House, was not in fact the house in which the Bard's mother grew up. The real **Mary Arden's House,** hitherto known as Glebe Farm, was actually nearby and (thankfully) already owned by the Shakespeare Birthplace Trust. ✉ *Wilmcote* ☎ *01789/204016, 01789/293455 for information on special events* ⊕ *www.shakespeare.org.uk* 🖃 *£5.50; combined ticket with Shakespeare's Birthplace Trust properties £13* ☉ *Nov.–Mar., Mon.–Sat. 10–4, Sun. 10:30–4; Sept., Oct., Apr., and May, Mon.–Sat. 10–5, Sun. 10:30–5; June–Aug., Mon.–Sat. 9:30–5, Sun. 10–5; last entry 30 mins before closing.*

★ ☾ Some 8 mi out of Stratford in the medieval town of Warwick, **Warwick Castle** fulfills anyone's most clichéd Camelot daydreams. This medieval, fortified, much-restored, castellated, moated, landscaped (by Capability Brown) castle, now managed by the experts at Madame Tussaud's, is a true period museum—complete with dungeons and a torture chamber, state rooms, and the occasional battle reenactment. ⊠ *Castle La. off Mill St., Warwick* ☎ *01926/495421, 08704/422000 24-hr information line* ⊕ *www.warwick-castle.co.uk* ✉ *Sept.–Feb. £11.25; May–July £12.50; weekends May–mid-July and daily mid-July–Aug. £13.50* ☉ *Apr.–July, Sept., daily 10–6; Aug., weekdays 10–6, weekends 10–7; Oct.–Mar., daily 10–5.*

### Where to Eat

£££££  ✕ **Quarto's.** Views of the River Avon and its resident swans add to the appeal of this attractive spot in the Royal Shakespeare Theatre, where you can dine decently before or after a play. The lounge offers pretheater canapes and champagne. The menu is contemporary British, so expect things like lamb with rosemary and goat cheese salad. ⊠ *Royal Shakespeare Theatre, Waterside* ☎ *01789/403415* ⌂ *Reservations essential* ⊟ *AE, MC, V* ☉ *Closed when theater is closed.*

★ £££  ✕ **Restaurant Margaux.** This chic French restaurant on two floors has a cozy bistro feel. The upscale menu highlights dishes like quail and foie gras ravioli with baby leeks, chargrilled tuna with crab beignet and saffron dressing, and pistachio and strawberry parfait. ⊠ *6 Union St.* ☎ *01789/269106* ⌂ *Reservations essential* ⊟ *MC, V.*

££–£££  ✕ **Lambs.** Sit downstairs in the no-smoking section to appreciate the hardwood floors and oak beams of this local epicurean favorite. The modern updates of tried-and-true dishes include roast chicken with lime butter and char-grilled sausages with leek mash. Daily specials keep the menu seasonal. The two- and three-course set menus are particularly good deals. ⊠ *12 Sheep St.* ☎ *01789/292554* ⌂ *Reservations essential* ⊟ *AE, MC, V.*

£–££  ✕ **Black Swan.** Known locally as the Dirty Duck, this is one of Stratford's most celebrated pubs—it has attracted actors since Garrick's days. A little veranda overlooks the theaters and the river here. Along with a pint of bitter, it's a fine place to enjoy English grill specialties, as well as braised oxtail and honey-roasted duck. You can also choose from an assortment of bar meals. ⊠ *Waterside* ☎ *01789/297312* ⊟ *AE, MC, V* ☉ *No dinner Sun.*

# WINDSOR CASTLE

Windsor Castle, the largest inhabited castle in the world, is the star sight of Windsor, a quiet Berkshire town. Windsor Great Park, however, shouldn't be forgotten; Eton College, England's most famous public school, with its Old Village, is a lovely walk across the Thames from Windsor; and there's also the kids' paradise of Legoland.

Windsor is the only royal residence to have been in continuous royal use since the days of William the Conqueror, who chose this site to build a timber stockade soon after his conquest of Britain in 1066. It was Edward III in the 1300s who really founded the castle, building the Norman gateway, the great round tower, and the State Apartments. Charles

II restored the State Apartments during the 1600s and, during the 1820s, George IV—with his mania for building—converted what was still essentially a medieval castle into the palace you see today. The queen uses Windsor often, spending most weekends here, often joined by family and friends. She's here when the Royal Standard is flown above the Round Tower but not when you see the Union Jack. Arrive early at the main entrance, as lines can be long.

## Exploring Windsor Castle

The massive citadel of **Windsor Castle** occupies 13 acres, but the first part you notice on entering is the **Round Tower,** on top of which the Standard is flown and at the base of which is the 11th-century Moat Garden. Passing under the portcullis at the Norman Gate, you reach the **Upper Ward,** the quadrangle containing the State Apartments—which you may tour when the queen is out—and the sovereign's Private Apartments. Processions for foreign heads of state and other ceremonies take place here, as does the Changing of the Guard when the queen is in. A short walk takes you to the Lower Ward, where the high point is the magnificent **St. George's Chapel,** symbolic and actual guardian of the Order of the Garter, the highest chivalric order in the land, founded in 1348 by Edward III. Ten sovereigns are buried in the chapel—a fantastic Perpendicular Gothic vision 230 feet long, complete with gargoyles, buttresses, banners, swords, and choir stalls. This is also where royal weddings usually take place, the most recent having been that of Prince Edward and Sophie Rhys-Jones in June 1999.

The **State Apartments** are grander than Buckingham Palace's and have the added attraction of a few gems from the queen's vast art collection: choice canvases by Rubens, Rembrandt, Van Dyck, Gainsborough, Canaletto, and Holbein; da Vinci drawings; Gobelin tapestries; and limewood carvings by Grinling Gibbons. The entrance is through a grand hall holding cases crammed with precious china—some still used for royal banquets. Don't miss the outsize suit of armor in the armory, made for Henry VIII. Make sure you take in the magnificent views across to Windsor Great Park, the remains of a former royal hunting forest.

One unmissable treat—and not only for children—is **Queen Mary's Dolls' House,** a 12:1 scale, seven-story palace with electricity, running water, and working elevators, designed in 1924 by Sir Edwin Lutyens. The detail is incredible—some of the miniature books in the library are by Kipling, Conan Doyle, Thomas Hardy, and G. K. Chesterton, written by the great authors in their own hand. The diminutive wine bottles hold the real thing, too.

In 1992 a fire that started in the queen's private chapel gutted some of the State Apartments. A swift rescue effort meant that, miraculously, hardly any works of art were lost, and a £37 million effort has restored the Grand Reception Room, the Green and Crimson drawing rooms, and the State and Octagonal dining rooms to their former, if not greater, glory. ✉ *Windsor Castle* ☎ *020/7321–2233 for tickets, 01753/83118 for recorded information* ⊕ *www.royalresidences.com* 🎫 *£12 for the Precincts, the State Apartments, the Gallery, St. George's Chapel, the Albert Memorial Chapel, and the Dolls' House; £6 when the State*

*Apartments are closed ☉ Mar.–Oct., daily 9:45–5:15, last admission at 4; Nov.–Feb., daily 9:45–4:15, last admission at 3; St. George's Chapel closed Sun. except to worshippers.*

### Where to Eat

£ ✕ **Two Brewers.** Two small, low-ceiling rooms make up this 17th-century pub where locals congregate. Children are not welcome, but adults will find a suitable collection of wine, espresso, and local beer, plus an excellent little menu with dishes from salmon fish cakes to chili and pasta. Reservations are essential on Sunday when the pub serves a traditional roast. ⊠ *34 Park St.* ☎ *01753/855426* ▭ *AE, DC, MC, V.*

# SIDE TRIPS A TO Z

*To research prices, get advice from other travelers, and book travel arrangements, visit www.fodors.com.*

### Bus Travel

FARES & SCHEDULES National Express coach lines runs buses from Victoria Coach Station to six of the towns in this chapter. Coaches depart for Bath (3 hours, 15 minutes) every 90 minutes; for Brighton (2 hours) hourly; for Cambridge (about 2 hours) hourly; for Canterbury (1 hour, 50 minutes) hourly; for Oxford (1 hour, 40 minutes) about every half hour; and for Stratford-upon-Avon (3 hours) about three times daily.

Take the Green Line bus to Windsor. It leaves from Stop 1 in front of the Colonnades Shopping Centre on Buckingham Palace Road, *not* from Victoria Coach Station. The fast direct service takes around one hour and runs hourly; the stopping services take up to 1½ hours or more. ⊠ Green Line ☎ 0870/608-7261 ⊕ www.greenline.co.uk. **National Express** ☎ 0870/580-8080 ⊕ www.nationalexpress.co.uk. **Victoria Coach Station** ⊠ Buckingham Palace Rd., Victoria SW1.

### Train Travel

FARES & SCHEDULES Trains run from Paddington Station to Bath (90 minutes, hourly departures), Oxford (55 minutes, half-hourly departures), and Windsor (45 minutes, departs half-hourly and requires one change). Direct trains leave Paddington for Stratford-upon-Avon (2 hours, 20 minutes) each morning; other routes depart from Marylebone (2½ hours) and Euston (2½ hours) stations and require a change at Leamington Spa. Direct trains for Windsor (50 minutes, departs every 30 minutes) depart from Waterloo Station. Trains depart King's Cross Station hourly for Cambridge (1 hour). Victoria Station is the point of departure for rail service to Brighton (50 minutes, hourly) and Canterbury (85 minutes, half-hourly). There is also service to Brighton (1 hour, departures every 15 minutes) and Canterbury (90 minutes, half-hourly) from London Bridge Station. ⊠ Railtrack ☎ 0870/580-8080 ⊕ www.railtrack.co.uk.

### Transportation Around the Countryside

Normally, the seven towns covered in this chapter are best reached by train. Bus travel costs less, but can take twice as long. However, train routes throughout Britain are often subject to delays as a result of engineering work being carried out on the national rail system. Wherever you're going, be sure to plan ahead for any day trip: check the latest timetables before you set off, and try to get an early start.

## Visitor Information

▸ Bath Tourist Information Centre ✉ Abbey Church Yard ☎ 0906/711–2000, 50p per minute) ⊕ www.visitbath.co.uk. **Brighton Tourist Information Centre** ✉ 10 Bartholomew Sq. ☎ 08457/573512 ⊕ www.tourism.brighton.co.uk. **Cambridge Tourist Information Centre** ✉ The Old Library, Wheeler St. ☎ 01223/457577 ⊕ www.cambridge.gov. uk/leisure/tourism.htm. **Canterbury Visitor Information Centre** ✉ 34 St. Margaret's St. ☎ 01227/766567 ⊕ www.canterbury.co.uk. **Oxford Information Centre** ✉ 15/16 Broad St. ☎ 01865/726871 ⊕ www.oxford.gov.uk/tourism. **Royal Windsor Information Centre** ✉ 24 High St. ☎ 01753/743900 ⊕ www.windsor.gov.uk. **Stratford Tourist Information Centre** ✉ Bridgefoot ☎ 0870/160–7930 ⊕ www.shakespeare-country.co.uk. **Warwick Tourist Information Centre** ✉ Court House, Jury St. ☎ 01926/492212 ⊕ www. warwick-uk.co.uk.

# UNDERSTANDING LONDON

# LONDON AT A GLANCE

## Fast Facts

**Type of government:** Representative democracy. In 1999 the Greater London Authority Act reestablished a single local governing body for the Greater London area, consisting of an elected mayor and the 25-member London Assembly. Elections, first held in 2000, take place every 4 years.

**Population:** City 7.4 million, metro area 11.2 million

**Population density:** 11,841 people per square mi

**Median age:** 40.6

**Infant mortality rate:** 5.7 per 1,000 births

**Language:** English. More than 300 languages are spoken in London. All city government documents are translated into Arabic, Bengali, Chinese, Greek, Gujurati, Hindi, Punjabi, Turkish, Urdu, and Vietnamese.

**Ethnic and racial groups:** White 71%, Indian 6%, other 6%, black African 5%, black Caribbean 5%, Bangladeshi 2%, other Asian 2%, Pakistani 2%, Chinese 1%

**Religion:** Christian 58%, non-affiliated 24%, Muslim 8%, Hindu 4%, Jewish 2%, Sikh 1%, other religion 1%, Buddhist 0.8%

*When a man is tired of London, he is tired of life; for there is in London all that life can afford.*
—Samuel Johnson

## Geography & Environment

**Latitude:** 51° N (same as Calgary, Canada; Kiev, Russia; Prague, Czech Republic)

**Longitude:** 0° (same as Accra, Ghana). A brass line in the ground in Greenwich marks the prime meridian (0° longitude).

**Elevation:** 49 ft

**Land area:** City, 67 square mi; metro area, 625 square mi

**Terrain:** River plain, rolling hills, and parkland

**Natural hazards:** Drought in warmer summers, flooding of the Thames due to surge tides from the North Atlantic

**Environmental issues:** Up to 1,600 people die each year from health problems related to London's polluted air. The city has been improving its air quality but is unlikely to meet goals it set for 2005. Only half of London's rivers and canals received passing grades for water quality from 1999 through 2001. Over £12 million ($22 million) is spent annually to ensure the city's food safety.

*I'm leaving because the weather is too good. I hate London when it's not raining.*
—Groucho Marx

## Economy

**Work force:** 5.3 million; financial/real estate 28%, health care 10%, manufacturing 8%, education 7%, construction 5%, public administration 5%

**Unemployment:** 6.9%

**Major industries:** The arts, banking, government, insurance, tourism

*London: a nation, not a city.*
—Benjamin Disraeli, *Lothair*

## Did You Know?

- With more than 7 million residents, London is the largest city in the European Union. It's among the most densely populated, too, following Copenhagen, Brussels, and Paris.

- London's ethnic mosaic includes communities of more than 10,000 people from 34 different countries.

- There are 481 foreign banks in the city, more than in any other world financial center. The London Stock Exchange deals with almost twice as many foreign companies as the New York Stock Exchange.

- Up to about £2,000 (about $3,680) of taxpayers' money can be used to purchase a wig for a London judge, who often still wears the antiquated accessory. Barristers and solicitors (lawyers) must pay for their own wigs and often buy them used.

- More than 100 species of fish, including smelt (which locals say has an odor resembling their beloved cucumber sandwiches), live in the Thames. In 1957 naturalists reported no signs of life in the river. The Thames looks brown because of sediment but is actually Europe's cleanest metropolitan estuary.

- Despite being surrounded by more than 5,000 pubs and bars, Londoners drink less than the average British resident. Twenty-three percent of men in London drank 22 or more units of alcohol per week from 2001 through 2002, compared with 27% in Great Britain as a whole.

- The Tube is the world's biggest subway system. With 253 miles of routes and 275 stations, it covers more ground than systems in New York, Paris, and Tokyo.

- City taxi drivers must pass a training test that requires between two and four years of preparation. Eight or nine of every ten applicants drop out before completion.

- The average home price in London is £210,100 ($386,580), about £75,000 ($138,00) higher than the average in the United Kingdom, and five times the average family income of first-time buyers. The average monthly rent for a one-bedroom apartment in private housing is £1,029 ($1,837).

# A LITTLE DRINK OR TWO

**V**ERLAINE (1873) CONSIDERED Londoners to be "noisy as ducks, eternally drunk," while Dostoevsky (1862) noted that "everyone is in a hurry to drink himself into insensibility." A German journalist, Max Schlesinger (1853), saw the inhabitants of a public house "standing, staggering, crouching, or lying down, groaning, and cursing, drink and forget." An observer closer to home, Charles Booth, noticed that drinking among women in the 1890s had materially increased. "One drunken woman in a street will set all the women in it drinking," he quotes one male inhabitant of the East End as saying. Nearly all women "get drunk of Monday. They say we have our fling; we like to have a little fuddle on Monday." All classes of London women seem to have been drinking, largely because it was no longer considered wrong for a female to enter a public house for a "nip." In the evening, children of the poorer classes were sent around to the local public house to have a jug filled with ale; as Booth reported, "it was constant come and go, one moment to go in and get the jug filled, and out again the next; none of the children waited to talk or play with one another, but at once hurried home."

Gentlemen drank as deeply and freely as the poor. Thackeray noted those "who glory in drinking bouts" with "bottle-noses" and "pimpled faces." "I was so cut last night" is one of the phrases he recalled.

In each year of the nineteenth century, approximately 25,000 people were arrested for drunkenness in the streets. Yet the conditions of life often drove poorer Londoners into their condition. One of them, a collector of "pure" (dog excrement) told Mayhew that he had often been drunk "for three months together"—he had "bent his head down to his cup to drink, being utterly incapable of raising it to his lips."

So even though the gin fever had subsided, and its shops closed down, its spirit—we might say—was continued in the "gin palaces" of the nineteenth century. These large establishments, clad in shining plate-glass windows with stucco rosettes and gilt cornices, were resplendent with advertisements lit by gas lamps announcing "the only real brandy in London" or "the famous cordial, medicated gin, which is so strongly recommended by the faculty." The fine lettering reveals the attractions of "The Out and Out!," "The No Mistake," "The Good for Mixing" and "The real Knock-me-down." Yet the exterior brightness was generally deceptive; the scene within these "palaces" was a dismal one, almost reminiscent of the old gin shops. There was characteristically a long bar of mahogany, behind which were casks painted green and gold, with the customers standing—or sitting on old barrels—along a narrow and dirty area beside it.

It might be noted here, too, that social observers believed drink to be "at the root of all the poverty and distress with which they came into contact." Again the emphasis is upon the unhappy conditions of the city itself, literally driving men and women to drink with its relentless speed, urgency and oppression. Of the skeletons investigated in St. Bride's Lower Churchyard, "just under 10 per cent had at least one fracture." It is also revealed, in the fascinating London Bodies compiled by Alex Werner, that "almost half of these were rib fractures, commonly caused by stumbling or brawling."

In the same period the breweries had become one of the wonders of London, one of the sights to which foreign visitors were directed. By the 1830s there were twelve principal brewers, producing, according to Charles Knight's London, "two barrels, or 76 gallons, of beer per annum for every inhabitant of the metropolis—man, woman and child." Who would not want to observe all this industry and enterprise? One German visitor was impressed by the "vast establishment" of Whitbread's brewery in Chiswell Street, with its buildings "higher than a church" and its horses "the giants of their breed." In similar fashion, in the summer of 1827, a German prince "turned my 'cab' to Barclay's brewery, in Park Street, Southwark, which the vastness of its dimensions renders almost romantic." He observed that steam engines drove the machinery which manufactured from twelve to fifteen thousand barrels a day; ninety-nine of the larger barrels, each one "as high as a house," are kept in "gigantic sheds"; 150 horses "like elephants" transport the beer. His awareness of the size and immensity of London is here reflected in its capacity for beer and, in a final parallel, he notes that from the roof of the brewery "you have a very fine panoramic view of London."

That emblematic significance was recognized by painters as well as visitors, and by the beginning of the nineteenth century there was established what London art historians have termed "the brewery genre." Ten years after the prince's visit, for example, Barclay's brewery was painted by an anonymous hand; the entrance is depicted, together with the thriving life of London all around it. To the right is the great brewhouse, with a suspension bridge connecting to the other side of the street. In the foreground a butcher's boy, in the blue apron typical of his trade, stands with another customer beside a baked-potato van; barrels of beer on sleds are being drawn by horses into the yard, passing a dray which is just leaving. In the street, to the right, a hansom cab is bringing in more visitors. It is a picture of appetite, with the meat carried on the shoulders of the butcher's boy as an apt

token of the London diet, as well as of immense energy and industry.

But there are other ways of conveying the immensity of the city's drinking. Blanchard Jerrold and Gustave Doré visited the same premises for their London: a Pilgrimage—"the town of Malt and Hops" as Jerrold called it in 1871—in order to see the brewing of the beer named Entire which assuaged "Thirsty London." Jerrold noted that against the great towers and barrels the working men "look like flies," and indeed in Doré's engravings these dark anonymous shapes tend to their beer-mashing and beer-making duties like votaries; all is in shadow and chiaroscuro, with fitful gleams illuminating the activities of these small figures in vast enclosed spaces. Here again the life of the city is like that within some great decaying prison, with the metal pipes and cylinders as its bars and gates. Jerrold, like the German visitor before him, looked over London "with St. Paul's dominating the view from the north," and apostrophized beer as the city's sacred drink. "We are," he remarked, "upon classic ground."

The gin palace was supplanted by the public house, which was the direct descendant of the tavern and the alehouse. Of course taverns survived in the older parts of London, known to their adherents for privacy and quiet, to their detractors for gloom and silence. Public houses continued the tradition of segregation, with saloon, lounge and private bars being distinguished from public bars and jug and bottle departments. Many pubs were not salubrious, with plain and dirty interiors and a long "zinc-topped" counter where men sat solemnly drinking—"You enter by a heavy door that is held ajar by a thick leather strap . . . striking you in the back as you go in and often knocking off your hat." Instead of the gin palace's long bar, the public house bar was characteristically in the shape of a horseshoe with the variously coloured bottles rising up within its interior space. The furniture was plain enough, with chairs and benches, tables and spittoons, upon a sawdusted floor. By 1870 there were some 20,000 public houses and beer shops in the metropolis, catering to half a million customers each day, reminiscent of "dusty, miry, smoky, beery, brewery London."

A stranger asking directions in 1854, according to The Little World of London, was likely to be told "Straight on till you come to the Three Turks, then to turn to the right and cross over at the Dog and Duck, and go on again till you come to the Bear and the Bottle, then to turn the corner at the Jolly Old Cocks, and after passing the Veteran, the Guy Fawkes, the Iron Duke, to take the first turn to the right which will bring you to it." In this period there were seventy King's Heads and ninety King's Arms, fifty Queen's Heads and seventy Crowns, fifty Roses and twenty-five Royal Oaks, thirty Bricklayers Arms and fifteen Watermen's Arms, sixteen Black Bulls and twenty Cocks, thirty Foxes and thirty Swans. A favoured color in pubs' names was red, no doubt complementing the analogy in London between drink and fire, while London's favorite number seemed to be three: the Three Hats, the Three Herrings, the Three Pigeons, and so on. There were also more mysterious signs such as the Grave Maurice, the Cat and Salutation and the Ham and Windmill.

The variety and plentitude of the nineteenth-century pubs continued well into the twentieth century, with the basic shape and nature changing very little, ranging from the munificent West End establishment to the sawdusted corner pub in Poplar or in Peckham. Then, in one of those paradoxes of London life, public houses became more mixed and lively places during the Second World War. The beer may have run out before the close of proceedings, and glasses may have been in short supply, but Philip Ziegler suggests in *London at War* that "they were the only places in wartime London where one could entertain and be entertained cheaply, and find the companionship badly needed during the war." There was an odd superstition that pubs were more likely to be hit by bombs, but this did not seem to affect their popularity; in fact, during the forced absence of men, women once again began to use pubs. A report of 1943 recorded that "they were often to be seen there with other women or even on their own." "Never had the London pubs been more stimulating," John Lehmann recalled, "never has one been able to hear more extraordinary revelations, never witness more unlikely encounters."

By the end of that war in 1945 there were still some four thousand pubs in the capital, and peace brought a new resurgence of interest. Novels and films have conveyed the atmosphere of pubs in the late 1940s and early 1950s, from the East End, where the men still wore caps and scarves and the girls danced "holding cigarettes in their fingers," to local saloons where what Orwell described as the "warm fog of smoke and beer" surrounded the "regulars."

*In London: The Biography, Peter Ackroyd engagingly traces the growth of London, from the time of the Druids to the beginning of the 21st century. He evokes the city's history, habits, and idiosyncrasies through anecdotes and the voices of its citizens. The result is darkly funny and alarming, insightful and entertaining.*

# COSMOPOLITAN COCKNEY VILLAGE

ONDON IS AN ENORMOUS CITY—600 square mi—on a tiny island, accommodating more than seven million inhabitants, one-eighth of the entire population of England, Scotland, and Wales, but to many travelers it never *really* feels big. It is fashioned on a different scale from other capital cities, as if, given the English penchant for modesty and understatement, it felt embarrassed by its size. Despite the apparent lack of space, building has almost always been out rather than up, and open space is widespread. Each of the 32 boroughs that compose the whole has its own character, lore, and rhythm. There is the heraldic splendor of Westminster, the chic of artistic Chelsea, the architectural elegance of Belgravia and Mayfair, the cosmopolitan charm of Soho, and the bellicose vestiges of Cockney East End—to name just a few. Stay here long enough and Professor Higgins' feat of deducing Eliza Dolittle's very street of birth from the shape of her vowels will seem like nothing special. It's a cliché, but London really is a city of villages.

London's contrasts can best be savored by strolling from one district to another. First pick a starting point such as Piccadilly Circus, face in the direction of the area of central London you want to explore, and start moving. To the north runs Regent Street, curving up one side of ritzy, mostly residential Mayfair. To the south is Lower Regent Street, leading toward Whitehall, the parks, and the palaces. To the east are Shaftesbury Avenue and Leicester Square, for theaters and Soho; to the west is Piccadilly itself, heading out to Hyde Park and Knightsbridge. This is also a great place to board a double-decker sightseeing bus—just remember to have some sort of protective wrap handy: atop these buses it's *always* windy.

That's one of the best things about the city: everything has been seen before, and history is forever poking its nose in. Whatever you're doing, you're doing it on top of a past layered like striated rock. You can see the cross sections clearly sometimes, as in the City, where lumps of Roman wall nest in the postmodern blocks of the street helpfully named London Wall. Walk toward the Thames to Cheapside, which you can tell was the medieval marketplace if you know the meaning of "ceap" ("to barter"), and there's the little Norman church of St. Mary-le-Bow, rebuilt by Wren and then again after the Blitz, but still ringing the Bow Bells. Then look to your right, and you'll be gobsmacked by the dome of St. Paul's. Of course, all you really wanted was to find a place for lunch—nearly impossible on a weekend in this office wasteland.

Instead of going weak-kneed at the city's sights, Londoners are apt to complain about its privations while pretending simultaneously that no other city in the United Kingdom exists. Edinburghers and Liverpudlians can complain 'til Big Ben tolls 13, but Londoners continue to pull rank with a complacency that amuses and infuriates in equal measure. London's sense of self-importance comes, in part at least, from the vein of water running through its center, which has always linked the city with the sea, and once gave British mariners a head start in the race to mine the world's riches and bring them home. The river proved convenient for building not only palaces (at Westminster, Whitehall, Hampton Court, Richmond, Greenwich) but an empire, too.

The empire dissolved, but the first Thames bridge is still there, in almost the same spot that the emperor Claudius picked in AD 43, and although the current drab concrete incarnation dates only from 1972, it's still called London Bridge. The Tudor construction was much more striking—a row of decapitated heads were supposedly stuck on poles above the gatehouse.

The old London Bridge lasted 600 years. Lined with shops and houses, it presided over a string of fairs *on* the Thames, when winters were colder and the water froze thick. Nowadays London rarely sees a snowfall, though Londoners talk endlessly about its possibility. People here are genuinely obsessed by the weather because there's so much of it, though most of it is damp. Snow varies the scenery, stops any Tube train with an overground route, makes kids of everyone with a makeshift toboggan and access to a park (99% of the population), and fosters a community spirit normally proscribed by the city's geography and its citizens' cool. Winters were colder as recently as the '60s, when waiting for the crust to thicken enough to skate on the Round Pond in Kensington Gardens—now good only for model-boat sailors and duck feeders—was only a matter of time.

The corollary to London's temperate winter, though, is a fresh confidence in summer sufficient to support herds of sidewalk tables. Holland Park Avenue no longer has the monopoly on a Parisian-style milieu. All over town, an epidemic of Continental-style café chains serving croissants and *salade frisée* has devoured the traditional tobacco-stained pubs serving warm bitter and bags of pork scratch-ings. Most of the remaining pubs have turned into faux-Edwardian parlors with coffee machines and etchings or, more recently, wood-floor bars serving flavored vodkas and Tuscan food. The change has been going on since the early 1990s, and it suits London, as does its momentous discovery that restaurants are allowed to serve good food in smart surroundings and not charge the earth.

London is increasingly a European city, as if England were no longer stranded alone in the sea. In fact, ever since airplanes superseded ships, this island race has been undergoing an identity crisis, which reached its apogee in the '70s when Prime Minister Edward Heath sailed the country irrevocably into the Common Market. Occasionally Britain still holds out against some European Community legislation or other, attempting to reassert differences that are following executions at the Tower and British Colonial supremacy into history. But however much the social climate changes, London is built on a firm foundation. Until the ravens desert the Tower of London—which is when, they say, the kingdom will fall—London has Westminster Abbey and St. Paul's and the Houses of Parliament, the Georgian squares and grand Victorian houses, the green miles of parks, the river, the museums and galleries and theaters, and 32 boroughs of villages to keep it going.

— Kate Sekules

# BOOKS & MOVIES

London has been the focus of countless books and essays. For sonorous eloquence, you still must reach back more than half a century to Henry James's *English Hours* and Virginia Woolf's *The London Scene.* Today, most suggested reading lists begin with V. S. Pritchett's *London Perceived* and H. V. Morton's *In Search of London,* both decades old. Three more up-to-date books with a general compass are: Peter Ackroyd's anecdotal *London: The Biography,* which traces the city's growth from the Druids to the 21st century ( ➪ see the excerpt at the beginning of this chapter), John Russell's *London,* a sumptuously illustrated art book, and Christopher Hibbert's *In London: The Biography of a City.* Stephen Inwood's *A History of London* explores the city from its Roman roots to its swinging '60s heyday. Piet Schreuders's *The Beatles' London* follows the footsteps of the Fab Four.

That noted, there are books galore on the various facets of the city. *The Art and Architecture of London* by Ann Saunders is fairly comprehensive. *Inside London: Discovering the Classic Interiors of London,* by Joe Friedman and Peter Aprahamian, has magnificent color photographs of hidden and overlooked shops, clubs, and town houses. For a wonderful take on the golden age of the city's regal mansions, see Christopher Simon Sykes's *Private Palaces: Life in the Great London Houses.* For various other aspects of the city, consult Mervyn Blatch's helpful *A Guide to London's Churches,* Andrew Crowe's *The Parks and Woodlands of London,* Sheila Fairfield's *The Streets of London,* Ann Saunders's *Regent's Park,* Ian Norrie's *Hampstead, Highgate Village, and Kenwood,* and Suzanne Ebel's *A Guide to London's Riverside: Hampton Court to Greenwich.* For keen walkers, there are two books by Andrew Duncan: *Secret London* and *Walking Village London.* *City Secrets: London* edited by Robert Kahn is a handsome little red-linen book of anecdotes from London writers, artists, and historians about their favorite places in the city. For the last word on just about every subject, see *The London Encyclopaedia,* edited by Ben Weinreb and Christopher Hibbert. HarperCollins's *London Photographic Atlas* has a plethora of bird's-eye images of the capital. For an alternative view of the city, it woud be hard to better Ian Sinclair's witty and intelligent *London Orbital: A Walk Around the M25* in which he scrutinizes the history, mythology, and politics of London from the viewpoint of its ugly ringroad.

Of course, the history and spirit of the city are also to be found in celebrations of great authors, British heroes, and architects. Peter Ackroyd's massive *Dickens* elucidates how the great author shaped today's view of the city; Martin Gilbert's magisterial, multivolume *Churchill* traces the city through some of its greatest trials; J. Mansbridge's *John Nash* details the London buildings of this great architect. Liza Picard evokes mid-18th-century London in *Dr. Johnson's London.* For musical theater buffs, Mike Leigh's *Gilbert and Sullivan's London* takes a romantic look at the two artists' lives and times in the capital's grand theaters and wild nightspots. *Rodinsky's Room* by Rachel Lichtenstein and Iain Sinclair is a fascinating exploration of East End Jewish London and the mysterious disappearance of one if its occupants.

Nineteenth-century London—the city of Queen Victoria, Tennyson, and Dickens—comes alive through *Mayhew's London,* a massive study of the London poor, and Gustave Doré's *London,* an unforgettable series of engravings of the city (often reprinted in modern editions) that detail its horrifying slums and grand avenues. Maureen Waller's *1700: Scenes from London Life* is a fascinating look at the daily life of Londoners in the 18th century. When it comes to fiction, of course, Dickens's immortal works top the list. Stay-at-home detectives have long walked the streets of London, thanks to great mysteries by Sir Arthur Conan Doyle, Dorothy L. Sayers, Agatha Christie, Ngaio Marsh, and Antonia Fraser. Cops and bad guys wind their way around 1960s London in Jake Arnott's pulp fiction books, *The Long Firm* and *He Kills Coppers*. Martin Amis's *London Fields* tracks a murder mystery through West London. For so-called "tart noir," pick up any Stella Duffy book. Marie Belloc-Lowndes's *The Lodger* is a fictional account of London's most deadly villain, Jack the Ripper. Victorian London was never so salacious as in Sarah Waters' story of a young girl who travels the theaters as a singer, the Soho squares as a male prostitute, and the East End as a communist in *Tipping the Velvet*. Late 20th-century London, with its diverse ethnic makeup, is the star of Zadie Smith's famed novel *White Teeth*.

There are any number of films—from *Waterloo Bridge* and *Georgy Girl* to *Secrets and Lies* and *Notting Hill*—that have used London as their setting. But always near the top of anyone's list are four films that rank among the greatest musicals of all time: Walt Disney's *Mary Poppins*, (complete with Dick Van Dyke's laughable cockney accent); George Cukor's *My Fair Lady;* Sir Carol Reed's *Oliver!;* and The Beatles' *A Hard Day's Night*.

Children of all ages enjoy Stephen Herek's *101 Dalmatians* with Glenn Close as fashion-savvy Cruella de Vil. King's Cross station in London was shot to cinematic fame by the movie version of J. K. Rowling's *Harry Potter and the Philosopher's Stone*.

The swinging '60s is loosely portrayed in M. Jay Roach's *Austin Powers: International Man of Mystery,* full of references to British slang and some great opening scenes in London. For a truer picture of the '60s in London, Michaelangelo Antonioni weaves a mystery plot around the world of London fashion photographer in *Blow-Up*. British gangster films came into their own with Guy Ritchie's amusing tales of London thieves in *Lock, Stock, and Two Smoking Barrels,* filmed almost entirely in London, and the follow-up *Snatch* with a comedic turn by Brad Pitt. Of course, the original tough guy is 007 and his best exploits in London are featured in the introductory chase scene in *The World is Not Enough*.

Sir Arthur Conan Doyle knew the potential of London as a chilling backdrop and John Landis's *An American Werewolf in London* and Hitchcock's *39 Steps* exploit the Gothic and sinister qualities of the city. St. Ermine's Hotel stands in for the 19th-century Savoy dining room in Oliver Parker's *The Importance of Being Earnest*. For a fascinating look at medieval London, watch John Madden's romantic *Shakespeare in Love*.

Two modern-day romantic comedies that use London as a backdrop are Peter Howitt's *Sliding Doors* with Gwyneth Paltrow, and Nick Hamm's sweet, romantic comedy about an American backpacker, *Martha Meet Frank, Daniel and Laurence (AKA The Very Thought of You)*. For a slice of Indian London, you can't do better than Gurinder Chadha's tale of a girl who wants to play soccer in *Bend It Like Beckham*.

# CHRONOLOGY

Note that the dates given for British kings and queens are those of their reigns, not of their lives.

ca. 400 BC  Early Iron Age hamlet built at Heathrow

54  Julius Caesar arrives with short-lived expedition

AD 43  Romans conquer Britain, led by the emperor Claudius

50  First London Bridge built

60  Boudicca, queen of the Iceni, razes the first Roman Londinium

ca. 100  The Romans make Londinium center of their British activities, though their capital remains at Camulodunum (now Colchester)

410  Roman rule of Britain ends

604  London's first bishop, Melitus, builds a cathedral in the name of St. Paul

700–800  Saxon trading town of Lundenwic (London) develops on the present site of Covent Garden and the Strand

886  Alfred the Great (871–99), king of the West Saxons, retakes the city; he is said to have "restored London and made it habitable"

1042  Edward the Confessor (1042–66) builds an abbey and palace at Westminster, and moves his court out of the City (London's original "square mile," now the financial district)

1066  William the Conqueror (1066–87), Duke of Normandy, wins the Battle of Hastings and is crowned William I

1067  William grants London a charter confirming its rights and privileges

1078  Tower of London construction begins with the building of the White Tower

1176–1209  After fire destroys the first London Bridge, a stone version is built by Peter de Colechurch

1191  First mayor of London elected

1265  First Parliament held in Westminster Abbey Chapter House

1314  Original St. Paul's Cathedral completed

1348–58  The Black Death kills one-third of London's population; 30,000 residents remain

1382  The Peasants' Revolt destroys part of the city

1476  In Westminster, William Caxton (1422–91) introduces printing to England

1529  Hampton Court given by Cardinal Wolsey to Henry VIII (1509–47); it becomes a favorite royal residence

1533   The Reformation: monasteries close and land goes to wealthy merchant families, creating new gentry

1558   Queen Elizabeth I (1558–1603) crowned

1568   Royal Exchange founded

1599   James Burbage (d. 1619) opens the Globe Theatre on the South Bank

1605   Unsuccessful Gunpowder Plot to blow up the Houses of Parliament

1637   Hyde Park opens to the public

1649   Charles I (1625–49) beheaded outside the Banqueting House on Whitehall

1660   The Restoration: Charles II (1649–85) restored to the throne after years of exile in Europe

1665   The Great Plague: deaths reach approximately 100,000

1666   The Great Fire: London burns for three days; its medieval center is destroyed

1675   Sir Christopher Wren (1632–1723) begins work on the new St. Paul's Cathedral

1694   The Bank of England founded

1712   Georg Friedrich Handel (1685–1759) settles in London

1732   No. 10 Downing Street becomes the prime minister's official residence

1739   London's second bridge is built at Westminster

1755   Trooping the Colour (parade to celebrate the monarch's birthday) first performed for George II

1759   The British Museum opens to the public

1762   George III (1760–1820) makes Buckingham Palace a royal residence

1785   *The Times* newspaper is first published, as the *Daily Universal Register*

1801   First census records 1,117,290 people living in London

1802   First gaslights on London streets

1829–41   Trafalgar Square laid out

1834   The Houses of Parliament gutted by fire (the present Westminster Palace built 1840–52)

1836   The University of London established

1837   Victoria (1837–1901) assumes the throne. London Bridge rail station opens

1849   Harrods opens as a small grocery store

1851   The Great Exhibition, Prince Albert's brainchild, held in the Crystal Palace, Hyde Park

1863   Birth of the "Tube": First underground railway runs between Farringdon and Paddington stations

1869   Albert Embankment completed, first stage in containing the Thames's floodwaters

1877   First Wimbledon tennis tournament

1888   "Jack the Ripper" strikes Whitechapel

1897   Queen Victoria celebrates her Diamond Jubilee

1901   Victoria dies. London's population reaches about 4,500,000

1909   Selfridges department store opens

1914–18   World War I: London bombed (1915) by German zeppelins (670 killed, 1,962 injured)

1936   The BBC begins television broadcasting in north London

1939–45   World War II: during the Blitz (1940–41 and 1944–45), 45,000–50,000 bombs are dropped on London

1946   Heathrow Airport opens

1951   The Festival of Britain lifts postwar morale

1952   Coronation of Queen Elizabeth II (born 1926)

1956   Clean Air Act abolishes open fires and makes London's "pea soup" fogs a romantic memory

1960–68   The Beatles, Twiggy, Mary Quant: "Swinging London" dominates the international music and fashion scenes

1965   Sir Winston Churchill's funeral, a great public pageant. Greater London Council established. First Notting Hill Carnival (now the biggest street fair in Europe)

1966   England wins the soccer World Cup in the final at Wembley, defeating West Germany 4–2.

1974   Covent Garden fruit-and-vegetable market moves across the Thames; the original buildings open in 1981 as a shopping and entertainment complex

1976   Royal National Theatre opens on the South Bank

1977   Queen Elizabeth II celebrates her Silver Jubilee

1981   Prince Charles marries Lady Diana Spencer in St. Paul's Cathedral

1982   July bombings in Hyde and Regent's Parks bring IRA violence to London

1983   The first female Lord Mayor takes office

1984   The Thames Barrier, designed to prevent flooding in central London, is inaugurated

1986  The Greater London Council abolished by Parliament; London's population almost 7 million

1991  One Canada Square, Britain's tallest building, opens at Canary Wharf

1994  The Channel Tunnel opens a direct rail link between Britain and Europe

1996  The Prince and Princess of Wales receive a precedent-setting divorce. The reconstructed Shakespeare's Globe Theatre opens

1997  "New Labour" comes to power, with Tony Blair as Prime Minister. Princess Diana dies in car crash at age 36 in Paris

2000  London welcomes the 21st century with the Millennium Dome. Ex-Labour Party rebel Ken Livingstone wins a convincing victory in the election to choose London's first elected mayor.

2001  The Millennium Dome closes, its future uncertain. Prime Minister Tony Blair is elected to a second term

2002  Princess Margaret, the queen's sister, dies at the age of 71; Queen Elizabeth the Queen Mother dies at age 101; Queen Elizabeth II celebrates her Golden Jubilee

2003  More than a million people march in central London against the second Gulf War. George W. Bush becomes the first American president since 1918 to be accorded the honor of a full state visit

# NOTES

# NOTES

# NOTES

# NOTES

# FODOR'S KEY TO THE GUIDES

America's guidebook leader publishes guides for every kind of traveler.
Check out our many series and find your perfect match.

## FODOR'S GOLD GUIDES
America's favorite travel-guide series offers the most detailed insider reviews of hotels, restaurants, and attractions in all price ranges, plus great background information, smart tips, and useful maps.

## COMPASS AMERICAN GUIDES
Stunning guides from top local writers and photographers, with gorgeous photos, literary excerpts, and colorful anecdotes. A must-have for culture mavens, history buffs, and new residents.

## FODOR'S CITYPACKS
Concise city coverage in a guide plus a foldout map. The right choice for urban travelers who want everything under one cover.

## FODOR'S EXPLORING GUIDES
Hundreds of color photos bring your destination to life. Lively stories lend insight into the culture, history, and people.

## FODOR'S TRAVEL HISTORIC AMERICA
For travelers who want to experience history firsthand, this series gives in-depth coverage of historic sights, plus nearby restaurants and hotels. Themes include the Thirteen Colonies, the Old West, and the Lewis and Clark Trail.

## FODOR'S POCKET GUIDES
For travelers who need only the essentials. The best of Fodor's in pocket-size packages for just $9.95.

## FODOR'S FLASHMAPS
Every resident's map guide, with dozens of easy-to-follow maps of public transit, restaurants, shopping, museums, and more.

## FODOR'S CITYGUIDES
Sourcebooks for living in the city: thousands of in-the-know listings for restaurants, shops, sports, nightlife, and other city resources.

## FODOR'S AROUND THE CITY WITH KIDS
Up to 68 great ideas for family days, recommended by resident parents. Perfect for exploring in your own backyard or on the road.

## FODOR'S HOW TO GUIDES
Get tips from the pros on planning the perfect trip. Learn how to pack, fly hassle-free, plan a honeymoon or cruise, stay healthy on the road, and travel with your baby.

## FODOR'S LANGUAGES FOR TRAVELERS
Practice the local language before you hit the road. Available in phrase books, cassette sets, and CD sets.

## KAREN BROWN'S GUIDES
Engaging guides—many with easy-to-follow inn-to-inn itineraries—to the most charming inns and B&Bs in the U.S.A. and Europe.

## BAEDEKER'S GUIDES
Comprehensive guides, trusted since 1829, packed with A–Z reviews and star ratings.

## OTHER GREAT TITLES FROM FODOR'S
Baseball Vacations, The Complete Guide to the National Parks, Family Vacations, Golf Digest's Places to Play, Great American Drives of the East, Great American Drives of the West, Great American Vacations, Healthy Escapes, National Parks of the West, Skiing USA.

At bookstores everywhere.                     www.fodors.com/books